HANDBOOK OF
WORLD FAMILIES

To Diane and Irene

HANDBOOK OF WORLD FAMILIES

EDITED BY
BERT N. ADAMS
University of Wisconsin, Madison
JAN TROST
Uppsala University, Sweden

SAGE Publications
Thousand Oaks ▪ London ▪ New Delhi

For information:

Sage Publications, Inc.
2455 Teller Road
Thousand Oaks, California 91320
E-mail: order@sagepub.com

Sage Publications Ltd.
1 Oliver's Yard
55 City Road
London EC1Y 1SP
United Kingdom

Sage Publications India Pvt. Ltd.
B-42, Panchsheel Enclave
Post Box 4109
New Delhi 110 017 India

· Printed in the United States of America

Library of Congress Cataloging-in-Publication Data

Handbook of world families / Bert N. Adams, Jan Trost, editors.
    p. cm.
Includes bibliographical references and index.
    ISBN 0-7619-2763-8 (cloth: acid-free paper)
1. Family. 2. Family—Cross-cultural studies. I. Adams,
Bert N. II. Trost, Jan, 1935-
HQ515.H3356 2005   2004013899

This book is printed on acid-free paper.

04   05   06   07   10   9   8   7   6   5   4   3   2   1

Acquisitions Editor:	Jim Brace-Thompson
Editorial Assistant:	Karen Ehrmann
Production Editor:	Diane S. Foster
Copy Editor:	Patricia Oman, Publication Services, Inc.
Typesetter:	C&M Digitals (P) Ltd.
Proofreader:	Scott Oney
Indexer:	Molly Hall
Cover Designer:	Michelle Lee Kenny

Contents

127722

Introduction

BERT N. ADAMS

JAN TROST

We often speak of *the* family, but there are many types of families. One can look upon the term *family* as a very complex word, with a great variety of meanings. Families can be studied from the perspective of a society and its organization. In many countries the law uses the term *family* to mean either the nuclear family of parents and minor children, or else blood relatives. Companies use various definitions of *family* to give discounts or bargains; they often advertise themselves as "family friendly." Also, the term family is used with various boundaries for employees' right to a leave of absence to grieve a deceased relative or following the birth of a child.

One can also look upon the term *family* from a small-group perspective and classify a specific group as family or not. For example, a single parent with a child may or may not be considered a family. Two parents living apart with a child alternatively living with each can be classified as a family or not. A married couple without any children can be called a family or not (for example, this couple may be asked, "When are you going to start your family?"). A cohabiting couple with a child may or may not be called a family. A family may be seen to include a large number of individuals related by blood or marriage. Such a group may be called the family, or the extended family, or the kin group. And so on.

One can also look at the term *family* from the perspective of the individual. Some persons see as members of their family only those related to them as parents, children, or siblings. Others see pets as family. Some include relatives such as uncles, aunts, and cousins. Still others consider (and label) close friends as family (Aunt Maurine and Uncle Roald may simply be close and long-term friends). The variety is enormous.

ORGANIZATION OF THE BOOK

Another way of looking at family or families is to see how the study of family is divided into subfields of related topics. The formation of relatively long-lasting relationships of same- or opposite-gender couples is one of the fields related to families. Some such relationships will be nonlegalized cohabiters, some will marry, and some will marry but be in a LAT (living apart together) relationship. Another field has to do with children being born (fertility) to a couple or a single person. The process of socialization is also a field to which family is related, as is the separation or divorce of cohabiting or married couples.

We know of books that are cross-cultural, but not necessarily comparative. At the outset of this project, we determined that to make it comparative, the format or outline of the chapters should be identical, or almost so. That way, the reader or student can look up a section and compare, for example, Chinese family formation with Indian, or Indian divorce with divorce in the United States. The major sections of each chapter follow this order: 1. Introduction; 2. Family Formation (or Pairing Up/Mate Selection); 3. Fertility and Socialization; 4. Gender; 5. Marriage; 6. Stresses and Violence; 7. Divorce and Remarriage; 8. Kinship; 9. Aging and Death; 10. Family and Other Institutions; and 11. Special Topics.

The 25 countries included in the volume are organized by world region. We have alphabetized the regions in the following order: Africa, Asia and the South Pacific, Europe, Latin America, the Middle East, and North America. Then, within these six regions, the countries included are also alphabetized.

Style and Expertise

As you begin to read a specific chapter, some variation from our outline may be found. Topics may be *omitted*. If the author has neither expertise nor available literature on, for example, violence or aging, they may leave it out. If the author sees his or her society's families as having no special or unique issue that deserves discussion, the Special Topics section will simply be left out. If the country's politics and economics have been covered in the Introduction, then Other Institutions may be omitted. Also, topics may be *combined*. Several authors see Gender and

Marriage as a single set of issues. If so, they are allowed to deal with them as 4 & 5, or together. Likewise, 6 & 7 have been combined (Stresses and Divorce) in a few cases, if the author chose to. Also, a topic or subtopic may be *added*. For example, the chapter on Cuba includes in its introductory section lengthy information on the revolution. Likewise, Kwang-Kyu Lee has included a lengthy treatment of South Korean history. Quite a few authors wrote a Conclusion (or Conclusions) as a way to end their chapter.

For some countries (and authors) there may be much information available for some topics, while for some others information may be very limited. For example, LAT relationships exist in many countries, but no information or data are available in some of these countries. In addition, the authors themselves may be experts on a certain issue—perhaps fertility or divorce—and in such cases the discussion of that issue may be more intensive. Our authors have written as comprehensively as possible, but there may be a certain internal unevenness in a chapter. Also, the authors have been allowed to change the heading of one of the eleven subsections, if they prefer.

The purpose is thus to utilize a set structure, but without forcing the author(s) to a rigid adherence. Their expertise is allowed to show through, as is the information available in a given society. We have also, while editing the English for readability, tried to avoid abandoning the style or "voice" of the author. It is our intent for both the author's expertise and style to be evident within the comparative outline.

Themes

You will in all likelihood find themes that run through many, if not all, the chapters. It is not our intention in this Introduction to extract all the important ones, but for your benefit we will note a few, distinguishing between (1) uniform themes; (2) variations on a theme; and (3) unusual but important ideas.

Uniform

Two of the most consistent cross-cultural themes are the rise in *divorce* rates and the decline in *fertility*. While the divorce rate may not have risen as much, nor the fertility rate declined as much in India as it has in many Western societies, the trend still holds. Another consistent set of findings concerns *gender* roles. Women's education and job opportunities are increasing, but women are still paid less and do more housework than men. While these trends have moved further toward gender equality in some societies than in others, the general trend holds. A fourth finding, often discussed under socialization, is the lessened *respect* shown by children toward their parents and other adults. While this may be less troublesome to certain Western societies than to those in Africa, the trend is close to universal.

Variations on a Theme

If you look at the Introduction (1) and section on Family and Institutions (10) of various chapters, you will find many discussions of family *policy*. The dramatic differences between Scandinavia, with its parental leave, and the United States can be compared with the policy of other societies. A second variation is on the theme of *cohabitation*. There are at least four situations in which nonmarital cohabitation occurs. There are the young premarried, the never married, the postdivorce, and the very poor. Each of these categories of cohabitors has a different set of reasons for living together without marrying.

A third set of variations has to do with family *violence*. You will find some societies

in this volume in which family violence is ignored, if not denied. There are others where certain types of violence, especially against women and children, are still close to being normative, or at least expected. Then there are societies that expect it to occur, but frown upon it—at least publicly. Finally, some societies do not expect it, and have even passed laws against it, but still find it occurring.

Not just in the Special Topics sections, but also in various other places, you will find intriguing or unusual issues that you will want to pursue further—both inside and outside this volume. For example, Kwang-Kyu Lee speaks of urban "neighborhoods without neighboring." By this he means that people may live close to each other without developing any sense of community. This is the sort of issue that may deserve further cross-cultural attention.

Caveat

This book includes chapters on 25 nations from around the world. That means, of course, that your favorite country—or the one you were most anxious to learn about—may not be included. There are several reasons why a particular country may be missing. First, it may simply be that we could not find an expert to write about families in that society. A second reason for omission is that we may have found an author (or authors), but were unable to get them to agree to write the chapter on their society. The third, and most disappointing, reason why a society may be missing is that a scholar agreed to write, but did not come through with his or her contribution. At some point we simply had to move ahead with completion of the project.

A good scholar can learn to understand another culture, but it is usually better to have authors who were brought up in the countries they are writing about. From the short biographies in the About the Contributors and About the Editors sections, you will see how successful we were at finding such authors. In fact, you will enjoy reading about the 34 authors of our 25 chapters. We cannot express enough appreciation to the scholars who have written the manuscripts now included in this *Handbook*.

This project has been 2 years in the making, and many more years as an idea. We believe the *Handbook of World Families* will be found useful by scholars and colleagues all over the world, by students in relevant and related fields, by professionals who work with families, whether as social workers or politicians, and by laypeople interested in family matters in societies other than their own, such as even by travelers who want to learn about the country to which they are going.

ACKNOWLEDGMENTS

The editors wish to thank James Brace-Thompson of Sage for his encouragement on this project. We also appreciate the hard work of our 34 authors, from many cultures and societies, whose efforts and scholarship have filled the chapters with information and insights. Finally, Karen Ehrmann and others at Sage have helped to make the finished product what it is.

—Bert N. Adams

—Jan Trost

Part I

AFRICA

CHAPTER 1

Families in Kenya

EDWARD K. MBURUGU

BERT N. ADAMS

1. BACKGROUND

The Republic of Kenya is situated on the upraised part of the eastern portion of the African continent, astride the Equatorial latitude. The northernmost part of Kenya (i.e., the Ilemi Triangle) is just above 5° north latitude, while the southernmost land (i.e., the small islands including Ras Jimbo to the south of Shimoni village, in Kwale District) is at 4°40′ south latitude. Longitudinally, Kenya extends from 33°83′ east longitude (i.e., from Sumba, Mfangano, Ilemba, and the Pyramid Islands on Lake Victoria) to 41°75.5′ east longitude (i.e., the location of Mandera Town). Currently, Kenya has an estimated population of 32.2 million, which is projected to increase to 33.4 million by 2005 (Central Bureau of Statistics [CBS], 2002, pp. 30–31). It covers an area of 582,646 square kilometers, of which only 2.3% is water: part of Lake Victoria and Lakes Turkana (6,405 sq km), Baringo (129 sq km), Magadi (104 sq km), and other smaller lakes.

Kenya is bordered on the south by Tanzania (the length of the international boundary being approximately 760 km), on the west by Uganda (approximately 720 km), on the northwest by Sudan (approximately 310 km), and on the north and east by Ethiopia (approximately 760 km) and Somalia (approximately 660 km). Kenya's southeastern extremity forms part of the Indian Ocean seaboard, which is approximately 495 kilometers long. On this coast is situated the magnificent seaport of Mombasa.

Geography

Kenya can be subdivided into six natural geographical-economic regions as follows: Coastal Belt and Plains; Duruma–Wajir Low Belt; Foreland Plateau; the Highlands— comprising Eastern and Western Highlands; Nyanza Low Plateau (part of the Lake Victoria Basin); and the Northern Plainlands. We will describe each of these.

The Coastal Belt and Plains

This is a narrow belt, generally below 152 meters (approximately 500 feet) above sea level. The land along this belt is famous for its tree crops, which include coconut palms, mangoes, oranges, cashew nuts, and sisal.

Duruma–Wajir Low Belt

This is an intermediate belt between the more humid coastal plain and the foreland plateau. It is a dry land that is now in use for group ranching. Along the Tana River valley, there is scope for more permanent agriculture through irrigation. Already irrigation has been initiated around Bura area. The main problem in land use is that the soils tend to be generally sandy, but in the higher parts such as Shimba Hills, cashew nuts, coconuts, and cassava are grown successfully, as has been demonstrated by the Shimba Hills settlement scheme.

The Foreland Plateau

This plateau has an altitude of 304 to 915 meters (approximately 997–3,002 feet) above sea level. It is a relatively narrow belt from the Mount Kilimanjaro foothills through the Taita Hills northward via Kitui to beyond Garba Tula. Settlement is confined to places where water can be obtained. Wildlife dominates the greater part of this region. The famous Amboseli Game Reserve and Tsavo National Parks are situated here.

The Highlands

This region forms the heartland of the Republic of Kenya. It is cool and, on the whole, malaria-free, and is the agriculturally rich part of the country. It is bisected by the Rift Valley into the eastern and western highlands. The central (or eastern) highlands and Mau escarpment to the west are the "breadbasket" of the country, growing food crops such as corn, wheat, potatoes, pulses, and many varieties of vegetables. Along with this, there is large-scale farming and export

farming, comprising the now famous tea, coffee, pyrethrum, dairy, and ranching for which Kenya is known. The modified tropical climate is healthy and energizing, and pleasant almost the year round.

The Nyanza Low Plateau

This is part of the Victoria Basin, dominated by the Kano Rift Valley, which runs west-to-east, with its western part (Winam Gulf) still part of the lake. The Kano Plain is suited for irrigation work. To the north are richly well-watered Kakamega, Vihiga, and parts of Siaya Districts, with their remarkably high rural population density. The higher parts of South Nyanza, like its northern counterpart, form equally rich agricultural land that has yet to be fully developed.

The Northern Plainlands

This region covers practically the whole of northern Kenya. It is united by its endless aridity, which has kept its human population low. Nomadic pastoralism is the normal mode of land use. The quality of the range has not been properly assessed, although efforts toward this realization have been made by the Integrated Project in Arid Lands (IPAL), a project supported by the United Nations Educational, Scientific, and Cultural Organization (UNESCO) since 1976. Northern Kenya is still suffering from the colonial neglect. Organized marketing and provision of facilities for the mobile pastoralists is urgently needed, as one way of reducing overstocking in a nonresilient and essentially fragile environment. This is necessary to arrest desertification, which is already threatening many parts of the region. Provision of modern infrastructure has begun in the region. The Kapenguria–Lodwar–Sudan, Isiolo–Marsabit–Moyale, and Isiolo–Wajir–Mandera roads have made the region much more accessible. The assistance being given to Kenya through development aid by a number of foreign agencies, in regions such as Turkana, Marsabit, and Samburu, should be encouraged and made part of national development goals.

The People of Kenya

It is often said that Kenya is a land of contrasts. This is not only true of the physical, geographical, and climatic conditions of the land, but also of the social, economic, and cultural character of its people. One of the most striking characteristics of the population of Kenya is its ethnic diversity, although 98.9% of the total population is of African origin and 99.7% of the total African population is of Kenyan origin, according to the 1999 census.

The various national population censuses have divided the African population on a linguistic basis. Interestingly, the social and cultural organization of the various ethnic groups is closely associated with the linguistic classifications. This is particularly the case when we consider variations in age and sex divisions of labor, as well as in cultural taboos and *rites of passage* to be observed by these linguistics groups. The largest of these is the Bantu-speaking group, which belongs to the Niger-Congo linguistic family. The Bantu in Kenya form about 65% of the total population. The present concentration of the group is largely south of an imaginary line from Mount Elgon on the west, southeast to Lamu on the Indian Ocean. In this part of the country the Bantu are found in varying concentrations in three main geographical regions: the Lake Victoria Basin, the East Rift Highlands, and the coastal belt. The central group, which is the largest, includes the Kikuyu, Embu, Meru, Mbere, Kamba, and Tharaka. The majority occupy the fertile Central Highlands extending from Nyambeni Hills in Meru and Mount Kenya

in the north to the slopes of Nyandarua. The coastal belt is dominated by Mijikenda people, who include Giriama, Digo, Duruma, Ribe, Chonyi, and Kauma.

The remainder of Kenya's Africans fall broadly into two other linguistic groupings: the Nilotic and Cushitic. The Nilotic is represented by Luo, Kalenjin, Maasai, and related peoples such as Samburu, Turkana, and Teso. The Luo occupy the Lake Victoria Basin, with the rural Luo concentrating in the lower parts of the western plateau draining into Lake Victoria. Away from the rural areas, the group is now well represented in main Kenyan towns. The Kalenjin-speaking and the related Maasai groups have historically been pastoral people, although farming now constitutes a major occupation of the groups.

The Cushitic group of languages represents only 3.4% of the total population of Kenya. The group falls into two distinct subdivisions. The larger subdivision includes the Somali-speaking group occupying most of the eastern portions of the arid and semi-arid northeastern areas of Kenya. The second subdivision is to be found in the western portion of the arid and semi-arid region, and includes mainly the Rendille and Orma-speaking peoples. The Cushitic-speaking people occupy a region that suffers from a serious moisture deficit with conditions unsuitable for agricultural activities.

The normative social structure of Kenya's societies includes patriliny, patriarchy, and polygyny, though Edmondo Cavicchi argues that in precolonial times the Kikuyu may have been matriarchal (Cavicchi, 1977). Kenya has a parliamentary government. Since independence in 1963, there have been three presidents: Jomo Kenyatta until 1979, Daniel T. arap Moi from 1979 to 2002, and Mwai Kibaki from 2002 to the present.

Much of the present chapter will draw on a study of kinship and families carried out by the two authors during the 1990s. Interviews were completed with 620 adult men and 644 women—84% of them being between 25 and 45 years of age, and two-thirds between 30 and 40. The study involved 300+ interviews with each of the following ethnic groups: the Mijikenda of the south coast, the Akamba of east-central Kenya, the Embu on the eastern slopes of Mount Kenya, and the Kikuyu of Nairobi and the central highlands. Some 63% of the respondents were rural, with only the Kikuyu being divided equally between rural and urban environments. It would be inaccurate to generalize about Kenya from these four societies, since the cattle herders (Samburu, Maasai) and the lake people (Luhya, Luo) are omitted. However, we will draw on other literature in speaking about Kenya as a whole.

2. PAIRING UP/MATE SELECTION

Courtship among the Luo is discussed by Ocholla-Ayayo:

> A girl is likely to have but one lover in a clan, thus reducing jealousy and conflict over a girl by counter claims. When a girl had a lover there was no interference, and it was known in the whole clan that such a girl is so-and-so's lover. But this did not prevent the girl from becoming married to others rather than to the lovers she had. (1976, p. 83)

A part of courtship is sexual experience. Both Kenyan men and women are likely to have first experience of intercourse prior to marriage. Prior to Kenyan independence, among the Nandi of Western Kenya, a communal dormitory accommodated six young couples (Snell, 1954, p. 67). Twenty years later, Goldschmidt reported that it was unusual, at least among the Sebei (on the Kenya–Uganda border) for a normal person to reach pubertal circumcision a virgin (1976, p. 203). If a girl becomes pregnant, the boy is

named, and the child is his, that is, part of his lineage—though he is not forced to marry the girl (1976, p. 204).

For women in the 1994 *Kenya Demographic and Health Survey* (KDHS), median age at first intercourse was 16.6 years, and 18.8 years for marriage. In the same survey, 64% of the men reported that they had had intercourse by age 18, but only 4% were married by that age. There are two regional differences worth noting. First, women in the Nyanza (Lake) region are younger than those of other regions both at first intercourse and at first marriage. Second, the coastal (Mijikenda) region, which is predominantly Muslim, is the only one in which age at first intercourse and at first marriage are virtually identical—an apparent indication of sexual and religious conservatism (KDHS, 1993, pp. 65–67, 156).

An important aspect of pairing continues to be *bridewealth* (once called bride-price), that is, money that passes from the groom's family to the bride's. Of our married respondents, 90% said that bridewealth has been, is being, or will be paid. Items included were very similar to Goldschmidt's list for the Sebei of Western Kenya: money, cows, goats, sheep, a water tank, clothing, millet, sugar, beer, honey, milk, bread, and salt (1976). More than a quarter indicated that the bridewealth consisted entirely of money, ranging from Sh 700 to Sh 70,000 (about U.S.$20 to $2,000 when the data were collected). Bridewealth amounts are often discussed in livestock equivalence. For example, one man said, "I was supposed to pay eight goats and two cows, but these were converted into Sh 10,000." The average value was approximately Sh 14,000, or U.S.$400. Thus, bridewealth seems to still be of significant economic value, rather than having become merely tokenistic or symbolic.

Neither urban residence nor education has thus far reduced either the prevalence or the amount of bridewealth. In fact, *all* our Kikuyu respondents who grew up in

Nairobi stated that bridewealth had been paid at their marriage. In fact, two of the largest bridewealths reported were paid by university-educated, lifelong Nairobians. In these and other urban instances, livestock was paid as well as money—indicating the continuing rural connections of the bride's family, the groom's family, or both.

Bridewealth, therefore, is an important indicator of marriage. Two other important aspects of bridewealth emerged from the authors' data: (1) continuing payment, and (2) "wives don't know." David Parkin notes that payment may continue for many years (1972), and J. L. Comaroff reported that it may be paid early on or over a period of years (1980, p. 217). Some of our respondents stated that either it had not yet been paid or was still being paid. On the second issue, quite a few of our women respondents said it was paid, but they had no idea how much. One woman stated that this was, in fact, the norm: "Normally the woman never knows the bridewealth amount."

It is important to note that the concept of *bridewealth* in African marriages fundamentally symbolizes a contract or a covenant between not only the bridegroom and the bride, but even more important between the clans of the two parties in marriage. No commercial interests were involved in bridewealth. Traditionally, there were standardized amounts of bridewealth payable in the form of a combination of goods such as cows, goats, sheep, honey, beer, millet, and milk, depending on the customary (i.e., "legal") requirements of the bride's ethnic group. Today, as we have noted, these goods are increasingly transformed into money equivalents. However, payments had to be made in installments approved by clan elders of the bride and the bridegroom.

Full payment of bridewealth was highly discouraged, although it was desirable to pay most of it (say 80%) before marriage. The remaining debt of bridewealth symbolized a continuing bond or social commitment between the relatives and clans of the two parties. Such a debt could outlast the lives of marriage partners to be paid by their children (often the eldest son) long after death of the father. Therefore, full settlement of bridewealth was ruled out by both parties, because it would imply an end to the relationship or covenant between the wife's and husband's clans and relatives with all the social, economic, and political benefits that were attached to the covenant.

A *wedding* may involve a traditional ritual ceremony or a modern church/mosque ceremony, both, or neither. Said one man: "There was no ceremony, but we are married because I paid the bridewealth." Bridewealth and polygyny are traditional patrilineal practices that indicate the value of a woman's productivity and reproductive capacity.

The vast majority of Kenyans marry at least once, but the normative history of Kenyan societies involves *polygyny,* or multiple wives. This, however, is a diminishing phenomenon. One-third of the fathers of our Kikuyu respondents were polygynous, while only 16% of the 30 to 40-year-old men have (or expect to have) more than one wife (Adams & Mburugu, 1994). According to the KDHS, the differences in polygyny are dramatic between regions. As recently as 1984, the percentages of Kikuyu, Kamba, and Meru/ Embu women in polygynous unions were 11, 15, and 14, respectively. In contrast, 41% of Luo women (near the Lake) and 40% of coastal Mijikenda women were polygynous (KDHS, 1994).

Polygyny is observed to be declining in Kenya. According to the 1977–1978 Kenya Fertility Survey (KFS), 30% of the currently married women were in polygynous unions. In the 1998 KDHS report it was shown that the incidence of polygyny had declined to 16% among the currently married women. The proportions of married women in polygynous unions in 1998 ranged from

29% among women with no education to 11% among women with at least some secondary education. This shows that education is a strong deterrent to polygynous marriages. Data for currently married men in 1998 show that 10% of them were in polygynous unions, but this varied widely according to the age of the man. For ages below 30, around 2% to 3% of men are in polygamous union compared with around 15% of men aged 40 and above (CBS, 1999, pp. 68–69).

According to the Kilbrides, writing in 1990, the advantages of polygyny are the following: (1) Economically, it provides a large pool of laborers, so that wage labor can be avoided; (2) it enhances the personal and political power provided to men, though Remi Clignet argues that it may also increase a woman's power (Clignet, 1970); and (3) men mentioned an emotional advantage, while women spoke of protection. The major disadvantages, according to both genders, include the following: (1) jealousy, envy, and/or hatred among cowives and their children, the result of the husband not sharing love and resources equally; and (2) disadvantages concerning religious and ceremonial activity (Kilbride & Kilbride, 1990, pp. 203–204).

Our polygyny-inclined Kikuyu respondents give several reasons for wanting multiple wives. "My wife and I do not have children, and they are the ones that make life a success—so a second wife may be necessary." Another man said, "When my wife grows old, I'll need a younger wife." The traditional norm was affirmed by another man: "I don't see anything wrong with many wives if one is capable of supporting them." Still another said "maybe," noting the tension between tradition and cost: "I don't think I have enough money, but with money it would be quite commendable." In rare instances, as Kayongo-Male and Onyango point out, a wife may ask her husband to get another wife if her work is too much (1984, p. 25).

According to the 1998 KDHS, older women are more likely to be in polygynous unions than younger women, and rural women are more likely than their urban counterparts. Substantial provincial variations in the practice of polygamy (polygyny) exist, with Central Province (dominated by Kikuyu people) having the lowest level of polygyny (4%) and Nyanza Province (dominated by Luo people) along with Coast Province (dominated by Mijikenda people) having the highest levels of polygyny (24% and 21%, respectively).

This leads to the reasons for monogamy. Several referred to Christian beliefs, saying "I have been saved." One man expressed the unwillingness of a woman to agree to polygyny: "I have a girlfriend I love so much I would like to take her as a second wife. However, she doesn't want to be a second wife." The vast majority of comments echo those of Michael O'Leary speaking of the Akamba: "With the rise both in the levels of acceptable standard of living and its cost, polygyny has become prohibitive even for the large cattle owner unless he also has substantial off-farm income" (1984, p. 123). It is not just cost in objective terms, but also rising expectations, that limit polygyny. (On this and other issues among the Akamba, see Ndeti, 1972.)

Not only is the prevalence of polygyny diminishing, but it is becoming less localized, so that kin and community control over the pairing process is reduced. For example, one wife may be in the rural area and another in the city—especially when the male is a city dweller. However, urban life itself reduces the prevalence of polygyny. Some authors, such as O'Leary, simply say cost is the primary problem (1984). Others, as noted previously, mention the Christian emphasis on monogamy. Helen Ware states that education works against polygyny, especially increasing the opposition of educated women (1979). Alfred Ukaegbo, writing about Nigeria, says that men still approve of it, but only the old and uneducated actually do it (1977). As we noted, however, such changes are taking place much more slowly among the Luo and Mijikenda than in the central highlands.

Another issue in partner selection is *hypergamy*—or the woman marrying a higher-status man. Little has been written about this, but in rural Kenya the bridewealth helps to balance the status of the parties and their kin. If the woman is of higher status, a marriage will require a larger bridewealth on the part of the man's family. In urban Kenya, however, hypergamy is likely. Educated urban males often express the desire for a rural wife (usually from their home region), because the educated urban woman is "too hard to control." Likewise, the high-status urban female may find it difficult to marry at all—though this is hardly unique to Kenya.

Besides being shunned by the educated urban male, the high-status urban female finds it difficult to marry due to three major reasons: First, she may desire to be free from control by a man and voluntarily choose to remain single and independent. In particular, she may desire freedom in reproductive choices and in the use of resources she generates. Second, she may fear losing face and esteem (both self-esteem and the esteem of others) if she marries the easily accessible low-status man. The societal expectation is that a woman should marry a man at least of equal status to herself, if not a man of higher status. To marry downward in status would lower the dignity and respect accorded to the woman. Third, the high-status urban female may be "too old" to compete with younger women in the prime years of marriage. At best, she can marry older men within her status group, but because these men are already married, she can only opt to marry as a second or third wife—an option she may find difficult to accept.

Although educated men avoid marrying high-status women, these men prefer strong friendship ties with the women to whom they secretly extend the rights of married women. In most cases, these men are already married but secretly maintain intimate relationships with high-status single women, by whom they proceed to have children without the knowledge of the wife. These forms of relationships have resulted in what is commonly known as "informal polygamy" or having "secret wives."

3. FERTILITY AND SOCIALIZATION: HAVING AND RAISING CHILDREN

Fertility Trends

The important measures of fertility are total fertility rate (TFR), children ever born (CEB), and fertility preferences and expectations. For each of these measures, it would be interesting to examine differentials by age, residence, province/region, and education—depending on the available data. In the 1970s, Kenya had the highest fertility level in the world. Since then, the country has undergone what could be considered one of the most dramatic fertility transitions in human history. The total fertility rate declined by 20% from about eight children per woman in 1977 to 6.6 children per woman in 1989. A further decline of 17% was recorded between 1989 and 1993, when the total fertility rate was estimated at 5.4 children per woman (Brass & Jolly, 1993; CBS, 1999). It is further shown that total fertility declined by 13% from 5.4 in 1993 to 4.7 in 1998 (CBS, 1999).

Provincial/regional differences show that Nairobi, with a TFR of 3.4 in 1993 and 2.6 in 1998, had the lowest fertility of any region, followed closely by Central Province, where the TFR was 3.9 and 3.7 in the respective years. On the other hand, Western Province, with a TFR of 6.4 and 5.6 in the respective years, had the highest fertility. The other provinces, namely Coast, Eastern, Nyanza, and Rift

Table 1.1   Mean Number of Children Ever Born by Kenyan Women by Data Source
(1989–1999)

Age Group	1989 Census	1993 KDHS	1999 Census
15–19	0.27	0.20	0.28
20–24	1.56	1.36	1.35
25–29	3.25	3.13	2.61
30–34	4.89	4.53	4.15
35–39	6.05	6.13	5.39
40–44	6.87	6.95	6.38
45–49	7.21	7.87	6.95

Valley, with TFRs of 5.1, 4.7, 5.0, and 5.3 respectively in 1998, fall between the two extremes of Nairobi and Western Provinces.

A major determinant of variations in fertility is education, a factor that largely explains fertility differentials by residence (urban vs. rural areas) and region. Regions such as Nairobi and Central Province are also regions dominated by the Kikuyu people, in which group women's education is considerably higher than in other groups. The central role of education in fertility differentials is shown in the 1993 KDHS and 1998 KDHS, where it is observed that women with no education had a TFR of 6.0 and 5.8, respectively, whereas women with secondary education or above had a TFR of 4.0 and 3.5 in the respective periods.

Children Ever Born

The average number of CEB, or lifetime fertility at the time of the census or survey, largely varies by age of woman. Age-determined variations can further be differentiated by ethnicity or region, and education. Age differentials in children ever born also indicate the momentum of childbearing. Table 1.1 shows mean number of children ever born according to age of woman during the 1989–1999 period.

The mean number of children ever born from the 1999 census shows a consistent decline compared with the 1989 census for all age-groups except 15 to 19 years. The decline is greatest among women aged 25 to 29 and 30 to 34 years, while the rise in age-group 15 to 19 is insignificant. Indeed, age-groups 20 to 39 years experienced a significant decline as follows: 13.5% for age-group 20 to 24 years, 19.7% for age-group 25 to 29 years, 15.1% for age-group 30 to 34, and 10.9% for age-group 35 to 39 years. On average, women in their late twenties, according to the 1999 census, have given birth to almost three children, women in their late thirties have had over five children, and women currently at the end of their childbearing years have had nearly seven children.

The average number of children ever born also varies by education, ethnicity, and type of residence. A general belief exists that education makes for lower fertility. Analysis of data from selected regions of Kenya show significant effects of education on CEB for both women and men (Mburugu & Adams,

Table 1.2   Mean Number of Children Ever Born by Women and Men Aged 39–45 Years From Selected Regions of Kenya by Levels of Education

Level of Education	Mean Children Ever Born	
	Women	Men
No education	4.7	5.6
Some primary	4.2	4.3
Completed primary	3.7	3.3
Secondary and above	2.6	2.6

2001). This is clearly shown in Table 1.2, where analysis is restricted to women and men aged 39 to 45 years.

A difference of slightly more than two children exists between women with no education and women with at least some secondary education. For men, the differences by education are even greater than for women, in part because of the greater likelihood of polygyny on the part of the less-educated men.

Ethnically, available data show that the mean numbers of children ever born among the Kikuyu of Nairobi and Central Province, the Akamba of Eastern Province, and the Mijikenda of Coast Province are 2.9, 3.5, and 3.6 respectively.

Concerning the type of residence, the median numbers of children ever born in urban and rural areas are 3.8 and 4.5, respectively. Yet, when education is controlled, most of the rural-urban difference disappears. Overall, it is not surprising that age accounts for most of the difference in fertility, but within age categories, the key factor is education.

Fertility Preferences and Expectations

The decline in fertility over the past 20 years is a consequence of declining desire for many children. An increasing number of married women no longer desire to have large families of six or more children and use contraceptives to avoid excess fertility. The ideal number of children has consistently declined from 6.2 in 1977, to 5.8 in 1984, 4.4 in 1989, and 3.8 in 1999 (CBS, 1999). It has been argued that the emerging concept of the "small family norm" is a product of severe social and economic strains as well as a product of the Kenya mass media, which has actively highlighted the many benefits of a small family vis-à-vis the problems of a large family in modern Kenyan society (Dow & Linda, 1983; Brass & Jolly, 1993; Westoff & Rodriguez, 1995).

Although the overall ideal family size has remained close to four children over the past decade, it increases with the actual number of living children. The mean ideal number of children increases from 3.3 among childless women to 5.1 among women with six or more children (CBS, 1999, pp. 85–86). (Of course, 5.1 is still fewer than they have!) There are several possible explanations for the relationship between ideal and actual number of children. First, to the extent that women are able to implement their preferences, those who want smaller families will tend to actually have them, and vice versa. Second, those who have large families may simply rationalize their family size. Third, older women with larger families may indeed have large ideal family sizes, as a consequence of the norm they acquired when growing up in the traditional social and cultural setting.

A most interesting expectation by women is based on the gender of the children they already have. Women with one boy at present expect to have 2.4 children; and if they have one girl they expect to have 2.7 children at completed fertility. For women with two boys or two girls, the expectations are 2.8 and 3.4 children, respectively. If they have three boys, they expect 3.3 children when fertility is completed, and with three girls and no boys, they expect four children—meaning that they will try once more to have a boy. This clearly shows a preference for boy children. However, by the time they reach four boys and no girls or four girls and no boys, women expect to have 4.5 children in either case. What this means is that the birth of a second or third girl, with no boys, results in their expectation of trying at least once more to have a boy. But a fourth girl results in many parents giving up the attempt to produce a male offspring.

Infertility

Infertility, whether primary or secondary, is not expected by couples who decide to marry in Kenya. Indeed the major reason for marriage, not only in Kenya but in other African societies, is to have children. A woman who cannot or decides not to have children is an object of pity in the family and the society at large. The percentage of women aged 45 to 49 who have never had children provides an indicator of the level of primary infertility, that is, the proportion of women who are unable to have children at all. It is estimated that primary infertility in Kenya is low—about 1%.

Infertility in Kenyan societies does not always result in divorce, though in some cases it does, while in others it results in seeking a second wife. Among the Nandi of western Kenya, "Childlessness in itself was not considered adequate grounds for divorce; there had to be indications of irretrievable breakdown or evidence of exceptional circumstances" (Langley, 1979). In our study of four societies in Kenya, one of the rural women respondents stated, "We divorced after two years because I was incapable of giving birth." Another woman said, "Since I can't give birth and people in my village know it, no man wants to be associated with me" (Mburugu & Adams, 2001).

The male response may be divorce, or it may be to seek a second wife. One rural man had this to say: "My relatives keep telling me to get a second wife, since mine is barren." Another man stated clearly: "I might marry another wife because we cannot have children and they are the ones that make life a success. Without them, life is useless." All these comments were made by rural respondents. These types of comments are much less likely to come from urban dwellers, especially the educated ones.

On Raising Children

Childcare is a challenging task for the increasing number of working women with young children, particularly in urban areas. A national survey of women in the reproductive years (i.e., aged 15–49) shows that slightly over one-half (52%) of employed women have a child under age 6 (CBS, 1999, p. 27).

On being asked to indicate the person who takes care of the child, 42% of the employed women who have a child under 6 said they look after their own child(ren) while at work, and 17% said they have relatives (other than husband) to look after their children. In 15% of the cases, another older child (usually female) minds the young child. Women with more education and who reside in urban areas (especially Nairobi) use a hired worker to take care of the young child, and are less likely to use some other child (male or female).

A study on childcare arrangements for children under 3 years of age in five Kenyan districts showed that different childcare arrangements were used in different environments. In Siaya and Kilifi Districts, mothers were the main caregivers. In Kericho District, mothers utilized institutional childcare services, since they could not simultaneously combine work with childcare. In Narok District, grandmothers were the main caregivers, while in the Nairobi slums siblings and child-minders were used (National Center for Early Childhood and Education [NACECE], 1992). In Laikipia District, it was found that 71% of the families with children aged below 6 years indicated maternal care to be the predominant childcare arrangement. This came in the form of maternal care at home (31%), maternal care at the farm (29%), maternal care at the business premises (9%), and maternal care at the employer's premises (2%). Childcare in nursery schools involved 17% of the families with children under age 6. Other types of childcare arrangements such as support by extended family (5%), support by siblings (4%), and house help (1%) were insignificant. The findings imply that as families become nuclear and schooling undercuts availability of siblings, only maternal care arrangements and the nursery school gain preeminence as childcare arrangements (Mwakera, 2003, pp. 28–30).

The options available for childcare are quickly changing from traditional forms of care to modern forms that entail social and economic costs. Traditionally, the rural mother is still to be seen carrying her baby to all manner of places including the marketplace, the river, the farm plot (*shamba*), village meetings, and so on, an example that is sometimes emulated by the mother in urban areas. If there is no reliable person to leave the child with at home, this trend remains the most

attractive option for both baby and mother despite the extra "load/weight" the mother has to bear. This way, the baby is wrapped in security and can feed on demand.

The urban environment, with its thick morning and evening traffic and long distances to cover to the marketplace or workplace, is not convenient for the mother carrying a baby. The urban society is also not tolerant of the inconvenience of baby/child company. In the words of a woman educator in Kenya: "A mother is almost always made to feel guilty that she brought her baby to church or meetings. It is as if the only outing a baby should have is to the MHC clinic" (Gachukia, 1989, p. 91).

Though diminishing in importance, the care of children through the extended family is widely practiced in rural areas. It is common to find a grandmother tending a compound and overseeing the welfare of young children while their mothers are attending other duties—a practice that is of mutual benefit to all parties involved. The elderly feel wanted and needed; they have something to offer. They command experience and have loving care to offer to the young and are experts in the socialization process. Furthermore, grandmothers, even the elderly, are good supervisors (Gachukia, 1989, p. 92). A few of our urban respondents indicated that their children are being raised by rural grandparents.

An important question we asked was whether parents see child raising as easier, harder, or about the same as when they were children. About 75% see raising children as more difficult, with the perception being even greater for rural respondents. Only 10% report that it is easier, with the rest believing it to be about the same. The primary complaint of those who find it harder has to do with expense. Expenses fall into three categories. First, there is the cost of education. Even the rural parents believe that their children need an education. School tuition is part of the cost, and another is school supplies, including uniforms. This brings us to a second expense factor: clothing. Not just school uniforms, but other clothing is costly today. The third expense factor concerns children's demands for the toys and treats related to modern urban life.

The second parental complaint is that children do not respect or listen to their parents as they once did. This concern, again, is not unique to Kenya. A general feeling on the part of parents is that lack of control over children is coupled with a lack of respect from the children. Several respondents noted that, when they were young, they entered a room on their knees when a parent or grandparent was present. Of course, any of the factors that make children more independent and self-reliant—such as education—are also related to a lessening of expressed respect.

Those few who indicated that child-rearing is easier today are almost all well-to-do urbanites, who can afford to pay for someone—usually a housegirl—to help with their children. This lessens the amount of time and energy the parent (primarily the mother) has to spend caring for children (Mburugu & Adams, 2001, pp. 30–31).

Another issue concerns discipline. On the physical disciplining of children, Kayongo-Male and Onyango note that

> [p]arents are more likely than other agents to use physical punishment. Beatings were usually given by fathers, though in polygamous households the mothers were more involved in physically disciplining children. (1984, p. 22)

4 & 5. MALES AND FEMALES: GENDER AND MARITAL RELATIONS

Traditionally, the patrilineal Kenyan male has had authority and power, yet this is not a simple issue. Niara Sudarkasa says that a certain amount of gender equality preceded colonialism and gave way to expatriate or colonial preference for dealing with males (Sudarkasa, 1994). One of our rural women said, "I am always under my husband's authority, but I have to make good decisions on how to run my shop." For polygyny, as the number of wives increases, the husband spends less time with each wife, and thus each gains more influence over her life and children. In addition, each subsequent wife tends to have less power than the previous one (Kayongo-Male & Onyango, 1984, p. 30).

According to the 2001 report, among the Mijikenda and Akamba, either the husband makes household decisions or a couple makes them together. When the respondents' comments about their decisions are compared with their perception of their own parents' decision making, it is obvious that there has been a change toward, but not to, equalitarianism. However, when couples decide together, it often means that they actually make decisions in separate domains, with the wife making child-rearing and a few household decisions.

When the husband is away, the wife becomes used to making decisions regarding property, finances, disciplining children, and the like. This makes it difficult to accept the husband's authority when he returns home (Kayongo-Male & Onyango, 1984, p. 63). These authors continue: While the urban woman may be the boss of her office, at home she is expected to be a "good African woman," defined as "one who keeps her household together, runs it efficiently, brings up the children, and welcomes anybody home with a wide smile on her face, and produces sons and daughters as God may allow" (1984, p. 69).

This point brings us to the fact that the gender division of labor, as noted by Kabwegyere (1982) and others is traditionally quite clearly demarcated. Iona Mayer describes the traditional separation of labor and activity among the Gusii:

> Men and women . . . were seldom if ever allowed to play the same parts, or play them in the same ways. Some roles and activities were reserved for one sex; only men could make ropes, or work with iron, only women could cook, tend the household fire, or brew beer. . . . Some were joint activities but the sexes had clearly articulated roles; in hut-building, men put up the framework, women plastered it. Many things were done by both sexes but done with a difference. . . . They routinely received different meat portions from the same animals. Their spheres were also divided in the literal sense of physical space. (1975, p. 266)

The particularly heavy duties that custom lays upon women are raising the children, providing food from the garden, doing most of the farm work, getting water and firewood, thatching and plastering huts, and carrying loads to market (Cavicchi, 1977). One of our rural male respondents made the power/division of labor distinction very clear: "Even if milk is boiling on the fire, I cannot remove it." The wife wakes up early to make sure "warm water is available for the husband's bath, and that the children are prepared for school" (Kayongo-Male & Onyango, 1984, p. 69).

The Kenyan research carried out by Mburugu and Adams shows that wives spend three times as many hours doing housework, and twice as much time caring for the children, as the husbands do. The differences in housework and childcare by gender are greater among the Mijikenda than among the Akamba. However, this is not accounted for by Akamba men being more likely to help, but by the fact that a substantial minority of Akamba households have paid help (Mburugu & Adams, 2001, p. 24).

The complexity of gender relations was made plain by Margarethe Silberschmidt in 1992. Writing about the Kisii of western Kenya, she questioned whether perhaps men had become the weaker sex. In 1900, she says, men's influence was due to control over women, herds, bridewealth, and heirs. But as men became migrant workers, their wage work was less important than women's agricultural productivity. In fact, says Silberschmidt, men's identity crisis often results in alcohol problems. Women produce *changaa*, men buy and drink it, and children's school fees are thus paid for by the women. Dignity, self-control, and wealth are unattainable for most men (1992, p. 247). Women may call men "heads" and "owners," but they believe that only women can plan. And while some women wish their men would die, without a man, the woman still has no status. "Even an alcoholic husband is better than none since, at least, the wife has access to his land" (1992, p. 253). While both genders have changed, women's changes have been emancipatory.

Land Use

Kenyan land is owned or controlled by the patrilineage. The rural woman joins the husband on his land. An important part of marital relations concerns the use of this land. Until independence, women did most of the cultivating, while men cleared land and boys looked after the livestock. As men move to the city, the women and boys have even more responsibility for the land. But if land use changes from subsistence to cash cropping or commercial farming, the man is likely to control both the land and the income derived therefrom. Beth Brockland says it simply: "Cash cropping was, and remains, largely seen as a 'male' activity in African societies" (2000, p. 19). Likewise, land previously available to women for subsistence agriculture has been gradually taken away and used for cash cropping. But, despite the distinction in land use by gender for subsistence and cash cropping, it is not as rigidly defined as it once was (Brockland, 2000, p. 25).

Satisfaction

Studies from many societies show that women are likely to be satisfied with their role in the family division of labor, despite the fact that they ordinarily do more work than men. This is due to a division of labor ideology. In the Mburugu-Adams research, more than one-half of the Akamba and Mijikenda women and men say they are satisfied with the division of labor (though not completely so). However, the Mijikenda women are less content than the Akamba with both their contribution and that of their husbands, though more than one-half are satisfied (Brockland, 2000, p. 34).

6. FAMILY STRESSES AND PROBLEMS

Other than occasional features on family issues (often concerning domestic violence) in newspapers and magazines, few major studies have been carried out on family problems in Kenya. However, Population Communications Africa (PCA) undertook a major study in 2000–2001 focusing on violence and abuse of women in Kenya. The survey covered some 1,664 women and girls aged between 17 and 77 years, together with two smaller matching samples totaling 445 men and boys in six of the eight provinces of Kenya (Johnston, 2002). The emphasis in the study was on the more overt and violent forms of abuse—physical and sexual abuse—without obscuring the fact that these types of bodily assault also carry an associated verbal (insult) component, which invariably combine to generate emotional abuse.

In general, the proportion of women who reported abuse in adulthood varied as follows according to type of abuse: physical abuse (52%), sexual abuse (41%), verbal abuse (64%), and emotional abuse (54%). On being asked to indicate whether the most recent physical and/or sexual abuse experiences was/were still continuing, 43% claimed the abuse to be currently ongoing, 52% claiming the abuse occurred with increasing frequency. Indeed, a telling example of physical abuse was reported in a newspaper article with the title "Battered for the Pill," which told of a wife who was terrorized by her knife-wielding husband, and for 4 hours was constantly bashed and beaten. The crime she had committed was to take (oral) contraceptives without his knowledge ("Battered for the Pill," 2001).

The patterns of abuse among married women show that 37% are abused daily, 21% on Christmas Day, 17% on payday (mostly end of month), 12% on weekends, and 8% on New Year's Day. Contrary to expectation, it seems that Christmas day is not always a day of peace and goodwill (Johnston, 2002, p. 20).

In Kenya, marriage brings young women into new extended family relationships. This is typically the case in rural areas. In doing so, marriage introduces a new set of potential and, too often, actual abusers. The predominant abusers reported by married women are husbands or partners, and mothers- and fathers-in-law. These three categories of within-family physical abusers are responsible for 62% of reported domestic violence. Second, the young wife's life is made physically uncomfortable by her own parents, cousins, grandparents, uncles, and aunts. Within the family, sexual abusers (often through unwanted sexual touch/rape) are husbands/partners, fathers-in-law, cousins (male, both sides), fathers, stepfathers, brothers-in-law, grandfathers (both sides) and uncles (both sides). It is to be noted here that the gender abuse of married women is a two-sided process. The abusers are males from the wife's family and from her husband's family-in-law. Also worth noting is that mothers-in-law are the leaders in verbal sexual insults and innuendos (Johnston, 2002, pp. 28–30).

The causes of abuse can be grouped into gender-role prescriptions and gender perceptions on culture and tradition. Kenyan married couples tend to have both similar and different perceptions of their ideal roles as husbands and wives. It is shown that Kenyan married men's perceptions of their role as an ideal husband were to protect the well-being of the family and household, to produce and provide for the family, to respond to the sexual desires of their wife/partner, and to provide their wife or partner with company and comradeship. On the other hand, their perceptions of the roles of an ideal wife were to produce and care for children, to prepare food for the family, to respond to the sexual desires of the husband, to provide marital/relational comradeship, to fetch water, food, and firewood, to keep the household compound tidy, and to buy and sell farm (*shamba*) products.

Kenyan women largely agree with their husbands that wives should be obedient—mindful and careful of their duties. The woman's perceptions of the role of an ideal wife were that she should be loyal and obedient to her husband (and his family elders), able to bear and raise children, careful of the welfare of children, mindful of her duties about the home and farm plot (*shamba*), and willing and able to care for family members who are sick (or disabled).

Thus the Kenyan men see themselves as the masters, protectors, and providers for the family. They perceive their wives to be their sexual and household servants. On the other hand, the Kenyan wives appear to want their husbands to be responsible. In return, they would be loyal and obedient subjects of their master, who they hope would treat them

well. It is worth noting that the women are focusing on values, feelings, and emotions.

Concerning culture and tradition, there are very significant differences in physical and sexual abuse and violence rates from different provinces. In Kenya, the provinces are largely coterminous with cultural (ethnic) groups. For example, Central Province consists of the Kikuyu people, Nyanza Province consists of the Luo people, Western Province consists of the Luhya people, and Coast Province consists of the Mijikenda people (though residential movement has made this somewhat less so). It is thought that differences in physical and sexual abuse are due in major part to varying cultural and traditional practices, which affect the social and economic status of women. The percentage of Kenyan women surveyed who reported physical and sexual abuse is shown in Table 1.3.

The traditions with a known impact on of women include the following: female genital mutilation, arranged marriage, dowry (brideprice), polygyny, wife inheritance, exclusion of women from decision making councils, and obedience/submissiveness.

About 55% of our married respondents indicated that they have at least one major marital problem. The most prevalent ones mentioned are decision making, finances, drinking, and beating (Mburugu & Adams, 2001, p. 27). Quite a few women indicated that their husbands drank heavily. This, in many cases, led to violence against the wife and children. Goldschmidt says that beating and quarreling are common, and the wife is expected to accept beating without complaint. However, the woman can use both her tongue and, traditionally, magic against her husband (1976, p. 227). Routine beatings are not grounds for divorce, but in our study one man, looking at it today, stated, "My wife left me because I beat her; I believe a woman should be beaten once in a while."[1]

A final issue noted by a few rural women was that their husband had a mistress in the

Table 1.3 Percentage Distribution

Province	Physical Abuse	Sexual Abuse
Central	71.5	67.4
Nyanza	58.2	51.4
Coast	47.8	38.7
Rift Valley	30.4	29.5
Nairobi	23.1	14.5
Western	21.8	12.6

city. This was also mentioned by some urban men—but as a fact, not as a problem.

7. DIVORCE, SEPARATION, AND REMARRIAGE

Divorce and separation are not as prevalent in patrilineal societies as they are in matrilineal, since in the latter the woman does not lose much in divorce (Kayongo-Male & Onyango, 1984, pp. 28–29). In Kenya the percentage divorced, according to the KDHS, is slightly over 4 for those ever married. Our study of the Kikuyu shows the percentage of those ever married who are either separated or divorced to be just over 7 (KDHS, 1994, p. 61; Mburugu & Adams, 2001, p. 28). As the Kilbrides note, divorce is a growing phenomenon in East Africa, especially in Nairobi (1990, p. 222).

Earlier we noted that infertility sometimes leads to taking a second wife. In some cases even a separation results in a new marriage: "If my wife refuses to come back, I might marry another one." However, instead of a second wife, infertility may bring a divorce. One of our rural female respondents said: "We divorced after two years because I was incapable of giving birth." Another woman

argued similarly: "My in-laws feel I should be divorced because I can't have a baby." A third stated: "Since I can't give birth and people in my village know it, no man wants to be associated with me."

While infertility is sometimes a reason given for the husband divorcing the wife, among the Nandi of western Kenya, it was not considered adequate grounds (Langley, 1979, p. 96). And, while customary divorce is exceptional today, modern court-sanctioned divorce occurs in cases of "repeated acts of adultery, refusal of conjugal rights, continuous quarrelsomeness, incompatibility of husband and wife, and conviction of the wife for sorcery" (Langley, 1979, p. 96).

As for reasons given by the wife, first, she may be unwilling to be beaten. As one man said, "My wife left me because I beat her; I believe a woman should be beaten once in a while." A second reason for the wife separating is her success and desire for equality. A rural Kikuyu stated, "Equality broke my marriage. My educated wife expected me to cook and wash clothes. This is unheard of in this society." Traditionally, as already noted, power was in the hands of the husband and his male relatives. However, today educated Kenyan women are less willing to tolerate this situation. They may separate from either an authoritarian *or* a dependent man. By a dependent man we mean one who has either no job or a poor job, and who is willing to live off of his wife's income. A woman with a good job simply does not need to put up with an unsatisfactory marriage. So the reasons for divorce in Kenya include the following: (1) childlessness, (2) family violence, (3) wife's economic independence and desire for equality, and (4) husband's economic dependence. Not surprisingly, the rate of divorce is lowest among Kenyan Muslims and is the next lowest for Catholics.

While divorce is more prevalent today than in the recent past, desertion is an alternative. Writing about the Kwaya of Tanzania, Huber says that it is "not very easy to meet an elderly man in Bukwaya who has not been deserted by one or more of his spouses, the same as elderly women staying with their first husbands are relatively rare" (1973, p. 167).

The taking of a second wife is more prevalent in Kenya than is a divorce and remarriage, though the latter does occur. One of our male respondents tried several marriages, and described the experience thus: "I have married three times. The first wife—the mother of my children—died. The second divorced me, and the third left me. Now I am alone; I have two relationships, but will never marry again." Thus, in many cases a divorce is followed by singlehood. One woman said, "I am so much happier than when I was married. I never used to have any freedom, and now I do."

8. KINSHIP

Kinship is an issue that has arisen from time to time in the preceding discussions, for example, in discussing child-rearing and land use. Kinship, says Jane Guyer, is "as important at the top of the social scale for maintaining privilege as it is at the bottom for

determining forms of poverty" and aid for survival (1981, p. 112).

Let us begin by saying more about the patrilineage, or the passing of property and privilege through the male line (see Lambert, 1956, on the Kikuyu). In an insightful discussion, Ivan Karp argues that "the fact that people hold to an articulated patrilineal ideology may not imply that groups are exclusively organized by this" (1978, p. 92). The key issue in patriliny is *inheritance*. Snell's discussion of the Nandi and Ocholla-Ayayo's of the Luo are particularly helpful. We will not try to cover all the issues raised by Snell, but here are some: (1) Property stays in the patrilineal clan; (2) cattle are inherited only by males; (3) the principal heir is the senior son, who is the executor; (4) if the beneficiary is a child, the property is held in trust; (5) in cases of polygyny, wives acquire seniority in order of marriage to their husband; (6) male personal items are inherited by sons, and female personal items by daughters; and, finally, (7) distribution takes place at the man's house with witnesses (1954, pp. 51–52).

Ocholla-Ayayo describes Luo land inheritance as follows:

> The senior son takes the centre portion of all the land of the homestead. (However) a youngest son may remain in the village of the father to care for him in his old age. His inheritance is the last property, called Mondo, and the remaining gardens of his mother. (1976, p. 129)

Ocholla-Ayayo goes on to discuss court cases in which land is disputed within the lineage. He also describes the *levirate* among the Luo. If a man dies without a male heir, the land reverts to his father's line. The wife may then produce an heir through her dead husband's brother, or she may call on "a close agnatic kinsman of her dead husband to cohabit and serve as genitor" (1976, p. 131).

The Mburugu-Adams data on the four Kenyan societies show that today there is substantial deviation from the patrilineal principle of land inheritance. In these data, 55% of the property belongs to the male, 30% to the adult female, and about 15% is owned jointly (2001, p. 19). Thus, the patrilineal principle, while still at work, is not as strong as it once was ideologically.

Besides inheritance, other kin issues exist. One is assistance—monetary and otherwise. O'Leary, speaking of the Akamba, says very simply, "one must assist kin and kin are expected to pull their weight in the relationship" (1984, p. 106). Poor kin and neighbors have their land ploughed for free, says O'Leary. A son-in-law "organized a *mwethya* of 34 people for his parents-in-law. . . . In so doing he was fulfilling affinal obligations as well as courting favors of his father-in-law who was an influential local leader" (O'Leary, 1984, p. 105).

Ferraro distinguishes between old-time Nairobians, new arrivals, and rural Kikuyu. Monetary assistance is greatest from the new arrivals, followed by the old-timers, and then the ruralites. Ferraro's plausible explanation is "the relative affluence (as well as the extent of participation in the urban market economy) of each of the three samples" (1973, p. 223). The new arrivals are likely to provide subsidies to their rural kin, making the economic disparity between urban and rural kin less than it would otherwise be. Most of the economic assistance to kin goes either to elder kinsmen or to school-age relatives who need help with school fees.

Another form of aid to school-age kin is housing. The authors know a coastal Kenyan who raised 29 teenagers during their secondary school years, because he was much better off financially than their parents.

The third issue in kinship, also discussed by Ferraro, is what he calls the "Kinship-Recreational Role Overlap" (1973, pp. 224, 226). Recreational activities include both prearranged visiting, either in town or in the village, and "the more fortuitous meetings of individuals in tea kiosks, beer bars, or on the street" (1973, p. 224). Prearranged visits are more frequent as "stopping-in" becomes less so—both in Kenya and in other parts of the world. Ferraro notes that it is sometimes impossible to distinguish the recreational component in actual situations. "For example, the man who goes . . . in search of employment will be interacting on two distinct, yet interrelated, levels, the economic and the recreational" (1973, p. 224).

One further factor that increases urban kin visiting is unemployment. Kin simply lack the opportunity to visit with coworkers. In addition, the unemployed are more dependent on kin for survival, as we noted earlier. Arguing with other writers, Ferraro concludes that urbanization has not truncated or substantially weakened kin ties. However, he was writing in 1973, and it is doubtful that the past 30 years have seen no weakening effect on lineage and kin ties in general.

What are the results of kin assistance? Kayongo-Male and Onyango summarize these well:

> The ethic of sharing resources within the extended family unit reduces the amount of accumulation of wealth and partially limits the formation of rigid class groupings. The wealthier family members are still expected to assist the poorer members by paying for school fees, providing accommodation for relatives who are at school or seeking work, or by offering small loans for various emergencies. (1984, p. 41)

9. AGING AND DEATH

In the previous section we noted the ways in which the elderly may be helped by their kin. Maria Cattell, writing about the Samia (part of the Luyia), describes the way in which sons and daughters care for and feed parents too old to work (1990, p. 382). Most often it is the last-born son who cares for the elderly or widowed mother, and sometimes the father.

The elderly give advice, though they are less likely to be listened to today than a generation ago. At death they are likely to be honored. However, recently disputes over burial location have gone to court, with the wife of a different ethnic group fighting to have her husband buried in her home area, instead of on the ancestral land.

10. FAMILY AND OTHER INSTITUTIONS

Economics

We have spoken of the economics of the patrilineage. However, Guyer notes that "land and labor are too narrow an interpretation of resources for African societies" (1981, p. 124). Commoditization and relations of production are hardly under the control of the patriline. As Guyer says, "The very difficult problem of understanding patterns of commoditization is particularly challenging to methodologies built around lineage or household or models of market penetration . . . or demand" (1981, p. 116).

Urban work gives young adults the financial capability to escape the power of the elderly. On the other hand, "large numbers of urbanites sell goods and services in a highly competitive situation with a minimum of capital investment and a narrow margin of profit" (Ferraro, 1973, p. 222). This means that the entrepreneur will often employ kin to work in their enterprises for a minimum of wages, but with housing and other services provided by the employer.

Another issue in the relationship between economics and family in Kenya is that "the family, through the husband, tends to limit the scale at which women can trade by altering responsibilities in response to women's trading income" (Kayongo-Male & Onyango, 1984, p. 43). The fact that female enterprises are limited, and that the husband may expect to control a wife's income, are reasons why an educated or successful Kenyan woman may be unwilling to stay in such a relationship, as we noted in the discussion of divorce.

Education

The three issues we will refer to in this section are gender differences, types of education, and university training. The presupposition in postcolonial Kenya has been that boys will receive more formal education than girls. This is, however, an oversimplification. Jean Davison reports that a minority of Kenyan mothers prefer to educate their daughters so they will not forget their families (1993, p. 333). Daughters, says Davison, will assist younger siblings and old parents, while educated sons become urban and forget family. But the majority still favor education for males. In fact, the 1994 KDHS reports that there is little difference by gender in the percentage of 6 to 15-year-olds in school, but for 16 to 20-year-olds the percentages are 52.2 for boys and 35.6 for girls (KDHS, 1994, p. 13).

While attitudes toward education for girls have improved, the preferred curriculum choices are still nursing or teaching (Davison, 1993, p. 336), and African education in general may be less than appropriate. School emphasis on the liberal arts does not prepare children for the technical skills needed today. But even a technical education "has not been useful to most children since the market for the skills acquired has not been growing at a similar pace." This also applies to commercial education (Kayongo-Male & Onyango, 1984, p. 92).

In fact, the relationship between education and the occupational marketplace is a well-known problem. Not only may the type of education be inappropriate, but education has outrun opportunity. Rees Hughes points out that for the decades of 1967 to 1987 "the University of Nairobi has grown in excess of 15% annually. Concurrently, private-sector employment has grown at 2.5% annually" (1987, p. 583). University graduates from high-status families are more likely to find high-status jobs than those from low socio-economic statuses (SES) backgrounds. The authors know of many university graduates who accepted temporary work as interviewers on their family research project, simply because full-time employment was unavailable. Thus, if education outruns opportunity, the result will be dissatisfied educated adults.

So while families see education as the "way up" for their offspring, it is not necessarily so.

Religion and Family

According to the KDHS, the Kenyan population is divided as follows in terms of religious affiliation: 31% Catholic, 60% Protestant, 5% Muslim, and 4% all others (KDHS, 1994, p. 17). Because the authors' research included the coastal Muslims, our percentages were 22% Catholic, 47.5% Protestant, and 27.5% Muslim (Mburugu & Adams, 2001, pp. 7–8).

In general, our respondents consider themselves to be religious, and while they may attend modern religious services, they are likely to engage in both traditional and modern rituals on special occasions, such as marriage, birth, and death.

11. SPECIAL TOPIC: AIDS

Though it is not unique to Kenya, AIDS is an important issue affecting families in east, south, and other parts of Africa. It is, of course, a heterosexual problem in Africa, and has left many children being raised by their grandparents. Africa is in great need of medical breakthroughs that will curb this scourge.

NOTE

1. The issue of wife-beating is hardly unique to Kenya. At a conference in India, a professional male was heard to say, "The problem is uppity women; the solution is beating them." He was, of course, criticized severely by the professional women at the conference. In the United States, a writer was commenting on the cutting off of funds for centers for battered women. She said, "There are some who favor a broken woman and an intact family over an intact woman and a broken family." So this issue is not unique to Kenya.

REFERENCES

Adams, B. N., & Mburugu, E. (1994). Kikuyu bridewealth and polygyny today. *Journal of Comparative Family Studies, 25*(2), 159–166.

Battered for the Pill. (2001, January 24). *East African Standard*, p. 4.

Brass, W., & Jolly, C. L. (Eds.) (1993). *Population dynamics of Kenya*. Washington, DC: National Research Council.

Brockland, B. (2000). *The division of labor by gender in Kenya: The cases of the Akamba and the Mijikenda*. Unpublished senior thesis, University of Wisconsin, Madison, WI.

Cattell, M. G. (1990). Models of old age among the Samia of Kenya: Family support of the elderly. *Journal of Cross-Cultural Gerontology*, 5, 375–394.

Cavicchi, E. (1977). *Problems of change in Kikuyu tribal society.* Bologna: EMI.

Central Bureau of Statistics. (1999). Nairobi, Kenya: Ministry of Planning and National Development.

Central Bureau of Statistics. (1999). *Kenya, Demographic and Health Survey.* Nairobi, Kenya: National Council for Population and Development.

Clignet, R. (1970). *Many wives, many powers.* Evanston, IL: Northwestern Press.

Comaroff, J. L. (1980). *The meaning of marriage payments.* New York: Academic Press.

Davison, J. (1993). School attainment and gender: Attitudes of Kenyan and Malawian parents toward educating girls. *International Journal of Educational Development*, 13, 331–338.

Dow, T. E., Jr., & Linda, H. W. (1983). Prospects of fertility decline in rural Kenya. *Population and Development Review*, 9(1), 77–97.

Ferraro, G. P. (1973). Tradition or transition? Rural and urban kinsmen in East Africa. *Urban Anthropology*, 2, 214–231.

Gachukia, E. (1989). The working mother and her child. In *Child abuse and neglect: Selected papers from the 4th Scientific Seminar of the Kenya Medical Women's Association, March 1989* (pp. 84–97). Nairobi, Kenya: Initiatives.

Goldschmidt, W. (1976). *Culture and behavior of the Sebei: A study in continuity and adaptation.* Berkeley: University of California Press.

Guyer, J. (1981). Household and community in African Studies. *The African Studies Review*, 24, 87–137.

Huber, H. (1973). *Marriage and the family in rural Bukwaya Tanzania.* Fribourg, Switzerland: University Press.

Hughes, R. (1987). Revisiting the fortunate few: University graduates in the Kenya labor market. *Comparative Education Review*, 31, 583–601.

Johnston, T. (2002). *Violence and abuse of women and girls in Kenya: A briefing book.* Nairobi, Kenya: New World Printers.

Kabwegyere, T. (1982). Determinants of fertility: A discussion of change in the family among the Akamba of Kenya. In J. C. Caldwell (Ed.), *The persistence of high fertility* (pp. 27–46). Canberra: Australian National University.

Karp, I. (1978). *Fields of change among the Iteso of Kenya.* London: Routledge and Kegan Paul.

Kayongo-Male, D., & Onyango, P. (1984). *The sociology of the African family.* London: Longman.

Kenya Demographic and Health Survey. (1993). Nairobi, Kenya: National Council for Population and Development (NCPD) and Office of the Vice President and Ministry of Planning and National Development.

Kenya Demographic and Health Survey. (1994). Nairobi, Kenya: National Council for Population and Development (NCPD) and Office of the Vice President and Ministry of Planning and National Development.

Kenya Demographic and Health Survey. (1998). Nairobi, Kenya: National Council for Population and Development (NCPD) and Office of the Vice President and Ministry of Planning and National Development.

Kilbride, P., & Kilbride, J. (1990). *Changing family life in East Africa.* University Park: Pennsylvania State University.

Lambert, H. E. (1956). *Kikuyu social and political institutions.* London: Oxford University Press.

Langley, M. B. (1979). *The Nandi of Kenya: Life crisis rituals in a period of change.* London: C. Hurst.

Mayer, I. (1975). The patriarchal image: Routine dissociation in Gusii families. *African Studies, 34*(4), 259–281.

Mburugu, E., & Adams, B. N. (2001). *Family and kinship in four Kenyan societies.* Nairobi, Kenya: Report to the Office of the President.

Mwakera, B. G. (2003). *Childcare arrangements made in Maina Village, Laikipia District, Kenya.* Unpublished masters thesis, Kenyatta University, Kenya.

National Center for Early Childhood and Education (NACECE). (1992). *A Report of the "Partnership and Networking in the Care and Development of Under Threes.* Nyeri, Kenya: Author.

Ndeti, K. (1972). *Elements of Akamba life.* Nairobi, Kenya: East Africa Publishing House.

Ocholla-Ayayo, A. B. C. (1976). *Traditional ideology and ethics among the Southern Luo.* Uppsala: Scandinavian Institute of African Studies.

O'Leary, M. F. (1984). *The Kitui Akamba: Economic and social change in semi-arid Kenya.* Nairobi, Kenya: Heinemann Education Books.

Parkin, D. (1972). *Palms, wine, and witnesses.* San Francisco: Chandler Press.

Silberschmidt, M. (1992). Have men become the weaker sex? Changing life situations in Kisii District, Kenya. *Journal of Modern African Studies, 30*(2), 237–253.

Snell, G. S. (1954). *Nandi customary law.* London: Macmillan.

Sudarkasa, N. (1994). Sex roles, education, and development in Africa. *Anthropology and Education Quarterly, 13,* 279–289.

Ukaegbo, A. O. (1977). Socio-cultural determinants of fertility: A case study of rural eastern Nigeria. *Journal of Comparative Family Studies, 8,* 99–116.

Ware, H. (1979). Polygyny: Women's view in a transitional society. *Journal of Marriage and the Family, 41,* 185–195.

Westoff, C. F., & Rodriguez, G. (1995). Mass media and family planning in Kenya. *International Family Planning Perspectives, 21*(1), 26–31.

CHAPTER 2

Nigerian Families

INNOCENT VICTOR OGO MODO

1. INTRODUCTION

Nigeria is a country made up of people of diverse cultures and ethnic nationalities. There are 372 linguistic ethnic groups that make up the country (Otite, 1990). It is therefore obvious that there are numerous family groups within Nigeria. The area now referred to as Nigeria was ceded to Britain during the Berlin Conference of 1884 when African territories were shared out among the colonialists. Nigeria became an entity in 1914 when the former British colony and protectorate of Southern Nigeria was amalgamated with the protectorate of Northern Nigeria.

Nigeria currently has a population of about 120 million people.[1] Given this large population and great ethnic and cultural diversity, it is often said that for every five Africans, one is a Nigerian. The country is a federation and is currently divided into 36 states with Abuja as the federal capital. There are three major ethnic groups, based on population. Each major ethnic group—the Ibo, Yoruba, and Hausa/Fulani—is made up of over 15 million people. It is clear that, apart from the three major ethnic groups of the country, many different, smaller ethnic groups may claim the majority in individual states. For example, the Tiv, with over 3 million people, are the major ethnic group in Benue State. In fact, there are more than 10 major ethnic groups in Nigeria that number more than 3 million people. One of the reasons for the country's division into states was to allay the fear of domination of the minor ethnic groups by the major ones.

The new Nigerian constitution of 1999 further placed each of the present 36 states into one of six geographical regions. This is to ensure that all states within a geographical region benefit equally in the allocation of resources for the development of each geopolitical region.

Size, Geography, and Economy of Nigeria

Nigeria has a total surface area of approximately 923,768 sq km (National Population Commission [NPC], 1998, p. 1). Nigeria lies between 4°1′ and 13°9′ north latitudes, and between 2°2′ and 14°30′ east longitudes. It is bordered in the north by the Republic of Niger, in the east by the Republic of Chad and Cameroon, and in the west by the Republic of Benin. The coastline along the Atlantic Ocean forms the southern border, which stretches about 800 km from the Badagry Inlet in the west to the Rio del Rey, which is east of the Cross River Estuary. The climate of Nigeria is influenced mainly by the rain-bearing southwest monsoon winds from the ocean and the dry, dusty or harmattan northeast winds from the Sahara desert. There are therefore two main seasons: the rainy and the dry. The rainy season lasts for about 7 months (April to October) in the southern part of Nigeria and only 5 months (May to September) in the northern part (Emedo, Maduka, & Oranekwulu, 1989, p. 17).

Nigeria is blessed with three main types of natural resources: underground minerals, forests, and water resources. Fossil fuels and metallic, nonmetallic, and radioactive minerals are the basic groups of mineral resources found in the country. Nigeria has always practiced a mixed economy of both public and private enterprises. The public sector remains dominant and serves as the main engine of growth. From the 1980s, especially after the second national development plan, private sector participation increased substantially and has continued to do so. Before the crude-oil boom of the 1970s, agriculture accounted for a high percentage of Nigeria's gross domestic product (GDP) and employed most of the working population. Since the 1970s, export of crude oil has been dominant and accounts for more than 80% of the total national revenue (NPC, 1998, p. 5). With less attention now being paid to agriculture, Nigeria has virtually become an oil-reliant monoeconomy.

Becoming Nigeria

Nigeria became a coherent cultural nation through the process of pairing up, that is, the coming together and blending of the different Nigerian ethnic families. Following the amalgamation of Northern and Southern Nigeria into a country in 1914, the British colonialists embarked on establishing durable economic structures to sustain the country. They encouraged the production of economic crops such as cotton and groundnut in the northern areas of Kano and Maiduguri; cocoa in the southwestern areas such as the Ijebu communities and Ekiti; rubber and palm oil plantations in midwestern areas around Benin City and Uromi; and palm oil plantations in the eastern parts such as Etinan, Abak, Arochukwu, Awka, and Oji River. The colonial government also started to intensely exploit some existing mineral resources, such as coal at Enugu and tin at Jos. The colonial government built an efficient railway system stretching from the economic crop evacuation centers to developed seaports at Lagos, Port Harcourt, and Warri (Udoka, 1996, pp. 33–50).

The Christian missionaries who, following the abolition of the slave trade throughout British territories by an Act of Parliament in 1833, had come into Africa side by side with British explorers and imperialists opened Christian missions and later schools in Nigeria (Fafunwa, 1974). For example, the Church Missionary Society (CMS) used an ex-Nigerian slave, Bishop Ajayi Crowther, to open missionary stations in Northern Nigeria from 1857. Some other missionary societies were also established by that time in Southern Nigeria. The Methodists started missions in Badagry by September 1842, the Church Missionary Society (Anglican) in Badagry by December 1842, Baptists in Badagry in 1850 and in Ogbomosho in 1855 (Akuma, 2002, pp. 110–115). British colonial administrators encouraged missionary societies to open up mission schools. They needed educated Nigerian men with the fear of God to assist in the colonial service. Boys' education started around 1842, but before 1925 some girls' colleges such as CMS Girls School at Lagos and Ijebu Ode had also been opened (Modo, 1994).

Virtually every school leaver was employed, in churches or Christian mission offices, railways, port authority offices, schools, law enforcement agencies, and so on. Virtually every ethnic family group was drawn into this colonial service. By 1930 the colonial administrative offices and economic centers of Lagos, Jos, Enugu, Kano, Lokoja, and Calabar had become centers of population. Although certain ethnic family groups owned much of and remained dominant in most of these cities, the smaller ethnic groups devised one way or another of living as a family within such cities. For example, there was daily interaction between the different ethnic families in the city of Lagos, in the workplace, markets, churches or mosques, on the streets, or in rented apartments. By 1911 the population of Nigeria was 16.05 million and that of Lagos was 70,000. By 1952–1953 the populations were 30.42 million and 270,000, respectively (NPC, 1998, p. 26).

The coming together of people from every ethnic family group into Lagos afforded these Nigerians the opportunity to understand one another. Though they competed for jobs and other necessities of life, living in these culturally diverse areas was a great opportunity for them to study, admire, and even criticize people of other ethnic groups or families (Ekpenyong, 1992, p. 77). There were obvious prejudices and ethnocentric feelings and behaviors among the people dwelling in Lagos. Since about 98% of what is now Nigeria was rural at that time (Modo, 1993), such Lagos dwellers went back to their rural villages and ethnic groups during the annual leave period with some positive but mainly negative stories about other ethnic groups they worked with. Those that later migrated to areas such as Lagos from the villages came armed with prejudices before actually meeting people from other ethnic groups or families. Centers such as Lagos or Jos were expected to be melting pots where different ethnic family members could assemble and tolerate one another, but, because of intense competition for jobs,

accommodation, schools, and so on, they were also centers for displays of ethnic prejudices and outright hatred.[2] It is little wonder that interethnic marriages are resisted today by most parents in Nigeria. Some usually say that people of other ethnic groups are tricky, cunning, and selfish, and they would not want their sons and daughters to have anything to do with them. Despite this, people from different ethnic backgrounds still pair up in marriage as members of the larger Nigerian community (Essien, 1996).

It is also important to note that most of the divorce cases that go to courts today are those involving interethnic couples. In Nigeria it is only when family members stand behind a wife that the husband finds it difficult to divorce her. It is also important to state that the success story of some interethnic marriages has encouraged others contemplating it. A typical example was that of the late Professor Sofola (from Yoruba) and the late Professor Zulu (Okwumabua) Sofola from Delta Ibo. They met as students and married in the United States in the 1950s amid opposition from the girl's father, who later pardoned her for the "crime" of marrying into another ethnic group. Both families and especially the younger brothers of Zulu have benefited immensely from such a marriage.[3] Nigerian families obviously have in the last quarter-century advanced beyond their ethnic boundaries. It is therefore necessary to know how children are raised in Nigerian society in addition to discussing how their parents pair up.

2. PAIRING UP

Culturally, Nigerians are polygamous or, rightly speaking, polygynous. Each man can marry as many wives as he is able, depending on his capacity to care for them and their children. The Nigerian Muslim man can take a maximum of four wives as a religious injunction (Hammudah, 1982). The Nigerian Christian man is expected to marry only one wife. However, if a Christian has married many wives before becoming converted to the Christian faith, he is not advised to divorce them. Traditionally, marital relationships begin with the acceptance of bridewealth from the family of the boy (suitor) by the girl's parents or relatives. This bridewealth (also known as bride-price, dowry, or dower) includes cash, kola nuts, clothing, and other items demanded for such occasions by the specific cultural group. The items and the amount of each item to be included are negotiable. The acceptance of such payment symbolizes that the girl's uxorial and genetricial rights (Mitchell, 1961) have been transferred to the boy and his family. This means that the girl in question becomes from that moment the wife of the boy on whose behalf the bridewealth has been paid. For the adherents of traditional religion, the ceremonies and festivities accompanying the payment of bridewealth signal the end of the wedding.

Christians proceed to the church and consummate this traditional marriage through a church wedding. The officiating minister in the church must begin by demanding to know if the traditional bridewealth (dowry) has been paid. Thereafter, he will want to see the parents or guardians of the couple. After satisfying himself that the couple's relatives sanction the marriage, he joins them in holy matrimony. The couple will, through this church marriage or consummation, become one until death.

Since the essence of marriage is for the continuity of the group or community, most societies devise cultural ways of ensuring this progeny where traditional methods fail. For example, among the Igbo—especially the midwest or delta Igbo—there is the concept of *Idegbe*. In a patrilineage where a husband and wife have all daughters, the family might persuade the only daughter or any of the daughters (if there are many) to remain unmarried but give birth to children for the family's name to be preserved (Modo & Essoh, 1997). The whole community will know that the girl has been placed in Idegbe. Any male friend should also know that no bridewealth is expected from him since the children she will give birth to will belong to her parents.

Among the same Igbo culture there is what could be called gynaegamy, or woman-to-woman marriage. An old lady who sees herself as the only survivor in a family might choose to preserve her family name by marrying a girl. She pays the bridewealth and the girl comes to live with her. She becomes the socially recognized husband of the girl. A healthy and stout young man could be invited from time to time to meet her and through that process children will be born into the aging woman's family.

Levirate is another marriage system that upholds family and lineage solidarity. It is believed among several ethnic groups in Nigeria—especially the Ibibio, Igbo, and Fulani—that women are married into families and lineage, and that marriages take place between two families and not just between the boy and the girl from such families. When a husband of a woman dies, culture demands that the junior brother of the late husband marry the widow of his elder brother. With the advent of Christianity, where Christians marry one wife only, it might not be possible for the married younger brother to take in the widow as a second wife. He will, however, care for the children of the woman and also for the woman if she remains unmarried.

Child betrothal is another method of acquiring wives and husbands in most cultural groups in Nigeria. When, for example, a baby girl is born, a friend of the father's could betroth his 4-year-old boy to this young girl. From there on, they see themselves as in-laws. It is a way of cementing friendship and also a technique of becoming related to the rich or big families. This system of engagement is dying out among the Igbo, Ibibio Idoma, Itshekiri, and Urhobo, especially with the high level of education children attain. A medical doctor may not agree to marry a restaurant waiter or a street cleaner to fulfill his father's marital agreement, which he did not enter into himself. However, child betrothal is still very much in vogue among the pastoral Fulani of Nigeria, since the practice fits into their pastoral way of life. At about the age of 7, when a pastoral Fulani boy is expected to become a herd boy, his father will give him some cattle in the presence of his agnates and other relatives. It is expected that for every herd boy there must be a herd girl who will milk the cows. The herd boy is then given a wife. He is betrothed to a little girl younger than him. The next step is to take away the little girl from her family into the boy's family. She is taken to the house of the boy's mother as her daughter-in-law. She grows up there but is prevented from having a sexual relationship with the boy until she sees her first menstrual period. From then on, she sleeps with the boy until she becomes pregnant (Stenning, 1960).

The last but not least marital system in Nigeria to be discussed is the Islamic system. In Islam marriage is considered a legal contract, so it is necessary to ensure that you really like and desire the person you wish to marry. The suitor makes a proposal of marriage to a girl or even to her guardian or parents. Once the proposal has been accepted, it becomes an engagement. It is believed that any girl to be married must have reached the age of maturity (puberty) where she can accept or reject a suitor. Islamic marriage is called mithaq (covenant) in the Holy Quran—a covenant between the husband and wife. The marriage must be well publicized and the *Nikah* performed in public. This contract is entered into in the presence of two male witnesses, one from each family. A sermon is usually delivered

before the Nikah, or proceedings of the ceremony, begin to give it the character of a sacred contract. The man thereafter gives dowry (*mahr*, or nuptial gift, bridewealth) to the girl, which is obligatory (Quran 4:24). The actual amount is determined by the social and financial position of the man and the wishes of the bride. The dowry must not be beyond the resources of the boy or his family. Islam does not require the sort of marriage in which gifts or feasts create a great burden (Mohammad, n.d., p. 25). The ceremony should be performed by an Aalim or pious person.

Muhammad (1997, p. 1a) explains the simple processes in Islamic marriage. A sermon is delivered by the Iman or someone else as the friends and relatives of both parties are assembled. The sermon must state fully the mutual rights and duties of husband and wife. At the end of the sermon an announcement is made that the man and the woman have accepted each other as husband and wife. The dowry is also announced at that time. The man and the woman are then asked if they accept this new relationship. Once the reply is yes, then the marriage ceremony is properly concluded. The whole audience will raise their hands and pray for the blessings of God on the newly wedded couple. Some sweets are then distributed before the guests disperse. A feast (*walimah*) then follows the consummation of this marriage.

In all, marriage is exogamous in Nigeria, except among the Fulani pastorals and the Kanuri who are endogamous, mainly preferring to marry their pastoral cousins. There are, however, rare cross-cousin marriages in some different ethnic groups, for example, the Ibibio, that could be classified as endogamous. When marriage is endogamous in some exogamous cultures it might be the result of incest, which is taboo. This could mean some rituals must be performed to please the community ancestors before such marriage relations are allowed.

3. FERTILITY AND SOCIALIZATION

Nigeria's diverse cultures have a strong patriarchal base. Apart from the Yako Society in Cross River State, which is double unilineal (Nwanunobi, 1992, p. 22), and the Ohafia Community in Abia State, which has some matrilineal traits, all other groups are patrilineal. In Nigeria's patrilineal societies, male children are valued more than females—especially since property normally passes from father to son. This belief affects the system of bringing up male and female children in a typical Nigerian traditional society. This point will be further stressed in the section on property and inheritance.

It is, however, necessary to say at this point that to avoid stress and strain within a young family it is important that a new wife be fertile, that is, she should be able to become pregnant within the first few weeks or months of being married and deliver the baby safely. However, Nigeria's healthcare delivery system is still very poor and Nigeria is also still about 70% to 80% rural (Modo, 1993).

Except for the general hospitals and primary healthcare centers in most of the 774 local government headquarters in the country, most of the rural villages do not have healthcare facilities. The good hospitals and well-equipped maternity wards are mostly in the cities and urban areas. The majority of women in rural areas resort to traditional birth attendants and traditional doctors when they are pregnant. Also, because of the acute nature of poverty in Nigeria, most of the urban poor cannot afford hospital fees. Therefore, they also patronize traditional doctors, some of whom are charlatans or fakes patrolling the urban area for selfish gains. Ikoh (2000, p. 35) observes that a pregnant woman who is poorly fed, malnourished, poorly clothed and housed, and exposed to a poor healthcare delivery system may be unstable emotionally. This negative state of mind could affect the personality of the unborn baby. It is therefore clear that the plight of Nigerian children begins from conception, because of the different hazardous conditions their mothers are exposed to during pregnancy.

Birth and Child-Rearing Practices

Inyang (1994) observes that up to 50% of Nigerian women prefer to deliver at home, attended to by a traditional birth attendant. Reasons for this include no nearby hospital, high hospital bills, and cultural practices such as those of the Cattle Fulani, who send a pregnant wife back to her parents for at least the first delivery. About 70% of Nigerians reside in rural areas, and the bulk of these people are farming families (Modo, 1993). Every rural family prefers that a wife give birth to a baby boy. The men need male children to assist in farm work. Such male children will eventually inherit the farms and family compounds. The women become anxious to give birth to male children in order not to be set aside and replaced by another woman. Even the urban and educated Nigerian men prefer male to female children. Some men cannot imagine their estates at Lagos or Abuja or their chains of companies being taken over by relatives instead of their sons when they die. Culturally, women do not inherit family property. It is assumed that such women will be married out. Relatives of a rich man who dies without a male heir will naturally clamor for his wealth and will not give a female child the opportunity to have even a pin out of her father's property unless the father has made a will and a lawyer is prepared to defend it (Okaba, 1997, pp. 19–29). Thus, when children are born, their socialization into their culture is expected to be total.

Child-rearing practices take into consideration what the family expects a child to become in the future. Families generally see their children as very great investments. They support parents in old age and become heirs. They also give a decent burial to their parents. Boys are expected to take over the family house and lineage title, while girls are expected to be married out to responsible men from neighboring clans or villages. Boys are therefore given training to be responsible future family leaders. Within the urban nuclear family, the boy is trained to see his father as his model. He is meant to develop manly character in every respect. The girl is made to watch her mother and become a good cook and be subservient in all respects. Within polygamous homes, mothers bring up their daughters in a way to protect their family's good name and so prevent being tagged the mother of spoiled girls that bring shame to the family. It is also agreed that the upbringing of the boys is mainly the joint effort of the women and the men. Serious cases of indiscipline on the part of a growing boy are referred to the father, who is normally outside the home most of the time. He is expected to be very hard on an erring boy (Agu, 1993, p. 30). In Nigeria different methods are used to maintain discipline: beating and whipping, scolding and threatening, denial of certain valuable privileges, restriction of play activities, imposition of extra domestic chores, exposing the child's behavior to his or her peers in school, and so on (Otite & Ogionwo, 1979; Onomuodeke, 2000). All these punishments aim at inculcating moral discipline in the child. The important morals include greetings of the elders, respect to elders, obedience, avoidance of lies, shunning pride, and being kind, humble, and upright.

Unfortunately most urban Nigerian families are losing these culture traits. In a situation where the father and mother work, the children are either left in the hands of housemaids or are put into childcare centers for the greater part of the day. Others are abandoned in boardinghouses even at the tender age of 3. Subsequently two groups of young generations of Nigerians are emerging. The first group is made up of young rural boys and girls immersed in Nigerian cultural systems who have sound moral upbringings. The second group is made up of urban boys and girls who are morally loose, disobedient, and very uncontrollable. Many such children ignore parents' advice and are only kept within bounds by their fear of the country's law enforcement agents, such as the police, army, and state security services.

4 & 5. GENDER ROLES AND MARRIAGE

From this socialization system, it is obvious that Nigeria is a gender-sensitive society. Whether this view is seen theoretically from the angle of biology or culture, the view still holds. From the biological standpoint, theorists such as Talcott Parsons, Robin Fox, and Lionel Tiger believe that women are different from men, and that accounts for the sexual division of labor in the society. On the other hand, Oakely (1974) and Friedl (1975) say that norms, values, and roles are culturally determined. In Nigeria both biology and culture determine gender roles. Nigeria is patriarchal and so men have greater rights over valued goods beyond the family circle. Physically, men perform more labor-intensive jobs than women and this marks them as the powerful group.

In the rural area of Nigeria where farming is the main occupation, men fell and burn off the trees and prepare the farms. They also plant yams and other root crops. Women plant some crops described as women's crops, such as cocoyam, in addition to growing vegetables. In riverine areas, men do deep-sea fishing, while women sell the fish caught. Among the pastoral Fulani, men take the stock for daily grazing, while women milk the cows and prepare butter. All these activities take into consideration the culture and the physique of the men and women. In the urban areas such as Lagos and Abuja, due to acquisition of Western or modern education, most men and women go out to work. While men engage in labor-intensive jobs such as carpentry, plumbing, or other white-collar jobs that demand high talent, most women engage in caring jobs such as teaching, nursing, pharmacy, and accounting. These are to a large extent jobs carried over from household chores. Some Nigerian women in cities also effectively combine the job of housewife with the aforementioned jobs, or even with selling provisions in front of the residential apartment.

In Nigeria, power in any family unit rests with the male head of the unit. He is the head of the nuclear compound or even the extended family unit. Indeed, in Nigeria gender roles have much to do with power, both social and spiritual. In extended family units, the lineage head is normally the oldest male member of the family. He adjudicates cases involving family members, including between husbands and wives of families within the lineage. For the adherents of traditional religion, such a lineage head has spiritual powers too. He is the oldest of the living family lineage members and is considered closest to the dead ancestors (Modo & Essoh, 1997). He is the person who offers acceptable sacrifices to the dead ancestors. He cannot, therefore, be bypassed by members of the lineage wanting to sacrifice and placate their ancestors (Bradbury, 1962, p. 127).

In Islam, men are considered more powerful than women. There is also the Quranic estimation of women's inferiority in intelligence (Quran 4:34a). Thus, wives deserve no better treatment than do naughty children whenever they misbehave. Husbands are advised to punish a recalcitrant wife by denying her sex for about a month or for her to be given a whipping (Quran 4:34b). Recently with the upsurge of Islamic fundamentalism following the introduction of the strict Sharia law system in some northern states of Nigeria (1999), Islamic women are even more devalued than before (Modo, 1998a, p. 99). The Nigerian Christian women also acknowledge the gender superiority of their husbands as stated in the Holy Bible. The head of woman is man (1 Cor. 11:3, 7–10). The Bible goes on to say that women were created for men. It would appear therefore that in both cultural and spiritual aspects of life Nigerian women are subservient to their male counterparts.

It is important to say that there is freedom of movement and also freedom of association in Nigeria. Because Nigeria is a secular state, every Nigerian is also free to practice his or her religion and no one can be coerced into another person's religion (Constitution of Nigeria, 1999). Nigeria is also a liberal and tolerant society; no one is denied his or her rights because of religious belief, ethnic nationality, social status, and so on. Many Nigerians by all standards are also educated and know their rights.

It is necessary to stress that Nigerian women are as educated and mobile as their male counterparts. In rural areas and also in the urban areas of Nigeria, which could be rightly described as the melting pot for the 372 ethnic groups that make up Nigeria, there are marital relationships not only between people from the same ethnic group but also between people from different ethnic groups, different religions, and even between Nigerians and foreigners.

Nigerians of all persuasions believe that marriage is an important event in the life of every man and woman. Boys normally begin to think seriously about marriage around the age of 25 and girls around the age of 18, if they have not already done so. Ideally Nigerians frown at very intimate relationships between a man and a woman who are not husband and wife, especially people believed to be cohabiting as some do in the cities. No Nigerian ethnic or cultural group can stand the shock of lesbian or gay practice. If any person belongs to such a community, he is presently operating underground. Every ethnic group has words and adages against such rare deviant behavior of any member of the society. There is therefore no marital relationship in Nigeria between homosexuals. Indeed, the penal code (Article 214) prescribes a 14-year imprisonment term for people having such carnal knowledge against the order of nature.[4]

6. FAMILY STRESSES AND VIOLENCE

Nigerian families are mainly patriarchal and patrilocal in residence. Family problems emanate mainly from cultural, psychological, and economic tensions in the society. Culturally, male children see themselves as owners of the family compound, as persons who will inherit the family assets and perpetuate the name of the family. Training of male children includes preparing them for family leadership and ensuring that they are able to provide not only for their future nuclear, but also the joint, families they will eventually head. Female children are brought up to be good and caring ladies. They should be ladies who will take proper care of their future husbands, their children, and other men of the homes they will be married into. From childhood, ladies are therefore trained in readiness for their leaving their family of birth. Their mothers have the sole responsibility of ensuring that daughters have this training (Nwaubani, 1997, p. 54)

In Nigeria today, most families give greater attention to the education of male children since they will perpetuate the family name. The girls could be sent to school if it is convenient economically. Girls are therefore made to understand that they are inferior to boys. Culturally this gender consciousness breeds gender violence in the home. Only a small proportion of Nigerian educated men imbibe the idea of equality between men and women. Most men beat their wives in the rural villages and even in the cities for expressing a different opinion on any issue or for challenging their actions. The proper adage is that women are expected to be seen and not heard. The boys in the home at times give respect to their senior sisters if they have any but beat up the junior sisters on every little exchange of words. Men believe that women talk too much, and their "medicine" is beating and flogging.

Psychologically, women are beaten at times for reasons not connected with themselves. A quarrel in the workplace or outside could make a husband so tense that the wife pays for it, probably for something as insignificant as not preparing the table on time. This is usually a transfer of aggression. When wives demand money for housekeeping or for household items, it could lead to a quarrel in which such wives are accused of being wasteful and inconsiderate of the economic pinch. This provides another opportunity for battering (Ganny, 1996, p. 38).

Some women also take pleasure in beating and "bossing" weak husbands. A wife who finds herself in such a position could beat the husband for offences ranging from failing to provide household items to an unsatisfactory sexual life. In the villages, such women are seen as bad and suitors are advised not to have anything to do with their daughters because it is believed that their female children will also be "husband beaters."

It is essential to stress that even in urban areas of Nigeria the idea of male and female equality or even the high level of education attained by both has not made family violence a thing of the past. Indeed the idea of equality infuriates some men so any economic or psychological problem may threaten the cultural sense of superiority in the man, which often results in family stresses and violence (Modo, 1998a, p. 100).

7. DIVORCE, SEPARATION, AND REMARRIAGE

Divorce and separation are very rare in the rural areas of Nigeria but frequent in the urban areas. The reason for this appears to be that in the rural areas every influential member of the lineage wades into the problem between the brother (the husband) and his wife. Culturally a woman is married into the lineage. The husband has only a uxorial right over her, that is, exclusive right for sexual intercourse and her domestic services. The lineage has genetricial rights over her. This means that her children belong to her husband's lineage and take their appropriate positions among lineage members and descendants (Mitchell, 1961). Wives, therefore, procreate for the lineage. Lineage elders normally wade into quarrels between a member of the lineage and his wife. No matter how hopeless the case is, they try all possible ways to maintain the marriage. Even a barren woman cannot be divorced. The husband could be allowed to marry another women but the first wife must live in the family house and still maintain her position among the wives of the lineage. Adultery is not rampant in the villages, as every person is known to every other person and keeps track of everyone's movement. Wife-beating is rampant, but women normally endure it because it is a shame to be separated from one's husband and children (Modo, 1998a).

When husbands and wives leave the village, they lose lineage surveillance and care. They go into a city where there is anonymity, where it is difficult for people to know intimately every other family within the neighborhood. One may not see one's lineage members in the city for months, and even if there is an existing village or lineage association in the city, one may not be compelled to attend. People living within one's neighborhood are normally members of different ethnic groups and at times foreigners or non-Nigerians.

I have said elsewhere that divorce in Nigeria is mainly an urban phenomenon (Modo, 1998b, p. 64). Reasons for divorce in these urban areas include adultery, desertion, stubbornness, arson, lack of love, and constant beating and battering. Table 2.1 documents divorce cases brought before the magistrate at Offot District Court, Uyo metropolis.

At Uyo metropolis, which is the state capital of one of the 36 states that make up the country, marriage problems are brought to the courts almost on a daily basis. Problems in marriages contracted through traditional systems and later church weddings are referred to customary courts or district courts for hearing. Those contracted through High Court registry go back to the High Court for hearing.

Table 2.1 shows that at Offot (one of five such courts at Uyo), within just 3.5 years of this new millennium, 15 cases had already been heard on adultery, with women being the defendants in 12 of the cases. Some women were accused of abandoning their poor or jobless husbands and openly clinging to their lovers. Some 15 cases were also heard on neglect. Some men refuse to take care of their wives and children but maintain their concubines and their children outside. Certain quarrels are blamed on extended family members. A man beats his wife on a daily basis and says the mother-in-law is a witch and the cause of his predicaments. Others seek divorce because of religious differences. Some women have refused to leave some Christian religious groups that some husbands and their relatives regard as cults and spiritually dangerous to their families. Other cases classified under wickedness include disposal of property of the mate without consent, setting fire to the clothes and other property of the wife, a wife threatening or attempting to poison food and encouraging a son to set upon his frail and jobless father.

Table 2.1   Reasons for Divorce at Offot District Court, Uyo

Year	Adultery	Neglect	Desertion	Constant Beating	Wickedness	Religious Differences	Witchcraft	Total
2000	4	3	3	2	4	1		17
2001	4	1	1	1	2			9
2002	5	7		3	2	2	1	20
2003	2	4	1	1				8
Total	15	15	5	7	8	3	1	54

SOURCE: Author's personal interview with the registrar, Offot District Court, Uyo metropolis. May 28, 2003.

Another study was conducted at Uyo metropolis on divorce cases. Okon (2001) interviewed 140 respondents at Uyo, among whom 60 had divorced their spouse. She found that the main cause of divorce is marital infidelity, especially adultery. Other causes include growing incompatibility between spouses, marrying for the wrong reasons, and permanent sexual disability such as impotence on the part of the man.

Okon (2001) also showed convincingly in her literature review that divorce is not only very common in other Nigerian cities but that is takes place for reasons similar to those in Uyo metropolis. From the foregoing, it could be estimated that for every 100 church weddings, five end in divorce. Magistrates normally allow divorce when it is obvious the couple can no longer live together.

Divorce Among Nigerian Muslims

The aforementioned divorce cases concern Christians. The divorce process in Islam is complex, so it becomes difficult for one to say whether the divorce rate is low or high. For example, in the southwest of Nigeria, which is predominantly made up of the Yoruba ethnic group, there are no Sharia or Muslim area courts, which makes it difficult to get court records on divorce.[5] Divorce, however, takes place quite often. A divorce pronouncement is made by the husband stating "I divorce you." With this statement, there must be a three-month period of waiting (*Iddat*), within which the man must feed and cloth her, but have no sex with her. It is expected that within this period the couple might reconcile, but after this period, divorce takes place. This divorce is still not the end. It is still revocable, and they can remarry again in the future. When "I divorce you" is pronounced three times in 3 months during her state of purity (not during menstruation) or pronounced three times at once, the divorce becomes irrevocable. This is why I said divorce in Islam is complex. Those thought to have divorced each other may be seen in the next few months as husband and wife again.

My fieldwork at Maradun (Bakolori dam area) (Modo, 1986) showed that in periods of economic stress the divorce rate could be very high among northern Muslims. From 1977, when Maradun men started to lose control of their irrigated farmlands as a result of the building of the Bakolori dam, women took control of caring for the home. They sent their daughters to sell cooked food to the dam construction workers. With the role reversal of women now taking care of the family, some women started divorcing their jobless husbands. Within the first quarter of 1978, as many as nine cases sent to New Marandun Area Court earned divorce. Apart from very turbulent economic periods, outright or irrevocable divorce among northern Nigerian Muslims cannot be said to be high even in this millennium (Modo, 1994).

However, when a northern Muslim or generally a Nigerian Muslim husband and wife agree not to live any longer as a couple, then the divorce process ensues. Both husband and wife are to be represented on a status of equality; a judge has to be appointed from his people and another from her people. The two are told to remove the differences and reconcile to each other. If agreement cannot be brought about, a divorce will follow, especially since divorce is the only remedy when a marriage fails to fulfill its objectives (Muhammad, 1997, pp. 38–39).

If no solution is found, the husband could pronounce "I divorce you" once, as stated earlier. After this pronouncement, her Iddat period begins. Within 3 months, the couple could reconcile, but if they do not, they separate and the Nikah bond is removed. The woman can then marry someone else or could also remarry this former husband. It is after the third pronouncement of "I divorce you" that the divorce becomes irrevocable (Masud, 2001). If the husband still requires her, the woman must first of all marry another husband and then divorce him before marrying her previous or first husband. Even if the divorce is irrevocable, the woman has the right to be maintained during her Iddat. She will be clothed, fed, and maintained. If she is pregnant, her Iddat period extends until the birth and she should still be given her recompense as she suckles his baby. Where the case is decided at the Islamic area or Sharia court, and divorce granted, the Iddat period will still be maintained (Muhammed, n.d.).

Separation

Separation for the married could be seen from three perspectives: after divorce, death of a spouse, and temporary separation. In Table 2.1, the nine cases brought before the magistrate in 2001 got their prayers for divorce granted. They became separated from their spouse. Death also permanently separates a husband from a wife, or vice versa. The third type of separation is temporal. In the different cultures of Nigeria, a husband and wife can keep away completely from each other for a long time if there is a case of adultery or any act that is considered taboo by the people. Among the Ibo, Ibibio, Itsekiri, and so on, there may be some rituals to be performed if the couple still continues to live as husband and wife. It is believed that adultery on the part of a wife if found out or ignored could lead to the death of the husband. There must, therefore, be certain rites or rituals to placate the ancestors of the patrilineage. The couple will remain separated until such rituals are performed. When a wife runs away from her husband, unless she has run to her husband's people, many cultural groups in Nigeria will not admit her back unless there is an elaborate rite of cleansing.

Remarriage

Among the different cultures of Nigeria, some people cannot remarry after separation. If a woman is constantly adulterous, or known to be a witch, or always fighting and quarreling, no suitor will approach her again because her deeds are known by all. Even when she travels away to a distant and completely different culture, those intending to marry her will still talk to her people. Her people will not hide her atrocities, especially since she might still continue with them and the new in-laws would think her character is characteristic of her people.

Remarriage for a young woman whose husband is dead is not very difficult, especially among the Christians or Muslims. The usual marriage systems described previously in both religions are applicable. An old woman having the same fate among the Christians might agree to marry if she has no grown children to take care of her. In that case, an old man who has similarly lost his wife might prefer to have her. In Islam she could easily be accepted by a man who has not yet married four wives and who has the capability to maintain four wives.

8. KINSHIP SYSTEMS IN NIGERIA

Two people are kin if one is descended from the other or if two of them are descended from a common ancestor (Onwuejeogwu, 1975). Nigeria is basically a patrilocal kingroup society. Each family lives in a village among lineage members or agnates that are consanguineally related. Nigerians mainly practice patrilineal kinship and so live patrilocally. Even among the Ohafia matrilineal clan in Abia State or among the people of Yako in Cross River State who practice a double unilineal system of kinship, residence is still patrilocal (Nwanunobi, 1992, p. 22).

Patrilineal families, lineage, and clans serve the function of socializing the young through imparting their culture, and meeting the member's religious, economic, and sociopolitical needs. Each kin group has its identifiable area in which the group lives, and trains its young ones in its language and culture. The kin group has its ancestral shrine, its totem, thus meeting the religious needs of members. The oldest members of the lineage are linked to their ancestors and are usually the medium through which the departed ancestors are properly worshipped (Onwuka, 1997, p. 40).

Family or lineage membership also helps people in marriage relations and political struggles within the broader Nigerian society. Marriages are mainly exogamous and membership of a well-respected lineage or clan ensures one an edge over other suitors for a girl well sought after. In modern Nigeria, with 372 ethnic groups made up of about 120 million people, membership of a strong or popular family, lineage, or clan in a populous ethnic group will give someone an advantage over others in the political leadership of the country.

Property and Inheritance

Kin groups are identified through their root or location, that is, land area, including farmlands, streams, and minerals. In Nigeria today, the ethnic families in the Niger Delta such as the Ogoni, Ijaw, and Ndokwa (Ukwuani) are determined that the government acknowledge their ownership right over the mineral (crude oil) in their land and accord them due recognition in terms of physical development and other benefits. The oil companies such as Mobil and Shell now give due recognition to the ethnic groups that live in their operating areas by offering university scholarships to their youths and also offering employment to job seekers.

Nigerian politicians cannot afford to ignore or neglect their kin group relations, especially their close kin, in this present political dispensation. For example, any Nigerian seeking election into the federal Senate, House of Representatives, or State Houses of Assembly must go down to his or her family (ward) to obtain nominations. This means that the first consent to run for such a political position must be obtained from one's family village ward. A politician who stays aloof from his or her family root cannot therefore advance politically in Nigeria.[6] Kinship ties not only enable people to have access to productive resources such as farmland, but also allow them to participate in political alliances and advance in the political leadership of the country.

In patrilineal societies there are certain rules that affiliate individuals to a definite set of kin. These are rules of descent. Patrilineal descent connects an individual to kinsmen who are connected to him through men only. This is a very common type of descent system. In this system every member of the patrilineage can trace his or her kinship relationship through males to a common ancestor. The system allows for orderly inheritance of property by primogeniture. The first male child inherits the property of his father or the family. The son is expected (in the event of his father having much property) to ensure that his other siblings benefit in some way from their father's property. If their father dies while the first son is a minor, their uncle or the lineage head could be in charge of the property until the oldest son is considered old enough to take over.

In rural communities where parents are farmers, and the rural family house is all the father can boast of, inheritance is not problematic. The first son supervises, for example, family palm trees and farmlands and supports other children through the sale of proceeds from the farms.

Where a father has much property, inheritance must be wisely handled to prevent schism and open confrontation. If a polygamous father dies leaving five houses in urban Lagos for the first son to manage and there are more than six other sons and about three wives, the situation is bound to be problematic. Moreover, it is not often that lineage elders of the family have such influence over such a compound family that they can adjudicate property problems.

However, with the advent of wills, parents who find themselves with much property try to will such property to different children before their death. Parents now take into consideration their female children when allocating property through a will. Even when such a father has only female children, he might will all the property to them before his death through a lawyer. This is to prevent his lineage agnates from taking over the property and allocating it to the female children's male cousins since in patrilineal cultures female children ought to be married out. This practice takes place among the Igbo, Ibibio, Itshekiri, Yoruba, Urhobo, Idoma Bini, and Nupe. However, among the Efik of Cross River State (a patrilineal society), first daughters have a place of pride in the family. The parents allow some of them to inherit family property and manage it for the rest of the children. Such ladies marry like other women but at a certain time in their lives they leave their husband and children and return to their ancestral home to manage the family property. Some of the women even persuade their husbands to live in their ancestral home matrilocally, even though the children of the family belong patrilineally to the man's lineage.

Among the pastoral Fulani, inheriting property does not constitute a great problem, because, as mentioned earlier, every male child at birth is given his own cattle by his father in the presence of his agnates during the naming ceremony. At the age of 7, when he is ready to become a herd boy, he is also given more cattle by his father in the presence of his relatives. He grows up with his flock and wife before separating into his own nuclear family (Stenning, 1960). There is, however, a clan in which married couples live partilocally but property is inherited matrilineally. In the Ohafia, a matrilineal clan in Abia State, children inherit from their mother's brother. Children see their mother's relatives as their agnates, while their father's people are distant kin with whom they can marry. With patrilineal societies as neighbors to the clan, it would appear that some members of the clan are resisting the matrilineal culture.

Finally, among the Yako of Cross River State (a double unilineal kin group), property is inherited from both the father's and mother's sides. Nonmoving property such as land could be inherited from the patrilineal kin with whom a man resides and movable property such as clothing, cars, and farming equipment could be inherited from the mother's side. In such a society, a man's mother's people have high regard for him just like his father's people do (Nwanunobi, 1992, p. 22).

In conclusion, since Nigerian descent groups are mainly partrilineal, property inheritance is from father to first son, and where there are inheritance problems, lineage elders normally wade in to ensure an amicable settlement.

9. AGING AND DEATH

Aging is a developmental and continuous process of change in the individual from conception to death (Beauvoir, 1972; Atchley, 1980; Cohen, 1994). Aging is associated with responsibility in the society. In Nigeria the aged generally are respected, because they are believed to be people specially endowed with accumulated wisdom. They are believed to have information about many unrecorded events that the national leaders may need for policy formulation and other important governmental and cultural reasons.

The aged in most contemporary Nigerian cultures, especially in the Igbo, Yoruba, Ibibio, and Urhobo, refers to men and women who are not only advancing in age but are achieving certain feats worth acknowledging. Even at the biological age of 70, cultural groups may not regard one to be old, especially if such a person is not among the influential ones or among the titled men of the community. In such a community, a person may be biologically old but culturally said to be young; and he may feel that he is young psychologically. In some rural communities, such men still go to the farms and engage in public tasks, and are known to still be marrying new wives.

Aging is also associated with longevity. In Nigeria, old women appear to live longer than their male counterparts. One can still find women aged 90 to 110 in some Nigerian rural communities, whereas it is difficult to find men aged 100. Kimmel (1980) observes that even at a very old age women appear to be more involved in social activities, religious organizations, and community groups than men. Bengtson et al. (1977) also observe that women differ from men in terms of widowhood. When a woman is widowed late in life, she is likely to find a group of similar widowed women who can provide support and a network of friendship. When an old man is widowed he is likely to find that he is greatly outnumbered by widowed women in the community.

Generally every Nigerian family group holds the old in high esteem, because they are a very valuable group. They offer useful advice especially in situations of war and emergencies, burial, marriage, and even coronation. Some Nigerian heads of state do invite chiefs and selected elders from all states of the federation for consultation to give legitimacy to a government decision that could cause agitation from some quarters.

In many Nigerian cultures, the old men are also the appropriate people to offer acceptable sacrifices to the ancestors, especially as they are regarded as near to such ancestors (Bradbury, 1962).

The Aged in Contemporary Nigerian Society

The impact of education and industrialization on the attitude of the Nigerian nouveau riche youths with regard to the aged is negative. The youths see themselves as wiser than the old people, who are seen to be illiterate, senile, unhealthy, and poor. This lack of respect stems from the fact that there is no government policy focused on aging and care of the aged.

In most rural areas of Nigeria, about 60% of the people are old men and women who can hardly support themselves financially (Modo, 1993). They include very old ex-farmers, those stricken with sickness, retired civil servants from corporations such as railways and national electrical power authorities, and ex-service men (army, police)—who are all very poor, with no income at all or very meager and irregular pensions.

Others are wives of these classes of men who are probably widowed and have little or no support from children. Some of the aged were in private enterprises before they left active service, so they are not entitled to pensions even at old age, thus compounding their problems. The main source of support for very old people in Nigerian families is physical attention by children. Some pensioners may not be able to use the money they are paid if their children do not send physical assistance, such as house help, to cook and tidy up. Nigeria has not adopted the culture of old people's homes for aged parents. Many of them are therefore lonely in the villages. Even those left in the cities do not fare better: Depending on how old they are, some of their grandchildren even fear them and suspect them to be witches and wizards, especially if any of their children have died before them. The youths see such elderly as a burden, and avoid them.

The problem of the elderly is also compounded by the fact that there is no comprehensive healthcare policy for Nigerians, including the aged. The government has no free medical services, so the aged must pay for treatment and this is especially difficult for people who have trouble paying for daily meals.

It was only recently (April 2003) that a church in Lagos (a non-governmental organization [NGO]) floated the idea of a home for the aged. About 24 non-church-related homes have already been built. This is a good beginning and worth commending.

Death of the Elderly

Death of the elderly in general is a time for thanking God for life well lived by the departed. It is also a great relief to family members and descendants who have waited for this event for years. Except for those who are terminally ill, it is difficult for anyone to think about death as imminent. Many people, therefore, fear to think of death and never think of death as something that will happen to them (Oluwabamide, 2000, p. 74). Besides, death is believed to be for the very old in the family. Any young man or woman who dies is believed to have been cut down by one force or another. Most Nigerian societies conduct different burial rites for the young dead and the aged.

Death means different things to different people. What it means to a people determines their approach to their own deaths and the deaths of others. Some see death as a destructive element, while others see it as a welcome release. Among the Edo-speaking people of Bini (Benin), young people who die have not fulfilled their destiny and so are known to be floating as ghosts. Older people, especially elders, should not, therefore, partake in their burial (Bradbury, 1962, p. 42). The death of an old man (Odion) is a cause for rejoicing. The children will endeavor to give him a befitting burial so that he can join his dead ancestors in the land of the dead (Erinbhin), thus taking his place among the "living" dead (Bradbury, 1962, p. 44). This is also the belief of other traditional religious adherents.

Burial rites among Nigerian Christian families are occasions for joy and celebration, because they believe that the soul of the dead has departed to be with the Lord Jesus Christ. Their relatives who are not Christians at times wonder how people could not be saddened by the departure of dear ones. However, there is still a deep sense of loss if a Nigerian Christian dies before the Bible age of 70 years (Psalm 90:10). People still weep, because the young ought not to die. When an old Christian who has accomplished much dies, the burial (the ceremony of putting a dead body into the grave) is always elaborate. It is an occasion for rejoicing and for feeding the guests and spectators and preaching and evangelizing to the area, and by doing so telling everyone present that a believer has just left to be with the Lord.

Some Christian sects may have 2 days of elaborate burial program, at times with an expensive coffin or casket to show how good God has been to the departed. To avoid indebtedness and to show honor, some groups, especially Catholics, demand that the dead be buried within 2 weeks of dying.

The Muslims also believe in paradise. They believe the soul of the dead Muslim has departed to await judgment. The dead body must be buried on the day of death or, in exceptional cases, the next day. Burial involves wrapping the body with new, white cloth and committing it to the earth. It does not involve the use of a coffin. They, however, have to pray for the dead after 40 days, and this is a time to request God to have mercy and permit the dead to go to paradise after judgment.

10. FAMILY AND OTHER INSTITUTIONS

The Nigerian family has really come a long way since it was the main building block of societal interactions, the socializing agent, and the industry with political functions, as it was in the old, precolonial Benin kingdom. Herding cattle, farming, leadership training, and other occupations such as blacksmith, carpentry, and military duties were initially learned in the home, or learned from lineage members already in such professions. In the politics and governance of such states, the most suitable excelled, especially since politics is the striving to share power or the striving to

influence the distribution of power either among states or among groups within states.

Since politics has to do with the acquisition and wielding of power within the larger social system, some families trained their members for political leadership positions. Precolonial states had different political institutions. For example, there were small or isolated societies, the largest political units of which were held together by kinship leaders. These leaders formed village councils and associations that wielded political authority, as among some Igbo groups. There was also the political system once described by Evans-Pritchard (1940, pp. 1–25) that consisted of societies that had administrative organizations ensuring greater differentiation among a usually large population, with economic and cultural heterogeneity and diversity, as among the precolonial families of the Benin kingdom. Some dominant families usually emerged as leaders, and in the Benin kingdom, a royal house emerged with its king (Oba) and its chiefs, subjects, and so on (Modo, 1996, p. 1). The economy of such governments depended on how they were able to reach out in trading or conquering other people as vassal subjects to provide tributes to the king and his people.

Present-Day Nigeria

The familial, political, and economic systems mentioned earlier experienced a great change during colonial rule. The leaders of the precolonial states in the Niger area (Nigeria) were forced to surrender their sovereignty and independence to Britain. The British army overran the Sokoto Caliphate in 1903 and introduced indirect rule there and in other areas. In areas where such authorities never existed and where decisions were taken collectively by village and family councils, Britain appointed chiefs (Sklar, 1963).

In the present postcolonial Nigeria, all the former traditional authorities and their governments have been maintained and have become think tanks that today's democratic government can consult on traditional matters. Nigeria has 372 ethnic groups (Otite, 1990), and except for those who became citizens through naturalization, all citizens belong to one of these ethnic groups. Postcolonial Nigerian families have changed from their traditional role; such families existed in kingdoms that could be said to be autonomous and independent. They traded and cooperated with people of other kingdoms and empires. Royal marriages were arranged between such friendly nations as Benin kingdom and Ile-Ife. The Benin kingmakers even at one time requested the Oni of Ife to allow his son, Oran-miyan, to rule over them during the kingdom succession struggle period (Stride & Ifeka, 1973, p. 162). In present-day Nigeria, the family serves the instrumental and expressive role of adequately preparing the children culturally and emotionally for incorporation into the Nigerian state (Parsons, 1959). Every family (nuclear or compound) trains its members to know the language of its ethnic group and distinguishes it from the other 371 ethnic groups, whose members they cooperate and compete with in the Nigerian job market.

Nigeria's educational policy includes prescribed schools one has to pass through to attain a certain level of employment or to occupy certain positions. Parents endeavor to train their children for such attainment through primary, secondary, and tertiary institutions. The majority of those who have lost their parents and who have no other relatives to move them along this social mobility route end up as laborers, messengers, and so on. The fathers perform the instrumental role of moving the children up, by using their earned income judiciously to provide education for the children. The wife provides the emotional or expressive support the man needs to achieve this purpose.

Every Nigerian family endeavors to bring up its children well, since they know that the children must compete for national positions, jobs, and recognition. They must fight for a piece of the national cake, since merit alone is not enough. Religion has become an instrument for positioning oneself in this place of honor. No matter how contentious this point appears to be, most people lose national jobs because such jobs are reserved for people from the specific religious denomination (Muslim or Christian) or cult of the Director General (or the powers that be). Indeed, before some well-respected Nigerians in positions of authority call for the removal or replacement of a problem figure, such as an indigenous coach of the national football team, or even Director General of the National Orientation Agency, they have a kinsman or someone of the same faith in mind for the position.

In spite of the numerous ethnic groups and the existing cultural diversities, the country has managed to move on as a united entity. After the initial political confusion of the early 1960s, the massacre of the Ibos in the north and west, and the ensuing Nigerian civil war (Nigerian-Biafra war) from July 1967 to January 1970, which claimed over 2 million lives, Nigeria has learned its lesson (Keay & Thomas, 1997, p. 91). Today there are cultural strings that have been woven to hold the country together in spite of its many ethnic and religious diversities (Modo, 1999). The 36-state structure is meant to allow each state to develop independently without being dominated by others. Federal government unity colleges for girls and boys have been built in all states of the federation: Children from different ethnic groups meet in such unity schools and learn about other cultures and peoples. Again, every Nigerian graduate of a university or polytechnic school around the age of 30 is expected to serve his fatherland for one year in the National Youth Service Corps (NYSC).

Such a youth is expected to be posted to a state other than his or her own for the service. The aim is to ensure that every youth in a leadership position knows something about other peoples and cultures of Nigeria. Indeed if a man and a woman (NYSC members) who come from two different ethnic groups are posted to the same state and decide to marry during that service year, NYSC authorities will finance their marriage. This is the extent to which the government will go to promote Nigerian unity. Again, the federal government has introduced a quota system for the recruitment of staff into the government's public service, the military, the police force, and corporations. The quota system enables equal numbers of citizens to be recruited from each of the 36 states into the government, to prevent, for example, one populous ethnic group such as the Hausa, Ibo, or Yoruba from dominating others in any one branch of the government, such as the army. The country has been divided into six geopolitical zones for its physical development. Cultural contiguity has been taken into consideration in this division. Any major development project could be sighted in a zone where something of such magnitude or type has not been built.

All these are efforts by the Nigerian state to move itself forward as a nation. Unfortunately some occupants of positions do not believe in the ideal and practice of unity and sharing. They believe in favoring their lineage members and their brothers. Some others believe in placing people in positions through bribery and corruption. Others show open prejudice against people from other ethnic groups, and try to keep them from the positions and resources within their power to dispense. The basic conclusion to all this is that Nigeria is rated by some as one of the most corrupt countries in the world. The present democratic government of Nigeria is very much aware of this perception and is doing everything possible to change things for the better. It is now embarking on a new national orientation on ethics for Nigerian society. To this end, a new bill on corrupt practices has been sent to the national assembly by President Obasanjo.

NOTES

1. Nigeria's present population of 120 million is projected from the 1991 census of 88,992,220 people at an annual growth rate of 2.8% (National Population Commission, 1998, p. 25).

2. Nigerians from different ethnic groups come together to compete for positions and for what they see as sharing the national cake. See Ekpenyong (1992, p. 151) for further details.

3. This example derives from personal knowledge of the family. The late Professor Zulu Sofola was my aunt.

4. Behind the Mask (2003) alleged that several gay men had been stoned to death since the introduction of Sharia law in the northern part of the country. According to it, a newlywed man, Abdullahi Jafara, has been arraigned before Sharia court for sodomy with two boys. This contravenes Section 133 of the Bauchi Sharia panel code (see http://www.mask.org.2A). Any gay or lesbian group claiming membership (Behind the Mask 1–10–2003 Page 1) in such a group in Nigeria is unrealistic, especially as every Nigerian culture repudiates homosexuality and would mobilize its members to destroy its threat.

5. I interviewed two Muslim scholars for this viewpoint: Lawal Abdulwaheed Bolande (June 13, 2003), a 2003 graduating student of sociology at the University of Uyo, and Azeez Ademola (June 16, 2003), a lecturer in the Agricultural Economics Department at the University of Uyo.

6. This is part of the Independent National Electoral Commission's guidelines to members competing for elective posts.

REFERENCES

Agu, S. O. (1993). Indigenous education in Igbo society. In J. O. Onwuka and Ahaiwe, S. C. (Eds.), *Nigerian heritage* (pp. 29–39). Okigwe: Whytem.

Akuma, J. E. (2002). *A handbook of Church history.* Aba: Assemblies of God Press.

Atchley, R. C. (1980). *The social forces in later life: An introduction to social gerontology.* Belmont, CA: Wadsworth.

Beauvoir, S. de. (1972). *The coming of age* (P. O. Brain Trans.) New York: G. P. Putnams and Sons.

Behind the Mask. (2003, June 10). Retrieved June 10, 2004, from http://www.mask.org.za.

Bengtson, V. L., Kesschau, P. L., & Ragan, P. K. (1977). The impact of social structure on aging individuals. In J. E. Birren and K. W. Schaie (Eds.), *Handbook of psychology of aging* (pp. 113–134). New York: Van Nostrand Reinhold.

Bradbury, R. E. (1962). Father and son in Edo mortuary ritual. In M. Fortes, et al. (Eds.), *African systems of thought.* London: Oxford University Press.

Cohen, L. (1994). Old age: Cultural and critical perspective. *Annual Review of Anthropology, 23,* 137–154.

Constitution of Nigeria. (1999). Lagos: Federal Government Press.

Ekpenyong, S. (1992). *The city in Africa.* Port Harcourt: African Heritage Research Center.

Emedo, A. B. C., Maduka, B. C., & Oranekwulu, S. C. (1989). *Comprehensive agricultural science for senior secondary schools.* Onitsha: Diamond Educational Publisher.

Essien, D. O. (1996). Some ethnic unions in the Old Calabar Province. *Ibom Journal of History, 1*(January), 63–74.

Evans-Pritchard, E. E. (1940). The Nuer of southern Sudan. In M. Fortes & E. E. Evans-Pritchard (Eds.), *African Political Systems.* London: Oxford University Press.

Fafunwa, A. B. (1974). *History of education in Nigeria.* London: George Allen and Unwin.

Friedl, E. (1975). *Women and men: An anthropological view.* New York: Rinehart and Winston.

Ganny, M. (1996). Domestic violence: The case of wife abuse and its effects on women's contribution to national development. In Y. Oruwari (Ed.), *Women, development, and the Nigerian environment* (pp. 37–49). Ibadan: Vantage Publishers.

Hammudah, A. (1982). *The Family structure in Islam.* Lagos: Islamic Publication Bureau.

Ikoh, N. F. (2000). The Nigerian child's background. In Q. I. Obinaju (Ed.), *The Nigerian child: His education in a sociological and psychological environment* (pp. 35–43). Lagos: IVY Press Limited.

Inyang, E. D. (1994). Traditional medicine: Orthodox medical perspective. In S. W. Peters, E. R. Iwok, and O. E. Uya (Eds), *The land of promise: A compendium* (pp. 229–236). Lagos: Gabuma.

Keay, M. A., & Thomas, H. (1997). *West African government.* London: Hutchinson.

Kimmel, D. C. (1980). *Adulthood and aging: An interdisciplinary development view* (2nd ed.). New York: John Wiley and Sons.

Masud, I. (2001). Divorce the Islamic ruling. *Dean Digest, 7*(5 July, August).

Mitchell, J. C. (1957). Aspects of African marriage on the copper belt of Northern Rhodesia. *Human Problems of British Central Africa, 22* (1–30).

Mitchell, J. C. (1961). Social change and the stability of marriage in Northern Rhodesia. In A. Southal (Ed.), *Social change in modern Africa.* Oxford: Oxford University Press.

Modo, I. V. O. (1986). *New Maradun—a creation of Sokoto–Rima River Basin Development Authority: An examination of place and impact of River Basin Development Authorities on Nigerian Development.* Unpublished doctoral dissertation, University of Nigeria, Nsuka.

Modo, I. V. O. (1993). Survival strategies of the rural poor: The case of Sokoto State. In J. A. Alao, et al. (Eds.), *Dimensions of rural poverty in Nigeria* (pp. 131–136). Ado Ekiti: Petoa Education Publishers.

Modo, I. V. O. (1994). *Issues in Anthropology.* Uyo: Dorand Publishers.

Modo, I. V. O. (1996). The royal culture of dynamic leadership and the maintenance of order and stability in pre-colonial Benin kingdom. *Ibom Journal of History, 1*(January), 1–10.

Modo, I. V. O. (1998a). Cultural devaluation of indigenous women in Sokoto metropolis: A cog in the wheel of sustainable development. In Y. Oruwari (Ed.), *Women, development, and the Nigerian environment* (pp. 99–105). Ibadan: Vantage Publishers.

Modo, I. V. O. (1998b). *Issues in Anthropology* (pp. 63–64). Uyo: Dorand Publishers.

Modo, I. V. O. (1999). A cultural panacea to the problem of malelessness in Igboland of Nigeria—The study of Ezechima clan. *African Anthropology, 6*(2 September), 99–105.

Modo, I. V. O., & Essoh, P. (1997). Social justice in Ibibio mortuary rites. In J. O. Onwuka and S. C. Ahaiwe (Eds.), *Nigerian Heritage* (pp. 101–116). Okigwe: Whytem.

Muhammad, E. P. (n.d.). *Kita abun Nikah—The book of marriage.* Lagos: Fatabram Nigeria Enterprises.

Muhammad, A. (1997). *Islamic law of marriage and divorce.* Offa: Hasbunallah Printing and Publishing House.

National Population Commission. (1998). *1991 population census of the Federal Republic of Nigeria.* Abuja: Author.

Nwaubani, O. O. (1997). Igbo traditional political system. In J. O. Onwuka and S. C. Ahaiwe (Eds.), *Nigerian heritage* (pp. 54–62). Okigwe: Whytem.

Nwanunobi, E. O. (1992). *African social institutions.* Nsukka: University of Nigeria Press.

Oakely, A. (1974). *Housewife.* London: Allen Lane.

Okaba, B. (1997). Ijo indigenous kinship and socio-political structure. In J. O. Onwuka and S. C. Ahaiwe (Eds.), *Nigerian heritage* (pp. 19–28). Okigwe: Whytem.

Okon, V. S. (2001). *The psychological effects of divorce on children: A case study of Uyo urban.* Unpublished bachelor's thesis, University of Uyo, Nigeria.

Oluwabamide, A. J. (2000). *The aged in African society.* Lagos: Nade Nigeria Ltd. and F. B. Ventures.

Onomuodeke, M. A. (2000). The child and the Nigerian traditional belief. In Q. I. Obinaju (Ed.), *The Nigerian child: His education in a sociological and psychological environment* (pp. 86–97). Lagos: IVY Press Limited.

Onwuejeogwu, A. (1975). *The social anthropology of Africa: An introduction.* London: Heinemann.

Onwuka, J. O. (1997). Agent and processes of socialization in traditional Nigeria. In J. O. Onwuka and S. C. Ahaiwe (Eds.), *Nigerian heritage* (pp. 40–53). Okigwe: Whytem.

Otite, O. (1990). *Ethnic pluralism and ethnicity in Nigeria.* Ibadan: Shaneson C. I.

Otite, O., & Ogionwo, W. (1979). *An introduction to sociological studies.* Ibadan: Heinemman Educational Books Ltd.

Parsons, T. (1959). The social structure of the family. In R. N. Anshen (Ed.), *The family: Its functions and destiny* (pp. 63–91). New York: Harper and Row.

Sklar, R. (1963). *Nigerian political parties: Power in an emergent African nation.* Princeton, NJ: Princeton University Press.

Stenning, D. J. (1960). Household viability among the pastoral Fulani. In J. Goody (Ed.), *The developmental cycle in domestic groups* (pp. 92–119). Cambridge, UK: Cambridge University Press.

Stride, G. T., & Ifeka, C. (1973). *People and empires of West Africa.* Lagos: Thomas Nelson and Sons Ltd.

Udoka, I. A. (1996). The role of private investors in the production of palm produce in South Eastern Nigeria: 1910–1995. *Ibom Journal of History, 1*(January), 33–50.

CHAPTER 3

Families in South Africa

Susan C. Ziehl

1. INTRODUCTION

South Africa has a population of just under 45 million and covers a land area of 1,219,090 sq km. This means that in terms of its population size, it is slightly larger than Spain and covers a geographic area equivalent to Spain, France, and Italy put together. There are nine provinces: KwaZulu-Natal, which has the largest share of the population (21%), followed by Gauteng (20%), the Eastern Cape (14%), Limpopo (12%), the Western Cape (10%), Northwest (8%), Mpumalanga (7%), Free State (6%), and the Northern Cape (2%). The climate varies considerably from an essentially Mediterranean climate in the Western Cape to a subtropical climate in KwaZulu-Natal and a dry summer-rainfall climate in Gauteng and the other northern provinces. From a topographical point of view, South Africa is characterized by a large, flat basin in the middle (known as the Karoo), which is bordered on the south and east by mountainous regions. Most of the population lives in the area between the mountains and the coast from Cape Town through to KwaZulu-Natal and in the Highveld/Gauteng area—principally, in and around Johannesburg.

South Africa is a culturally diverse society. There are 10 official languages, the most widely spoken being IsiZulu (native language to 24% of the population), followed by IsiXhosa (18%), Afrikaans (13%), English (8%), and Setswana (8%). The other official languages (Sesotho, Xitsonga, Siswati, Tshivenda, and IsiNdebele) are mother tongues to less than 8% of the population. Apartheid-style classification of people into population groups is still maintained today for official and other purposes, and in terms of this, 79% of the population is black/African, 10% is white, 9% is colored, and 3% is Indian/Asian (Statistics South Africa, 2003).

The economy of South Africa has changed considerably over time. It started as an essentially agrarian economy and moved toward one in which mining (gold and diamonds) played a significant role (in the late 19th century). Today, mining and agriculture account for only a small part of gross domestic product (GDP). At present, manufacturing and services are the major economic sectors.

South Africa has a long history of colonial conquest (Britain and the Netherlands) and frequent wars between the colonists and the indigenous people, which was followed by the period of Apartheid, during which separate homelands or bantustans were created and assigned to some of the major African ethnic groups and laws were passed to keep the races apart in the rest of the country. Subsequent to the 1994 elections and the coming to power of the African National Congress (ANC), the various homeland areas were reincorporated into South Africa and a Constitution and Bill of Rights, which guarantee equality for all, were enacted.

2 & 8. PAIRING UP AND KINSHIP

While South Africa is made up of numerous different ethnic groups, all the various black communities (which constitute the vast majority of the population) belong to the same linguistic family[1] and share certain commonalities in their kinship and marriage systems. Consequently, their family and domestic arrangements are similar (Preston-Whyte, 1976, p. 177): (1) All black communities in South Africa are patrilineal in the sense that descent and property are passed down through the male (agnatic) line; (2) while a woman is permitted only one husband, men are allowed to marry numerous wives (polygyny); (3) there is the principle that a woman joins the house of her husband upon marriage (patrilocal post-marriage residence); (4) the transfer of bridewealth is seen as an essential part of marriage; and (5) great importance is attached to ancestral spirits, both in terms of everyday life and life-cycle events such as births, maturation, marriage, and death (Preston-Whyte, 1976, p. 179).

There are, however, important differences. In this regard, it is useful to distinguish between two broad categories or clusters: Nguni-speaking communities and Sotho-speaking communities. The former include the Xhosa, Mfengu, Zulu, Swazi, and Ndebele communities, which are located primarily in the southeastern parts of the country. Sotho-speaking communities are found primarily in the northeast and include the South Sotho, Western Sotho/Tswana, and North Sotho/Pedi communities.[2] One of the main differences is that among Nguni-speaking communities, lineages and clans form a very important part of both the social structure and the kinship system. As noted, descent is always reckoned patrilineally. This means that all people who are related to each other via the male link form a lineage. Lineage segments are usually the basis for "residential clustering" (Preston-Whyte, 1976, p. 178). Even though (in rural areas) homesteads are spread over hillsides and separated by fields and grazing land, they are connected to each other by means of the agnatic/male bond—brothers tend to live in close proximity to each other. Each lineage has its own head (usually the genealogically senior male). In Zulu he is called *inkhulu,* and the lineage segment is referred to as the *umndeni* or *umzalo.* Each lineage segment forms a corporate group that, as a collectivity, has rights to livestock and land (Preston-Whyte, 1976, p. 185). Members of lineages are expected to respect each other, meet on important occasions (such as marriages and funerals), and consult with each other on issues of mutual concern. They are also expected to accept the rulings of the lineage segment head (headman) in matters of dispute.

Clans differ from lineages in that they have greater depth since they include all people who are related to a common distant ancestor or mythical figure via the male line. All Nguni communities practice exogamy, and the clan is the basis of the exogamous rule. In other words, a man and a woman who share the same clan name may not marry. They may also not marry anyone who shares the same clan name as both sets of grandparents. Since residential groupings are formed on the basis of lineages (segments of clans), this means that Nguni men must move outside their local community to find wives. It also means that marriage is the alliance of clearly defined and separate descent groups and results in the linking together of numerous and distant groups. Another consequence of clan exogamy is that a clear distinction is kept between relatives by blood (consanguines) and marriage (affines). Members of each of these groups are treated very differently and play different roles at ritual ceremonies. More particularly, there are various avoidance customs (*ukuhlonipha,* or show respect) that a married woman is expected to adhere to. For example, she is not permitted to utter her father-in-law's name or any word that may contain syllables or sounds that are present in his name. She may also not walk close to the kraal where the ancestral cattle are kept (Meqeke, 1999).

It is with regard to marriage rules that one finds the greatest difference between Nguni- and Sotho-speaking communities. What is permitted by the latter is "unthinkable" for the former (Preston-Whyte, 1976, p. 193). More specifically, in Sotho communities, men may marry relatives on their mother's side. In fact, there is a preference for cousin marriages (the mother's brother's daughter, in particular). One of the consequences of this marriage system is the merging of consanguineal and affinal relatives (blood and marriage). If a man marries a cousin on his mother's side, then his uncle (mother's brother) is also his father-in-law (Preston-Whyte, 1976, p. 193). Another consequence is the blurring of the boundaries between descent groups and a reduction in the importance of lineages and clans. It also

has implications for residential groupings. In contrast to the Nguni pattern of scattered homesteads linked through the male line, Sotho communities show a preference for living in villages that contain both agnates and cognates (Preston-Whyte, 1976, p. 185).

The transfer of bridewealth is a custom that is common among all black South African communities. The generic term is *lobola,* a Zulu term (Xhosa: *ikhezi*; Tswana: *bogadi*). *Lobola* has both an economic and a symbolic significance. Traditionally it was measured in heads of cattle, the number being decided after a lengthy process of negotiation between the lineage segment of the bride and that of her future husband. Today, it is usually paid in the form of cash. In contrast to the dowry system, where the parents of the bride confer capital and goods on the bride at her wedding, bridewealth refers to the transfer of assets from the kin group of the groom to that of the bride (Goody, 1976). It is more appropriately called *childwealth,* since it is a means through which the groom's family compensates that of the bride for the loss of control over her reproductive capacity (Ziehl, 1997). It thus emphasizes the importance of fertility in African societies. No marriage is seen as complete until children (particularly sons) are born, and various mechanisms exist (sororate and levirate) to ensure that this aspect of the marriage contract is observed even when the wife proves infertile. Although lobola cattle become the communal property of the bride's lineage segment, it is also part of a circulatory system, since cattle received for a daughter's marriage can then be used to secure a marriage for her brother. In this sense brothers and sisters are often referred to as cattle-linked (Preston-Whyte, 1976, p. 180).

In most, if not all, black South African communities, children are expected to attend initiation schools on reaching puberty. These usually involve a period of exclusion from the rest of the community and the endurance of hardship. Initiation schools usually take place in winter, and one of the common hardships that initiates are expected to endure is bathing in a cold river. Another purpose of initiation schools is the teaching of the values and norms of the society at large. Paramount among these values is respect for elders and the principle of seniority (which does not necessary follow chronological age). During initiation, male circumcision is practiced among all but the Zulu and Venda (van Warmelo, 1976, p. 58).[3] It is often thought that the attendance at an initiation school marks the attainment of adulthood. However, as van der Vliet (1976, p. 240) points out, it is only the first step in a long process. In the case of a man, adult status is only really achieved after the birth of an heir, and a woman may have to wait until the death of her husband and his elder brothers before enjoying the rights and privileges associated with adulthood.

As noted, polygyny is permitted in all black South African communities. This does not mean that at any one time the majority of men are polygamous. Rather, it is only the wealthiest of men that can afford numerous cattle payments and thus acquire numerous wives.

In all societies, households (or houses) change their composition as people are born, mature, marry, and die. However, the domestic life cycle in traditional African society (whether based on monogamous or polygamous marriage) is more complex than that commonly found in the West or what Goody (1976) refers to as Eurasian societies. The following is based on an adapted version of Preston-Whyte's application of Fortes's "typical cycle of family development" to South Africa:[4] In the case of monogamous marriage, the first stage (preliminary) involves the marriage of a couple and the birth of their children. The second stage (expansion) occurs when sons marry and bring their wives to live with their parents, while daughters move to their husbands' homesteads. When sons have children, this creates a three-generational extended family. The stage of dispersion (stage three) occurs when the oldest male and his wife die and some or all of the brothers set up independent homesteads. The final stage (replacement) occurs when the sons' grandchildren are born and the whole cycle repeats itself.

In the case of polygamous marriages, the domestic life cycle is, of course, even more complex—the main difference being that during the stage of dispersion (stage three), households split according to the ranking of the sons' mothers (Preston-Whyte, 1976, pp. 183–184).

In sum, the kinship system practiced by black South Africans is patrilineal and patrilocal, marriage is accompanied by bridewealth, and polygamy is permitted. This contrasts with the Eurasian kinship system practiced by the rest of the population, which is bilateral (except for the inheritance of surnames) and neolocal (a couple sets up an independent household upon marriage), and, except among those of the Muslim faith, in which only monogamy is accepted.

3. FERTILITY AND SOCIALIZATION

Although the fertility rate has declined significantly in South Africa, fertility is still highly valued, as manifested in the continued acceptance and practice of the *lobola* custom—even among educated women. Today, it is seen as a sign of the man's seriousness in making a marriage proposal and therefore emphasizes the value attached to a wife as well as children.

Around the middle of the 20th century, South Africa commenced the process of demographic transition. Between 1950 and 1960 the crude death rate dropped substantially (from 20 to around 12 deaths per 1,000 of the population) and was below 10 in the 1990s (Mostert, 1998, in Ziehl, 2002). The birth rate also started declining in the 1950s but at a much slower pace than the death rate: from about 42 in 1950 to 38 in 1970 and then to about 26 in the 1990s. The decline in the fertility rate was even more dramatic. On average, South African women were having six children in the 1960s, fewer than five in the 1980s, and fewer than three in the 1990s (Mostert, 1998, in Ziehl, 2002, p. 59). The prior decline in infant mortality is undoubtedly one of the explanations for the significant decline in fertility in South Africa. The infant mortality rate (IMR) dropped sharply between 1945 and 1955 (from 140 to just above 80) and then more slowly after that. It was estimated at just above 40 in 1995 and just below 60 in the period 1995–2000 (Mostert, 1998, and United Nations, 2001, in Ziehl, 2002, p. 60).

As noted, the family pattern traditionally followed by the majority of South Africans is the extended family pattern. This means that in traditional society children would have been socialized in a context that includes relatives other than their immediate biological parents. Does this still pertain today? Answering this question is extremely difficult, given the dearth of research on family life in South African society as a whole. There are numerous small-scale, community- and village-level studies but none that encompass South Africa as a whole. The only available data come from national censuses—a problematic source of information, particularly as far as family life is concerned. The main problem here is the way in which the question relating to the relationship between individuals in households is phrased (see Ziehl, 2001). The census nevertheless remains the only source of national data on families and will thus be used here.

According to the 1996 census, 12% of the total South African population was living in a household headed by a grandparent. When one compares the black and white communities on this issue, one notices important differences. In the case of white communities (which, as noted, follow the Eurasian pattern), the respective percentage is only 0.5 compared with 13% in the case of black/ African communities. This gives some indication of the persistence of uniquely African family patterns in a modern environment. Similarly, when one compares the distribution of household structures in South Africa with that found in Great Britain, one notices significant differences. More particularly, whereas the vast majority of households in Great Britain (86%) fall within one of the phases that make up the (conventional) nuclear family pattern, this applies to only about one-half of South African households. It is also noteworthy that in South Africa, it is far less common for couples to live on their own than is the case in Great Britain (11% vs. 28%) and far more likely for individuals to live in single-parent or extended-family households (35% vs. 11%) than is the case in Britain. From this, one can conclude that in South Africa a child is far more likely to be socialized in a context that excludes a parent (usually the father) but includes other relatives (grandparent, aunt, etc.) than is the case in the West. (See Tables 3.1 and 3.2.)

4 & 5. GENDER ROLES AND MARRIAGE

Like all societies, South Africa is stratified along gender lines. Since the coming to power of the ANC government, enormous strides have been made in the area of policy and structures dealing with gender issues. Official structures that have been put in place are the Commission on Gender Equality (an independent body that reports to parliament); the Office on the Status of Women (located in the office of the president); and the Committee on the Quality of Life and Status of Women (a joint monitoring committee of parliament). A number of laws have also been passed with the purpose of promoting gender equality—most notably the Employment

Table 3.1   Relationship to Household Head by Population Group (Individuals) According to South Africa Census 1996 (Percentages)

Total	Black	"Colored"	Asian	White	Unspecified	Total
Head of household	22	24	24	35	17	23
Husband/wife/partner	10	15	19	25	11	12
Son/daughter	40	41	42	32	39	40
Brother/sister	4	2	2	1	2	4
Father/mother	1	1	2	1	1	1
Grandparent	1	0	0	0	1	1
Grandchild	13	10	5	1	10	12
Other relative	4	5	5	2	4	4
Nonrelated person	2	3	1	3	9	2
Unspecified	3	1	0	1	5	2
Total	100	100	100	100	100	100

SOURCE: Ziehl (2001).

Equity Act of 1998, which provides for affirmative action and the prohibition of unfair discrimination based (inter alia) on gender. Furthermore, significant achievements have been made in the area of education. Today, rates of enrollment in educational institutions are similar for men and women, as are educational levels attained. (See Figure 3.1 and Table 3.3.) Indeed, at universities and technikons (the equivalent of polytechnics), women presently outnumber men.

Despite these improvements, gender disparities remain. Women are less likely to be employed than men. According to the results of the 2002 Labour Force Survey, about one-half of women aged 15 to 65 were not economically active, compared with about one-third of men in the same age category (Table 3.4). And among those who are economically active, women earn less money than men. As indicated in Figure 3.2, 19% of women were earning less than R200.00 per month compared with 9% of men. That figure also shows that 23% of men were in the top income bracket compared with 14% of women. Industrial and occupational segregation are also prevalent. Certain industries (mining, transport, and construction) are heavily weighted in favor of men, while other industries (services and private households) are the major employers of women (Figure 3.3). In terms of occupational segregation, only 30% of managers are female, while 64% of clerks are female (Table 3.5). Similarly, 87% of plant and machine operators and assemblers are men. Women are also more likely to be in informal as opposed to formal employment, and therefore are less likely to receive fringe benefits such as medical coverage and unemployment insurance.

Table 3.2   Comparison of Household Structures: Great Britain and South Africa

Type of Household	Great Britain 1998	South Africa 1996
Single person	28	18
Couple	28	11
Nuclear family	30	27
Nuclear Family Pattern	*(86%)*	*(56%)*
Single-parent household	10	22
Extended-family household[a]	1	13
Individual with relatives (other than child)	0	4
Unrelated adults	3	2
Other	0	2
Total	100%	100%

SOURCES: Great Britain: Giddens (2001, p. 176). South Africa: Author's calculations from raw data from census 1996.

a. Various permutations of extended family households.

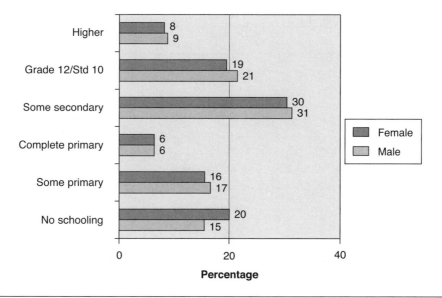

Figure 3.1   Educational Levels by Sex, Ages 20 and Older

SOURCE: Statistics South Africa (2003).

Table 3.3 Enrollment in Educational Institutions by Sex (Persons Aged 5–24) According to South Africa Census 2001 (Percentages)

	Male	Female	Total
Not attending	27.8	29.1	28.5
Preschool	3.0	3.0	3.0
School	66.4	64.8	65.6
College	0.9	1.1	1.0
Technikon	0.7	0.8	0.8
University	0.8	1.0	0.9
Adult education center	0.1	0.2	0.1
Other	0.2	0.2	0.2
	100.0	100.0	100.0

SOURCE: Statistics South Africa (2003).

Table 3.4 Labor Market Status by Sex (15–65 Years)

	Male	Female	Male	Female
	Thousands		Percentage	
Not economically active	4,897	7,217	36.71	49.31
Working	6,184	4,841	46.36	33.08
Unemployed	2,259	2,577	16.93	17.61
Total	13,340	14,635	100.00	100.00

SOURCE: Statistics South Africa (2002b, p. 7).

Official definition of unemployment: Not working and has not taken active steps to find employment in previous 4 weeks.

These inequalities in the areas of work and income are mirrored in inequalities in the division of labor within families. In this regard, Time Use Surveys show that women spend far more time on unpaid work such as housework, caring for others, and fetching water and fuel. Indeed, according to the 2000 Time Use Survey, women were spending an average of 215 minutes per day on these tasks, whereas the comparable

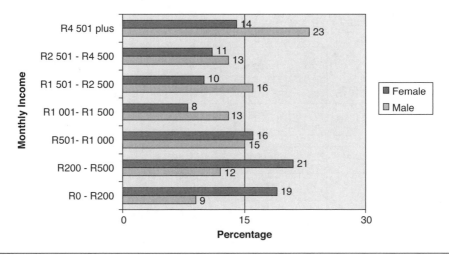

Figure 3.2   Income by Sex (15-65 Years)

SOURCE: Statistics South Africa (2002a).

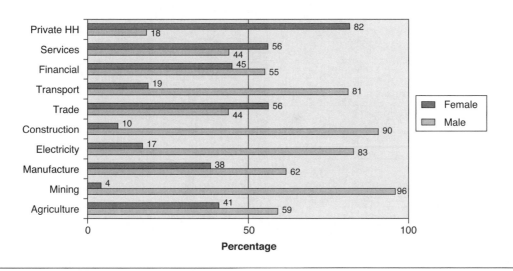

Figure 3.3   Industry by Sex

SOURCE: Statistics South Africa (2001, Table 3.4.1, p. 29).

figure for men was only 84 minutes (Figure 3.4). Given the gender inequalities both within and outside families outlined previously, it is difficult to conceptualize families as unitary entities in which all share the same experiences and have the same interests. This situation persists despite the enormous strides that have been made in the policy arena and the fact that today South Africa has one of the largest representations of women in parliament.

6. FAMILY STRESSES AND VIOLENCE

Families are often conceptualized as "havens in a heartless world," as a refuge from the

Table 3.5   Occupation by Sex (Census 2001)

	% of Occupation		% of Males and Females	
	Male	*Female*	*Males*	*Females*
Legislators; senior officials and managers	70.45	29.55	6.50	3.81
Professionals	57.38	42.62	6.87	7.13
Technicians and associate professionals	44.44	55.56	7.32	12.78
Clerks	36.10	63.90	6.77	16.75
Service workers; shop and market sales workers	64.70	35.30	11.32	8.63
Skilled agricultural and fishery workers	74.66	25.34	3.58	1.70
Craft and related trades workers	85.23	14.77	17.77	4.30
Plant and machine operators and assemblers	87.00	13.00	13.15	2.75
Elementary occupations	44.79	55.21	20.36	35.08
Undetermined	55.69	44.31	6.36	7.07
Total	58.29	41.71	100.00	100.00

SOURCE: Statistics South Africa (2003).

brutal, uncaring, bureaucratic world outside (Elliot, 1986; Lasch, 1971). However, since the 1970s, it has become apparent that families are also places where violence occurs and where individuals abuse each other. As Cooper (1971) indicates, family members often form alliances with some member(s) and strategize against others in an effort to obtain from them whatever they want. Sometimes the violence and abuse are subtle and hidden, other times overt and brutal.

In the 1980s, South Africa experienced a spate of family murders. These are cases in which an adult (in most cases a father) kills his wife and children and then commits suicide.

These occurred primarily in the white community and can be seen as a manifestation of the belief/ideology that wives and children are an extension of the husband/father. In the mind of the man, his wife and children cannot survive without him and therefore, before committing suicide, he decides to "save" them from shame and destitution.

Between 1994–1995 and 2002–2003, reported instances of rape (and attempted rape) per 100,000 people initially increased and then declined to almost the same level as in 1994–1995, giving an overall change of −0.43% in the rate of rape (Table 3.6). Over that period, the rate of child abuse declined

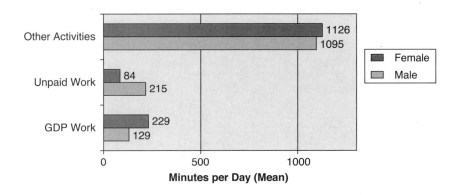

Figure 3.4   Time Use: 15–65 Years

SOURCE: Statistics South Africa (2002b).

until 2001–2002 but then rose sharply to 10.6 per 100,000 of the population in 2002–2003. Focusing mainly on the fact that the number of rape and child-abuse cases reported to the police increased between 1994–1995 and 2002–2003 by 17% and 56%, respectively (Table 3.6 and Figure 3.5), the question of domestic abuse and abuse against women has received wide-spread media attention. Comparison of official data on crime in South Africa with that of other societies for which Interpol has records has led to the labeling of South Africa as "the rape and murder capital of the world." It is, however, important to remember that Interpol only publishes crime statistics for 89 of the roughly 200 countries in the world. Moreover, Interpol specifically warns against intersocietal comparisons due to the various inconsistencies in the definitions and reporting of crimes. In a similar vein, Elliot (1996) points out that in the course of the 20th century there has been a tendency to broaden the scope of what is included under the label of abuse and violence, making the documentation of trends with respect to these issues particularly difficult. She further indicates that, depending on the definition used, studies in Britain show prevalence rates of child sexual abuse that range from 3% (narrow definition) to 46% (broad definition, which includes noncontact). Comparable

figures for the United States are 6% (narrow definition) and 62% (broad definition) (Elliot, 1996, p. 56).

Against this background, it is extremely difficult to analyze and interpret the trends with respect to crime rates generally (but rape and child abuse, in particular) within the South African context. It is possible that any of the increases identified (with regard to child abuse, for example) are an indication of a greater tendency to report those crimes rather than an indication of an increase in the actual number of such crimes occurring in relation to the size of the population concerned. The idea that an increasing tendency to report may play an important role in our understanding of official crime statistics finds support in the fact that the 1994 democratic election was accompanied by a heightened awareness of issues that had previously been seen as secondary to the national question—most notably, gender issues.

Instances of child-rape have also received widespread attention in the media. While it is difficult to fathom the physiological possibility of such horrific crimes (particularly the three cases of the rape of babies that have been reported), it is again difficult to know whether these are old social perversions or new phenomena. If the latter is the case, then it needs to be seen against the background

Table 3.6   Selected Crimesin in South Africa (1994–2003)

	Rape[a]		Child Abuse		Murder	
	Number	Ratio[b]	Number	Ratio[b]	Number	Ratio[b]
1994–1995	44,751	115.8	3,070	7.9	26,832	69.5
1995–1996	49,813	126.2	2,634	6.7	26,637	67.5
1996–1997	51,435	127.5	2,264	5.6	25,782	63.9
1997–1998	51,959	126.0	2,297	5.6	24,588	59.6
1998–1999	49,679	117.9	2,173	5.2	24,875	59.0
1999–2000	52,891	122.9	2,497	5.8	23,823	55.3
2000–2001	52,872	121.0	2,487	5.7	21,683	49.6
2001–2002	54,293	121.8	2,648	5.9	21,180	47.5
2002–2003	52,425	115.3	4,798	10.6	21,738	47.8
1994–2003	17.10%	−0.43%	56.28%	34%	−19%	−31.22%

SOURCE: SAPS Crime Statistics (2003).

a. Included attempted rape.
b. Per 100,000 of population.

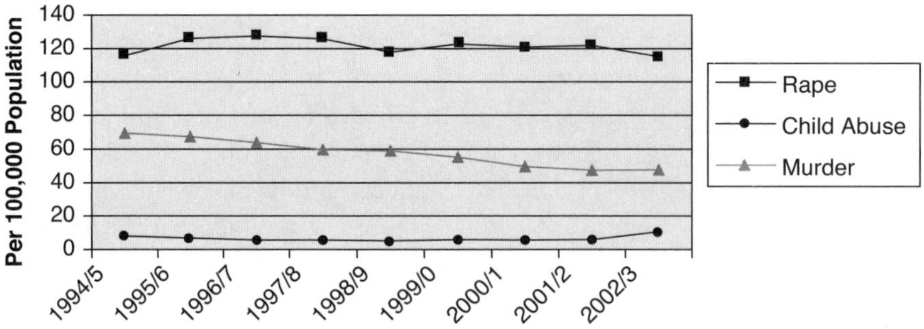

Figure 3.5   Selected Crimes in South Africa (1994–2003)
SOURCE: SAPS Crime Statistics (2003).

of the heightened awareness of the dangers of sex, which have been part of anti-AIDS campaigns. In terms of the latter, sex has come to be associated not only with danger but with death, and some men have reacted by having sex with virgins to avoid becoming infected. Far more thought and analysis need to be devoted to the question of crime rates generally and domestic abuse in particular before we can make any definite pronouncements on whether these phenomena are more common today than in the past or more common in South Africa than elsewhere.

Within the field of family studies there has been a debate about whether family violence should be seen as a function of individual pathologies, of sociostructural forces, or as a consequence of patriarchy. Proponents of the first position argue that family violence (whether it be wife or child abuse) is committed by people with personality disorders such as excessive jealousy, an inability to control impulses, being sadistic, passive-aggressiveness, and holding rigid gender stereotypes (Elliot, 1996). In terms of this approach, the solution is to treat the individuals concerned through various forms of psychotherapy. The second approach moves the focus away from the individuals concerned to the family (as a network of relationships) and the broader society. Here, the focus is on the particular stresses and frustrations that lower-class families face, as well as the culture of violence, which is said to predominate in these sections of society. For example, in terms of the conventional sociological approach, family violence is seen as a function of blocked opportunities that prohibit individuals from attaining socially desirable goals and, in turn, predispose them to taking their frustrations out on their families. The third approach draws heavily on feminist literature and criticizes the others for not placing adequate emphasis on the fact that women are disproportionately the victims of domestic violence and men, the perpetrators (Elliot, 1996). South African research gives some support to the latter position.

Unfortunately the South African Police Service does not provide data on the sex of perpetrators or victims of crime. By contrast, victim-of-crime surveys provide some, though limited, information on this issue. According to the 1998 City Victim Survey conducted in Cape Town, the majority of victims of all crimes (54%) were male (murder,

robbery, burglary, etc.). However, the same study shows that women were far more likely than men to suffer from sexual assault and sexual harassment. More particularly, the survey showed that no male respondents and 32 of the female respondents (0.04%) indicated that they had been victims of sexual assault.[5] It further showed that the majority of victims knew their assailants (43% by name and 20% by sight) and that only a minority of cases involved strangers. Furthermore, 44% of the assaults occurred in the home and a further 16% in a residential area—the vast majority taking place at night (83%). In only 20% of the cases did the sexual assault occur in the public realm (i.e., a place of entertainment, an open space, or on public transport) (Camerer, Louw, Shaw, & Scharf, 1998).

Another study (Violence Against Women in Metropolitan South Africa) involved interviewing women who had experienced various forms of domestic abuse. Since this study focused only on women who sought help after having experienced abuse, it cannot be used to determine prevalence levels. It does, however, show the various types of abuse that women suffer. In this regard, the study found that 90% of the women had experienced emotional abuse, 90% physical abuse, 71% sexual abuse, 58% economic abuse, and 43% all four types of abuse (Bollen, Artz, Vetten, & Louw, 1999). With regard to the place where the abuse occurred, the study found that in the majority of cases it occurred in the home of the victim (52.4%), that of the perpetrator (19.2%), or the home of a friend or family member of the victim or perpetrator (9.4%). In the remainder of the cases, it occurred in an outdoor public place (11.2%), an indoor public place (6.7%), or at work (1.1%) (Bollen et al., 1999). From this data, it would appear that there is a close association between domestic violence and gender and that the family is a haven (for some), a prison (for others), or a combination of both (Elliot, 1986).

7. FAMILY LAW AND DIVORCE

Prior to 1994, family law in South Africa operated in terms of a dualistic system. One set of laws applied in the three principal *bantustans* or homeland areas and another (civil law) in the rest of the country. In terms of the latter, which is based primarily on the Marriage Act of 1961, marriage is regarded as the union of one man and one woman "to the exclusion of all others" (Cronje, 1994, in Ziehl, 1997, p. 49) and was only regarded as valid if conducted by a marriage officer or magistrate. Ministers of only a limited number of religious organizations were permitted to act as marriage officers. By contrast, in the former Ciskei, Transkei, and Bophuthatswana, African customary marriages and therefore polygamy were regarded as valid and legal. Some of the consequences of the nonrecognition of African customary marriages outside of the homelands were that the children were regarded as illegitimate and spouses had no right to inherit *intestate* from one another. Since 1994, when the homeland areas were reincorporated into South Africa, this state of affairs has been called into question, in part, because the constitution declares that "everyone has the right to freedom of conscience, religion, thought, belief, and opinion," thus clearing the way for the recognition of "marriages concluded under any tradition or a system of religious personal or family law" (South African Constitution, 1996, Section 15).

In 1998 the Recognition of African Customary Marriages Act was passed (Act No. 19539). This act provides for the recognition, legalization, and registration of marriages concluded according to African custom—whether polygamous or not. It further provides that when a man wishes to take on an additional wife, he must apply to court for approval of a written contract that regulates the distribution of the matrimonial property on his death or at the dissolution of the marriage(s) concerned. In considering the application, the court will take note of the fact that customary marriages concluded after 1994 are deemed to be in community of property (unless excluded by an antenuptial contract) and effect the "equitable distribution of the property" after having taken account of the circumstances of the family groups concerned (Act No. 19539).

Steps have also been taken to bring Muslim marriages within the ambit of South African family law. A bill is presently before the Minister of Justice that makes provision for the registration and legalization of monogamous and polygamous marriages concluded according to Muslim rites legal in a court of law of the *Talaq* and *Faskh* (decrees for the dissolution of marriages).

A number of other developments have occurred in the field of family law, and the legal realm more generally, in recent years. For example, the "Natural Fathers of Children Born Out of Wedlock Act" was passed in 1997 (Act No. 18502). It was largely a response to the 1983 Child Care Act, in terms of which fathers of children born outside marriage enjoyed no rights toward those children but were obliged to pay for their maintenance. In consequence, there was no legal obligation to obtain permission from or inform such fathers of impending or actual adoption placements. In terms of the new act, such fathers may apply to the court for rights of access, custody, or guardianship, and in granting or refusing such an application the court will take account of the "best interests of the child" after having considered, inter alia, the relationship between the mother and the father as well as the father and the child. It further provides that an application for the adoption of children born out of marriage will not be granted unless the court is satisfied that the biological father has been given reasonable notice of the impending adoption (1997, § 6.1, p. 4). Other developments have included the establishment of a law commission to investigate "domestic partnerships" (project 118). There have also been a number of court cases that indirectly affect family law. For example, the National Coalition for Gay and Lesbian Equality and others successfully sued the Minister of Home Affairs claiming that the Alien's Control Act (Act 96 of 1991) was unconstitutional since it permitted an individual in a heterosexual marriage to enter the country with his or her spouse but denied this to partners in a gay relationship (Constitutional Court, Case CCT 10/99). Similarly (Judge) Kathy Satchwell success-fully challenged the Judges Remuneration Act, which denied pension and medical ben-efits to her gay partner. The outcome of these and other cases suggest that South Africa is on its way toward recognizing a variety of family situations: heterosexual and homo-sexual, legal and nonlegal, monogamous and polygamous. The sociological implications of these developments have yet to be fully understood.

CONCLUSIONS

South Africa is a society ripe for research and analysis—particularly as far as family life is concerned. It has recently experienced a major transformation of its political system. The introduction of democracy has called into question old ways of doing things and has led to the introduction of new policies and laws aimed at reflecting or effectuating the changes that have occurred in the political realm. How these new policies have actually affected peoples' lives remains to be seen. Since the 1990s South Africa has also experi-enced a major HIV/AIDS epidemic. This has placed enormous strain on the health system and led to numerous debates about how this disease is or is not affecting the society and families in particular. Unfortunately a national survey of families and households has yet to be undertaken. This would provide the necessary reference point for discussion and analysis of how family life has changed in postapartheid South Africa.[6]

Table 3.7   Marital Status: 20 Years and Over (Percentages)

Never married	39.46
Married: cvil	28.78
Married: traditional	12.11
Married: polygamous	0.10
Living together	9.12
Widowed	7.04
Separated	1.22
Divorced	2.16
Total	100.00

SOURCE: Statistics South Africa (2003).

NOTES

1. They are collectively known as Bantu languages. The term *Bantu* has fallen into disrepute but still remains the only scientific term used in linguistics and anthropology to refer to the languages spoken in Southern Africa.

2. The Venda, Tsonga, and Lemba communities do not fit neatly into the Nguni–Sotho divide.

3. It is said to have been abandoned by the Zulu when initiation schools were replaced by military schools in the 19th century.

4. Whereas Preston-Whyte identifies three stages and two phases, I will use four stages: preliminary, expansion, dispersion, and replacement.

5. It is accepted that men may be reluctant to admit to being the victims of domestic abuse due to the fear of stigmatization. For a debate on male vs. female abuse see Aulette (1994).

6. Today, as previously, polygamous marriages are rare. See Table 3.7.

REFERENCES

Aulette, J. R. (1994). *Changing families.* Belmont, CA: Wadsworth.

Bollen, S., Artz, L., Vetten, L., & Louw, A. (1999). *Violence against women in metropolitan South Africa: A study on impact and service delivery.* Monograph No. 41, September 1999. Pretoria: Institute of Security Studies.

Camerer, L., Louw, A., Shaw, M., & Scharf, W. (1998). *Crime in Cape Town: Results of a city crime victim survey.* Monograph No. 23, April 1998. Pretoria: Institute of Security Studies.

Cooper, D. (1971). *Death of the family.* Harmondsworth, UK: Penguin Books.

Elliot, F. (1986). *The family: Change or continuity.* London: Macmillan.

Elliot, F. (1996). *Gender, family and society.* London: Macmillan.

Giddens, A. (2001). *Sociology.* Oxford, UK: Polity.

Goody, J. (1976). *Production and reproduction: A comparative study of the domestic domain.* London: Cambridge University Press.

Lasch, C. (1971). *Haven in a heartless world?* New York: Basic Books.

Meqeke, R. (1999). Rainbow jurisprudence and the institution of marriage with an emphasis on the recognition of Customary Marriages Act 120 of 1998. *Orbiter, 52.*

Mostert, F. W. (1998). *International trademark treaties and agreements.* New York: INTA.

Preston-Whyte, E. (1976). Kinship and marriage. In W. D. Hammond-Tooke (Ed.), *The Bantu-speaking peoples of southern Africa* (pp. 177–210). London: Routledge & Kegan Paul.

SAPS Crime Statistics. (2003). Retrieved October 22, 2003, from www.iss.co.za/CJM/stats0903.

Statistics South Africa. (2001). *Labour force survey. February 2001.* Statistical Release P0210. Pretoria: Government Printers.

Statistics South Africa. (2002a). *Labour force survey. September 2002.* Statistical Release P0210. Pretoria: Government Printers.

Statistics South Africa. (2002b). *Women and men in South Africa—Five years on.* Pretoria: Government Printers.

Statistics South Africa. (2003). *Census 2001. Census in brief.* Report Number 03-02-02 (2001). Pretoria: Government Printers.

van der Vliet, V. (1976). Growing up in traditional society. In W. D. Hammond-Tooke (Ed.), *The Bantu-speaking peoples of southern Africa* (pp. 211–245). London: Routledge & Kegan Paul.

van Warmelo, N. J. (1976). The classification of cultural groups. In W. D. Hammond-Tooke (Ed.), *The Bantu-speaking peoples of southern Africa* (pp. 56–84). London: Routledge & Kegan Paul.

Ziehl, S. C. (1997). Law, family ideology and multiculturalism in South Africa. *African Sociological Review, 1*(2), 41–59.

Ziehl, S. C. (2001). Documenting changing family patterns in South Africa: Are census data of any value? *African Sociological Review, 5*(2), 36–62.

Ziehl, S. C. (2002). *Population studies.* Cape Town: Oxford University Press.

Part II

ASIA AND THE SOUTH PACIFIC

CHAPTER 4

Australian Families

DAVID DE VAUS

1. INTRODUCTION

European settlement in Australia commenced in 1788 with the establishment of a British penal colony. Colonization led to the destruction of the cultures of the indigenous nomadic population so that by 2001 just 2.3% of the population classified themselves as indigenous Australians. Throughout the 19th century until the end of World War II in 1945, most of the population growth consisted of immigrants from Britain and their descendents. After 1945, there was a sharp growth in immigration but the sources of immigration became more diverse, with a wider range of white European immigrants coming to Australia. In the early 1970s the abandonment of the White Australia Policy meant that an immigration policy that had restricted migration to white and mainly European immigrants was replaced by a less discriminatory policy. This led to more migrants from Asian countries settling in Australia. By 2001, 28% of all Australians were born overseas. Relatively high rates of immigration from diverse sources, together with a national policy that has supported "multiculturalism," has resulted in a country that has been increasingly characterized by cultural diversity and tolerance of this diversity.

Australia is nominally a Christian country with 68% acknowledging adherence to a Christian religious group. While most people once were associated with mainline Protestant churches and the Catholic (Irish) Church, the increasing ethnic diversity is being reflected in greater religious diversity. European migration has seen the growth of Catholicism and Orthodox religion, and migration from the Middle East and Asia has seen the growth on non-Christian religions. At the same time, there has been a steady growth in the proportion of people having no religious adherence and a steady decline in religious participation.

While rural industry remains an important part of the Australian economy, the economy is nevertheless dominated by the manufacturing and service sectors. Australia is a large and sparsely settled continent that is just slightly smaller than the area of the 48 contiguous states in the United States. Most of the 19 million Australians live in urban areas in the coastal regions of southeastern Australia.

Table 4.1   Family Types, Australia (1976–2001)

	1976 (%)	1981 (%)	1986 (%)	1991 (%)	1996 (%)	2001 (%)
One-parent family with dependent children	6.5	8.6	7.8	8.8	9.9	10.7
Couple only	28.0	28.7	30.3	31.4	34.1	35.7
Couple with dependent children	48.4	46.6	44.8	44.4	40.6	38.6
Couple with nondependent children	11.1	10.0	10.9	9.5	9.0	8.4
Other families	5.9	6.0	6.2	5.9	6.4	6.5
Total	100.0	100.0	100.0	100.0	100.0	100.0

SOURCE: Australian Bureau of Statistics (2001c, 2002b).

With the exception of indigenous Australians, longevity in Australia is among the highest in the world. Women can expect to live until 82.4 years of age and men can expect to live until 77 years of age. Nevertheless, compared with many European countries, Australia still has a relatively young population profile. Currently 12.6% of the Australian population is aged over 65 and 1.3% is aged over 85.

Family Types

Although the nuclear family is the typical family form in Australia, there remains a great deal of family diversity. Furthermore, there is widespread evidence of change in the types of families being formed (Table 4.1). As far as household-based families are concerned, 82.8% of families in 2001 contained a couple—a decline from 87.2% in 1976. In 2001, 38.6% of families consisted of couples with dependent children—down from 48.4% in 1976. A further 8.4% of families consisted of couples with a nondependent child. In addition to families containing a couple, 10.7% of families in 2001 consisted of a single parent and a dependent child and a further 4.7% consisted of a lone parent and a nondependent child.

Single parents with dependents have become more common since 1976 when 6.5% of families were single parents with dependent children. This change from 6.5% to 10.7% represents a 65% growth in this family type in just 25 years. The other family type that has grown sharply in these same 25 years has been the couple-only family, which has grown from 28% to 35.7% of all families—a 29% growth.

2. PAIRING UP

The ways in which Australian adults partner are both diverse and changing. Most partnering that results in a couple living together is heterosexual partnering. According to the

Table 4.2   Changes in Levels of Being Unpartnered (1986–2001)

Age	Female			Male		
	1986 (%)	*1996 (%)*	*2001 (%)*	*1986 (%)*	*1996 (%)*	*2001 (%)*
20–24	61	73	76	80	85	87
25–29	33	43	47	47	57	59
30–34	23	30	34	29	38	41
35–39	20	27	30	23	30	34
40–44	21	26	29	21	27	31
45–49	22	27	30	21	25	29

SOURCE: 1986 and 1996 figures from Birrell and Rapson (1998) based on special matrix tables from the 1986 and 1996 census. 2001 figures from Birrell and Rapson (personal communication) based on special matrix tables from the 2001 census.

2001 national census (Australian Bureau of Statistics [ABS], 2001b), of all couples who lived together, 99.5% were heterosexual. Just 0.26% were gay couples and 0.21% were lesbian couples.

There is widespread acceptance in Australian society of sexual relationships between unmarried males and females. Just 11% of Australian adults say that premarital sex is wrong (Rissel, Richters, Grulich, Visser, & Smith, 2003). However this support for premarital sex seems to be largely approval of sex between committed couples—almost 60% of adults disapprove of casual premarital sex. Monogamy in marriage and committed relationships is generally expected, with 78% of adults believing that having an affair when in a committed relationship is always wrong (Rissel et al., 2003).

aged 20 to 49 who are partnered at any given point of time. In each age group, substantially fewer men and women were partnered (either married or cohabiting) in 2001 than in 1986 (Table 4.2). For example, in 1986 just 23% of women aged 30 to 34 were without a partner. By 2001 this percentage had risen to 34%. Among similarly aged men, the percentage unpartnered increased from 29% to 41% over the same period. This decline in partnering has been interpreted by Birrell and Rapson (1998) as stemming from the increasing mismatch of available men and women. Women are becoming more educated and more able to earn an income, while economic restructuring has made it difficult for many men to take on the breadwinner role. As such, the "available" men are not very attractive as partners for the "available" women.

Decline in Partnering

Since the mid-1980s, there has been a steady decline in the proportion of people

Cohabitation

Cohabitation—living together in an intimate relationship without being formally married—has become a common form of partnering in Australia and is widely accepted. Only a quarter of the adult population disapproves of a couple living together even if they do not intend to marry, and only a quarter think that it is not a good idea for a couple to live together before marrying (Kelley, Evans, & Zagorski, 1998). Cohabitation has steadily increased from 1981, when 4.7% of couples were cohabiting, to 2001, when 12.4% were cohabiting. This trend shows no sign of slowing down. Cohabitation is especially common among stepfamilies, where 54% of couples with children under the age of 18 are cohabiting rather than formally married (ABS, 2001b).

A change that is even more dramatic than the growth of couples cohabiting is the sharp increase in the proportion of Australians who cohabit at some point. Of people who marry for the first time, 72% lived with their partner before they married. This is a sharp increase from 16% in the early 1970s and 43% in the early 1980s. The upward trend in premarital cohabitation shows no sign of slowing down.

Cohabiting relationships can have one of three outcomes. The couple can continue to cohabit in the long term, the relationship can end, or it can convert to marriage. Long-term cohabitation is the least common outcome. It is far more common for a cohabiting relationship to convert to marriage than to continue in the long term as a cohabiting relationship. Of women who began to cohabit in the late 1970s, 64% had married their partner within 5 years. However, the proportion of cohabiting couples who go on to marry is declining. By the early 1990s, just 41% had married their partner 5 years later.

Break-ups are also common in cohabiting relationships and seem to be becoming even more common. In the early 1970s, 22% of cohabiting women reported that their relationship had ended in a break-up within 5 years. By the mid-1990s, 40% of cohabiting couples had broken up within 5 years.

Marriage Decline

As cohabitation has become an increasingly common form of partnering, at least for a portion of a couple's relationship, marriage has become less common. In 1971, 64.5% of the population over the age of 15 was married. By 2001 this had declined to 51.4%. This decline is due to a range of factors including the aging of the population, but it is also due to a decline in marriage, even among that part of the population considered to be of marriageable age. In 1966, for example, 84 out of every 1,000 never-married women aged 25 to 29 got married. In 2001 this rate had more than halved to just 40 per 1,000. Among men the comparable decline was from 69 per 1,000 to 29 per 1,000.

One of the reasons fewer men and women in their late 20s are marrying now is that they are delaying marriage (see below), but there are two other reasons for the declining marriage rate. The first has already been mentioned—the increase in cohabitation. The second reason is that there has been a decline in the percentage of people who are partnered. Between 1981 and 2001, there has been a decline of 8 percentage points in the number of people who are married. One-half of this decline is due to the increase in cohabitation. The other one-half is due to fewer people being partnered at all (Figure 4.1).

The decline in the proportion of adults who are partnered is not because people are not partnering at all or even because they are delaying forming live-in relationships. Indeed, there has been very little change in the age at which people are developing live-in relationships. If the age by which 75% of adults had had a live-in relationship is

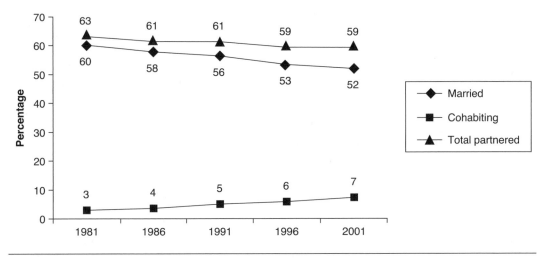

Figure 4.1   Percentage Married, Cohabiting, and Partnered (1982–2001)

SOURCE: Reproduced from de Vaus, Qu, and Weston (2003a).

considered, there has been very little change over the years. Of men born since 1952, there has been a consistent pattern whereby 75% had been in a live-in relationship by the age of 27 or 28. Among women the same pattern applies—of women born since 1952, 75% had been in a live-in relationship by the age of 24. This pattern has been quite consistent across the years.

In other words, while fewer people are partnered at any particular point of time, this does not mean that they are not forming live-in relationships or that they are even delaying forming these relationships. The main factor seems to be that younger people are not *sustaining* these relationships. Younger people are cohabiting rather than marrying when they are relatively young and these cohabiting relationships are more likely than marriages to end. This in turn means that at any point of time, more people are unpartnered.

The increasing practice of cohabiting before marrying and the relatively higher rate of break-up of cohabiting relationships appears to be associated with delays in marriage. Certainly, both men and women

are marrying much later than they once did. In Australia the average age of marriage reached its lowest point in the mid-1970s when women typically married by the time they turned 21 and men by the age of just over 23. Since then, the average age of first marriage has steadily increased to almost 27 for women and almost 29 for men in 2001. Teenage marriage has virtually disappeared.

Love is almost universally seen to be the appropriate basis for marriage in Australia. Arranged marriage is rare and confined to particular ethnic groups. Nevertheless, there is a clear social patterning to the way in which people find partners. It is usual for women to be either the same age or younger than their male partner. Just 15% of marriages involve men marrying older women. There is also a very strong pattern whereby men and women marry people within their own ethnic group. Furthermore, there is a pattern whereby men "marry down"—that is, they marry women with equivalent or lower education, earning power, and occupational status but rarely marry women of higher education, earning power, or occupation.

3. FERTILITY AND SOCIALIZATION

Fertility

Fertility behavior has undergone considerable change in the latter part of the 20th century. One change has been the unraveling of the requirement of marriage as a social prerequisite for having children. This unraveling is evident in the rising rate of ex-nuptial birth.

Ex-Nuptial Births

There has been a sharp rise in the proportion of births to unmarried mothers (ex-nuptial births). Just after the second world war, about 4% of births were to unmarried mothers. By the mid-1970s this had increased to 10%. By 2001, 31% of all births were to unmarried mothers (ABS, 2002a). Not all of these ex-nuptial births were to single mothers. Ex-nuptial births consist of births to single mothers and to those in cohabiting relationships. In 2001, approximately 12% of all births were to single mothers (Australian Institute of Health and Welfare [AIHW], 2003a; de Vaus & Gray, 2004). Births to cohabiting parents are doubling every decade. In 1970, 2% of births were to unmarried but cohabiting couples. By 1980 this had increased to 4%, by 1990 to 8%, and by 2001 to 18% (de Vaus & Gray, 2004).

In addition to the unraveling of the link between marriage and having children, there have been other significant changes in fertility behavior.

Fertility Delays

A second change has been that women are delaying having children. The median age at which women have children in Australia is now 30 years of age—a considerable increase from 25.5 in 1970, when women were having children at an earlier age than at any other time in the 20th century. On average, women now have their *first* child when they are aged 27.6

years. Increasingly women are waiting until they are well into their thirties before they have their first child. In 2000, almost a quarter of all births to women aged 35 or older were first births—up from 16% just 10 years earlier. Relatively few babies are now born to young mothers. While 220 per 1,000 women aged 20 to 24 had a child in 1960, just 58 women per 1,000 in this age group had a child by 2001.

Fertility Decline

A third change has been that women are having fewer children. Fertility peaked in 1961, with the average woman having 3.5 children. By 2001 this rate had halved to 1.73 children—the lowest rate on record. The sharpest declines occurred in the 1960s and 1970s, when the contraceptive pill and abortion became more widely available and more women were staying in the paid workforce. Since the early 1990s, fertility has continued to decline, but at a much slower rate than in the 1960s and 1970s. Fertility decline also has meant that relatively few women (less than 2%) now have five or more children. An increasing number of women, especially those with higher education, are predicted to remain childless, with levels of childlessness being projected to double from current levels of 12% to around 25% (ABS, 2000b; Rowland, 1998).

Socialization

Child-rearing and socialization of children is seen primarily as the responsibility of parents—especially mothers. Two-thirds of Australian parents consider parenting to be their own business and reject the right of governments or anyone else to tell them how to rear their children.

Child-Rearing Values

Independence for both boys and girls is highly valued. Virtually everyone agrees that children should be encouraged to express their opinions, question things, and be curious, and two-thirds agree that a 13-year-old should be learning to be independent of his or her parents. There is general support for a child's right to privacy, with most adults (90%) saying children should have their own room. At the same time, most people feel that it is the parent's responsibility always to know the whereabouts of a 13-year-old and most (86%) believe that children of this age need strict, well-established rules. The characteristics adults see as most desirable in children are those associated with being a "good person," being honest, having good manners, having good sense and sound judgment, being considerate, and trying hard (de Vaus, 1995).

Although adults play down the importance of gender-specific behavior for children, there is—in practice—a traditional gendered division of domestic labor. Boys do less around the home and their main activities are restricted to "male" tasks such as mowing lawns. Girls do more and undertake the routine tasks such as bed-making, dishes, cooking, vacuuming, and laundry. Both boys and girls resent being asked to do a household chore that "belongs" to the opposite sex (Dempsey, 1992).

Although families regard the way they rear their children as their own business, parents nevertheless expect and receive support by governments in the task of rearing children. Government support is mainly provided by means of financial assistance to help families meet the cost of raising children and to help partly compensate families when a parent leaves the workforce to raise children. Governments also contribute to the socialization of children through a free or heavily subsidized education system.

Time Spent With Children by Mothers and Fathers

Caring for young children is a gendered activity. Mothers spend far more time caring than do fathers. Compared with partnered fathers, partnered mothers in families with a child under the age of 15 spend 2.6 times more time per day on childcare activities (6.5 hours for couple mothers compared with 2.5 hours for couple fathers); 4.3 times more time on attending to children's physical and emotional care; twice as much time playing, reading, talking, or watching TV; over six times as much time related to the children's schooling; and three times more time transporting children or traveling on their behalf (de Vaus, 2004).

Part of the reason fathers spend less direct time with their children is that they are much more likely than mothers to be working full time. However, even among mothers and fathers who both work full time, mothers still spend about four times as much direct time per child than fathers in raising their children.

Values and beliefs partly underlie the different roles of mothers and fathers. Although one national survey of fathers found that 96% of fathers believed that mothers and fathers should have an equal responsibility in bringing up children, they did not necessarily mean that mothers and fathers should do the same things (Russell et al., 1999). Two-thirds of men in the survey indicated that they believed that "mothers are naturally better nurturers and therefore more suited to raising children than men" and over one-half (54%) believed that preschool children needed their mothers more than their fathers.

When asked what they felt their two most important parental contributions were in socializing their children, fathers stressed their educational and instrumental learning contributions. The most common responses were "self-control and self-discipline" (36%), "attitudes and values" (35%), "education and learning" (34%), and "interests and sport" (32%). Relatively few fathers saw their main contributions in terms of "expressions of love and care" (4%), "personality" (5%), or "emotional stability and well-being" (8%) (Russell et al., 1999).

Childcare

While parents have the main responsibility for caring for their children, they do not do this on their own. As children grow older, the direct care provided to children from parents declines as other groups and agencies play a bigger role in the lives of children. One of the changes in recent decades has been the increasing role of other people in assisting parents with their childcare responsibilities. As more mothers have continued to be employed, there has been a need to help mothers combine their employment and parenting responsibilities. The rise of single-parent families also has led to the need to provide assistance to single parents in meeting the needs of their children.

As more mothers are in the paid workforce (see below), parents use formal and informal childcare to assist with the task of rearing their children. Although one-half of all children aged 11 or younger in 2001 received no formal or informal childcare[1] apart from parental care, a third received at least some informal childcare and a quarter received at least some formal childcare.

Formal childcare has become much more widely used in recent years. Between 1984 and 2002, the percentage of children under the age of 11 who received regular formal childcare doubled from 12% to 25%. Over the same period, the percentage receiving informal childcare has remained relatively stable. The proportion of children being cared for exclusively by their parents declined from 62% to 51% (ABS, 2003).

Caring for Children After Separation

Caring for children after separation is an important part of child-rearing in contemporary society. By the time children reach the age of 15, approximately 25% of them have a parent living elsewhere. When parents separate, most children (88%) live with their mother. Many continue to have significant contact with their father but a third of fathers lose contact with their children altogether after separation. Relatively few children (between 3% and 10%) are in shared care arrangements where they live with each parent for at least 30% of the time (Smyth & Parkinson, 2003).

Despite the fact that children disproportionately live with their mothers after separation, there is widespread belief among both divorced and nondivorced adults that both parents have an ongoing responsibility for the care, socialization, and financial support of children after separation (Funder & Smyth, 1996). Obligations of nonresident parents to help support dependent children are enshrined in law, and the Child Support Scheme provides a mechanism for collecting financial contributions from nonresident parents according to their designated capacity to pay child support.

Children Leaving Home

Most children continue to live with at least one of their parents until their late teens. While children begin to leave home from age 18 onward, over two-thirds of 18- to 19-year-olds continue to live with their parents. The rate of leaving home accelerates in the early 20s so that only 41% of 20- to 24-year-olds still live with their parents. By the time they are in their late 20s only about 16% of children still live with their parents. Daughters typically leave home earlier than do sons, but in recent years both sons and daughters have been delaying their departure from the family home. Of those that do leave, almost one-half return to live at home for a period. The emerging pattern of delaying leaving home and returning home reflects a pattern of extended education, difficulty in obtaining ongoing and well-paid work, relationship breakdown, and the increased cost of housing.

4. GENDER ROLES

Different gender roles in families can be indicated in a number of different ways. One way is by examining differences in time use of men and women.

Time Use

Regardless of the type of couple family examined, men spend more time per day in paid employment than women. Among partnered men and women with dependent children, men, on average, spend twice as much time per day on paid work (5.55 hours compared with 2.25 hours).[2] In each type of couple family, partnered women do more domestic work than men—in most cases at least twice as much. Women in couple families with dependent children also spend much more time than men on childcare (Table 4.3).

When the total time that partnered men and women spend on these three activities (paid employment, domestic work, and childcare) are combined, the total time spent by women in most family types is similar to that of men (Table 4.3). The main exception is in couple families with dependent children, where mothers spend a total of 11.6 hours per day on a combination of paid work, domestic work, and childcare compared with fathers who spend an average of 9.7 hours per day on these activities.

As well as doing more domestic work, partnered women and partnered men do very different types of domestic work. For example, among men and women in couple families with dependent children, women do most of the cooking, laundry, and other housework, while men and women do similar amounts of outside work (gardening and home maintenance). A disproportionate amount of men's domestic work is outside work, while a disproportionate amount of women's domestic work is inside work (Dempsey, 1997; Baxter, 1997).

Workforce Participation

The second area in which differences in gender roles are evident is in levels of workforce participation of men and women. While mothers with young children have increasingly become involved in the paid labor force, it remains the case that mothers are much less likely than fathers to be in the paid workforce.

Gender differences in workforce participation are most noticeable when children are young. Of partnered parents with a child aged 0 to 4, just 15% of mothers worked full time in 2002 compared with 84% of fathers. When children are this young, one-half of all partnered mothers are out of the paid workforce altogether (compared with 10% of fathers). A third of mothers with preschool-aged children are employed part time (Figure 4.2).

As children grow older and go to school, mothers begin to return to the workforce. However a third of partnered mothers whose youngest child is aged 5 to 9 are not in the paid workforce. Partnered mothers with children of this age are more likely to work part time (41%) than full time (26%). Fathers with children of this age are mainly employed full time (82%).

The gender differences in workforce participation become less marked as children grow older, but the differences are nevertheless still large. Of mothers whose youngest child is aged 15 to 24 (a dependent student), a quarter remain out of the workforce (compared with 12% of fathers). These mothers have only one-half the full-time employment rate of comparable fathers (41% compared with 81%).

Table 4.3   Average Hours per Day (Total Time) on Various Activities (by Family Type and Gender)

Hours per Day (Total Time)	Couple Only <35		Couple Only 35–64		Couple Only 65+		Couple With Dependent Children		Couple With Only Nondependent Children	
	Female	Male	Female	Male	Female	Male	Female	Male	Female	Male
Employment	5.10	6.26	2.11	4.66	0.13	0.44	2.25	5.55	2.88	4.69
Domestic work	2.08	1.21	3.95	2.10	4.15	2.86	3.36	1.48	3.47	1.53
Childcare	0.10	0.11	0.43	0.19	0.26	0.12	5.99	2.66	0.32	0.09
Total	7.28	7.57	6.49	6.95	4.54	3.42	11.60	9.69	6.67	6.31

SOURCE: Australian Bureau of Statistics (1997).

Total time includes time devoted primarily to the child and secondary time, which includes supervision of children while undertaking other activities.

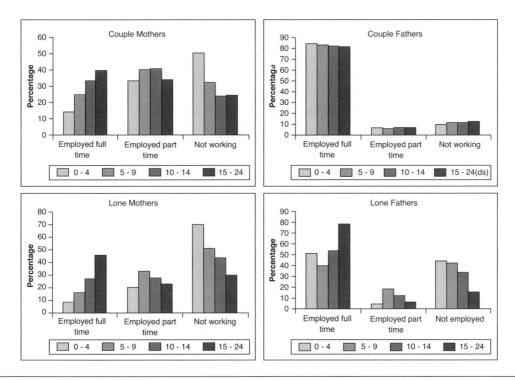

Figure 4.2   Employment of Lone and Couple Parents by Age of Youngest Dependent Child (June 2002)

SOURCE: Australian Bureau of Statistics (2002b).

Despite the considerable gender differences in workforce participation of mothers and fathers, there is evidence that these gender-based differences in parental employment are declining. For example, between 1983 and 2002 the percentage of partnered mothers with dependent children who are in the paid workforce has increased from 42% to 63%. Among single mothers, the labor-force participation has increased from 32% in 1983 to 48% in 2002 (Figure 4.2).

Power and Decision Making

The third area in which gender differences in families are often evident is in decision making. Most adults say that husbands and wives should jointly make decisions (de Vaus, 1995), a considerable change from the 1950s, when there was widespread acceptance of the legitimacy of men's traditional authority in the home (Dempsey, 1997). However, the belief in equal decision making is by no means always translated into practice.

Dempsey's (1997) research on inequality in Australian marriages shows that for husbands and wives joint decision making does not mean equal power. He reports that for many couples, joint decision making means being consulted or each partner making decisions in a particular sphere of competence, or in implementing decisions that the main power holder has delegated. He demonstrates that, despite attitudes to the contrary, husbands more often have the final say in important decisions, especially those involving a large expenditure. The majority of wives in his study only made decisions on their own that involved little or no expenditure, and normally they were simply implementing rather than making the decision. Typically the decisions made by women related to areas associated with their traditional areas of responsibility such as shopping, arranging social activities, and minor decisions regarding children. Dempsey demonstrates continuing inequality in decision making within Australian marriages but does observe that the inequality appears to be less in the 1990s than it was in the 1950s.

5. MARITAL RELATIONSHIPS

Marriage and family are no longer part of the same package. While a married couple is normally considered to constitute a family, it is certainly the case that marriage is not a necessary component of being a family. Even though the most common family form consists of a married couple with or without children, social changes mean that more and more families do not include a married couple.

An increasing proportion of couples consist of a cohabiting couple rather than a married couple (see earlier discussion on partnering). Of partnered adults with dependent children, 10% were not married in 2001. Furthermore,

well over one-half of cohabiting adults aged in their 30s have dependent children living with them (ABS, 2001b).

The nature of marriage relationships also has changed. While lifelong marriage is still widely regarded as the ideal and the large majority of people within any age group have had only one marriage or marriage-like relationship, there is a significant number who have had two or more marriages or de facto marriages (Table 4.4). For example, in 1996, while 78.6% of those in their 30s who had ever been married (or de facto married) had had just one relationship, 21.4% had had two or more such relationships. Almost 5% had had three or more such relationships (ABS, 1996a).

Many families do not include a married or even a cohabiting couple. One of the significant changes in Australian families since 1976 has been the steady growth in single-parent families. Single-parent families with dependent children make up 22% of all families with dependent children. Single parents with dependent children make up almost 11% of all families (ABS, 2001b).

While the majority of single-parent families are the result of relationship breakdown, an

Table 4.4   Number of Times Married or de Facto Married (by Age, 1996)

Number of Times Married or de Facto Married	18–29 (%)	30–39 (%)	40–49 (%)	50–59 (%)	60–69 (%)	70+ (%)	Total (%)
1	85.3	78.6	76.0	77.5	83.9	86.9	80.4
2	11.7	16.6	18.3	17.5	13.5	11.3	15.5
3 or more	3.0	4.8	5.7	5.0	2.5	1.8	4.2
Mean	1.19	1.28	1.31	1.29	1.19	1.16	1.25
N	1,107	2,180	2,025	1,459	1,101	1,151	9,023

SOURCE: Australian Bureau of Statistics (1996a).

increasing percentage of children are born to a single mother. In 1950, 2% of children were born into a single-mother family. By 1975 this had increased to 7.3%, and by 2001 it had increased again to 11.6% of all births (de Vaus & Gray, 2004).

The widespread practice of cohabitation and the degree of marriage breakdown means that many families consist of a married couple in which at least one person has been married previously. In Australia in 2000, just two-thirds of marriages consisted of two parties neither of whom had been married previously—a considerable decline from the figure of 86% in the early 1970s.

Despite the many changes in marriage, monogamy remains a basic expectation in Australian marriages. The Australian Family Values Survey (de Vaus, 1995) asked Australian men and women to identify the things they thought were important for a successful marriage. Monogamy was stressed as the single most important attribute, with 90% of adults—regardless of age—saying that extramarital sex is always or nearly always wrong (de Vaus, 1997).

In recent years there has been a greater acceptance of same-sex relationships. Nevertheless, over 60% of adults oppose regarding same-sex couples the same as married couples. In no part of Australia are same-sex relationships treated the same as marriages. However, a system of registering same-sex relationships has been introduced in one Australian state (Tasmania). Nevertheless, in some legal jurisdictions, same-sex relationships are treated in law the same way as opposite-sex relationships. Some legal protections are becoming available for partners of same-sex relationships, but these are not of the same order as for partners in registered marriages.

Marriage remains a popular institution in Australia, with less than 20% of Australian adults saying that it is an outdated institution (World Values Survey, 1995). Despite the decline in the married population in recent decades, most people do eventually marry—at least for a time. On the basis of 1997–1999 trends, it is expected that 72% of men and 77% of women will marry at some point.

These estimates are lower than those just 12 years earlier, when 79% of men and 86% of women were predicted to marry (ABS, 2002c). Marriage rates are declining and people are delaying marriage. These delays and the increasing levels of cohabitation mean that men and women are spending a declining proportion of their lives as married people. Based on 1997–1999 trends, men are estimated to spend just one-half of their life after the age of 20 as a married man and women are estimated to spend just 47% of their life after the age of 20 as a married woman (Table 4.5).

Are Marriages More Stable Than Cohabiting Relationships?

Cohabiting relationships are more likely than marriages to break up. Figure 4.3 shows that in the early 1990s, for example, 40% of cohabiting relationships of women had ended within 5 years of commencing the relationship. Over the same period just 12% of marriages ended within 5 years.

In the early 1970s fewer cohabiting relationships broke up within 5 years than in later periods. In 1970–1974, 28% of cohabiting relationships of men and 22% of those of women had ended within 5 years—a somewhat lower figure than in the early 1990s. Among cohabiting women, but not men, there has been a consistent trend since the early 1970s for cohabiting relationships to become less stable and to break up within 5 years.

How Many Long-Term Cohabiting Relationships Are There?

Relatively few cohabiting relationships endure as cohabiting relationships in the

Table 4.5   Predicted Duration of Marriages and Probability of Marrying

Based on Trends in	Proportion of Life After Age 20 in Married State		Probability of Ever Marrying	
	Male (%)	Female (%)	Male (%)	Female (%)
1985–1987	61.2	56.8	79.3	85.6
1990–1992	57.3	52.7	76.5	81.7
1997–1999	50.4	46.8	71.4	76.6

SOURCE: Derived from Australian Bureau of Statistics (2000c).

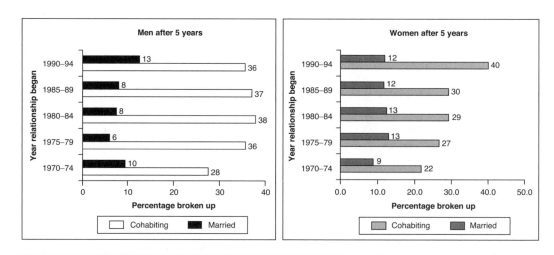

Figure 4.3   Percentage of Cohabiting Relationships and Marriages Broken Up After 5 Years (by Gender)

SOURCE: HILDA Wave 1, FACS (2001).

long term—most end in break-up or marriage. Of those who began first cohabiting in the 1970s, less than 1% were still cohabiting in the same relationship in 2001. Of those who first began cohabiting in the early 1980s, just 2.3% were still cohabiting with the same partner by 2001. Of those who first began cohabiting in the early 1990s, 8.6% were still together as a cohabiting couple by 2001. While this

percentage is higher than for those who began cohabiting in the 1970s, it partly reflects the fact that these couples have had less time to either break up or marry by 2001 than those who began cohabiting in the 1970s.

Regardless of when people began cohabiting, the majority of the relationships convert to marriage. However, the proportion converting to marriage is steadily declining. It is not certain why this is so, but it is likely that as cohabitation has become more widespread, more people are entering such relationships with the intention of it being short term. In addition, as more people cohabit, the move into cohabitation may be becoming more casual and attracting people into relationships that, when cohabitation was less common, would not have been even considered.

Increasing Employment in Families

Increasingly, as mothers participate in the paid workforce, more and more couple families with dependent children are becoming dual-worker families. In 2002, 57% of all couple families with dependent children were dual-worker families where both parents were employed. In 22% of families both parents were employed full time (Figure 4.4). The level of dual-worker couple families in 2002 represents a considerable increase from 1983, when just 40% of couple families with dependent children were dual-worker families. Most of the growth in dual-worker families is due to the increasing number of families in which one parent works part time and the other works full time.

Employment levels also have grown among single-parent families with dependent children. In 1983, 37% of single parents were employed. By 2002, this had grown to 51%. Most of this employment growth among single parents is due to a doubling of the level of part-time work among lone parents (Figure 4.5).

These increased employment levels in families have many real benefits but can also add to the time stresses on families and the

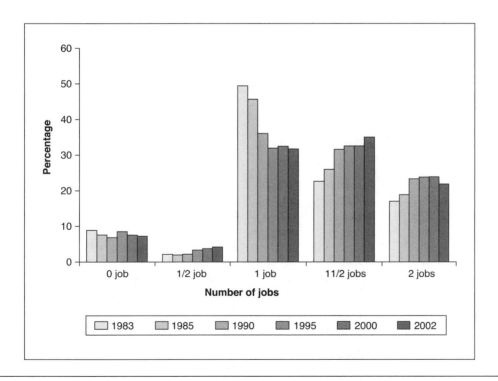

Figure 4.4   Number of Jobs in Couple Families With Dependent Children (1983–2002)

SOURCE: The figures are adapted from those provided in Renda (2003), which were based on ABS labor force surveys in various years.

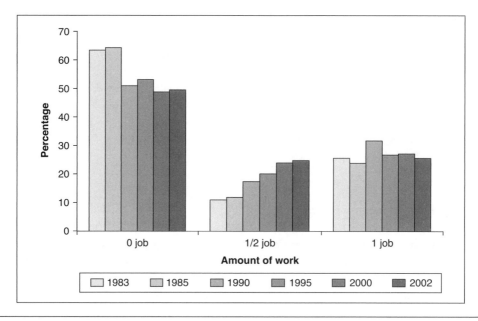

Figure 4.5   Number of Jobs in Lone-Parent Families With Dependent Children (1983–2002)

SOURCE: The figures are adapted from those provided in Renda (2003), which were based on ABS labor force surveys in various years.

difficulties in achieving a satisfactory balance between work and family responsibilities.

Self-Care

At the political level, Australia has seen a substantial reshaping of the welfare state in recent decades. Increasingly, governments are seeking to reduce the financial demands of the old welfare state and are expecting families to take a greater responsibility to manage their own welfare. Governments will assist, but much more emphasis is being placed on partnerships between individuals, families, community, and government. These policy changes are evident in much tighter targeting of income support for single parents and greater expectations that single parents will gain employment to help support themselves. A greater emphasis is being placed on individuals to provide for their own income and

care in old age. Families are being expected to play a bigger role in looking after their own family members. Increasingly, young people are being required to contribute to the costs of their own education.

Work–Family Balance

Maintaining a balance between the demands of the workplace and family is an important source of stress in Australian families. The difficulty of balancing these demands is associated with a range of changes in the wider society.

Economic restructuring, which has been directed at improving the competitiveness of Australian industry in an increasingly globalized economy, has meant that productivity demands have increased substantially in the workplace. These increased demands have meant that many workers are now working longer hours than in the past and are working less family-friendly hours than once was the case.

Most of the employment growth in the late 20th century was in the area of part-time and casual employment and in the service sector of the economy. This has meant that more family members undertake shift work, weekend work, and work on public holidays, leaving less time to spend with families.

Industrial reforms and the increasing casualization of the labor force means that jobs are less secure and that employment conditions are less attractive. Much of the increase in labor-force participation of women in recent decades has been in part-time and casual employment. These jobs frequently have poorer employment conditions in terms of access to family leave, maternity leave, and flexible start and end times than have traditional full-time jobs. Furthermore, the levels in organizations at which many women have taken employment are the levels at which family-friendly conditions are less available (Gray & Tudball, 2002).

Delayed Transitions

Transitions to adult independence are increasingly being delayed. Young people are now having to extend their education and are taking longer to obtain stable, full-time employment. Changes to the way in which young people partner mean that early relationships are relatively likely to break down. Family formation being postponed, deferred labor-force entry, and the increasing cost of home ownership all mean that the transition to adulthood is being delayed.

These delays have consequences for both young people and their parents. It means that young adults remain financially dependent on their parents longer and are living at home longer (Kilmartin, 2000; ABS, 2000a). Lifestyle differences between young people and their parents can be brought into sharp relief as young adults continue to live with parents and can strain relationships between young adults and their parents (Hartley, 1993).

6. STRESSES AND VIOLENCE

Family Stresses

The rate of family change and the level of marriage and family break-up suggest that families face many stresses. As an integral part of the wider society, families are not insulated from wider social and economic changes. While a family may be a "haven in a heartless world" (Lasch, 1977), family dynamics and the pressures facing families will be affected by social changes. Poor economic times, economic restructuring, societal value changes, and wider social movements (e.g., feminism, gay rights, child rights, etc.) will affect the ways families function.

Financial Strains

The costs of home ownership are just one of the financial strains faced by contemporary families but are a significant source of financial stress. Between the mid-1970s and the late 1990s, the real cost of purchasing a home has more than doubled *in real terms*. This means that the costs of purchasing a home now take twice the share of a family income. This has resulted in delays in purchasing homes. In the early 1970s, 61% of adult Australians were purchasing a home by the age of 26. By the mid-1990s just 31% were purchasing a home by age 26. Subsequent sharp increases in housing costs will have made this position even worse.

Where families have entered into home ownership, the cost of purchasing and maintenance requires more than one income. This has the effect of either delaying having children or mothers combining working with child-rearing. The demands of combining work and family responsibilities lead many women to work the "double shift" (Hochschild, 1989).

It is not just housing costs that lead to financial strain. Changed expectations of a reasonable standard of living and the costs associated with two jobs (childcare, clothing, additional food, transportation, etc.) all add to the financial strains on families. Most families with young children report feeling highly stressed financially and report spending more money than they earn. The 1998–1999 Household Expenditure Survey indicated that of couple families with dependent children, 17% spent more money each week than they earned—that is, they were either living off savings or gifts from others or going into debt. Almost 30% of single parents were spending more each week than they were receiving.

Children represent a significant financial cost to families and, despite the rewards of children, these costs can create substantial financial strains on families. Recent estimates (Percival & Harding, 2003) are that to raise two children to adulthood parents will spend almost $500,000 (Australian) (2002 dollars) on children and forego earnings of over $170,000 because of time out of the labor force caring for children (Gray & Chapman, 2001).[3]

Financial stress is more common among the growing proportion of single-parent families, with 41% of single parents with dependent children experiencing high levels of financial stress (McColl, Pietsch, & Gatenby, 2001). Of couple families with dependent children, 14% experience high levels of financial stress.

Time Stress

The lack of money creates financial stress, but lack of time also can be highly stressful. In trying to avoid financial stress, families can experience high levels of time stress. Women report more time stress than do men. Thirty-nine percent of women report being often or always rushed, compared with 32% of men. However, the level of time stress among both women and men depends very much on their stage in the family/life cycle (Figure 4.6).

Gender differences in time stress are particularly pronounced among families with children (Figure 4.6). In the 1997 Time Use Survey (ABS, 1997), mothers with dependent children reported very high degrees of time stress. Of partnered women with dependent children, 55% said they were often or always rushed. This percentage was higher than for men or women at any other life stage (Figure 4.6).

The main reasons given for time stress relate to work and family demands. More than one-half (52%) of those who reported high levels of time stress identified work–family balance as a key source of time stress. As indicated earlier, mothers with dependent children are especially likely to report being highly time-stressed. Part of the reason for this is the pressure of combining work with family commitments. Figure 4.7 shows that two-thirds of partnered women who worked full time and had dependent children were highly time-stressed. Working part time did not seem to reduce substantially the levels of time stress, since 61% of partnered women who worked part time and had dependent children were time-stressed. Those not in the labor force reported much lower levels of time stress than those in paid work, but 43% of these nonemployed mothers still reported high levels of time stress. It is notable in Figure 4.7 that partnered fathers of dependent children reported substantially less time stress than the mothers—even when they had similar levels of workforce participation as mothers. Of the full-time employed parents, 14% more mothers than fathers were highly time-stressed; among the part-time employed, 33% more mothers were time-stressed, and among the not employed, 16% more mothers were time-stressed.

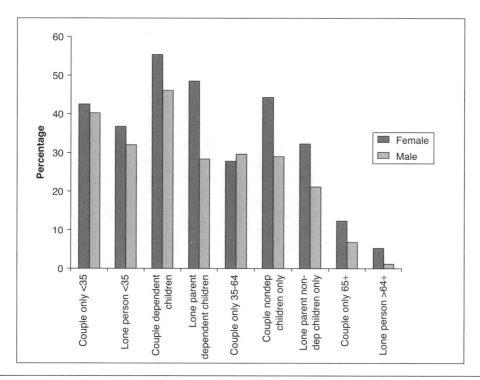

Figure 4.6   Percentage Feeling Often or Always Rushed (by Family Stage and Gender)

SOURCE: Australian Bureau of Statistics (1997).

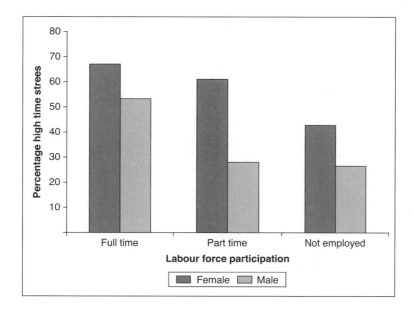

Figure 4.7   Percentage With High Time Stress by Gender and Labor Force Participation (Couples With Dependent Children, 1997)

SOURCE: Australian Bureau of Statistics (1997).

Mental Health

Mental health disorders represent a further important stressor in many families. Lack of resources and support for people with mental disorders mean that many families must deal with the problems of mental health without adequate support. Family stresses surrounding the breakdown of marriages and relationships are evident in the higher rates of mental disorders among separated and divorced adults and children in single-parent and stepfamilies (de Vaus, 2002). Table 4.6 shows that the rate of mental disorders in divorced and separated adults was double the rate of mental disorders in those who were married.

The type of family in which children live is associated with their mental well-being. Children and adolescents in step- and blended families and in single-parent families have a higher incidence of a range of common mental health disorders than those in intact families (Table 4.7).

Overall, both male and female children in blended and stepfamilies and single-parent families have at least double the rate of three disorders (depression, conduct disorder, and attention deficit/hyperactivity disorder) than children and adolescents from intact families.

Violence and Child Abuse

Domestic violence and child abuse are topics that are now openly acknowledged as a widespread social problem. Estimates of violence between partners vary widely depending on definitions, samples, and the time frame over which the incidence is measured. The most recent national estimates indicate that in the previous 12 months, 2.4% of partnered women reported having been the victim of physical violence from their male partner and 5.7% of partnered men reported having been the victim of physical violence from their female partner (ABS, 1996b; Headey, Scott, & de Vaus, 1999). Lifetime rates are higher than this. In a 1996 national survey, 7.6% of women reported that they had been the victim of physical violence from a male partner at some point (ABS, 1996b).

Child abuse and neglect within families is also a matter of widespread concern. Rates

Table 4.6 Disorder by Marital Status

	Disorder Type					
	Mood (%)	Anxiety (%)	Drug (%)	Alcohol (%)	Any (%)	N
Married	5.1	9.0	1.3	5.0	13.5	6,680
Divorced/ Separated	12.8	18.9	2.4	9.1	25.1	1,413
Gamma	0.12*	0.12*	0.14*	0.14*	0.16*	

SOURCE: Australian Bureau of Statistics (2002c). Table adapted from de Vaus (2002).

*$p < .001$.

Table 4. 7   Mental Disorder of Children and Adolescents Aged 6–17 (by Family Type)

Disorder	Family Type		
	Intact (%)	*Step/Blended (%)*	*Sole Parent (%)*
Males			
Depressive disorder	3.2	6.6	6.1
Conduct disorder	3.0	9.4	7.3
ADHD	13.2	21.6	20.6
Females			
Depressive disorder	2.0	5.1	8.7
Conduct disorder	1.3	3.1	1.6
ADHD	5.6	11.8	9.6

SOURCE: Sawyer et al. (2000).

of substantiated child abuse vary in different jurisdictions in Australia. Nevertheless, in 2001–2002, in the main jurisdictions, the rates of substantiated abuse (sexual, physical, emotional, and neglect) for children under the age of 16 ranged from five to eight children per 1,000 (AIHW, 2003b).

Overseas and Australian evidence indicates that child abuse and neglect is more common in single-parent, step-, and blended families than in intact families (Tomison, 1996). In 2001–2002 almost 18% of child abuse substantiations related to children in step- or blended families. Since only about 10% of children live in such families, this figure means that the percentage of substantiated cases of child abuse and neglect in step- and blended families is almost twice as high as would be expected given the percentage of children living in step- and blended families. Almost 44% of substantiated cases of child abuse occur in single-parent families, while just 18% of children live in single-parent families. A quarter of substantiated child abuse takes place in intact families—a much lower rate than would be expected given that three-quarters of children live in such families (AIHW, 2003b).

7. DIVORCE, SEPARATION, AND REMARRIAGE

Divorce Rates

The divorce rate has increased from 4.1 per 1,000 married women in 1970 to 12.0 in 2000 (ABS, 2002c), with the bulk of change occurring soon after the introduction of no-fault divorce under the Family Law Act in 1975. After the introduction of the act, divorce rates rose to 19 per 1,000 married women in 1976 but had declined to around 12 per 1,000 by 1980 and have remained close to that level since then. Despite the decline in divorce rates 5 years after the introduction of no-fault divorce, the divorce rates after the act are approximately three times higher than they were

Table 4.8   Percentage of Marriages Ending in Divorce After 5, 10, 15, 20, and 24 Years of Marriage (by Year of Marriage)

Year of Marriage	Duration of Marriage				
	5 (%)	10 (%)	15 (%)	20 (%)	24 (%)
1975–1976	6.9	17.1	23.2	28.3	31.9
1980–1981	7.7	17.7	25.2		
1985–1986	7.5	18.1			
1986–1987	7.6	18.7			
1987–1988	7.9	19.0			
1988–1989	8.6	19.8			
1989–1990	8.6	20.4			
1990–1991	8.3				
1994–1995	8.8				

SOURCE: Australian Bureau of Statistics (2000c).

before its introduction (Carmichael, Webster, & McDonald, 1997).

While divorce rates indicate the number of marriages that end in any given year, they do not indicate the chances of a person's marriage ending. The cumulative chance of a marriage ending increases the longer a person has been married. The risk of divorce also depends on the period in which people married.

Of marriages that took place in 1975–1976, 32% had ended in divorce 24 years later (i.e., by 1999). Table 4.8 shows that of those marrying in 1975–1976, 6.9% had divorced within the first 5 years, 17.1% within the first 10 years, 23.2% within the first 15 years, and 28.3% within the first 20 years. Of those who married more recently, there is a slightly enhanced risk of divorce within 5 or 10 years of marriage than for those who married in 1975–1976.

While the cumulative divorce rate increases the longer a couple has been married, the highest risk of separation and divorce occurs in the early years of marriage. Of all marriages that eventually end in divorce, one-half have ended in their final separation within the first 8 years. Divorce, on average, follows 3 years later. A third of marriages that end in divorce have ended in the final separation within the first 4 years (ABS, 2001a).

Focusing on divorce rates masks some of the changes in relationship breakdown. While the divorce levels have been relatively stable during the last two decades, more adults have been cohabiting. The breakdown in these relationships is not identified by the divorce statistics, but ignoring the breakdown in these relationships will underestimate the extent of relationship breakdown and probably masks an overall increase in separations.

Children's Experience of Parental Separation

One of the major concerns about divorce and separation is the impact of parental separation on children. In Australia approximately 1 million children under the age of 18 have a biological parent living elsewhere. Research evidence indicates that, as a group, children who experience parental separation have poorer outcomes on a variety of measures including social and emotional behavior, educational and economic outcomes, aggression, adult substance use, quality of family and intimate relationships, mental health, and divorce risk in adulthood (Pryor & Rodgers, 2001). These poorer outcomes do not, by any means, apply to all children who experience parental separation and the effects are generally relatively small.

Over the course of their childhood children face the potential of a number of family disruptions as parents separate, live as a single parent, repartner, and possibly separate again. Of children born into an intact family (i.e., parents were married or cohabiting) between 1976 and 1983 (and thus turned 18 between 1994 and 2001), 74% continued to live in an intact family until age 18. Twenty-six percent of these children experienced the separation of their parents. Because some children are born into a single-parent family, a total of 30% of children spend at least some of their childhood without at least one biological parent living with them.

Parental separation, periods in a single-parent family, and periods in a stepfamily mean that children potentially experience a number of disruptions to their living arrangements over the course of their childhood. However, 71% of children live in the same family living arrangement for their whole childhood (either with both parents or with a single parent for their whole childhood). Of the 29% of children who experience a disruption in their childhood living arrangements, just over one-half live in two family arrangements over the course of their childhood and the balance live in three or more living arrangements.

In other words, while parental separations are becoming more common, it remains the case that the large majority of children live all their childhood without experiencing separation. Of those that do experience such disruption, more than one-half experience just one such disruption.

Premarital Cohabitation and Divorce

Premarital cohabitation has been associated with an enhanced risk of subsequent divorce (Glezer, Edgar, & Prolisko, 1992; de Vaus, Qu, & Weston, 2003b). For example, a recent national Australian survey found that 16% of people who did not live together before they married had finally separated 10 years later. Of those who did live together before marrying, 27% had separated 10 years later (Table 4.9).

This somewhat counterintuitive pattern has been found in many studies and in most Western countries. However, the greater proneness to divorce among those who cohabit before marrying is not because they cohabit but because of the types of people who, in the past, have chosen to live together before marrying. The people who in the past lived together before marrying were also those who have the characteristics that are associated with greater proneness to divorce (e.g., come from family background of divorce, are less religious, etc.). If it were not for these different characteristics of adults who choose to cohabit before marrying, couples that cohabit before marrying would not be more divorce prone (de Vaus, Qu, & Weston, 2003b).

Table 4.9   Percentage Finally Separated After 5, 10, 15, and 20 Years of Marriage
(by Premarital Cohabitation)

Years Since Marriage	Couples Living Together Before Marrying (%)	Couples NOT Living Together Before Marriage (%)
5 years (married 1990–1994)	19	10
10 years (married 1985–1989)	27	16
15 years (married 1980–1984)	37	26
20 years (married 1975–1979)	46	30

SOURCE: *Household, Income and Labour Dynamics in Australia survey,* Australian Government Department of Family and Community Services, 2001.

Single-Parent, Step-, and Blended Families

One of the consequences of divorce and separation is the consequent diversity of family structures. The most common consequence of divorce and separation where children are involved is the formation of single-parent families and of step- and blended families.

Single-parent families are those in which a parent and at least one of their natural or adopted children live. Of all families with dependent children in 2001, 22% were single-parent families. This represents a sharp growth since 1975, when just 7.5% of families with dependent children were single-parent families. In most of these single-parent families (88%), children live with their natural mother.

While the majority of single-parent families are formed as the result of parental divorce or separation, some are formed when a single woman has a child. The percentage of children born into a single-parent family has increased steadily since the second world war. In 1950, 2% of children were born to a single woman. This has steadily increased so that for children born in 2001, 11.6% were born to a single woman (de Vaus & Gray, 2004).

For children to be part of a single-parent family at one point in time does not mean that they spend their whole childhood in a single-parent family. On average, children who ever live in a single-parent family do so for about 6 years by the time they reach the age of 18. Furthermore, the proportion of children living in a single-parent family at any particular point of time understates the proportion that ever lives in a single-parent family. Of children born between 1976 and 1983, 27% spent some time in a single-parent family by the age of 18 (de Vaus & Gray, 2003).

Step- and blended families also are formed as the result of divorce and separation. A stepfamily is a family containing a couple and at least one child that is the natural child of just one parent but includes no natural children of the couple. A blended family consists of a couple and at least two children. One child will be the natural child of just one parent and one child will be the natural child of the couple.

In 2001, 5.5% of couple families with children under the age of 18 were blended families and 4.4% were stepfamilies—a total of 9.9%. Of children born between 1981 and 1985, 16.6% spent some of their first 15 years of life living in a step- or blended family (de Vaus & Gray, 2004). Those that do live in such a family, do so on average for 7 years.

Children and Parental Divorce and Separation

Just over one-half of all divorces involve children under the age of 18 (ABS, 2002c). Following divorce or separation, almost a third of fathers lose contact with their children for one reason or another. In 1997, 41% of nonresident parents had at least fortnightly contact with their children and a quarter had at least weekly contact (ABS, 1998). Repartnering of either the resident or nonresident parent after separation reduces the amount of contact that nonresident parents have with their children. Between 3% and 10% of parents share care of their children following divorce or separation (defined as at least 30% of care provided by each parent) (Parkinson & Smyth, 2003).

Remarriage Following Divorce

In 2000, 34% of all marriages involved at least one partner who had been previously married—up from 1967 when the comparable figure was just 14%. In 2000, 15% of all marriages were of two previously married people and a further 19% of marriages included one person who was remarrying.

The chance of remarrying after a marriage has ended depends very much on whether the marriage ended by divorce or by the death of a partner. Divorcées are far more likely than widows to remarry. Based on patterns of remarriage in 1997–1999, it is predicted that 58.2% of divorced males will eventually remarry and 48.7% of divorced women will eventually remarry.

While remarriage is one option after divorce, it is by no means the only option. Cohabitation, living without a partner, and living alone are other common alternatives. Living alone is a more common arrangement than cohabitation following divorce. In 2001, just 18% of divorced adults were cohabiting. The rest were either living without a partner or were living as a single parent (ABS, 2001b).

8. KINSHIP

Multifamily Households

Most people have families that extend beyond their immediate nuclear family. However, in most Australian households these other family members live in separate households. Only 1.8% of Australian households contain more than one nuclear family and just 3.1% of families live in multifamily households.[4] A further 4% of families live in extended-family households.[5] In most of the households that contain more than one nuclear family, the families are related.

Multifamily households are clustered among particular sectors of the community and are mainly formed for people at a particular stage of the life cycle when the standard nuclear, single-family household is unable to deal with particular family circumstances (e.g., marriage breakdown, an elderly or ill older person).

Single-parent families are more likely than couple households to be part of a multifamily household. In 2001, of people in single-parent families, 4.7% lived in multifamily households compared with just 1.6% of couples with dependent children and 2.7% of couples without children. This is likely to be because of the relative poverty in which many single-parent families live. Sharing households is one way of reducing living expenses. Multifamily households also provide an easier way in which families can share other resources such as care, skills, and company.

Multifamily households are much more common among some ethnic and cultural groups than others. Indigenous Australians (12.6%) and Australians born in Southeast Asia or China are the most likely to live in multifamily households (7.4%), while non-indigenous Australians and those born in the United Kingdom or Western Europe are the least likely to have this living arrangement.

Extended Family Beyond the Household

The fact that few families share the same household does not mean that extended family networks do not exist or are not important. There is strong evidence that family networks beyond the household are an important part of many lives and the support and assistance exchanged between these family networks is an important part of the social glue that helps bind society together.

These extended family networks are an important source of childcare and elder care (Walker, 1997). Grandparents are the single most widely used type of childcare in Australia (ABS, 2003), and family members are a fundamental part of the care support system of the frail elderly who either live in their own home or live with their children (Millward, 1998). Assistance between adults and their parents flows both ways. However, more support and assistance flows from the older generation to the young generation than vice versa. The exception to this is for the relatively brief period when some parents become frail and dependent (de Vaus & Qu, 1998). A survey of 50- to 70-year-olds found that 91% provided emotional support and help to adult children, 72% provided financial assistance to adult children,

and 83% provided other practical help to adult children (Millward, 1998; Wolcott, 1998).

Parental divorce can disrupt extended family networks and intergenerational supports. Divorced parents receive less help from their grown children than do married or widowed parents. Furthermore, divorced parents provide less support to their grown children than do married or widowed parents (Rezac, 2002; Millward, 1998). Divorced and separated older people also have less contact with their grown children than do other parents (Millward, 1998). Divorce is especially likely to disrupt extended family ties and supports if a divorced parent has repartnered (Millward, 1998).

Intergenerational ties are more active when young children are involved. When children are aged 0 to 4 years old, adults have the most contact with their own parents, siblings, and other extended family members. Once the children have all reached school age (5 years or older), contact with these extended family members declines substantially (Millward, 1996). This is partly because many mothers return to the workforce once their youngest child goes to school, which, in turn, limits the amount of time for contact with other family members.

Women are more active than men in maintaining contact with the extended family. For this reason women have often been described as the "kin-keepers." Adults typically have more frequent contact with their mothers, and mother-daughter contact is the most frequent of all interfamily contacts. Caring is an important part of extended family interactions, and women are much more likely than men to provide day-to-day childcare or elder care. This is not to say that men are not part of these extended family networks but simply that women are the more active players in these networks and rate these family ties as more important than do men (Millward, 1996; Wolcott, 1998).

9. AGING

Population Aging

Like most other countries, Australia's population is aging. Population aging occurs where the population, on average, becomes older. Population aging is not a new phenomenon. It has been occurring for at least the last 150 years in Australia. In 1861 only about 2% of the population reached the age of 65. By 2001, close to 13% of the population lived to this age. By 2041, a quarter of the population is expected to be aged 65 or older.

Population aging is due to two factors operating at once—people living longer and having fewer babies. Increased longevity means that there will be more multigenerational families that include grandparents and great-grandparents for a larger part of a child's life. The declining fertility discussed earlier also contributes to the aging of the population. As fewer children are born, older people make up a larger share of the total population.

Population aging is one reason behind the changing profile of Australian families. It means that families with dependent children constitute a smaller share of all families, and couple-only families and single-person households compose an increasingly large share of families and households.

Caring for Older Family Members

The bulk of care for older frail family members is undertaken in the community by family members with the support of a range of government-supported services. Relatively speaking, few older people are in long-term institutional care. Table 4.10 shows the percentage of older people living in private homes and institutions. Of all people aged 65 or over, just 8% were living in institutions in 2001. Even in the oldest age-group (85 and older), less than a third (31%) lived in an institution.

The chances of older persons entering institutional care increases as they grow older. Those that survive to an old age have a relatively high likelihood of spending some time in a nursing home or other aged-care facility. At the age of 65, men have a 29% chance of ever spending some time in a permanent aged-care facility some time in the future. Because of their greater longevity, women face a greater probability of, at some point, entering a permanent aged-care institution (46% chance). Men who survive to their 90th birthday have a 54% chance of spending some time in institutional care, while similarly aged women have a 69% chance of entering permanent institutional care (Table 4.11).

Table 4.10   Living Arrangements of Those Aged 65 and Over (2001)

	65–69	*70–74*	*75–79*	*80–84*	*85+*	*All*
Private home	97.4	96.3	94.0	87.7	69.1	91.9
Institution	2.6	3.7	6.0	12.3	30.9	8.1

SOURCE: Australian Bureau of Statistics (2001b).

Table 4.11 Probability of Ever Entering Into Permanent Care in an Aged-Care Home, Australia (by Age and Sex, 1999–2000)

	Current Age (Years)						
	65	70	75	80	85	90	95
Males	0.29	0.31	0.34	0.39	0.46	0.54	0.54
Females	0.46	0.48	0.51	0.56	0.62	0.69	0.75

SOURCE: Mason, Liu, and Braun (2001).

On average, older men who go into permanent institutional care do so for between 2 and 2.5 years. Women typically spend longer in a permanent aged-care facility—normally about 4 years (although this is shorter for very old women, who are in care for between 2 and 3 years).

CONCLUSION: THE FUTURE

There can be little doubt that Australian families have changed a great deal over the past century and over the past 25 years in particular. Changes will continue into the future. Predicting the directions of future family change is a risky business. Since families are not isolated from the wider society, family change will depend on the direction of change in other social institutions and within the Australian culture. Future Australian families will be shaped by economic changes; the forces of globalization; the direction of religious change; changes in social values and the growth of individualism; educational changes; technological, medical, and legislative developments; and demographic changes. The particular way in which these social institutions change will be crucial to the way in which families change.

Some guesses about the future shape of families can be extrapolated from trends that are already evident. Perhaps the thing that can be anticipated with some confidence is that there will be an increasing diversity of family forms in which people live across their life course. This trend to diversity is likely to flow from the broad cultural trend by which individuals expect to shape their own life course rather than simply follow a strict set of social rules. The development of free-market economies, the decline of religion, and the emphasis on individualism mean that there will be increasing diversity in the ways in which people "do family." Rather than simply fit into a particular family type, "designer families" or "do-it-yourself" families will become more common.

We can therefore anticipate the following:

- There will be an increase in the proportion of people that choose to never marry.
- More people will live alone at all stages of the life course.
- More people will remain unpartnered for more of their life.
- Of those who are partnered, there will be an increasing diversity in the way in which people partner. We can expect that more people will choose to live together, at least for a time, without marrying.
- Same-sex relationships will become more accepted both socially and legally, and advances in medical technology will mean that an increasing share of same-sex couples will have children.

- Having children without being married will become more and more acceptable. More couples will have children without being married and more single women will have children without any intention of partnering.
- There will be a continuing growth of single-parent families, and more children will spend part of their childhood in a single-parent family.
- Although there is not much evidence of an increase in divorce, the rise in cohabiting relationships will mean that more and more people will have more than one live-in relationship during their life.
- Fertility is unlikely to recover to replacement levels (2.1) and is unlikely to rise much at all in the foreseeable future.
- Families will continue to be smaller and more women will remain childless.
- Mothers will continue to return to and remain in the paid workforce.

Many of these changes are already evident, and it is difficult to see what wider social changes will reverse the current direction of changes in families.

One way of thinking about the ways in which families will change in the future is to think of two opposing sets of factors affecting families. On the one hand, families will have to continue to cope with the centrifugal forces of individualism and fragmentation that characterize contemporary society (Bauman, 2003). These are the forces that emphasize that relationships and commitments cannot and should not be permanent—that ties must be loose so that they can be untied—so that we can "move on." These contemporary forces work against the notion of long-term commitment, obligation, and togetherness that is implied by the notion of marriage, family, and child-rearing. Relationships are conditional on them working "for me." Rather than a relationship being "till death us do part," a relationship is "until further notice."

Nevertheless, the fragility of these relationships can create anxieties and a sense of aloneness and meaninglessness that, in turn, can encourage people to look for tighter bonds and a sense of meaning and purpose in relationship. The limits of individualism can negate some of the centrifugal forces of postmodernity and create a centripetal force that favors family formation and connection. Families in the future will be shaped by the way in which they respond to these opposing forces in contemporary society toward individualism and fragmentation on the one hand and for connection and belonging on the other.

NOTES

1. Informal childcare is nonregulated childcare that includes care from family members (apart from parents), friends, neighbors, and baby-sitters. Formal care is regulated care out of the child's home and includes long-day family care, crèches, before- and after-school care, and kindergarten.

2. These averages are based on 7 days a week over a whole year.

3. The median full-time male wage in 2002 was $789 per week.

4. A multifamily household contains two or more families. A family, as defined by the ABS, consists of "two or more persons, one of whom is at least 15 years of age, who are related by blood, marriage (registered or de facto), adoption, step, or fostering, and who are usually resident in the same household."

5. An extended-family household consists of one family plus at least one other relative such as a grandparent, aunt, uncle, or cousin when these other relatives do not form a separate family unit within the household.

REFERENCES

Australian Bureau of Statistics. (1996a). *National survey of wellbeing and mental health, confidentialised unit record file, 1996.* Canberra: ABS.

Australian Bureau of Statistics. (1996b). *Women's safety, Australia, 1996, Catalogue No. 4128.0.* Canberra: ABS.

Australian Bureau of Statistics. (1997). *Time use survey, 1997, confidentialised unit record file.* Canberra: ABS.

Australian Bureau of Statistics. (1998). *Family characteristics, Australia, 1997, Catalogue No. 4442.0.* Canberra: ABS.

Australian Bureau of Statistics. (2000a). *Australian housing survey: Housing, costs characteristics and conditions, 1999, Catalogue No. 4182.0.* Canberra: ABS.

Australian Bureau of Statistics. (2000b). Special article: Lifetime childlessness. In *Australian demographic statistics: September quarter 1999, Catalogue No. 3101.0* (pp. 8–9). Canberra: ABS.

Australian Bureau of Statistics. (2001a). *Marriages and divorces, Australia, 2000, Catalogue No. 3310.0.* Canberra: ABS.

Australian Bureau of Statistics. (2001b). *Population of census and housing, customised matrix tables.* Canberra: ABS.

Australian Bureau of Statistics. (2001c). *Year book, Australia, 2001, Catalogue No. 1301.0.* Canberra: ABS.

Australian Bureau of Statistics. (2002a). *Births, Australia, 2001, Catalogue No. 3301.0.* Canberra: ABS.

Australian Bureau of Statistics. (2002b). *Census of population and housing, selected social and housing characteristics, Australia, 2001, Catalogue No. 2015.0.* Canberra: ABS.

Australian Bureau of Statistics. (2002c). *Marriages and divorces, Australia, 2001, Catalogue No. 3310.0.* Canberra: ABS.

Australian Bureau of Statistics. (2003). *Child care, Australia, 2002, Catalogue No. 4402.0.* Canberra: ABS.

Australian Institute of Health and Welfare. (2003a). *Australia's mothers and babies 2000, AIHW Catalogue. No. PER 21.* Sydney: AIHW National Perinatal Statistics Unit.

Australian Institute of Health and Welfare. (2003b). *Child protection, Australia, 2001–2.* Canberra: AIHW.

Bauman, Z. (2003). *Liquid love: On the frailty of human bonds.* Cambridge, UK: Polity.

Baxter, J. (1997). Gender equality and participation in housework: A cross-national perspective. *Journal of Comparative Family Studies, 28*(3), 220–247.

Birrell, B., & Rapson, V. (1998). *A not so perfect match: The growing male/female divide, 1986–1996.* Clayton: Centre for Population and Urban Research, Monash University.

Carmichael, G. A., Webster, A., & McDonald, P. (1997). Divorce Australian style: A demographic analysis. *Journal of Divorce & Remarriage, 26*(3,4), 3–36.

Dempsey, K. (1992). *A man's town: Inequality between women and men in rural Australia.* Melbourne: Oxford University Press.

Dempsey, K. (1997). *Inequalities in marriage: Australia and beyond.* Melbourne: Oxford University Press.

Department of Family and Community Services (FACS). (2002). *Household, Income and Labour Dynamics in Australia (HILDA) Survey, 2001.* Confidentialised Unit Record, File.

de Vaus, D. A. (1995). Australian family values survey, unit record file.

de Vaus, D. A. (1997). Family values in the nineties: Gender gap or generation gap? *Family Matters, 48*(Spring/Summer), 5–10.

de Vaus, D. A. (2002). Marriage and mental health. *Family Matters, 62*(Winter), 26–32.

de Vaus, D. A. (2004). *Diversity and change in Australian families.* Melbourne: Australian Institute of Family Studies.

de Vaus, D. A., & Gray, M. (2003). Family transitions among Australia's children. *Family Matters, 65*(Winter), 10–17.

de Vaus, D. A., & Gray, M. (2004). Childhood transitions. In D. A. de Vaus (Ed.), *Diversity and change in Australian Families.* Melbourne: Australian Institute of Family Studies.

de Vaus, D. A., & Qu, L. (1998). Intergenerational family transfers: Dimensions of inequality. *Family Matters, 50*(Winter), 27–30.

de Vaus, D. A., Qu, L., & Weston, R. (2003a). Changing patterns of partnering. *Family Matters, 64*(Autumn), 10–15.

de Vaus, D. A., Qu, L., & Weston, R. (2003b). Premarital cohabitation and subsequent marital stability. *Family Matters, 65*(Winter), 35–39.

Funder, K., & Smyth, B. (1996). Family law reforms and attitudes to parental responsibility. *Family Matters, 45*(Spring/Summer), 10–15.

Glezer, H., Edgar, D., & Prolisko, A. (1992). *The importance of family background and early experiences on premarital cohabitation and marital dissolution.* Paper presented at the International Conference on Family Formation and Dissolution: Perspectives from East and West, Taipei, Taiwan, Republic of China.

Gray, M., & Chapman, B. (2001). Foregone earnings from child rearing: Changes between 1986 and 1997. *Family Matters, 58*(Autumn), 4–9.

Gray, M., & Tudball, J. (2002). *Family friendly work practices: Differences within and between workplaces.* Melbourne: Australian Institute of Family Studies.

Hartley, R. (1993). Young adults living at home. *Family Matters, 36,* 35–37.

Headey, B., Scott, D., & de Vaus, D. (1999). Domestic violence in Australia: Are women and men equally violent? *Australian Social Monitor, 2*(3), 57–62.

Hochschild, A. (1989). *The second shift.* New York: Avon.

Kelley, J., Evans, M. D. R., & Zagorski, K. (1998). International social science survey 1998: Australian module. Available from Australian Social Science Data Archives, Australian National University.

Kilmartin, C. (2000). Young adult moves: Leaving home, returning home, relationships. *Family Matters, 55*(Autumn), 34–40.

Lasch, C. (1977). *Haven in a heartless world.* New York: Basic Books.

Mason, F., Liu, Z., & Braun, P. (2001). *The probability of using an aged care home over a lifetime (1999–00).* Canberra: AIHW.

McColl, B., Pietsch, L., & Gatenby, J. (2001). Household income, living standards and financial stress. In Australian Bureau of Statistics (Ed.), *Australian economic indicators, June 2000, Catalogue No. 1350.0* (pp. 13–32). Canberra: ABS.

Millward, C. (1996). *Australian extended family networks.* Unpublished master's thesis, La Trobe University, Melbourne.

Millward, C. (1998). *Family relationships and intergenerational exchange in later life* (Working paper No. 15). Melbourne: Australian Institute of Family Studies.

Parkinson, P., & Smyth, B. (2003, February). *When the difference is night and day: Some empirical insights into patterns of parent-child contact after separation.* Paper presented at the 8th Australian Family Research Conference, Melbourne.

Percival, R., & Harding, A. (2003, February). *The costs of children in Australia today.* Paper presented at the 8th Australian Family Research Conference, Melbourne.

Pryor, J., & Rodgers, B. (2001). *Children in changing families: Life after parental separation.* Oxford: Blackwell.

Renda, J. (2003). Polarisation of families according to work status. *Family Matters, 64*(Autumn), 16–21.

Rezac, S. J. (2002). Intergenerational assistance in Australian families: The role of parental family structure. *Journal of Family Studies, 8*(1), 24–37.

Rissel, C., Richters, J., Grulich, A., de Visser, R., & Smith, A. (2003). Sex in Australia: Attitudes towards sex in a representative sample of adults. *Australian and New Zealand Journal of Public Health, 27*(2), 118–123.

Rowland, D. T. (1998). The prevalence of childlessness in cohorts of older women. *Australasian Journal on Aging, 17*(1), 18–23.

Russell, G., Barclay, L., Edgecombe, G., Donovan, J., Habib, G., Callaghan, H., & Pawson, Q. (1999). *Fitting fathers into families: Men and the fatherhood role in contemporary Australia.* Canberra: Department of Family and Community Services.

Sawyer, M. G., Arney, F. M., Baghurst, P. A., Clark, J. J., Graetz, B. W., Kosky, R. J., Nurcombe, B., Patton, G. C., Prior, M. R., Raphael, B., Rey, J., Whaites, L. C., & Zubrick, S. R. (2000). *The mental health of young people in Australia.* Canberra: Mental Health and Special Programs Branch, Commonwealth Department of Health and Aged Care.

Smyth, B., & Parkinson, P. (2003, March). *When the difference is day and night: Insights from HILDA into patterns of parent-child contact after separation.* Paper presented at the HILDA Conference, University of Melbourne.

Tomison, A. M. (1996). *Child maltreatment and family structure* (Child Abuse Prevention Discussion Paper No. 1). Melbourne: National Child Protection Clearing House, Australian Institute of Family Studies.

Walker, A. (1997). *Australia's aging population: How important are family structures?* (Discussion Paper No. 19.) Canberra: NATSEM.

Wolcott, I. (1998). *Families in later life: Dimensions of retirement* (Working Paper No. 14.) Melbourne: Australian Institute of Family Studies.

World Values Survey. (1995). *World Values Survey.* Confidentialised Unit Record File.

CHAPTER 5

Chinese Families

Xuewen Sheng

1. INTRODUCTION AND DESCRIPTION

For most Chinese people, family (*jia* or *jiating*) is a simple as well as a complex concept. It is simple because everybody has a family (or families) and thus knows what it is. It is complex because different individuals have different explanations about families. Quite often, the answer to the question, "What is a family?" is "it depends. . . ." In traditional Chinese society, family was another name for a patriarchal clan, including not only its current members but also its ancestors enshrined and worshiped in clan halls, and a set of feudal orders and ethical codes among kinships, based on Confucian doctrines. In contemporary China, the meanings of family may vary from person to person. From the perspective of politicians (such as Mr. Yaobang Hu, former leader of the Chinese Communist Party), family, rather than the individual, is the "basic cell" of the society. In the view of administrators, a family is a household within which a group of people live at a given period of time for resident registration or census. Meanwhile, a rural peasant may think of his house, land, and livestock as part of his family, and family

in the mind of an urban dweller may include the networks of direct kinship spreading outward in the city. In addition, family may mean mom, dad, and a playground to a little child; a small but warm, comfortable, and affective home to a young newly married couple; raising up children and supporting the aged to a middle-aged person; or all her children and grandchildren to a retired senior.

Despite these variations, Chinese academics have commonly accepted a more institutionalized concept of family—"[F]amily is an essential unit of social life, which is tied through relationships of marriage, blood, and adoption" (*Chinese Encyclopedia: Sociology*, 1991, p. 102)—and taken the "household" approach to operationally define family in their empirical studies. From a rigorous scientific point of view, by highlighting the instructional feature of family only, this definition is too general to cover other natures of family, such as biological (MacIver, 1937), cultural (Lowie, 1934), interactional (Burgess & Locke, 1960), and structural-functional (Parsons, 1955). Moreover, the "household" approach underrepresents the real cultural connotations of Chinese families, given that most Chinese people consider family as something more than a household. Therefore,

I will adopt these family definitions with caution in this chapter by emphasizing the following: (1) the continuity and change of the cultural traditions of Chinese families, and (2) the diversity of contemporary Chinese families, particularly the significant differences between urban and rural families.

Background

China is a country of 1.3 billion people, 31 regional areas, and 56 nationalities. About 40% of Chinese people live in urban areas, while the remaining 60% live in rural areas, according to official statistics (National Bureau of Statistics, 2001a). As is shown in the 5th National Population Census data, in the year 2000, the average family size (persons per household) of China was 3.44 (p. 93) with a standard deviation of 0.39, representing a moderate variation among 31 provinces, autonomous regions, and municipalities in the country. In general, families are smaller in metropolises and larger in rural and autonomous regions. For instance, the average family sizes in Beijing, Shanghai, and Tianjin were 2.91, 2.80, and 3.09, respectively, while the numbers in Tibet, Hainan, and Xinjiang were 4.77, 4.07, and 3.68, respectively.

Obviously, with this average size of families, the typical Western notion that most Chinese people live in joint or large families is thoroughly discredited (Cohen, 1978). Although the descriptions of large patriarchal families have long been a major focus of classical Chinese literature (e.g., *The Red Chamber* and *Four Generations Under One Roof*; Cao, 2002), large families with several generations under one roof have never been the dominant family pattern in Chinese history. By analyzing 71 available household registration records ranging from 2 A.D. to 1911, Chinese historians found that the average family size across Chinese history was 4.95, with a standard deviation of 1.61 (R. Pan, 2002). It appears that, throughout

history, the dominant family size was four to seven people (55 times), accounting for 77.5% of the 71 records. "With a local community of 4 to 7 people," as Fei pointed out, "it is absolutely impossible to form those large families" (1981, pp. 85–86). Practically, maintaining large families needs certain social and economic conditions (Cohen, 1978). With a poor agricultural economy, high fertility and high mortality rates, low life expectancy, and frequent wars, pestilences, and famines, ancient China provided very limited ground for large families to develop, although favored by its cultural traditions.

As argued by Laslett and Wall (1972) and Hareven (1977), the industrialization and modernization processes served as a main engine for speeding up the process of downsizing of families, reducing the number of stem-families, as suggested by a functionalist modernization hypothesis (Christensen, 1964). In the past century, industrialization has changed the Chinese demographic structure dramatically. At the beginning of the 20th century, the rural population accounted for more than 90% of the total Chinese population. However, as more and more people moved into the industrial sectors, the rural proportion declined to 88.00% in 1953, 80.61% in 1980, 73.59% in 1990, and 63.78% in 2000 (National Bureau of Statistics, 2001a, p. 93). Accordingly, the average urban household size fell from 3.89 in 1985 to 3.50 in 1990, 3.23 in 1995, and 3.13 in 2000 (p. 305). Similar rural trends have taken place also, although they are not as dramatic. The average household size of rural residents decreased from 4.80 in 1990 to 4.48 in 1995 and 4.20 in 2000 (p. 322).

In addition to the processes of industrialization and modernization, the population control campaign launched in the1980s has also been responsible for the rapid shrinking of Chinese families. As China's population policy requires that couples have only one child, the national birth rate declined rapidly from 22.28 in 1982 to 15.23 in 1999 (National Bureau of Statistics, 2001a, p. 91). Given the fact that the one-child policy was more successful in urban areas than in rural areas, the current birth rate is slightly lower in urban areas than in rural areas (13.18 compared with 16.13). As a result, the three-person families consisting of a father, a mother, and an only-child have become one of the major patterns of Chinese families, especially in urban areas. According to the Fourth National Census, these three-person families accounted for 23% of total Chinese families, 30% of urban families, and 20% of rural families (adopted from Y. Ma, Wang, Sheng, & Shinozaki, 1994).

Family studies conducted in recent decades confirmed that Chinese families have experienced a smooth transition to smaller and nuclear families. With data collected from 5,075 married women in Beijing, Tianjin, Shanghai, Nanjing, and Chengdu, the Five Cities' Marriage and Family Study was the first large-scale research project on Chinese families conducted since sociology as an academic discipline was reconstructed in China in the early 1980s (Y. Liu & Xüe, 1987). By investigating the patterns of respondents' original families at the time of their marriage, this study was able to trace the changes in family patterns since the 1930s. Findings from this study showed that the nuclear family had long been the dominant family pattern in Chinese cities, and its proportion increased gradually from 55.6% in or before the 1930s, to 57.9% in the 1960s, 67.1% in the 1970s, and 69.28% in the early 1980s (Five Cities' Marriage and Family Study Project, 1985, p. 484). The proportion of stem-families as the second major family pattern, however, remained roughly the same or decreased slightly across the last century, from 25.7% in the 1930s to 21.0% in the early 1980s (p. 484). Another study of 1,920 Beijing residents in the early

1990s (Y. Ma et al., 1994) presented similar findings: The proportion of nuclear families was 65.4%, while the proportion of stem-families was 20.3% (p. 100). As far as family patterns in rural areas are concerned, two large-scale social surveys conducted in the late 1980s revealed a trend similar to the one in urban areas. A study on current rural families in China collected data from over 7,000 rural families in 14 provinces across China, and showed that, from 1978 to 1986, the proportion of nuclear families increased from 64.4% to 68.7%, while the proportion of stem-families decreased from 25.8% to 19.7% (Y. Liu et al., 1993). Similarly, by surveying 2,799 rural families in six city suburbs and provinces, another project (J. Lei, Yang, & Cai, 1994) found that, during the same period of time, nuclear families increased from 69.3% to 74.1%, while stem-families decreased from 24.7% to 23.7% (p. 79).

As yet, Chinese cultural attitudes favor large families, although most Chinese people are actually living in separate, small households. This is not only reflected in Chinese literature, but also in ordinary peoples' ideas about family. As revealed by *A Study on Life and Consciousness of Contemporary Urban Families in China*, even though not necessarily living together, 40.4% of the respondents tended to consider their married children (son or daughter) as family members, 75.5% of them thought their parents or in-laws were family members, 23% of them reported their brothers or sisters as family members, and 16.9% of them included their grandchildren as family members (Y. Ma et al., 1994, p. 105). A large family is still an ideal, if not a reality, in contemporary Chinese society.

2. PAIRING UP

Traditionally, a marriage in China was based solely on "the command of parents and the good offices of a matchmaker," which emphasizes matching socioeconomic statuses between the two families. Thus, marriage is actually an issue of connecting the political, social, and economic resources between the two families, rather than a result of love and affection between the two married parties. In most cases, the married parties did not choose their spouses, and they were not supposed to meet each other until the wedding.

In contemporary China, however, the arranged marriage has become all but obsolete. According to the Five Cities' Marriage and Family Study (1985, p. 307), through the 50 years from the 1930s to the 1980s, the percentage of arranged marriages in urban China dropped off from 54.7% to 0.9%, and the percentage of married couples that were introduced by relatives decreased from 24.4% to 15.8%, while so-called free courtship, including married couples introduced by friends and by oneself, increased from 15.3% to 50.8% and from 4.99% to 32.8%, respectively. In addition to these historical trends, findings from a study on women's status in contemporary China revealed some diversity in mate selection between over 9,000 urban and rural respondents. While the percentages of absolute arranged marriages were very low in both urban and rural areas (1.09% and 2.01%, respectively), more urban mates were selected "by oneself" than rural (41.09% compared with 14.86%), while more rural mates were selected by the "introduction of parents and relatives" than urban (49.07% compared with 16.02%) (Institute of Population Studies, 1994, p. 99). As far as the final determination of the marriage is concerned, although the majority of marriage decisions in China were made "by myself with parent permission" (urban: 33.00%; rural: 23.77%) or "by myself with the permission from parents and parents-in-law" (urban: 58.86%; rural: 48.68%), rural respondents were more likely to report the decisions made "by parents with my agreement" (20.20%) than were urban

respondents (3.17%) (p. 114). It seems that, compared with urban parents, rural parents still have more involvement and more power over their children's mate selection.

This women's status study also found that, instead of emphasizing the matching of socioeconomic statuses between the two families, in contemporary China more consideration has been given to mates' personal factors such as educational level, occupation, appearance, moral standing, and temperament. However, while the majority of respondents (50.29%) placed "moral standing" as the main consideration for their mate selection, urban respondents tended to give more weight to educational level (15.31%) and occupation (8.71%) than did rural respondents (3.72% and 3.08%), and male respondents were more likely to select their mates based on "appearance" (urban: 15.02%; rural: 26.94%) than were female respondents (urban: 6.60%; rural: 18.52%) (Institute of Population Studies, 1994, p. 123). This urban-rural difference reflects the reality that educational level and occupational prestige gradually become more important indicators of personal socioeconomic status in urban areas than in rural areas due to the rapid development of modern technologies in urban China.

China used to be a country that encouraged early marriage. Throughout the history of ancient China, the most common lawful age of marriage was 16 years old for boys and 14 years old for girls. During the period of the Republic of China (1912–1949), the lawful marriage age was raised to 18 for boys and 16 for girls, although early marriages were still very common at that time (P. Zhang, 1993). In 1950, the new republic's first marriage law raised the lawful marriage age to 20 for boys and 18 for girls, and the marriage law published in 1981 again raised the lawful marriage age to 22 for boys and 20 for girls. Along with legal enforcement, there have been developed governmental policies that strongly encourage "later marriage, and later childbirth" in the past 50 years in China. As a result, the average first marriage age in China has been increased substantially. According to official statistics, the average first marriage age of Chinese women has risen from 18.57 (urban: 19.16; rural: 18.44) in 1949, to 22.66 (urban: 24.93; rural: 22.07) in 1982 (Research Institute of All China Women's Federation and Research Office of Shanxi Provincial Women's Federation, 1991). In 1996, the average age of first marriage (for both men and women) in China was 24.02 ("The Age of First Marriage," 1998). Early marriages have largely been eliminated, though they have resurged somewhat since the 1980s in some poor rural and minority areas (R. Li, 1992; Yan & Shi, 1995; P. Zhang, 1993) due to the loosening of social control resulting from the dissolution of the commune system.

The marriage ceremony was one of the most important ceremonies in traditional Chinese society. Until the end of the Qing Dynasty (1911), China had practiced the civil marriage ceremony system. In the period of the Republic of China, both the civil marriage ceremony system and the marriage registration system were applied (Tao & Ming, 1994). Since 1949, the marriage registration system has become the major practice in Chinese marriage. In addition to official registration, the most common marriage ceremony in contemporary Chinese civil society is the wedding dinner party, where relatives and friends are invited to celebrate and recognize the marriage. The size of the wedding party is dependent on the social and economic status of the marriage couple and their families. Since the 1990s, there has been a growing concern about the rapidly increasing cost of marriage in China, including the expenses of purchasing furniture, clothes, and a wedding party. A survey conducted by the Zero Point Survey Company showed that in Chinese metropolises such as Beijing, Shanghai,

Wuhan, and Guanzhou, the average expense of marriage increased from 161.43 RMB Yuan in the 1930s and 1940s, to 1,282.71 RMB Yuan in the 1970s, 5,486.51 RMB Yuan in the 1980s, and 21,082 RMB Yuan in the 1990s ("The Match of Wedding," 1997). This survey also reported that more marriage expenses were paid by married parties themselves (44%) and less of them were supported by parents (31%). Other studies conducted in Tianjin (Hao & Wang, 1994), Shanghai (Luo, 1992), and Chengdu (H. Ma, 1997) revealed a similar trend of increase in marriage expenses. The cost of a new marriage has risen rapidly in recent years, according to official reports. The current average cost for a young couple's wedding in Shanghai is 150,000 RMB Yuan (US$18,000), excluding the cost of an apartment ("Wedding Costs on the Rise in Shanghai," 2002). In general, the increase in marriage expenses, on one hand, reflects the growth in people's living standards. On the other hand, the sense of competition in marriage cost often makes a young couple spend most of their and their parents' savings at the beginning of the marriage and may cause potential troubles for their future family lives.

To some of the young couples, marriage means the beginning of a new family household, while for others it is just an addition to their parents' family households. The study on women's status in contemporary China (Institute of Population Studies, 1994, p. 107) presented dramatic differences in residential status at marriage between urban and rural wives. While a majority (58.39%) of urban wives lived alone with their husband, only 27.91% of rural wives did so. In contrast, 65.40% of rural wives lived in their parents-in-law's home, while only 31.67% of urban wives did so. It appears that urban couples tend to be more independent after marriage than are rural couples, and the patriarchal family norm is still stronger in rural areas than in urban areas. However, this is only partially true. Many living arrangements may, in fact, be made under some practical considerations. For instance, the over-crowded housing conditions in large cities often force young couples to live apart from their parents if they can find their own houses, while the same reason may force others to crowd into their parents' home for a period of time until they find somewhere to stay. In rural areas, because family properties such as land, productive materials, houses, and livestock belong to all family members, living apart from the parents' home means separating family properties and will even-tually weaken the family's productive capa-bilities. Thus, the married sons (along with their wives and children) normally stay with their parents for a period of time until some-thing (e.g., the death of parents, major family conflicts, employment mobility of some members, etc.) happens in the family that forces them to separate (Z. Liu, 1996). Although most married couples will have their own houses near their parents' homes, and they may also officially be registered as individual households, they do not nor-mally consider themselves as separated from parents' families.

3. FERTILITY AND SOCIALIZATION

China has experienced a remarkable transi-tion from a country with high fertility, high infant mortality, and low life expectancy to a country with low fertility, low infant mortal-ity, and high life expectancy over the past 50 years. These trends can be attributed to the development of the social economy, the popularization of modern techniques of maternal and child hygiene, the viability of reliable contraception, and the enforcement of government policies and legislation related to population control. Until the end of the 1940s, China held a gross fertility rate of 5.813, an infant mortality rate around 20%,

and a life expectancy of 34 years (29.8 years for men and 38.3 years for women). The same indexes have been changed dramati-cally since the 1950s, to 1.9, 3.2%, and 70.1 years in 1999, respectively (Research Institute of All China Women's Federation and Research Office of Shanxi Provincial Women's Federation, 1991). A direct conse-quence of these trends in the Chinese popu-lation is the transition from high birth rates, high death rates, and high natural growth rates to low birth rates, low death rates, and low natural growth rates.

It is widely recognized that the well-known one-child policy has played a critical role in the dramatic decline of population growth in China, along with other factors. Although the championing of population control began as early as 1962 in China, its impact was not substantial until the one child per couple policy became fully operational in the early 1980s (Kallgren, 1985; Wolf, 1986). The policy was enforced mainly through adminis-trative channels and work units, resulting in a great diversity in actual practices of imple-menting the policy among provinces, cities, and work units (The Research Project on the Efficiency of Implementing Family Planning in China, 1996). The amount of penalties for extra births and rewards for couples with one child has varied greatly from one area to another (G. Feng & Hao, 1992). In general, the one-child policy has been implemented more successfully in urban areas than in rural areas, and in minority areas even more (Bianco, 1981; X. Chen, 1985; Poston & Gu, 1984), with the result of reducing the popula-tion by an estimated total of 250 million at the end of the last century. The population repre-sented by only-children climbed to 50 million in the early 1990s, accounting for one-fourth of the Chinese population aged 0 to 9, accord-ing to the 1990 census data. In 1995, about 95% of the preschool children in urban China, more than 90% of children in kinder-gartens, and 60% of the university freshmen were from only-child families. One negative outcome of the policy results from the Chinese preference for male children over female children. Consequently a large number of female children have been abandoned or gone unregistered (Ching & Penny, 1999). In the year 2002, China published its first law of family planning, and birth control was for the first time put into legislation.

The potential implications of the one-child policy for family life are significant. The policy has reduced the size of Chinese families. Another long-term consequence of this policy has been the formation of a 4-2-1 pattern of kinship in China (Sheng, 1992). That is, in the foreseeable future, a child's kinship would include only his or her parents and grandparents without any other relatives such as brothers, sisters, nephews, or cousins. It also means that a couple would have to support or care for two, four, or even six older couples as well as their own child without support from other relatives. In addition, the one-child policy also creates a generation of "little emperors," children who have not had to share with siblings the attention of their parents and grandparents. With the expectation of succession of family lines and of support for later life, parents and grandparents tend to devote a great deal of their resources to their only-child or grandchild. This provides an unprecedented and advanced developmental opportunity for the new only-child generation. However, these children could be easily spoiled to the point of selfishness and self-centeredness, with little sense of family obligation and expectation of caring for others (K. Chen, 1986; "China's Lifestyle Choice," 2001; Huang, 1992; Ji, Jiao, & Ring, 1993; Jiao, Ji, & Ring, 1986, 1996; Wan, Fan, & Lin, 1994; Wan, Fan, Lin, & Jing, 1994).

Chinese parents, who are deeply influenced by the Confucian tradition, consider education as the major means of socializing young children and have high expectations for their children's academic achievement. Over the past 50 years, the Chinese education system has been expanded substantially. In 1950, there were only 193 universities/colleges, 5,123 secondary schools, 384,000 primary schools, and 1,799 kindergartens (similar to preschools in Western society) in China. With a half-century's efforts, these numbers have increased to 1,041 universities/colleges, 93,935 secondary schools, 553,622 primary schools, and 175,836 kindergartens in 2000 (National Bureau of Statistics, 1999, 2001b). Now, about 45% of Chinese children aged 5 or younger are in kindergarten, about 60% of rural children are in 1-year preprimary school classes, 99% of school-age children are in schools, and almost all of them will go to secondary school (*China Education Yearbook*, 1998). The remaining 1% represents the children living in poor, remote, rural and mountain areas who are still struggling for educational opportunities. Although the one-child policy has taken some pressure off of the school system at the primary level, the needs for postsecondary opportunities are expanding for several reasons.

Higher education has long been very competitive in China. To send their children to universities or colleges so that they can eventually find good jobs, build up successful careers, and have a good future, Chinese parents start preparing their children from birth. Thus, the typical picture is that, as soon as the mother is pregnant, the father starts looking for fetus education tapes for his baby to hear. After the baby is born, the parents begin to follow the suggestions for toys for the baby and check his or her developmental situation all the time. When the baby is 2 or 3 years old, they begin to send him or her to kindergarten. The parents begin to think about early intellectual development. Some parents start to buy such things as musical instruments and intellectually stimulating toys, and look for tutorial classes for their children. After children are of school age, the parents have more worries. They pay money for their children to enter a good school. They help children with homework. They take care of everything in their children's daily lives to allow them to study and achieve. In general, only-children's parents try to do everything they can for their children, all the time.

However, compared with this great devotion, the techniques of parents training their children are critical. A survey by the Zhejiang Academy of Social Sciences (Zhu, 1992) shows that 55% of the parents consider the school achievement of their children as the most crucial thing for their families. More than one-half of the parents report that they are likely to beat their children if they fail an examination. Most (68%) of the parents want their children to obey whatever the parents ask of them. In addition, parents of only-children push very hard on their child to study. As one survey conducted by the *Beijing Daily* (Man, 1993) shows, besides studying on weekdays, about 80% of the interviewed pupils are asked by parents to take certain spare-time training classes during the weekend—including classes in math, writing, computer, piano, arts, and so on. One sixth-grade pupil said that on Sundays he had to take math class at 7:30 A.M., and then take his music and piano class at 10:15 A.M.; in the afternoon, he had to take his English class and orchestral music. At the end of the interview, he said that his biggest wish was to have a good sleep on Sunday. His situation is not unusual in urban China, according to this survey.

Chinese families now provide only-children with superior training, compared with the training of older generations. However, they push them toward intellectual achievements more than toward the development of appropriate social values and norms or the cultivation of initiative and creativity.

Thus, one should not be surprised by the fact that the only-child generation seems more advanced in intellectual development but is more problematic in personality development. To have a better outcome in terms of individual development of the only-child generation in China, improvement of social and family environments must be seen as an essential step.

4. GENDER ROLES

Since ancient times, the Chinese have thought that the idyllic division of gender roles at home was so-called "men plough the fields and women weave" and "the husband sings and the wife follows." However, this was hardly a reality over the 2000 years of feudal society in China. From Confucianism to the feudal ethical codes developed in the following dynasties, Chinese ideology and ethics were built on patriarchy and man's domination and on the oppression and subordination of woman, characterized by the rules of "three obediences and four virtues" (obedience to father before marriage, to husband after marriage, and to son after husband's death; morality, proper speech, modest manner, and diligent work) (G. Liu & Zhao, 1994). The Confucianism ideology and ethics were not challenged until the beginning of the 20th century by the "May Fourth" movement of 1919, an anti-imperialist, antifeudal, political and cultural movement, and liberation of Chinese women has only been gradually reached in recent decades.

In contemporary Chinese society, women, by law, have the same rights as men in political, economic, educational, and social and family life. At the social level, pursuing equality between men and women has long been one of the main goals of the Communist Party and government. One of the remarkable changes in women's social status has been the rapidly increasing participation of women in the labor force since the 1950s. Until the end of the 1940s, the majority of Chinese women were excluded from the job market, and it was estimated that there were only 610,000 female workers in China, accounting for 7% of the total labor force (S. Lei, 1995). This proportion has increased to 40.5% in 1960 and 45.2% in 1999, according to World Bank statistics (National Bureau of Statistics, 2001b). Most women are currently working in agriculture (76.1%, compared with 69.1% for men), while another 13% of them are in the manufacturing industry, and the remaining 10.6% are in the service industry, based on the statistics of 1995 (National Bureau of Statistics, 2001b).

In terms of family life, women have gained freedom to choose a marriage, use their own surname, and inherit family properties, which could ensure them equality with their husbands at home. With universal full-time employment in urban areas, wives are able to be independent economically from their husbands and to become important contributors to family income. As shown in the study on women's status in contemporary China (Institute of Population Studies, 1994), although most wives had a slightly lower income than their husbands, working wives shared equally or had even more power over family matters. In terms of economic control, 76.25% of the respondents reported, "husband and wife control and arrange the income together," whereas 10.35% of them reported "wife controls the income," and only 3.79% of them reported "husband controls the income." Also, more sharing was found in decision making about consumer goods, helping children with their education, employment, and mate selection.

Compared with the sharing of family decision making, however, there is more gender segregation between wife and husband in doing housework. Wives seem to dominate more in tasks such as purchasing food and

cooking (65.73%, compared with 17.51% of husbands), shopping (66.06%, compared with 20.48% of husbands), washing clothes (80.23%, compared with 9.95% of husbands), cleaning rooms (73.63%, compared with 13.38% of husbands), and taking care of children (54.72%, compared with 6.40% of husbands). Husbands are more likely to handle such heavy jobs as purchasing coal and changing gas tanks (for cooking) (64.22%, compared with 5.53% of wives) and purchasing grain (65.58%, compared with 21.72% of wives). Another study (Y. Ma, Liu, Sheng, & Meng, 1992) on working mothers of 2,000 kindergartners in Beijing, Shanghai, and Xian revealed similar findings of gender roles in Chinese cities. By sharing power in family decision making, wives have more control in managing the family economy (29.4%, compared with 9.4% of husbands) and saving and investment (18.1%, compared with 8.5% of husbands).

It appears that current gender roles of urban Chinese couples are preconditioned by the universal employment policy and characterized by the increase of women's power in family decision making. However, women's liberation has never been without a price—the dual burden of employment and family life (Stockman, Bonney, & Sheng, 1995). The fact is that urban wives have to do the major domestic labor while they are engaged in full-time employment outside the home. As the society has been making the transition from a socialist planned economy to a capitalist market economy since the 1980s, jobs have become more competitive and unstable, and women have become the main targets (70%) for layoffs or early retirement (Zhong, 1994). Thus, concerns about women's gender roles inside and outside families have long been and continue to be a hot topic for debate in Chinese public and academic circles (Tan, 1995).

In rural China, there is no clear distinction between whether or not a person is employed, because at some level all work contributes to the overall economic effort. Because the old collective economy of the people's commune was replaced by the economy of contracted farmers in the 1980s, productive activity became a private matter of individual families. The only distinction in agricultural activities, therefore, is working on the land and working at home. According to the study on women's status in contemporary China (Institute of Population Studies, 1994), 71.08% of rural husbands (compared with 30.15% of wives) were working mainly on the land, while 69.87% of wives (compared with 7.80% of husbands) were working mainly at home. Even though working in different areas, a majority of husbands (84.83%) and wives (87.81%) contributed all of their income to their families. Rural husbands are mainly responsible for the land, including plowing, seeding, fertilizing, irrigating, and harvesting. Rural wives take the major responsibilities of housework, compared with their husbands. These include cooking, washing, taking care of children, feeding chickens and ducks, feeding pigs, and purchasing daily necessities in town. With this gender division of labor, rural couples also seem to share in family decision making in such matters as house building, purchasing household durable consumer goods, when to have a baby, when to start the children's education, and purchasing betrothal gifts or dowry for daughters.

In recent years, more and more rural migrants have gone to urban areas to look for jobs. This occupational migration has created a large number of living apart together (LAT) families in rural China. Normally, the husbands and older children (both sons and daughters) work temporarily in construction, service, and light industries in nearby towns and cities to bring cash back to support their families, while women and seniors stay on the land. There has been an emerging pattern of gender roles among rural

families; that is, "husband works in town and wife plows in the field." Some researchers (e.g., Meng, 1995) suggest that this pattern provides women more opportunities to control productive activities (because of the absence of husbands); this, in turn, raises women's sense of self-esteem and independence. However, I would argue that it is a greater challenge for women to handle both land work and household tasks than it is an opportunity for independence.

5. MARITAL RELATIONSHIPS

Although major family surveys conducted in past decades frequently reported that the majority of Chinese couples considered their marital lives as happy, there has always been a question about the criterion of happiness that people are applying. Similarly to people in other societies, Chinese husbands, as "main breadwinners," are expected to bring more money home, and Chinese wives, while also working outside the home, are supposed to perform as a "good wife and loving mother." However, ideas regarding how good an income a man should gain to be a good husband and how nice a woman should be to be a good wife and mother vary significantly from one respondent to another. Thus, having a mutual understanding, care, and adjustment between wife and husband is critical for healthy marital relationships.

Available research data on marital relationships (Institute of Population Studies, 1994) showed that in urban areas 20.85% of wives and 31.12% of husbands expected their spouses to improve mutual understanding, and 18.32% of wives and 15.94% of husbands wanted their spouse to show more consideration and care. The same data for rural couples are 17.69% (of wives) and 23.37% (of husbands) for the former, and 11.28% (of wives) and 12.92% (of husbands) for the later. This implies that about two of every five Chinese couples have problems in their mutual understanding and mutual caring for each other.

These problems may be seen as a side effect of current expectations of gender roles, which can lead both wives and husbands into a vicious circle of unhappy relationships. That is, the more the husband and wife focus on their gender roles, the more they demand understanding and caring from each other, but the less they are actually able to give them to each other. As shown in a study of 2,170 couples in Beijing (J. Liu, 1991), mutual understanding and caring were highly correlated with marital satisfaction ($r = 0.37$), and lack of mutual understanding and caring was a major reason for dissatisfaction in conjugal relationships. It was suggested by some scholars (e.g., Wu, 1995; Stockman et al., 1995) that traditional gender role expectations need to be replaced by some more equalitarian, flexible, and realistic expectations for roles of husband and wife, to balance the contradictions between work and family life.

Need of sexuality is an important part of mutual understanding and caring. In general, sexual and affectionate expression and intimacy are considered basic characteristics of a successful marriage (Michael, Gagnon, Laumann, & Kolata, 1994). Until recent decades, sexuality had been a closely guarded secret of married couples, and most Chinese people felt ashamed to talk openly of sexuality. Sex education was poorly developed before the 1990s in China, the assumption being that people learn sexual behavior by themselves. Recognized as an important turning point, the so-called China Kinsey report (cf. Kinsey, Pomeroy, & Martin, 1948) was the first large-scale survey on sexuality and was conducted by D. Liu (1992). He collected information on sexual perceptions and behaviors from 23,000 respondents across 15 provinces in China. According to this study, Chinese husbands

initiated sexual behavior and wives were likely to be more passive. For the question "Who usually initiates sexual intercourse?," 63.7% of husbands and 71.9% of wives reported "husband initiates." The percentages answering "both (wife and husband) initiate together" were 20.8% for husbands and 15.4% for wives. Although 55.5% of urban couples and 66.6% of rural couples were "very satisfied" or "satisfied" with their sexual life, the credibility of these satisfaction rates are open to question, given the fact of men's normative domination in sexual behavior in China. As reported in a study conducted in northeast China in the 1980s, among 1,000 divorced couples, 47% of husbands and 17% of wives listed an "unharmonious sexual life" as a primary reason for the divorce. Similarly, another analysis of divorce cases in Shanghai in 1983 reported that 23% were caused by unharmonious sexual life. Available evidence also showed that an unharmonious sex life reduced the likelihood of pregnancy and quite often led to marital conflicts. By analyzing more than 40,000 clients of a pregnancy consultation service over 5 years, a study in the early 1990s reported that about a quarter of the sterility cases resulted from problems in sexual behaviors (data adapted from R. Pan, 2002).

Effective communication between husband and wife is another way to increase mutual understanding and caring. It includes spending time together, frequently exchanging ideas, caring about spouse's feelings, and so on. By collecting information from 1,985 married couples in Beijing, J. Liu's study (1991) reported that about 67.5% of couples frequently spend leisure time together, about 58% of them frequently exchange ideas, and about 80% of them care about each other's feelings. This study also showed significant correlations between a couple's communication and their marital satisfaction. G. Zhang, Lei, and Liang's study (1996) suggested that efficient communication between wife and husband was heavily influenced by their perception of gender roles. Traditional views of gender roles were negatively associated with frequent communication ($\beta = -.169$), whereas modern views on gender roles tended to increase communication between wife and husband ($\beta = 0.035$).

Mutual understanding and caring may also be expressed in arrangements such as sharing housework and pursuing a more egalitarian power structure at home. As discussed previously, with certain kinds of specialization, Chinese husbands are generally willing to share some household tasks and powers in family decision making with their wives. Available evidence shows that sharing housework and family power equally is an important factor for marital satisfaction, especially for dual-employment couples. According to J. Liu's study (1991), among the three patterns of housework division—wife does more, husband does more, and couple equally shares—the proportions of both wife and husband satisfied with marriage are 27%, 30%, and 36%, respectively. Equally sharing couples, therefore, had higher satisfaction rates than couples in the other two patterns. Instead of husbands' dominant power in family decision making, a current concern focuses on a wife's power over her husband in some large Chinese cities such as Shanghai, Beijing, and Guangzhou. A study in Shanghai reported that wives tended to have more power than their husbands in managing the family economy (wife control: 30%; husband control: 7.5%) and on overall family decision making (wife control: 31.1%; husband control: 8.7%) (Xu, 1992). Wives in this emerging pattern of marital relationships were called "strong women" who tend to bring in more money and carry on more housework in their families. It appears that the traditional pattern of gender roles inside the family is being challenged.

6. FAMILY STRESSES AND VIOLENCE

Family life is never without stresses. Adapting and managing stresses properly leads the family to a new stage of life with a stronger set of ties. According to the study on women's status in contemporary China (Institute of Population Studies, 1994), slightly less than one-third of Chinese couples reported no stresses, and the others reported three main conflicts between wives and husbands in their family lives: children, housework, and family economy. About 44% of urban couples reported children's issues as the main reason for conflict, compared with 30% of wives and 3.5% of husbands in rural areas. About 12% of urban couples reported housework as their main reason for conflict, while 20% of wives and 17% of husbands did so in rural areas. About 4% of urban and 10% of rural couples reported family economy as the main reason for their arguments.

To some couples, the birth of a new baby means love and happiness, while to others, it means burden and responsibilities. A survey of parents of newborn babies showed that by the time husbands heard the news of their wives' pregnancies, 52.8% of them felt their lives coming into a new turning point, 22.8% of them felt their burden becoming heavier, 18.8% of them felt very happy, and 4.1% of them felt they were unprepared. Because of the one-child policy, many Chinese families have only one child, especially in urban areas. The only-child naturally becomes the focus of the family, influencing the couple's daily interaction, communication, division of housework, and daily life arrangements. Misunderstandings and disagreements among family members regarding children may become a source of family stresses. Based on this survey, the conflicts between urban wives and husbands around children's problems increase as the child grows older and decrease as the child becomes a young adult. In rural areas, because wives take the major responsibility of raising children, they reported many more conflicts about children than their husbands. Another feature of rural couples is the low percentage of both wives and husbands who report the child(ren) as the main reason for conflicts: 1.14%, compared with 32.64% of urban couples.

Issues about housework are another important source of stress, especially for husbands and wives who both work full time outside the home. The problem includes conflicts between wife and husband on who should do what and how to do it. The same study (Institute of Population Studies, 1994) also reported that in the first few years of marriage, urban couples met greater challenges on housework. After this period of time, conflicts around housework seemed to decrease. In rural areas, conflicts around housework seemed consistently low across the life span. However, the proportions of rural wives and husbands who perceived housework as a major source of conflict were very low, indicating that normative patriarchy kept complaints from being expressed.

The family economy seemed less likely to be a source of stress for urban couples (wife: 3.45%; husband: 3.91%) than for rural couples (wife: 9.09%; husband: 9.85%), according to this survey. This may simply be because urban residents are generally better off than rural residents in terms of family income. Besides this factor, there have been some social changes in the past years in both urban and rural China that may create stresses for families and require adjustment between wives and husbands. In urban areas, due to widespread layoffs in state-owned businesses (where most urban residents worked), thousands of urban families have faced challenges regarding their economic well-being. Instead of continuously waiting and looking for jobs in state-owned business, about 23% of urban families are taking a

"one family, two (employment) systems" approach. That is, one person keeps working in a state-owned business and the other one looks for a job in private enterprise (Nan & He, 1997). The advantage of this approach is that families can benefit both from state-owned businesses for their stability of employment and from private businesses for their higher salaries. In rural areas, as the prices of agricultural products remain low in China, more and more rural husbands go to nearby cities to look for jobs, while their wives remain on the land and take care of homes and farms. This strategy functions in overcoming some of the economic stresses on rural families, but may create other tensions between wife and husband because of long-term separation.

Family violence may be seen as an extreme solution to family stresses. Although reports about family violence often appear in the mass media, very little serious scientific research has been done on this in China. Jun's survey (1994) in some coastal cities revealed that 80% of the surveyed families had at least one experience of family violence, 40% of them serious or very serious violence, including couples fighting with each other, physical abuse of wife (or husband), and the beating of children. The cases of wife abuse accounted for about 50% of family violence. In another survey conducted by the Beijing Marriage and Family Association (Y. Li, 1995), 21.3% of husbands reported having beaten their wives at least once, and 15.2% of wives reported having beaten their husbands at least once. These studies suggested that marital violence in China happens in a great proportion of families.

Besides marital violence, child abuse is another widespread problem in China. A survey conducted by the Zhejiang Academy of Social Sciences (Zhu, 1992) revealed that more than one-half of the parents of young children reported that they were likely to beat their children if they were being lazy in their studies or failed an examination, and 68% of the parents reported they used force to make their children obey whatever the parents said. In addition to general abuse, in rural areas many girls and disabled boys, if not aborted, face orphanages or second-class lives concealed from the world and with reduced chances of schooling and healthcare because of the widespread preference for boys and the demands of labor on the land (Ching & Penny, 1999).

One of the important reasons for widespread family violence in China is the acceptance of traditional cultural and civic values. In traditional China, people believed that "a family should have rules, as a country should have laws." Deeply rooted in Confucian ethics, these family rules set up standards for regulating family members' behaviors (R. Wang, Li, & Shao, 1993). Punishment would be applied in the case of any family member breaking these rules. Therefore, physical abuse was considered a family matter rather than a public issue. The victims of family violence usually felt hesitant to report these cases because of the widely accepted idea, "don't give publicity to scandals of your family." The public tends to avoid becoming involved in family conflicts even when they are aware of the violence. As shown in a study on marital violence, in only 15% of marital violence cases was there outside intervention (Jun, 1994). Physical punishment of a child is commonly recognized as a way of discipline, "a filial son comes under sticks." Abusive parents have not been seen as criminals but as responsible. Some parents even give schoolteachers the right to punish their children in case they perform badly in school. Although there are a number of laws developed in recent years against family violence, the general public still holds the idea, "don't bother to advise a fighting couple, because they will get along and have dinner together soon." It seems that changing attitudes and behaviors around the issue of family violence will need a long-term campaign in China.

7. DIVORCE, SEPARATION, AND REMARRIAGE

In traditional China, divorce and remarriage were men's privileges and monopoly, characterized by the joint enforcement of feudal ethics and laws. The historic ethics about divorce were built on the beliefs that "husband is the sky while wife is the land" and "the land has no reason to leave the sky away." According to *Baihutong: Marriage*, "even if husband is bad, wife is not allowed to divorce him." Associated with these moral principles, feudalist marriage laws prohibited women's rights to divorce and separate. For instance, *Tang's Statute: Family and Marriage* (Tang Dynasty: 618–907 A.D.) stipulated the following: "wife who leaves without the permission of husband, two years' imprisonment; who, as a result, remarries, double imprisonment." In contrast, a man can legally have several wives and divorce them at any time without any penalty, but only if he follows certain legal procedures or civil customs. The most important divorce pattern that existed in China for thousands of years was the so-called *chuqi* (divorces wife), which allowed a man to divorce his wife for any of the following seven reasons: disobeying parents, no sons, licentiousness, jealousy, foul disease, talkativeness, and stealing (Tao & Ming, 1994). With only a few exceptions (e.g., mourned husband's brother/sister for 3 years, husband is richer now than at the time of his wedding, and the wife has no one to rely on after divorce; *Tang's Statute: Family and Marriage*), men have had the absolute right of divorce.

In addition, the Confucian view of chastity required women to "marry only one man for life-long." Thus, after the divorce or death of a husband, women were not encouraged to get remarried, even when they were in financial difficulties. The phrases "good woman does not serve two husbands" and "hungering (because of losing support from husband) is a small thing but losing chastity is a big thing" were the moral models set for widows at that time. Although feudal laws did not prohibit the remarriage of ordinary women (but did prohibit wives of officials from remarrying), they, to a certain extent, served as enforcement of the Confucian ethic against women's remarriage. For instance, according to Ming Comprehensive Law (1358–1644 A.D.), "civil widows, whose husband died 30 years ago and who were over 50 years old without remarriage, will be rewarded with a silk banner as praise, and released their families from corvée." In practice, the association of laws and ethics prevented a large number of women from remarriage for thousands of years in China.

Contemporary Chinese women have gained equal rights with men for divorce and remarriage. However, because China had long practiced a fault system of divorce, until the end of the 1970s, an actual divorce was rarely approved without long-term intervention and mediation by work units, and with complex court trials aimed at identifying the guilty party. This set of barriers explains why China's divorce rates were so astonishingly low at that time, accounting for only 2% of all marriages (adapted from Nass & McDonald, 1982). A substantial change in the Chinese divorce system occurred in 1980, marked by the publication of the new marriage law, which replaced the fault system with a no-fault system by adding "emotion come to rupture" as a key reason for no-fault divorce and by developing effective divorce registration agencies.

As a result of this amendment to marriage law and other social changes caused by the introduction of a market economy (e.g., the growing awareness of independence among women, increasing social interaction, the acceleration of employment mobility, the introduction of Western values toward marriage and divorce, etc.), China's divorce rates have increased dramatically in recent decades (H. Zhang & Tong, 1997). According to official statistics (Ministry of Civil Affairs of China, 2002), the crude divorce rate (number of divorces vs. number of population) increased from 0.35% in 1978 to 1.2% in 1988, and to 1.98% in 2001. The increment of general divorce rates (number of divorced couples vs. number of new married couples) was even more remarkable: from 4.76% in 1978 to 7.28% in 1988, and to 15.53% in 2001. In other words, there was one divorce for every six new marriages in 2001, compared with one divorce in 20 new marriages 20 years ago. In general, urban divorce rates are much higher than those of rural areas. For instance, the divorce rates of Beijing and Shanghai were 34.87% and 33.83%, respectively, in 2001, while the rates in Henan, Anhui, and Shandong were 11.10%, 7.80%, and 9.10%, respectively.

There have been two well-documented features of current divorce in China (Xu, 1994; P. Zhang, 1995). One is the increasing percentage of court cases and decreasing percentage of administrative registration cases. This trend reflects a wilder awareness of using legal means to protect one's rights in marital dissolution. Another trend of current divorce is that about 70% of all divorce cases were initiated by females, showing the increase in women's awareness of independence and control over their marital life (Y. Liu, Wang, & Hao, 1992; Xu, 1994). It seems that, unlike before, in most cases, women divorce their husbands rather than being divorced by their husbands. Data on the causes of individual divorces vary from one study to another. By analyzing available studies, P. Zhang (1995) generalized some common reasons leading to divorce in China, including the following: (1) conflicts in character traits between wife and husband, (2) wife abuse, (3) long-term conflicts on domestic tasks (e.g., controlling family finance, division of housework, educating children, etc.), (4) out-of-marriage affairs, (5) husband's failure to support the family, (6) husband's bad habits or crime, (7) disharmony in sexuality, (8) disharmony with other family members, and (9) husband's discrimination.

Accompanying the increase of divorce rates has been the growth of remarriage rates since the 1980s. According to official statistics (Ministry of Civil Affairs of China, 2002; Z. Wang, 1999), the total numbers of remarriage registration have increased from about 500,000 in 1985 to 1.12 million in 2001. Accordingly, the proportion of remarriages in total marriage registrations has increased from 3% in 1980 to 14% in 2001. There were more remarriages in urban than in rural areas (e.g., Beijing: 29.93%; Shanghai: 28.84%; Tianjin: 25.69%, in comparison to Anhui: 5.26%; Henan: 9.02%; Guizhou: 6.08%), based on the statistics of 2001. Available data also show that divorced women are more likely to get remarried (3 out of 4) than are divorced men (1 out of 3) (P. Zhang, 1995).

Although divorce and remarriage have been widely accepted by Chinese society, it is more difficult for senior citizens to get remarried than for the younger generations. There have been two major obstacles to remarriage of the elderly: the influence of traditional ethics and the opposition of adult children (Lu, 1994; S. Ma, 1991; Q. Wang, 1988). Many female elderly refuse to get remarried because of the traditional idea of "being faithful to one's husband to the end." Many others feel shame to be remarried because of the belief that courtship and sexuality are something belonging to young people; thus, remarriage causes a senior to lose face with children, relatives, and neighbors. Many adult children oppose having their parents remarried because they are afraid to be ridiculed for not taking filial responsibility seriously. Many others oppose it because of inheritance. Among remarried senior families, conflicts between two sides of children and relatives on various family issues often push the new marriages toward dissolution.

8. KINSHIP

In traditional Chinese society, kinship was included in the patriarchal clan system—a social group held together through blood and geological relationships and feudal ethics and functioning as a social control and management agency in rural areas. Usually, there were one to several clans in each village, each of which was titled by the same family name and might include several kinship groups. Tao and Ming (1994) outlined three important characteristics of traditional Chinese kinship. First, it placed patriarchal clan relatives in the superlative position above all kinship ties; second, it favored father's kinship and neglected mother's kinship, distinguished as direct and indirect relatives; third, it emphasized the ethical codes among relatives, which focused on the absolute authority of the older and the responsibilities of the younger. In general, kinship includes clan relatives, outside relatives, and wife's relatives. Clan relatives are the most significant, including parents, brothers and sisters, and wives, along the patriarchal line. Outside kinship refers to the relatives of the mother's clan, including mother's parents, brothers and sisters, and nephews and nieces. The wife's relatives are mainly the wife's parents, brothers, and sisters (Tao & Ming, 1994).

The socialist revolution marked by the establishment of the People's Republic of China in 1949 fundamentally destroyed the feudal clan system in China through land reform and socialist industrialization. Then, the political power of the clan system in rural society was taken over by the new local and grassroots governmental agencies, such as people's communes, production brigades, and production teams. By gaining freedom from the feudalistic clan system, Chinese kinship abandoned its dominant patriarchal features and became more egalitarian between father's and mother's relatives.

In contemporary China, kinship performs some important functions in the household economy, mutual communication, and mutual support in people's family lives. By summarizing recent research findings, R. Pan (2002) generalized the following major functions of kinship in urban areas today: (1) economic exchanges; (2) daily life support; (3) care of elderly, children, and patients; (4) emergency services and life security; (5) communication and emotional support; and (6) services on important family events such as weddings and funerals.

Economic Exchanges and Transfers

Economic exchanges and transfers occur mainly between direct relatives (parents and children), including upward and downward flow of money and materials. In a family survey conducted in 27 provinces and cities in 1991, 64.5% of respondents reported supporting parents economically with an average of 30 Yuan per month, and 37% of them reported receiving economic support from their parents regularly (25 Yuan per month on average), plus some informal support such as paying rent, electricity, and phone (6%), eating at parents' home without payment (18.7%), often receiving materials from parents (25.5%), and receiving special payment from parents for important events (23.8%). In contrast, the economic support from indirect relatives took place only during such important family events as weddings, funerals, illness, and childbirth.

Daily Life Support

According to a survey of 181 families in Tianjin, to save time and costs, about 86% of adult children often go back to their parents' home for meals; most parents cohabiting with adult children often help children with daily household tasks; in return, adult children usually help their parents with such difficulties as buying heavy items, travel, and taking medication.

Care of Elderly, Children, and Patients

As reported in a study of 17 families with a hospital bed at home for elderly with chronic diseases, there was always kinship care and a support network in each family, including cohabiting members (2.31 per family) and separated members (5.06 per family), composed of adult children and grandchildren.

Meanwhile, the survey of 181 families in Tianjin reported that 20% of adult children sent their children to the grandparents' homes for daily or weekly care, with 12% of the childcare in the husband's parents' homes and 8% in the wife's parents' homes.

Emergency Services and Security

Kinship can also be a resource for emergency services and security, represented in disaster and emergency situations when kin provide help and support. In a survey of 27 provinces and cities, 19% of families reported that their relatives had helped each other to deal with emergency situations, and 4.6% of them felt that kinship gave security to their lives.

Communication and Emotional Support

Communication and emotional support were more common among kin than among other relationships. About 76.8% of the respondents in the survey reported having frequent communication and emotional support with their kin, according to the survey of 27 provinces and cities.

Services at Important Family Events

Services at important family events usually are time and labor jobs, and kinship members are normally the major source of such support. Twenty percent of the respondents in the survey reported experiences of providing these kinds of services for their relatives. (Preceding data are adapted from R. Pan, 2002).

Other Aspects of Kinship

In addition to these general functions, kinship has played an increasingly important role in productive activities in rural China since economic reform started in the 1980s. As the right of land use was assigned to individual families after the reform, production became a critical task for the survival of rural families. The demands of labor and cooperation during busy times have strengthened kinship ties and increased the importance of indirect kinship. A study of families in Tangdong village of Fujian province (Mai, 2002) revealed that, once there is need of support, people are most likely to ask close relatives for help before asking far relatives and friends. About 48% of financial support, 41% of help on public relation, 78% of labor support, and 42% of information support were from cousins of the father's side, while the percentages of these four supports received from cousins from the mother's side were 25%, 34%, 14%, and 29%, and from friends were 27%, 25%, 8%, and 29%. These supports will, on one hand, benefit rural families in their productive activities. On the other hand, they encourage the reemerging of the old clan system in rural China, given the current loosening of governmental control of rural areas as the result of the weakening of the commune system (Mai, 2002).

The separation and inheritance of family property is another aspect of the kinship system. Traditional Chinese culture placed the inheritance of status first and the inheritance of property second. Family properties, including both movable and unmovable, belonged to all family members, and the head of a family had only the right of using the properties. Thus, if no family member was separated until the parents died, there was no such thing as private property for parents to give to a specific individual. In terms of inheritance, traditional Chinese society emphasized inheritance by law more than inheritance by will, reflecting the intervention of government and feudal ethics in inheritance behaviors (Tao & Ming, 1994). In general, traditional inheritance law and ethics had two important principles. First, family properties were only divided and inherited along patriarchal lines, normally by brothers and their sons. Second, women had no inheritance rights from their parents or their parents-in-law.

In contemporary China, these feudal laws and ethics were abandoned. The marriage law published in 1950 stated, "Husband and wife have right of mutual inheritance." The new inheritance law published in 1985 declared, "male and female have equal right of inheritance" and "spouse, children, parents, brother and sister" all have rights to inheritance. Along with these law enforcements, there have been great changes in people's values and practices of inheritance. By analyzing the data from the study on women's status in contemporary China, Sun (1996) pointed out three characteristics of inheritance in China. First, the traditional idea of male-only inheritance has weakened. As evidence, about 40% of urban respondents and 27% of rural respondents agreed with the idea of dividing family property equally between sons and daughters. Second, more people tended to relate inheritance to aged support (properties "should go to whom are willing to take more responsibilities for aged parents": 50% of urban and 35% of rural respondents). Third, rural respondents were more traditional than urban respondents. For instance, 36.63% of rural respondents agreed with "mainly give to sons," while only 6.8% of urban respondents did so.

In practice, urban residents are likely to use the new laws to protect their rights of inheritance because of their higher level of education and their easier access to legal consultants and court services in cities. In rural areas, where the general education levels are lower and lawsuits and consultants are not often available, local custom and traditional ethics still play important roles in inheritance. According to Z. Liu's study (1996) in Xinleitou village, Hebei province, the division and inheritance of family properties were still based mainly on customs and traditions, even though the new law was 10 years old. As Z. Liu described, once married adult children decide to be separate from their parents, family property has to be divided among sons (not daughters). There normally was a ceremony held during the slack season, when seniors of the clan, close relatives, or officials of the village were invited as witnesses. Starting from the oldest son, sons in turn picked up their own part of family property through drawing lots that were carefully discussed among relatives and were supposed to be equal. Then, they had to sign a formal lease for this division, and witnesses had to sign as well.

Commonly, the leases of this village contained two major parts: (1) the detailed division of family properties including house, house-base, saving, production materials (land, machines, and livestock), and debts; (2) special agreements such as the dowry for unmarried daughters, fees for caring for the disabled or for schooling of younger family members, the temporary property of parents

and its inheritance after parents' death, the ways of supporting aged parents (including daily life, housing, medications, funerals, etc.), and so on. To villagers, this lease is one of the most important law documents, which should be kept very carefully and passed from generation to generation (Z. Liu, 1996).

9. AGING AND DEATH

In recent decades, the Chinese population has accelerated its pace toward becoming an aging society. According to official statistics, the proportion of Chinese people aged 65 years old or above increased from 4.41% in 1953 to 6.96% in 2000, close to the definition of an aging society (7% or above). Actually, some developed Chinese cities and provinces, such as Shanghai (11.53%), Beijing (8.36%), Tianjin (8.33%), Jiangsu (8.76%), Zhejiang (8.84%), and Chongqing (7.90%) have already gone far beyond this international standard for an aging society (National Bureau of Statistics, 2001a). This trend is expected to be more significant in the foreseeable future, reaching an overall aged proportion of 16.8% by 2020 (United Nations, 2003).

Along with this aging trend, there has been an increasing concern about old people's lives, both inside and outside families, given that the rapid industrialization, modernization, and other socioeconomic changes in the past decades have challenged the traditional values and practices for later life and for family support to the aged. Deeply rooted in the traditional agriculture economy, Chinese culture favored the aged for their political and economic power, their specialized knowledge, and their experiences of life. Filial piety, as one of the important family norms, has dominated Chinese families for thousands of years. The elderly expect to be spiritually respected and materially supported by their offspring, and family has long been the major resource for supporting the aged in Chinese society. However, in recent decades we have seen: (1) the shrinking pool of family support to the aged caused by the implementation of the one-child policy and by the speeding up of occupational mobility; (2) the devaluation of old techniques and skills because of the innovation of new technology and the development of new industries; (3) the instability of pensions and employment-based welfare benefits in urban areas, caused by the transition from the socialist planned economy to a market economy; and (4) the loss of collective welfare benefits for elderly in rural areas, resulting from the dissolution of the commune-based welfare system. Overall, we have seen an increase in the relative poverty of the aged population and an underdevelopment of the social welfare system for the aged in China (Tang, 2002; "What Shall We Do About Supporting 40 Million Old Women?," 2001).

Nevertheless, the majority of Chinese elderly are still living with their children, as reported by several national sample surveys (e.g., Hu & Ye, 1991). According to the *Survey of Chinese Aged Population*, in 1988, 82.2% of old people (aged 60 years old or above) were living in two- (29.2%), three- (50%), or four-generation (3%) families (Tian, Xiong, & Xiong, 1991). More specifically, the nine-city survey of old people (Hu & Ye, 1991) reported that, among 7,000 urban aged respondents, 17.6% of them were living in husband-wife families, 15.9% in nuclear families, 42.1% in stem-families, 7.2% in grandparents-grandchildren families, and 2.3% in extended families (Hu & Ye, 1991). Among those who were living with adult children, 67% were married sons staying at their parents' home, and 14% were married daughters staying with parents. It is noticeable that not all elderly cohabiting with their adult children were being supported or cared for by children. Instead, 28.3% of them lived together because married children did

not have their own houses, 15.7% were helping married children with housework, and 4.4% of them were together because children needed financial help from them. While 44.8% of the elderly preferred to have married children living with them, another 35.1% of them would like to live separately, but close to their children's homes.

It appears that as coresidence continues to be the emotional core of support relationships between parents and adult offspring in mainland China, there are tendencies to live closer to and keep in frequent contact with each other even when not living together. As Unger (1993, p. 40) argues, Chinese "parents who live apart from their married children still tend to maintain very close mutual contact, more than would be the norm in most Western societies." A commonly held ideal in China for the distance between parents and children is "a distance that keeps a soup warm." Bian, Logan, and Bian's study (1998) in Shanghai and Tianjin found that 9% of non-coresident children live in the same neighborhood (3 minutes walk) as the parents, and 48% live within at least the same district (20 minutes walk). The usual frequency of intergenerational communication is that about 25% of parents have at least daily contact with their children, most parents (80%) see their children at least every week, and there is only a small difference between the contact with sons and daughters. According to this study, the intergenerational assistance flows still mainly upward rather than downward. About 55% of the parents reported receiving regular help from offspring, whereas about 25% of the children received regular help from parents. Similarly, the nine-city survey of old people (Hu & Ye, 1991) has shown that, while there was an upward flow of financial support (41%), there also was a flow of cash transfers (21%) from the older to the younger generations.

These studies have also revealed that the elderly were highly respected by their offspring (over 80%) and there were very few reporting no respect or abuse (Tian et al., 1991). In terms of the older generation's authority inside the family, urban elderly seem to have more power in the family economy than rural elderly (Tian et al., 1991). It appears that older people's economic power inside families is associated with their contribution to the family economy. The more income the elderly bring into the family, the more control the elderly have. Most urban elderly have their pensions to contribute to the family, whereas most rural elderly have no pension and make fewer contributions to productive activities after they become older, thus having less power over the family economy. Besides family economy, Chinese elderly also have a certain power in a variety of family issues. According to the nine-city survey of old people (Hu & Ye, 1991), 42% of urban elderly have decisive power over important family issues, and 43.2% of them have a word to say about those issues. Another 60% of urban elderly report playing a great role in family issues in general. A noticeable change in the family power of the elderly is that only 8.2% of respondents reported having decisive power over their children's marriage, and 10.8% reported having decisive power over children's studying and professional development.

According to the sampling survey on the Chinese aged population (Tian et al., 1991), 16.3% of Chinese elderly were in "very good" health in 1988, 28.3% were in "good" health, 27.9% were "just so-so," 17.6% were "worse," and 9.3% were "worst." In general, women were more likely to report a "worse" or "worst" condition than men, and urban elderly were more likely to report a "worse" or "worst" condition than rural elderly. However, this does not necessarily mean rural elderly have good nutrition (or proper food) and better medical conditions. Actually, rural elderly tend to have more serious problems with their medication than do urban elderly. While 68% of urban elderly reported "no problems" with medication, only 5.27% of rural elderly did so. The fact is that, without social welfare, almost all rural elderly (94.69%) have to pay all of their medication fees by themselves, while only 26.73% of urban elderly do so.

Malignant tumors, cerebrovascular disease, heart trouble, respiratory disease, and trauma and toxicosis were ranked in 2002 as the five major reasons for death of Chinese elderly, accounting for 83% of the total deaths (National Bureau of Statistics, 2001a). There were significant differences between urban and rural elderly in terms of the ranks of these diseases. The rank for the urban elderly was as follows: (1) malignant tumor, (2) cerebrovascular disease, (3) heart trouble, (4) respiratory disease, and (5) trauma and toxicosis. In comparison, the rank for the elderly in rural areas followed this pattern: (1) respiratory disease, (2) malignant tumor, (3) cerebrovascular disease, (4) heart disease, and (5) trauma and toxicosis. The differences again reflect the fact that medication is less available in rural areas than in urban areas. While the urban elderly mainly deal with more complicated diseases, common and frequently occurring diseases such as pneumonia, bronchopneumonia, emphysema, and asthma are still the major killers of rural Chinese elderly.

10. FAMILY AND OTHER INSTITUTIONS

The Chinese family, as a social institution, is interdependent and interactive with other social institutions such as social politics, economics, and education. China is one of the countries in the world in which families were heavily influenced by the dynamics of social politics in the 20th century. The successive political struggles and national and international wars in the first half of the century drove out hundreds and thousands of families, while the endless political movements and social reforms in the second half of the century intervened in people's family lives a great deal. Under the control of radical politics during Mao's time, families were divided based on their class origins. While the communist party cardholder's families, workers' families, and poor peasants' families were favored by politics, families of landlords, rich peasants, counterrevolutionists, bad persons, and right deviationists were oppressed by society, and their members often faced difficulties in job searching, gaining education, and other aspects of social and family lives.

As part of the social and political control system, household registration (*hukou*) has been used for centuries in China since imperial times (Duttom, 1992). Initially, this system was developed mainly for tax and convée purposes. However, it has been institutionalized since the middle of the last century by the development of a series of household registration-based measures that catered to the demands of socialist social control and the planned economy through regulating population mobility, employment, education, and food and goods supplies (Cheng & Selden, 1994). Under this system, families were identified as either "agricultural" or "nonagricultural," and the approved resident locations were classified as either "urban" or "rural" in specific cities, towns, or villages (Christiansen, 1991; Mallee, 1995). As a result, residential mobility was severely restricted. Only a very small group of people and their families could make an official transition from rural to urban or from towns to large cities by joining the army, or by gaining a place in higher education or governmental agencies. Thus, urban or rural registration became hereditary, inherited from the mother, and could only be changed under limited and specific conditions (Q. Zhang, 1988; Chan & Zhang, 1998; Stockman,

2000). Fundamentally, this system deprived numerous families of their right to pursue a higher standard of living. For example, many couples and families had to live-apart together for many years, because their members came from different resident registration areas (L. Pan, Yuan, & Hu, 1992). Although current social changes, resulting from socioeconomic reform and the rapid growth of the economy in China, have eliminated some functions of the resident registration system (e.g., coupons for food and goods, local registration-based employment, etc.), some of its regulations are still in force and continue to influence people's family lives (Stockman, 2000).

In addition to the institutional systems such as resident registration, innovations in social policy have long been an important force of political intervention in family lives. One of the most influential social policies in the late 20th century has been the one-child policy. Since this policy became fully operational in the 1980s, Chinese family size has rapidly become smaller. By the year 2000, China held a family size of 3.13 for urban and 4.20 for rural families (National Bureau of Statistics, 2001a). This policy has caused discussion recently of the possible shrinkage of the family support pool of relatives for the aged (Sheng, 1992). Another concern resulting from this policy has been developmental issues of the single-child generation. It is widely noted that this group of children has had better conditions for advanced cognitive achievement but has some weaknesses in their personality development (X. Feng, 1993, 1994; Gao, 1992). More serious problems related to the policy have been the strong opposition from peasants in rural areas, which resulted in a widespread phenomenon of abandoning, abusing, and killing baby girls and disabled children (Ching & Penny, 1999).

Chinese families have also been tied strongly with their members' employers. Until recent years, rural families were organized as the members of production teams of communes. They had to rely on the teams or brigades for their production, income, housing, education, welfare, and medication (Stockman, 2000). Usually, all of the families in one village belonged to a production team or brigade. In fact, a commune and its suborganizations (brigade or production team) served not only as an economic unit but also as a grassroots governmental agency in rural areas, communicating with families intensively on a daily basis. This joint unit of government and production currently has been replaced by a village government agency due to the dissolution of the communes since the early 1980s. The new agency has released itself from the productive functions of the commune and given rural families more freedom to control their economic lives. Similarly, each of the urban working units (e.g., companies, factories, schools, etc.) had been a comprehensive organization that covered production, business, education, housing, childcare, welfare, and medication, serving its employees and their families. These functions, however, have been gradually transferred to other social institutions in recent years because of the introduction of the market economy. In general, both communes in rural areas and work units in urban areas used to have strong control over their members' family lives in the past, but their influence has decreased recently due to ongoing social and economic changes.

Due to the heavy involvement of women in the labor force (43%), public childcare and educational facilities such as day-care centers, preschools, and kindergartens have been well developed in China in the past decades. The absolute numbers of these facilities have increased from 1,799 in 1950 to 181,368 in 1998 (National Bureau of Statistics, 1999). A large part of these facilities were run by work units and communes before the 1980s and have been gradually transferred to public institutions since then. The popularization of childcare and education institutions has partially released Chinese working couples from their daily childcare tasks and enabled them to devote themselves to their careers. Nevertheless, in recent decades Chinese parents have tended to make more and more investments in their children's education, starting from primary schools, because to most Chinese, education is the only channel to obtain good jobs and to develop careers in an increasingly competitive society (X. Feng, 1993). Universally, the child's education has become a daily routine and a central topic in most Chinese families, including regular contact with schoolteachers, helping children with homework, looking for additional tutorial classes and interest groups, sending children to and picking them up from school, and so on (Man, 1993; Zhu, 1992). As Chinese education has gradually transferred from a welfare-based system to a market-based system in recent years, Chinese parents have begun to worry about their children's education fees, especially the cost of higher education. This will likely change the consumer structure of Chinese families in the foreseeable future.

CONCLUSION

Family as a social institution has never developed in a vacuum. The dynamics and variations of Chinese families can, to a certain extent, be seen as reflecting the fundamental changes in Chinese society across the 20th century, and the current geocultural, geopolitical, and geosocioeconomic conditions of China in a global context. For thousands of years, Chinese families had remained "super stable" structures dominated by patriarchal clan ideology and Confucian doctrines (Z. Wang, 1999). The historical events taking place in the 20th century, such as the collapse of the Qing feudal dynasty, the establishment of the republic, the successive wars, the new republic, the radical communist movements, and the recent social and economic reforms, all had a profound influence on the development of Chinese families. As China has been changing from a poor feudal agricultural society to a modern industrial society involved in globalization, Chinese families have gained more flexibility in their lives and shown a new face to the world.

Understanding Chinese families from a life-course perspective (Hareven, 1977) will allow us not only to distinguish the current trends but also to predict the possible future directions of Chinese families. Given the fact that China is currently experiencing the transitions from a socialist planned economy to a capitalist market economy, from a rigid political and ideologically controlled society to an increasingly open-minded and lawful society, and from a poor Third World country to a fast-growing, developing country, it is reasonable to expect that Chinese families will present the following features in the foreseeable future:

- A gradually improved living standard. Being aware of the remarkable difference in living standards from Western society, the demand for higher living standards will continue to increase among Chinese families. This will stimulate families to seek out more of such things as better housing, motor vehicles, electronic equipment, nutritional food, proper medicines, and a beautiful environment. This will eventually raise the general standard of life in Chinese families.
- An increasing diversity in family structures. While nuclear families and stem-families will still be the dominant patterns of Chinese families, the proportion of other family patterns such as single-person families, empty-nest families, single-parent families, cohabitation families, reconstituted families, and gay and lesbian families will increase constantly as they tend to be more tolerated and acceptable to the society.

- An increasingly active family network. Although families are becoming diverse and smaller, the connections and interactions among generations and direct kin will become more active because of the availability of modern communication technologies (e.g., telephones, Internet, etc.), public and private transportation, and the increasing demand for cooperation in daily lives and economic activities.
- A greater accessibility of choices in mate selection, marriage, divorce, and remarriage. While love and affection will still be the basic criteria for a desirable marriage, the importance of educational level and occupational privilege will increase. Marriage, divorce, and remarriage will become easier, and the rates of divorce and remarriage will continue to increase.
- A more realistic division of gender roles. Because of the rapid growth of private enterprises and family businesses, the distinctions between housework and employment will become less clear. More couples will divide their gender roles based on the practical needs of family lives rather than biological or ideological considerations.
- A more flexible support system for the aged. Family will likely perform as a main mediator rather than a main agent for supporting the aged. This will involve using family networks, paid social services, and available institutions to share the responsibilities for elderly care.

It is expected that China will experience many great social changes in the first part of the 21st century—as will Chinese families. It seems that, in this increasingly globalizing world, Chinese families will share more commonalities with families in other societies, as well as continue to perpetuate some fundamental characteristics rooted deeply in Chinese cultural traditions. Thus, I close this chapter with my best wishes for more healthy, harmonious, and happy families in China in the future.

REFERENCES

Bian, F., Logan, J. R., & Bian, Y. (1998). Intergenerational relations in urban China: Proximity, contact, and help to parents. *Demography, 35*(1), 115–124.

Bianco, L. (1981). Birth control in China: Local data and their reliability. *China Quarterly, 85*(1), 119–137.

Burgess, E. W., & Locke, H. J. (1960). *The family*. New York: American Book Co.

Cao, X. (2002, reprint). Hong Lou Meng [The story of the stone, or The dream of the red chamber] (in Chinese). Beijing: People's Literature Press.

Chan, K. W., & Zhang, L. (1998). The Hukou system and rural-urban migration in China. Retrieved October 31, 2003, from http://csde.washington.edu/pubs/wps/98-13.pdf.

Chen, K. (1986). *A study of current only-child families in China: A survey of 1180 families in the urban and suburban areas of Beijing*. ASP Association Paper.

Chen, X. (1985). The one-child population policy, modernization, and the extended Chinese family. *Journal of Marriage and the Family, 47*(1), 193–202.

Cheng, T., & Selden, M. (1994). The origins and social consequences of China's Huhou system. *China Quarterly, 193*, 644–668.

China's Lifestyle Choice: Changes to the famous one-child policy miss the point. Who will care for a graying population? (2001, August 6). *Time, 158*(5), 32.

Ching, Y. C., & Penny, K. (1999). China's one child family policy. *British Medical Journal, 319*(7215), 992.

Christensen, H. T. (1964). Development of the family field of study. In H. T. Christensen (Ed.), *Handbook of marriage and the family* (pp. 3–32). Chicago: Rand McNally.

Christiansen, F. (1991). Social division and peasant mobility in mainland China: The implication of the *hu-kou* system. *Issues and Studies, 26*, 23–42.

Chuhun nianling [The age of first marriage]. (1998, March 25). *Chinese Population Daily*, p. 2.

Cohen, M. L. (1978). Developmental process in the Chinese domestic group. In A. P. Wolf (Ed.), *Studies in Chinese society* (pp. 183–198). Stanford, CA: Stanford University Press.

Duttom, M. (1992). *Policing and punishment in China: From patriarchy to "the people"*. Cambridge, UK: Cambridge University Press.

Fei, X. (1981). *Shengyu zhidu* [Fertility system]. Tianjin: Tianjin People's Publishing House.

Feng, G., & Hao, L. (1992). Qianguo 28 ge difang jihuashengyü tiaolie zongshu [A summary on regulations of family planning in 28 local areas nationwide]. *Population Studies, 4*, 28–33.

Feng, X. (1993). Pianjia yü xianshi: Dushengzinü jiaoyu wenti de diaocha yü fenxi [Bias and reality: A survey analysis of issues on only children's education]. *Sociological Studies, 1*, 90–96.

Feng, X. (1994). Dushengzinü jiating: Yizhong xide shenghuo fangshi [Single-child families: A new life style]. *Journal of Social Science, 5*, 28–32.

Five Cities' Marriage and Family Study Project. (1985). *Zhongguo chengshi jiating* [Urban Chinese families]. Jinan: People's Press of Shandong.

Gao, W. (1992). Guanyü dushengziniü de jiankang, xüexi he shenghuo zhuangkuang de diaocha [Survey on the health, learning, and living conditions of single children]. *Journal of Population Studies, 6,* 40–44.

Hao, M., & Wang, J. (1994, February 8). Xinhun yü Zhufang [Wedding and housing]. *Chinese Women's Daily,* p. 6.

Hareven, T. K. (1977). Family time and historical time. *Dardalus, 106,* 57–70.

Hu, R., & Ye, N. (Eds.). (1991). *Zhongguo jiu da chengshi laonianren zhuangkuang chuyangdiaocha* [The sampling survey on the current situation of old people in nine large cities in China]. Tianjin: Tianjin Educational Press.

Huang, L. (1992). Guanyü jiatingyinsu dui zinü gexifazhan de diaochafenxi [The survey analysis of the influences of family factors on children's personality development]. *Journal of Demography, 2,* 49–52.

Institute of Population Studies. (1994). *Sampling survey data of women's status in contemporary China.* Beijing: International Academic Publishers.

Ji, G., Jiao, S., & Ring, Q. (1993). Expectancy of Chinese parents and children's cognitive abilities. *International Journal of Psychology, 28,* 821–830.

Jiao, S., Ji, D., & Ring, Q. (1986). Comparative study of behavioral qualities of only children and sibling children. *Child Development, 57,* 357–361.

Jiao, S., Ji, D., & Ring, Q. (1996). Comparative development of Chinese urban only children and children with siblings. *Child Development, 67,* 387–395.

Jun, L. (1994). Hunyin baoli: tantan wenti yü tuice [Marital violence: Issues and responses]. *The Family, 3,* 15–18.

Kallgren, D. (1985). Politics, welfare and change: The single-child family in China. In E. Perry & C. Wong (Eds.), *The political economy of reform in post-Mao China* (pp. 131–156). Cambridge, MA: Harvard University Press.

Kinsey, A., Pomeroy, W. B., & Martin, C. E. (1948). *Sexual behavior in the human male.* Philadelphia: Saunders.

Laslett, P., & Wall, R. (Eds.). (1972). *Household and family in past time.* Cambridge, UK: Cambridge University Press.

Lei, J., Yang, S., & Cai, W. (Eds.). (1994). *Gaige yilai zhongguo nongcun hunyin-jiating de xibianhua* [The changes of marriage and the family in the Chinese countryside since the reform of the economic system]. Beijing: Peking University Press.

Lei, S. (1995, July 18). Zhongguo funü jiefang jishi [The history of Chinese women's liberation]. *Chinese Women's Daily,* p. 1.

Li, R. (1992). Duiyü renkoupucha shujü zhong youguan zhongguo zaohun xianzhuang de zhubufenxi [A preliminary analysis of census data on the current situation of early marriage in China]. *Population and Economy, 3,* 9–12.

Li, Y. (1995, February 28). Beijingren de hunyin meiman ma? [Are the marriages of Beijing people happy?]. *China Women's Daily,* p. 4.

Liu, D. (1992). *Dangdai zhongguo ziwenhua: Zhongguo liangwanli "xingwenhua" diaochabaogao* [Sex culture in contemporary China: Survey report of 20,000 cases on "sex civilization" in China]. Shanghai: Shanghai Sanlian Press.

Liu, G., & Zhao, S. (1994). *Shilun lijiao zhong nüxing de diwei weti* [Issues about women's position in feudal ethnic codes]. *Jiangxi Social Science, 9,* 63–65.

Liu, J. (1991). *Beijingshi fuqiguanxi yianjü* [A study of conjugal relationships in Beijing]. *Population & Economics, 84*(3), 38–47.

Liu, Y., Pen, Y., Ma, Y., Dai, K., Sheng, X., Wang, J., & Sun, W. (Eds.). (1993). *Dangdai zhongguo nongcun jiating* [Contemporary families in rural China]. Beijing: Social Science Documentation Publishing House.

Liu, Y., Wang, Y., & Hao, F. (1992, August 22). "Xiufu" zai dangjin de zhongguo nongcun ["Divorce husband" in contemporary rural China]. *Peasants' Daily*, p. 8.

Liu, Y., & Xüe, S. (Eds.). (1987). *Zhongguo hunyinjiating yanjü* [The study of marriage and family in China]. Beijing: Social Science Documentation Publishing House.

Liu, Z. (1996). Nongcun jiatingcaichan de fegejicheng [The division and inheritance of family property in rural families]. *Sociological Studies, 5*, 93–96.

Lowie, R. H. (1934). *An introduction to culture anthropology*. New York: Farrar Y. Rinehart.

Lu, X. (1994, September 20). Laonian zaihun de xinliyali yü kunhuo [Seniors' psychological pressures and puzzles in remarriages. *China's Social Daily*, p. 3.

Luo, K. (1992). Shanghai qingnian jiehun feiyong de paoxi [An analysis of wedding expenses of Shanghai youth]. *The Overview, 3*, 12–13.

Ma, H. (1997, January 19). Zhongguoren de dongfang: Guanyü jinnianlai jiehunfeiyong de diaocha [The Chinese wedding house: A survey on wedding expenses in the past years]. *Digits, 1409*, p. 8.

Ma, S. (1991). Nongcun laonianren zaihun de zhiyüe yinsu fenxi [An analysis of the constraints on the remarriage of rural seniors]. *Society, 11*, 14–15.

Ma, Y., Liu, Y., Sheng, X., & Meng, C. (1992). *Funü jiuye yü jiating: Zhongri bijiaoyanjiu diaochabaogao* [Women's employment and family: A comparative study between China and Japan]. Beijing: Social Science Documentation Publishing House.

Ma, Y., Wang, Z., Sheng, X., & Shinozaki, M. (1994). *A study on life and consciousness of contemporary urban families in China: A research in Beijing with comparison among Bangkok, Seoul, and Fukuoka*. Kitakyushu: Kitakyushu Forum on Asian Women.

MacIver, R. M. (1937). *Society: A textbook of sociology*. New York: Farrar Y. Rinehart.

Mai, W. (2002). Zhongguo nongcui jiazushili fuxing de yuanyin tanxi [An exploration of the reasons for the reemerging of clan forces in rural China]. *Sociology, 2*, 78–80.

Mallee, H. (1995). China's household registration system under reform. *Development and Changes, 26*, 1–29.

Man, G. (1993, April 21). 80% xiaoxuesheng zhoume shangke [80% of pupils go to Sunday schools]. *Beijing Daily*, p. 3.

The match of wedding. (1997, January 24). *Southern Weekend*, p. 4.

Meng, X. (1995). "Nagengnüzhi" yü zhongguo nongzun nüxing de fazhan ["Men work in town and women plow in the field" and the development of rural Chinese women]. *Social Science Fronts, 1*, 248–251.

Michael, R., Gagnon, J., Laumann, E. O., & Kolata, G. (1994). *Sex in America: The definitive survey*. Boston: Allyn & Bacon.

Ministry of Civil Affairs of China. (2002). *Zhongguo minzheng tongji nianjian* [China Civil Affairs' Statistical Yearbook]. Beijing: China Statistics Press.

Nan, Y., & He, X. (1997, January 18). Yijialiangzhi yü, haoguo rizi [One family, two systems, and happy life]. *China Youth Daily*, p. 8.

Nass, G. D., & McDonald, G. W. (1982). *Marriage and the family*. Reading, MA: Addison-Wesley.

National Bureau of Statistics. (1999). *Comprehensive statistical data and materials on 50 years of new China*. Beijing: China Statistical Press.

National Bureau of Statistics. (2001a). *China statistical yearbook: 2001*. Beijing: China Statistics Press.

National Bureau of Statistics. (2001b). *Guoji tongji nianjian: 2001* [International Statistical Yearbook: 2001]. Beijing: China Statistical Press.

Pan, L., Yuan, H., & Hu, J. (1992). Chongtu yü zhangai: Woguo fuqi liangdifenjü xianxiang tanxi [Conflicts and barriers: The phenomenon of couple living apart together in China]. *Economy and Society*, 1, 97–100.

Pan, R. (2002). *Shehui bianqian zhong de jiating: Jiating shehuixüe* [Families in social transition: Sociology of family]. Tianjin: Tianjin Academy of Social Science Press.

Parsons, T. (1955). The American family. In T. Parsons & R. Bales (Eds.), *Family, socialization and interaction process* (pp. 3–34). Glencoe, IL: Free Press.

Poston, D., & Gu, B. (1984). Socioeconomic differentials and fertility in the provinces, municipalities and autonomous regions of the People's Republic China. Circa 1982. *Texas population research center paper*. Series 6: Paper No. 6.011. Austin: University of Texas.

Research Institute of All China Women's Federation and Research Office of Shanxi Provincial Women's Federation. (1991). *Zhongguo funü tongji ziliao* [Statistics on Chinese women]. Beijing: China Statistical Press.

The Research Project on the Efficiency of Implementing Family Planning in China. (1996). Jiceng nongcun jihuashengyü zhixing qingkuang de diaochayanjiu [A research survey on the implementation of family planning in rural areas]. *Population Research*, 20(1), 30–40.

Sheng, X. (1992). Population aging and the traditional pattern of supporting the aged. In *Proceedings of Asia-Pacific regional conference on future of the family* (pp. 66–71). Beijing: China Social Science Documentation Publishing House.

Stockman, N. (2000). *Understanding Chinese society*. Cambridge, UK: Polity Press.

Stockman, N., Bonney, N., & Sheng, X. (1995). *Women's work in East & West: The dual burden of employment and family life*. London: UCL Press.

Sun, S. (1996). Dangdai zhongguo funü jiatingcaichan jichengqian de weiguan yanjiu [A micro study on the inheritance rights of family property among contemporary Chinese women]. *Population & Economics*, 99(6), 48–53.

Tan, S. (1995). Funü yanjiu de xinjinzhan [Recent developments in womens' studies]. *Sociological Studies*, 5, 66–74.

Tang, J. (2002). Dangqian zhongguo chengshi pinkun de xingcheng yü xianzhuang [The emerging and current situation of poverty in urban China]. *Sociology*, 6, 16–21.

Tao, Y., & Ming, X. (1994). *Zhongguo hunyin jiating zhidushi* [The history of Chinese marriage and family system]. Beijing: East Press.

Tian, X., Xiong, Y., & Xiong, B. (1991). *Zhongguo laonian renkou shehui* [Chinese aging population society]. Beijing: China Economics Press.

Unger, J. (1993). Urban families in the eighties: An analysis of Chinese survey. In D. Davis & S. Harrell (Eds.), *Chinese families in the post-Mao era* (pp. 25–49). Berkeley: University of California Press.

United Nations. (2003). *United Nations. World population prospects.* Retrieved October 31, 2003, from http://esa.un.org/unpp/p2k0data.asp.

Wan, C., Fan, C., & Lin, G. (1994). A comparative study of certain differences in individuality and sex-based differences between 5- and 7-year old only children and non-only children. *Acta Psychologica Sinica, 16,* 383–391.

Wan, C., Fan, C., Lin, G., & Jing, Q. (1994). Comparison of personality traits of only children and sibling school children in Beijing. *Journal of Genetic Psychology, 155*(4), 377–388.

Wang, Q. (1988, September 3). Yige zhidezhuyi de shehuiwenti: Chengqü laonianren zaihun wenti diaocha [A noticeable social problem: Survey on the remarriage of urban seniors]. *Labor's Daily,* p. 4.

Wang, R., Li, X., & Shao, L. (1993). Zhongguo gudai de jiagui [Family rules in ancient China]. *Journal of Liaoning Normal University* (Social Science Edition), 6, 1993.

Wang, Z. (1999). 1998–1999: Zhongguo hunyinjiating zoushi yü xiuding <hunyinhai> de taolun [1998–1999: The trends of Chinese marriage and family, and the discussions around the revision of the *Marriage* Law]. In *1999 nian: Zhongguo shehui xingshi fenxi yü yüce* [The analysis and prediction of social situations in China: 1999] (pp. 214–228). Beijing: Chinese Social Science Documentation Press.

Wedding costs on the rise in Shanghai. (2002, August 23). Xihua News Agency Website p. 1008235h7149.

Weilai 4000 wan gugua laonian funü de yanglao wenti zenmeban? [What shall we do about supporting 40 million widowed old women in the future?]. (2001). *Population Studies (Beijing), 5,* 50–59.

Wolf, A. (1986). The preeminent role of government intervention in China's family revolution. *Population and Development Review, 12*(1), 101–116.

Wu, Z. (1995, April 28). Nanxingguan zhipei xia de nanren and nüren [Men and women under the control of male culture]. *China Youth Daily,* p. 6.

Xu, A. (1992). Zhongwai funü jiating diwei de bijiao [A comparison of the family positions of Chinese women and women abroad]. *The Society, 1,* 12–15.

Xu, A. (1994). Lihun yü funü diwei [Divorce and women's position]. *Chinese Women, 7,* 21–24.

Yan, M., & Shi, R. (1995). Shixi woguo 80 niandai zaohun shuliang huisheng de yüanyin [Exploring the reasons for the re-increasing numbers of early marriage during the 1980s]. *Sociological Studies, 5,* 97–101.

Zhang, G., Lei, T., & Liang, H. (1996). Xingfu hunyin jiqi xiangguan yinsu de yanjiu [The study about happy marriage and relevant factors]. *Sociological Studies, 4,* 106–116.

Zhang, H., & Tong, L. (1997). Zhuanxingqi zhongguo chengshi lihunlü shangsheng de shehuixüe sikao [A sociological thinking about the increase of the divorce rate in Chinese cities during the period of social transition]. *Learning and Exploring, 108*(1), 92–98.

Zhang, P. (1993). Zhongguo weifa hunyin xianzhuang fenxi [An analysis of current illegal marriages in China]. *Sociological Studies, 5,* 79–91.

Zhang, P. (1995, March 27, April 6, & April 13). Zhongguo funü de hunyin zhuangkuang [The marital situation of Chinese women]. *China Women's Daily,* p. 4.

Zhang, Q. (1988). Basic facts on the household registration system. *Chinese Economic Studies, 22*(1).

Zhong, Y. (1994, October 16). Shehui zhuanxing: Funü huijia? [Social transition: Should women back home?]. *Peasant Daily*, p. 4.

Zhongguo dabaike quanshu: Shehuixue [Chinese encyclopedia: Sociology]. (1991). Beijing: Chinese Encyclopedia Press.

Zhongguo jiaoyü nianjian [China education yearbook]. (1998). Beijing: People's Education Press.

Zhu, G. (1992, December 16). Qiangqüan yü niai: Shaoer chengzhang de tiandi [Forcing and spoiling: The natural enemies of child development]. *Chinese Women's Daily*, p. 3.

CHAPTER 6

The Contemporary Indian Family

J. P. SINGH

Family is fundamental to society, as the society begins and ends with the family because of its special role in the processes of biological and social reproduction. The family as a social institution or as a primary group assumes a special significance, especially in the case of a traditional society. One can easily imagine how central the study of family is in sociology, particularly in the context of India. It is indeed hard to offer a generalized view of the Indian family, as the subject is quite complicated for the reason that Indian society is very vast and is characterized by bewildering complexity. It has numerous facets, and drawing of universal generalizations is an intricate and hazardous task, because of the existence of substantial variations between regions, between rural and urban areas, between classes, and finally, between different religious, ethnic, and caste groups.

Prima facie, the Indian subcontinent looks like a single cultural region, but an in-depth analysis of Indian society suggests that it is a congeries of microregions and subcultures, with crucial sociological differences. These are discernible with respect to the level of female literacy, sex ratio, age at marriage of girls, dissolution of marriage, female workforce participation rate, marital practices, gender relations, and authority structure within the family. Furthermore, institutions that significantly affect the lives of women in the family are confined to certain groups inhabiting particular areas. For instance, polyandry continues to be practiced by the Khasa of Jaunsar Bawar, and hypergamy by the Rajput north of the Vindhyas, the Khatri and the Jat of the Punjab, and finally, by the Patidar and the Anavil Brahmin of Gujarat. Matriliny is practiced not only by the high-caste Nayar and a few other groups in Kerala, but also by the Khasi, the Garo, and the Pnar tribes in the northeastern hill areas.

In fact, inter-regional and intragroup differences are not the only hazard. In a country

Thanks are due to Emeritus Professor John C. Caldwell and Pat Caldwell, Demography and Sociology Program, Research School of Social Sciences, Australian National University, Canberra, ACT, Australia, and Sachchidananda, Chairman, A. N. Sinha Institute of Social Studies, Patna (Bihar), India, for offering useful comments and suggestions on an earlier draft of this paper. However, the usual disclaimer applies.

such as India with a long, checkered, recorded history, the existence of a body of literature, sacred and secular, proves obtrusive especially as it sanctions present conduct, directly or indirectly, by reference to ideals and rules that are expressed in it. The corpus of literature is, however, a heterogeneous one, and it abounds in inconsistent, if not contrary, ideas, ideals, rules, beliefs, and practices. The important point to note is that the ideals of conduct and the behavior of people continue to be influenced by various sets of considerations both within and outside of the family. Yet, underlying the variety, there is also a notable degree of similarity in family relations. In this chapter the discussion is essentially confined to features of family that characterize Indian society generally. The family bears a characteristic Indian stamp because of the widely shared ideal model for family relations and because of the common value system as well as a common perspective of hierarchy.

1. INDIA: A BRIEF INTRODUCTION

Considering the fact that India is a vast country with enormous diversity, there is need for a brief discussion of certain broad facets of the country. India's population was estimated to be around 1.068 billion in 2003, spread over slightly more than one-third the geographical size of the United States, registering an annual growth rate of 1.7%. India is characterized by an imbalanced sex ratio of 107 males per 100 females. From 361 million at the time of independence, the population reached 1 billion in 2001, registering nearly a threefold increase in 50 years. Every year about 18 million people were added to India's population between 1991 and 2001, compared with 16 million annually between 1981 and 1991. In other words, each year India's population increases by the equivalent of the number of inhabitants of Ghana,

Australia, Mozambique, or Saudi Arabia. The vast majority of Indian people still live in villages, primarily depending on agriculture to eke out their living. Merely 28% of the total population was recorded as urban dwellers in the 2001 census. The expectancy of life at birth is estimated to be 65 years for females and 63 years for males in 2003. The age structure continues to be favorable to high fertility (current total fertility rate [TFR] is 3). Of the total population, 33% falls under age 15, 62% in the 15 to 64 group, and another 5% is in the 62+ age-group.

India as a free republic came into being only recently, in the mid-20th century, but India is home to one of the world's oldest civilizations. The Indian subcontinent's rich cultural history presents a kaleidoscope of linguistic and religious groups. The major ethnic groups are Indo-Aryans (72%), Dravidian (25%), and Mongoloid and others (3%). The diversity of language and culture across 28 states and 7 union territories makes India a unique country among the nations of the world. In fact, 150 years of British rule or interventions brought the country together as one geographical entity for the first time, but at the end of that rule, India was partitioned into two countries (India and Pakistan) on the basis of a strong religious feeling.

All the coastal states, including the landlocked states of the northeastern region, tend to have their own language. There are 18 official languages and at least 50 regional tongues. A great variety of official languages recognized under the constitution continue to hinder communication among the people of different regions, especially in rural areas. The most common language is Hindi, spoken by nearly one-half of India's population, particularly in states of the northern, western, and central zones. English enjoys associate status but is the most important language for national, political, and commercial communication. Hindustani is a popular variant of

Hindi/Urdu spoken throughout northern India but is not an official language.

Although Indians are quite religious, India has no official religion. About 81% of Indians profess Hinduism. The share of minorities, particularly Muslims and Christians, in the Indian population has been steadily rising because of the poorer adoption of family planning measures and the policy of religious conversion pursued by Christian missionaries taking advantage of the state's secular policy. The share of Muslim population has gone up from about 10% to nearly 12% during the postindependence period, resulting from a relatively higher rate of fertility. Christians and Sikhs constitute about 2% each of the total population. Other religious communities together, primarily Jains, Buddhists, and animists, constitute 2%. Many Indians are worried about the possible shift in balance of political power as a result of the gradual decline in the proportion of Hindu population from about 85% in 1951 to 81% in 2001.

According to the Anthropological Survey of India, published under the People of India Series, the country comprises 4,635 distinct castes/communities dispersed over the different states and union territories of India. The country has been subdivided into 91 identifiable cultural regions marked by a distinct language/dialect, territorial identity, and cultural variations with diverse levels of economic development (K. S. Singh, 1992). The fact that India is a highly plural society needs no emphasizing. In fact, there are many societies that are characterized by huge pluralities or diversities, but they are more discernible in India than elsewhere because of the uneven economic development and modernization in India. Hence, what is true in one section may be untrue in others.

Indian society has long been characterized by vastly disparate socioeconomic classes. Because of age-old sociocultural prejudices and discriminatory practices, India's constitution protects its citizens against discrimination on the basis of religion, race, caste, sex, or place of birth. Yet, modern-day India shows the impact of the traditional caste system that has so long dictated the behavior and life chances of individuals in society and the social structure generally at a broader level.

In traditional India, the untouchables classified as scheduled castes, or now called *dalits,* occupied the lowest rung in the hierarchical Hindu social order. Untouchables were considered unclean because they had to adopt mean and menial jobs as a means of livelihood, such as tannery, carrying carcasses of domestic animals, cleaning sewerage, lanes, and latrines, and so on. Thus they were destined to live in poverty and suffer overt discrimination from caste Hindus for centuries. Because an individual's caste is ascribed at birth and cannot be altered, an untouchable could never hope to move into the higher echelons of society under any circumstances without affirmative action pursued by the state.

After independence, the Indian government abolished untouchability in the Constitution of India and actively tried to do away with past injustices through affirmative actions. Those affected have been allotted a certain percentage of seats in admission to educational institutions, public employment/services, national and state legislative bodies, and local self-government bodies, such as municipal corporations and village *panchayat.* Despite this, they still occupy the lowest of the socioeconomic strata in general. There are 471 scheduled castes, whose members make up about 17% of the national population.[1]

Yet another disadvantaged group that has also been favored for similar preferential treatment under the Indian Constitution is that of the scheduled tribes, which include people ethnically distinct from the mainstream population. There are about 350 scheduled tribes that constitute about 8% of the national population.[2] Most members of these ethnic groups, or *tribals,* live in extremely primitive conditions in remote, hilly areas of central India stretching from Maharashtra and Gujarat in the west to western Bengal and Orissa in the east, covering almost the whole of the northeastern states. In general, tribals live in underdeveloped or forest-clad areas and have limited prospects for improving their lot.

As regards literacy, the Indian population is quite disadvantaged. India is one of the least literate societies in the world. About 50% of the world's illiterate people live in India. There were altogether 328 million illiterates in the country at the 1991 census, marking an addition of about 22 million in a decade. At the 2001 census, of 296 million illiterates in the country, 253 million (excluding members of the population aged 0–6) lived in rural areas, which is greater than the total population of any country in the world, except China and the United States.

In the 2001 census, 65% of the people (excluding those below age 7) were recorded as literate in the country, but there is high gender disparity in literacy levels. Men are much more likely than women to know how to read and write—76% of men were enumerated as literate in 2001. However, female literacy has risen steadily from 8% in 1951 to 54% in 2001. An encouraging fact is that the gender disparity in the level of literacy has been steadily declining over the years at the national level (J. P. Singh, 2002b, pp. 471–482). However, the differential in male/female literacy is still substantial (i.e., 22.2 percentage points) according to the 2001 census.

The Indian family may not show uniformity in its character at the national level as in many smaller countries. Therefore, as stated previously, it is very hazardous to present a generalized view about the Indian family system. Yet another problem with this subject is that no national- or state-level surveys on family that can be used as definitive evidence to draw national-level generalizations have been conducted. Though this chapter depends heavily on the census and the National Family and Health Surveys (NFHS) 1 and 2, it also seeks to piece together widely scattered ethnological studies as supplementary evidence on households/ families to corroborate the arguments, despite the fact that there is inherent difficulty in drawing generalizations from such heterogeneous sources. In view of these facts, it is important to qualify that observations made about the Indian household or family in the subsequent discussion are true in broad terms only. Herein no effort has been made to prove or disprove any contention; rather, the chapter primarily presents a summary view of the contemporary Indian family in broad terms. Distinction between family and household has been kept in mind throughout the chapter, as all families are households but all households may not constitute families. A single member or two or more unrelated persons may make up a household, but not a family.[3]

The Form of the Indian Family

To a social scientist, the phrase *Indian family* has usually meant the joint family, especially the Hindu joint family system ever since the pioneering work of Henry S. Maine appeared in 1861. He projected the Indian joint family as the living example of the earliest ancient form of the human family whose outline can be discerned in early Europe (Maine, 1972). Ever since then, much has been written on the subject, and controversies still abound on this subject.[4] So, let us begin with the conceptual aspect of this term at the outset. The traditional joint family has been defined as "a group of people who generally live under one roof, who eat food cooked in one kitchen, who hold property in common, participate in certain family worship, and are related to one another as some type of kindred" (Karve, 1965, p. 8). Though

Karve's definition of joint family has possibly remained the most popular one to this date, there have always remained controversies around what constitutes an ideal joint family, because it has been defined in different ways by ethnographers, depending on which of the common features are selected as essential. Freed and Freed (1982, p. 190) have observed that the "joint family controversy is . . . bedeviled by problems of definition." Let us briefly touch on the important elements of joint family here to understand the current scenario relating to the nature of the existing Indian family system.

Common residence, commensality, joint ownership of property or coparcenary, cooperation, patri(viri)locality (except in parts of southern India), and the fulfillment of obligations toward kin, and ritual bonds, have been commonly outlined as the central criteria for defining what constitutes a joint family. As the debate on various levels of jointness has persisted for a long time, there is need to place bare facts relating to the bases of jointness in a family as they exist in contemporary India, so that one can readily sort out to what degree a particular element is jointly shared by the members of the Indian family now. All the important elements are dealt with one by one. Some social scientists, on one hand, have taken common residence and commensality (eating together) as the defining criteria. In a traditional joint family, its members had a common hearth; they cooked their food collectively and so ate food from the same kitchen. This was inevitable because they were working and living together on their ancestral property generation after generation. But now there are cases where different members of a joint family reside independently from their ancestral home because of their varying means of livelihoods. Thus the criteria of common residence and so also common hearth or kitchen have shattered. But such split-up households with independent sources of income and expenditure are still regarded as a single joint family by many anthropologists because of the common ancestral property and kinship bond.

On the other hand, some scholars have taken coparcenary as the essence of jointness, irrespective of the type of residence and commensality, but coparcenary can be an important criterion only when there is a system of common purse, as an element of economic dependence among members of a family unit is the cornerstone of an ideal joint family. Since different collateral members, if working outside agriculture or other traditional callings, tend to work and reside independently from their ancestral homes, the element of joint ownership of property has also eroded. Because of rising individualism or selfishness, different brothers, and particularly their wives, do not let others know about their actual earnings. Income has become a personal or private affair even where there exists a joint household at the ancestral place (J. P. Singh, 2003, pp. 53–70). In fact, such households can at best be called pseudo or marginal joint families.

Despite huge, noticeable changes in the character of the joint family system, what still survives is cooperation and a sense of belonging of different members of different households to a common family or line. There are also families whose members may be located in far-off places and may not have property in common, but they nonetheless identify themselves with a particular family, cooperate in rituals and ceremonies, render financial and other kinds of help, and cherish a common family sentiment and abide by the norms of joint living. They are also bound together by periodic propitiation of the ancestors. The members perform a *shraddha* ceremony, in which the senior male member of the family propitiates his dead father's or mother's spirit, offering it the *pinda* (ball of cooked rice) on behalf of all the members.

Another ritual bond among the joint family members can be common deity worship. In many parts of southern India, each joint family has a tradition of worshipping a particular village deity. Vows are made to these deities in times of joy or trouble. The first tonsure, donning of the sacred thread, marriages, and so on are celebrated in or near the deity's temple. Srinivasa of Tirupathi and Subramanya of Palani are two well-known Hindu deities who have a large number of southern Indian families attached to them (Srinivas, 1980, p. 71). Such ritual bonds among different households are considered to be an important component of a joint family by some anthropologists. It is, however, hard to classify such fractured households as a joint family on the basis of common ritual bonds, as it is difficult to assess or evaluate the strength of traditional ritual bonds among the members of a family under the changed circumstances. Commonality of social and cultural obligations does not make a constellation of isolated nuclear families a true joint family. As a matter of fact, the dislocation of different nuclear families has weakened the old familial ties, resulting from spatial distance and diverse sources of living and personalized forms of saving. In a joint family setting, every working person actually works for everybody else, and hence everyone is prepared to share everyone's responsibility and liability to the best of one's ability or capability. The word *joint* always stands for a team spirit as well as collective endeavor to protect and further the interests of all the members of a family.

On the whole, a joint family has to be taken to mean a patrilineal, patri(viri)local, property-owning, coresidential, and commensal unit comprising three or more generations, wherein the oldest male is the head of the family (popularly called *Karta* in Hindi). The rights and duties in this type of family are laid down to a great extent by the ordering principles of family hierarchy based on age and sex. Such essential elements as common residence and commensality may not be regarded as essential conditions to constitute a joint family under the changed circumstances. But, again, this conception of joint family may not be unanimously accepted. The notion of joint household should not be separated from the notion of joint family in a strict sense, but in the case of a joint family, where different coparceners own independent households, there must be a common purse to meet everyone's responsibility and liability in the larger family if any exigency warrants doing so. Most Indian villagers share only this notion of a joint family. Most rural households survive as nominal or marginal joint families essentially because different brothers reside at diverse places with their wives and children. They have their own independent sources of income and expenditure and assemble for the short term on certain festivals and family rituals. The conceptual aspect of joint family has been dealt with at a greater length by Madan (1962), Shah (1998), and most recently by J. P. Singh (2003) elsewhere, recording the immense diversity of views.

Nuclearization of the Joint Family

It is commonly believed that joint family has been the characteristic feature of Indian society. But the contention has been contested by many family scholars. There is no need to address the whole range of debates on the joint family in India, as the full discussion on the subject is available elsewhere (J. P. Singh, 2003, pp. 53–70). The available evidence simply suggests that it has not been the most dominant type of family system in India. It has been observed that the joint family was never really prevalent in India on a large scale, that, as in China, it occurred only among a limited number of people— landed peasantry and certain trading castes and community (Levy, 1949, pp. 55–58).

It was hardly ever present among landless people, service castes, *dalits,* or tribal populations, which together have constituted the largest chunk of India's population. Mandelbaum has noted that the incidence of joint family is associated with the nature of occupation of the people:

> Family occupation affects family form throughout the land. Village surveys from different regions show that families who own and cultivate their own land tend to remain together longer as multicouple families than do noncultivating landowners and still longer than do landless laborers of the same locality. Hence at any one time owner-cultivators tend to have a higher proportion of joint families. (1972, p. 50)

This kind of family, which characterized the landed castes for so long, could not and need not go on indefinitely under the changed circumstances. There are both physical and social limitations to its continuance. Different brothers or their sons are not under the same social obligation to stay together as true kindred. The fission of the larger family is an unavoidable social event. One of the earliest explorations into the size and composition of rural families based on a survey of 12,030 families selected from 74 villages from India's western zone conducted by the Gokhale Institute of Politics and Economics (Pune) during 1947–1951 demonstrated that only 32% of all families consisted of two or more couples (Dandekar & Pethe, 1960, pp. 189–199). This obviously implies preponderance of nuclear families even half a century ago in rural India. Studies of joint families in a historical perspective by ethnographers have distinctly shown that the life span of the joint family has become increasingly shorter over time in the face of a new economic order and demographic regime (J. P. Singh, 1984, pp. 86–95; 2001, pp. 229–248).

Recent census data have revealed that it is the nuclear family, not the joint one, that predominantly characterizes the Indian family system. According to the 1981 census, nuclear families constituted 68% of all households, and the single-member or lone-parent household (or eroded families) composed about 11%. The stem and joint family together could claim 20% of all households at the 1981 census. After a lapse of two decades, that is, at the 2001 census, the share of single-member or lone-parent households remained more or less the same, but the share of households comprising only one married couple increased to 70.4% and the percentage of stem and joint families together further came down to 18.5. It is very surprising that such a glaring piece of evidence from censuses about the preponderance of nuclear family had been glossed over or played down by the advocates of the persistence of the joint family in India. The 2001 census has definitely provided evidence of a further decline in the importance of the joint family system, as households comprising three or more married couples account for merely 5% of the total households (Table 6.1).[5] One may wonder on what basis Madan (1962, 1999) and Shah (1998) built up their case so strongly and persisted with their views for about four decades when the available data from one census after another, in addition to data from various surveys, have clearly been in contravention with their arguments. It seems their views remained quite popular in academic circles of Indian sociology and anthropology for a long time, partly because both these scholars worked in one of the premier academic institutions of the country—Delhi University—until they superannuated from the job and partly because their views are contrary to those of Western scholarship, that is, that urban-industrial civilization tends to weaken extended family ties. A discussion on the subject at a greater length can be seen elsewhere in one of the recent publications of the author (J. P. Singh, 2003, pp. 53–70).

Table 6.1   Percentage Distribution of Couples per Household in India in 1981 and 2001

	1981 Census	2001 Census
No. of Couples per Household	Percentage of Households	Percentage of Households
<1[a]	11.4	11.2
1	68.1	70.4
2	15.1	13.5
3	4.1	3.4
4	1.0	1.0
5+	0.3	0.5
	100.0	100.0
Households (N) =	128,439,820	191,963,935

SOURCE: Census of India (1981).

Note: The computation does not include houseless households and households unspecified by number of couples per household. The married couples constituted 114,227,084 in 1981 and 220,389,861 in 2001 censuses.

a. This includes single-member households as well as those households with more than one member, but without spouse.

Although there is no need for supplementary evidence to corroborate the preceding argument regarding the disappearance of the joint family, the size and composition of households are also briefly highlighted to further substantiate the views relating to disintegration of the joint family. The available data on household size and composition from the NFHS-1 provide clinching confirmation of the nuclearization of stem or joint family, no matter how liberally one prefers to define joint family (see Table 6.2). The data suggest that no more than 5% to 6% of all families or households live as a joint household. Large stem or extended families, which include a couple with married sons or daughters and their spouses, as well as a household head without a spouse but with at least two married sons, daughters, and their spouses, constitute about one-fifth of the total households in India.

On the basis of past trends, it is believed that with further industrial development, rural to urban migration, nuclearization of family, and the rise in the incidence of divorce, the proportion of single-member households is likely to increase steadily, as in other industrializing societies. The states that have a higher level of urbanization tend to have a higher proportion of single-member households. The cultural climate of India has always been strongly opposed to the notion of divorce or separation, spinsterhood, unwed mothers, and the gay or lesbian way of life. Hindus believe strongly in the inevitability of marriage and they are, in fact, relatively more rigid in the case of females, with minor exceptions in parts of western Bengal and southern India.

Table 6.2   Nature and Composition of Household and Family in India (1992–1993)

Type of Household/Family	Explanations	Percentage	
		Rural	Urban
1. Single-member household	Respondent found alone at the time of enumeration.	2.5	3.5
2. Nuclear family	(a) Household having a couple with or without nonmarried children; and (b) household having a single spouse, but with nonmarried children (eroded family).	47.5	53.0
3. Stem nuclear family	(a) Household head and spouse with or without nonmarried children but with other relations; (b) household head without spouse but with other relations of whom only one has spouse; and (c) household head without spouse, with or without nonmarried children, but with other nonmarried/separated/divorced/widowed relation.	22.5	20.5
4. Large stem or extended family	(a) Household head and spouse with married son(s)/daughter(s) and their spouses; and (b) household head without spouse but with at least two married son(s)/daughter(s) and their spouses.	21.5	19.0
5. Conventional joint family	(a) Household head and spouse with married brother(s)/sister(s) and their spouses with or without other relation(s) including married relation(s); and (b) household head without spouse but with at least two married brothers/sisters and their spouses with or without other relations.	6.0	4.0

SOURCE: Compiled from NFHS-1 (1994).

Note: This classification of family has been done from both a sociological and a demographic angle. It differs from the sixfold anthropological classification of family done by Kolenda (1987, pp. 11–12), namely, collateral joint family, supplemented collateral joint family, lineal joint family, supplemented lineal joint family, lineal collateral joint family, and supplemented lineal-collateral joint family. It is not really clear what useful purposes such typologies serve. In fact, many classifications of family forms are logically impossible.

The purposes of the National Family Health Survey were such that it covered married women only. Single-member households with male respondents were left out. Hence, it shows a lower proportion of single-member households than the census data in Table 6.1. This has consequently inflated the percentage distributions in the subsequent categories of family. Therefore, the census distributions, despite certain inherent limitations, are more authentic representations of household distributions across the country than the NFHS data.

The NFHS-1 data have revealed some remarkable facts about family structures cross-classified by education, religion, ethnicity, occupation, ownership of land, geographical location, and so on. The data have borne out the fact that there exists a positive association between level of education and the incidence of the nuclear family. At the same time, it is also true that the incidence of nuclear families is much greater among scheduled tribes and scheduled castes although their level of literacy is quite low. They have recorded a much lower incidence of joint family than other categories of people. Similarly, landless people tend to record a greater proportion of nuclear families than land-owning people (Niranjan, Sureender, & Rao, 1998, pp. 287–300).

The states and union territories that have a relatively higher proportion of tribal people in their population or have attained a higher level of urbanization tend to record a greater proportion of single-member households and nuclear families than others. About the scheduled tribes, K. S. Singh (1997b, p. 9) has categorically reported that the dominant form of the tribal family is nuclear (91.4%). The joint or extended type of family, except for certain cultivating groups, has never been popular among them, as it appears from various other ethnographic studies. Kolenda, who did extensive research on the family in India since 1949, tried to ascertain whether joint families were more characteristic of higher castes or lower castes. On the basis of her empirical investigations, she concluded the following: "[J]oint families are least characteristic of untouchables and more characteristic of Sanskritized caste" (Kolenda, 1968, p. 390). But, as a matter of fact, the incidence of joint family has hardly anything to do with the ranking of individual castes in the social hierarchy. It is the ownership of land rather than caste status that determines family types. Since the higher castes are often characterized by higher levels of land ownership there

is an apparent positive association between caste ranking and joint family (Dasgupta & Hennessey, 1999, pp. 561–577). In certain parts of southern India, Brahmins may be an exception to the generalization relating to the strong relationship between land ownership and the incidence of joint family, as at some level of land ownership Brahmins are more likely to live in joint families. In addition to land, caste also seems to have some bearing on the nature of family type. All the predominantly forest-clad and hill states and union territories such as Himachal Pradesh, Meghalaya, Nagaland, Sikkim, Arunachal Pradesh, Goa, Daman and Diu, Andaman and Nicobar Islands, and Lakshadweep have recorded from one-tenth to one-fourth of the single-member households in urban areas. It is much higher than the national average of 8% (Chakravorty & Singh, 1991). Geographical condition sometimes also seems to determine the size of household or family.

Rural to urban migration is mostly dominated by young adults, and the migrants are more likely to move alone than with other members of the family, giving rise to a significant proportion of single-member households in urban India (J. P. Singh, 1985, pp. 69–87; 1988, pp. 87–99). Joint families are breaking up more prematurely than in the past. Based on a meticulous study of nine villages in Karnataka, Caldwell, Reddy, and Caldwell (1984, p. 222) reported that 41% of all households were partitioned when fathers were still alive. The percentage is higher in the case of northern Indian villages where there is no system of marriage (or *vivah*) between close kinsmen. This is visibly evident from the rising incidence of bride-burning, divorce, and violence against women in northern India generally.

Notwithstanding individual differences among the members, the joint family was a much more serene organization in olden days, for the head of the family was a quite commanding person who ironed out any intra- or interfamilial differences. Education among the young, or their increasing ability to secure work elsewhere, has posed a continued threat of partition. This has meant reduction in the pyramidal control structure of the traditional joint or stem family. Studies of western Bengal villages on ethnographic lines have also pointed out the preponderance of nuclear households (Dasgupta, Wetherbie, & Mukhopadhyay, 1993, p. 356).

The emergence of financially independent, career-oriented men and women who are confident in taking their own decisions and crave a sense of individual achievement has greatly contributed to the disintegration of the joint family. Female discord, particularly between mother-in-law and daughter-in-law or among daughters-in-law, is considered to be the prime factor behind the partitioning of the family or household. There is a proverb in Kannada that says that a thousand moustaches can live together, but not four breasts. With the rise in female education and individual autonomy, discord between brothers is gradually increasing. In the course of their study, Caldwell et al. (1984, pp. 223–224) noticed that disputes were more common between brothers than between sons and fathers.

Sometimes disputes also originate in suspicions of unequal parental treatment and favors. Daughters-in-law are considered major disputants because they are essentially aliens in the household. Females are socialized in one setting and live with others in another. Therefore, dissension among women is considered the principal reason for the disintegration of the joint or extended family in India. However, it has often been noticed in northern Indian villages that the women who in their younger years urge their husbands to separate from the joint family are commonly the same persons who later as mothers and mothers-in-law or grandmothers are most unwilling to see their joint family split in their lifetime.

On the death of the patriarch, the disintegration of the stem or joint family becomes imminent if there are persistent problems or constant tensions within the family. This fact is true more in the northern than the southern zone, and more true of Hindus than of Muslims because of the system of cross-cousin marriage among southern Indian Hindus and parallel cousin marriages among Muslims. When a girl marries her maternal uncle, she enters a household that her mother lived in before marriage and her mother-in-law is actually her grandmother. When a Hindu girl in southern India marries her father's sister's son or her mother's brother's son, she joins a household in which her mother lived before marriage and which she has subsequently visited with her mother, and her father-in-law is her uncle and mother-in-law her aunt. When a Muslim girl marries her father's brother's son, she does not even change residence if it is a joint family. However, marriages between relatives are continuing to decline for various reasons (Caldwell et al., 1984).

Rise in the partition of households does not always mean a rise in tension or bitterness within the family. It is a sign of greater willingness of young couples to argue and to press for further partition of households. Conditions that were tolerated in prepartition days only a generation ago are much less likely to be tolerated now. This is a consequence more of a rise in the spirit of individualism than of anything else. But people tend to remain in joint families longer when economic factors are favorable. The poorest and the lowest tend to have fewer joint families (J. P. Singh, 1984, pp. 86–95; 2001, pp. 229–248). Nuclearization of the joint family has given rise to a massive increase in the number of independent households, fragmentation of landholdings and business complexes, the number of court cases relating to the division of property, and a decrease in the size of homesteads. A new type of family based on close emotional bonds, enjoying a high degree of domestic privacy preoccupied with rearing of children, is surfacing as a dominant form of family.

Progressively greater contact of traditional Indian society in general with new cultural and family legislation and economic and political orders over the years has caused the Indian family system to pass through fresh experiences. Both families and individuals have slowly but surely tended to look for a new social identity in a relatively more open setting. Such experiences and challenges, however, have not been smooth and undemanding. They have given thrust to the transition of the Indian family from a consanguineal orientation to a conjugal orientation, which is by and large a historical inevitability, as Goode (1963) observed in his comparative study of family in five different areas of the world. Changes, as they are evident from the preceding, have covered a large part of Indian society, but many more changes in various aspects of the Indian family structure are yet to come about, as there are still conspicuous differences between the familial system of a metropolis and that of a small town and also between the familial system of a small town and that of a village community. Here it may be noted once again that a little more than three-fourths of Indians still live in villages.

2. THE SYSTEM OF PAIRING UP OR MATE SELECTION

Since time immemorial the system of Indian cultural values regarding sex has been such that a premarital relationship of any kind, or even frequent social interactions, between young boys and girls has been highly discouraged. Even now young boys or girls seldom exercise their rights in matters of mate selection, especially in the vast rural community. The practice of child marriage (prepuberty marriages) that has been in vogue right from ancient times has possibly deterred the system of pairing up, as is commonly found elsewhere. The pairing-up system has been in vogue on a very limited scale only among certain aborigines or scheduled tribes. In fact, generally people do not expect even young married couples to interact or mix freely with each other outside of their home in the presence of others, or in the presence of their own parents at home.

There are three striking features of mate selection in India. First are the rules of endogamy, which indicate the groups from which a person is expected to find a spouse. Second are the rules of exogamy, which prohibit a person from marrying into certain groups. The rules of endogamy and exogamy are both linked mainly to the caste or kinship structure. Third, marriages in India are mostly arranged by the parents or, in their absence, by elderly close kin. Let us discuss these features of marriage briefly.

Endogamy

Indian society has traditionally been highly endogamous. The rules of endogamy require an individual to marry within a specified or defined group of which he or she is a member. The group may be a subcaste, caste (or *jati*), clan, or ethnic or religious group. Religious and caste endogamy are two of the most pervasive forms of endogamy in India. In India there are innumerable castes that are divided into numerous subcastes, and further divided into subsections—each one of them endogamous. The endogamous unit, for many Hindu subcastes, consists of a series of kin clusters living in a fairly limited geographical area. The operation of the rules of endogamy shows discernible variations by region and religion.

The endogamous character of Hindu marriages is steadily changing. Civil marriages are on the gradual rise. Though legally permitted, inter-religious marriages are not commonly arranged or popular, while marriages across subcastes or castes have become a common event in Indian cities. The role of parents in arranged marriages is on the gradual decline. The age-old requirement that marriage has to occur within the same subcaste is no longer a cherished value of Hindus. The parents are fully prepared to recognize the nuptial bonds of their sons and daughters across the subcastes. Evidently such a process of secularization of marriage has ascended steadily with the rise in urbanization and the spread of modern education.

Polygamy, more particularly, polygyny, has been a salient feature of the Indian family. It has been more popular among Muslims than Hindus. The polygamous males often derive support from age-old scriptures and mythological stories, but mainly those who had no issue from the first wife practiced such marriages. The preference for sons has been strong because in a patrilineal society only a son can continue the family line. Sons are needed also because they provide succor to their parents in their old age. This fact has been well explained in some demographic explorations (Mutharayappa, Choe, Arnold, & Roy, 1997), but the practice of polygamy, particularly among Hindus, is virtually extinct, with some exceptions of scheduled castes. K. S. Singh (1997b, p. 7) has reported, "Two hundred and sixty-five of the scheduled castes (35.2%) allow polygyny." However, it does not mean that all of them essentially practice it. The enactment of the Hindu Marriage and Divorce Act in 1955 and its amendment in 1976 played an important part in this process. Bigamy has been made a penal offence among Hindus. With the rise in education, the incidence of polygyny has declined even among the Muslims, despite the fact that such marriages have gotten full cultural and legal sanction. The scheduled

tribes are somewhat different from others with respect to marriage. While monogamy is the predominant form of marriage, there are a large number of tribes practicing sororal polygyny and nonsororal polygyny (K. S. Singh, 1997b, p. 8).

Related to endogamy is the practice of consanguineous marriage, which has been one of the notable features of a large segment of Indian society. Through the ages, the system of cross-cousin and cross-uncle/niece marriages has been the most favored kind of marriage in southern India. The most desirable mate for a man has been his own sister's daughter or mother's brother's daughter (Driver & Driver, 1988; Nair, 1978, pp. 121, 131). However, such marriages have remained taboo among a large majority of Hindus in northern India (P. S. S. Rao, 1983). The Hindu Marriage Act (1955) prohibits marriage among close relatives—called *sapinda* marriage. The *sapinda* relationship extends as far as the third generation in the line of mother and the fifth in the line of father.[6] In northern India only Muslims, certain scheduled castes, and scheduled tribes tend to observe consanguineous marriages.

K. S. Singh (1997b, pp. 8–9) has reported that most of the tribal groups follow consanguinity of both types, such as marriage with the father's sister's daughter, the mother's brother's daughter, and the elder sister's daughter. As many as 359 scheduled tribes (56.4%) allow marriage with the mother's brother's daughter and 259 allow marriage with the father's sister's daughter. (Here the number of scheduled castes far exceeds 350 because certain tribes are found in more than one state and are enumerated in each state and union territory separately.) Of these, 84 tribes also permit an uncle-niece alliance. Such consanguineous marriages are reported from all tribal areas in southern, central, and northeast India. The incidence of such marriages is much less in the northwest. Marriage with parallel cousins is practiced among 23 tribes. Contrary to the general belief, as circulated by Karve (1965), K. S. Singh (1997b, pp. 8–9) has observed that the incidence of cross-cousin marriages is far more widespread than was earlier believed. In addition to sororate and levirate marriages of both types—senior and junior—tribes are also unique in their institution of polyandry of the fraternal type.

The National Family Health Surveys have shown that there has been appreciable decline in consanguineous marriage, especially in Dravidian India. At the national level, nearly 15% of the ever-married women have married blood relatives. In Tamil Nadu and in some parts of Karnataka and coastal Andhra Pradesh only 25% to 50% of the marriages are of the consanguineous type, and on the West Coast consanguineous marriages are less frequent and account for only 10% to 20% of all marriages. In the rest of India, consanguineous marriages are extremely rare, generally as low as 2% (Bhat & Zavier, 1999, pp. 3021–3024). A study conducted by Richard and Rao (1994, p. 17) in Tamil Nadu has borne out that consanguineous marriages have declined, with the rate of decline being greater in urban than rural areas. Conversely, the data also imply that nonconsanguineous marriages have increased quite markedly, and the amount of increase is still much greater in urban areas.

Exogamy

Rules of exogamy are complementary to those of endogamy. Hypergamy is a kind of exogamous marriage wherein rules prohibit marriage between members of certain groups. The prohibition may be so narrow as to only include members within the elementary family (i.e., marriage between a brother and sister or parent and child), or so wide as to include all those with whom genealogical kinship can be traced. The definitions of these groups, however, show variations by caste, region, and religion. Under the rules of hypergamy, girls marry boys of higher status. Those who follow this rule always seek for men having higher social status than their own for the marriage of their daughters. It is also a rule whereby marriage takes place or is generally arranged within the same caste but between a girl of a lower subcaste and a boy of a higher subcaste. This is possible because each caste is divided into several subcastes that are again divided into hierarchically ordered groups. It is quite clear that the rules of hypergamy operate within the confines of each endogamous group.

As a matter of fact, neither hypergamy nor hypogamy was ever a popular kind of marriage across the country. It was more a contextual than a large-scale empirical reality. The practice of hypergamy has been found among such groups as the Rajput and the Jat of northern India, Anavil Brahmin and Patidar of Gujarat, and the Maithil Brahmin of Bihar to some extent. It has also been found among the Nayar, Kshatriya, and Ambavasi of Kerala.

The system of exogamy has also shown a spatial or regional characteristic. For instance, among the Rajputs of Uttar Pradesh, traditionally girls were given in marriage from the east to the west direction within the same subcaste. This has been so because the Rajput clans were associated with a geographic region and the prestige of Rajputs of the western region is considered progressively superior to that of the eastern side. But, by and large the hypergamous marriages, whether across caste or subcaste, are not favored by the parents or guardians of boys or girls.

Rules of exogamy are also found to operate at the village level. In northern India, a girl born within a village is considered the daughter of the village and, hence, she cannot marry a boy from the same village. This is known as village exogamy. Village endogamy is discouraged also because of commonality of lineage. But the practice of village exogamy does not lead to severing of the relationships between a woman and her family of origin, because of the continuing bonds of kinship relationships. A husband is always treated as the most esteemed or respected guest not only in the family of his wife but also among all the close kinsmen of her parents throughout his life. In southern India, the exogamous unit in one's own generation is defined by one's own sisters and brothers and real and classificatory parallel cousins. The Moplah Muslims of North Malabar in Kerala live in matrilineal units and among these the matrilineage is the exogamous unit. Lineage exogamy also exists among the Muslim Gujjars of Jammu and Kashmir (Srinivas, 1980, p. 56). Among the Nayars, who are a matrilineal group, a girl can never marry her mother's brother.

Arranged Marriages

The majority of marriages in India are still fixed or arranged by parents or elders on behalf of and with or without the consent of the boy or the girl involved. When a marriage is fixed by parents or elders, it is called an arranged marriage. This is in contrast to marriage by personal choice (such a marriage is popularly known as a love marriage in India). In some cases elements of both these types of selection of spouse can be found together. There has never been any room for romantic marriage in Indian society on the line of Western societies. The choice of spouse cannot be left to the decision of the young if rules of marriage alliance are to be effectively carried out. The restriction placed on free interaction between a boy and a girl in India is yet another factor that does not allow marriage by self-choice.

Though the measure of participation in choosing one's life partner has shown variations between different groups, by and large, marriage arranged by parents and elders is the most prevalent form of selection

of a spouse in contemporary India. For the majority of high-caste Hindus, matching of horoscopes (charts relating to one's birth under certain astrological calculations) constitutes an important element in the final choice of a marriage partner. Today, apart from astrologers matching the horoscopes of a boy and a girl, computers are also used to match horoscopes. Among the Muslims, the parents, elders, or *wali* (guardian or custodian) arrange a marriage.

Though most marriages continue to be arranged by parents, elders, or *wali*, the pattern of choosing one's spouse has undergone some modifications today. Very often, the boy is consulted and his consent is sought. Parents or elders do not think it essential to ask the girl whether she approves the match, but in cities educated people seek the consent of their sons and daughters about the choice of preferred partners, and the time of ceremonization of marriages. Marriages are even arranged through newspaper advertisements for both the boy and the girl.

In the past the young trusted their parents and watched, with peripheral interest, the matching of horoscopes, the meeting of families, and finally the meeting of the two parties to the future union. A large percentage of these marriages seemed to work, and if they did not, very few knew about the dissolution of marriage. In conventional families, the wife's subservient attitude curbed her individuality, and she was prepared to take the backseat while the husband devoted his time to his career. Whatever might have been the path leading to a marriage, arranged or otherwise, there were societal pressures, and the onus was on the couple to keep the marriage together. As should be expected, with the lapse of time, marked changes have occurred in all these affairs of family life. The practice of matching horoscopes, however, especially among caste Hindus, is still in existence, though the educated people do not seem to have much faith in it. Hindu marriage was once regarded as a sacrament, ordained and imperative, that every normal man and woman should undergo, but now there have occurred far-reaching changes in the attitudes of people toward marriage.

As mentioned before, now boys and girls, contrary to the old practice, are beginning to assert their wishes in mate selection. Parental decisions are no longer supreme in all cases. Changes concerning erosion of the authority of the old guard, particularly in matters of mate selection, are occurring among educated rural people as well.

Arranged marriages commonly last longer than romantic marriages, as the couple's families constantly stand behind each other. The families invite each other on all social and religious occasions and also tend to exchange gifts. If any need arises, they also help each other in case of crisis or calamity. If the relationship between the couples is about to go haywire leading to desertion or dissolution of the marriage, parents of both spouses make concerted efforts to resolve the crisis, considering it a personal problem in their own life. Such is not usually the case with romantic marriages. Hence, such marriages are likely to be more fragile. They tend to get dissolved on minor matters when parents on both sides do not intervene, if they had not played a major role in the formation of such a marriage alliance. Nevertheless, the females may still ultimately fall back on their parents as their lifelong supports. However, remarriages of such women, if not impossible, are still quite problematic.

Marital Practices and Dowry

Marriage has received special attention in Hindu religious scriptures, as the Hindu traditions are set against promiscuous expression of sex. Marriage provides sustenance to the family system, as fertility outside marriage is unthinkable. Marriage is also essential for continuation of the line and smooth transfer of inheritance. But because of diverse sociocultural practices, marital practices are also quite varied. Rituals relating to the traditional Hindu marriage once used to be quite elaborate, but now they have undergone conspicuous changes. In this regard, Srinivas has made the following observation about southern India:

> The manner in which wedding ritual has been abbreviated is interesting. Formerly, a full-blown Brahmin wedding would last between five and seven days. Now, however, much of the non-*Sanskritic* and folk ritual, traditionally the exclusive preserve of women, is being dropped. There is even an increasing tendency to compress *Sanskritic* ritual into a few hours on a single day. (1977, pp. 125–126)

The prevailing situation in northern India is not much different from the preceding. Countless marriage rituals have been omitted or abbreviated. Now people are generally found disinclined to adhere to all the minute rituals laid down for marriage. People do not have either time or money to observe all the rituals strictly, and, therefore, they have developed liberal attitudes toward them. Priests also do not insist on their observance. In fact, many priests performing marriage rituals have forgotten the scriptural practices by now. In temples the process is faster still. These priests are found to be engrossed in making fast bucks rather than in solemnizing marriage strictly according to the traditional Hindu scriptures. Kerala's situation may be somewhat different, as traditionally marriage had no religious significance in Kerala.

There are some other significant changes in the nuptial practices in rural areas, as well as in urban areas. Rules of residence (from matrilocal and bilocal to patrilocal) have changed. The predominant rule of residence is patrilocal, as out of 4,635 communities in the country, 4,517 communities follow patrilocal residence for women after marriage. Rules of divorce have also become quite flexible. In 596 communities, there has been a change in the rules of inheritance, and in 186 rules of succession have changed (J. P. Singh, 1984).

With the massive expansion of mass communications, the impact of Hindi cinema and TV serials on Indian marriage practices has become so profound that variations in marriage practices across castes, communities, and regions are steadily evaporating into thin air. Homogeneity in marriage practices is slowly but surely taking on a pan-Indian look. Wedding receptions, a purely alien practice, for instance, have emerged as a widespread and common postmarriage event, particularly in urban India. Such events are usually organized either to amass gifts or to show off one's valued position—or both—to others. In general marriages are occasions for conspicuous spending. In addition to kinsmen, to give expression to family status, all sorts of persons, even ordinary acquaintances, as well as professional colleagues, members of one's club, well-known caste men, bureaucrats, politicians, and even unfriendly neighbors, are invited to attend the marriage ceremony. Care is taken that many cars are parked outside the wedding halls. The hospitality is usually on the lavish side. The bride's kin are a little more eager to impress everyone, while the groom's kin and other guests are only too eager to find fault. However, their praise is keenly sought by the bride's family. Expenditure on the marriage ceremony is one of the prime means of acquiring, demonstrating, or validating the high status of the family. Temporal assets alone do not automatically bestow higher status. Thus, the Indian marriage practices are progressively undergoing the process of secularization.

As dowry (or groom-price) or bride-price is a very essential consideration of marriage, no discussion on Indian marriage can be complete without some discussion of dowry. The dowry is not to be confused with *stridhan* (it is a gift given to a woman by her natal kin or by her husband at or after marriage), as it is completely owned by the woman and not by her husband. The practice of dowry (*dahej* or *daj*) has become the archetypal institution of modern Indian society. It is neither an ancient nor a medieval phenomenon. Being an important precondition, the process of dowry-giving or -taking commonly precedes the actual ceremonization of marriage, and in some cases dowry and its problems also continue in one form or another beyond the actual event of the ceremony.

Marriage of a daughter is so essential and inevitable in Indian society that parents are put under extreme pressure to meet any feasible demand to get their daughters married. Parents themselves are generally so worried about the happiness or future of their daughters that they do not mind giving a handsome amount of dowry even after they are married, no matter whether that money comes from moneylenders at a heavy interest rate, through the sale of property, or by some foul means. Dowry has assumed such an alarming proportion that the number of cases of bride-burning and bride-torture,[7] both mental and physical, in law courts is rising, and the media are agog with ever-increasing numbers of such instances. The fact is that most cases are either not pursued in law courts or covered through the media because they are tolerated and suppressed for one reason or another.

To be capable of offering or meeting a big amount of dowry to marry one's daughter or sister, or to be eligible to ask for a hefty dowry for the sake of marrying one's son or brother, is a matter of social pride. This pride comes from being able to demonstrate what one has acquired in recent years through hard work. These days it is taken as an important indicator of the social honor of family in the community. The dowry has become a status symbol in view of the rising economic prosperity of the people. It is because of this fact that dowry is gradually covering southern India, where bride-price and consanguineous marriages had been the most common practices for a long time. Castes and communities that did not traditionally demand or take dowry freely insist on dowry now (Caldwell, Reddy, & Caldwell, 1983; Caplan, 1984). The situation has come to the point that a marriage can hardly take place without a dowry. Right from the birth of a daughter parents start to worry about saving money for her marriage.

Rise in the practice of dowry has accounted for a rise in nonconsanguineous marriages in southern India. Caldwell, Reddy, and Caldwell (1982, pp. 706–707) have observed that in rural southern India marriages are moving from bridewealth to dowry, resulting in diminution of the proportion of marriages between relatives. This transition, however, first occurred in urban areas and gradually percolated to rural areas. The system of dowry has also become popular among the Christians of southern India (Caplan, 1984, pp. 216–233). Persons practicing bride-price are looked down on by dowry takers. They are dubbed backward or primitive. The main reason for such labeling is that it was quite widespread among non-twice-born castes and, until recently, among most scheduled tribes, both in pre-British India and British India until the 19th century. An observation made in the report of the National Committee on the Status of Women in India seems useful: "Changing from bride-price to dowry is an attempt to improve the social status of family or group, because dowry is associated with the higher social groups" (Indian Council on Social Sciences Research [ICSSR], 1975, p. 24).

A recent survey covering 10,000 respondents from 18 states conducted by the All India Democratic Women's Association (AIDWA) and the Indian School of Women's Studies and Development (ISWSD) presents a disquieting view of the prevalence of dowry in India. The report suggests that dowry has gained social legitimacy across all communities and regions. It is not an upper-caste phenomenon anymore, but has become a common practice in all sections of society—scheduled tribes, scheduled castes, the most backward castes, and Muslims all over the country. Over 1,000 tribal women interviewed in Assam, Tripura, and Orissa have indicated that the traditional practice where the groom had to give a bride-price has been completely reversed. Now the bride's parents have to offer cash and jewelry to the groom's parents. All the women respondents from Kamrup, Barpeta, Dibrugarh, Dhubri, and Sonitpur districts in Assam responded that this appears to be a distressing trend, especially when the Assamese women have never been regarded as an economic liability for their parents (*Times of India*, 2002, p. 4). It has been reported by Shanti Kak, the Director of the ISWSD, that the practice of dowry has spread to remote rural areas of such states as Kerala and Tamil Nadu, where it was infrequent.

All the scheduled castes, scheduled tribes, the other backward classes, and Muslim female respondents from Tripura unanimously observed that this was originally a largely upper-caste phenomenon there, but now it has trickled down to all sections of their society. The poorer sections of society who own no land to sell or mortgage for the sake of money are being forced to resort to moneylenders to borrow money at exorbitant rates of interest to get their daughters married. Once among the Tripura tribals, grooms had to act as unpaid laborers in the bride's house for a stipulated period of time. This was to compensate for the economic loss to her parents resulting from marriage, which was known as *jamai pratha*, but now this has evaporated into thin air in the face of the dowry system.

The survey has also revealed how even urban Muslim families are under the grip of dowry. The majority of Muslim spinsters interviewed in Delhi insisted that their parents should give dowry for them, as they would not have an opportunity to get a share of their parents' property once they are married. Muslim females interviewed elsewhere expressed similar views.

The practice of dowry is still not identical or uniform across communities or regions, because of the considerable cultural diversity across India. For instance, it is still not so common among the scheduled tribes. What is generally common among tribal communities (535) is the practice of bride-price in cash or kind or in both (K. S. Singh, 1997b, p. 8). Similarly, bride-price has been popular among scheduled castes, but they are gradually drifting toward the practice of dowry. To quote K. S. Singh (1997a, p. 7), "The incidence of bride-price is reported from 247 communities, while 303 have taken to dowry." Compared with dowry, the amount involved in bride-price is quite meager. Scheduled castes as well as scheduled tribes, particularly those settled in towns and cities, are gradually moving away from bride-price to dowry, seeking to emulate the lifestyle of affluent caste Hindus.

3. FERTILITY AND SOCIALIZATION

The Indian value system has always been quite pronatalist, favoring natural fertility. In other words, Hindus and Muslims have traditionally been in favor of a large family size with many sons and daughters. But now, men and women, especially Hindus, in consultation with each other, seek to have fewer children. Women are encouraged to take increasingly greater interest in regulating the reproductive processes. At the societal level, 96% of currently married women know about some methods of family planning and 47% of married women practice some method of family planning to regulate conception. Decline in the natural fertility of over 7 children per woman to the current total fertility rate of less than 3 in urban areas clearly indicates the increasing role that women are playing in determining family size through translation of their knowledge of family planning into practice (NFHS-1, 1994). Women, together with their partners, are obviously making crucial decisions in matters affecting the interest of society in general, as well as their own. Couples are independent or autonomous in decision-making processes. Such was never the case before, at least on such a large scale. People are no longer having children without thought or because of social pressure, but because they truly want them. Formally and manifestly, the birth of a boy is a more auspicious event than the birth of a girl. It is altogether a different matter that parents assert in public that they do not love their daughters less than their sons.

The NFHS-1 (1994) revealed a very strong preference for sons in India. Preference for a son is deeply rooted in the cultural traditions of Indian society, and it is markedly more prevalent in the northern, western, and central regions than in the southern zones of the country (Bhat & Zavier, 1999, p. 3021). As the preference for sons in Indian society is quite strong, girls are often reported as neglected within the family. Neglect of female children is so serious that an unusually higher incidence of mortality among females than males is reported. A girl child may be so neglected from her childhood that she comes to expect very little from her life. By the time she becomes an adult, she tends to lose all self-worth or respect for herself. She is conditioned to accept the humiliation heaped on her. She is expected to combine the many roles of income provider, super-mother, efficient housekeeper or obedient or submissive wife, and daughter-in-law. If she, especially in rural northern India, slips up in any one role, she is cursed or taken to task. For such a state of affairs, men alone are not responsible; rather, other adult females are also partly liable (Singh, 2002a, p. 166).

Sons are highly valued in India because parents have a variety of vested interests in them. Sons usually live with their parents after marriage and contribute to the family income. Sons provide vital financial support to elderly or ill parents, who often have no other source of income at the end of their life. Daughters move away at marriage and transfer their allegiance to their husbands' families. Parents in general can expect little financial or emotional support from daughters after they leave the parental home. The structure of patriarchy, as in other parts of southern Asia, remains firmly in place in India. It has been held that "the culture of patriarchy is deeply entrenched in the region and gender biases are held not only by men but also by women" (Mahbub ul Haq Human Development Centre [MHHDC], 2000, p. 3).

Girls are much less likely to be enrolled in school than are boys. Girls' representation decreases as they move up the educational ladder and drops precipitously at the university level. Girls are also more likely than boys to be chronically absent from school, or to drop out altogether, as poor mothers tend to rely on their children to care for younger siblings, perform farm work, or earn wages. Girls are expected to help their mothers in household chores and in childcare from an early age. Among middle- and upper-class Indians, gender discrimination in matters of education, however, is not so likely (J. P. Singh, 2002a, p. 166).

Female education is not promoted so much in India because, among other reasons, many parents fear that education will make a girl less attentive to household chores and less willing to obey both her parents and her husband. These doubts are institutionalized

in the familial value system more across northern India, where parents of educated girls must offer a high amount of dowry to attract a better-educated man. Yet another important reason is that a large number of educated women do not enter the paid workforce and offer reciprocal support to their natal households because of social restrictions on their mobility.

Gender discrimination in matters of education and health is, however, much less among the tribal people than among caste Hindus and scheduled castes (or ex-untouchables). In the low-caste poor family, women make significant economic contributions to the sustenance of their family and therefore they assume an important place in it.

Now let us discuss the process of socialization in general. As elsewhere, family is the first and foremost agency of cultural conditioning for children. They encounter readymade ways of doing things first in their family. Children learn the fundamentals of their society and culture initially with the help of their parents within the family circle. As the children are the junior members of the family, they are taught deference and obedience. Children are also taught about pollution and purity in the daily round of household activities. Parents constantly seek to make their children capable of performing the roles normally expected of their parents in the given community, but in cities all parents expect their children to do still better than what their parents have accomplished in their lives. As soon as children are able to speak, they are taught the hierarchy of relations both inside and outside the family. If they do not listen to their parents, the most common form of punishment for them is scolding. The usual way is to call them by derogatory names, but among the low-caste rustic people, they are also called obscene names. Mothers can scold both sons and daughters, but fathers commonly avoid scolding their daughters. If that is not enough, children are also hit by their parents—and the grandparents, if present in the family, come to the children's rescue. Battering of children is a common sight in village primary and middle schools.

The relations between parents and offspring normally change as they grow into adolescence. Parents are expected to act more liberally toward their sons and daughters as they grow older. There is a clear-cut division in the role of parents as agents of socialization on the basis of sex because of the gender-based division of labor in society. As girls grow in age, distance between father and daughter steadily increases. In general, sons and daughters are trained to perform two different but complementary roles in society. Males are supposed to do mostly nonhousehold chores, and hence the father takes special care to pass on his knowledge and experience to sons to make them successful and enterprising in life. Similarly, as girls are supposed to do household chores, they are trained to be good mothers and housewives, and the onus of such training usually rests with the mother or the grandmother in the family. This is true more of rural than urban families, and more of the poorer than richer sections of society.

As the nature of family has changed, change is visible in the role of the family as an agent of socialization. In the past, children enjoyed security of a kind unknown today. In extended or joint families, they were always assured of playmates and attention. Growing up under the joint care of adults made them feel responsible for, and cared for by, all the extended members of the family, besides their own parents. Children in a large family were children of all the male members in the parental generation. It was not uncommon for an aged aunt or granduncle to spend her or his last years happily in the home of a nephew. Now children are placed in an entirely different situation.

In urban areas both male and female members of the family may go for gainful employment outside their home. In some families the parents may live temporarily with their son's wife and children. In some others, members of the wife's family may live with the couple and mind the children for a short time. With both the husband and wife going outside the home for gainful employment, and with the absence or limited availability of childcare facilities, the presence of kin members to look after the home and children is useful for the smooth functioning of many a household. However, there are also working couples who prefer to live in nuclear families and who fear or resist interference from kin and try to organize their households with professional help from outside the family—such as cooks, maidservants, or crèches.

In metropolises in recent years there has been a manifold increase in the mother's role in relation to children within the family. It is she who monitors children's homework and tutors them in areas of weakness or laziness. Mothers dropping and picking up children—from school or coaching classes in computer, cricket, or tennis—by bus, moped, scooter, and car, is a common sight these days. True, some fathers have shaken off age-old male chauvinism and begun to help with housework and child-rearing, but it is the woman who shoulders a "man's weight" in these labors and responsibilities. In many cases the mother is the primary agent of socialization.

The result is that children in modern nuclear families look on the mother as a greater friend and intellectual companion than the father. "Mom, please convince Dad, he won't understand," is a frequent remark or cry from the young in middle-class urban families. Interestingly, centuries of male domination and sheltered existence have not suppressed women's ability to move with the times. In many matters she is far more progressive than the male, with a greater capacity to adapt to change. She may even help her children keep up with their pop/rap/jazz/rock and sports icons. Modernization, globalization, and the economic shifts across the world have swept away many of the safeguards protecting human relationships, and modern urban women have been quick to realize that children must be trained to face the world, where hostilities are as much on the increase as opportunities.

There are also cases where working mothers are not able to discharge their usual and expected obligations toward their offspring. The emerging culture of working women or career women in cities has enhanced the distance between parents and children. Obviously, latchkey children of working couples are strangers to the sense of security enjoyed by their own parents. With the diminished role of family as an agent of socialization, juvenile delinquency is on the increase in cities. The system of surrogate mothers or the Montessori and kindergarten systems of schooling have proved to be a very poor substitute for family as an agent of socialization (J. P. Singh, 2002c, p. 51). Surely the problem has not taken on serious proportions so far even in urban areas, as career women are still a very small proportion of Indian women.

4 & 5. GENDER ROLES AND MARRIAGE

The role of women outside the family also needs to be covered here, as their external activities considerably affect their status and roles within the family. In general, most women are still not encouraged to work outside the home. For a long time, India has been described as a hidebound society. The spheres of women's and men's activities have tended to be sharply separated, especially in rural northern India, where the system of *purdah* (the veiling and seclusion of women) is still in vogue. This has kept women, particularly those belonging to well-to-do upper and intermediary castes, close to the household. Women practicing *purdah* can have only very limited visits and contacts outside the kinship circle. Hence, females have always been discouraged from working outside the home. Even now there are people who discourage female members of their family from working outside the home. In addition, it is also true that, with the improvement in economic conditions, some people prefer to withdraw the women from work, particularly those who do not hold any high office or earn enough money to contribute greatly to family expenses. However, a large number of Indian women are found to be working outside their homes, and others are prepared to. This is obvious from the heaps of application forms by female candidates for different jobs in response to advertisements for employment in both the private and public sectors.

One can get some idea about the nature of participation of women in the workforce from the 2001 census materials. Tribal women have recorded, as the census data show, a much greater participation in the workforce than women of nontribal societies. Similarly, Christian and Hindu women tend to record higher levels of workforce participation than Muslim women. In general, women in southern India show a higher level of workforce participation than in northern India.

Women in urban India are found in many different roles. With female literacy in India at 54% in the 2001 census, it is not unusual to see women working as clerks, typists, receptionists, nurses, doctors, school and college teachers, lawyers, police, social workers, and social activists. Women may assume still greater public roles in society than what we see today. They have a lower workforce participation rate because there are not many suitable opportunities for them outside the home (J. P. Singh, 1996, pp. 56–70). However, some argue that women are less likely to seek employment because of their inherently strong attachment to family and household responsibilities. The problem for women is that they must fit schooling, jobs, or political activity around those family roles.

On the whole, with the rise in education, urbanization, and opportunity for proper employment, women are much freer now to come out of their homes with a view to meeting family expenses. According to the 2001 census, of the total working population of urban areas, about 17% is female, which is higher than earlier census figures. In terms of the percentage distribution, this may not appear a substantial proportion, but in absolute terms it is a big number (15.6 million). This suggests that every sixth woman in the working-age group is gainfully employed outside her home. Most working women (about 72%) are engaged in industries, trade and commerce, and different categories of the service sector, and of the remaining 28%, one-half are in household industries and another one-half in the primary sector (see Table 6.3). At the national level, there were 4.5 million female employees in the organized sector according to the Employment Review

(1995–1996) of the Ministry of Law (Government of India). This suggests that a good proportion of women are capable of economic autonomy. In fact, women would have shown a much higher level of workforce participation rate had there not been so much unemployment in the country. Nonetheless, this marks a huge change in a society such as India where the women have always been discouraged from working outside the home. There is hardly any reason why the trend toward women's employment will not continue in the future.

With the rise in education and gainful employment in the open market, women have acquired a new face and more effective role in their family. Now considerable changes are noticeable in the traditional role of women. Once the priority for young women was the husband, but now it has shifted to include their careers, and in addition deep resentments tend to surface when the husbands are loathe to take part in household chores. Stay-at-home women who give up careers to be good mothers and homemakers find this role daunting and frustrating, as they have to meet the demands of

Table 6.3   Distribution of Female Main and Marginal Workers in Urban India (2001)

Occupations	Population	Percentage
Cultivators	664,429	4.3
Agriculture laborers	1,720,546	11.0
Household industry workers	2,016,258	12.9
Other workers (including industry, construction, trade and commerce, transport, storage and communications, and other services)	11,191,484	71.8
Total workers	15,592,717	100.0

SOURCE: Based on Census of India (2001).

little children and cope with the never-ending drudgeries of housework single-handedly. The woman's fatigue and pent-up frustration is heaped on her husband, producing inevitable distance in the marriage. The changing roles of Indian women are believed to have created problems of adjustment in marital life.

Certain women who were brought up by their parents all along to be conformist women have tended to become rebellious under the new urban milieu, which would not have been the case four or five decades ago. The phenomenon of gender consciousness has increasingly become a predominant feature of metropolitan families these days, especially with well-educated working women. The women have started to assert themselves for gender equality not only because of the rise in their education or greater openness in the urban milieu but also because they have joined the new house with a hefty amount of dowry. On the up-and-coming family life in Indian cities, J. P. Singh (2002c, p. 48) has observed that the new-image woman, bewildered by the revolt, when she has been brought up all along to be a conformist woman who regards her husband as the most important factor in her life, intimidates the husband. A partial answer to this lies in mothers bringing up their sons to accept the fact that gender roles are changing and that men and women have to share the burden of work and child-rearing, tempered with tolerance and understanding, if the marriage is to work. With the present-day work pressure of city life, understanding each other's needs, giving one another space, and having a healthy respect for each other is of paramount importance.

In totality the changes in man–woman relationships described in the previous paragraphs are undoubtedly dramatic. There was a time when a husband was expected to be his wife's superior and received symbolic and actual deference from her. At meals the woman customarily served the men first, and ate only after they had finished and risen. A wife, in all her relations with her husband, was expected to adhere to the scriptural ideals of being a *pativrata,* one who is faithful and follows her husband's will and authority in all respects. A wife customarily followed behind her husband when the two walked together. She avoided uttering his name lest it be taken as disrespectful. She greeted him ritually with gestures of respect and deference. A woman was supposed to be deferent as wife. Such patterns of familial life are, in fact, still noticeable in India, especially in parts of rural northern India, where the impact of urbanization and westernization and the spread of modern education continue to be very little or low.

6. DOMESTIC TENSIONS AND VIOLENCE

Violence within family settings is primarily a male activity. The prime targets are women and children. In the Indian context, women are of special concern, as they have been victims of humiliation and torture for as long as we have written records of Indian society. Despite several legislative measures adopted in favor of women during the 20th century, the spread of modern education, and women's gradual economic independence, countless women have continued to be victims of discrimination and violence (J. P. Singh, 2002a, p. 168). Increasing family violence in modern times has compelled many social scientists to be apologists for the traditional joint family—as happy and harmonious, a high-voltage emotional setting, imbued with love, affection, and tenderness. India's past has been so romanticized by certain social scientists that they have regarded the joint family as the best form of family. Thus, the ongoing disintegration of joint family is not taken as a promising sign of progress or social development.

In all societies there are cultural institutions, beliefs, and practices that undermine women's autonomy and contribute to gender-based violence. Certain marriage practices can disadvantage women and girls, especially where customs, such as dowry and bridewealth, have been corrupted by consumer culture. In recent years, for example, dowry has become an essential part of the marriage transaction in India, with future husbands or their parents demanding ever-increasing dowry both before and after the marriage. Dowry demands can escalate into harassment, threats, and abuse; in extreme cases, the woman is killed or driven to suicide, freeing the husband to go for another marriage and dowry (Jha, 1998; V. Rao, 1997; Schuler, Hashemi, Riley, & Akhter, 1996). It was reported by the Government of India (2002) that nonpayment or curtailment of dowry resulted in 4,148 cases of dowry-death in India in 1990. Uttar Pradesh, Maharashtra, western Bengal, and Madhya Pradesh accounted for 77% of such cases. Delhi alone recorded 421 cases in 1980, 568 in 1981, 619 in 1982, 423 in 1987, and 441 in 1997.

Marriage traditions are such that they undermine the ability of women to escape abusive relationships. For example, many parents in India are reluctant to allow their daughters to return home for fear of having to pay a second dowry or gift, whereas in bridewealth cultures, women's parents must repay the man if their daughter leaves the marriage. With the rise in the level of education and exposure to mass media, women tend to have greater awareness of the notion of gender equality, faith in the effectiveness of legal action to protect their rights, and confidence in such institutions as family courts and certain voluntary organizations working for women. Despite such facilities, many cases of violence are still not reported or recorded for various reasons, even in cities. Cases of domestic violence, such as wife-battering and forced incest with the women of the household, are so personal and delicate that they are seldom reported to the police or law courts.

There are data showing that 40% of women in India have experienced violence by an intimate partner. These stark figures underline the fact that, although the home and community are places where women provide care for others, they are also where millions of women experience coercion and abuse. A study of five districts of Uttar Pradesh has revealed that 30% of currently married men acknowledge physically abusing their wives (UNC, 1997). Similarly, the multisectoral survey done by the International Clinical Epidemiologists Network (INCLEN) has recently reported that two out of every five married women reported being hit, kicked, beaten, or slapped by their husbands. About 50% of the women experiencing physical violence also reported physical abuse during pregnancy.

A strange fact brought to light by the NFHS-1 is that the majority of Indian women accept the use of force to discipline them. Three out of five women believed that wife-battering was justified, particularly when they neglected the house or child. Women are socialized within such a dominant patriarchal value system that they accept the right of husbands to use force to discipline them, especially when the wife violates traditional gender norms. The high level of acceptance of wife-beating in Indian society also suggests that women feel powerless against such violence, and therefore most of them accept it without any tangible protest (J. P. Singh, 2002a, pp. 170–171).

Why do women face violence at the hands of those who are supposed to provide them security? The range of causes varies from not cooking on time to mismanagement of the household to neglect of children. In short, nonadherence to gender roles and responsibilities leads to violence. Violence, or the threat of it, is used very often to ensure discipline, which either maintains gender roles or prevents changes in gender relations. For example, alcohol and dowry have long been associated with violence, but then, why is it that men only beat their wives and children after drinking? Why is it that women have to contribute a host of material possessions to establish and maintain their status within the matrimonial home? Both these phenomena reflect women's subordination, a strongly endorsed gender role in society.

There are other sources of family tensions as well. Under the new socioeconomic scenario, parents' expectations for children have become greater than before, with inter-familial competitions and rivalries for ever-increasing accomplishments for a better family image in the society. In general, now parents intend to accomplish things in their life through their children that they themselves did not achieve. Children are put under great stress and strain to score high marks at school to meet the ever-increasing challenges of a fiercely competitive world of education and employment. In addition to helping their children achieve high goals of life, women have to work harder with a view to attaining economic independence and maintaining a high standard of living for their family.

7. DIVORCE, SEPARATION, AND REMARRIAGE

Divorce is not tolerated by the Brahmanical law books and does not have the sanction of priests. Hindu law, codified by the English with help of the Brahman savants, withheld recognition of divorce. Except for most scheduled tribes, the dissolution of marriage has been quite uncommon and infrequent in India for a long time, but now legal divorce is permissible. Despite legal sanctions, Indian marriages are relatively more stable than in

the industrial West. Hindu marriage, except among scheduled tribes, is taken as a lifelong union for the couple, as it is a sacrament, rather than a contract between the couple to live in a social union so long as is cordially feasible. Even in the event of frequent mental and physical torture, most Indian women persist in marriage, since remarriage of divorced or separated women has been quite difficult. Morality relating to sex is so highly valued that every male wants to marry a virgin girl only. In the past, Hindus demanded prenuptial chastity on the part of both, but now it is by and large limited to females. In fact, both boys and girls try to find out secretly about each other's premarital sex life. Virginity is regarded as the girls' greatest virtue and a symbol of respectability. In addition, there are several other reasons for the relatively greater stability of Indian marriages.

Census data have revealed that divorced and separated women had never constituted even 1% of all women between ages 15 and 49 during the 1961–1991 census. The NFHS-2 (2000), conducted during 1998–1999, has also recorded that divorced and separated women constituted merely 1% of the total married women. The statistics, however, may not hold so strongly in the case of cities, in which a consistent rise has been reported in the incidence of divorce.

There has been a significant change in attitudes toward marriage in the recent past. Marriage is no longer held to be a divine match or a sacred union in the urban milieu. Now it is more like a transfer of a female from one family to another, or from one kinship group to another. The marriage is no longer sanctified as it was in the past, and is viewed only as a bonding and nurturing lifelong relationship and friendship.

Some believe that in India there has been so much talk of gender equality without adequate supporting changes that the relationship between wife and husband has become more tense than before, despite the fact that the level of education, family income, and rationality has improved. The incidence of divorce in a country such as India, with norms of sustenance and forbearance, is reported to have increased in metropolises. A Chennai-based legal practitioner has reported that up until 1988 only one civil court was earmarked for divorces under the Hindu Marriage Act. Today, three family courts work overtime to deal with petitions from all religious groups (Radhakrishanan, 1999, p. 37). While divorce is practiced both among scheduled castes and scheduled tribes, the incidence of divorce in recent years is reported to be on the decline among the scheduled castes (K. S. Singh, 1997a). With respect to the incidence of divorce, the tribal communities have been more liberal than others. Divorce is permitted in 93% of the tribal communities, as is the remarriage of a widow. Either party can seek divorce (K. S. Singh, 1997b, p. 8).

Where gender roles are defined, it is easier to conform to a pattern, but with the gradual emancipation of women, women's economic independence, Western influences, and new value systems learned from peer groups or passed on by parents, marriage in urban India has assumed a new face. Marriage counselors, formerly derided, have today assumed much importance in guiding couples through stormy seas and in averting the imminent pain of divorce. Today in cities there is disenchantment with the system of arranged marriages.

Women tend to be more concerned about their marriages than men, and in the event of problems, they are expected to go for counseling. They are expected to take the lead in resolving conflicts, and when they give up the effort, the marriage is generally over. Men feel that women's expectations are immense, and the men cannot please them however hard they may try, despite a sizable contribution to the family. Men are under pressure to improve their financial contribution, share in raising the children, and provide emotional support to the wives. With tremendous pressure at work, men confront emotional exhaustion. The simpler role of husbands in the past has now been made more complex, but the emotional needs of a woman are different: She wants a soul mate, someone who can understand her needs, someone who is caring and who will take care of her when she is unduly stressed.

Many people believe that the remarriage of widows is a serious problem in India, largely for the caste Hindus. The incidence of widow remarriage is estimated to be much higher than Indian sociologists and social anthropologists have believed. Bhat and Kanbargi (1984) have estimated that about one-third of ever-widowed women are currently remarried. This proportion is bound to be still higher in urban areas. This may be a very startling demographic fact for the conventional Indian sociologists working on micro qualitative data. They have long argued that Indian society is so tradition-bound that widow remarriage is a rare event, ignoring the fact that remarriage of young widows has never been uncommon among low castes and tribal populations. The statistics provide clinching evidence that the Indian value system with respect to widow remarriage has experienced tremendous changes with the rise in education and level of development. All parents, particularly urban, strive to remarry their daughters if they become widowed below age 30 or 35, though remarriage of such women is not easy.

In today's shifting values and changing times, there is less reliance on marriage as a definer of sex and living arrangements throughout life. There is a greater incidence of extramarital relationships, including openly gay and lesbian relationships, a delay in the age at marriage, higher rates of marital disruption, and more egalitarian gender-role attitudes among men and women. It is reported that in big metropolises a new system of live-in arrangements between pairs, particularly in the upper stratum of society, is steadily emerging as a new kind of family life. Anyway, high divorce rates, inter alia, connote that marriage is an institution in trouble, or else expectations are so high that people are no longer willing to put up with the kinds of dissatisfactions and empty-shell marriages that the previous generation tolerated. High rates of remarriage clearly mean that people are sacrificing their marriages because of unsatisfactory relationships. Nevertheless, the majority of Indian marriages are still resilient and lasting, whereas in many industrialized societies one-half apparently break up—for seemingly trivial reasons.

8. SYSTEM OF INHERITANCE AND KINSHIP

The position of women both inside and outside the family and the bond of relationships between family members can be usefully understood from the rights of inheritance, because economic rights are one of the most basic rights. As the matter now stands, the female members are not included in the category of the coparcener in a Hindu family. Earlier they had rights of residence and maintenance only as dependents. In 1937 legislation was effected to confer the same right, that is, the right of inheritance of property, on a Hindu widow as her son would have in the asset or property of her deceased husband. The act enabled her to benefit from income only from the immovable property of her husband during her lifetime.

Until the passing of the Hindu Succession Act (1956), two systems of inheritance dominated among patrilineal Hindus. Under one system, known as the *Mitakshara* school, prevalent in almost the whole of Hindu India, except for Bengal and matrilineal Kerala, a son inherits property rights in his father's ancestral property from the moment of his birth.[8] The father cannot give away any part of this property to the detriment of his son's interest. Under the other system, known as the *Dayabhaga* school, prevalent mainly in western Bengal and Assam, the father is the absolute owner of his property and has an absolute right to alienate his son or daughter from the property.[9] In practice, women have few inheritance rights, which adversely affects their position in the family. Women are unlikely to bring land or wealth to their families through inheritance.

Among the patrilineal Hindus, some movable property is given to the daughters at the time of marriage as *stridhan*. With the passing of the Hindu Succession Act of 1956, a uniform system of inheritance was established. The individual property of a Hindu male, dying intestate (having made no will), passes in equal shares between his son, daughter, widow, and mother. Male and female heirs have come to be treated as equal in matters of inheritance and succession. Another important feature of this legislation is that any property possessed by a Hindu female is held as her absolute property, and she has full power to deal with it as she likes. This has also given a woman the right to inherit from the father as well as from the husband. However, the benefit conferred on a woman is limited compared with the rights of the male members who have gotten rights as coparceners in the ancestral property by birth. Daughters are not yet coparceners and have no birthrights, but in Kerala inheritance was from mother to daughter, from brother to sister's children, rather than from father to son. This was not unusual, as the Nayar women stayed in their natal household after marriage.

Marked changes are noticeable in the kinship system too. The extended or joint family was based on a long-lasting bond between the members. It was meant to be much more than an arrangement of convenience. The joint family as a cohesive force was an ideal social unit for well-to-do landed families of rural India, until subsistence itself became difficult and materialistic values or individualism crept in. Though the joint family or joint household in rural areas survives in a skeletal or nominal form as a kinship group, many adults have migrated to cities either to pursue higher education or to secure more lucrative jobs. Some simply eke out a living outside their traditional callings, but in any case the kinship bonds still survive, though not with the same intensity. Many urban households are really offshoots of rural stem or joint families. A joint household in the native village is the fountainhead of nuclear families in towns. Members of such families meet at the time of certain festivals or social ceremonies, either in towns or in native villages as the case may be, even if relationships among them are not so cordial—though for all practical purposes they constitute independent households.

There is a sense of unity, solidarity, and mutual support when the brothers are under the firm authority of their father or when they confront a threat from outside the family. But since parental authority has steadily weakened, brothers are not as united as they traditionally were, and are often found to rub each other the wrong way and find reasons for heated debates. While among poor, low-caste families different brothers may have little in common to quarrel about, their wives are found to argue among themselves about trifles, often leading to separation of property and kitchen. The relationship between brother and sister is usually more stable and affectionate. He keeps up the relation after his sister has married and has left her natal home. He always tries to assist her in case of need, open-handedly and open-heartedly. He gives more to her than he receives from her. Rivalry figures little in

brother-sister relations. In northern India a brother may be an occasional visitor to his sister's house, but a father who may remain in constant touch with his daughter and son-in-law rarely visits his daughter in her married home. The common belief is that the one who has given his daughter to the other family must not take anything from them, not even food. In cities, however, such belief has nearly evaporated into thin air.

Now distinct changes are evident in the case of familial networks. Kinship networks have become smaller and obligations are decreasing in intensity with the rise of individualist sentiments. Personal interests of individuals are becoming so central in life that attachment to relatives outside the family is gradually diminishing. This is natural, because when the brothers are separated from brothers and parents are separated from their sons, a strong kinship bond cannot be expected to survive, as the self-interests of individuals become paramount. Conjugal family ties are becoming more *intense* than they were in the past, and yet at the same time they have become more *fragile*, giving rise to a greater incidence of separation and divorce in urban areas.

The younger generation appears to be less attached to distant kin than is the older generation. With the rise in prevalence of nuclear families, there has been a substantial increase in the influence of woman's natal family on her married family. Many people are closer to their fathers-in-law than to their own parents. Care, however, is taken that all kinsmen are invited to attend the marriage ceremony. The closest kin are expected to take part in the marriage ceremony compulsorily. Other related families should send at least one representative if they want to keep the kinship bond alive. They should participate through giving gifts, performing of services, or just being present for the occasion. At the same time, it is also true that now family friends and professional colleagues outnumber kinsmen at the time of marriage. This is the real test of one's association or friendship with others.

9. TRADITIONAL AUTHORITY, AGING, AND DEATH

Once, the authority within the family was chiefly in the hands of the senior male member of the family. The general attitude of family members toward the traditional patriarch was mostly one of respect. Loyalty, submissiveness, respect, and deference over the household were bestowed on him. These attributes also encompassed other relationships in the family, such as children to their parents, a wife to her husband, and younger brothers to their older brothers (Gupta, 1978, p. 72). Within a household, no one was supposed to flout the will of his elders. Contrary to the situation elsewhere in the country, in the case of Nayars, the mother's brother was the elder, and he was the head of family. It was he who was expected to carry authority and enforce discipline over his nephew. The Nayar boy had to give the same deference and instant obedience to the head of his mother's family as the boy in northern India gives to his father.

If grown-up sons did not wish to follow a parental mandate for some reason, they usually found ways to circumvent rather than to contradict it. Perhaps gray and bald himself, the son still conceded that his father and grandfather were his wise and experienced counselors. The daughter-in-law was assured of the genuine concern of her mother-in-law in all matters affecting her children. The joint or extended family did not allow the neglect or disregard of elders. The age- and sex-graded hierarchy was quite strong. To quote Gore (1965, p. 216), "The men have the more decisive authority in the traditional Indian family as compared with women, and elders have greater authority as compared

with young persons." He has further observed that a difference of a year or two in age is sufficient to establish firmly who is the formal superior. Even now in some rural locations younger members are required to show respect to the older members, and can hardly question the authority or decisions taken by elders even when it directly concerns them.

Among the women, the patriarch's wife was the paramount authority. In fact, women's positions depended on the position of their husbands in the household. The wife of the household head or mother-in-law was in charge of the household. Her word was law. Her decisions were made for the entire family, not for the welfare of the individuals in it. Young women in the family were expected to be dutiful and obedient. Self-assertion, even in bringing up one's own children, was blasphemy. Even now in a patriarchal family, conventional women exercise much less authority than men, especially in rural areas.

In sum, family members used to accept all major decisions of the elders for the family as infallible. Flouting paternal authority was not common. Boys were granted little freedom. They had no choice but to follow the footsteps of their fathers. Though the patriarch used to have consultation with younger brothers and cousins, the decision of the head had to be final and supreme. Sons neither participated in deliberations nor questioned the decision of their elders. If the adult or married son wanted to do anything on his own, he always expected consultation. Avoidance of consultation was seen as disobedience and disregard. There was a time when it was an exception and not the rule for a girl to enter college. Usually she was married off as early as possible to a groom selected by the family elders.

With a view to comprehending the nature of changes that have come about or understanding the difference between the ideals of traditional household heads and present-day household heads, one may have a close look at the poignant description of the ideals of family elders in the autobiographies of two great modern Indian personalities. Mahatma Gandhi (1940, p. 11), for instance, has written quite truthfully that he was married at the age of thirteen and had a very intense relationship with his wife, but nothing in his role as a husband could be allowed to come in conflict with that of a devoted son: "I dared not meet her in the presence of the elders, much less talk to her." He added that at the time of his father's death, he was with his wife rather than by the side of his ailing father. He wrote that his unfilial behavior remained a blot that he had never been able to efface or forget.

Yet another example is from the life of Rajendra Prasad, the first president of India, who hailed from a landowning family in North Bihar. He has written in his auto-biography that his young wife, along with other women in the family, was kept in the strictest kind of *purdah* seclusion. He met his wife only during his school holidays and then he had to sleep apart from her. In the middle of the night, his mother used to send a maidservant to wake him up to send him to his wife's room, but he had to be back in his own bed before others awakened in the morning (Prasad, 1957, pp. 22–23, 238–239).

A sea of change has occurred in the relationships between father and son and also between brothers themselves. Countless civil or even criminal suits involving parents and sons are in progress in Indian courts, and the number is steadily rising. Parents are often proved wrong in making choices for their children. Many parents avoid discussions with their adult sons. Parents are also abused in public or sometimes even battered. Now the younger generation, particularly those with modern education, do not show the same reverence that their fathers used to have for their parents. Sometimes the traditional

values system does momentarily surface in the behavior of family members, especially on the occasion of family rituals relating to birth, marriage, and death, or on the occasion of a get-together in the event of some serious familial crisis.

It appears from census data that of all the households in urban India, 70% are of ages below 50. Of these, 15% are less than 30 years. Similarly, according to the NFHS-1 (1994), household heads below 50 and 30 compose 64% and 11%, respectively (NFHS-1, 1994, p. 46). This suggests two important trends: erosion of the authority of the traditional patriarch in the family and separation of sons from parents and brothers, if any. In both rural and urban areas, young people tend to be free from their family of orientation, especially when they get married and have a suitable means of livelihood.

Unlike the traditional patriarch, the present-day head of the family has a continuous process of consultation with his wife and adult sons and daughters if they share a common household. Now the son, in the case of a stem family, is more likely to protest if the father takes independent and unilateral action on behalf of his son. To ensure familial peace and harmony, particularly in old age, the elderly father prefers to do things in consultation with his young sons and daughters-in-law. The decision-making process has become more collective and dispersed than before. Age-graded hierarchical authority has diminished in its importance at both the familial and societal levels. The constellation of relations within the family has also undergone considerable changes.

About rural southern India Caldwell et al. (1982, p. 701) observed, "The younger couples do not seem to wrest decision-making powers from the old during overt conflict, but rather the old increasingly retire from various arenas of decision-making." In fact, the situation has changed so much now that people of the adult generations do not enjoy a common household. The process of nuclearization of the family may not be a painful event for the aging parents. Everybody likes a hassle-free family life. Furthermore, parents do not expect much return on their investment from earning sons.

Aged parents, who formerly used to look to their eldest son or other sons for support in old age, are now adjusting themselves to the new demands of family life by making economic provisions for their old age. Even in a city parents and married sons may reside separately. Another trend in family life in India is that girls are prepared to support their parent or parents in old age, and it is possible to find a widowed mother or parents staying with a married daughter (mainly, in the absence of sons) to help her manage the household.

Some parents in their old age aspire to live with a son in the city, but when the son takes his parents to live with him, the result is not always a happy one. The old are particularly unable to come to terms with the new lifestyles and values of their sons and daughters-in-law or their offspring—they are so completely at variance with their own. This leads to ambivalence and dilemmas. Some grandparents prefer to return to their traditional homes. When one partner dies, the loneliness can become unbearable, nor can the widow or widower look to the stem family for support as in the old days. Nieces and nephews are so scattered across the country that their hectic life admits no one outside their own tight circle.

Many parents of the present generation will have to get used to spending their last phase of life alone in the absence of their offspring, who live in far-off places. The transition of authority from the old to the young carries with it less of that responsibility that was once a part of most human cultures for many centuries. Old-age homes, and the young leaving the parental nest, are going to

be a usual way of life in the postmodern phase of India. Despite all these new experiences, most Hindu parents still find a spiritual immortality through their sons. Their future life here and hereafter is blessed through the sons and their religious and social behavior. A son is essential to perform the last rite marking the end of the human career of the individual. It is known as the *antyesthi* or the funeral rite performed at death. It is essential to ensure entrance of the father into the realm of the ancestors (*pitris*). This is followed by *sraddha* (a ritual sacrifice to the dead performed a certain number of days after the funeral) offered by a son, preferably the eldest one, so that the departed soul can transmigrate to heaven or rest in peace.

Current troubles inside and outside the family are genuine, but we should never forget that many of the most vexing issues confronting us as men and women, parents and children, derive from the very benefits of modernization—benefits too easily taken for granted or forgotten in the fashionable denunciation of modern times. There was no problem of the aged in the past, because most people never aged; they died before they got old. Nor was adolescence a difficult stage of the life cycle when children farmed and education was a privilege of the rich. And when most people were hungry illiterates, only the rich could worry about sexual satisfaction and self-fulfillment. Modernization surely brings trouble in its wake, but not many would like to trade the troubles of our era for the ills of earlier times (J. P. Singh, 2002c, p. 52).

10. FAMILY AND OTHER INSTITUTIONS

Although parents, particularly fathers, have played the primary role in the formation of the marriage alliances of their sons and daughters for a long time, their role seems to have diminished in importance under changed circumstances. These days, marriage has become so expensive that it is often arranged or sorted out by social and cultural organizations. Many such organizations have sprung up among different castes and communities that help in matchmaking for marriage either individually or collectively. Marwaris, Punjabis, and Sindhis, in particular, are quite well known for such activities in various Indian cities. The parents who are economically hard-pressed contact these organizations to get details of suitable grooms for their daughters. The parents of the girls communicate with the parents of prospective grooms with the usual enquiries through the go-between. At times such organizations also coordinate meetings of prospective brides and grooms along with their parents. In such meetings people are introduced one by one to the mass gathering by means of a public address system. Further negotiation and final ceremonization of marriage can take place with the help of such organizations, or the concerned parties themselves can conclude the marriage independently at a mutually agreed on place. Voluntary organizations also conduct mass marriages annually at a low cost. They provide a wedding dress for a poor bride and a free feast on the day of the mass marriage. Some parents take advantage of such nontraditional facilities and agree to the mass marriage. Such establishments initially started in temples in big cities and have now spread to small towns. This is found in both northern and southern India (Raja, 1991; Richard & Rao, 1994, p. 26).

Retired parents living with their children are not so common in Indian cities. Old-age homes are no longer a bizarre concept in Indian cities. The demand exceeds the supply, which that gives rise to commercialization of the worst kind in running such homes.

CONCLUSION

The evidence and arguments recorded in this chapter have borne out that many aspects of the conventional Indian family have spectacularly changed in the last century. A new emerging demographic scenario provides the most impressive and crucial confirmation of change. Changes that have surfaced are the outcome of interplay of various factors and forces at work, such as the rising pressure of population, westernization, spread of the urban-industrial ethos, secularization of occupations, modernization, and state intervention through legislation over a long period of time. In fact, decline in fertility, rise in the level of female literacy resulting in greater autonomy of women, greater work participation of women outside the home, preponderance of household heads in the younger age-groups, and a rise in the age at marriage of females are both cause and consequence of structural changes in the family.

The conventional family consisting of the housewife-mother, breadwinner father, and sons' families is now a statistical minority, especially in cities. The nuclearization of the joint family is by and large a *fait accompli*. The number of fissioned families is rising and the size of traditional joint or extended families has become gradually smaller. Nevertheless, sons continue to fulfill their traditional ritual obligations toward their parents.

Kin marriages are becoming less and less common. There is a general trend toward the free choice of a spouse. Rights of women as well as children are becoming more widely recognized. New economic and political developments have started to generate a higher degree of individualism and equality between the sexes. In sum, the Indian family, as elsewhere, is in transition from a consanguineal orientation to a conjugal orientation, and the reversal of this trend is highly unlikely. Taken alone, none of the particular changes that have been described amounts to a transformation of the family, but taken together, the changes are certainly dramatic.

NOTES

1. *Scheduled castes* is a frequently used category referring to a group of people identified by the government of India as being historically disadvantaged. The number of such groups is substantially lower than the total of 1,734, as given in the census reports of different states, because a large number of scheduled castes are common to several states. As different government publications give different figures, the exact number is not really known. But the given number is believed to be close to the truth.

2. *Scheduled tribes* is a frequently used category referring to a group of people identified by the government of India as being historically disadvantaged. The number of such groups is substantially lower than the total of 461, as given in the census reports of different states, because a large number of scheduled tribes are common to several states. As different government publications give different figures, the exact number is not known. But the given number is believed to be close to the truth.

3. The term *household* contains elements of coresidence and commensality, not necessarily kinship relationship. The kinship relationship is the key ingredient of family in addition to coresidence and commensality.

4. The first comprehensive trend report in the field of Indian sociology and anthropology was prepared by the Indian Council for Social Science Research in the 1970s, which specifically devoted a chapter to family and kinship systems (Dube, 1974). It is not unusual that many of the observations made in this chapter are in contrast with those made in the survey report. Such divergence in observation is in part due to the fact that changes have taken place in the Indian family during the last three decades, and in part due to the fact that nearly all works done on the subject so far, whether by sociologists or anthropologists, were narrowly focused and ethnographic in nature. Although enough census materials existed in the past, family scholars did not use them to verify their assertions or draw national-level generalizations. The reviewer, Leela Dube, herself an anthropologist by training, pieced together different fragmentary ethnographic studies, made even more difficult by her complicated style of presentation. She did not use large-scale secondary data to incorporate conclusions drawn by other authors. This study, as stated earlier, is heavily based on the census and national-level survey materials. We have used ethnographic studies simply as supplementary evidence, and have drawn conclusions that we feel are representative.

5. In Table 6.1 the single-member households constitute 8% of all the households in the 1981 census, while the NFHS-1 data suggest merely 3% during 1992–1993. Here one should not try to construe that the percentage of single-member households or eroded family declined over the period of a decade. This discrepancy is mainly because the survey was primarily designed to cover couples, resulting in a slight underenumeration of the eroded family. Therefore, the percentage of single-member households is underreported.

6. The term *sapinda* means (1) those who share the particles of the same body and (2) people who are united by offering *pinda*, or balls of cooked rice, to the same

dead ancestor. Hindu lawgivers have not given a uniform definition of the kinship groups within which marriage cannot take place. Some prohibit marriage of members within seven generations on the father's side and five generations of members from the mother's side. Some others have restricted the prohibited generations to five on the father's and three on the mother's side. Several others have permitted the marriage of cross-cousins (marriage of a person with his father's sister's children or mother's brother's children).

7. When the dowry amount is not considered sufficient or the expected demands are not met easily, the bride is often harassed, abused, and tortured. "Dowry violence" does not refer directly to marriage-related payments made at the time of the wedding, but to additional payments demanded after the marriage by the groom's family where the husband systematically abuses the wife to extract larger transfers. The dissatisfied husband takes recourse to domestic violence to show his displeasures with the marriage to extract additional transfers from the wife's family by credibly threatening her with separation if no transfers are made.

The woman as a bride is the softest and surest means of extracting the maximum amount of money or property from her parents to enhance one's economic position in society, since the bride is helpless in her new home and physically so powerless that she cannot retaliate against the coercive behavior of others. Not many women are brave enough to divorce their husband on the ground of frequent mental or physical torture, since they have nothing to fall back on in a traditional and poorly developed country such as India. Since divorce is the toughest choice or option for her, under no circumstances can she move back permanently to her parent's home. Violence is used as a mechanism to extract further transfers from the bride's family. Brides' parents keep giving out the money hoping that everything will be all right, but unfortunately the demands keep increasing. Dowry harassment is far more prevalent in extended and stem families than in nuclear or joint families. It may be a matter of concern for one and all that in spite of the specific legal provisions, dowry deaths and bride-burnings become frequent headlines of the Indian dailies.

8. *Mitakshara*, which means measured words, is a commentary on *Yajnavalkya Smriti* written by Vijnaneshwar—an ascetic who lived in the region of the Chalukya king Vikramaditya of Kalyani in Andhra, who ruled during the period 1070–1126 A.D. This is the chief textbook of Hindu law. Incidentally in all *Smritis* there is a section on inheritance. Under this, each male is entitled to an equal share of the family property from the moment of his birth and hence all brothers are coparceners.

9. Primarily based on *Manusmriti*, Jeemutavahana, whose time is probably 1090–1130 A.D., wrote a book on inheritance. The book is called *Dayabhaga*, which means division of inherited property. It had authority in Bengal, Assam, and eastern Bihar. It postulates that all married sons should live together and share property with their parents and also remain together after the death of their parents.

REFERENCES

Bhat, P. N. M., & Kanbargi, R. (1984). Estimating the incidence of widow re-marriages in India from census data. *Population Studies, 38*(1), 89–103.

Bhat, P. N. M., & Zavier, F. (1999). Findings of national family health survey. *Economic and Political Weekly, 34*(42–43), 3008–3032.

Caldwell, J. C., Reddy, P. H., and Caldwell, P. (1982). The causes of demographic change in rural South India: A micro approach. *Population and Development Review, 8*(4), 689–727.

Caldwell, J. C., Reddy, P. H., and Caldwell, P. (1983). The causes of marriage change in South India. *Population Studies, 37*(3), 343–361.

Caldwell, J. C., Reddy, P. H., and Caldwell, P. (1984). The determinants of family structure in rural South India. *Journal of Marriage and the Family*, (February), 215–229.

Caplan, L. (1984). Bridegroom-price in urban India: Class, caste and dowry evil among Christians in Madras. *Man, 9*, 216–233.

Census of India. (1981). *Household tables, Series 1 (India)*. New Delhi: Office of the Registrar General India.

Census of India. (1991). *Final population totals: Brief analysis of primary census abstract, Series 1 (India)*. New Delhi: Office of the Registrar General India.

Census of India. (2001). *Provisional population totals, Series 1 (India)*. New Delhi: Office of the Registrar General India.

Chakravorty, C., & Singh, A. K. (1991). *Household structures in India* (Census of India 1991, Occasional Paper 1). New Delhi: Registrar General and Census Commissioner.

Dandekar, V. M., & Pethe, V. (1960). Size and composition of rural families. *Artha Vijnana, 2*(3), 189–199.

Dasgupta, S., et al. (1993). Nuclear and joint family households in West Bengal villages. *Ethnology, 32*(4), 339–358.

Dasgupta, S., & Hennessey, S. (1999). Caste, Class and family structure in West Bengal villages. *Journal of Comparative Family Studies, 30*(4), 561–577.

Driver, E. D., & Driver, A. E. (1988). Social and demographic correlates of consanguineous marriages of South India. *Journal of Comparative Family Studies, 19*, 229–244.

Dube, L. (1974). Sociology of kinship. In M. N. Srinivas, M. S. A. Rao, & A. M. Shah (Eds.), *ICSSR: A survey of research in sociology and social anthropology* (Vol. 2, pp. 233–366). Bombay: Popular Prakashan.

Freed, S. A., & Freed, R. S. (1982). Changing family types in India. *Ethnology, 21*(3), 189–202.

Gandhi, M. K. (1940). *The story of my experiments with truth* (M. Desai, Trans.). Ahmedabad: Navajivan Publishing House.

Goode, W. J. (1963). *World revolution and family patterns*. London: Free Press of Glencoe.

Gore, M. S. (1965). The traditional Indian family. In M. F. Nimkoff (Ed.), *Comparative family systems* (pp. 209–231). Boston: Houghton Mifflin.

Government of India. (2002). *Crime in India 2000*. New Delhi: National Crime Records Bureau, Ministry of Home Affairs.

Gupta, G. R. (1978). The joint family. In M. S. Das & P. D. Bardis (Eds.), *The Family in Asia* (pp. 72–87). London: George Allen & Unwin.

Indian Council of Social Sciences Research. (1975). *Reports of the National Committee on the Status of Women in India. Summary Report*. New Delhi: Indian Council of Social Science Research.

Jha, M. R. (1998). India: *Chappal*, sticks and bags. In L. Marin, H. Zia, & E. Soler (Eds.), *Ending domestic violence: Reports from the global frontline*. San Francisco: Family Violence Prevention Fund.

Karve, I. (1965). *Kinship organization in India*. Bombay: Asia Publishing House.

Kolenda, P. M. (1968). Region, caste and family structure: A comparative study of the Indian joint family. In M. Singer & B. S. Cohn (Eds.), *Structure and change in Indian society* (pp. 339–398). Chicago: Aldine.

Kolenda, P. M. (1987). *Regional differences in family structure in India*. Jaipur: Rawat Publication.

Levy, M. J. (1949). *The family revolution in modern China*. Cambridge, MA: Harvard University Press.

Madan, T. N. (1962). The Hindu joint family: A terminological clarification. *International Journal of Comparative Sociology, 3*(1), 7–16.

Madan, T. N. (1999). The Hindu family and development. In P. Uberoi (Ed.), *Family, kinship and marriage in India* (pp. 416–435). New Delhi: Oxford University Press.

Maine, H. S. (1972). *Ancient law*. London: Everyman Edition.

Mandelbaum, D. G. (1972). *Society in India*. Bombay: Popular Prakashan.

MHHDC. (2000). *Human development in South Asia* (Mahbub ul Haq Human Development Centre). Karachi: Oxford University Press.

Mutharayappa, R., Choe, M. K., Arnold, F., & Roy T. K. (1997). *Son preference and its effect on fertility in India* (NFHS Subject Reports No. 3). Mumbai: International Institute for Population Sciences.

Nair, P. T. (1978). *Marriage and dowry in India*. Calcutta: Minerva Associates.

National Family Health Survey (NFHS)-1. (1994). *India: Introductory Report*. Mumbai: IIPS and ORC Macro.

National Family Health Survey (NFHS)-2. (2000). *India*. Mumbai: IIPS and ORC Macro.

Niranjan, S., Sureender, S., & Rao, G. R. (1998). Family structure in India—evidence from NFHS. *Demography India, 27*(2), 287–300.

Prasad, R. (1957). *Autobiography*. Bombay: Asia Publishing House.

Radhakrishanan, S. (1999, September 5). Marriage in crisis. *The Hindu Sunday Magazine*, pp. 37–39.

Raja, M. K. D. (1991). Cult of mass marriages. *Indian Perspectives, 4*, 35–37.

Rao, P. S. S. (1983). Religion and intensity of inbreeding in Tamil Nadu, South India. *Social Biology, 30*, 413–421.

Rao, V. (1997). Wife-beating in rural South India: A qualitative and econometric analysis. *Social Science and Medicine, 44*(8), 1169–1197.

Richard, J., & Rao, P. S. S. (1994). Changes in consanguinity and age at marriage. *Demography India, 23*(1), 15–28.

Schuler, S. R., Hashemi, S., Riley, A., & Akhter, S. (1996). Credit programs, patriarchy and men's violence against women in rural Bangladesh. *Social Science and Medicine, 43*(12), 1729–1742.

Shah, A. M. (1998). *The family in India: Critical essays*. New Delhi: Orient Longman.

Singh, J. P. (1984). The changing household size in India. *Journal of Asian and African Studies, 19*(1–2), 86–95.

Singh, J. P. (1985). Marital status differentials in rural to city migration in India. *Sociological Bulletin, 34*(1–3), 69–87.

Singh, J. P. (1988). Age and sex differentials in migration in India. *Canadian Journal of Population Studies, 15*(1), 87–99.

Singh, J. P. (1996). The sociology of women and work. In J. P. Singh (Ed.), *The Indian women: Myth and reality* (pp. 56–70). New Delhi: Gyan Publishing House.

Singh, J. P. (2001). Changing village, family structure and fertility behavior: Evidence from India. *International Journal of Contemporary Sociology, 38*(2), 229–248.

Singh, J. P. (2002a). Social and cultural aspects of gender inequality and discrimination in India. *Asian Profile, 30*(2), 163–176.

Singh, J. P. (2002b). The state of universal education in India. *Journal of Educational Planning and Administration, 14*(4), 471–482.

Singh, J. P. (2002c). Urbanization of family in India. *The Eastern Anthropologist, 55*(1), 39–55.

Singh, J. P. (2003). Nuclearization of household and family in urban India. *Sociological Bulletin, 52*(1), 53–70.

Singh, K. S. (1992). *People of India: An introduction.* Calcutta: Anthropological Survey of India.

Singh, K. S. (1997a). *The scheduled castes: People of India* (Vol. 2). New Delhi: Oxford University Press.

Singh, J. P. (1997b). *The scheduled tribes: People of India* (Vol. 3). New Delhi: Oxford University Press.

Srinivas, M. N. (1977). *Social change in modern India.* New Delhi: Orient Longman Ltd.

Srinivas, M. N. (1980). *India: Social structure.* New Delhi: Hindustan Publishing Corporation.

Times of India. (2002, September 8). p. 4.

UNC. (1997). *Uttar Pradesh male reproductive health survey 1995–96.* The Evaluation Project). Chapel Hill: Carolina Population Center, University of North Carolina at Chapel Hill.

CHAPTER 7

South Korean Families

Kwang-Kyu Lee

1. DESCRIPTION, HISTORY, AND BACKGROUND INFORMATION

Korea divided into two nations after World War II: in the south, the Republic of Korea, and in the north, the People's Republic of Korea. South Korea follows the democratic system in politics and the free-market economic system. North Korea follows the communist-type control system. This chapter describes families in South Korea, about which there is much data to analyze. South Korea is known as one of the newly industrialized societies in East Asia (NIEs) or one of the four "little dragons of East Asia."

Korea was under Japanese colonial rule from 1910 to 1945. Five years after liberation from Japan, there was a war between the south and north in the early 1950s, which continued for about 3 years. The Korean War brought catastrophe to the landscape, destruction of industries, and enormous casualties. Subsequently, North Korea was influenced by Russia and especially by China, and South Korea by the United States.

From the ashes, South Korea began to recover and industrialize. The first 5-year plan, which began in 1962, concentrated on light industry. By the third 5-year plan,

concentration was on heavy industry and petrochemicals, which marked a defining period in South Korea's industrialization. The rapid development of industries in South Korea was called the "miracle of Han River."

The population of South Korea increased from 20 million in 1945 to 40 million in 1986. Besides the growth of population, urbanization is seen in the fact that the ratio of rural to urban was 7:3 in 1945, but had changed to 2:8 by 1986. Now the rural population is less than 20%. Thus, Korea was a typical agrarian society until the 1960s, and is now a typical industrial society. Not surprisingly, social changes during these periods have included those in the family.

Family change is easily observed in three aspects: family size, family structure, and the situation of the family. Large extended families, once the ideal, have shifted toward small nuclear families in recent years. We will deal further with family changes after introducing additional sociopolitical issues.

Sociopolitical Changes

The era of nation-building saw two political systems develop in drastically different ways in the north and south. When the Korean War began in 1950, 16 nations supported the Republic (South Korea) and China backed North Korea. After 3 years of intensive fighting, there had been no significant alteration of the border between the two Koreas.

In South Korea the founding father of the first republic, Syngman Rhee, was forced to step down from office after massive student demonstrations spread throughout the country in 1960. The second republic, headed by Yun Boseon, was cut short by a military coup in 1961. General Park Chung-Hee was the leader of the coup d'état, and in December 1963, he was inaugurated as president of the third republic. Park was strongly devoted to the economic development of the nation.

During the third 5-year plan (1972–1976), South Korea began to manufacture steel, automobiles, ships, heavy machinery, chemicals, and electronic goods. The target goal was to reach $10 billion in exports. A remarkable achievement during this period was the development of high-tech electronics. By the mid-1980s, Korea (from now on Korea refers to South Korea) had become one of only three countries in the world having the ability to manufacture 286-bit silicon chips.

This period also marked the appearance of a new class of wealthy Koreans. The most affluent came to be known as *chaebol* or conglomerates. This new class was composed of the elite families who owned and managed groups of companies that exerted monopolistic control over product lines and industries. Among the 50 chaebol groups, the most famous are Samsung, Hyundai, Daewoo, LG, and SK.

In the 1970s, President Park Chung-Hee launched the Saemaul, or New Community, movement. Rural areas were, in effect, developed into more modern, urban landscapes. Traditional thatch-covered roofs were replaced with tin or tile, and modern bathrooms and kitchen facilities were installed, among other renovations. Park's New Community movement was aimed at instilling awareness in rural villagers about the rapidly changing environment of Korea; a motto of diligence, self-help, and teamwork was often employed during this period.

In 1972 Park single-handedly amended the constitution to retain his position as president during the fourth republic. The Yushin Constitution also ascribed unlimited power to Park in restricting civil liberties. According to the new laws, Park had the power to mobilize the whole population for purposes of national security, and to set wages and prices to accommodate economic needs. Collective bargaining and collective action were not permitted under any circumstances.

A widespread citizens' revolt against the government arose as a response to the Yushin Constitution and the Park regime. Demonstrations led by students and other citizens were effectively suppressed by an extensive police network, however. The ubiquitous Korean Central Intelligence Agency (KCIA) had agents stationed at every conceivable site of potential resistance. A hegemonic blanketing of political ideology centered on "peaceful industrialization" aimed to suppress any alternative thought. The regime came to an abrupt halt when Park was assassinated in October 1979 by his trusted follower and director of the KCIA, Kim Chae-Kyu.

Besides the Saemaul movement, there were significant social changes during the period of industrialization. One area that was markedly affected was the rate of population growth. After the Korean War, a baby boom accounted for an increase in population from 24 million in 1960 to 37 million in 1980, and to 46 million in 2000. And, as noted previously, the ratio of rural to urban changed from 7:3 to 2:8.

Besides rural-to-urban migration during industrialization, Koreans also emigrated to other countries for job opportunities and education. In the mid-1960s, as the result of new immigration laws passed by the United States, Koreans were able to immigrate to the U.S. in significant numbers. Koreans also began to settle in parts of South America. In addition, during this period more than 8,000 miners and 12,000 nurses moved to West Germany as contract workers.

Currently, there are over 7 million Koreans living in 150 different nations. Approximately one-half of the overseas Koreans emigrated after 1965. In the present day, there are over 2 million Koreans residing in the United States, 2 million in China, 800,000 in Japan, 500,000 in the Commonwealth of Independent States (CIS), and 100,000 in South America.

The export-led development of the 1960s and 1970s forced laborers to sacrifice for their companies. In manufacturing industries, working conditions were deplorable. Laborers often had to tread carefully in the workplace since they had to contend with employers who distrusted and mistreated them.

Students became involved in labor issues during the first 3 years of Chun's presidency, and the May 1980 Gwangju uprising became a horrific event, as students and citizens were massacred by police. Demonstrations continued, with protesters demanding better working conditions, social security, higher wages, health insurance, and protection against gender discrimination. The labor movement was characterized by substantial female participation.

In late 1983, Chun's regime loosened its policies and withdrew military police from university campuses, where most demonstrations had occurred. Chun also strategically released political prisoners in an effort to gain public favor for the upcoming elections.

Several groups concentrated their efforts on constitutional revision. However, on April 13, 1987, President Chun declared that he would no longer tolerate discussion of constitutional revision. To counter this, university professors issued a public statement criticizing and opposing Chun's statement. Laborers, students, artists, writers, and religious leaders soon followed suit.

In June 1987, the chairman of the Democratic Justice Party (DJP), Roh Tae-Woo, issued an eight-point proposal on democratic reform. A series of violent labor conflicts arose within weeks of Roh's announcement. Labor strikes spread throughout various industries in southern cities such as Ulsan, Busan, and Changwon.

The presidential election was held in December 1987. Roh was leader of the DJP, and factional strife within the opposing party gave Roh the needed impetus to win the election and become inaugurated as the sixth president. Roh, a former general, was a close friend of Chun's.

During Roh's term, while the trade union movement began to decline, middle-class-led social movements were on the rise. From the beginning of his term, there was a tremendous increase in social movements, including environmental, anti-nuclear, consumer advocacy, feminist, and civil consciousness.

In 1992 Kin Young-Sam was elected as the first civilian president in more than three decades. Kim launched a series of unprecedented political, economic, and social reforms. During the 1990s, many nongovernmental organizations (NGOs) began to focus on social justice and the environment.

The collapse of one of the conglomerates, Hanbo, had a spiraling effect on other big businesses as they, too, began to face insolvency. Foreign banks and investors pulled their investments from Korea, which placed the country on the brink of defaulting on its foreign debt obligations. On December 3, 1997, the International Monetary Fund (IMF) agreed to provide a $57 billion aid package. Korea was thereafter under the control of the IMF.

The impact of the financial crisis was devastating to Korea in a number of ways. Rising unemployment, business fallout, severe

Table 7.1 Gross National Income (GNI) and Gross Domestic Product (GDP) Growth in Korea

	GNI	GDP	GNI in US$
1978	24,119.2	24,233.1	1,399
1980	37,032.2	37,788.5	1,598
1985	79,170.4	81,312.3	2,229
1990	178,628.3	178,796.8	5,886
1995	376,316.4	377,349.8	10,823
2000	514,635.4	517,096.8	9,628

cuts in wages, homelessness, and family breakdown were just some consequences of the IMF crisis. President Kim Yong-Sam failed to resolve the crisis and has the legacy of being the most unpopular president in Korean history.

In December 1997, Kim Dae-Jung was elected the eighth president of Korea. This was the first time in Korean political history that there had been a peaceful transfer of power from the ruling to the opposition party. Kim, who had run before, was successful in his fifth bid for the presidency in 1997.

Kim inherited the IMF crisis and began to work on it before his inauguration. Various conditions were attached to the loans, and the financial and corporate sectors were restricted. Kim pushed for rapid capital and trade liberalization. The crisis finally passed 3 years into Kim's term. Kim was also involved in peace talks between South and North Korea. He visited Pyongyang and signed a declaration in 1999 that promised normalization between South and North Korea. For his meritorious efforts, Kim was awarded the Nobel Peace Prize in 1999.

The 1980s and 1990s marked a period of democratization, corresponding with rapid economic development. This period also saw the significant expansion of the Korean middle class. While the political sector sill lagged in terms of achieving democratic ideals, the mass media and civil groups served as a check against gross injustices. The economic and social growth of this period is summarized in Table 7.1.

2. PAIRING UP AND FUNCTION OF THE TRADITIONAL FAMILY

As a typical Asian society, marriage in Korea was traditionally arranged. The bride's and groom's parents arranged the marriage between the families through a go-between, so the future couple had no opportunity to meet before the wedding ceremony. This has gradually changed so that the future bride and groom now have many chances to meet before the final decision.

The family in traditional society had many functions. Korea was a typical agrarian society in the past and the family was the economic unit of production and consumption. Agricultural tasks depended mainly on the labor of the family members, even though they exchanged labor with their neighbors or hired laborers at the busiest times, such as rice transplanting or harvest.

In this sense, the family was its own reason for existing, and members cooperated to maintain the family under the family head.

The family was, therefore, the main source of the social security of the individual, especially in the case of old people. Continuity of the family depended mainly on the birth of several sons who would carry on the family.

The most important function of the family in traditional society was ancestor worship. The first son had a responsibility to perform ancestor ritual up to the fourth generation—namely, the great-great-grandparents, great-grandparents, grandparents, and parents. The direct-descent male offspring had an obligation to participate in the ritual service of ancestor worship. The ritual followed Confucian thought and indicated Korea's Confucian past.

3. FERTILITY AND SOCIALIZATION

In agrarian societies, the family depends mainly on the labor of its members. The more the offspring at home, the better the family's future. Therefore, the traditional family wanted as many children as possible to produce more strength in the future. The ideal number of offspring in the past was two or three sons and one or two daughters. Usually, the first son had an obligation to live with his parents, while younger sons lived separately after marriage. Another joy of life for the parents was to have a son-in-law by their daughter's marriage.

In 1955 the average Korean family size was 5.29 persons. Now the average number in a family is 3.51 persons, which means fewer than two children. There are now very few three-generation families, which was a fairly prevalent form of Korean family in the past.

Parents both help to form the personalities of boys and girls and teach them the skills of housekeeping. Parents pay close attention to the moral education of their offspring, because they have responsibility for the behavior of their children even after they become adults.

The first and foremost responsibility for children's upbringing is on the mother. The mother feeds the baby until he or she becomes 2 or 3 years old. A mother used to feed her baby every time he or she cried. She entered or left the house with the baby on her back, wrapped in a baby quilt. When the elder sister became 6 years old, it became her responsibility to help the mother by carrying the younger sibling on her back.

In traditional society, the children grew in a free atmosphere, and toilet training was relatively stress-free. Adults tolerated the behaviors of children, because children were considered simply immature and half-grown.

Today, school begins at age 8. Primary school continues for 6 years, followed by 3 years each for middle and high school and 4 years of college and university.

4 & 5. GENDER ROLES AND MARITAL RELATIONS

In traditional society, the husband and father was the undisputed head of the family. He represented the family in activities outside the home, and his authority within the family was supreme. Housework used to, and still does, belong largely to the wife, whose tasks consist of cooking, laundering clothes, and attending to the children. There was a clear division of family roles in the past. Therefore, the husband was called the "outside master," and the wife the "inside master."

In traditional society, the relationship between husband and wife was so vertical that the husband was esteemed by his wife, who used honorific language toward him, while he used crude language and talked roughly toward her. The husband was treated to better foods out of respect. Also, the father and family head occupied a separate room, usually located outside the main building, while the wife occupied the central room in the main building. This separate location of husband and wife symbolized that the father had authority over the space, and the mother had authority over family affairs.

However, recent changes have been introduced by industrialization, so that marital relationships and the roles of husband and wife have changed from vertical toward horizontal. The husband concentrates his time and energy on bread winning, and has less time to function as family head than before. Furthermore, all family affairs rely on the housewife. For example, the housewife takes part in various kinds of outdoor activities, such as visiting offices and banks or taking children to school. Thus, the modern family is characterized by mother- or wife-dominated family management. As a result, there is a perception of the "fatherless complex" in the modern Korean family.

6 & 7. CONFLICT, DIVORCE, AND REMARRIAGE

Because of rapid industrialization and modernization, there are many social problems in Korean families. The Confucian traditional family has undergone dramatic changes. The urban family has lost a sense of neighborhood or psychological neighboring, even though it has many visible neighboring houses. It is said that the modern family is isolated.

There are many disharmonies of attitude and behavior among family members, and between institutions and individuals. For example, the marriage type has changed from arranged marriage to free choice. Many marriages of younger people end in divorce.

The more complicated situation is conjugal relationships. There are three different types of conjugal relationships: (1) The husband is conservative, while the wife is progressive; (2) both have much freedom of choice; and (3) the husband and wife are in traditional gender-role agreement. The hardest problems occur in the first type of family. The conservative/progressive type usually results from an educated and successful wife and a husband who prefers a housewife.

Traditionally, the man would not go into the kitchen, because it is the woman's territory. Following this tradition, if a man in the living room asks his wife for a cup of water, she will get it, even if she has come back from her office and is now working hard in the kitchen preparing dinner.

As shown in Table 7.2, the divorce rate has increased tremendously in recent times. It was 0.4 in 1970 and increased to 1.1 in 1990, and 2.5 in 2000. Two aspects characterize recent divorces. The majority of divorces involve young couples within the first 3 years of marriage. However, some older couples, 60 years old, divorce after the marriage of their last child. The old woman does not want to serve her husband with a traditional style of life, wanting to have her own life in the later years. An old woman still has work to do at home; however, there is little for the old man to do. Therefore, he is likely to depend totally on his wife in their old age.

Because of divorce, there are many single parents nowadays. The life of a single woman with one or two children after divorce is not easy in Korea, even though there are more equal opportunities between the sexes than formerly. There are no statistical data, but a popular topic in drama is the remarriage of young men and women.

In the last 10 years, there has appeared in Korea the single mother before marriage. This was not tolerated in the past when Confucianism was dominant in society. The unmarried mother is shameful not only for herself, but also for all the family. Recently the number of single mothers has increased and is estimated at more than 100,000. This is interpreted as a reflection of recent changes in the sexual morals of Korea.

8. KINSHIP AND GENERATIONS

Korea is a typical patrilineal society. In traditional society, the property was divided among the sons after the father's death.

Table 7.2   Marriage and Divorce Rates

	1970	*1975*	*1980*	*1985*	*1990*	*1995*	*2000*
Marriage	295,137	283,226	403,031	376,847	399,312	398,484	334,030
Divorce	11,615	16,453	23,662	38,838	45,694	68,279	119,982
Divorce rate	0.4	0.5	0.6	1.0	1.1	1.5	2.5

In that case, the first son inherited one-half of the family property, whereas the other sons succeeded to the rest divided equally. The first son was responsible for his parents, performing ancestor worship rituals. The daughters received a dowry, but not family property.

The younger sons lived with their parents for several years after their marriage, but had to leave the parents' house to establish their own branch families. Therefore, there was one main family and several branch families for each of the sons.

The separated branch family is a totally independent unit economically and socially. However, these branch families are not free from participating in ancestor worship, which is performed by the main family.

Confucianism emphasizes the ritual service for the ancestors as the most important aspect of filial piety. This ritual service at home is performed on commemoration day and is valid to the great-great-grandparent generation. That means the first son performed the ritual for his father, grandfather, great-grandfather, and great-great-grandfather. On each occasion, the direct offspring had to participate in the ritual. Thus, the third cousin belongs to the category of *dang-nae*. This is also the unit of mourning obligation after the death of a cousin. Kinship terminology is limited to these boundaries, and the generation principle is carried out within this boundary.

The lineage organization usually has a written document for its organization and activities. Lineal organizations have common properties, such as a common graveyard, common house, pavilions, and rice fields. There is a chairman who is elected by a general assembly of the lineage. The chairman nominates two assistants, one property controller, and one ritual service man.

The lineage organization, *mun-jung*, fixes the date of the ritual service for ancestors at the grave, up to the fifth ancestor. Some lineal organizations include several hundred ancestors' graves, and have branch lineages for the ritual no matter how many graves there are. The ritual service at the grave has to be finished within the month of October by the lunar calendar. This ritual service is an important event for bringing together the lineage members who share the same family names.

During industrialization, ancestor worship at home declined due to the busy urban life, whereas the ritual graveside service increased because of lineage property being connected to local elections.

9. AGING

A recent issue in modern society is aging. The percentage of Korean people more than 65 years old was 3.5% in 1975, but by 1995 it had increased to 6%. Life expectancy for women was 73 in 1985 and 77 in 1995. For men it was 70 years in 1995.

Table 7.3 shows the percent age breakdown by various demographic/social categories for those over 65 years of age in Korea in 1975 and 1995.

Table 7.3   Demographic Statistics of Aging in Korea

		1975 (%)	1995 (%)
Sex	Male	37.11	37.06
	Female	62.89	62.94
Age	65–69	44.28	39.61
	70–74	27.26	29.10
	75–79	17.05	17.16
	80+	11.41	14.12
Education level	None	84.27	54.13
	Primary school	11.79	31.31
	Middle school	1.76	6.14
	High school	1.20	4.77
	College+	0.98	3.39
Marriage status	Never married	0.07	0.02
	Couple	43.99	47.77
	Dead partner	55.76	51.62
	Divorced	0.17	0.41
Economic activity	Work	17.66	24.7
	No work	92.34	75.3
Occupation	Manager	1.60	1.90
	Specialist	0.65	1.52
	Engineer	0.61	2.16
	Officer	5.64	0.81
	Shopkeeper	1.73	7.71
	Farmer	87.16	76.03
	Worker	2.60	9.82

You will note that at both time periods, far more elderly are women than men. The percentage of those with no formal education dropped from 84% of the elderly in 1975 to 54% in 1995. Also, in 1995 there were more people still living in couples, and there were also fewer farmers than 20 years earlier.

Farmers, of course, have no end of working in Korea. However, the percentage who are farmers diminished from 87% in 1975 to 76% in 1995. In general, working in physical activities declined and mental activity increased.

The main problem of aging in Korea is the responsibility of the eldest son for aged parents, whether he has enough space at home or has the economic capability to care for them. In Korea there are very few homes for the aged. And even though there are a few aging homes, offspring think that sending their parents there is shameful.

11. SPECIAL TOPIC: MATERIAL CULTURE

As the result of industrialization, material culture influences family life. The younger people prefer to buy a nice car instead of (or before) a house. Oftentimes better clothes, house ornaments, and house utensils are the goals they seek.

The modern house type also influences conjugal and family relations. Traditionally, there were different levels and purposes for each room in the house. For example, there was a holy place for a god image, an authority space used to preserve some precious things, and a lower space for other—especially female—activities. However, a modern house is designed according to the principle of equality, so there is not likely to be a different-level design. This idea of equal living space is related to the fact that the traditional family head (the husband and father), as mentioned previously, has suffered a great loss of authority, which is no longer as important for family unity or for the education of children.

CONCLUSION

South Korea is well-known for its rapid development. It was a colony until the end of World War II. It was liberated but divided into two nations. Our focus has been on South Korea. This was one of the poorest countries in the world after 3 years of war. It achieved industrialization—"miracle of Han River"—under the strong leadership of President Park, with the strong will of hardworking people, and some help from foreigners.

After industrialization, the Koreans spent two decades seeking to democratize. Led by students, then blue-collar workers, and then by the white-collar middle class and the intelligentsia, Koreans concentrated their energy on capitalism and fought for freedom and equality. Now Korea is a highly developed nation economically and politically.

Because of rapid industrialization and modernization, there are many problems in the family. The Confucian traditional family underwent severe change. The family has become small in size. The urban family has lost a sense of neighborhood, even though there are many neighboring houses.

There are many disharmonies between attitude and behavior among family members. For example, the marriage process changed from arranged to personal choice. Also, there are many divorces, especially among younger couples, because the selection of a marriage partner is based on both the old style of outside conditions and interference and on personal characteristics.

The roles of husband and wife in the traditional way of life are hard to carry into the modern family. Traditionally, the man should not enter the kitchen, because it is the woman's territory, but recently husbands and wives have begun to share housework, which can bring about companionship, reconciliation, or conflict.

In the traditional family, there were many intermediaries in and outside the family. In the modern family, there are no (or few) intermediaries between husband and wife to help resolve conflicts. Tensions and conflicts in the modern family may escalate and may easily lead to a divorce.

The modern urban family has lost many important functions, such as educational, religious, recreational, and economic/producing functions. Many of these functions are taken over by the secondary institutions of society. The most complex problem is educational function. The young wife may have little idea about modern child-rearing. Young people are very likely to have more education than their parents, lessening their respect for parents. And, since personal maturity and social experiences are not central to formal education, the parents cannot advise their children. This causes considerable discontinuity in families.

One important issue in modern families is aging. The small modern family is unable to carry out the old traditions of social welfare for family members, but the nation still depends on the care of the elderly by family members. Some welfare facilities exist, but the offspring do not send their parents to such homes, even though some parents may want to go. There is also the opposite case, that is, the parents do not want to go to public facilities, but the offspring send them anyway. The old concept was that parents are to be cared for by their sons and daughters.

Imitating the upper class, there are some efforts to bring back mutual respect between husbands and wives, good home education (socialization) of children, good economic life, and respect for and harmony between family members. However, change is never easy to deal with.

BIBLIOGRAPHY

Armstrong, C. (Ed.). (2002). *Korean society: Civil society, democracy and the state.* London: Routledge.

Brandt, V. (1971). *Korean village between farm and sea.* Cambridge, MA: Harvard University Press.

Choi, J.-S. (1965). *A study of the Korean family.* Seoul: Minjug Sukwan.

Cumings, B. (1997). *Korea's place in the sun: A modern history.* New York: Norton.

Deuchler, M. (1992). *The Confucian transformation of Korea.* Cambridge, MA: Harvard University Press.

Janelli, R., & Dawnhee, Y. J. (1982). *Ancestor worship in Korean society.* Stanford, CA: Stanford University Press.

Kim, C.-S. (1992). *The culture of Korean industry.* Tucson: Arizona University Press.

Kim, T.-K. (1964). *A study of a consanguineous village.* Daegu: Institute of Shilla and Kaya Culture.

Korean Cultural Anthropological Association. (2001). *Questioning, exploring and shaping the Korean family system at present.* Seoul: Korean Cultural Anthropological Association.

Korean Family Studies Association. (2000). *Families in aging society.* Seoul: Korean Family Studies Association.

Korean Family Studies Association. (2003). *State, labor market, family.* Seoul: Korean Family Studies Association.

Kwon, T.-H. (1977). *Demography of Korea.* Seoul: Seoul National University Press.

Lee, H.-C. (1967). *Urban family.* Seoul: Royal Asiatic Society.

Lee, K.-K. (1975). *A structural analysis of Korean family.* Seoul: Iljisa.

Lee, K.-K. (1977a). *A historical study of Korean family.* Seoul: Iljisa.

Lee, K.-K. (1997b). *Korean family and kinship.* Seoul: Jipmoondang.

Lee, K.-K. (1981). *Psychological problem of Korean family.* Seoul: Iljisa.

Lee, K.-K. (2003). *Korean traditional culture.* Seoul: Jipmoondang.

Lee, M.-G. (1973). *Structure and change of Korean rural society.* Seoul: SNU Press.

Osgood, C. (1951). *The Koreans and their cultures.* New York: The Ronald Press.

Wang, I.-K. (1982). *Korean rural development studies.* Seoul: Pakyongsa.

Wells, K. (Ed.). (1995). *South Korea's Minjung movement: The culture and politics of dissidence.* Honolulu: University of Hawaii Press.

CHAPTER 8

Taiwan's Families

YU-HUA CHEN

CHIN-CHUN YI

1. INTRODUCTION

Taiwan is located in the Western Pacific with a total land area of about 36,000 sq km. Hills occupy three-fifths of the island. The plains and basin areas are major political, cultural, industrial, and commercial centers. In 2003 Taiwan had a population of 22.5 million. With the exception of aborigines who mainly inhabit the mountainous central and eastern parts of the island, Han Chinese compose roughly 98% of Taiwan's population. Early Han Chinese immigrants left their homes in southeastern coastal China in the 17th and 18th centuries and were mostly from two groups: Fukienese and Hakka. These two groups are about 85% of the Han population, with the Fukienese outnumbering the Hakka by about three to one. The last ethnic group of immigrants to Taiwan were government officials and soldiers of the ruling party—Kuomingtang (KMT)—after the Civil War in mainland China in the late 1940s (Government Information Office [GIO], 2003c).

Despite geographical separation from the mainland, early settlers brought a variety of Chinese cultural practices with them to Taiwan. Specifically, the Chinese family and kinship institutions that early immigrants relied heavily on for means of subsistence and development were essential parts of social life. Families were viewed as the primary social units, and the interests of individuals were generally secondary to those of the family. The extended family continued to be the ideal residential arrangement for these settlers, whereas the kin necessary for making up a larger family were generally not available at that time. Nevertheless, elders were accorded great respect and exercised extensive authority over younger family members.

With hard labor and intensive cultivation, Taiwan quickly became a stable agricultural society and later entered the global industrialized circle. During this historical process, the impact of large-scale social and economic transformation on family life has always been a research focus. As noted by Western sociologists, a special feature of the Taiwanese family is that unusually rapid social changes occurred in a relatively short period of time and thus provide a valuable opportunity to study the effect of such changes on family life without having to document centuries of history (Marsh, 1996; Thornton & Lin, 1994). In this chapter, we will present major features, starting from family formation to dissolution, throughout the life courses of the Taiwanese family.

2. PAIRING UP

The traditional Chinese marriage system was characterized by the overwhelming power of parents. Marital decision was undoubtedly the first step to demonstrate parents' control of this important family issue. To have complete dominance over the younger generation, romance and courtship among youth were strictly forbidden. Compatibility between two marrying families in terms of socioeconomic status, cultural background, and the implied value system was the top priority in a marriage match (Yi & Hsung, 1994). Hence, marriage was a process of agreements and rituals rather than an interpersonal event, and a family-based decision rather than a personal choice. Due to these concerns, most parents arranged and directed marriages for their children and the idea that prospective mates should come from similar economic and social backgrounds has been maintained for decades.

With the drastic transformation from an agrarian society to an industrial society after World War II, several important but traditional family functions have been replaced by modern institutions in Taiwan. The rapid increase in educational attainment, more premarital nonfamilial employment, and off-family living experiences of young people together change their relationships and interactions with parents and peers. Therefore, the younger generation has become more involved in mate selection and participates in marital decisions. According to a series of nation-wide surveys, the percentage of parent-arranged marriages declined from over 60%

in the 1950s to slightly over 10% in the early 1980s (Thornton & Lin, 1994). The 2001 *Taiwan Social Change Survey* shows that more than 50% of all marriages are now decided entirely by the couples themselves (Chang & Fu, 2002). While young people now get involved in the mate selection process in their own social networks, Taiwanese parents continue to have an important role in the marriage process. A great majority of young people date and marry only with parental approval. It is clear that most parents still have the final say in the marital decision.

The prevalence and timing of marriage in Taiwan have also been greatly changed during the past century. In 1905, 47.3% of Taiwanese women aged 15 to 19 had married and most men married by their middle 20s. At age 30 and above, the number of women who had been married was over 99% (Thornton & Lin, 1994). Marriage was nearly universal among men and women in the first half of the 20th century, but this was disturbed following an influx of mainlanders in the late 1940s. While there were many married couples in the group of newcomers, there were also a substantial number of unmarried young men in the military. The imbalanced sex ratio at this period produced a marriage squeeze, making it difficult for men, in particular for veterans, to find a potential partner. Table 8.1 shows that 42.5% of men were single in 1976, while only 31.2% of women were single. This substantial gap between genders has narrowed in recent years because of the natural replacement of population and the adoption of foreign brides. We will discuss this new social phenomenon in a later section of this chapter.

Economic and social changes have led to later marriage in Taiwanese society. By the end of 2002, the average age of first marriage reached 26.8 years for women and 31.0 years for men. The official statistics also show that a growing number of men and women in their 30s have never married. The single population, being an

Table 8.1   The Marital Status of 15-Year-Olds and Above by Sex: 1956–2002

	Single		Married		Divorced		Widowed	
	M	F	M	F	M	F	M	F
1956[a]	40.1	29.5	55.1	58.3	1.0	0.9	3.7	11.3
1966[a]	47.7	33.6	48.0	56.4	1.7	1.2	2.6	8.8
1969	41.9	29.1	54.8	61.9	0.8	0.7	2.5	8.3
1976	42.5	31.2	54.3	60.7	0.9	0.9	2.3	7.2
1981	40.6	30.4	56.0	61.5	1.2	1.1	2.2	6.9
1986	39.0	27.7	57.0	61.7	1.7	1.6	2.3	6.9
1991	38.0	29.6	57.2	61.0	2.4	2.4	2.5	7.1
1996	38.3	30.0	56.4	58.9	3.1	3.3	2.2	7.8
2001	37.4	30.4	56.0	56.3	4.3	4.8	2.3	8.6
2002	37.1	30.4	56.0	55.7	4.6	5.1	2.3	8.7

SOURCES: *1956 Household Census Report*. Vol. 2, Bk. 2 (from Table 2, Population by Sex and Marital Status). Taipei, Taiwan: Ministry of the Interior, Executive Yuan, Republic of China (in Chinese). *1966 Household Census Report*. Vol. 2. Bk. 2 (from Table 2: Population by Sex and Marital Status). Taipei, Taiwan: Ministry of the Interior, Executive Yuan, Republic of China (in Chinese). *1969-2002. Taiwan-Fukien Demographic Fact Book* (from Table 7: Year-End Population by Age, Sex and Marital Status for Hsiens and Cities of Taiwan-Fukien Area). Taipei, Taiwan: Ministry of the Interior, Executive Yuan, Republic of China.

a. Data of 1956 and 1966 refer to Taiwanese people who were 12 years old and above.

unconventional choice, has caught much attention. A closer scrutiny of the earliest and latest census data shows the proportion of women in their early 30s who had never married increased from 0.8% in 1905 to 11.6% in 2000. While this may only be a continuation of the shift toward later marriage, it may also represent the beginning of a trend toward lifelong singleness.

Social mechanisms to counteract the undesirable single status reveal interesting phenomena. Informal estimates indicate there are numerous matchmaking services available for a variety of marital needs. Generally they fall into two types: television shows that introduce groups of men and women to each other and let individuals select partners from the field, and the so-called *super*

matchmakers who introduce potential mates on a one-to-one basis, exemplifying the role of traditional matchmakers (S. Wu, 2001). In addition to the availability of these popular services, several official agencies have also entered the business of matchmaking by providing spaces and opportunities for interested participants. It appears the social norm still regards being single as an undesirable status, and both public and private forces are involved in the legitimate cause of alleviating this difficulty.

The extent of crossing social strata to marry someone with a different level of educational attainment has been taken as an indicator of societal openness. Using data from 23 countries, Ultee and Luijkx's (1990) empirical study indicates that industrial societies differ in their levels of educational homogamy. In this regard, it is suspected that the traditional Chinese norm of family compatibility in the marriage match is losing its importance in modern Taiwanese society. Comparing 1975 and 1990 data, an overall trend toward increased educational heterogamy in Taiwan can be ascertained (Raymo & Xie, 2000). With more educational opportunities available for women, scholars also find that marriage is less likely as amount of schooling increases (Tsai, 1996; R.-M. Tsay, 1996). However, it should be pointed out that although the strength of ethnic homogamy has decreased over time (Tsai, 1996), a positive association between husband's and wife's social classes is still found (R.-M. Tsay, 1996).

3. FERTILITY AND SOCIALIZATION

Taiwan has been an important destination for migrants from mainland China since the 17th century. The earliest census recorded the island's population as 3.12 million in 1905, and this figure nearly doubled to 6.02 million in 40 years. The aftermath of the Chinese Civil War brought a massive influx of military and civilian workers from the mainland and the population was quickly increased to 7.39 million in 1949. As a result, the natural rate of population increase peaked at 3.84% the next year. The baby boom during the postwar years added considerable population pressure on Taiwan's economy (see Figure 8.1). The government was thus prompted to launch a family planning program with substantial help from American population experts, and later the program was seen to be one of the most effective models in reducing excessive fertility.

Family Planning Program

The beginning of significant fertility decline occurred in the late 1950s, but this demographic trend actually accelerated after the introduction of the family planning program in the early 1960s. The Taichung

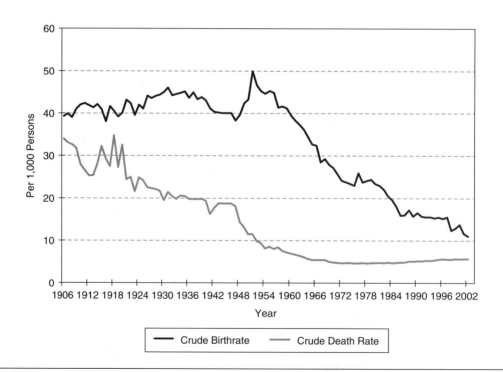

Figure 8.1 Crude Birthrates and Crude Death Rates of Taiwan Population: 1906–2002

Experiment was developed and structured by Ronald Freedman (then the coordinator of the Taiwan Family Planning Institute) in 1962–1963, applying a classic experimental design to family planning. The program was appraised as a success because it considered the receptivity of the population to family planning, as well as the importance of the diffusion of new ideas within society, the program was since formally launched in 1964. This experiment has thus been labeled as a landmark in demographic and social science research.

In line with sociological perspectives, the Taiwan Family Planning Institute conducted a series of surveys—Knowledge, Attitude, and Practice of Contraception in Taiwan (KAP)—that went far beyond questions of fertility and contraceptive use, and explored key issues such as married women's employment, educational attainment, family relationships, and important social indicators of changing values as important determinants. The unique value of this data set is not only that it allows further analyses regarding emerging demographic trends and the changing social factors behind them, but also that it has demonstrated an independent effect of a family planning program on reducing fertility beyond the socio-economic factors that often impose themselves on fertility decisions (Freedman, 1987).

The official statistics show there were a total of 246,758 newborns in 2002, with an average age of biological mothers of 8.2 years, and 31.9 for biological fathers (an increase of 1.2 and 1.8 years for mothers and fathers compared with 1992). Referring to the total fertility rate of the year 2002, each Taiwanese woman of childbearing age is estimated to give birth to 1.34 babies. Increased education, delayed marriage, and relatively fewer potential mothers between ages 20 and 34 together have led to a reduced birthrate. Figure 8.2 shows an interesting relationship of total fertility rates to marriage and divorce rates of Taiwan from 1994 to 2002. As can be

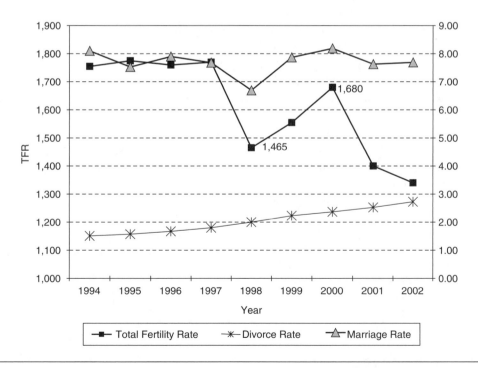

Figure 8.2 Changes in Total Fertility Rates, Marriage Rates, and Divorce Rates in Taiwan: 1994–2002

seen, fluctuations in total fertility rates are significantly correlated with marriage rates in recent years, with a sharp decline in 1998 (the year of the Tiger of the Chinese Zodiac—a year earmarked for war, disagreements, and disasters of all kinds), and a sudden increase in 2000 (the year of the Dragon—a desirable year for marriage and birth in the family). The marriage rates resumed a relatively normal range while total fertility rates continued declining afterward. Divorce rates, on the contrary, have shown a stable increase since 1994. The close gap between marriage and divorce rates and their possible impact on the family system has certainly become a most important issue for family scholars in Taiwan.

It should be pointed out that 40 years ago the primary goal of Taiwan's population policy was to maintain a reasonable population growth and particularly to encourage young men and women to get married and raise children at *suitable* ages. The intention was clearly to prevent the population from rapid degeneration and aging. As a consequence, the birth rate indeed declined with the help of full-scale family planning since 1964, as well as with the positive approach to the implementation of population control measures. In 1987 and in 1992, the U.S. Population Crisis Committee rated Taiwan's population program as the best among the world's developing countries (Ministry of the Interior [MOI], 2003b). However, whether Taiwan's population will continue to decline is a complex question.

According to Freedman and his colleagues,

the question of whether fertility preferences will fall further probably depends for the most part on the extent to which traditional family relationships are eroded. But even a further erosion need not carry fertility and fertility preferences to lower levels, since Taiwan's fertility is at Western levels, which have leveled off near or below replacement levels now for some years. (Thornton & Lin, 1994, p. 304)

A related factor is that in an age of individualism, many young people choose to be childless. Typical Chinese notions such as "producing a male heir to continue the family line," "suppressing oneself for the sake of the family," or "raising children as an insurance for old age" are no longer strong appeals to the younger generation. In response to possible population decline and aging, the government has readopted its old policy slogan "Two children are just right," and in recent years more positive measures such as birth paychecks and educational support have been proposed to encourage more births in Taiwan.

Gender Imbalance

According to the KAP surveys, the mean preferred number of children for married women was 4.0 in 1965, while 20 years later this figure had decreased to an average of 2.4. Along with the downward shift in the trend of preferred number of children, there was a decrease in the preference for sons, too (Thornton & Lin, 1994). Nevertheless, the preference for male descendants is recurring again as young newlyweds favor only one (male) child for economic and lifestyle reasons. In 1965, only 6% of potential mothers preferred their first child to be a boy. By 1991, the percentage rose to 52%, indicating a clear resurgence of son preference. Among the 246,758 births registered in 2002, there were 110 boys for every 100 girls. More specifically, the figures for 2000 illustrate a vivid social reality. Among families having more than one child, the sex ratio was 107 for the firstborn, 108 for the second child, 119 for the third, and 135 for the fourth baby (GIO, 2003a). These figures tell a clear story that strong son preference is still existent among Taiwanese parents and may result in an unnatural gender imbalance in the near future.

With the advancement in new reproductive technologies, a very low fertility rate is theoretically compatible with the strong son preference. Several women's organizations (including Awakening Foundation and Taiwan Women's Link) and medical professionals have suggested that the situation is a result of the 1985 promulgation of the Genetic Health Law, which allows abortion 24 weeks after pregnancy if the fetus is found to have a congenital defect. The law may have been misused by medical staff as a pretext for performing otherwise illegal abortions. However, the social cost of the resultant imbalanced sex ratio deserves serious attention. Living in a context of patriarchal cultural norms, to have a male heir remains a prevailing trajectory for Taiwanese families. Whether the future marriage market will be disturbed by the gender imbalance is yet to be evaluated, but the son preference itself has already brought immediate harm to women's status in the private sphere (C.-L. Wu, 2002).

Socialization

Taiwanese society in the past was primarily organized within family units. The family provided its members the basic socialization and training necessary to live in the community in which the individual was embedded. Generally, the male household head exercised considerable authority and pooled/distributed resources and responsibilities to his family members. Outside the household, the major interactions were mainly confined to extended kinship. The convergence of individual and family interests was commonly reinforced by social norms emphasizing family loyalty and commitment (Thornton & Lin, 1994).

Since the 1960s, a large-scale social and economic transformation has occurred in various processes of industrialization, urbanization, educational expansion, and modernization. The centers of individual activities have been shifted from familial settings to other social institutions including schools, dormitories, factories, governmental agencies, and mass media (Marsh, 1996). As a result, while the family is still seen as the primary agent of childhood socialization, other family functions such as being a provider of information and training for children have declined and been replaced. Through a 9-year compulsory education system and the mass media, children and adolescents receive unconventional beliefs and values originating from Western societies. Furthermore, the transformation of the labor-pooling family economy into a wage-pooling family economy (Thornton & Lin, 1994) makes it necessary for people to work outside their household boundaries. The availability of new ideas and rearrangement of economic activities present lifelong socialization processes involving many different social forces that influence our lives and alter our self-images.

4. GENDER ROLES

Gender roles have experienced drastic changes over the past 100 years. Taiwan is no exception. The patriarchal norm as well as its subsequent code of conduct for women imposed a strict confinement for women's social participation. Being submissive to father before marriage, then submissive to husband after marriage, and to sons after widowhood vividly pictures a traditional woman's role over the family life course. However, the mandatory 9-year education for both genders since 1968 has laid a foundation for changing gender roles in Taiwanese society. With higher education possible, more women are taking advantage of elementary and junior-high schooling, and have thus greatly enhanced their employment opportunities (Yi, 2002). The last three decades evidenced an unprecedented increase in female labor force participation with an average rate of

35.5% in 1970 and 46.0% in 2000. The possible impact of women's employment on the gender division at home and in society needs further investigation.

Japanese Colonial Government: 1895–1945

With no specific intention to change traditional beliefs and practices regarding gender inequality, the Japanese government adopted few meaningful policies that led to an advancement of women's social status. For example, the abolishing of foot binding and the establishment of primary schooling for both genders after occupation in 1895 were meant to make full use of Taiwan's manpower during wartime by assimilating and acculturating young Taiwanese women. Although these measures significantly improved young women's roles generally, within the family it was the son who still had access to valuable but insufficient educational opportunities. Nevertheless, a small number of career women, mainly doctors, nurses, and teachers, were trained during that era. The influence of education on gender roles was perhaps revealed most clearly in allowing both sexes to become aware of the unequal gender division and to expose them to the modern egalitarian thinking. But, in general, Taiwanese women continued to live to meet their traditional obligations, owing to the shared patriarchal ideology between Japanese and Chinese cultures (Yu, 1995).

The Republic of China Administration in Taiwan: 1949–Present

From the 1950s, a small number of elite women with higher education were elected as people's representatives because the Republic of China (ROC) Constitution reserves a fixed proportion of positions for women in various elections (called the "Reserved Seat System for Women"). Although the constitution grants women equal opportunities to participate in politics and education, the early KMT government neither allocated sufficient resources nor set effective policies for promoting women's status. As a consequence, Taiwanese women are still underrepresented and less likely to be promoted in the public sphere (Chou, 1997; Liang, 1999), and the dominant patriarchal practices toward women have changed very slowly (Shieh, Lo, & Su, 1997).

In contrast, the overall educational attainment of women has reached a record high in recent years. At the end of 2001, 53.7% of junior college students and 47.8% of college and university students were women. Two decades earlier, the figures were 37.3% and 36.4%, respectively. Corresponding with advancement of women's education, a large number of women have been entering the labor force (Yi, 2002). For married women, the increase between 1983 and 2003 is from 35.5% to 47.3%. Regardless of marital status, almost one-half of Taiwanese women are now regular wage earners and help to support their families.

The Export-Oriented Economy and the Female Labor Force

Industrialization in Taiwan was and continues to be fueled by a large reserve of women. Because the export-oriented economy is heavily dependent on foreign capital and trade, the government must maintain a favorable investment climate, including political stability and low wage rates, to ensure that foreign capital does not seek cheap labor elsewhere. Scholars have argued that Taiwan's economic success resulting from the past export-oriented growth strategy was related to a system of male-dominated industrial structure that in turn affected women's subordinated and inferior status in general (Diamond, 1979; Gallin, 1984a,

1984b, 1990; L. Cheng & Hsiung, 1992; Chow, 1997). As a result, a married woman's primary roles are defined as those of wife and mother. Regarding the public productive roles, women are demanded only to play secondary and supportive roles.

Therefore, to delineate Taiwanese women's inferior status and roles requires an exploration of the intertwined relationship between capitalism and patriarchy. In a context where formal and informal sectors coexist in the labor market, women are increasingly dependent on wage work because of the devaluation of women's lower-paid informal and unpaid household work. However, conforming to the strong demand of fulfilling wife and mother roles, married women actually have few advantages in the formal labor market compared with single women. If the contribution to the family economy is viewed as an important means for family status attainment in a capitalist society, this tendency somewhat reflects the difficulty of married Taiwanese

women in seeking to improve their domestic status (Hsiung, 1996). They face double disadvantages from constraints at home and at the workplace.

In spite of the double burdens carried by working wives, it has been documented that the significant rise of female labor-force participation in Taiwan can be attributed to married women's employment, especially those with small children (Yi, 2002). Comparing mothers with school-age children and with preschool children, Table 8.2 shows that the latter group reveals a much higher increase between 1983 and 2003: 33.4% to 53.5% versus 35.7% to 44.7%. It means mothers with children under 6 years old actively participate in the labor force and have contributed to the overall rise in female labor-force participation.

However, it does not imply that having preschoolers at home is no longer a definite barrier impeding married Taiwanese women's employment. Their labor-force participation

Table 8.2 Married Women's Labor-Force Participation (LFP) Rates in Taiwan by Children's Age: 1983–2003

Year	Overall LFP	All Children Above 6 Years Old			All Children Under 6 Years Old			Childless
		Subtotal	All Children Older Than 18	Children 6–17	Subtotal	All Children Under 6	All Children Under 3	
1983	35.53	35.70	25.24	43.98	33.40	30.64	—	48.89
1988	42.66	41.82	30.20	52.23	42.29	40.83	—	56.55
1993	44.39	43.78	31.32	55.76	42.99	41.50	41.73	59.71
1998	46.50	44.20	31.28	59.23	49.60	48.73	46.84	65.58
2003	47.34	44.69	32.39	62.02	53.46	53.90	53.96	64.30

SOURCES: *1983–2003 Report on the Manpower Utilization Survey in Taiwan Area.* Taipei, Taiwan: Directorate-General of Budget, Accounting and Statistics, Executive Yuan, Republic of China. *1983 and 1998* (from Table 4: Married Women's Labor Force Participation Rates in Taiwan by Children's Age, p.7). *1993, 1998 and 2003* (from Table 14: Married Women's Labor Force Participation Rates in Taiwan by Children's Age, pp. 24–25).

rate in contrast with those having school-age children (i.e., aged 6–17) is clearly much lower. In effect, the participation rate of mothers having school-age children is approaching married women without children (62.0% vs. 64.3%). In other words, once children enter the educational system, mothers are relatively free from childcare and are able to focus more on their own careers. Before that, the young children's demands are constant and may impose restrictions on married women's employment decisions.

Unlike older women, who are more likely to act in accordance with social and cultural norms, younger generations of women are making every endeavor to pursue higher education and to commit themselves in the labor force as competitively as their male counterparts. However, it is less certain how the majority of Taiwanese view women's

productive and reproductive roles. According to three waves of the *Taiwan Social Change Survey* (Chang & Fu, 2002), Table 8.3 represents the attitudinal change on gender roles in the past decade. As can be seen, while there is still substantial uncertainty about women being breadwinners rather than homemakers, women's employment is actually encouraged and its possible negative consequence to family life has been somewhat devalued. Specifically, as in most other countries, 64.0% agree that an employed mother is harmful to her preschool children (a 9% increase in 10 years), but regarding the woman herself, 51.0% report that a full-time job will interfere with the woman's family life (a 9.7% drop in 10 years), and 76.3% agree that having a job is the best way for a woman to become independent (an 11.2% rise in 10 years). It is clear that by 2001, the

Table 8.3   Change of Attitudes About Gender Roles Among Taiwanese: 1991, 1996, and 2001

	Agreement (%)		
	1991	1996	2001
If a mother were employed outside the household, it would have a negative impact on her preschool-age kids.	54.8	71.6	64.0
The family life of a working woman will always be interfered with by her full-time job.	60.7	60.4	51.0
For women, it is more meaningful to be a breadwinner than a homemaker.	37.8	43.1	49.9
For women, the best way of becoming independent is to have a job.	65.1	71.8	76.3
Husband's major role is a breadwinner and wife, a caregiver.	54.6	56.1	50.7

SOURCE: *Report on Taiwan Social Change Survey IV–2*. 2002 (p.187–188). Taipei, Taiwan: Office of Survey Research, Academia Sinica, Taiwan. (In Chinese.)

public had accepted a young mother's employment, although only one-half will endorse her job as the major role for her as well as for her family.

5. MARITAL RELATIONSHIPS

After marriage, Taiwanese women often quit jobs and become either informal workers or housewives (Yi & Chien, 2001). Beyond the economic system, Confucian culture and most of the state-sponsored family and women's projects have long played important roles in perpetuating the patriarchal ideology (L. Cheng & Hsiung, 1992).

While more Taiwanese women are achieving higher educational levels and are making substantial contributions in the public sphere, it is uncertain whether married women enjoy equal relationships with their husbands at home. Empirically, the status of a married woman in the family often refers to her status relative to her husband's, and it might best be understood as a reflection of the difference in marital power between spouses (Steil, 1997). The division of labor at home, decision-making processes and outcomes, and conflict resolution utilized in domestic disputes have served as valid indicators of women's family status or marital power in numerous reports (Blood & Wolfe, 1960; Kolb & Straus, 1974; Shehan & Lee, 1990; Yi, 2000). In the following discussion of marital relationships among Taiwanese couples, our discussion will focus on these three major dimensions.

The division of labor within the family has been a main focus of family studies, because it reflects the gender relationships in a society and reproduces the gender relationship itself (Coltrane, 2000). Scholars have documented that the division of household labor in Taiwan is affected by each spouse's resource inputs, gender ideology, and the power relationship between the spouses (Lee, Yang,

& Yi, 2000). The typical traditional gender division of household chores is still found in rural Taiwan, regardless of wives' own resources and gender ideology (Tang, 2003). According to the empirical findings of the 2000 *Taiwan Social Change Survey,* slightly more than 50% of married women quit jobs temporarily or permanently to fulfill their obligations as wives, mothers, and daughters-in-law (Chang & Fu, 2002). Due to the impact of socioeconomic development, smaller family structures, including nuclear and stem families, have become the major family types in contemporary Taiwanese society (Yi & Lu, 1999). It is expected that husbands will be more likely to share household tasks in the nuclear family than in larger family structures.

Joint decision making has been a major pattern among Taiwanese couples (Y.-H. Chen, Yi, & Lu, 2000; Yi & Yang, 1995). Using an integrated framework considering both resource exchange processes and the social practices of the patriarchal system, Y.-H. Chen and Yi (2003) find generational, educational, and attitudinal differences explaining most of the variation of women's family decision-making power. These effects are particularly significant among younger women with a college education and those holding less traditional sex-role attitudes. In addition, married women in the family enterprise who are wives, mothers, and workers simultaneously are found to enjoy higher family decision-making power.

With a varied migration history, Taiwan is composed of older and newer migrants from various regions of China. Marriage across ethnic boundaries is common and marital power is found to be affected by spouses' ethnic backgrounds. Y.-H. Chen and Yi (2003) also point out that male mainlanders are more likely to grant their wives higher decision-making power than their Fukienese and Hakka counterparts. This finding implies that egalitarian ideology may be more acceptable among mainlanders. Although anthropological studies argue that Hakka women have higher family status (Chuang, 1994), significant evidence from island-wide representative surveys supporting this argument is yet to be ascertained.

It is evident that marital communication and marital satisfaction are highly related to women's family status and marital power. While the Western U-shaped marital satisfaction pattern is not dominant in Taiwanese society, couples tend to exhibit overall lower satisfaction as life stage progresses (Yi, 1991). Regarding conflict resolution in marriage, it is found that conventional and conservative couples (e.g., rural and older) report less conflict (Yi, Yang, & Tsai, 1992). Husbands with higher education and higher marital commitment reveal negotiation patterns in marital conflict. In contrast, employed wives are more likely to report no communication during conflict (Yi et al., 1992). The gender differences suggest that the interplay between patriarchy and personal resources jointly affect a wife's conflict resolution pattern in Taiwan. Further studies indicate that couples who communicate during marital conflict are more likely to adopt the joint decision-making pattern at home (Yi, Lu, & Pan, 2000). Marital communication not only contributes to marital satisfaction but also results in more egalitarian interaction among couples.

6. FAMILY STRESSES AND VIOLENCE

Like other governments in the world, the Taiwanese government is committed to protect the rights of all citizens, irrespective of their sex, religion, race, class, or party affiliation. Nevertheless, discrimination against women, especially violence against women, continues. Domestic violence and sexual harassment remain serious problems in Taiwan, according to the latest annual report on human rights released by the U.S. Department of State (USDS, 2003). Child abuse is another significant problem mentioned.

Family violence has always been around in Taiwan (J.-D. Tsay & Wu, 2001). The challenge to promote women and children's protection programs lies in the traditional belief that all family affairs are private (Yi, 1997). If domestic violence is a family affair, then outsiders have no right to get involved. Further, wrong impressions such as the belief that only abnormal men will abuse their wives, children, and the elderly bring additional obstacles to the program. The vague distinction between private and public spheres has actually prevented "domestic violence" from becoming a public issue.

Following the 1999 enactment of the Domestic Violence Control Law, 21 city and county governments established domestic violence protection centers with a major goal of protecting women, children, and senior citizens from domestic violence. Services set up by the Ministry of the Interior include a 24-hour hot line, emergency assistance, shelter, medical treatment and examination, counseling for victims, legal assistance, and education and training for professionals. In 2002 the local centers consulted a total of 71,613 persons, followed up cases of 36,120 persons, helped obtain 8,727 court protection orders, and assisted in obtaining emergency shelter for 1,663 persons. With regard to gender, adult females are more likely to be victims of domestic violence than their male counterparts, but in the case of children and the elderly, both genders have an almost equal likelihood of being victims (Table 8.4). Since most spousal abuse is reported by victims in contrast with reports by others, in the case of child and elderly abuse, it is not surprising that Taiwanese reports of domestic violence are mainly wife abuse. More

Table 8.4   Service Targets of the Domestic Violence Prevention Center's Hot Line by Gender: 2002

Service Target	Both Sexes	Male	Female
Children	4,590	2,103	2,487
Spouse	26,329	1,016	25,313
Elderly	1,262	547	715
Others	4,409	1,045	3,364
Total	36,590	4,711	31,879

SOURCE: *2003 Annual Statistic of Domestic Violence Prevention Center.* Ministry of the Interior, Executive Yuan, Republic of China (in Chinese). (Retrieved from http://www.moi.gov.tw/home/index.asp)

self-protection education needs to be implemented, at least for schoolchildren.

The Ministry of Justice also participates in the protection of women and children against violence. According to the law, prosecutors are allowed to take the initiative in investigating complaints of domestic violence without waiting for the filing of a formal lawsuit. Although some cases are successfully prosecuted, strong social pressure often discourages abused women from reporting incidents to the police, to avoid the disgrace imposed on the families afterward. Worst of all, recent studies indicate that women who have received resettlement or legal assistance from local prevention centers are likely to face risk of divorce eventually (F.-L. Chen, 2001; Lin, 2003). Again, normative constraint plays a significant role in the handling of family violence in Taiwan.

7. DIVORCE AND REMARRIAGE

Although it has been argued that women's economic independence gives working women more freedom to reject dysfunctional marriages in most industrial countries (Bianchi,

Subaiya, & Kahn, 1999), there is still a lack of direct evidence to support this association in Taiwan. Statistics released by the government indicate that the crude divorce rate has increased more than three times in the past 20 years, from 0.8 couples per 1,000 persons in 1981 to 2.7 in 2001. Over the same period, the crude marriage rate has shown a decrease after reaching an all-time high of 9.6 couples per 1,000 persons in 1981, due mostly to baby boomers arriving at marriage ages, falling to 7.6 in 2001. These records indicate a declining trend of marriage, in contrast with increasing divorce in Taiwan.

Analyzing the household registration system established by the Japanese, Lee, Thornton, and Lin (1994) find that divorce was relatively common in Taiwan at the beginning of the 20th century. It may be attributed to the relatively weak lineage organizations of early settlers migrating from the mainland. Following the improvement in health and in family lineage, marital dissolution decreased continuously through the end of the 1960s. However, educational expansion and urbanization in the early 1970s contributed to an important reversal of the declining trend (Lee et al., 1994). In particular, the divorce rate increased rapidly in the 1990s. Although Taiwan's divorce rate is still not as high as in most Western countries, it is only lower than that of Korea among Asian societies (Hsueh, 2003).

In Taiwan, husbands' extramarital affairs are often responsible for the marital dissolution, which in turn produces more single-parent families headed by divorced mothers. While recent research has shown the high cost for single mothers of adjusting to their postdivorce life (L. Cheng, 1999), it is less clear whether marital dissolution places children at a greater risk for delinquency or emotional problems. Studying seventh graders and their mothers in northern Taiwan, C.-I. Wu (2000) finds that, regardless of the family structure, the majority of teenagers show only minimal involvement in delinquent behaviors. In other words, there is no definite association between family disruption and adolescent behavioral problems.

In 2000, after the review of the civil law on family relations code, the Ministry of Justice approved various proposed legal revisions concerning divorce, remarriage, and related matters. The revisions make it easier for either party to file for a divorce when it becomes difficult for the couple to continue living together. The law also paves the way for loosening the current ground for divorce, including the provision that couples must have separated for at least 5 years before filing for divorce. Benefiting from protective laws as well as from personal higher education, women have become more resourceful and have taken a more liberal view on marriage.

Remarriage after divorce, however, is not as equal as the law permits. In 2002, the remarriage rate for Taiwanese men was 50.9 per 1,000 persons and only 16.6 per 1,000 persons for women. The average remarriage age also shows a significant gender gap in that men are 44.3 years and

women are 36.3 years of age. Obviously, fewer women than men got remarried after divorce or widowhood. It is not surprising that under the patriarchal norm, men have been expected to remarry so as to fulfill their breadwinner's role. Women, accordingly, are expected to remarry if they have small children. Remarriage in Taiwan has gradually been accepted, but much research is still needed to delineate its possible impact on the traditional family system and family relations between lineages.

8. INTERGENERATIONAL RELATIONS AND KINSHIP

Nowadays, it is not difficult to find the news in Taiwan portraying angry and heartbreaking elderly parents accusing children of not taking care of them. Meanwhile, an increasing number of seniors have sought an independent life and campaigned to strengthen medical care and social welfare for the elderly. Two opposing perspectives address this question. On one hand, modernization theory contends that industrialization and urbanization lead to a weakening of extended kinship (Goode, 1963). On the other hand, demographic studies propose that it is the result of the demographic transition rather than of modernization that results in the dominance of the nuclear family (Laslett, 1995). Taiwan has experienced both declining extended kinship and the rise of nuclear families. Which argument applies better to Taiwan?

To answer this question, it is necessary to begin with an examination of the core concept of filial piety in the Chinese society. The cultural concept of filial piety has been widely accepted to explain the very existence of intergenerational relationships, parental support, and children's commitment to their elderly parents. Under this core doctrine, children must obey and respect their parents and support them in old age unconditionally. Adult children, particularly the eldest son, are obligated to provide their elderly parents with financial and emotional support. Therefore, multigenerational coresidence was the ideal in China (Lai & Chen, 1980). Even if the son did not live with his parents, filial piety still imposed obligations on him, as pictured by an old Chinese proverb—"Parents rear sons for old age; people store up grains for famine."

Another related aspect of the Chinese family system is the kinship network. In the 18th century, lineage was weaker because the large localized family lineage of the mainland mostly did not survive the migration to Taiwan, where settlers came either as individuals or in small family units. At that time, bases of mutual aid were mainly one's native place in the mainland, the community temple, or the common surname organization instead of powerful lineages (Marsh, 1996). In other words, the function of kinship was apparently not adequate to meet demands and was therefore temporarily replaced by these other social organizations. Nevertheless, kinship continued to be an essential social network for early immigrants, and many important social and productive activities received support from kin groups. Overall, family and kinship was the central structure of the Taiwanese society in past centuries.

In contemporary Taiwan, the importance of filial piety and its impact on intergenerational solidarity and the kinship network has constantly been questioned. According to Yeh's (1997) long-term psychological studies, the traditional material or concrete manifestations of filial piety have always changed with the times and the environment. Over the past 20 years, the original authoritarian parent–child relationship has obviously weakened as a result of industrialization, urbanization, democratization, and diversification (Yeh, 1997). Although the practice of dictatorial parenting is losing ground within

the household, the reciprocal filial piety focusing on harmonious intergenerational relationships still maintains its significance (Yeh, 1997; Yi, 1994).

One way to delineate intergenerational relations is to examine patterns of coresidence and financial support to elderly parents. This is because filial piety can be indicated by the real practice between generations. Based on two waves of survey data, Marsh (1996) found that the Taiwanese were significantly less likely in 1991 than in 1963 to express normative obligations toward their parents. More specifically, by asking respondents to consider the ideal pattern from three perspectives—namely, parents, adult children, and their own future preference—Yi and Chen (1998) showed that adult children are more likely than their parents to endorse coresidence and economic support. Normative expectations apparently impose strong pressure on children. With regard to personal preference, 44% of respondents favor separate living arrangements as well as economic independence in old age. Not depending entirely on children for elderly support has gradually become an accepted practice between generations in Taiwan.

Despite the strong preference for the ideal of an extended family, in the 1990s approximately 60% and 27% of Taiwanese households were categorized as nuclear family and stem family, respectively (Yi & Lu, 1999). From elderly parents' standpoint, Yi and Chen (1998) found that coresidence between elderly parents and one or more married children (64%) has been the dominant mode in Taiwan. Although more people express the preference for, and expectation of, economic independence in old age, children's support as a major financial source for the elderly (61%) remains the prevailing practice (Yi & Chen, 1998). Yi and Chen also point out that factors accounting for the support pattern include the adult child's financial resources, family composition, and filial obligation.

Speaking of the changing nature of kinship, Thornton and Lin, in their study on social change and the family in Taiwan, indicate the following:

> The family chain has been weakened so that young people now place less emphasis upon the family chain than do their elders. Relatively more emphasis is now placed on nuclear family relationships than on the larger network of kin relationships that includes the ancestors and unborn children. (1994, p. 402)

This contrast between generations is valid. However, the very fact that coresidence continues to be a major support pattern for Taiwanese elderly implies that intergenerational relations will maintain its significance as the basis for social bonds in Taiwan.

9. AGING AND DEATH

Since fewer and fewer babies are born each year, Taiwan will soon become a graying society. The life expectancy in Taiwan is rising. In 2002, according to official statistics, the average life expectancy at birth was 73.1 years for men and 79.0 years for women. Population over the age of 65 also exceeded 8.9% and is still rising. The index of aging, calculated by dividing the number of people over 65 years old by the number under the age of 15, was 42.6%. It is clear that Taiwan is becoming an aging society and is encountering various problems a typical aging society confronts, such as labor shortages, a high ratio of elderly to workers, and increasing national expenditure on health care.

The national population policy and guidelines on Taiwan's aging problems were revised by the Ministry of the Interior and approved by the Executive Yuan in November 1992. Contrary to past family planning programs that aimed at curtailing population growth, the revised policy proposes a moderate increase in population. To decelerate the increase in the percentage of elderly, "Two children are just right" has re-emerged as the current family planning slogan.

The increase in longevity has changed relations in the family. Not only is it possible for three or four generations to exist at the same time, but grandparenthood has also become a vital phase in the family life cycle (Lauterbach, 2003). For a society such as Taiwan, where the social security system is still inadequate, family must compensate in times of crisis, including aging and death (Hsieh, 2000). As family members grow older and remain healthy, a substantial amount of intergenerational interactions is possible. Although it has been suggested that the aging process may be easier in a cultural context where elders are respected with their life experiences and wisdom (Hsu, 1971), this is certainly not the most appropriate statement for Taiwan. Treating the elderly as a burden rather than an asset in the family often accompanies the geographical separation resulting from employment in urban areas. For many elderly Taiwanese women, taking care of a son's household chores has become part of a necessary living arrangement (Hu & Chou, 1996). Without economic independence, aging does not bring the filial respect normatively expected, but rather an undesired feeling of "serving" the next generation (Hu & Chou, 1996).

In the Chinese tradition, the hope is that death will occur at home, not in the hospital. Consequently, aging and death have been ordinary phenomena in family life. The mourning period afterward has specific and rigid rituals to symbolize loss of family members, particularly the death of parents and grandparents. In a family's bereavement, children are not hidden from the ongoing rituals, and thus the death of loved ones can be a real-life experience extended for a certain period of time in the family. However, with modern medical facilities available, dying outside of the home has become more frequent. The subsequent ritual has been simplified and the funeral is often contracted to professionals. In other words, while aging remains an important family development, death is increasingly a separate event that takes place in a nonfamily setting.

11. SPECIAL TOPIC: THE INTERCULTURAL MARRIAGE

Since the 1990s, a new form of family has emerged in Taiwan, namely families with foreign brides. This wave of immigration consists of females from China and from Southeast Asia, especially from Vietnam and Indonesia. In 1998, marriages between Taiwanese men and foreign women accounted for only 6.2% of all new marriages, but the figure soared to approximately 25% in 2002 (GIO, 2003b). According to data published by the Ministry of the Interior, there are about 100,000 Southeast Asian and 168,000 Chinese immigrant spouses currently residing in Taiwan, and 90% of them are female. Together, they constitute about 1% of the island's population (23 million). Although that figure may seem negligible, a major worry for policymakers is the fact that, despite relatively low fertility, about 8% of Taiwan's newborns were mothered by Southeast Asian and 4% by Chinese women in 2002 (Liu, 2003).

The intercultural marriage is by no means a new phenomenon in Taiwan. Before the 1980s, most intercultural marriages were unions between Taiwanese women and Americans or Japanese husbands. After the 1980s, the situation reversed. With the economic takeoff and the massive internal migration from rural to urban areas, the socioeconomic position of Taiwanese women

quickly improved. Two groups of Taiwanese men suffered in the marriage market from this development. Many blue-collar male workers or farmers who remain in the countryside have a harder time finding marriage partners. In addition, older veterans who migrated to Taiwan from China in the aftermath of the Chinese Civil War were single and were relatively less marriageable owing to the lack of property and family support. Both groups have the need to marry and to have descendants. Hence, rural men started to look for spouses from less developed countries in Southeast Asia (Hsia, 2000). As for veterans, once travel permission across the Taiwan Strait was granted in the 1980s, mainland China became the most suitable provider of marriage partners (Chao, 2003).

Due to the heavy demand for foreign brides, many commercialized marriage brokers specializing in matchmaking foreign women and Taiwanese men flourished in small towns and rural areas. However, existing differences in culture and values within the couples have resulted in less stable marriages and high divorce rates in these commercialized marital arrangements. According to a survey targeting foreign brides who ever asked for assistance from social workers and policemen (Bureau of Social Affairs [BSA], 2002), it is shown that foreign brides are much more likely to be victims of domestic violence than their Taiwanese counterparts. In most cases, these victims are economically disadvantaged homemakers who lack citizenship and other resourceful information in Taiwan. The same survey also found that proficiency in Chinese appears to be a prerequisite for foreign brides to report domestic violence and seek help.

In addition to the issue of domestic violence, other major concerns regarding the influx of foreign spouses center on their children's educational problems. Since most foreign brides are less educated and are not equipped with Chinese-language abilities, they are unable to monitor their children's schoolwork as most Taiwanese parents do. As a consequence, these children not only have poor language skills, but they also often exhibit general maladjustment at school (Hsia, 2000). The problem is exacerbated by the inferior socioeconomic status of fathers. To meet basic needs and to sustain their families, men who married foreigners are more likely to work overtime than others. They are not able to perform the expected parental role in home education either. The lack of family resources, both economic and emotional, has resulted in serious inadequacies for children of intercultural marriages, and this is certainly the most urgent public issue in Taiwan (Liu, 2003).

Facing related problems caused by the substantial proportion of foreign brides, the government is finally reacting and is planning to implement several new programs to help foreign spouses and their children to adjust to life in Taiwan (MOI, 2003a). Since forming marriages is a fundamental family value in Taiwan, unless the difficulty of finding spouses can be solved for the lower social classes, foreign brides will continue to have a market. It is therefore more practical to alleviate potential social problems by actively initiating various resource programs for these needy families than to wait until the difficulty becomes insurmountable in the future.

CONCLUSION

In the foregoing discussion, we have represented major aspects of family life in contemporary Taiwanese society. With a solid cultural heritage of familism, family issues—including structure, organizations, and processes of formation and dissolution—are among the most researched topics in Taiwanese family sociology. These research interests are due to the existing context of rapid social and economic transformation (Yi & Lu, 1999). While the attitudes and practices toward elderly parental support and son preference remain constant, it is less possible to predict precisely the continuity and change in other features of family life, such as parenthood and marriage. Specifically, the trend to late marriage and the introduction of foreign brides have somewhat modified the timing and form of marriage. The former may eventually create a substantial increase in lifelong singleness and the latter has attracted plenty of attention and debate on its possible negative consequences on the family and the overall society. The low fertility rate in recent years also deserves serious attention. The Taiwanese government is revising its population policy and reproductive measures, as it is expected that the total fertility rate will remain at a low level if there is no significant improvement in the major socioeconomic indicators.

REFERENCES

Annual Statistic of Domestic Violence Prevention Center, Ministry of the Interior, Executive Yuan, ROC.

Bianchi, S. M., Subaiya, L., & Kahn, J. (1999). The gender gap in the economic well-being of nonresident fathers and custodial mothers. *Demography, 36,* 195–204.

Blood, R., & Wolfe, D. (1960). *Husbands and wives.* New York: The Free Press.

Bureau of Social Affairs. (2002). *Survey report on foreign brides as victims of domestic violence in Kaohsiung County.* Taiwan: Kaohsiung County Government.

Chang, Y.-H., & Fu, Y.-C. (Eds.). (2002). *Taiwan social change survey: Report on survey 4–2* (in Chinese). Taipei, Taiwan: Institute of Sociology, Academia Sinica.

Chao, A. (2003, January). *Gender politics of cultural citizenship: A case study of marriage between mainland brides and glorious citizens in Taiwan.* Paper presented at the Annual Meeting for Cultural Studies Association of Christchurch Art Centre, New Zealand.

Chen, F.-L. (2001). Private violence and public obligation: Discussing the structural factors of violence against women (in Chinese). *NTU Social Work Review, 4,* 243–280.

Chen, Y.-H., & Yi, C.-C. (2003, July). *Do couple data matter? A comparison on marital power of three Chinese societies.* Paper presented at Seminar on Marital Dyadic Relationship, Sun Yat-Sen ISSP, Academia Sinica, Taipei, Taiwan.

Chen, Y.-H., Yi, C.-C., & Lu, Y.-H. (2000). Married women's status in the family: An example of decision-making patterns (in Chinese). *Taiwanese Journal of Sociology, 24,* 1–58.

Cheng, L.-C. (1999). The process of asset accumulation and intergenerational delivery with the female-headed family (in Chinese). *NTU Social Work Review, 1,* 111–147.

Cheng, L., & Hsiung, P.-C. (1992). Women, export-oriented growth, and the state: The case of Taiwan. In R. Appelbaum & J. Henderson (Eds.), *State and development in the Asian Pacific Rim* (pp. 233–266). Beverly Hills, CA: Sage.

Chow, E. N.-L. (1997). Economic development, patriarchy, and intra-household dynamics: The case of high-tech workers in Taiwan. In V. Demos & M. T. Segal (Eds.), *Advances in gender research* (Vol. 2, pp. 145–181). Greenwich, CT: JAI Press Ltd.

Chuang, Y.-C. (1994). *Family and marriage: Hokkien and Hakka villages in north Taiwan.* Taipei, Taiwan: Institute of Ethnology, Academia Sinica.

Coltrane, S. (2000). Research on household labor: Modeling and measuring the social embeddedness of routine family work. *Journal of Marriage and the Family, 62,* 1208–1233.

Diamond, N. (1979). Women and industry in Taiwan. *Modern China, 5,* 317–340.

Freedman, R. (1987). The contribution of social science research to population policy and family planning program effectiveness. *Studies in Family Planning, 18,* 57–82.

Gallin, R. S. (1984a). The entry of Chinese women into the rural labor force: A case study from Taiwan. *Signs, 9,* 383–398.

Gallin, R. S. (1984b). Women, family and the political economy of Taiwan. *Journal of Peasant Studies, 12,* 76–92.

Gallin, R. S. (1990). Women and the export industry in Taiwan: The muting of class consciousness. In K. Ward (Ed.), *Women workers and global restructuring* (pp. 179–192). Ithaca, NY: ILR Press.

Goode, W. J. (1963). *World revolution and family patterns.* New York: The Free Press.

Government Information Office. (2003a). *A brief introduction to the Republic of China (Taiwan).* Retrieved May 26, 2004, from http://www.gio.gov.tw/taiwan-website/5-gp/brief.

Government Information Office. (2003b). *Marriages with foreign spouses rising.* Retrieved May 26, 2004, from http://th.gio.gov.tw/show.cfm?news_id=18522.

Government Information Office. (2003c). *The Republic of China yearbook—Taiwan 2002*. Retrieved May 26, 2004, from http://www.gio.gov.tw/taiwan-website/5-gp/brief.

Hsia, H.-C. (2000). Internationalization of capital and trade in Asian women: The case of foreign brides (in Chinese). *Taiwan: A Radical Quarterly in Social Studies, 39*, 45–92.

Hsieh, M.-E. (2000). The impact and experience of adult children as caregivers for their disabled parents (in Chinese). *NTU Social Work Review, 3*, 1–36.

Hsiung, P.-C. (1996). *Living rooms as factories*. Philadelphia: Temple University Press.

Hsu, F. (1971). *Under the ancestors' shadow: Kinship, personality and social mobility in China*. Stanford, CA: Stanford University Press.

Hsueh, J. C.-T. (2003). The marital change and its social impact in Taiwan (in Chinese). *National Policy Forum, 2*. Retrieved May 26, 2004, from http://www.npf.org.tw/monthly/0303/theme-245.htm.

Hu, Y.-H., & Chou, Y.-J. (1996). Women and the three-generation household: An exploration of economic dependence and living struggle among elder women. *Journal of Women's and Gender Studies, 7*, 27–58.

Kolb, T., & Straus, M. (1974). Marital power and marital happiness in relation to problem solving ability. *Journal of Marriage and the Family, 36*, 756–766.

Lai, T.-H., & Chen, K.-J. (1980). Historical and demographic perspectives of the Chinese family size (in Chinese). *Chinese Journal of Sociology, 5*, 25–40.

Laslett, P. (1995). The family in the industrializing east and the industrial west. In C.-C. Yi (Ed.), *Family formation and dissolution: Perspectives from east and west* (pp. 1–32). Sun Yat-Sen ISSP Book Series (36). Taipei, Taiwan: Academia Sinica.

Lauterbach, W. (2003, March). *Changes in the intergenerational structure and relations in families across the life course: The case of Germany*. Paper presented at the International Conference on Intergenerational Relations in Families Life Course, Institute of Sociology, Academia Sinica, Taipei, Taiwan.

Lee, M.-L., Thornton, A., & Lin, H.-S. (1994). Trends in marital dissolution. In A. Thornton & H.-S. Lin (Eds.), *Social change and the family in Taiwan* (pp. 245–263). Chicago: The University of Chicago Press.

Lee, M.-L., Yang, Y.-J., & Yi, C.-C. (2000). The division of household labor: Employment reality or egalitarian ideology? (in Chinese). *Taiwanese Journal of Sociology, 24*, 59–88.

Liang, S.-L. (1999). Limitation and advancement of female government officials in Taiwan (in Chinese). *TPSI Report, 85*, 41–47.

Lin, Y.-L. (2003). Domestic violence prevention and divorce: Dilemma in the ideas and assessing situation in the Law of Domestic Violence Prevention (in Chinese). *Taiwanese Journal of Social Welfare, 4*, 17–50.

Liu, L. (2003). Foreign spouse influx: Boon or bane? *Taipei Journal*, Oct. 31–Nov. 07, 2003. Retrieved May 26, 2004, from http://publish.gio.gov.tw/FCJ/past/03110771.html.

Manpower Utilization Survey. (2004). Directorate General of Budget Accounting and Statistics, Executive Yuan, ROC.

Marsh, R. M. (1996). *The great transformation: Social changes in Taipei, Taiwan since the 1960s*. Armonk, NY: M. E. Sharpe.

Ministry of the Interior. (2003a). *Handbook of social welfare resources available for foreign and Chinese brides*. Taiwan, Republic of China: The Ministry of the Interior, Executive Yuan.

Ministry of the Interior. (2003b). *Population affairs administration.* The Ministry of the Interior, Republic of China. Retrieved May 26, 2004, from http://www .moi.gov.tw/moi/english/e-3.asp.

Raymo, J. M., & Xie, Y. (2000). Temporal and regional variation in the strength of educational homogamy. *American Sociological Review, 65,* 773–781.

Shehan, C. L., & Lee, G. R. (1990). Roles and power. In J. Touliatos, B. F. Perlmutter, & M. A. Straus (Eds.), *Handbook of family measurement techniques* (pp. 420–441). Newbury Park, CA: Sage.

Shieh, V., Lo, A., & Su, E. (1997). Families of employed mothers in Taiwan. In J. Frankel (Ed.), *Families of employed mothers: An international perspective* (pp. 213–235). New York: Garland.

Statistics of Household Registration. (2003). Department of Civil Affairs, Ministry of the Interior, Executive Yuan, Taiwan, ROC.

Steil, J. M. (1997). *Marital equality: Its relationship to the well-being of husbands and wives.* Thousand Oaks, CA: Sage.

Taiwan Social Change Survey. (2003). Office of Survey Research, Academia Sinica, Taipei, Taiwan.

Tang, S.-M. (2003). A comparison of the differences between dual-earner families living in metropolitan and non-metropolitan areas on the household allocation and the sense of housework fairness (in Chinese). *Taiwanese Journal of Rural Studies, 1,* 109–140.

Thornton, A., & Lin, H.-S. (1994). *Social change and the family in Taiwan.* Chicago: The University of Chicago Press.

Tsai, S.-L. (1996). The relative importance of ethnicity and education in Taiwan's changing marriage market. *Proceedings of the National Science Council, ROC, Part C: Humanities and Social Sciences, 6,* 301–315.

Tsay, J.-D., & Wu, S.-H. (2001). Planning and prospect for prevention of domestic family violence (in Chinese). *Community Development Journal, 94,* 5–17.

Tsay, R.-M. (1996). Who marries who? The association between wives' and husbands' educational attainment and class in Taiwan. *Proceedings of the National Science Council, ROC, Part C: Humanities and Social Sciences, 6,* 258–277.

Ultee, W. C., & Luijkx, R. (1990). Educational heterogamy and father-to-son occupational mobility in 23 industrial nations: General societal openness or compensatory strategies of reproduction? *European Sociological Review, 6,* 125–149.

U.S. Department of State. (2003). Country reports on human rights practices— 2002. Retrieved May 26, 2004, from http://www.state.gov/g/drl/rls/hrrpt/2002/ 18240.htm.

Wu, C.-I. (2000). Family structure, parenting practices and adolescent conduct problems (in Chinese). *Taiwanese Sociological Review, 4,* 51–95.

Wu, C.-L. (2002). The new reproductive technologies and gender politics in Taiwan, 1950–2000 (in Chinese). *Taiwan: A Radical Quarterly in Social Studies, 45,* 1–68.

Wu, S. (2001). Catch me a catch: Singles reach for a match. *Sinorama, 26.* Retrieved May 26, 2004, from http://www.sinorama.com.tw/ch/show_issue.php3?id= 2001109010040C.TXT&page=1.

Yeh, K. H. (1997). Changes of Taiwan people's concept of filial piety (in Chinese). In L. Y. Cheng, Y. H. Lu, & F. C. Wang (Eds.), *Taiwanese society in the 1990's* (pp. 171–214). Taipei, Taiwan: Institute of Sociology, Academic Sinica.

Yi, C.-C. (1991). A preliminary study on marital adjustment in Taipei area (in Chinese). *Proceedings of the National Science Council, ROC, Part C: Humanities and Social Sciences, 1,* 151–173.

Yi, C.-C. (1994). *Change of family values in Taiwan: Child-rearing practice and elderly parents' support.* Paper presented at the International Symposium on Families as Educators for Global Citizenship, UNESCO, Budapest.

Yi, C.-C. (1997). How to format the family policy? An example for building family protection network (in Chinese). In H.-F. Hsieh (Ed.), *Family welfare and family policy in a controversial era* (pp. 1–29). Taipei, Taiwan: Soochow University.

Yi, C.-C. (2000). The transition of family structure and female's domestic status in Taiwan. In National Science Council, Taipei, Boon Office (Ed.), *Conference Prague 1999, Transitional societies in comparison: East Central Europe vs. Taiwan* (pp. 227–250). Frankfurt: Peter Lang.

Yi, C.-C. (2002). Taiwan's modernization: Women's changing roles. In P. Chow (Ed.), *Taiwan's modernization in global perspective* (pp. 331–359). Wesport, CT: Praeger.

Yi, C.-C., & Chen, Y.-H. (1998). Present forms and future attitudes of elderly parental support in Taiwan (in Chinese). *Journal of Population Studies, 19,* 1–27.

Yi, C.-C., & Chien, W.-Y. (2001). Continuing employment of married Taiwanese women: A compromise between the family institution and the labor market (in Chinese). *Taiwanese Sociology, 1,* 149–182.

Yi, C.-C., & Hsung, R.-M. (1994). Mate selection networks and the educational assortative mating in Taiwan: An analysis of introducer (in Chinese). In C.-C. Yi (Ed.), *The social image of Taiwan: Social science approaches* (pp. 135–178). Sun Yat-Sen ISSP Book Series (33). Taipei, Taiwan: Academia Sinica.

Yi, C.-C., & Lu, Y.-H. (1999). Who are my family members? Lineage and marital status in the Taiwanese family. *The American Journal of Chinese Studies, 6,* 249–278.

Yi, C.-C., Lu, Y.-H., & Pan, Y.-K. (2000). Women's family status: A comparison of the family power structure in Taiwan and China. In C. D. H. Harvey (Ed.), *Walking a tightrope: Meeting the challenges of work and family* (pp. 91–116). Hampshire, UK: Ashgate Publishing Ltd.

Yi, C.-C., & Yang, W.-S. (1995). The perceived conflict and decision-making patterns among husbands and wives in Taiwan. In C.-C. Yi (Ed.), *Family formation and dissolution: Perspectives from east and west* (pp. 129–168). Sun Yat-Sen ISSP Book Series (36). Taipei, Taiwan: Academia Sinica.

Yi, C.-C., Yang, W.-S., & Tsai, Y.-L. (1992). Factors affecting conflict management patterns among spouses: A comparison between husband, wife, and conjugal sample (in Chinese). *Chinese Journal of Sociology, 16,* 25–54.

Yu, C.-M. (1995). *Professional women in Taiwan under Japanese rule* (in Chinese). Unpublished doctoral dissertation, Institute of History, National Taiwan Normal University, Taipei, Taiwan.

Part III

EUROPE

CHAPTER 9

Families in Austria

RUDOLF RICHTER

SANDRA KYTIR

1. INTRODUCTION

Austria is located in southern, central Europe. Geographically, its territory encompasses both the Eastern Alps and the Danube region and has a land surface of 83,858.3 sq km (32,369 sq miles). Located within a temperate climatic zone with influence of the moderate Atlantic climate in the west and the influence of the continental climate in the east, Austria includes a wide variety of landscapes and flora. About 46% of its surface area is wooded. Austria's landscapes range from the mountain peaks of the Alps to hilly landscapes and plains. The foothills of the Alps and the Carpathians as well as the Vienna Basin in the east are the principal areas of settlement and economic activity.

According to census data for 2001, Austria has 8.1 million inhabitants, of whom approximately 98% speak German. Austria has common borders with eight other countries: Germany and the Czech Republic in the north, Slovakia and Hungary in the east, Slovenia and Italy in the south, and Switzerland and Liechtenstein in the west. At the end of World War I, the Austrian-Hungarian monarchy disintegrated mainly as a result of forces of nationalist self-assertion and as a consequence of the Versailles treaties. In 1918 Austria finally was proclaimed a republic.

Austria's population is quite heterogeneous. Czechs, Slovaks, and Hungarians reside in eastern Austria and in the capital of Vienna. There is also a small Croatian and Slovenian minority around the southern regions, but at present immigrants from the former Yugoslavia and Turkey exceed these original minorities. About 10% of the Austrian population are immigrants.

There are six ethnic groups officially recognized in Austria. In terms of religious allegiances, 78% of Austrians are Roman Catholic, and 5% are Protestant. Some 4.5% of the population belong to another faith, and 9% do not belong to any religious group.

While the alpine regions in the west are agriculturally oriented, the eastern part of Austria was urbanized and industrialized early on. In 1995 Austria joined the European Union.

Demographic Description

Austria is considered a typical social welfare state with low rates of infant mortality (0.5%), an extensive system of social security, high quality of life, and high life expectancy. In terms of demography, Austrian family patterns are quite characteristic of advanced and modern industrialized societies. The number of marriages is declining; at the same time, the number of divorces is rising. The fertility rate is rather low. In Austria about 2 million people are married or cohabiting. More than one-half of them (about 55%) have children. The number of single parents is steadily increasing and is now up to about 400,000.

While the importance of marriage has definitely decreased, one might say that the importance of family as an institution has increased. Family and children mean a lot to Austrian people and more than 80% see it as one of the most important aspects of their life. This might explain why the number of families, including cohabiting couples, with children, as well as single parents, has risen in the last decades. While in 1971 there were about 2 million families, in 2001 there were 2.3 million families. Furthermore, the number of families with children has also risen from 1.3 million to 1.4 million.

However, the fertility rate, in at 1.31 in 2001, is quite low. In this context, it is interesting that although couples, and especially women, usually would like to have two children or more, in most cases they have only one. There is no real explanation for this gap between wishes and practice. It is probably due to a combination of factors such as the economic situation, individualistic values, and experiences with the first child (first-child "shock," according to Nave-Herz, 2002). Nevertheless, social scientists found that couples' wish for children has decreased, and it has become normal to have one or even no child. If this development continues,

the fertility rate will further decrease, and the decline will not be balanced by immigrant families living in Austria, who have more children than Austrian families.

At this point we should say that reported data and demographic developments in this chapter refer mainly to data from the 1960s and the 1970s. More recent figures show more dramatic changes.

2. PAIRING UP

It is remarkable that a relatively small amount of data exists about the process of pairing up or finding a partner in Austria. Youth research in Austria suggests that socializing mainly takes place in school and other educational institutions rather than in cafes, discos, or in the street.

In Austria during the 1950s and 1960s, it was quite common for young people to be members of youth groups, such as voluntary associations, and political or religious institutions. However, since political and religious institutions have been losing their credibility during the last decades, they are now less important in the process of pairing up. Young people may also socialize with peers in the context of sport activities, but few engage in a sports club.

Modern facilities such as the Internet are beginning to play an important role in the process of pairing up. However, it seems that singles platforms are considered a game rather than a serious means of socializing and pairing up among young people. Conversely, the Internet seems increasingly to be of use for people between 30 and 40 years of age to approach other people. However, there exist no representative studies dealing with this phenomenon.

In young people's minds, values such as family and friends play an essential role and are of great importance for their well-being. According to the *Vienna Youth Health*

Report in Austria (2002) aside from the family, whose importance remains stable, friends represent the most important social reference group for young people. (See also Großegger, 2001.)

More than 50% of young people in Austria between the ages of 15 and 24, especially girls, wish for a permanent partnership and plan for children in their 20s or 30s. Boys and some girls in their teens prefer to enjoy youth before seriously pairing up and beginning a family. Generally speaking, young people connect partnership to faithfulness, trust, and having fun, but cohabiting seems unimportant to them at this time.

Studies on adolescent sexuality indicate that most adolescents first have sexual intercourse between ages 16 and 19. This has not changed noticeably during the last 25 years. At the age of 16, 50% of adolescents have already had sexual intercourse, and about 25% will first have intercourse after the age of 18. In Austria the number of teenage mothers is negligible and decreasing.

While in the late 1960s and early 1970s people married at the age of about 20, at present they marry closer to 30. Consequently, the mean age at the time of marriage has risen considerably. This is due to the fact that people prefer to date someone without sharing a household or living together in nonmarital cohabitation or marrying right after having met. The time delay of marriage creates a new phase in life, the so-called postadolescence or early adulthood that is very characteristic for young people in Austria between ages 20 and 30. They might have a partner, but they are not likely to live together. Some cohabit, but this does not mean that they are getting married. They find themselves in an ambivalent situation, trying to be independent while in constant touch with their parents.

In Austria young women leave their parental home for the first time on average at the age of 20, and young men leave about 2 years later at the age of 22.5 (Pfeiffer & Nowak, 2001). Figures from the *Family and Fertility Survey* (Doblhammer, Lutz, & Pfeiffer, 1996) show that 23% of men born between 1966 and 1970 had not moved out of their parents' home by the age of 30. Some young people return to their parental home later on as a consequence of separation or financial difficulties.

3. FERTILITY AND SOCIALIZATION

In Austria nearly all children (98.3%) are born in a hospital. Austria has a very low fertility rate. In 2001 it was at 1.31, corresponding to a reproduction rate of 0.63. This decline in population provokes severe sociopolitical problems, which at present are intensely discussed by politicians, social scientists, and other experts.

Although the fertility rate is higher among immigrants, who represent about 10% of the Austrian population, this will not make up for the population loss within the scope of the next generation. This development has far-reaching consequences for the pension schemes in Austria, which are based on the transfer of insurance contributions from the working population to retirees. On the other hand, it can be argued that a smaller population of young people would save expenses in relation to childcare or the educational system.

Low fertility remains a fundamental characteristic of the country's family system, and family policy consults fertility rates for family-related decisions. Low fertility results from multiple political, social, and economic factors that have an important impact on people's preferences: the feasibility to combine work and family, financial circumstances, need for personal freedom, housing conditions, and the perception of society as child-friendly. In Austria a large number of care institutions are available, and on average 80% of children between 3 and 6 years old attend kindergarten.

Socialization mainly takes place in the family and in school. School is obligatory for 9 years. After 4 years of primary school, secondary schools, vocational schools, or grammar schools are available. Most children attend school for a total of 12 years and in so doing obtain a general qualification for college or university entrance.

In Austria education is marked by tolerance and cooperation between children and their parents. Parents feel that it is important to make their children responsible, independent, and tolerant persons having good manners. However, only one-quarter believe that children's obedience is crucial to child-rearing.

4. GENDER ROLES

Gender roles and gender differences in society constitute an important research topic. Let us summarize some crucial points. At present 15% of children below 15 live in single-parent households. In 93% of the cases, children live with their mother.

Although women tend to search for a man with an equal or higher level of education, they increasingly marry men with lower levels of education. This is due to the increasing number of women in the tertiary educational system, which exceeds that of men (Schwarz & Spielauer, 2002).

The distribution of household chores is considered one of the most useful indicators of the disparities between men and women. In the 1970s the Austrian government argued that household chores should be distributed equally between partners. However, household chores are still mainly done by women, even though changes have taken place. While in 1983 about 75% of men reported that they would not do any chores, in 1995 it was down to 60%. This change can partly be explained by the increasing

number of men living in single households during the last decades, and also, of course, by the increasing number of men participating in the doing of chores.

The *Family and Fertility Survey* (Doblhammer et al., 1996) shows age differences in this matter. Young men are more willing to do household chores than older men. Furthermore, it is indicated that the portion of work done by men may be overestimated. For example, 50% to 75% of men report that their spouse does the cooking, while 70% to 90% of women say they do the cooking. Therefore, percentages based on questionnaires rather than on daily protocols are quite imprecise, though they may indicate trends concerning the distribution of housework. The general findings are quite stable: Household chores are mainly done by women, and young men do significantly more chores than older men. Shopping, for example, seems to be done equally by men and women between 30 and 39 years old.

It is remarkable that the distribution of household chores significantly changes after birth of the first child. Men do fewer household chores than before, neglecting activities such as cooking, shopping, cleaning, washing, and ironing. Marital satisfaction of both men and women decreases when children are born (Rollet & Werneck, 2001, p. 132). Although these data are from 1992, they have not lost their timeliness and the results still hold today. Considering job and housework together, women work on average 1 hour more than men regardless of how many hours they work in paid labor.

Childcare requires a lot of time, and usually women care for their children. Most men are only periodically involved and play, dress, or swaddle their children on an irregular basis. Because of this irregularity, men spend less absolute time in childcare than women do. And, as we have said, young men care more for their children than older men.

Parental leave is mainly claimed by mothers. Although 19% of men can imagine taking leave at least for a short time, only about 2% actually do. As a new qualitative study indicates (Gräfinger, 2001), there are several social factors having a significant impact on men's attitudes toward parental leave. Most men argue that the main reason for not taking parental leave is their substantial income and the risk of being considered a loser. Most men feel that their employer would not embrace their parental leave. However, men who did take parental leave report that they surprisingly had far fewer difficulties than they had expected. In addition, it is interesting that men's parents and parents-in-law do not want their son or son-in-law to stay at home and care for his children. Sisters-in-law are more agreeable to the idea, and when men take parental leave, they are surprised by how many household chores have to be done.

Such results are beginning to lead to public debate, and while most studies researching the combination of family and work focus on women's perspectives, recent studies are taking into consideration men and their points of view.

Although Austrian law allows parents a maximum of 3 years of parental leave on condition that men take at least 6 months, only very few men take this opportunity. As a result hardly any family utilizes the full 3 years of leave.

As part of the discussion of the division of household chores, family research also deals with the question of how partners negotiate the division of work. Mikula and Freudenthaler (2002) researched the distribution of household chores from a psychological point of view. His secondary analysis of data of the *Family and Fertility Survey* (Doblhammer et al., 1996) shows that about one-third of women perceive the division of household chores as unjust. This feeling strongly relates to the time spent on chores by women themselves. Furthermore, women desire their partner to come off well in comparison to other men—and the better he performs, the more women are comfortable with the actual division.

Marital status and income also contribute to the evaluation of equity. In comparison to unmarried women, married women feel the division of chores to be more unjust, and the lower their income, the more dissatisfied they are. Therefore, the perception of equity or inequity strongly depends on women's social relations and their social network rather than on real differences and inequalities. However, in most partnerships the distribution of household chores does not lead to any fundamental conflicts.

One of the most essential functions of the modern family is the care of its members, especially of children and the elderly. In 1999 it was estimated that this work would be valued at € 58 billion if counted as wages, including hours of overtime. About 80% of this work is done by women. In contrast to other European countries, it is remarkable that women in Austria and Germany find it particularly difficult to combine work and family, although modern childcare facilities are available and family policies are among the most advanced in Europe (European Commission, 1996).

This result might be due to the prevailing idea that children have to be cared for by their mother—and only by their mother. Because of this social norm, most women feel constrained to care for their children and stay at home—at least as long as their children are below 3 years of age. Value studies researching people's opinions about how women's professional life affects the well-being of their children found that the majority of men and women living in a partnership think that the relationship between the mother and her children is not affected unfavorably by occupation. In 1996, 75% of women and 66% of men agreed with this. However, by contrast, 71% of men and 65% of women are of the opinion that it is better that men are the breadwinners and women care for the children (Bacher & Wilk, 1996, pp. 175f).

Although gender roles have begun to change fundamentally during the last decades—in some families both parents work part-time or the father even cares for the children and the mother works—it is still widely expected that women care for their children while men go to work. This is why most women feel guilty when trying to combine work and family if their child is in a childcare institution.

5. MARITAL RELATIONSHIPS

Traditional roles lose their importance and partners continually have to negotiate and arrange their relationship in everyday life. Emotional closeness and mutual understanding are found to be of great importance for successful partnerships.

Although violence in families can be found, it is not common. In most cases, even separations and divorces are consensual and are accomplished deliberately and in a rational way.

Marital satisfaction changes in the course of marriage, usually resembling a U-curve. At the beginning, marital satisfaction, mutual love, and affection are very high. At the time of childbirth, partners' contentment with their marriage significantly declines. This is partly due to the fact that men desist from doing household chores. When the second child is born, men work longer and spend even less time at home with their family. When children reach puberty, satisfaction falls to the lowest point. Bit by bit satisfaction rises again and marital relationships reach a high level of intimacy and common understanding again in the empty-nest stage (Austrian Family Report, 1999).

Couples without children face a similar pattern. However, childlessness sometimes causes severe conflicts. On the one hand,

affection, good communication, love, and tenderness as well as sexuality are very important for childless partnerships. On the other hand, young couples in particular try to maintain their individuality and freedom to pursue professional goals and other activities advancing their personal development.

6. FAMILY STRESSES AND VIOLENCE

Partnerships perpetually have to meet new challenges in their everyday lives. Numerous studies indicate that children constitute an important stress factor, in particular for women who try to combine work and family, job and childcare. Depending on the availability of part-time jobs and childcare facilities, the effort to combine work and family can be a very stressful task. At present there exist numerous childcare facilities in Austria for children over 3 years of age, but very few institutions that care for children under the age of 3.

In Austria, children go to school in the morning and in the early afternoon. Consequently, childcare after school requires deliberate time management in families where both parents are working full-time. Some schools offer after-school day care, which, however, is difficult for low-income families to afford. Children's school achievements represent another possible stressor. In fact, many pupils find studying rather demanding and Austrian families spend a lot of money for private tutorials.

Discrepancies between parents on how to bring up their children might also represent an important stress factor, though no relevant studies yet exist.

Recapitulating, stress may cause domestic violence, though not always. In the majority of cases, violent hands are laid on children and women, although men are sometimes mistreated.

The *Vienna Youth Health Report* (2002), a representative study of young people between ages 15 and 24 living in Vienna, indicates that 11% of young girls and boys experience physical violence. However, there exist significant gender differences. Whereas boys are more often physically attacked, girls rather experience verbal and psychic violence. Furthermore, boys report that two-thirds of violence originates from their father. Conversely, girls experience 58% of violence from their mother. Ten percent of both boys and girls report having been threatened with being sent to an "approved" school. However, more than 50% say they are allowed to criticize their parents, and one-third of the interviewed boys and 44% of the girls say that their parents allow contradiction.

The data on violence differs in various studies. Depending on the definition of violence, the number of people having experienced violence (at least in the form of slaps) is as high as 80%. Psychic violence is very difficult to measure.

Newspapers and other media increasingly report sexual harassment. Out of 622 reported cases of physical violence against children within 1 recent year, 259 were sexual. In most cases, the abused children are below 10 or 11, meaning below puberty. These data were collected from doctors in 1994. There is no clear profile of the abuser. Therefore, violent behavior and sexual harassment might relate in part to the attitude toward sexuality rather than to social milieus.

Concerning violence against women, it is estimated that 5% to 10% of women experience violence in their partnership. Major crimes against women are often committed out of jealousy. Low income, financial difficulties, and alcohol abuse also play a significant role in such crimes. The increasing number of reported cases in recent years can presumably be explained by the greater willingness of women to report them, rather than

an effective rise of violent crimes, and there is a law in process that will define sexual harassment within marriage as a crime. This will have significant consequences on criminal proceedings.

7. DIVORCE, SEPARATION, AND REMARRIAGE

Divorce: Data and Development

In Austria the rate of divorces has considerably risen during recent decades. Actually the divorce rate is at 46% and is expected to remain stable at this level. However, this does not mean that 46% of marriages are going to end in divorce. The divorce rate takes into account the number of divorces and the number of marriages and relates them to each other. Therefore, the divorce rate automatically rises as the marriage rate falls. This is exactly what has happened during the last three decades.

Divorced families have become a natural constituent part of Austrian society. While only 1.1 of 1,000 inhabitants divorced in 1961, at the turn of the 21st century, 2.5 of 1,000 inhabitants were divorcing in a single year. In absolute numbers, this meant 8,000 divorces in 1961 and 20,600 in 2001.

The typical age at the time of divorce has risen from the early 30s to the late 30s. This can largely be explained by the higher age of people at the time of marriage and by the increasing duration of marriages. At present, marriages in Austria last an average 9.5 years. However, we find that most divorces take place within the first years of marriage and that the number of divorces reaches its peak in the fourth year.

Many people who divorce marry again. About 60% of divorced people under the age of 30 remarry. However, after the age of 30 years, there are significant gender differences: Fifty-five percent of divorced men but only 46% of divorced women marry again within 10 years after divorce. Generally, partnerships after remarriage are lifelong, and very few people divorce a second time.

Separation of Unmarried Couples

Whereas the number of marriages has declined, nonmarital cohabitation has become more and more popular. However, it is very difficult to give exact figures and to analyze the quality and duration of these relationships. People living together in cohabitation are for the most part in their 20s. Following the definition of cohabitation as living together and sharing a household with a partner over months, the number of unmarried people living together is in all probability underestimated. Furthermore, there exist various forms of cohabitation, since both partners can live in one household during the week but can visit their parents separately or together on weekends. They can also live together in one household, but one or both partners can still officially live in their parents' household. In this way nonmarital cohabitation precedes marital cohabitation rather than replacing it. The *Family and Fertility Survey* (Doblhammer et al., 1996) shows that more than 50% of cohabiting couples marry after 6 years of cohabitation.

In the context of these developments, the number of nonmarital births has risen considerably since the late 20th century. While in 1960 13% of children were born out of wedlock, in 2001 33% of children were born to an unmarried mother. In contrast to the former practice that couples married when they were expecting a child, it is common at present that they remain unmarried or marry later on.

At this point it might be interesting to go back about 100 years. During the 19th century, Austria was an agricultural society, with more than 70% of the population involved in agriculture. At that time men could only marry when their parents' property and house were handed down to them. This was usually at the age of 30, when the old farmer was about to die. Thus, the age at the time of marriage was the same as nowadays.

Furthermore, marriage was strongly connected to income and property. This is why maidens and farm laborers of the lower classes could not marry. However, they had children and consequently the rate of extramarital births was rather high—even though for different reasons than these days.

In many ways, cohabiting couples resemble married people in sharing similar values such as fidelity. However, the risk of separation is higher than among married couples. The Austrian law still differs for married couples and couples living together in nonmarital cohabitation. Consequently, different legal obligations and rights apply. However, the law that applies in the case of divorce/ separation of families and cohabitors has largely been equalized concerning the maintenance obligation, the amount of alimony for children, and the custody of children.

New Forms of Living Together as a Consequence of Divorce

As a consequence of numerous patterns of cohabitation and the increasing number of divorced families, new forms of family structure are emerging. These are the single-parent family, the stepfamily, and the patchwork family.

Single-parent families may be the result of separation of unmarried or of divorced couples. At a young age it often happens that men leave their partner because of an unintentional pregnancy and the woman's decision to give birth to their child. At higher ages single parents are mostly an outcome of divorce. While young single mothers are often financially suffering and on the verge of poverty, single parents in their 40s are self-supporting and better off.

Remarriage often results in stepfamilies, which represent about 6% of the Austrian population. Patchwork families are families in which children of previous and present marriages live together. Unfortunately, there are no statistical data on the number of step- or patchwork families in Austria.

LATs as "Separated Marriage"?

Whereas remarriage was the common practice when divorce rates were beginning to increase, at present a new kind of partnership is seemingly about to emerge—so-called LATs (living apart together relationships). Couples are living in different households, regardless of whether they are married or not. This might be for professional or for personal reasons. They might think that living in separate households will strengthen their partnership rather than weaken it. It is very difficult to figure out how many people are living in such an arrangement. This is especially true when young people forming a couple but living in their parents' homes are counted among LATs. However, these young couples do not represent the typical LATs. LATs are rather a form of partnership at a higher age when both partners follow individual careers, or other biographical experiences have led to this form of living apart together.

How Children Are Affected

About 20% of children up to the age of 19 are affected by the divorce of their parents. There is a multiplicity of recent studies dealing with long-term consequences of divorce. However, many studies interpret the data from an ideological point of view, focusing on either the disadvantages or advantages of divorce, while neglecting the other aspects.

In the first place, it is quite evident that children suffer after divorce for several months or even years. However, we also have to question the impact of an existing but conflict-filled partnership on a child. Furthermore, we might also consider the economic effect of separation or divorce. Children raised by single parents have a higher risk of poverty. However, this risk strongly relates to the age and employment of the single parent. It can also be argued that divorce and remarriage extend the children's social networks.

The right of custody, which allows courts to decide on the basis of specific criteria with whom the child will live, constitutes an essential but often contentious issue in the course of divorce. Before joint custody of children was adopted in 2001, only one parent was entitled to have custody. Joint custody certainly allows children to more easily maintain a good relationship with both parents after divorce. Consistent with Haller (1998), who focused on the risk of separation and divorce among people whose parents divorced, the quality of the relationship between parents and children after divorce is crucial for the well-being of children and their later partnerships.

8. KINSHIP

In Austria, the word *family* usually refers to nuclear families consisting of parents and their children, or single parents and their child or children.

In Austria, relatives have no legal obligations and hardly play any role in the education of children. In most families relatives apart from grandparents only meet occasionally at momentous occasions, such as birthdays or Christmas. However, the frequency of family reunions depends on the quality of relationships as well as spatial distance. Living more than 30 minutes travel time apart lowers the chance of meeting frequently.

Kinship and its minor role in Austria can be demonstrated by considering the law of succession. Generally speaking the nearest relative inherits. In most cases these are spouses and children or their descendants. If there are no near relatives to whom the inheritance can be handed down, the decedent's siblings, nephews, or nieces will inherit. If they are not available, the grandparents or their descendants will inherit. Partners, parents-in-law, brothers-in-law, and sisters-in-law have no right to inherit by law. However, this only applies if there is no last will and testament in which the descendant explicitly expresses his wishes for the inheritance. Finally, although law of succession differs between spouses and nonmarried partners, this has no consequences for their children, who are in any case inheritors.

Concerning marriage there are some rules that are mainly meant to prevent incestuous relationships between relatives. Consequently the marriage of relatives by blood is prohibited, which means that father and daughter, grandparent and grandchild, siblings, and stepsiblings are not allowed to marry.

9. AGING AND DEATH

Aging

In Austria most elderly are in good health until about age 75. Demographics indicate gender differences in life expectancy. While women's life expectancy has been about 82 since the beginning of the 21st century, men are expected to live 76 years. As a result of this difference, the proportion of widowed women is higher than that of widowed men. While about 51% of women aged over 75 live alone, only 17% of men at the same age outlive their wives. Consequently, there are more elderly women than men who require continuous healthcare. In many cases their daughters, 20 to 30 years younger, take on their care.

The majority of elderly are not affected by poverty because of the Austrian pension scheme, which allows people to receive an adequate pension. However, the amount of pension depends on a person's profession and former income. Therefore, people with low income such as unskilled workers, women, and the self-employed have a higher risk of poverty. In Austria about 17% of all households live at the poverty level. Forty-two percent of these households are households of old people.

It might be interesting to note that people reach their highest level of income between ages 50 and 60, by which time they have worked for many years and their children have moved out. It is worth mentioning that the transfer of social and economic resources from aging people to the young generation is higher than the other way around, even when the necessary care of older people is taken into consideration. (See Rosenmayr, 2000, p. 236.)

Elderly people are embedded in generational relationships and are therefore seldom isolated. About 50% of families consist of three generations, and 27% of four generations. In many families, grandparents actively take part in family life and some 40% of the elderly live with their children or children-in-law, and another 23% live nearby.

The relationship between grandparents and grandchildren is reportedly very good, and even better than between grandparents and their own children. At this point, it is worth mentioning that individuals tend to rate their personal relationship to other generations better than they perceive intergenerational relationships between young and old people in general. A total of 38% of Austrians fear that intergenerational relationships will decline. Pessimism prevails particularly among the age-group of 46- to 60-year-olds, 48% of whom fear that the situation will deteriorate, as compared with 32% of those 45 and under.

Over the last decade, public opinion has changed considerably with regard to old people. In 1989, only 35% called on old people to renounce their rights and interests and to make way for young people. Ten years later 53% had the same opinion. Even older people support this idea, at least at the verbal level.

At the macro level the proportion of the total national payroll redistributed to the parents' and children's generations is a useful indicator for the quality of intergenerational relations. In Austria, some 22.8% of the total payroll, plus a substantial contribution from the federal budget, is paid as old-age pensions to the retired. Only 3% of the total payroll is spent on family allowance to children.

In most cases, the elderly can expect emotional, social, or material help from their family. Old people are usually cared for by their daughters. Employment is the main reason (far more frequently than any other) why people do not want to or are not able to care for their parents. Incidentally, this is cited more often by employed women than by men.

If children care for their elderly parents, they do so for reasons of gratitude or obligation rather than for the abstract reason of family solidarity. It seems that the more parents helped their children, the more they can count on their children's help later on.

Looking at all age-groups in society, young people experience more situations that require help than do elderly. They need someone to talk to, to do housework and repairs, to look out for each other in case of illness, and so on. The *Generations Study* of 1998 concluded that conflict between generations is more apparent in the public media and social policy discourses than in the family sphere itself (Majce, 2000).

Death

Cancer and diseases of the cardiovascular system are the main causes of death in Austria these days. The process of dying mainly takes place in hospitals, nursing homes, and other institutions, though about one-third die at home. The percentage of people (66%) dying in a hospital is highest in the 70- to 74-year-old age group. With a further increase in age, the proportion of people dying in a hospital decreases so that among people aged 95 and above only about 40% die in a hospital, and nearly as many (38%) die at home. The number of people aged 75 and above dying in nursing homes has risen significantly since 1990.

The process of dying is much more institutionalized in urban areas than in rural areas, and it is considered "advanced" to leave dying people to caring institutions, where it is assumed that they will receive adequate help and support. Consequently, families often exclude old family members because they feel they do not know how to cope with the process of dying. Therefore, many families avoid facing death, which means that dying persons often experience fear and isolation. The hospice movement tries to offer emotional support and professional care so that those dying away from home and family will have some sense of dignity.

It is internationally accepted that women deal better with their partner's death than do men, whose mortality risk increases significantly after the death of their wife/partner. In most cases women regain a reasonably normal life after shock, grief, and mourning. However, it often takes longer than a year to accept one's partner's death and to adapt to the new situation.

10. FAMILY AND OTHER INSTITUTIONS

Family policy is one of the central political issues in Austria. Within the European Union, it is assigned to the individual countries and not under the responsibility of the European Commission. We will discuss some crucial developments of the Austrian family policy since the Year of the Family in 1994.

The Family Fund (FLAF)

The Family Fund, which was introduced in 1954, constitutes an effective tool to support families by financing specific family-policy measures at the federal level. Family allowance, for example, is intended to cover the maintenance costs of children. Over the past 20 years, the Family Fund has increasingly developed into an instrument to finance an even greater range of family policy measures, but has failed to tap new financial resources. Its main resource is a payroll tax of 4.5%[1] (6% before 1980).

In 1999, 60% of the Family Fund's expenditures were designed for family allowance (compared with some 88% in 1970). Another 20% was primarily intended to be used for other measures such as parental leave and the mother–child booklet scheme of payments in return for medical checkups (compared with 2.8% in 1975). Finally, 9% is intended for children's free travel to school and free schoolbooks. Since 2001 the Family Fund also covers family-related research studies.

Depending on the individual's income, a specific percentage of payroll tax is transferred to the FLAF. The fund's distributive effect includes a strong vertical component: up to the sixth income decile, households with children are the net recipients. The lowest quarter contributes 9.8% of the fund's revenues and receives 29% of its expenditures; the top quarter contributes 44.7% and receives 19.2%.

In 2001 the Austrian government enacted a law that transformed the previous child benefit, which was intended to support parents who worked before parenthood, into a general benefit payable to all parents regardless of whether they were employed or not. Consequently, students may receive the child benefit.

At present the child benefit is at €430 per month for up to 30 months. In case the father also takes a leave for 6 months, the child benefit is allocated for a further 6 months. For additional income, a ceiling of about €1,136 per month has been introduced. Although the childcare benefit is very controversial and holds the risk that women are likely not to work anymore, at present there is no political party pleading for its abolishment. Besides, evaluations have shown so far that the childcare benefit has only minor effects on women's participation in the workforce, while it reduces poverty.

In 2003 a new pension scheme was established that implies substantive changes to both the private insurance system and the state-run insurance system. In Austria the central problem is that many employees retire quite early. Consequently, only one-third of people between 55 and 65 who are able to work actually are working. The new scheme envisages a continual rise in the retirement age, and will not allow people to go on early pension. In addition, the years women spend caring for their children are counted among preretirement years.

Counseling and Parental Education

These days families and family members face changes that frequently exhaust their capacities. Therefore, a supportive and preventive backup system is of great importance. Family-counseling and parental-education systems currently in place undertake this task of supporting families. Counseling is provided in accordance with the 1974 Act to Promote Family Counselling. In 2000 there were about 305 family-counseling centers with a staff of about 2,000 counselors available in Austria.

Over time most centers have become specialized, focusing on specific target groups and specific contents. They range from educational counseling to marriage counseling and their work concentrates on problematic issues related to relationships, separation/divorce, and education. In many cases, interdisciplinary teams have been very successful. As a consequence, many counselors dream of so-called multifunctional centers that offer a variety of different psychological and social services. These "one-stop shops" could provide help for many family-related problems.

At the federal level, parental education has been neglected so far, although there has been some improvement since the Year of the Family in 1994. Finally, the federal government substantially increased funding for parental education from €0.22 to 2.2 million in 2000.

Family Audit

In Austria the government encourages the so-called Family Audit. At the beginning, the Family Audit was intended to analyze firms with regard to their family friendliness and later on it was extended to communities and villages.

The priority objective with regard to firms is the improvement of the work and family interface. Firms that participated and reached a high standard of family friendliness were honored by the government, which labeled them "family-friendly firms."

Communities are also subject to extensive analysis of their family and child friendliness. Following such analysis, programs for improvement are implemented. The participation of inhabitants and children in particular is essential to ensure success. In 2003 the first family-friendly community was honored by the Austrian government.

NOTE

1. For 2001, revenues under this title are expected to be €3.2 billion, out of total fund revenues of €4.4 billion.

REFERENCES

Austrian Family Report. (1999). Bundesminsiterium für Umwelt, Jugend und Familie (Hrsg). Österreichischer Familienbericht 1999. Zur Situation von Familie und Familienpolitik in Österreich. 4. Österreichischer Familienbericht: Familie zwischen Ansprich und Alltag. Vienna.

Bacher, J., & Wilk, L. (1996). Geschlechtsspezifische Arbeitsteilung—Ausmaß und Bedingungen männlicher Mitarbeit im Haushalt. In M. Haller et al. (Eds.), *Österreich im wandel* (pp. 165–187). Oldenbourg: Verlag für Geschichte und Politik.

Demographisches Jahrbuch. (2001). Vienna: Bundesanstalt Statistik Österreich.

Doblhammer, G., Lutz, W., & Pfeiffer, C. (1996). *Family and fertility survey.* Vienna: Austrian Institute for Family Studies.

European Commission. (1996). *Equal opportunities for women and men in Europe?* Eurobarometer 44.3. Strasbourg: Eurostat.

Friesl, C. (1991). *Österreichische jugend-wertestudie.* Vienna: Austrian Institute for Youth Research.

Gräfinger, E. (2001). *Die Welt von innen. Männer in Karenz.* Vienna: Dipl. Arbeit an der Universität Wien.

Großegger, B. (2001). "Beziehungswerte"—Freunde, Partnerschaft und Familie in den Werte-Sets Jugendlicher In C. Friesl (Ed.), *Experiment Jung-Sein. Die Wertewelt österreichischer Jugendlicher* (pp. 42–72). Vienna: Czernin Verlag.

Haller, M. (1998). *Scheidungsfolgen—Die langfristigen Auswirkungen von erlebter Scheidung auf die Lebenserführung unter besonderer Berücksichtigung der ersten Lebensgemeinschaft.* Working Paper 7. Vienna: Austrian Institute for Family Studies.

Majce, G. (2000). Generationenbeziehungen und Generationenverhältnisse. In Federal Ministry of Social Security and Generations, *Ältere Menschen—Neue Perspektiven* (pp. 106–163). Vienna: Federal Ministry of Social Security and Generations.

Mikula, G., & Freudenthaler, H. H. (2002). Division of tasks and duties and the perception of injustice: The case of household chores. *Psychologische Beiträg*, 4(44).

Nave-Herz, R. (2002). *Familie heute: Wandel der Familienstrukturen und Folgen für die Erziehung* (Vol. 2.), überarb. u. erg. Edition. Darmstadt: Primus-Verlag.

Pfeiffer, C., & Nowak, V. (2001). *Transition to adulthood in Austria*. In M. Corijn & E. Klijzing (Eds.), *Transitions to adulthood in Europe* (pp. 43–66). Dordrecht: Kluwer Academic Publishers.

Rollet, B., & Werneck, H. (2001). Einstellungen, Rollenverhalten und Berufstätigkeit bei Erst- und Dritteltern in Österreich. In H. Nickel & C. Quaiser-Pohl (Eds.), *Junge Eltern im kulturellen Wande: Untersuchungen zur Familiengründung im internationalen*, (pp. 123–136). Weinheim: Juventa.

Rosenmayr, L. (2000). Neue Daten und Thesen zur Generationenfrage. *SWS Rundschau*, 3(40), 229–248.

Schwarz, F., & Spielauer, M. (2002). *The composition of couples according to education and age. An analysis in the context of FAMSIM—Family microsimulation model for Austria.* Working Paper 26. Vienna: Austrian Institute of Family Research.

Vienna youth health report. (2002). Vienna: Bereichsleitung für Gesundheitsplanung u. Finanzmanagement, Gesundheitsberichterstattung, Magistrat d. Stadt Wien.

Werneck, H., & Rollett, B. (2001). Sozialer Wandel und Familienentwicklung in Östereich. In H. Nickel & C. Quaiser-Pohl (Eds.), *Junge Eltern im kulturellen Wandel* (pp. 61–72). Weinheim und München: Juventa.

CHAPTER 10

Belgium's Families

Wilfried Dumon

1. INTRODUCTION

Belgium often is compared with the saxophone, which was created by Belgian musician Adolphe Sax in 1846, 13 years after the creation of the country. The saxophone is characterized by its complexity; it is difficult to play, but, if handled well, has a pleasing sound. Belgium (population about 10 million) is a federal state composed of three language communities: Dutch speaking, French speaking, and German speaking. In the Belgian vocabulary, they are referred to as the *communities*, each headed by a (cultural) government that handles cultural matters and education as well as issues concerning welfare—including family welfare and health. This cultural division is paralleled by a partitioning of the country into three regions: Flanders (northern part), Wallonia (southern part), and Brussels (central part), representing about 60%, 40%, and 10%, respectively, of the population.

The regional governments attend to economic matters, including employment and housing. The regions, except for Brussels, nearly overlap with the language communities, with the result that the cleavages tend to reinforce each other. Consequently, policies related to families including childcare (a community matter) and policies geared to balance family, work, and citizenship (a regional matter) tend to become increasingly divergent. In addition to the differences in policies between the language communities and the regions, the federal government, which administers taxes and social security (including child allowances), adds to the complexity of policies, especially regarding family matters. Ever since Belgium turned into a federal state in 1988, the power as well as the impact of the regional cleavages, more particularly concerning family matters, have tended to increase steadily, at the expense of the federal level. In this respect Belgium can serve as a textbook example of the trend of *decentralization of family policies*, already documented as a European tendency by the European Observatory on Family National Policies in 1994.

For some decades, the language border (Dutch/French), constitutionalized in 1963, has been identified as a demographic border. However, some recent research does not support this hypothesis, which can be characterized as more political than scholarly. Yet, concerning specific family-related behavior such as mate selection, the language communities tend to act as almost segregated communities. A second major cleavage in Belgium relates to religion, which in Belgian vocabulary is referred to as *philosophical orientation*. Belgium is predominantly a (nominal) Catholic country. The second most prevalent religion is Islam, due to the immigrant population (13%). As a result, the religious division is not by denomination, but between Catholics and the so-called freethinking (or in the Belgian vocabulary, *humanistic*) part of the population. Although unbalanced, with 47.4% (Catholics) and 8.5% (freethinking), this cleavage has played a crucial role in Belgian society, as expressed by family-related policies and legislation on areas such as abortion, divorce, euthanasia, and so on. Yet, due to the secularization process, these differences are gradually losing their impact on policies. An example of this is the introduction of same-sex marriage in June 2003, which was marked by a remarkable silence and absence of almost any reaction by the Church (Catholic) or any other partisan organization. Yet, as to behavior concerning family matters (including sexual behavior), religious affiliation still tends to play a role in many life-course events, such as childbirth (baptism), marriage (church ceremonies), and so on.

The sharp, well-marked, and institutionalized regional division of Belgian society is reflected in data gathering and scholarly research activities. As a result, most research, including on family matters, exclusively relates to one region or another and fails to provide information on the country as a whole, making reporting on Belgium as a nation challenging.

2. PAIRING UP

The marriage market in Belgium can be characterized as segmented. Mate selection resulting in marriage is heavily preconditioned by residential propinquity as well as by a kind of linguistic apartheid. Linguistic homogeneity data for 2001 was as follows: Flanders, 96.15%, Wallonia, 93.3%, Brussels, 8.45%, reflecting a strong degree of intermarriage within the language communities, with marriage with non-Belgians outnumbering marriages among Belgians belonging to different language communities. The data suggest that singles select singles (89%).[1] Yet, this might be due not so much to personal preference as to the structure of the marriage market, in terms of availability as well as in terms of age structure. The latter factor, age structure, is intriguing since the age discrepancy between women and men remained almost unchanged over the last decades, with men being 2 years and some months senior to their selected mates. This might still give some indication that males take the initiative in selecting a partner; however, it might also be the result of persons of the same age-group in the marriage/partner market already being engaged or already living together or even being married. At any rate, one can postulate that the age discrepancy between men and women might serve as an indicator that equity between men and women on the marriage market has not yet been fully achieved. It could suggest that men remain the predominant initiators of contacts, or in contrast it could suggest that women prefer their partners to be somewhat older or more mature.

As to mixed marriages, for example, a Belgian citizen selecting a non-Belgian partner, the absolute numbers tended to remain rather stable over the last decade. Yet, the share of mixed marriages in the absolute number of marriages has increased in the last decade. The *percentage* of mixed marriages has risen significantly: from some 10% (10.63%) in 1990 to more than 15% (16.79%) in 2001, an increase of more than 50%. More particularly, the share of Belgian men selecting a non-Belgian (immigrant) partner has increased considerably. As a result, there is almost a balance between foreign men and foreign women marrying Belgians. This contrasts with the situation, only one decade ago, when foreign men selected Belgian women, but Belgian men hardly had access to the immigrant female population on the marriage market. This development could suggest a greater liberalization of the marriage market and thus an increased degree of "integration" of foreigners (immigrants) residing in Belgium. However, it also could suggest a greater internationalization of the marriage market, stimulated by the European integration, enhanced by increased international mobility (tourism) and scholarly exchanges such as Socrates programs (student exchanges)— that is, a Europeanization of the marriage/ partnership market.

The process of pairing up is not well documented in Belgium. Only for Flanders (the northern part of Belgium) are some longitudinal data available, due to the successive fertility surveys that were conducted in Flanders in the style of NEGO (Relation and Family Formation in Flanders) (Corijn, 1995; Cliquet, 1996). The last data collection dates back to the early 1990s; thus, the results tend to be outdated. Yet, the processes described may still hold some value. More particularly, elements focusing on timing may still be valid. One element concerns gender differentiation: Women tend to engage in a stable partner relationship at a younger age than do men. Moreover, the time span to engage in a stable relationship by men is more extended, which means for men a specific time for starting a stable relationship is difficult to identify. Regardless of gender, the age to start a stable relationship does not seem to change considerably. In contrast, timing constitutes a significant variable: The late starters seem to postpone a stable relationship. This process is even more pronounced for men than for women. An early starter is someone who first engages in a stable relationship at around 18 years

of age for women and 17 for men; the definition of a late starter is someone who first enters a stable relationship at 21 years of age for women and 25 for men. In addition, the data suggest that before entering into a stable relationship, both men and women customarily were previously engaged in relationships they defined as "love relationships."

Although the research evidence is not abundant, the general impression is that pairing up for lasting relationships in Belgium can be considered rather traditional. Partners tend to match in terms of culture (language) as well as in terms of social ranking.

3. FERTILITY AND SOCIALIZATION

One way to look at these issues is to see fertility in terms of child quantity and socialization in terms of quality.

Reproduction

For decades now, the fertility rates have tended to be below reproduction rates. Until recently, this sustained decline in the fertility rate was not a matter of much debate in the public forum. If some voice was raised in the media, the concern was specifically directed toward the differential decline between the language regions: Flanders/Wallonia. Although currently some attention is being paid to this situation, the Dutch-language press (such as *De Standaard*) almost exclusively reports on the situation in Flanders, and the French-language press (such as *Le Soir*) reports on the situation in Wallonia and Brussels. Concern tends to be community-specific rather than national.

Low fertility, as well as low birthrates, result in small families. About one-half of children in the 3 to 5 age bracket have siblings. About one-third of the children in the 6 to 11 age-group live in a household with two or more siblings (Vernaille & Lodewijckx,

2001; Lodewijckx & Vernaille, 2003). In Belgium, as in other Western European countries, the number of children living with married parents is declining. The distinction between marriage and cohabitation is becoming almost irrelevant, except for one group: children living in a one-parent family. Research evidence suggests that children (0–17) in the latter situation tend to enjoy more autonomy and feel as accepted and supported by their mothers as children in two-parent families, but they have experienced more negative communication patterns between their parents (Van Peer, 1993).

The number of children living in one-parent families, at least for some time during their life course, has increased. This increase was remarkable between 1990 and 2000. In the age bracket 0 to 17, less than one in ten lived in a one-parent family in 1990; in 2000 that figure read ±15% (Lodewijckx, 2002a). As in many other Western societies, due to later age at first parity, children currently live with parents who, on average, are older (Lodewijckx, 2002b). A rather new phenomenon in this respect is that men in second or third relationships might become fathers at age 60 or over. Although this phenomenon has almost no demographic bearing, it produces new challenges on two accounts. First is a sociopolitical question on age-limit—until what age is one entitled to become a parent. Second, how will children cope with parents as old as grandparents?

In Belgium children tend to be a rather scarce product, so they receive a lot of attention and in return are expected to fulfill high expectations of their parents.

Nurturance

At birth, all children are monitored by health workers as part of a program of "care for mother and child." Babies and their mothers receive house calls by health workers, followed by monthly visits by mother and child to a healthcare center, where the baby is examined by medical doctors and health workers. This is a service available to all families, so there is no stigma attached. Almost all mothers, especially young mothers, take advantage of this service. A bonus of the system is that mothers learn from each other's experiences. Fathers are less visible in this picture. The services traditionally were, and still are, predominantly medically oriented; recently, however, the perspective is widening toward a broader concept of parenting.

As already mentioned, issues such as child policy fall under the supervision of the language communities—thus, the orientation tends to be divergent. In the largest region (the Flemish), all new parents receive a monthly "Brieven aan ouders" (Letter to Parents) containing information and advice about parenting. One regular feature of the letters relates to breast-feeding, which is a common practice and is becoming more popular. Recent data suggest that about two-thirds of mothers start breast-feeding, and about one-quarter of children aged 3 months are still nurtured exclusively by their mother. The nutrition situation of babies is considered adequate and some mothers are thought to be rather overconcerned about the nutrition of their babies (Lenaers & Goffin, 2002).

In fact, the two concepts, nurture and nutrition, seem to overlap. However, this idyllic representation obscures the other side of the picture—the evidence concerning child abuse and neglect. More particularly in Belgium, the Dutroux affair (1998), in which high officials were involved in pedophilia and assassinations of young children, still overshadows the issue and still traumatizes the Belgian self-image. A brutal awakening followed. Ever since, physical and sexual abuse of children is brought into the open and extensively covered by the mass media. The handling of child abuse and neglect in Belgium reflects the involvement of society in parenting. The idea that "my home is my castle" has been broken open and society is looking into this fortress and is concerned about domestic affairs. In Belgium—as in many other European countries—child abuse has been transferred from the judicial sector to the welfare sector, more particularly to the medical sector—a mix of medicosocial concern. Central in dealing with problems are the so-called confidential MDs, serving as centers of monitoring and reporting as well as treatment. Although the organizational format is somewhat different in the Dutch- and French-language communities, their overall mode of operation is rather similar.

The data suggest that reporting child abuse and neglect is on the increase. This does not necessarily reflect an increase in the number of cases but rather that detection is becoming more adequate. In reporting child abuse and neglect, the informal sector (kin, friends, neighbors) by far outweighs the formal sector (school, welfare workers, etc.). The data further suggest that children in the age bracket 3 to 6 are the most vulnerable. In contrast to other forms of domestic violence, adequate figures indicating incidence are not available. In 2002 in one region (Flanders), about 6,000 cases of child abuse and neglect were documented, representing about 1% of all children in that region (de Grendele, 2002).

Raising of children in Belgium is not entirely a family matter. To a large extent, socialization is a community matter. Even at a comparatively early age, children are taken care of by others (substitute parenting). As can be expected, the age of the child constitutes the most crucial variable. Three age brackets— 0 to 3, 3 to 6, and 6 and over—mark sharp differences in the provision of care, as well as education. Most of the relevant data are provided by regional authorities, so it is difficult to get figures for the country as a whole. The largest region, Flanders, covering about 60%, provides reliable data at regular intervals

about the actors involved in the socialization of young children. Figures reported for 2002 suggest that babies 0 to 3 months old are almost exclusively cared for by their parents (typically the mother). However, from the third month on, a substantial number—about one-third—are regularly taken care of by nonparents. They are taken either to crèches or to so-called care mothers. When children reach the age of 6 months, more than one-half of them are taken into care on a regular basis. The formal care outweighs the informal care. Indeed, crèches and day-care mothers offer about two-thirds of all care (Het Kind in Vlaanderen 2002), and informal caregivers— predominantly grandparents—account for about one-third. Caregiving is almost exclusively taken up by women. Currently, this situation is evaluated as undesirable and thus in early 2003 government-sponsored campaigns were launched to abolish these "women's bastions," and men were portrayed as suitable and competent caregivers.

At the age of 3, children tend to be transferred from crèche to regular school and become integrated into the educational system. In Belgium, almost all children attend school at the age of 3. The figures for children attending school in 1999 are as follows: 93.8% of all children aged 6 to 12 attend school on a regular basis, that is about 50% on a full-time basis, and about 50% on a more than full-time basis—they stay in the school overtime (unpublished results from the panel study on Belgian Households [PSBH].) This implies, as a rule, that children are taken care of by the school system before school hours and even more often after school hours.

Schools run from Monday through Friday, with Wednesday afternoons and weekends free. As a result, in Belgium the debate on childcare services is heavily focused on after- and out-of-school care. Although children in Belgium are compelled to attend school up to the age of 18, and thus experience a long school career, currently some politicians advocate an even earlier entrance age. Some social arguments are voiced: Low-income families tend not to send their children to kindergarten as frequently as do other parents. In general, research data over and over again suggest that parents are satisfied with the schools (Verhoeven, Devos, Stassen, & Warmoes, 2003). More particularly, parents of preschool children attending kindergarten-in-school are over-represented in the category of satisfied customers. The term *customers* is adequately chosen since the parents do not fully participate in parent-teacher associations and more particularly in school boards, which are guaranteed by law.

Lately parenting is becoming more and more a public concern of the regional authorities, the so-called language communities. To some extent, parenting has become a matter of the sociopolitical debate. In general terms, this development might serve as an example of the advanced stage of the secularization process in Belgium—where the role of the church is being taken over by the state. Another popular hypothesis, recently often voiced, links the heavy approach to parenthood to the fertility rates. Since children are becoming a rather "rare good," parenting is taken more seriously.

4. GENDER ROLES

One of the early empirical research projects on the family in Belgium, published in 1968, heavily focused on family organization, for example, the division of labor and power inside the family. A clear picture emerged. Men were occupied and integrated in the labor force; women tended to be housewives (de Bie et al., 1968). The data were collected during 1961 to 1962. Half a century later, one can state that the breadwinner family is now almost unrepresentative of the Belgian family, as has been documented by Van

Dongen (1993, 2001). The old division of husband/father/provider and wife/mother/housewife/caretaker has become a thing of the past. This so-called Parsons model, characterized by sharp division of labor—instrumental role: male; expressive role: female—is gone, but it has not been replaced by one dominant new model. Currently in Belgium one can identify two major models competing for attention: In the first model, both of the partners are engaged in the labor market on a full-time basis. In the second model, the male partner/husband works full time and the female partner/wife is employed part time. Both models represent about 30% of Belgian couple-families. The breadwinner model represents somewhat less than one-quarter of all Belgian cohabitation families, married as well as unmarried. Other forms do occur, but they are difficult to put into categories, except for one: both of the partners being employed part-time. Moreover, families representing these plural minority models tend to reorganize themselves into one of the modal forms. In contrast, the three major models are characterized by stability. Yet, in one of the dominant groups—the two earner/two income families—the full-time status of the female partner sometimes evolves into a part-time activity. This is often due to motherhood (a first child, a second child). The reverse transfer form—part-time to full-time—occurs as well, but not as frequently (Jacobs, De Maeyer, Back, De Bruyn, 2000).

In Flanders, 2003 data indicated that the gap in education as well as in the activity rate between women and men has been bridged (Vrind, 2002). This occurs in a context where public awareness on this issue is raised and the mass media extensively report on any research evidence suggesting that active participation of mothers in the labor market does not constitute a handicap for the adequate raising of children. These developments are reflected by employment and family policies focusing heavily on balancing the three poles: work, family, and citizenship. Yet, women outnumber men in reporting problems in their efforts to reconcile family and work. This subjective parameter is paralleled by objective measurements. Indeed, research evidence suggests that mothers in dual-career families experience time pressure to a higher degree than their partners. Even highly educated childless couples experience time pressure, since in addition to busy work schedules they tend to be highly active in their leisure time (Moens, 2003).

As in any other Western society, in Belgium domestic division of labor is seen, but on the hit parade of "new men," men who undertake household tasks that have traditionally been the exclusive domain of women, Belgium scores rather well—third place in Europe. The unequal distribution of domestic duties is considered to be unfair and, moreover, there is ample room for improvement. Also, in Belgium, as in many other countries where equality has become a value in itself, many studies have been conducted to demonstrate the gender imbalance, and many initiatives have been taken to narrow or even bridge the gap. Commonly, two indicators are applied to measure the difference: (1) time spent on household tasks, and (2) number of tasks carried out. As to time, in 2003 the figures were as follows: In couple-families, women spend 23 hours per week on household chores, compared with 8 hours spent by men. In other words, women invest about three times more of their time in household work than do men. In addition, three-quarters of the tasks are done by women and one-quarter are done by men. These objective accounts contrast sharply with the values men claim to adhere to, as well as with subjective assessments of behavior. Men tend in overestimate their involvement, and women tend to underestimate the degree of sharing of their husband. This might be based on the value structure shared by both genders:

equality and distribution of paid as well as of unpaid labor. As repeatedly demonstrated in research data, men are assessed to be able to perform tasks formerly stigmatized as gender specific, such as laundry. Yet, distribution of tasks is not the only or most adequate variable of emancipation, as suggested by the new thinking on emancipation and the emergence of new concepts such as differentiation (Jacobs et al., 2000).

The big question is focused on the young generation: Do they act differently from former generations? Does the behavior of new fathers contrast with that of their fathers? Does the new father exist? Recent research evidence suggests that "new fathers" are rare: They still tend to perceive themselves mainly as breadwinners, but emotionally they are focused on the child and are able to express themselves; only a minority of them take an equal or greater share in raising the child. So the new fathers do exist, but they still are to be considered rare (Mortelmans, 2002; Mortelmans, Ottoy, & Verstreken, 2003).

Lately, a rather symbolic gender issue became the focus of sociopolitical debate. In early 2001, the system of allocation of surnames was declared discriminating, outdated, and patriarchal. There was even an appeal to the highest court, which ruled that, although the system in itself was not discriminatory, it was up to the legislature to change the system. The debate continued until the end of 2003, when a new government decided to look into the matter and to take action. The debate was fueled by press reports about children born to women separated from their husbands who still had to carry the surname of the ex-husband. This was perceived as unjust. Public opinion polls show a majority of the population being in favor of altering the system to the effect that the name of the father should not automatically be carried by his child. The question remains open as to whether the authorities or the parents should be the ones who decide on the name.

The issue of gender roles has gained priority in the sociopublic debate to the extent that new mores have been adopted. In contrast, behavior patterns seem to be more resistant to change. The latter issue is gender specific: Women tend to be more flexible and adaptive than men. The former enter into/remain in the labor market, whereas their partners lag behind in adapting to the new type of family organization. Paradoxically, these matters are perceived by the actors as private arrangements, yet the public authorities—legislative, executive, and even judicial—enter into these domains and exert power. The division between the private and public domain is changing. This balance is not unidirectional. One example: Free choice of surname undoubtedly would constitute another element of family empowerment. On the other hand, although the two-career/two-income model is almost becoming socially, culturally, and economically imperative, it hardly reflects the free choice of partners.

5. MARITAL RELATIONSHIPS

In Belgium, as in almost any other Western society, multiple forms of marital or marital-like relationships have existed for quite some time. Yet, Belgium is probably one of the few countries in the Western world, if not the only one, where at least three types of marriage, or marriage-like relationships, are institutionalized. All three models are not merely recognized but formally institutionalized: marriage, cohabitation, and marriage of same-sex couples. Other forms, such as living apart together (LAT) relationships, are to some extent recognized but not (yet) institutionalized. Lately, however, public attention has focused on the reverse situation: singlehood. In the media, more particularly in the press, attention is paid to their growing number (quantity), as well as to their lifestyle (quality). One of the key issues relates to timing, the age at which youngsters leave the parental home.

Marriage

The most striking characteristic of current marriage trends is late marriage. In one decade the average age has increased for men from less than 30 years to over 33 years, whereas for women it has increased from 27.5 up to more than 30 years. This increase is due not only to remarriage after divorce or after widowhood but also significantly to a relative advanced age at first marriage. Indeed, for that category, in the last decade the marriage age raised from less than 27 years to more than 29 for men, and from about 25 years to almost 26.5 years for women. This increased age pattern continues, and the phenomenon has not caused any concern. However, the falling marriage rate has made front-page news. Nevertheless, both events are related by definition.

In 1992 about 60,000 weddings were registered; 10 years later, in 2002, the total was approximately 42,000, a shortfall of one-third (National Statistical Office, n.d.; see also National Statistical Office, 2002). Lately, the rate of the decline is leveling off. Often the question is raised as to whether this process should be put in terms of postponement or in terms of rejection. The answer is not clear, since one cannot write history before it takes place, but it is not unlikely that both elements play some role. Postponement makes for temporarily lower figures in the marriage statistics. On the other hand, rejection would have a long-lasting effect. However, a very important factor relates to the structure of the population. The marriage-age cohort in Belgium each year becomes more and more reduced as a result of the falling birth rate two and almost three decades ago (National Statistical Office, n.d.).

Up to the 1960s, almost all Belgians had a double wedding due to the so-called

Napoleon Concord in Belgium, in which the relationship between church and state was institutionalized: one in church, preceded by one at the mayor's office. Customarily, the latter was a sober formality and the former was a great event where the bride and groom and guests were dressed according to the occasion. Lately, church weddings are in sharp decline. The number dropped from about 50%(49.2%) in 1998 to 44% in 2000, a time span of only 2 years (unpublished data provided by Secretariaat van de Bisschoppenconferentie, Brussels, 2003; see also Dobbelaere, 2001). The dramatic decline of pomp and glory was counterbalanced over a larger period by the rituals at the occasion of the civil ceremony in the town hall. Nowadays, in most towns and cities the wedding ceremony is conducted with greater solemnity and an appropriate decorum. Weddings still are highly visible in society; customarily they are celebrated with great pomp and tend to be widely announced and well attended.

Unmarried Cohabitation

As to unmarried cohabitation, official statistics concerning registered cohabitation are hardly available. By October 2002, this number amounted to 13,972. The distribution over the country is rather skewed: some 11,000 in Flanders, 2,600 in Wallonia, and 400 in Brussels (Maldague, 2003). Statistics about nonregistered cohabitation do not exist, by definition, though some data are provided by survey research. However, the more recent data only apply to one region, Flanders. Moreover, the data relate to *premarital* cohabitation. Of all persons getting married (1961–1966) in Flanders, somewhat more than one-third had experienced some form of premarital cohabitation: men, about 36%; women, about 34% (Corijn, 1999). The phenomenon of postmarital cohabitation, succeeding divorce or widowhood, is not covered

in these figures, although there are some indications that cohabitation in Belgium is even more frequent among the latter. So the information on current unmarried cohabitation is meager, incomplete, and partial. Since the age bracket is limited to persons aged 45 years old, hardly any adequate information is available on cohabitation after marriage, divorce, or separation. Yet, as stated previously, some indications suggest that in Belgium cohabitation does occur even more frequently among those groups than among youngsters. As to profile, cohabiters tend to be overrepresented among the lower-educated, the nonpracticing Catholics, and especially among non-Catholics. The phenomenon tends to be more an urban than a rural one. At least that was the situation in the early 1990s. The data suggest that Belgium, compared in this respect with other Western European countries, more particularly with its neighbors France and the Netherlands, tends to lag somewhat behind. Moreover, if one compares the situation in the beginning of the last decade with the more recent data, one could speculate that Belgium was a very late starter.

In society at large, any difference between cohabiters and married persons is gradually fading away. Children born out of wedlock, formerly, even until the 1950s, were characterized as illegitimate or even bastards; these terms are seldom employed any longer. Legally, as well as factually, there is little difference anymore, and the distinction between children born in wedlock and born out of wedlock is becoming totally irrelevant. Yet, there are still some reminders, such as in the vital statistics published by the federal statistical office. In contrast to regional statistics, which originated later, the bulk of information in the federal statistics relates exclusively to legitimate children. For example, the breakdown by rank, timing in the life cycle, and so on apply only to legitimate births. As a result, the official statistics on natality and fertility tend to be inadequate.

Singles/One-Person Households

In the last decade, the number of house-holds has increased dramatically. In Belgian statistical jargon, a household is labeled a family. It is composed of all persons living under the same roof. The percentage of the statistical category "singles" has increased over the last decade (Jan. 1992–Jan. 2002) by 16% (National Statistical Office, n.d.; Lodewijckx, 2001). The distribution of these households is heavily skewed as to sex; female-headed one-person households largely outnumber the male-headed one-person households. Three factors have contributed to this sharp increase: (1) expanded longevity; (2) better health of the aged, enabling them to live by themselves for a longer of time; and (3) the improved economic condition of the elderly, which allows many of them to live independently rather than stay with their children. This situation is paralleled by a cultural norm. For decades now, "living-in" situations of young couples with parents, and conversely of old persons living with their offspring, have been called outdated. This situation is supported by the development of new social policy and new instruments of policy, such as the expansion of home services including catering, nursing, and household-help services, geared at serving the elderly population with the explicit target of keeping them at home as long as possible.

Although the federal statistical office (NIS/INS), even in its official briefing, labels persons living in one-person households as singles, there is no indication that these persons have no steady social or sexual rela-tionships. In fact, LAT relationships, by defi-nition, require that the persons engaged in such a relationship live in separate (one-person) households. Up to now, the incidence of LAT relationships has not been very well documented. However, an educated guess would suggest that these relationships are increasing rapidly, or are at least becoming very visible in society. The impression is that these relationships are over-represented in older age brackets.

In Belgium many forms of marital relation-ship exist simultaneously. Yet, as in any other Western society, these different forms can be characterized as the expression of a particular lifestyle in a particular phase of the life course of a person rather than as the expression of opposite ethical or social attitudes resulting out of deep cleavages within the society.

6 & 7. DIVORCE, REMARRIAGE, AND STRESSES

Divorce

In the vital statistics on the 15 member states by Eurostat (Statistical Office of the European Union), Belgium tends to occupy a middle position. One exception is divorce. In that statistic, Belgium has ranked first for almost a decade. Even according to the most recent data, for the calendar year 2002, the divorce rate in Belgium continues to increase, in contrast to quite a few other member states where the divorce numbers tend to decline. For quite a while, the high figures could be attributed to a catch-up effect, but lately the steady high level has put even the most experienced observers at odds. The public awareness of this phenomenon was raised in 2001, when for the first time in Brussels divorces outnumbered weddings. In the subsequent year, 2002, this trend was con-firmed. Although both events refer to totally different cohorts, this event caught the public imagination. Front-page headlines stated that three out of four marriages ended in divorce.

The absolute number of registered divorces increased from about 20,000 in 1991 to about 30,000 in 2001. As a rule, demographers do not pay great attention to absolute figures, yet from a sociological point of view, they are very important, since the absolute number of cases makes for social visibility of the phenomenon. Moreover, the absolute number is vital in relation to the acceptance of the phenomenon and its transformation from a problem into a social issue. The terms *broken home* and *broken relationship* are hardly ever mentioned in Belgium, and one could suggest that the term *divorce* be replaced by *turnover of partners*. The crude divorce rate, indicating divorces per 100,000 inhabitants, raised from about 2.0 in 1991 to about 3.0 in 2001 (National Statistical Office, n.d.; see also National Statistical Office, 2002). This measure would be totally relevant if the population structure remained stable. However, it does not, so in an aging population, even stable crude rates would suggest an increase in the divorce rates for the simple reason that the oldest section of the population has a lower risk (or chance) of becoming divorced.

A more adequate indicator is provided by the total divorce rate, or the final divorce rate. The total divorce rate provides an indicator of the chance/risk a couple would have to divorce under the condition that all other demographic parameters, such as marriage rates, terms of divorce, and so on, remain stable. Although these conditions seldom apply, the crude divorce rate still provides a rather fair measurement, and it can be characterized as a fair indicator for international or inter-regional comparison. The total divorce rate in Belgium was 18.4 in 1980, 30.6 in 1990, and 45.1 in 2000, meaning that the marriage cohort of 1980 had one chance in five to experience a divorce, the cohort of 2000 almost one in two. The mere magnitude of these figures suggests they might be biased. And so they are, since, as stated, they would only hold if timing remained stable. If the duration of marriage before divorce is decreasing, the chance of divorce tends to be overestimated; if timing is increasing, the rate of divorce tends to be underestimated. Actually, timing is decreasing, so divorce is overestimated. The third measure—final divorce—might prove to be more trustworthy. This indicator does not measure chances of getting divorced but actually registers divorces happening. It would be perfect, if there were no drawback—history

can be written only after the events have occurred. Thus, divorce can be registered only after the marriage has ended. If this measure is not predicted, the mere figures might suggest some (rapid) change, as illustrated in Figure 10.1 (Van Hove & Matthijs, 2002).

It is a paradox that the country showing the highest divorce rates in Europe institutionally still maintains one of the most out-of-date legal divorce procedures. Unlike almost any other member state of the EU, Belgium has not yet adopted a system of faultless divorce. Currently, two quite separate divorce procedures are simultaneously in vogue: divorce on certain grounds and divorce by mutual consent. The former procedure is heavily guilt-oriented. Divorce itself is a sanctioning mechanism with heavy emphasis on retribution: alimony and child support. Currently the so-called grounds for divorce include adultery, gross insult, and actual separation. Gross insult is the most invoked reason. In case of actual separation, the person who left the mutual home is presupposed to be the guilty party. Divorce on certain grounds, by definition, is evidence (content) oriented. In contrast, the procedure—mutual consent—is heavily formal, that is, procedurally oriented. The latter can be characterized as a mirror image of the wedding. It consists of the couple appearing, in person and together, before the judge and expressing their firm intention to end the marriage. This element as well as the time factor (reconciliation period) are the imposed ingredients of the procedure. In the 1980s and 1990s, several measures were introduced to simplify the formerly long and rather complex procedure. As a result, the balance between the two procedures changed dramatically. In 1980 the bias was considerably in favor of divorce by mutual consent. In 1960 80% of the requests for divorce were fault based, and 20% by mutual consent; in 1990 the former still outnumbered the latter—about 60% versus 40%—but in 2000 the situation was totally reversed: Less than 25% were

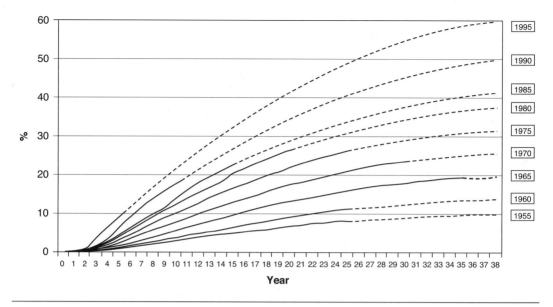

Figure 10.1   Observed and Estimated Longitudinal Divorce Rates per Marriage Cohort in Belgium
(1955–1995)

fault based, and more than 75% were by mutual consent (National Statistical Office, n.d.). However, it was not until 2003 that the government formally announced its intention to introduce a new bill more in line with the current trend: faultless divorce. Parallel with the evolution in procedure in the public domain, changes were also occurring in the private sphere: Divorce mediation became fashionable. The aim was to reduce antagonistic behavior and to attempt to make the divorce process less emotional and somewhat more rational. In the late 1990s and the early years of the new century, some legal provisions came into effect. This movement is not yet totally integrated into the legal procedure, but it is not unlikely that some forms of divorce mediation will be inluded in the legal provisions introduced in the forthcoming bill on faultless divorce.

Remarriage

Although the number of divorced persons is increasing, the number of remarriages is (slightly) declining too, but, in absolute numbers, the figure is not as sharp as that of first marriages. As a result, the share of divorced and widowed persons in the total marriage figures is increasing considerably. It has increased from about one in four (25%) in 1991 to one in three (33%) (National Statistical Office, n.d.). This factor also partially explains why the number of church marriages is declining, since the church is not offering services for divorced persons. Some divorced persons do stay single; quite a few, however, engage in cohabiting or in a LAT relationship. The latter do not figure in any official statistics, so in some respect vital statistics on marriage increasingly tend to lose their validity and are no longer an adequate parameter of singlehood, let alone loneliness.

Over the last two decades, divorce in Belgium has become an accepted fact of life, an event not unlikely to occur in a married person's life course. This generalization can be taken more seriously if one takes into consideration the factual separation of married persons, as well as persons living in a close relationship such as marriage-like cohabitation and LAT relationships. Therefore, the concept of *partner turnover* might better describe what is happening in our society. Belgium tries to come to terms with this transitional phase in the life course, through so-called mediation procedures. Currently, in addition to mediation, the emphasis is on coparenting—with great concern for the role of men, not in their role as ex-husbands but in their role as fathers. In other words, the emphasis is on the kinship relationship rather than the partner relationship. Public concern in these matters overtakes private arrangements, in contrast to the partner relationship, where private arrangements tend to overshadow public concern.

8. KINSHIP

In Belgium, the term *family* refers to kinship. In this sense, family is more than a safe haven in a heartless world. Even in this new century, family represents a stronghold in Belgium, serving beyond its function as a safety network.

Familialism is not (yet) an inappropriate term and neither does it refer to inappropriate behavior. In economics, politics, and social life, familialism is tolerated to a degree that one could qualify as acceptance.

Family business is a common phenomenon. Even in big business, family has its place, in terms of capital (shareholders) and management. However, in recent decades, executive officers who are family members have gradually been replaced by professionally trained non–family members. In medium-sized and small companies, however, family is still important. Small enterprises, and more particularly farming, still tend to be heavily family-oriented. Though not as prevalent as in farming, the emphasis on family is not totally absent in the labor market. In large companies, the employment strategy of preferential hiring of family members has

become obsolete and is almost totally replaced by hiring done by professional outside agencies such as recruitment firms. Family ties still prove strong in job selection and search for employment, though. Job spotting, providing information, and lobbying are some of the strategies used by family members in favor of their kinsmen (and women).

Familialism as a practice isn't foreign in the political arena. Although hardly any political dynasty is as visible as the Kennedys in the United States, father-son and father-daughter teams are not uncommon in the executive as well as in the legislative branches of political power. For example, lately it was documented that almost one-quarter of all mayors and heads of towns and cities in Belgium are sons of fathers heavily involved in politics, many of them holding a political office (Steyers & Reynaert, 2003). This situation is not party-specific but is common practice in all political families, as the large political organizations are called in Belgium. It has been so since the creation of Belgium in the late 19th century and seems to be an accepted fact of life and a normal procedure that seems to be expanding rather than being curtailed.

In the social domain, one outstanding variable can be identified: Women are the gatekeepers and the initiators in informal social contacts (friends, neighbors), as well as in maintaining and activating kinship contacts. It is a paradox that in a society characterized by weakening of the husband–wife tie, kinship relations still constitute ties that bind, as expressed by visiting patterns and exchange of material and nonmaterial goods. As a result, kinship still yields the most significant others.

Since heritage taxes are under the jurisdiction of the regions, hardly any figures for Belgium are available. Tentative research evidence suggests that from one out of three to two out of five couples sign a marriage contract before a notary, regulating heritage in case of death or divorce.[2] This contract agreed to before the wedding can often be characterized as a ritual dance, since it more or less reflects the social status of the persons involved. In all other instances, heritage is regulated by law, which often has been adapted to changing social mores.

In the beginning of this century, voices were raised to make it possible for couples to let their grandchildren benefit directly from heritage—thus bypassing their children. The arguments referred to increased longevity. Up to now, no steps have been taken to realize this idea. However, heritage is an important matter in Belgium, and the passing over of material wealth formerly through weddings (virtually) and through death (actually) now is being challenged due to the fact that marriage itself is on the decline. The family patrimonium is replaced more and more by the his and her patrimonium. This autonomization of capital goods is in line with the already outdated law of 1976 regulating familial patrimony, stressing the absolute equity of the two spouses.

Familialism as an element of social networking yields material and nonmaterial benefits for the persons involved. However, there is a price to be paid—ties bind. This holds for the persons involved and has a more important effect for the persons outside the group. Those persons outside the group are restricted to the resources of their own kinship network. In this sense, family acts as one constituting element of the ongoing social stratification in Belgian society.

9. AGING AND DEATH

In Belgium, as in all Western societies, increased longevity has a tremendous impact on family life, as well as on family structure. In 2000, life expectancy for women was 81.48 years and for men 75.65 years (National Statistical Office, n.d.). The increase in longevity is not expressed exclusively in terms of quantity, that is, additional years added to life, but, even more spectacularly, in qualitative terms—increased wealth and well-being in the last period of the life course.

As documented in the aforementioned figures, gender represents *the* crucial issue in aging. Women outlive men. This quantitative issue is paralleled by a qualitative aspect. Generally, men receive more care and women provide more care. However, these differences are changing and becoming somewhat less dramatic. The aging situation of both genders is still in a transitional phase.

Changes in the Belgian household in the last decade have been extensively documented for Flanders. The gender difference in mortality is most clearly connected to marital status, even controlled for age. The figures for 2000 suggest that in the age bracket 85 to 89, about one-half of the men still live with their wives, whereas only 10% of the women still live in a marital relationship (Audenaert, 2000). This can be due to the simple fact, as shown by mortality statistics, that men pass away while still married and most women outlive their partners. There is an additional line of reasoning suggesting that men are less able to cope with widowhood than women and that they profit disproportionately from the marital relationship, as suggested by Durkheim and recently advanced by current demographers such as Hu and Goldman (1990). Whatever the case, due to prolonged longevity, more and more persons are married for a longer period in their life course. In other words, the last phase of the family life cycle has become more extended.

In the last decade (1990–2000), the trend was that the number of widowed decreased and the number of married persons increased. The number of persons being cared for in nursing homes is increasing, as is the number of very elderly. In this respect, a paradoxical situation is developing regarding gender difference: Statistical data suggest that—in absolute and relative numbers—women tend to move to nursing homes not at a later age, which might be expected on grounds of increased wealth and decreased health, but at younger ages. This paradox is to be understood easily if one looks at the decline of persons living with relatives. In Flanders, the latter situation is becoming almost atypical. Still, 13.5% of all women (vs. 8.9% of men) in 1990 in the age bracket 85 to 89 were living with relatives (Audenaert, 2000). In 2002 the figures fell to 7.7% and 3.8%, respectively, suggesting a profound change in family organization and a dramatic change of relationship between generations occurring over a relatively short time span—one decade.

In Belgium the policy regarding care of the elderly is a regional matter, to the effect that policies tend to differ somewhat between the language regions. Yet one can identify a common trend to the effect that, although to different degrees, the policies are aimed at keeping the elderly at home as long as possible. In this respect, a sharp distinction should be made between medical and nonmedical care. This is due to many reasons but with one particularity for Belgium: Medical care is a federal matter and nonmedical care is a regional (language-community) matter. Two elements in medical care are somewhat Belgium-specific. First, general practitioners, family doctors, still make house calls. This means that to a certain degree doctors are likely to be aware of family situations, and moreover, in many instances, the doctor attends to all family members. Therefore, a large number of elderly persons are covered by some—almost informal—medical supervision. Second, a large medical care network linked with medical insurance companies has been developed and offers nursing services

as an integral part of medical insurance. This system is part of the social security system covering almost all citizens, and therefore the services are free of charge. This is in contrast to medical doctors, who operate under a fee-for-service system. Their fees are largely reimbursed, and the total amount of medical expenditure a year is capped at a fixed amount, according to net income. As to nonmedical care, currently two types of help or assistance are offered: cash or in-kind. In Flanders in 2001, a new element of social security was introduced called "(in)dependence assurance." All citizens have to contribute and all are covered by the system. Its aim is to enable persons "in need of severe care" to buy nonmedical care services provided in the formal market or in the informal sphere (kin, relatives, family, friends). The degree of need is measured by a medical checklist. One year later the system was expanded to include nursing home care. This event points to some competition between formal and informal care. The vested interest in healthcare, the residential sector, tends to overpower the informal sector. It also shows the imbalance in power between care providers and care receivers. The so-called (in)dependance insurance was introduced with the idea that it would enhance the autonomy of the persons in need of (severe) care.

Nonmedical services offered, in kind, include the following: (1) household help and more particularly housekeeping services, (2) catering services, and (3) odd-job services. More particularly, senior help services can be qualified as effective in helping the elderly to stay at home for a prolonged time. Even more important than the formal help is the informal help. Recent measures such as the (in)dependence insurance somewhat blur the division between the formal and informal sector, so that there is a trend evolving from competition to cooperation between the two sectors.

Death/Bereavement

Universally, death is family related—it tends to bring families closer together, enhancing family ties at the moment one family bond, the marital system, is coming to an end. In Belgium two family-related issues are currently a focus of sociopolitical debate: avoidable death and the opposite, euthanasia. Both issues are to some extent family related.

In Belgium the overwhelming majority of persons do not die at home but in nursing homes or hospitals. After passing away, they usually are transferred to a funeral home. In most cases, the funeral itself consists of a religious ceremony attended by the immediate family and other relatives, friends, and neighbors. Lately, the so-called palliative nursing movement advocates that persons should have the option to die at home. In addition, palliative services are being developed in hospitals so that terminal patients are more likely to pass away in a more humane setting. An increase in persons dying at home is not yet visible in any statistic. In 2003 a bill legitimizing euthanasia was passed in Belgium. The provisions of that bill are person oriented rather than family oriented, with the relationship between patient and medical doctor at the core of the bill. Indirectly, though, in many cases family is very much involved. As to avoidable death, one particular form tends to become socially unacceptable—accidents, more particularly traffic accidents. Another form becoming more and more the focus of attention is suicide, in particular suicide by elderly men. The social response is suicide prevention. Compared with the rest of Europe, Belgium has a relatively high suicide rate.

Aging of the population and more particularly the creation of an important group of old elderly (very elderly) represent a rather new phenomenon. Belgian society has not yet been able to fully grasp the magnitude of this event, let alone come to terms with it. Up to now, it is stated in terms of a problematic issue rather than in terms of a challenge.

10. OTHER INSTITUTIONS: FAMILY POLICY

In Belgium, unlike in some other countries, family policy has been an issue in domestic policy ever since World War I. Family matters have been a legitimate issue in politics for a long time. Family occupies a central place in the sociopolitical debate and in parliament and is a central issue debated by the different political parties. In the long history of family policies, three major phases can be identified: (1) economic family enabling policy, (2) service building, and (3) family empowerment policy. Although these three phases occur sequentially, they do not follow each other and they do not replace each other. Each new dimension is added to the policy already in vogue. The family enabling policy consists of policies geared at income maintenance for the family. It was instrumental in supporting a particular type of family—the breadwinner family. The two main instruments in this policy are tax deductions (for the spouse as well as for the children) and child allowances. This policy is not geared toward helping the deserving poor. On the contrary, it is geared toward the blue-collar worker. Its aim is to *enable* him to provide for *his* family, that is, *his* wife and *his* children. A second feature of this policy is its demographic component. It can be characterized as a pronatalist policy. Some Western European countries, such as Belgium, paid a heavy toll in World War I, as shown by a reduction of the population. In the 1960s and 1970s, a new branch of family policy developed. In that period cabinet ministers holding the portfolio family emerged. Emphasis was given to establishing services for families. Two kinds of services can be identified: (1) educational (parent/partner oriented), and (2) care service (child/family oriented). Educational services offer information on contraceptives and family counseling services. Care services include providing childcare, for example, crèches and provisions offering family household help in case the wife/mother was unable to take care of the family, for instance, in the case of illness or another pregnancy. In short, these provisions were for part-time and partial family replacement. In contrast to the economic enabling policies, these new instruments were not in line with but were cross-cutting the natalistic demographic policy. The new policy was not geared toward men but focused on women. A third wave of family policy was developed in the 1980s and 1990s. *Time* became the central issue. Balancing family and work was at the core of this policy. This policy was not bipolar, that is, concerned only about family and work, but tripolar, concerned about family, work, and citizenship. Time for self-development was recognized as an essential factor of life. *Quality* became a central objective for which governmental authorities and the corporate world were held responsible. A striking feature of this third wave is that men were identified as constituting part of the problem. The "new man," the "new father," is an ideal. According to the new norms, there is a lot of room for improvement and change of behavior by fathers/husbands/partners—in fathering as well as in doing household tasks. Among the new elements introduced in family policy, parenting has become a central issue, as has care. Parenting and care are considered the core business of families. Three rather new elements are characteristic for this last period: (1) The number of actors in family policy is increasing. Next to government (national, regional), the corporate world is involved. The latter includes employers and their organizations and employees and their organizations—in short,

the so-called social partners. (2) A second element, family policy, is still heavily oriented to the able, productive section of the population. The unemployed, the nonactive part of the population, are not the focus of attention. (3) In contrast with the previous waves, the third wave of family policy recognizes the resilient power of families and their capacity to cope with problems. As a result, families are gaining power in dealing with other institutions such as schools (the education system), hospitals (the medical system), and the market sector (families in their capacity as consumers). Family empowerment has become a keystone of family policy.

The three elements constituting current family policy have a differentiated impact on family life. The impact of financial support to the family, in terms of tax relief and child allowances, has diminished over time on two accounts. First, their relative importance is diminishing. Second, but more important since these instruments are geared at the breadwinner family, they tend to lose their impact on the two-income/two-career family. In this respect, the term *family policy* is to be replaced by *families policies*. Actually, current policies recognize the plurality of family forms. The second type of instrument has resulted in the creation of a vast group of family professionals. In this respect, family has become recognized as an element with great potential to expand the labor market. Many measures relating to family therefore can be qualified as employment policies. In this sense, family policy has become families policies. The third wave of family policy establishes that families no longer are considered mere objects of policies but are also recognized as reactive elements, for example, as partners. They are recognized as being able to cope with social challenges, as posed by demographic changes (e.g., aging population) and new socioeconomic demands (such as adapting to the knowledge-based society).

CONCLUSION

Belgium, situated geographically and socially in the middle of the European Union, offers a schoolbook example of the European family, which is in the process of a profound change. Three processes of change can be identified as follows: (1) A dramatic change in family organization, from a command structure to a negotiation dynamic. The model family, a cultural (normative) concept, regulating the division of power and task allocation by gender and age is gradually being replaced by a structure emphasizing equity and equality. (2) A shift in the balance between the public and private domain shows that in many respects families are gaining power in society. The authorities (the political system), the market (the economic system), and the third sector (the sociocultural sector) are adapting to the changing family structure in terms of a growing acceptance and recognition, valuing different family structures (single-parent families, cohabitation, reconstructed families). (3) Last but not least are changes in demographic parameters (e.g., longevity) as well as in social parameters. The emergence of the knowledge society based on dramatic changes in the information and communication systems (social, medical, genetic) confront families with new challenges. In coping with these new challenges, the development of families in Europe tends to be characterized by convergence more than by divergence.

NOTES

1. Calculations by the author are based on data provided by the National Statistical Office (2002).

2. Based on statistics provided in paper presented at the XVIIIe Journées d'Etudes Juridiques Jean Dabin. Louvain-la-Neuve, March 13–14, 2003. See also Valenduc (2003).

REFERENCES

Audenaert, V. (2000). *Transities in de huishoudelijke situatie van ouderen.* Brussels: Centrum voor Bevolkings- en Gezinsstudies (CBGS).

Cliquet, R. (Ed.). (1996). *Gezinnen in de verandering.* Veranderende gezinnen. Brussels: CBGS.

Corijn, M. (1995). *De overgang naar volassenheid in Vlaanderen. Resultaten van het Nego V-onderzoek.* Brussels: CBGS.

Corijn, M. (1999). Ongehuwd samenwonen in Vlaanderen. *Bevolking en Gezin,* 28(2), 173–179.

de Bie, P., et al. (1968). *Het echtpaar. Een sociologische studie.* Antwerpen: Standaard Wetenschappelijke Uitgeverij.

de Grendele, H. (2002). *Meldingen kindermishandeling. Cliëntenregistratie bij de vertrouwenscentra.* Rapport 2002. Brussel: Kind en Gezin.

Dobbelaere, K. (Ed.). (2001). *Verloren zekerheid. De Belgen en hun waarden, overtuigingen en boudingen.* Lannoo: Tielt.

European Obervatory in Family National Policies. (1994). *Decentralisation and gearing the various policy levels to the private/public divide.* Proceedings of the workshop, Bordeaux, October 8–10, 1993. Brussels: Commission of the European Communities.

Het Kind in Vlaanderen 2002. (2003). Brussels, Belgium: Kinden Gezin.

Hu, Y., & Goldman, N. (1990). Mortality differentials by marital status. *Demography, 27*(2), 233–250.

Jacobs, T. S., De Maeyer, M., Back, M., & De Bruyn, S. (2000). Arbeidsverdeling, bij samenwonende koppels in België: Diversiteit, dynamiek en emancipatie. *Bevolking en Gezin, 29*(1), 33–58.

Lenaers, S., & Goffin, I. (2002). *Onderzoek naar de voedingssituatie van jonge kinderen.* Diepenbeek: Limburgs Universitair Centrum, SEIN.

Lodewijckx, E. (2001). *Huishoudens in België. Een ontsluiting van de rijksregistergegevens.* Brussels: CBGS.

Lodewijckx, E. (2002a). *Steeds meer Kinderen met oudere ouders.* Retrieved, March 3, 2002, from http://www.cbgs.be, Uit het onderzoek, Kinderen enjongeren.

Lodewijckx, E. (2002b). *Steeds minder Kinderen wonen bij een gehuwd paar.* Retrieved July 3, 2002, from http://www.cbgs.be, Uit het onderzoek, Kinderen enjongeren.

Lodewijckx, E., & Vernaille, N. (2003). Kinderen in hun gezinnen: Een sociodemografische schets. In B. Van Den Bergh et al. (Eds.), *Tienertijd. Communicatie, opvoeding en welzijn in context 10- tot 18-jarigen, ouders en leerkrachten bevraagd.* Leuven: Garant.

Maldague, J. (2003, March). *Statistiques relatives à la cohabitation légale.* Paper presented at XVIIIes Journées d'Etudes Juridiques Jean Dabin, Louvain-la-Neuve.

Moens, M. (2003, September). *Handelen onder druk. Tijd en tijdsdruk in Vlaanderen.* Paper presented at the 25th IATUR Conference on Time Use Research, Brussels.

Mortelmans, D. (2002). *De transformatie van een man in een vader. De gevolgen van een eerste kind op het leven van een man, in Vaders in soorten.* Tielt: Lannoo.

Mortelmans, D., Ottoy, W., & Verstreken, M. (2003). Een longitudinale kijk op de gender-verdeling van huishoudelijke taken. *Tijdschrift voor Sociologie, 24*(2/3), 237–259.

National Statistical Office. (2002). *Bevolking en Huishoudens. Huwelijken en Echtscheidingen in 2001.* Brussels: NIS.

National Statistical Office. (n.d.). http://www.statbel.fgov.be.

Steyers, K., & Reynaert, H. (2003). *Political recruitment and career of mayors in Belgium.* Paper presented at European Consortium for Political Research, Marburg.

Valenduc, C. (2003, March). *L'évolution du patrimoine des ménages.* Paper presented at XVIIIe Journées d'Etudes Juridiques Jean Dabin, Louvain-la-Neuve.

Van Dongen, W. (1993). Nieuwe krijtlijnen voor gezin, macht en maatschappij. Een geïntegreerde benadering. In B. Van Den Bergh et al. (Eds.), *Tienertijd. Communicatie, opvoeding en welzijn in context 10- tot 18-jarigen, ouders en leerkrachten bevraagd.* Leuven: Garant.

Van Dongen, W. (Ed.). (2001). *Beroepsleven en gezinsleven. Het combinatiemodel als motor voor een actieve welvaartsstaat?* Leuven: Garant.

Van Hove, T., & Matthijs, K. C. E. (2002, November). *The socio-demographic evolution of divorce and remarriage in Belgium.* Unpublished paper presented at a seminar titled Divorce in Cross-National Perspective: A European Research Network, Firenze.

Van Peer, C. (1993). Kinderen en echtscheiding. Verschillen in perceptie van de opvoedingscontext tussen kinderen in éénoudergezinnen en kinderen in andere gezinnen. In B. Van Den Bergh et al. (Eds.), *Tienertijd. Communicatie, opvoeding en welzijn in context 10- tot 18-jarigen, ouders en leerkrachten bevraagd* (pp. 298–363). Leuven: Garant.

Verhoeven, J., Devos, G., Stassen, K., & Warmues, V. (2003). *Ouders over scholen.* Antwerpen: Garant.

Vernaille, N., & Lodewijckx, E. (2001). *Kinderen en Huishoudens in België. Een tabellenboek gebaseerd op rijksregistergegevens van 31/12/1996.* Brussels, CBGS.

VRIND. (2003) Onderwijs en vorming, *VRIND 2003. Vlaamse Regionale Indicatoren* (pp. 121–162). Brussels, Belgium: VRIND Publicaties. Retreived from http://aps.Vlaanderen,be/statistick/publicaties/stat_Publicaties_vrind2003.htm

CHAPTER **11**

The Czech Family

Ivo Možný

Tomáš Katrňák

1. INTRODUCTION

The Czech Republic is a small European nation of about 10 million people with a long history of statehood. The natural demarcation of the state's borders by a line of mountain ranges explains why it is among the states with the historically oldest borders on the continent. Because of its central geographical position, the basin of the Czech Kingdom was the battleground for many European wars, including religious conflicts during the disintegration of medieval Europe. Imperial alliances never moved the borders of the Czech Kingdom, but repeatedly annexed the state as a whole; the Czech state was much too small to be partitioned like Poland.

History and Development
of the Czech Family

The Catholicization
of the Czech Family

Two foreign annexations were especially important for the development of the Czech family into its present form. The first relevant annexation occurred after the Westphalian Treaty (1648), when the predominately Protestant populace of the Czech Kingdom was annexed by the Catholic Habsburg monarchy. The property of the Protestant aristocracy was expropriated and they were forced to emigrate, and the country was forcibly re-Catholicized. For the next three centuries the Czech family was governed by canon family law. Its basic cultural layout was that of a Catholic family.

Since the beginning of modern history, the Czech family has exhibited all the characteristics of the Western European family type: a high degree of autonomy of the nuclear family in relation to the network of relatives, entry of both men and women into their first marriage fairly late in life, and the virtual impossibility of dissolving a marriage. Other applicable customs included those of primogeniture and the subsequent neolocality of the families of younger siblings. Men had to gain economic independence and women a dowry before they could marry, hence the high percentage of people who never married. Due to its geographical location, which caused early and dense urbanization, property ownership patterns in the Czech lands never included communal tilling of land. Great importance was placed on trade and crafts. Both of these factors enhanced the individualism of the European tradition, which also influenced family patterns.

In the late 18th century, the enlightened Emperor Joseph II issued his edict of religious tolerance (1781), allowing people to declare adherence to faiths other than the state-promoted Catholicism. He also enacted a new marriage act (1793) that allowed mixed marriages and gave Protestants and Jews the right to end their marriages by divorce. For Catholics, that is, the majority of the populace, the dissolution of marriage continued to be practically impossible.

Secularization

Developments leading to the loosening of family ties and secularization were enhanced in the 19th century by relatively early and rapid industrialization of the Czech lands, and the development of a strong industrial proletariat. As a result, the same problems appeared in the Czech lands as those that can be found in the historical sociology of the family in the Industrial Revolution.

After World War I, the Czech Kingdom ceased to exist by emancipating itself from the disintegrating Austrian-Hungarian Empire, and the Czechs and the Slovaks (and large German and Hungarian minorities) established a new democratic state together: the Czechoslovak Republic (1918). One of the first pieces of legislation discussed in the parliament of the newly created state was the family act. It allowed civil marriages, and thus gave Catholics the right to divorce. Furthermore, by recognizing civil marriages, a new family was established. During the long absence of men from home during the war, their wives gave birth to children fathered by other men. Their biological fathers had not

been allowed to marry the mothers of their children, even though they admitted paternity. At that time, about 100,000 couples were waiting for the opportunity to divorce (Klabouch, 1962). After the postwar situation stabilized, the divorce rate during the interwar period remained stable at a relatively low level. About 10% of marriages ended in divorce. A second demographic revolution had taken place, and the modal number of children per family became two.

The Communist Coup and Its Consequences

The annexation of Czechoslovakia to the Soviet Empire, which expanded into Europe after World War II, lasted almost the entire second half of the 20th century and had a profound influence on the Czech family. In the beginning, the Communist revolution (1948) regarded the institution of the family with disfavor; the Communist party, with its monopoly on power, considered it a competing loyalty. It waged an intensive propaganda campaign against the "selfishness of the bourgeois family," and considered the family historically outdated. It broke the power of the family economically by expropriating family property. The paternalistic state took on some of the family's traditional responsibilities: It promised state-built flats to all young families, built a network of nurseries and kindergartens where children could be left for the day from the age of 3 months and could be boarded during the week from 6 months. The state mobilized women into full-time employment in nationalized firms, built a network of workplace canteens in public sector companies where employees were served subsidized meals, and also supported collective leisure activities in a network of company hotels and recreational facilities.

Changes in the structure of ownership soon moved the Czech family closer to the East European family model in some respects. It became most apparent with the decreasing age at first marriage and birth of first child. The traditionally high marriage rates became even higher (unmarried persons had no chance to obtain a flat); people entered into marriage very early in life, and women became mothers at an earlier age. In the 1950s, the modal age at primiparas dropped to 22 years, and remained there until after the fall of the Communist regime in the late 1980s. The illusion of "eternal youth" that state paternalism offered to young couples by taking over some of their responsibilities was very attractive.

The offer of the "socialist way of life," however, soon proved deceptive; the paternalistic state was unable to keep its promises to the family in some fundamental respects. This was particularly true with regard to the notion of an inexpensive council flat for every family. The post-war housing shortage showed no signs of abatement, and in spite of large-scale construction of satellite housing estates, it became more and more difficult for young families to obtain a flat of their own. The allocation of flats became influenced by political and economic corruption and personal connections. With both spouses gainfully employed, the failing retail system was a major problem. It was necessary to stand in long queues even for staple foods such as meat and vegetables. Modern household appliances (refrigerators, washing machines, televisions) were only available through corruption and personal connections. The nurseries proved economically unsustainable because their rapidly spreading infections and high sickness rates caused mothers to spend a substantial amount of time away from work caring for sick children. Thus, the state had to bear the losses caused by both mothers' absences from work and keeping sick children's places in nurseries available. For that reason, practically all weekly boarding nurseries were discontinued, and, starting from the 1960s onward, the

number of places for children up to 3 years of age in day nurseries began to be significantly reduced.

The Crisis of State Paternalism

The crisis in the caretaking functions of state paternalism robbed families of all illusions, and made them mobilize their own reserves. With the absence of the traditional structures of economic capital in the Western model, the value of social capital networks came to the forefront. In times of trouble, the family proved to be the best *survival kit*. The unsuccessful attempt at an at least partial escape from the Soviet Empire in 1968 was rapidly suppressed by the Warsaw Pact invasion. The blatant puppet government, which was installed following the invasion, no longer needed to, nor was able to, cover up the gap between Communist ideology and reality. What the Czechs and Slovaks lived under in the Czechoslovak Socialist Republic in the 1970s and 1980s was officially called "really existing socialism." The regime's attitude toward the family had changed. The family was now supported, because family values carried with them a retreat from the inadequate public political space to the private sphere. An emphasis on collective nurseries was replaced with an extension of the maternity leave period and relatively generous child benefits. In the politically frustrated population, these benefits stimulated a significant increase in the birth rate in the 1970s, with which Czech society countered trends in Western European countries.

The Communist rhetoric was consistently collectivistic. Its collectivity was not, however, experienced in the same manner as that of the collectivity of the family. It was the collectivity of the system, of socialist society, of the party, of work co-ops and youth groups. In reality the political system was individualistic; "false collectiveness" was fabricated in the media and in all that was uttered in public spaces. The expediency of that construction became increasingly evident, as did its hidden aim of paralyzing the possibility of spontaneous collective action.

With the total occupation of the public semantic space, it was not possible for any political discourse to develop. Collective political action was impossible. In spite of that, as the decades passed and the regime aged, a strangely ambiguous situation crystallized in Czech society. There was a shift in the balance of power: from a situation in which the world had to defend itself against a sovereign system imbued with brutal power to a situation in which the weakened system found it more and more difficult to fend off the world. The atomized society spontaneously restructured itself into discrete egalitarian family networks on one hand, and hierarchical networks of personal connections and corruption on the other. A special anti-establishment collectivity began to emerge, in which the family played a very important role. One could sum up the 40-year history of socialism in the Czech lands by concluding that the socialist state started by expropriating the roles and functions of the family, but was ultimately colonized by it.

Thus, the false representation of reality in the rhetoric of the Communist party–controlled press proved to be doubly false: First, while collectivistic, it in fact manipulated people toward individualism. Second, the system was unable to function without the support of social capital, which is necessary to generate collectivity—albeit collectivity of a completely different order, in which the family played a key role.

Return to the Western Family Model

The opportunity to capitalize on the results of economic activity was returned to the Czech family by the political coup and economic transformation of the 1990s. Small businesses in the retail and service sectors were privatized; some were given back to the descendants of the original owners. Real estate was also restituted. It was again possible to start, or engage in, private business. In 1992, the peaceful division of the Czechoslovak Republic into two democratic states—the Slovak Republic and the Czech Republic—took place. The Czechs thus returned to the historical boundaries of the Czech Kingdom. With the return of a market economy and the restitution of private property, the Czech family quickly returned to the Western family model. However, it still exhibits the characteristics of the institutional dependence caused by a half-century with little private ownership of the means of production and a command rather than a market economy.

2. PAIRING UP AND LIVING TOGETHER

The first phenomenon to reassume the West European model was the pattern of pairing up. The opportunity cost of early parenthood rose sharply with the opening up of society and the economy. It was again possible to travel abroad or start a business, and university education was more accessible. After the change in the political regime, the decision to get married and have a family lost its uniqueness as one of the very few opportunities to make an authentic free decision. The boom in consumption opportunities was not accompanied by an adequate increase in purchasing power, and consumption aspirations began to markedly exceed a realistic level. Young people began to postpone marriage and parenthood, and the age of primiparas and age at first marriage began to shift closer to the historically traditional age in the Czech lands. This process took place throughout the 1990s and is continuing in the first decade of the 21st century. It seems that large numbers of people who postponed marriage are entering into it in their 30s.

Decrease in Marriage Rates and Unmarried Cohabitation

Czech society in the entire second half of the 20th century was characterized by very high marriage rates. The 2001 census found that among 55 to 60-year-olds, only 5.1% of men and 2.8% of women had never married. Girls married around the age of 20, and men only 2 or 3 years later. After the change of political regime, however, there was a sharp drop in the rate of first marriages. While in 1990 the marriage rate among men was 91.1%, in 2001 it was only 65.4%; the marriage rate among women fell from 96.2% to 72.3% during the same period.

The decrease was mainly the result of a marked drop in marriage rates among the youngest age-groups; the probability of marriage among people less than 25 years of age dropped by more than 50% in the first decade after the change of political regime. Marriages among teenagers, which had been quite common (in 1990 almost 30% of brides and 10% of bridegrooms were under the age of 20), have all but disappeared. Nowadays only 1% of bridegrooms and less than 6% of brides are not yet 20 years old at the time of their first marriage. The marriage rate among older age-groups did not increase even in the late 1990s; therefore, if the 2001 marriage rate remains constant, in the future 35% of men and 28% of women at the age of 50 will have never married (Paloncyová, 2003).

The aforementioned statistical extrapolation should be read with caution, as it contains hidden contradictions. On one hand, one should bear in mind that it was calculated at the time of a rapid increase in age at first marriage. Very young brides from the early 1990s are already married and thus do not increase the first marriage rates, while slightly older women are postponing marriage. If those postponed marriages take place before the end of the first decade of the 21st century, it can be expected that marriage rates will increase somewhat. Thus a slight increase in marriage rates in the 25 to 30 age range since 2001 can be predicted.

Marriage Continues to Enjoy High Status for Czechs

Research into attitudes among representative samples of the population has repeatedly shown that a considerable majority of the younger generation consider married life the most suitable type of family. About 80% of young men and women from the cohort of adults under the age of 30 agree with the statement that "people who want to have children should get married" (Hamplová & Pikálková, 2002). Although we cannot assume that marriages postponed in the 1990s until later in life would bring about a return to an extremely high marriage rate, a significant number of men and women from that generation will enter into at least one marriage.

This trend will clash with the other growing trend toward unmarried cohabitation—and gradual change in its character. In the 1980s, the setting up of a family proceeded in the following sequence: (1) pairing up, (2) sexual intercourse, (3) if it were a long-term relationship, a sporadic and gradually decreasing use of contraception, (4) unmarried cohabitation if the housing shortage allowed, (5) conception of a child, and (6) when the woman found that she was expecting, the wedding would follow. The traditional notion that a pregnancy can be legitimized by marriage was still very strong. Nine out of 10 children were born to parents within wedlock, but one-half of first children were born within 8 months after the wedding, that is, were conceived before the wedding day. As evidenced by the high marriage rate, unmarried cohabitation was generally considered a "test marriage." In the early 1980s, about one-third of engaged couples lived together before getting married, and the average premarriage cohabitation period lasted

12 months. This phenomenon was more frequent in larger rather than in smaller cities, and its frequency was negatively correlated with the socioeconomic status of the couple (Možný, 1987; Možný & Rabušic, 1992).

The sequence of steps leading to the setting up of a family and the character of cohabitation began to change in the early 1990s. The need to legitimize births through marriage has decreased, and the number of pregnant brides has dropped by one-fifth in the last 10 years. Unmarried cohabitation is largely accepted by the general public, and, in demographic surveys, three-fourths of the population aged 18 to 65 say that it is makes sense for people who want to marry to cohabit first. Eight out of 10 young people under the age of 30 believe that it is acceptable for two people to cohabit, even if they are not planning to marry each other.

Being tolerant of others is one issue, but one's own life project is a different matter all together. As a personal choice, cohabitation is not considered the best option by even the youngest generation: Only one in 10 unmarried respondents hold that he or she wants to have that type of relationship, and over 80% of cohabiting individuals maintain that they plan to marry their partner at some time in the future. The 2001 census found that in the 25 to 29 age range, 40.4% of men and 59.5% of women were married (and 4.4% and 7.8% of men and women, respectively, were divorced). By the age of 28, less than 20% of women had never married. Surveys have shown that about one-third of unmarried women of that age have no steady partner, and that about one-third of those who do have a steady partner nevertheless do not cohabit (Hamplová & Pikálková, 2002).

The Housing Situation

Independent living is still outside the realm of possibility for many individuals and couples. In the 2001 census it was found that

780,000 Czech families, that is, one in five, live in the same household (in the same flat or house) as their parents, relatives, or entirely unrelated persons. For over one-half of these, this arrangement is not due to personal choice. The opportunity for partners to cohabit is heavily influenced by the possibility of securing independent accommodation. For many of the younger generation, cohabitation, as a "test marriage," is a precondition for marriage and setting up a family. Access to independent accommodation is an important precondition for entering into marriage, preceded only by economic independence. Age and independent accommodation are, of course, prerequisites for having a baby (Kuchařová, Nedomová, & Zamykalová, 1999).

In addition to wider life opportunities, another factor that keeps young people from setting up stable partnerships and households is the housing shortage, which became even more acute after the fall of the old regime. Securing independent accommodation no longer depends on the allocation of state-built flats, or on building a house oneself. Flats have become a commodity, and their availability is limited by the market. While price regulation of construction materials and labor has been abolished, rent has remained regulated. The result has been a sharp decrease in capital investment in residential housing. With fewer than two flats built per 1,000 inhabitants in the 1990s, the Czech Republic is among European countries with the fewest flats built per capita. Because demand outstrips supply, the prices of flats and houses have risen even beyond the means of young people from the professional classes. Banks secure mortgages with guarantees that young people cannot offer, and local council housing projects have become very limited. Investment in housing only began to grow after 2001 when, with Czech accession to the EU, people began to view property as a good investment. That, of course, prompted further increases in the cost of housing for those who wanted to buy or rent flats and houses, not as an investment, but as a place to live.

For many years to come, the housing shortage will remain one of the factors limiting cohabitation and the setting up of households. It will also play a negative role in the marriage rates and birthrates among those from the generation of Czechs who would have normally been setting up a household and a family at the time of the economic and political transformation that followed the collapse of the Communist system in 1989.

3. FERTILITY: CHANGES IN REPRODUCTIVE BEHAVIOR AND VALUES

The Czech population, along with populations in other East and Central European societies, underwent a second demographic transition about one generation later than their Western counterparts. In Western countries, modified family behavior patterns began to appear in women born in 1950 and later; in Eastern Europe these modified family behavior patterns began to emerge in women born in 1970 and later.

While in Western countries new values, norms, and attitudes were developed during periods of social stability, in post-Communist countries these occurred during periods of profound economic and social transformations. It is not clear whether groups exhibiting the same formal demographic parameters are also identical in their value orientations; they may in fact represent different cognitive processes and responses to different variables. It may not be possible to make more certain interpretations for several more years (Rychtaříková, 2002, p. 125).

Research on the younger generation's values and priorities has shown to date a markedly traditional orientation in their pairing-up patterns. For both men and women, the most demanded characteristic in their ideal life partner is a good attitude to children, followed by "sense of family life," "responsibility and honesty," "a good upbringing," and "tolerance." The same values were ranked highest by both men and women. Individualization and competitiveness in particular appear near the bottom half of the list, and are traditionally gender differentiated: Women more often reported that they expect decisiveness from men with regard to career success, ambition, and good financial and material conditions, while men traditionally reported that they expect women to be good-looking (Kuchařová et al., 1999; Hamplová & Pikálková, 2002).

Postponing Parenthood, Decreasing Birthrates, and the Rise in Illegitimate Births

Trends in the birthrate indicate a possible change in attitudes and expectations. In the 1970s, when the birthrates plummeted in most European countries, the Czech Republic experienced a major baby boom. The Czech family, shaken by the 1968 Warsaw Pact invasion by six armored divisions and the subsequent occupation of the country, was, paradoxically, strengthened. People retreated into the privacy of their own homes and had children. The large cohort of women, those born during the post–World War II baby boom, were at an age when they were deciding whether to have their second or third baby. This contributed to the marked increase in birthrates. The probirth measures, introduced by the reformist government of "socialism with a human face" in the late 1960s, also played a role. Experts estimate that about 500,000 more children than usual were born in about an 8-year period of increased natality—an increase from the usual 140,000 babies born annually to over 190,000.

The strong profamily climate in the 1970s can also be documented by the low ratio of children born out of wedlock. When birthrates peaked between 1974 and 1975, only 4.4% of babies were born to unmarried women. It was probably the historically lowest level of illegitimacy ever in the Czech lands—Bohemia and Moravia. There are no indications that this might be repeated in the foreseeable future.

Change in Reproductive Strategies Brought About Change in the Political Regime

The generation that began establishing families after the turn of the century was very large. In the early 1980s, families having three or more children became scarce, and Czech families have been having fewer and fewer children ever since. However, it was expected that the total numbers of births would increase, even against a declining total birthrate, when girls from the large generation born in the mid-1970s reached childbearing age. That did not occur.

After the change of regime, the birthrate in the Czech Republic first dropped sharply, but in the mid-1990s it stabilized at about 90,000 births annually (instead of the usual 120,000). The most dramatic decrease—about three-quarters—was recorded among teenage mothers. The number of mothers in their 20s, who until then were responsible for about 80% of births, also dropped significantly. Additionally, the proportion of 30-year-olds who have not had a child tripled in the 1990s (from 6% to 18%), and it is still growing.

The political changes in 1989 brought about a change in life strategies. This change has also significantly affected reproductive strategies. Two changes have been documented, and a third is surmised. First and foremost, Czech families, just like their Western European counterparts a generation earlier, generally have one rather than two children, and the number of large families is dwindling. Second, Czech men and women set up a family much later now than they did under the previous political regime. The period of political "normalization" following the Soviet invasion, when Czech women gave birth to their firstborns most frequently at 21, has ended. In that period Czechs had the second youngest primiparas in Europe, preceded only by Turkish women. In the early 1990s, the Czechs began to postpone the birth of their firstborns, and the average age of primiparas grew in the first decade after the revolution by 2.5 years, reaching 24.9 in the year 2000.

In comparison with other European countries, Czech women still become mothers at a very young age. However, a large proportion of the generation born around 1975, who will turn 30 around the year 2005, have yet to give birth to their first child. As has been demonstrated with regard to marriage rates, postponed births, just like postponed marriages, may still be realized in the second half of the first decade of this century.

It would not be safe to link the expected projections on birthrates to marriage rates. An increasing number of young couples, or young women, do not equate parenthood with marriage. Thus, a marked change is a steep increase in the percentage of children born out of wedlock. Between 1989 and 2002, the proportion of children born out of wedlock tripled; since 1975 it has increased fivefold. In the year 2002, 25% of children were born to unmarried mothers (see Figure 11.1).

Social Stratification of Proportion of Children Born out of Wedlock

The distribution of children born out of wedlock is not uniform across all age-groups. The highest incidence is among teenage mothers. While about two-thirds of children born to mothers under 20 are born out of wedlock, less than one-seventh of children

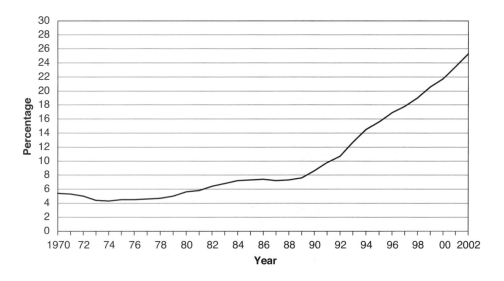

Figure 11.1 Proportion of Live Births Outside of Wedlock in the Czech Republic (1970–2002)
SOURCE: *Populační vývoj Ceskí republiky 2001* (2002).

born to mothers between 25 and 30 are illegitimate. But because of the marked drop in the birthrate among teenagers, the total number of illegitimate children born to women from that age-group is actually smaller than those born to mothers over the age of 30. Children born out of wedlock are not only those born to women who have never been married. One-fourth of the births are to women who had previously been married and are now divorced. As a result, 40% of children born out of wedlock in the Czech Republic are not first children.

This trend has been gathering strength. In the 1990s the number of third or later children born in wedlock has dropped by 45%, while the number of third and subsequent children born out of wedlock has increased by 32%. Almost one-fifth of illegitimate children are now their mothers' third or fourth child.

The explanation for this age stratification is social rather than demographic. The ratio of children born to unmarried mothers largely depends on their education, and that trend became increasingly prominent during the 1990s. In the Czech Republic, 70% of children born to mothers with elementary education only are born out of wedlock. The ratio of illegitimate children decreases with each subsequent level of formal education obtained, and only 11% of children born to mothers with a university degree are illegitimate (see Figure 11.2).

In the Czech Republic, having children out of wedlock is not an expression of a liberal spirit. If it were, it would be positively correlated with increasing education, and not the opposite. Instead, it is linked to lower socioeconomic status and less cultural capital. This seems to be corroborated by the fact that the highest ratios of unmarried mothers are not found in university centers and large cities but in economically backward border regions with a high proportion of unskilled jobs in the local economy, as well as a high level of unemployment, racial crimes, and suicides, in addition to other evidence of social disorder.

The right to unmarried motherhood is one of the important values in liberal discourse in the Czech Republic. Birth statistics, however,

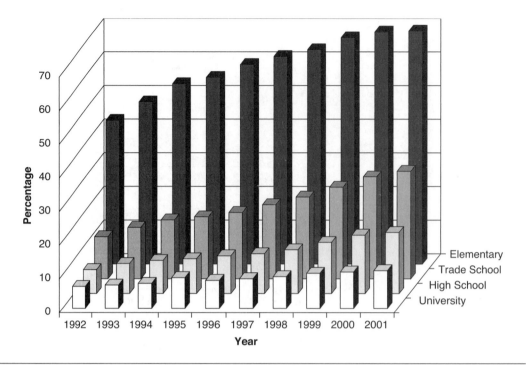

Figure 11.2   Proportion of First Children Born out of Wedlock in the Czech Republic, According to Mother's Education

SOURCE: *Pohyb obyvatelstva* 1992–2001. ČSÚ, Praha 1991–2001.

show that educated women, who support and contribute to that discourse, do not use that right themselves. Unmarried motherhood is more attractive for the less educated populations who encounter it in its degenerated form in the mass media, such as tabloids and television.

Increase in the Number of Single People, One-Member Households, and Single-Parent Families

The third emerging change is the formation of a socially important group of childless single people. This group includes divorced men, who may or may not have already fathered a child but do not live in the same household with him or her, and women who may or may not have been married, but have children.

The last five Czech national censuses have shown a continuous decrease in the number of family households (i.e., households comprising a couple, with or without children). Such households represented three-quarters of all Czech households in the mid-20th century, but now represent only 55%. On the other hand, there has been a dynamic growth in the number of one-member households, which increased from 16% to 30% over the same period. The number of single-parent households (a single parent living with at least one child) has risen from 8% to 14% (see Figure 11.3).

A further inspection of the age and gender structure of one-member households shows it as an important new trend in family behavior. In the Czech Republic, one-member households were traditionally predominately those of widows. Although life expectancy has

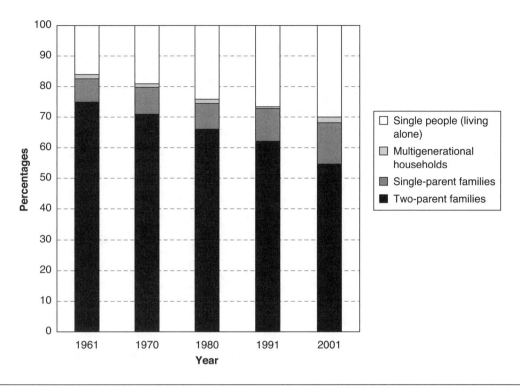

Figure 11.3   The Structure of Families and Households in the Czech Republic (1961–2001)

SOURCE: *Sčítání lidu* (2002).

increased significantly (particularly in the past 10 years, and particularly for women), the number of widows has remained constant. The increase in the number of one-member households is due to the growing cohort of young people living alone. Their contribution to the total number of one-member households has tripled over the period monitored, and the raw number has increased sevenfold. This group is primarily composed of young men, either bachelors or divorcés: Only 16% of women who live alone are under the age of 35, compared with 31% for men. Forty-three percent of women who live alone are aged 70 or older, compared with only 13% of men.

Because young women living on their own very often have a child (or children), they are not one-member households; households consisting of a child (or children) and one parent are included in Czech statistics as single-parent families or households. Over the past decade, this has been one of the fastest-growing types of household. Currently about 15% of the population of the Czech Republic are members of single-parent families. Eighty-five percent of such families are headed by a woman, most frequently a divorcée. More single-parent families than any other type of family live in a flat with another family, usually with grandparents. Mothers provide assistance to their daughters who have become single parents, and who are encountering financial and housing problems, by sharing their home and income with them. Sometimes the grandmothers themselves are also divorced, thus creating a marginal but growing subculture of families managed by women for several generations. Women who have grown up and been socialized in such families often tend to set up the same kind of families themselves. The younger women living in such households often have a partner who does not live with them in the same household.

This pattern of family relationships is the second most frequent Czech version of the living apart together (LAT) relationship, which is not due to personal choice, but rather to the housing shortage. It is particularly characteristic for young and middle-age people. Sporadic surveys indicate that the number of these families is on the increase. The greatest proportion of Czech LAT relationships is still made up of elderly couples and pensioners. In these cases, the two partners live in their own homes, which they want to maintain, so that in the event that the relationship breaks up, they would have a place to live.

In spite of its growing frequency, the single-parent family is still viewed as a less than ideal solution. Although it may enhance the variety of Czech family life, it remains a marginal and often temporary solution for the majority of the population. The situation is rather different for Roma families.

Czech Roma Families

The history of the 20th century is responsible for the fact that the Czech state—distinctly multinational and multicultural in character at the time when the Czechoslovak Republic was established in 1918—became quite a homogeneous nation with regard to ethnicity, culture, and nationality. First the Germans living along the borders with Germany waged a successful campaign for the unification of these territories with Adolf Hitler's Third Reich in 1938. The remaining Czech territory was occupied by Hitler's troops in 1939, and subsequently became a protectorate of the Reich. Slovakia set itself up as an independent state, and lost its territories settled by the Hungarians. Finally, the large Jewish minority in the Czech lands and in Slovakia was exterminated by the Germans. After the collapse of Nazi rule, the Czechs, whose state had been reestablished within its original borders, expelled the German minority with the assistance of the victorious Allies (1945–1946). After the fall of the Communist regime, the Czechs peacefully parted ways with the Slovaks (1992). Virtually all the families that remained in the territory of the Czech Republic were Czech families.

The only significant exception was Roma families. The size of the Roma community in the Czech Republic is not large. Experts estimate that there are about 250,000 Roma in the country (2.5% of the total population); this is several times less than in neighboring Slovakia, Hungary, or Romania. However, even the Roma community has not been in the Czech Republic very long: Before World War II, there were only about 6,000 to 9,000, usually traveling, Roma in the Czech Republic. Most of them, however, were killed in the Holocaust. Thus, the present Roma are mostly second- or third-generation immigrants.

Roma families differ markedly from the Czech majority, although they are beginning to approximate the majority. Whereas the Czechs have already undergone their second demographic transition, the Roma are still undergoing their first. Extensive networks of relatives, and a strong influence of patriarchs and matriarchs, are still very much alive in Czech Roma families today. The cultural pattern for setting up a family tolerates, and even presupposes, the beginning of the sexual life 2 or 3 years before it is common among the majority population. For the Roma, sexual intercourse before the age of consent (15 years) is not culturally illegitimate—hence it is neither reported nor prosecuted. The use of contraceptives is much more limited than among the majority Czech population, and Roma mothers are therefore markedly younger. Compared with other Central and Eastern European countries with major Roma populations (Romania, Hungary, Bulgaria, Slovakia), the number of Roma families with only two or fewer children in the Czech Republic is relatively high (almost one-half of all households), and there are almost twice as many childless Roma families as in the other countries. On one hand, this is the result of higher life expectancy, and hence a greater relative number of older Roma in the Czech Republic, and a higher share of young households that have assumed the same reproductive strategies as the majority population. The lower birthrate is also due to substantially lower numbers of married teenage Roma (about 15% in the Czech Republic compared with 40% to 50% in other countries).

However, that is a relatively recent development:

> [M]arried Roma women with children had on average 5 children by the end of their reproductive age (in the 45 to 49 age group), while the corresponding figure for the Czech women was only 2.17 children. In poorer Roma settlements in Slovakia (which was part of common state of Czechoslovakia for the decisive part of their reproductive years) the number of children per family reaches 7.8. (*The Roma*, 2002, p. 25)

Younger Czech Roma exhibit the majority trend toward unmarried partnerships. They are voluntarily childless less often than the majority Czech population. In the Czech Republic 80% of first children born to mothers with basic education are illegitimate. These mothers are largely Roma women.

The large number of Roma women with only basic education is due to the traditionally low value attached to formal education for children (and girls in particular) in traditionally oral Roma culture, but also due to mistakes in educational policies, and the prejudices of the majority population

in the Czech Republic. According to the Organisation for Security and Co-operation in Europe (OSCE), the Czech government reports that "approximately three-fourths of Roma children attend special schools for children with minor mental defects, and more than 50% (some estimates are close to three-fourths) of all pupils attending special schools are Roma children" (Report, 2002, p. 77). The high ratio of Roma children in schools that provide only basic education is attributable both to prejudices of Czech teachers who diagnose cultural differences as mental deficiency and to Roma mothers' belief that a school with lower demands and a larger number of Roma children is better for their offspring. This belief is further strengthened by prejudices of the majority population that the Roma fail vis-à-vis more sophisticated career aspirations, not because they are ill-prepared to cope with them, but because they are Roma.

These young basic school leavers exhibit high drop-out rates in their further vocational education, and up to 80% of them are long-term unemployed. They form street gangs as teenagers and live on petty crime, and, more recently, have also been active in the drug culture and prostitution. Girls often become pregnant early in life and are uncertain about the father of their child; thus, the cycle of social disorganization repeats itself. This cycle, which is found most among new immigrants from the East, greatly affects and disrupts the social patterns of the Roma who have been settled in the Czech Republic for several generations and built up a way of life compatible with the majority population. In spite of major efforts on the part of the authorities and social workers supported by international organizations, the Roma's progress has been both slow and uncertain. If given intensive social assistance, they often fall into the trap of dependency.

Compared with the Roma from comparable post-Communist countries, the Czech

Roma enjoy the highest standard of living and longest life expectancy. They have their own political representation and publish their own magazine written partly in Romany (far from all Roma can speak their language). In the Czech Republic there are no usual squalid Roma settlements; most of the Roma are more or less dispersed in urban areas, where they form only relatively small neighborhoods. Compared with the majority population, however, they have a markedly lower standard of living, the highest unemployment, the least formal education, the highest rate of incarceration, and the shortest life expectancy. At present they represent the greatest social problem for society.

4 & 5. GENDER ROLES, MARRIAGE AND FAMILY, AND THE ECONOMY

The Universal Employment of Women

The ground plan of the Czech family's social habitus is defined by the fact that for more than three generations nearly all Czech women have been employed, mostly on a full-time basis. Since the mid-20th century, almost one-half of the Czech economy has been dependent on the female labor force. This fact has generally been taken for granted, and has influenced Czech lifestyles for decades.

The roots of the present situation go back to the 1950s when women were mobilized to join the workforce through massive political bullying. When the Communist party seized power in 1948, it set the universal employment of women as an important party doctrine. This policy was not only based on the ideology that a person's dignity rests on being employed, but also on the wish to mobilize the economic resources of the Communist block in Stalin's preparation for a possible third world war. Last but not least, it was part of the effort to weaken the social

importance of the family, which was viewed as a competing loyalty to the party.

The result of intensive political pressures was that very soon up to 97% of women were employed for almost the entire period of their adult economic life. Many women responded to the radical opening of the labor sector with enthusiasm because it presented the opportunity to gain higher qualifications, to expand social contacts, and to earn the feeling of autonomy and self-confidence. At that time, the majority of women entered employment without professional training, which was reflected in the types of jobs they took. However, they soon acquired the necessary skills and some developed careers.

The vast majority, however, stayed in simple and poorly paid jobs. At the same time, new acute problems emerged in their homes. Few husbands were ready to shoulder a significant proportion of the housework and to move away from existing patriarchal roles. As a result, quite a few gainfully employed women and mothers began to consider themselves victims of fraud: Their jobs, instead of liberating them, created a double burden for them. They found it nearly impossible to reconcile their responsibilities at home and in the workplace. This overburdening, combined with their disgust at ideological bullying and the fact that it was impossible to open a public discussion about their problems, often led them to romantic daydreaming about the stress-free lives of housewives in the "good old days" (Stinbauerová & Helus, 2002).

Women of that generation are still alive and, through their daughters and granddaughters, exert a lot of influence over contemporary Czech society. Studies conducted after the 1989 revolution and change of regime confirmed the existence of the residual effects of that process among women of all generations. In practice, however, Czech women have refused to give up the autonomy gained through employment, even though they are no longer forced to enter employment by ideological pressures.

The generations of women that have entered society from the 1960s onward have gradually been better qualified, and, starting from the 1970s, equally represented at universities. From the 1960s onward, women made up more than 50% of graduates from medical and law schools, and far outnumbered men at teacher-training colleges. They remained a minority at technological universities, which attracted significantly fewer women than men.

Unemployment did not emerge as a social phenomenon in the Czech Republic until the mid-1990s. Because it had not exceeded 3% for half a century, and was not even reported during the communist government, the economically active population had no prior experience with this phenomenon. In the second half of the 1990s, unemployment in the Czech Republic gradually grew until it leveled off at 10%. The proportion of women in the unemployment figures fluctuates around 55%. Older women, who are largely unskilled, women returning from maternity leave, and women from rural areas where it is difficult to find work near home compose a disproportionately large share of the unemployed. In such circumstances it makes more financial sense to collect unemployment benefits and look after young children than to commute to work (Sirovátka, 1997).

Working Mothers

The situation in Czech families is characterized by the fact that Czech women have held full-time jobs for three generations, even while they were caring for small children. Maternity leave is guaranteed by legislation in the Czech Republic. It is one of the longest maternity leaves in Europe, having been repeatedly extended since the mid-1970s. Since 1993, every woman with a child is entitled to a family allowance of 69% of her salary for the first 6 months after childbirth, and 1.1 times the official minimum for subsistence in the form of maternity social benefits for another 3.5 years. Furthermore, her employer is obliged to allow her to return to her previous position at any time during the first 3 years.

Surveys of young women show that most of them plan to stay home with their children until they are 6 years old (Kuchařová et al., 1999). However, a substantial number do not even make use of the full legally guaranteed maternity leave, but return to employment before their youngest child reaches the age of 4. Two years after a birth, one-third of mothers have returned to employment. Only one-fourth of mothers take advantage of the full 4 years legal maternity leave (Páloncyová, 2002). Mothers usually return to work full time because there are not enough part-time jobs on the labor market. Furthermore, their original employers are not required to consent to shorter working hours when mothers return to the positions reserved for them. Returning to work, whether full time or part time, entails an immediate end to maternity and social benefits.

Over 80% of economically active women in the Czech Republic work full time, that is, the legal standard of 42.5 hours a week, and 3% hold a second job. In comparison with many member countries of the Organisation for Economic Co-operation and Development (OECD), part-time employment is exceptional in the Czech Republic (only 60% of women in the United States, 20% in Germany, and 10% in Denmark work more than 40 hours a week). Only 1% of women of an economically active age are housewives in the classical sense on a permanent basis. About 8% of the female workforce is in the home on a temporary basis (Fischlová, 2002).

Surveys have repeatedly shown that being "just a housewife" is rejected in the Czech Republic as counter to the need for independence. At the same time, however, Czech women declare that looking after children is a higher priority for them than a professional career. That may also be the reason why they largely accept that men hold higher positions in the workplace and also receive better salaries. They are not, however, willing to forsake holding a job for the benefit of their husbands' careers (Stinbauerová & Helus, 2002).

Pay Discrimination Against Women

The Czech Republic applies all laws passed in the EU to protect women against discrimination in the workplace. In areas where local legislation is given precedence, Czech laws generally tend to be stricter than most European laws.

Real income analyses nevertheless indicate that women are clearly undervalued in the workforce. The extent of this undervaluing in the Czech Republic is similar to that in other EU countries. The coefficient for the macroeconomic difference in pay is 86.2 (the ratio of women in employment to the ratio of salaries drawn by women to the total). This would have ranked the Czech Republic the fifth best among the fifteen EU countries in the second half of the 1990s.

Throughout the 1990s, women's average salaries were between 77% and 73% of the average for men, and changes in the extent of the pay differential mirrored fluctuations in economic prosperity. In the Czech Republic, income inequality is to a large extent the heritage of the calculated control of salaries and employment rates during the period of central planning. Very low salaries were set in sectors that could easily employ women, or that were considered economically inferior (light industry, education, healthcare, and even agriculture, banking, and the court system). This was intended to discourage the entry of men, who were needed in sectors where it would be more difficult for them to be substituted for by women. The conservative communist regime was able to accept a female doctor, but not a female engineer. Students at law schools were mostly women because the regime did not hold law in high esteem. The demand for legal services in the new open society soon rectified lawyers' fees and salaries; however, the work of teachers and physicians in hospitals, which remains in the public sector, continues to be undervalued relative to other countries.

In the national economy as a whole, the greatest pay gap is at the expense of women from the middle generation, and the smallest pay gap is among the youngest working generation. Higher education pays off for men more than for women: The average income of a male university graduate in 2000 was 2.43 times that of a worker with elementary education only; the same ratio for women was 1 to 2.08. A female university graduate's average salary before tax was only 65% of that of her male counterpart. This is to a large extent due to the continuing high numbers of female graduates in education and healthcare, and also to the huge differences in salaries between men and women in upper and top management.

Some factors also indicate that higher average salaries paid to men reflect the higher value of the work they do. These factors primarily include the higher percentage of men in more demanding and highly skilled professions, the fact that men work overtime more frequently and generally log more working hours, women's career breaks and absences from work due to childcare (maternity leave, caring for their children when ill, paid and unpaid leave), and women's higher share in family and household duties as compared with men. The consequence of this, in the Czech Republic and elsewhere, is a lower accumulation of expertise and less stable professional careers among women (Fischlová, 2002). However, Czech women, like women in other OECD countries, are continually moving closer to the male model of economic activity.

When changes in the economic and political system in the early 1990s brought about opportunities to start private businesses, Czech women, long accustomed to economic autonomy, quickly grasped them. The ratio of female to male entrepreneurs shows a predominance of the latter (the ratio of self-employed women to men is 1 to 6; 2% of women are self-employed, as compared with 13% of men, and 2.2% of female business owners employ other people, as compared with 5.8% of male business owners (*Pohyb obyvatelstva*, 1992–2001). The figures for men and women are, however, not more disparate than in other EU countries, which have a long uninterrupted tradition of free enterprise, and the gap is narrowing.

Gender-Based Division of Housework and Childcare

Although no one in the Czech Republic remembers anything other than the dual-income family model and universal employment of women, the complementary model of male and female roles has remained intact, and about two-thirds of the population subscribes to it. It is not, however, the only model. Images of family models have gradually diversified over the last 50 years, but it was only possible to articulate different models and engage in public discourse on them since last decade's reestablishment of an open society. In particular, women with higher education, for whom the male model of economic activity is a matter of course, seek family models that entail an equal distribution of childcare and housework between both spouses.

Within mainstream social consciousness, Czech men do consider female aspirations to professional fulfillment and social engagement as fully legitimate. Men admit that women have the capability, aptitude, and skills to be successful in their professional and public lives. At the same time, however, Czech men do not depart much from expectations of women as traditional housewives and mothers. On the other hand, despite being quite vocal in expressing their interest in being liberated from the bonds of family responsibilities, women defend their irreplaceable position in the family. Over one-half of women respondents in demoscopic surveys say that looking after the family is the woman's job; the number of men holding the same opinion is not substantially higher. Over three-quarters of women believe that women care more about their family and children than do men, and two-thirds of men agree with them.

Sociological research into the real division of housework and childcare show that in the majority of Czech households, routine chores are done by women. Such chores are primarily the man's domain only in exceptional cases. In this respect, the Czech Republic resembles countries such as Germany and England. The proportion of Czech households where housework and childcare are equally shared is slightly higher than in other post-Communist countries, but substantially lower than in countries such as the Netherlands (Krížková, 1999). On the other hand, in Czech families in which the family budget is not managed by both spouses (about a third of households), it is the woman who controls the finances. It is exceptional that this is the man's role. In a third of Czech households, it is also the woman who completes the income tax returns (in another third they are completed by the man, and in the remaining third they are completed either by both spouses or neither) (Fischlová, 2002).

6. STRESSES, VIOLENCE, AND CONFLICT IN THE FAMILY

As in all developed societies, no form of violence within the family is legitimate in Czech society. However, as everyone knows, it does occur. As distinct from many other Western societies, the existence of the phenomenon was barred from public discourse for many decades. Communist propaganda tried to present a positive picture of a happy society, and thus, in a paranoid manner, suppressed information about the existence of social problems and manifestations of social pathology. No negative manifestations were acceptable for public discourse, even with regard to private and individual characteristics, such as violence in the family.

The Communist party's loss of monopoly in public discussion brought about the opportunity for public discussion of violence in the family. Despite the efforts of feminist authors, it is still treated as a marginal observation in the media. The topic is poorly covered, even in research. Representative demoscopic surveys show that about one-half of the population acknowledge that they are aware of incidents of domestic violence. However, every seventh woman (and every eighth man) admits that their partner occasionally behaves toward them in a way that could be defined as violent. The slight difference between violent behavior by women and men would certainly require a more thorough research effort in which the extent of violence and related incidents and differences in the definition of violence would be monitored. In respect to the long history of the economic emancipation of Czech women, a lower rate of passivity among women in violent conflicts can be expected than in a society without such a history. In current Czech society, domestic violence is generally considered to be a private matter. Roughly one-fifth of women and one-third of men consider it appropriate to ignore domestic violence in their surroundings, because they consider it to be a private problem (Kuchařová & Zamykalová, 1996, p. 66).

Sexual harassment is also a relatively new topic for public discussion and research in the social sciences. Recent research has reported that 29% of women and 8% of men in the Czech Republic have experienced sexual harassment (Kuchařová & Zamykalová, 1996). Over one-half of the population is tolerant toward most expressions of sexual harassment, with the exception of sexual blackmail of women employees by their superiors. In the current social climate, sexual harassment is often addressed by avoidance strategies; there is fear of an unfavorable reaction and secondary victimization.

Political Representation of Women

Devastated by the absence of a civic society for a half-century, political culture is difficult to rebuild. This also applies to the political representation of women. The Communists maintained a set level of 30% women deputies in their puppet parliaments. That was part of the external presentation of the system as a "people's democracy." It had no practical implications. The elections were rigged and manipulated, and the parliament had no real political powers. When it regained its authority in 1989, political plurality was reestablished and the first free elections took place. The proportion of women in the parliament fell to 15%, a common level throughout Europe, and has remained so.

The number of female members of parliament is low, and most of them work in less important committees, generally connected with humanitarian issues such as social policy, healthcare, education, and culture. The unconvincing track record in equal opportunities policy and the marginalization of the so-called feminine agenda are usually attributed to the fact that men hold an absolute majority of the key positions in public life. Nonetheless, female Czech politicians have not found an approach to that agenda, and they "behave like men" in political life. Thus, the areas where women play an important or specific role (family, schools, healthcare) are politically administered from a male point of view, although the proportion of women among administrators is high. The cautious attitude of female deputies toward female issues and equal opportunities policies stems from the fact that the man is viewed as the norm in politics, even by women, and political behavior is not linked with gender. Women politicians want to be seen, first and foremost, as politicians, and not as women in politics.

The representation of women in the Czech executive branch also remains very low; there are only one or at most two female ministers in the 15-member cabinet. At regional and local levels, however, the number of women in politics is higher. The number of female mayors, particularly in smaller towns, is relatively large, and the *Association of Female Mayors in the Czech Republic* supports their identity and makes them a political power to be reckoned with. It also indicates the practical focus of women in politics: Politics at the local administrative level is more concerned with resolving the day-to-day problems of the electorate than with playing the power game.

The growing frustration with politics among Czechs is in part due to political intrigue and lack of accountability to voters. The 97% turnout in the first elections after the 1989 revolution dropped to 58% in 2002. The parliament is the least trusted of all public institutions in the eyes of the population. Still, Czechs have maintained trust in the free press. Analysis of the mass media discourse in the Czech Republic has shown (Havelková, 1999) that the public's dissatisfaction with the domestic political scene is acquiring a gender dimension, the specific content of which can be summarized as follows: Men are immature and greedy for power, and women are potentially more sensible but lacking self-confidence and interest in power. In the context of calls for more women in politics, the traditional image of

women has therefore been expanding and changing in a remarkable way. Not only are the professional capacities of women more or less taken for granted, but there are expectations that women could bring to politics attributes traditionally ascribed to mature manhood, such as rationality, courage, and determination. At the same time, however, women in high political positions are required to project traditional feminine qualities and aspirations. These very high expectations and demands on women politicians are associated with the primary orientation of discussion toward the benefits women might bring to politics (cultivation and refinement), and neglect of the issue of the benefits politics might bring to women. As yet, discussion has not shifted from the purely cultural level to the level of the theory of democracy or active citizenship, let alone the context of social policy.

7. DIVORCES AND REMARRIAGES

The Czech Republic is among countries with the highest divorce rates. Over the past 50 years, the divorce rate has continually increased (see Figure 11.4). In the Czech Republic today, as in Denmark, Norway, Great Britain, and Austria, four out of 10 marriages end in divorce. In larger cities, the ratio is five out of 10, and in towns and villages, it is three out of 10 (*Populační vývoj*, 2002).

The continual growth in the divorce rate from the 1950s to 1999, when there was a sharp temporary decrease (see Figure 11.4), was primarily due to the simplicity of the divorce process. Divorce law in Czechoslovakia prior to 1989 was both extremely liberal and not further complicated by the judicial process. Divorce was not difficult, because marriage was defined as a secular affair, not legitimated by anything more that the wishes of the two partners.

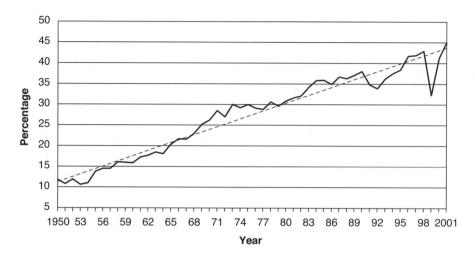

Figure 11.4 Total Divorce Rate in the Czech Republic (1950–2001)

SOURCE: *Populační vývoj* Ceské republiky 2001 (2002).

Divorce was thus defined as a natural part of a marriage conceived on this basis, and many marriages ended in it, even if there may have been other possible solutions to problems between spouses. Considerations of jointly owned property did not influence the decision to divorce, because the Communist system did not allow families to accumulate property. Furthermore, the universal employment of women meant that divorcées were not dependent on alimony. However, child custody battles were often long and bitter because childcare and custody agreements were not essential preconditions for the granting of a divorce. Disputes over custody and guardianship were more frequent than disputes over property.

Czech divorce law was rewritten in 1998, after more than 30 years. (The last divorce laws were enacted in 1964.) The new laws made divorces easier on one hand, but were stricter on the other. They introduced divorces based on mutual agreement between spouses. If a married couple have settled child custody issues, divided joint property, and have not lived together for at least 6 months, they can ask the court for a no-fault divorce without indicating the reason for the break-up of the relationship. The law has also enabled divorce in the case of "dead marriages" (in which the couple have not lived together for more than 3 years), even without the consent of one spouse. On the other hand, the new legislation has banned divorces within the first year of marriage, and those that would be counter to the interests of minor children. After the interests of children have been considered, the divorce process may be started. The only cause for divorce in Czech marriage law is a qualified breakdown of the relationship between partners. The new legislation came into force in 1999, and the divorce rate fell by 10%. It was only a temporary decrease; in 2000 the divorce rate essentially returned to pre-1999 levels, and indicators show that since 2001 it has been on the increase again (see Figure 11.4).

Highest Divorce Rate: First Years of Marriage

Most divorces in the Czech Republic take place during the first 5 years of marriage, and then the rate falls for each further year of marriage: The longer the marriage, the lesser the likelihood of divorce. Along with the decrease in marriages among very young persons came a decrease in the number of divorces in the first 3 years of marriages, particularly in cases where the marriage had not been adequately considered in advance, as was often the case for pregnant teenage brides. In 1990 most divorces took place in the third and fourth years of marriage, but in 2000 they had shifted to the fourth and fifth years. There was a corresponding increase in the age of spouses at the time of divorce. In 1991 the average age at divorce was 33 for women and 36 for men. In 2000 the figures were 36 for women and 38 for men (*Populační vývoj*, 2002).

Low Age at Marriage: High Divorce Rates

The earlier Czech men and women enter into marriage, the more likely they are to end the marriage in the divorce courts. Two-fifths of women who marry before age 20 get divorced; however, the figure is only one-third for women who get married around age 25, and just one-fifth for those who get married after age 30 (*Pohyb obyvatelstva*, 2001).

This relationship is to a certain extent influenced by level of education. In Czech society, young people who leave school immediately after high school enter into employment around age 18. Those who carry on to study at university enter the work world at around age 23 or 24. With the end of the caretaker state, marriages among couples who are not economically independent have fallen sharply, and marriages among students have all but disappeared. Those with trades or a high school education, who entered directly into employment, have a greater probability of entering into marriage sooner than those with a university education. Thus, they also have a higher

probability of their marriages ending in divorce.

Divorce Rates Among Those With Less Education

In the Czech Republic, the divorce rate is strongly influenced by the level of education of spouses. Traditionally this has only been true for women. In older cohorts, we find more divorced women than men. It was the case only for women that the higher the level of education, the greater the likelihood of divorce. There was no differentiation in the of divorce rate among men with respect to this variable, but the situation changed for the cohort born between 1940 and 1950. The relationship between the divorce rate and education among women reversed; the higher the level of education, the less the likelihood of divorce. Among men the reverse happened, and a strong differentiation according to education appeared: The higher the level of education obtained, the greater the number of divorces (see Figure 11.5).

High Divorce Rate for Marriages With Young Children

At the end of the 1990s, nearly two-thirds of all divorces in the Czech Republic were among marriages where there were minor children. The most divorces were among families with one child (about two-fifths), and the divorce rate decreased as the number of children increased (*Populační vývoj*, 2002).

In terms of the number of years of marriage that elapse before a divorce, divorces among families with minor children occur later than among those without. The highest divorce rate among couples with children occurs 5 to 8 years after marriages, but after 2 to 3 years among those without children (*Populační vývoj*, 2002).

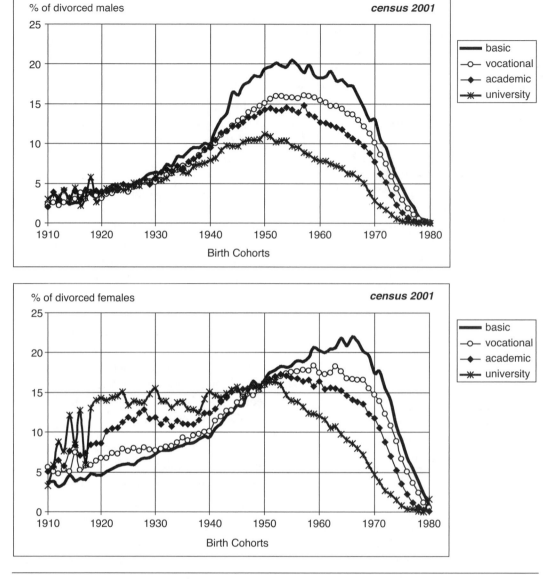

Figure 11.5 Percentage of People Divorced, by Birth Cohorts (1910–1980)

SOURCE: *Sčítání lidu* (2002).

Emphasis on Personality Conflicts as a Reason for Divorce

Women file for divorce far more often than men in Czech society. At the end of the 1990s, 68 women filed for divorce for every 32 men who filed (*Populační vývoj*, 2002).

Women, however, are often only legalizing reality, in which men have already left the family. If they are not divorced, they cannot expect child support or alimony, which are set and enforced by the divorce courts. The law provides for the possibility of suing one's own (current) spouse for alimony in the event that he or she does not distribute income equitably within the family. However, such cases are rare, and the defendant usually responds by filing for divorce. Of the 10 possible grounds for divorce that are recognized by the courts, both women and men cite personality conflicts most frequently. This ground has gradually become more popular for both sexes since the 1970s, even though, during the 1980s, alcoholism and infidelity competed on the men's side, and other grounds (officially listed as "other reasons") on the women's side. Since 1989 character differences, as grounds for divorce, have continued to grow: In 2001 more than one-half of divorces filed had this stated as the grounds (*Pohyb obyvatelstva*, 2001). Even though we know that this is only one of 10 acceptable grounds for divorce, we can assume that causes for divorce do not much differ from those that are perceived as legitimate. It can also be seen that the number of men and women who find it impossible to stay in a marriage due to character differences has increased since the changes in Czech society after 1989, and the move from collectivist rhetoric to individualist rhetoric.

Expected Trends in Divorce

In the future we can expect two phenomena in divorces in the Czech Republic: an increase in divorces among older partners and a general decrease in the divorce rate as a whole. The shift in peak frequency of divorce to an older age-group can be expected due to the increasing age at marriage. Data from the end of the 1990s, when compared with data from the end of the 1980s, already indicate this trend. The decrease in the divorce rate should follow the decrease in the marriage rate, which has been taking place since the beginning of the 1990s. However, this expectation has not been fulfilled. Cohorts with low marriage

rates are already reaching the age at which a high divorce rate would be expected, but, as shown in Figure 11.4, the divorce rate in the Czech Republic returned to its previous high rate after 1999, and has even begun to grow again since 2001.

8. INTERGENERATIONAL SOLIDARITY AND RELATIONSHIPS, AND PERCEPTIONS ABOUT THE FAMILY AMONG GENERATIONS

A relatively high level of intergenerational solidarity and assistance are traditional elements of the Czech family. This is, to a certain extent, a direct result of the organization of society before 1989, which continues in a different form today.

Intergenerational Dependency Before 1989

The so-called generational sandwich effect—potential conflicts in caretaking role expectations between parents and children on the one hand, and between parents and grandparents on the other—had a specific form in the pre-November (prerevolution) society. There was social pressure for a small age difference between generations, the result of which was the prevailing low age at becoming a parent. Mothers did not dissuade their daughters from early parenthood. Rather, they encouraged them to get married as soon as possible after reaching the legal age (18 years). If this happened, and the daughter gave birth around age 21 or 22, the mother would become a grandmother in her mid-40s, while still at the peak of her economic and social capacity—when she could help her daughter a great deal. Because it worked, the modal age at primiparas was 21 to 22 for two generations in the Czech Republic.

During the period when the "economics of scarcity" prevailed, assistance and aid within the family, from the mother to the daughter's family, was very significant. Parents supported their children's families financially, provided for them materially, supplied them with services that, in the centrally planned economy, were otherwise unobtainable, and generally helped them with the running of a young household. They primarily assisted with caring for children, because mothers of young children were generally in full-time employment.

This need decreased as the children became independent. If they were born early, this happened when their mothers' mothers were in their 50s, healthy, and in full physical and economic strength. The period of motherhood for their daughters came to an end in time for them to help their own mothers, who had meanwhile reached a geriatric age and had begun to be dependent on them. The middle generation, therefore, avoided the difficulties of simultaneously caring for the young (their daughter's and son's families with small children) and the old (their parents).

This instinctive strategy for managing the "sandwich effect" was not only a fundamental element of intergenerational solidarity prior to 1989, but it was also, to a certain extent, the backbone of the whole of the pre-November Czech society. It occurred as a reaction to the political machinery and state institutions, which could not be sufficiently relied on during the course of one's life (Možný, 1991).

Weakening of Intergenerational Dependence After 1989

During the course of the 1990s, the web of connections between the family of origin, one's own nuclear family, and older relatives ceased to be essential in Czech society. Young people experience less of a need to rely on their parents' social connections for property and services, as compared with the pre-1989 period. Women are now becoming mothers on average between the ages of 22 and 27, which is less than ideal with regard to the fact that their parents are becoming grandparents around the age of 55, at the time when they are faced with the need to help their own parents in old age.

Intergenerational Solidarity After 1989

The current weakening of dependence among the generations in the Czech Republic certainly does not mean that intergenerational solidarity has died. However, the change in regime has brought about changes in its form.

Recent research has shown that current generations do not prefer that young newlyweds live in the same household as their parents. However, the vast majority live in close vicinity to their parents and grandparents. Czechs move infrequently, and when they do, they generally move only small distances. Only one-fifth of newlyweds lived in a multigenerational household with their parents at the turn of this century; however, over one-half lived in the same city or town, on average less than 30 minutes from their parents (Páloncyová, 2003). Thus, the relationships between families can function similarly to those as if they were living together, but present less reasons for intergenerational conflicts, which are frequent problems in multigenerational households.

In Czech society, the predominant form of intergenerational solidarity is emotional. This presents itself in the form of frequent contacts, primarily among daughters, mothers, and granddaughters. The father plays a relatively small role in intergenerational relationships. Emotional solidarity most often comes in the form of moral and psychological support: advice, consolation, reassurance, and pep talks. In general terms, emotional solidarity amounts to the passing on of personal experiences with a relative or relatives. Besides this, such support is also related to help with the household, or more concretely, older generations help younger generations with their children and the younger generation helps the older generation in times of illness. Material support is provided only sporadically, if at all, and usually from the older generation to the younger (Možný, Pridalová, & Bánovcová, 2003; Páloncyová, 2003).

9. THE AGING CZECH POPULATION AND FAMILY LIFE

Czech society, like all European societies, is aging. The proportion of older people in the population is increasing. Older people have specific lifestyles, specific values and expectations, and special demands and needs with regard to social and economic security. Even the family life of older people has its own characteristics. During the Communist regime, no research was conducted into these trends, and the situation has not improved significantly over the past decade.

The global measure set a threshold of 8% of a population over the age of 70 as the sign of an aging population. This threshold was already crossed in the Czech Republic in the middle of the last century. By the middle of the 1970s, the proportion of elderly persons in the Czech population increased further. This was a relative aging; the average life expectancy was lengthened by a decrease in child and infant mortality. Mortality in older age-groups remained high, particularly among men. The mortality rate for Czech men in the 55 to 59 age range in the 1970s was one of the highest in Europe. The high mortality rate among men in this age-group characterized all Communist states. It was related to lifelong frustration in the command economy, the poorly functioning health system, and the abuse of alcohol and nicotine.

The demographic crisis, next to the economic and political crises, revealed that the system could not be maintained, and the old political elite did not have a solution for these problems—if they were even conscious of them.

Since 1989 the quality of healthcare has improved as the lifestyle of the population has changed. As a result, the mortality rate has fallen, and life expectancy has increased. At the beginning of the 1990s, the average life expectancy in the Czech Republic was 68 years for men and 75 for women. By 2001, life expectancy for men had increased by 4 years, to 72, and by 3 years for women, to 78 (*Populační vývoj*, 2002). With this trend, the Czech population has separated itself from other post-Communist countries, where there has been a stagnation or even a worsening in mortality.

11. SPECIAL TOPIC: GENERATIONAL CHANGES IN CONCEPTIONS OF COHABITATION AND FAMILY LIFE

Views of family life in Czech society vary with generation. The older the generation, the greater the emphasis placed on family values and family life. In contrast, the younger generation places more emphasis on individuality, personal success, and the right to make individual decisions. Of all the living generations, personal differences from the family of origin is most acceptable to the younger generation; by this we mean enforcing one's own choices and emphasis on one's own life, which are not overly linked to ties with relatives and extended family. However, family and married life are, at the same time, highly valued by young Czechs. They view it as an opportunity to show that they do not just live for themselves, that they are not simply public persons, oriented toward personal gain and competition on the open market. In seeing the family as a source of pleasure and as giving meaning to life, young people are similar to their parents and grandparents; however, they differ in their interpretations and perceptions of the family.

The current family has a low number of children and is less focused on joint activities with extended family. It is more focused on joint activities, equal opportunities for both partners, and an equal distribution of housework between the genders.

They perceive as optimal a family model that is not in conflict with the outside world and the work world, positive coexistence, and satisfied partners. In contrast, they reject the model of the family in which only one partner is satisfied, and accept that a dissatisfied partner should be able to leave the family without excessive difficulty. Thus, the family is easily dissolved (Katrňák, 2002; Hamplová, 2000).

REFERENCES

Fischlová, D. (2002). *Analýza rozdílů ve výši pracovních příjmů mužu a žen–navržení modelového postupu zjištování podílu diskriminace.* Praha: VÚPSV.

Hamplová, D. (2000). Postoje k manželství a rodicovství. In L. Fialová, D. Hamplová, M. Kucera, & S. Vymetalová (Eds.), *Predstavy mladých lidí o manželství a rodicovství* (pp. 67–98). Praha: Slon.

Hamplová, D., & Pikálková, S. (2002). Manželství, nesezdaná soužití a partnerský vztah. In Z. Mansfeldová & M. Tůcek (Eds.), *Současná česká společnost: Sociologické studie* (pp. 127–147). Praha: Sociologický ústav AV CR.

Havelková, H. (1999). The political representation of women in mass media discourse in the Czech Republic, 1990–1998. *Czech Sociological Review, 7*(2), 145–163.

Katrňák, T. (2002). Proměny české rodiny v devadesátých letech. In V. Smékal & P. Macek (Eds.), *Utváření a vývoj osobnosti* (pp. 227–246). Brno: Barrister & Principal.

Klabouch, J. (1962). *Manželství a rodina v minulosti.* Praha: Orbis.

Krížková, A. (1999). The division of labour in the Czech hoseholds in the 1990s. *Czech Sociological Review, 7*(2), 205–214.

Kuchařová, V., Nedomová, A., & Zamykalová, L. (1999). *Predpoklady snatkového a rodinného chování mladé generace.* Praha: VÚPSV.

Kuchařová, V., & Zamykalová, L. (1996). *Aktuální otázky postavení žen v CR.* Praha: VÚPSV.

Možný, I. (1987). K některým novým jevům v kulturně legitimních vzorcích rodinných startů. *Demografie, 29*(2), 114–123.

Možný, I. (1991). *Proč tak snadno . . . Některé rodinné důvody sametové revoluce.* Praha: Slon.

Možný, I., Přidalová, M., & Bánovcová, L. (2003). *Hodnota dětí a mezigenerační solidarita.* Brno: VÚPSV.

Možný, I., & Rabušic, L. (1992). Unmarried cohabitation in Czechoslovakia. *Czechoslovak Sociological Revue, 28,* 107–117.

Paloncyová, J. (2002). *Rodinné chování mladé generace.* Praha: VÚPSV.

Paloncyová, J. (2003). *Změny ceské rodiny. Mladá generace a demografický vývoj.* Praha: VÚPSV.

Pohyb obyvatelstva v roce 1992 až v roce 2001 (1991–2001). Praha: CSÚ.

Populační vývoj České republiky 2001. (2002). Praha: Katedra demografie a geodemografie PF UK.

Report on the situation of Roma and Sinti in OSCE area. (2002). High Commissioner on the National Minorities. The Hague: OSCE.

The Roma in Central and Eastern Eureope: Avoiding the dependency trap. (2002). Bratislava: UN Development Programme.

Rychtaříková, J. (2002). Minulá a současná diferenciace reprodukce v Evropě. In Z. Mansfeldová & M. Tuček (Eds.), *Současná česká společnost: Sociologické studie* (pp. 107–126). Praha: Sociologický ústav AV CR.

Sčítání lidu, domu a bytu 2001. (2002). Praha: CSÚ.

Sirovátka, T. (1997). Sociální a ekonomické faktory marginalizace na pracovním trhu v České republice. *Sociologický Časopis, 33*(2), 169–188.

Stinbauerová, R., & Helus, Z. (2002). Ženy a dívky ve světě práce a ve škole: Od tradičních vzorců vnímání sebe a druhých ke "genderovému pojetí"—směrování k optimalizaci šancí. In R. Steinbauerová, E. Koliadis, & Z. Helus (Eds.), *Qualität durch qualifikation* (pp. 17–42). Brno: Paido.

CHAPTER 12

Finland's Families

Hannele Forsberg

1 & 10. FAMILY IN THE CONTEXT OF INDIVIDUAL RIGHTS AND SOCIAL CITIZENSHIP

Geographically, Finland shares long stretches of borderline with Sweden and Russia. In the south, beyond the Baltic sea, the closest neighbors are the Baltic republics, Poland, and Germany. In the north there is a small stretch of shared border with Norway. The roots of the nation state are in the class-based civil war of 1918, followed by Russian domination until the collapse of the Soviet Union in 1991. Culturally and mentally Finland is part of the West.

Finland may be described as a highly developed, equal society combining a welfare state and a technologically oriented information society (Castells & Himanen, 2002), in whose public policy individual rights and social citizenship, linked to the maintenance of the welfare state, are important principles. Family and close relationships have an important role especially as an arena of informal intimacy, nurturing,

care, sharing, and affection (Reuna, 1997). Public authorities are responsible for many tasks related to social security, care, and nurturing, but in recent times the significance of the family has increased in this respect.

Finland joined the European Union in 1995. It's land area is fairly extensive, but the country is sparsely populated. An important proportion of the population lives in the south in or around the capital or in other growth centers. At the beginning of 2003, there were slightly over 5.2 million inhabitants in Finland, the majority of whom speak Finnish and share a homogeneous cultural background. A growing number of inhabitants, still only about 2%, are immigrants. The largest groups among these are Russians and Estonians. Immigrant groups also include people from Sweden, Somalia, the former Yugoslavia, Iraq, the United Kingdom, Germany, Iran, the United States, Turkey, China, Vietnam, and Thailand. Immigrants typically live in the largest cities (Väestötilastot, 2003).

Measured by various indicators used in public policy, Finland is considered one of the most equal countries in the world. As an example, Finnish women were the first in Europe to receive the right to vote; at the moment, the president of the republic is a woman, as was the previous prime minister. Similarly, in matters concerning the rights of children, Finland is a pioneering country.

The Finnish family is difficult to understand without some clarification of the concept of the welfare state. Finland is considered an example of the so-called Nordic model, in which the welfare policy is primarily implemented by the state and the local authorities (municipalities). The structure of industry was long dominated by agriculture and small-scale farming. In the agrarian way of life, men, women, and children took an equal part in productive work. The bourgeois nuclear family established in other parts of Europe, based on paid work by the husband, the privacy of the family, and the nurturing role of the woman at home, never became prevalent in Finland, where towns were small and prosperity was accessible to few (Pylkkänen, 1999, p. 26). The changeover from the agrarian society to an industrialized service society took place in Finland almost without intermediate stages, as late as the 1960s and 1970s (Takala, 2002, pp. 8–9). This was the stage that strengthened the welfare state project; the placing of the state's welfare task in an important position.

The expansion of the welfare state to children's day care and free school meals supported the increased prevalence of women working for pay (though it was not rare even before the advent of public day care for children). The expansion of public services offered new jobs for women and made it possible for them to work outside the home. As early as 1960, almost one-half of Finnish mothers held a paid job outside the home (Takala, 2002, p. 12). Little by little, the family

model based on two breadwinners was built into the Finnish system. The normative lifestyle came to be based on two paychecks; the family with one breadwinner gains no financial advantage if one of the spouses remains a homemaker. Single parents are also expected to have a paid job (Julkunen, 1999).

The principle of universality contained in the Nordic welfare state model had its own influence on family and close relationships, by underlining individuality and equality between the sexes and the social groups. The fact that social security benefits were individual, not based on the family, and that social security is universal, not just dependent on paid work, has guaranteed the individualization and independence of people. Individualization has also been promoted by the fact that grown-up children are not legally required to support their parents or to bear responsibility for their care, as is the case in many countries of Southern Europe, for instance. All citizens have equal rights to the education, healthcare, and social services provided by public authorities; such services as children's day care, old people's homes, and maternity clinics are meant for all citizens, not just for the lowest social groups. The welfare state is considered to have liberated women in particular from unpaid care work and to have enabled the economic independence of women. The implementation of these ideas has been possible thanks to a high rate of taxation, which has enabled the redistribution of income and which requires social citizenship, solidarity as an institutionalized value. The system has been accompanied by a fairly equal distribution of income and a low incidence of poverty (Anttonen & Sipilä, 2000, pp. 54–89).

However, the social revolution in the 1990s placed new challenges before the Finns. The deep economic recession, the ensuing unprecedented burst of economic growth, related particularly to the information technology boom, globalization, integration into the information society, and then the waning of the rapid growth with certain negative results are some of the milestones of this change. Around the same time, debate on the accelerating pace of working life, the hectic way of life, and the strain caused by this on family life increased. Psychological ill health, especially as regards children and young people, repeatedly hit the headlines. Despite widespread support by the citizens, the welfare state faces strong pressures to change. The globalization of the economy and global competition, associated with demands to decrease taxation, create external challenges. The aging of the population, migration into the growth centers, unemployment rates that are fairly high on the European scale, and the challenges of developing the service system create internal pressures to change. A crucial concern is the financing of the welfare state. By now it is obvious that there is more reliance on market-based services, on family and individual responsibility, and, more than before, on the third sector. Instead of citizens' social rights, what have been emphasized in recent years are cutbacks and decreases (Kantola & Kautto, 2002). In particular, families with children are considered to be the "losers," while it is noted that the differential between families doing well and those doing less well is increasing (Bardy, Salmi, & Heino, 2001). The idea of social citizenship is facing new problems. It remains to be seen how, and with what emphasis, the family will be noted when the new directions of the welfare state are determined.

2. PAIRING UP

Finnish society takes a fairly liberal attitude toward individual choices regarding pairing up. Sexual morals have become more permissive, and the religious ethic guided by the Christian tradition and the Church is no longer predominant. Nor do the views of the family or outsiders necessarily weigh heavily on decisions concerning pairing up (Reuna, 1997, p. 27). It must, however, be noted that even if individual autonomy has become stronger, there still exists a wide array of external authorities governing people's ways of life. Legislation, church, the media with its plethora of experts or other idols, the educational system, and the research results from various disciplines provide guidance, advice, evaluations, and norms that affect people's choices—often in conflicting directions (Määttä, 2002, pp. 40–41). These cultural rules defining the process of pairing up have a general influence on the forming of families. As in all Western countries, the status of coupledom has become stronger, and it has become a phenomenon in itself (Jallinoja, 2000, pp. 10–11; Määttä, 2002, p. 38). This is due to the strengthening of individualism and the trend that consists of justifying a wide range of lifestyles.

Coupledom and the associated striving for the feeling of being in love and for compatibility have become significant matters. An important aspect often stressed is that the feeling is personal in character, individual, and unique. Falling in love is the starting point of modern coupledom, but falling in love is not only reserved for the relationship between two spouses. One is allowed to fall in love several times, only a few of which will lead to long-term relationships. Intimate relationships with the opposite sex start at an earlier age than before, but correspondingly, the settling down to a permanent relationship occurs at an older age (Jallinoja, 2000, pp. 38–82). Marriage is equated with a permanent relationship, but cohabitation can also be defined as permanent (Reuna, 1997, pp. 26–30).

On average, Finnish women marry for the first time at the age of 29, and men at the age of 31. In the 1960s people married 5 years younger than today (Jallinoja, 2000,

p. 63). Unlike in Southern and Eastern Europe, for example, where moving away from one's childhood home is linked to the completion of studies and the first permanent relationship, young Finnish adults often live alone after moving away from their childhood home. This is made possible through the social security system, which includes a system of housing allowances. On average, girls move away from home at the age of 20, boys at the age of 22 (Families 2001, 2002, p. 55). Living alone creates a different culture for intimate relationships than living with one's parents.

This development has brought about an increase in the number of romantic partners, especially since romantic friendships begin at an earlier age than before. The increased number of romantic partners can be interpreted as emphasizing a genuine choice, since the partner can be selected from among several candidates during a period of about 10 years. As more and more people are of the opinion that they are not going to "settle down" or "start a family" before they are 30, new cultures of heterosexual relationships have also begun to emerge. One of them is the so-called dating culture, manifested by young women as well and based on an absence of romantic emotions, whose proponents enjoy sex but consciously avoid falling in love and commitment (Jallinoja, 2000, pp. 63–67). More traditional cultures of romantic friendships naturally coexist with these. However, there is an increase in the sexual autonomy and activity of women in particular and in public debate on these topics. The background to this is formed by the free access to advice on contraception, the development of contraceptive methods, and the right to abortion (Määttä, 2002, pp. 40–41). Despite the diversification of romantic friendship cultures, the young—as indeed people of all ages—emphasize the importance of family and close relationships in their lives (Harinen, 1998, p. 426).

Some of the young cohabit at least some length of time with different sex partners, and only get married with the conception of children; other couples of various ages never marry, but live in cohabiting relationships that may be of long duration. The legislation takes a fairly liberal stance on several types of unions, even though the status of a marriage relationship continues to be the strongest.

The crucial role of coupledom is also shown by statistics. The majority of the statistical families consist of coupledom families based on the marriage (32% of all identified family forms) or cohabitation of two adults (12% of all family forms). Families including a couple outnumber families formed by parents and underage children (36% of all family forms) (Families 2001, 2002, pp. 42–44). In March 2002, fairly late in comparison with the other Nordic countries, it became possible to legally register a partnership between same-sex couples. During the first year, about 456 such couples were registered, 207 of whom consisted of women and 249 of men (Parisuhdetilasto, 2002). Parallel to coupledom, living alone is very frequent as well. Out of all households, the share of one-person households is 38% (Families 2001, 2002, p. 56). In addition to the young, elderly people also live alone most typically. In spite of the increase in living alone, the majority of Finns live in a couple at some point in their lives (Määttä, 2002, p. 13).

It has been suggested that the essential criterion for choosing a permanent partner these days is compatibility. This is above all equated with matters related to lifestyle and worldview. The assessment of compatibility is a way of preparing for the unavoidable risks of a permanent relationship, since it is generally known that it may fail. This is a matter of the morals of risk awareness in a society emphasizing individuality, a precaution that strives for an optimal personal choice in a selection process that has become very long in duration (Jallinoja, 2000, pp. 68–82).

3. FERTILITY AND SOCIALIZATION

Number of Children Decreases

As in many other industrialized Western countries, the number of childbirths has continuously decreased. The urban way of life, secularization, the need for self-actualization, women's long educational careers, the demands of working life, the prevalence of precarious employment, the higher age of giving birth, and the lack of a permanent partner are factors that leave less and less space for the desire to have children (Paajanen, 2002). Nevertheless, birthrates in Finland are among the highest in Europe (Takala, 2002). On the one hand, a policy that supports families with children is assumed by some to improve birthrates, while, on the other hand, others assume it has no effect on the matter (Paajanen, 2002, p. 86).

At the moment, the average number of children in Finnish families is just under two. The ideal number of children is somewhat higher, 2.4 children on average (Paajanen, 2002, p. 33). It is estimated that about 10% of children have no siblings in their families. At the end of 2001, the proportion of children under 18 was about 20% of the population. During the past 20 years, the number of children has remained relatively stable, but it is expected to decrease slightly, since the number of women at a fertile age is going down (Kartovaara & Sauli, 2000, p. 12). The share of women who remain childless either willingly or involuntarily is estimated to be 15% to 20% (Families 2001, 2002, p. 51). The average age of first-time mothers has increased, especially the number of first-timers over 35 years of age (Vikat, 2002). It appears that the better a woman's education, the older she will be at the birth of her first child (Nikander, 1992). The so-called teenage mothers are rare in Finland. In 1998 the number of mothers under 18 years of age giving birth was 254 in the whole country.

The same year, 800 abortions were given to girls under 18 years of age (Kartovaara & Sauli, 2000, pp. 94–95).

The possibility of contraception and individual choice means that children who are born are nowadays the result of conscious choice and therefore expected. Even though the types of family forms have increased, the majority of children live with married parents. However, the number of children living with a single parent or in a stepfamily after the parents' divorce and remarriage continues to increase, and especially so with older children. Similarly, the number of children born to cohabiting parents has increased continuously (Kartovaara & Sauli, 2000, p. 29). The legal status of children has been safeguarded so that it is not dependent on the type of family. It has become culturally more important that children maintain contact with the absent parent, and this increases the number of family relationships and homes a child may have. A similar effect is caused by the increase of families with heterogeneous cultural backgrounds (Bardy et al., 2001, p. 26). Most Finnish children live in urban environments. Seventeen percent of all children live in the four large cities of the Helsinki metropolitan area (Kartovaara & Sauli, 2000, p. 15).

Shared Responsibility for Upbringing and Socialization

In Finnish society, the upbringing and socialization of children occurs not only in family and close relationships, but also in relationships with various social institutions, such as the day-care center, the school, the healthcare system, the media, the parents' jobs, and so on. In a society of many professional people, the society as a whole participates in the bringing up of children in many ways. It has been stated, with some oversimplification, that the parents are the silent partners in the business of upbringing, while the experts monitor, advise, and guide the child and the parents from before birth up to adulthood (Hoikkala, 1993, p. 47). In the moral sense, however, the primary responsibility for upbringing is considered to rest with the child's own parents and family.

An essential characteristic of modern parenthood is held to be the striving to avoid hierarchical command relationships. The relationship with the child should be something that foreshadows equality rather than a relationship based on authority. However, the placing of limits and the creation of security are important principles. Communication, talking, and discussion are keywords (Hoikkala, 1993, pp. 47–61). Children's rights to participation, protection, sufficient resources, individuality, and personal inviolability are important principles also recorded in legislation. Corporal punishment, earlier used as a means of upbringing, is prohibited by law.

The majority of Finnish children below school age are cared for by their mothers in their own homes. The maternal and parental leave period of almost a year is long in international comparison. Thanks to the fairly good financial benefits, it enables the home care of children below 1 year of age. Even after this, most families with small children continue to care for the children at home for a few months, supported by the child home-care allowance available to all children below 3 years of age (Anttonen, 2003). Fathers also have an individual entitlement to a paternal leave of 18 days and the opportunity of taking parental leave (158 days). After the period of parental leave, the father has the further opportunity of caring for the children at home instead of the mother, drawing the child home-care allowance. Except for the brief paternal leave of a few days, fathers rarely take up the opportunity of caring for their child at home (Rantalaiho, 2003). Similarly, employing a child-minder

at home is very rare. Children who are not cared for at home are placed in a day-care center, family day care, or private care. The most common form of care is municipal day care (Kartovaara & Sauli, 2000, pp. 134–136). No matter which form of care is selected for children under school age, the emphasis in childcare is on nurturing rather than on pedagogic or educational activity (Anttonen, 2003).

Children spend a large part of their childhood at school. All Finnish children, even if severely disabled, are obliged to participate in education. With few exceptions, children begin school at 7 years of age (Kartovaara & Sauli, 2000, p. 139). The younger schoolchildren usually go to school on their own and after school they spend time alone or with friends in and near their homes. The general security, the hot meal provided at school, and the social norm that allows children to spend time alone have made this possible until recently. Elsewhere in Europe, such a situation might be seen as neglecting the children. Lately, however, the time spent alone by small children has been highlighted as a social problem. The present government has included on its agenda an act that would guarantee supervised afternoon care for first- and second-graders. Attempts to solve the problem include a project that experiments with a new structure of the school day, with lessons interlaced with leisure pursuits to avoid the problems caused by the parents' absence. The debate has not focused much on the positive meanings contained in children's peer activities and their free and autonomous activity.

In principle, all children complete at least the 9-year comprehensive school. About 95% of them move on to the upper secondary school or to vocational education. Even after this, one-half of each age-group continues their studies (Kartovaara & Sauli, 2000, p. 139). Although, in principle, the educational system provides the same opportunities to all children, in practice the parents' level of education has a cumulative effect on the child's level of education (Kartovaara & Sauli, 2000, p. 148).

Besides time spent at school, the school-children's daily lives consist of homework, friends, leisure pursuits, and, increasingly, the use of various media such as TV or computers. The latter also contribute to the socialization of children alongside the more traditional agents. The school days are unbroken, for lunch is eaten at school, not at home, as is the case in many other countries. Time-use surveys indicate that school-children rarely have paid jobs (Pääkkönen & Niemi, 2002, pp. 19–31). However, work done by children is often invisible. Part-time paid work, summer jobs, and other seasonal jobs, such as paper distribution, childcare, cleaning, and working in shops are typical jobs of children. Children's work is not nec-essarily linked with poverty; rather, modern children want to work to have more oppor-tunities for consumption independent of their parents (Strandell, 2001, pp. 90–93). Consumption is actually a domain in which the boundaries of adults' and children's worlds are blurred.

Another domain where the boundaries between adulthood and childhood are blurred is the media culture and information technology. Since children may be more experienced as IT users, the role of adults as the authorities of socialization, the mediators of knowledge and experience, may be chal-lenged in certain situations. On the other hand, children's basic needs and their depen-dence on adults have not disappeared even with the move into an information society (Forsberg & Pösö, 2001).

At the beginning of the 21st century, child-hood in Finland has begun to appear increas-ingly problematic. In recent years public debate has focused strongly on psychological ill health, loneliness, substance abuse, and exclusion of children and young people.

Attention has been focused on new types of social problems, such as the contribution of the Internet to crimes perpetrated by or on children. Many adults are confused and uncertain about these new phenomena. The concern easily turns into talk of a crisis of parenthood: parents who have disappeared, are absent, or are worn out by the hectic pace of work. Suggested measures easily concen-trate on the upholding of the authority of parents and other responsible adults. It is rare to see an approach in which the new phenomena are not studied from individual angles but from structural viewpoints. In the latter case, the problems of childhood are seen as manifesting a transition toward a new social status of childhood. There are signs that the polarity between childhood and adulthood is lessening, and childhood as a particular space, taking place in designated localities, is disappearing. Studying children as active agents, as social participants—also as essential partners in socialization—is a part of this new turn (Strandell, 2001).

4. GENDER ROLES

From the 1960s onward, gender equality has been a crucial goal of Finnish social policy. The aim has been to expand the field of activity of women in particular and to develop a day-care system enabling this. In consequence, Finnish women have attained rights earlier than women in many other countries, and have participated actively in working life and other activity—while still bearing a considerable responsibility for their families. Parallel to expanding the women's field of activity, men have been encouraged to participate in domestic work and child-care. The underlying intention has been that by this means, the children would internalize a concept of equality between the sexes (Vuori, 2003, p. 51). Despite the striving for equality, the culture still contains many elements that discriminate against women, and new backlashes have occurred. In recent years it has been asked increasingly loudly whether gender equality is only superficial and, at bottom, only a delusion. Despite full-time jobs, women bear the main responsibility for the care of the family and home, violence against women in the home is surprisingly common, and the labor market is gender segregated and there is a considerable pay differential between men and women.

The value and attraction of paid work is great, and it has a significant effect on family relationships. Mothers participate in working life clearly more often than non-mothers on average. Women and mothers not only have jobs, but increasingly are also committed to their work, thus seeming more similar to men in this respect (Jallinoja, 2000, p. 14). Women in white-collar jobs and women managers in particular have felt that the job requires an increasing amount of time and energy, pushing domestic tasks into the background (Kivimäki, 2003, p. 193). Studies have shown that the pressures toward profitability and flexibility that have lately become an intrinsic part of working life, manifested as short-term contracts and part-time work, as well as unemployment and the hectic pace of work with the resulting negative phenomena, have affected women more than men (Bardy et al., 2001, pp. 54–57), and this is also visible in family life. A new phenomenon is that younger and younger children are brought into day care for fear of the mother losing her job. However, it is only the mother who regulates her commitment to work for the benefit of the family. The mothers of small children in particular use their parental leaves, take up part-time jobs, or avoid working long hours (Kivimäki, 2003, p. 190). In contrast, the family appears to have less effect on the father's work, at least in the sense of limiting the amount of work done. Among all employed persons, the fathers of small children work the longest hours (Bardy et al., 2001, p. 57).

However, fatherhood is associated with many hopes of increasing gender equality; the image of the times as presented by the family debate is the desire to combine the domains of the man and the home (Hoikkala, 1998, p. 75). General interest in fatherhood has, surprisingly, lessened the mothers as a focus of interest (Vuori, 2003). The goal is that parenthood be shared and men participate in childcare and life equally with the women. Especially during the 1980s and 1990s, fatherhood was in the forefront as a family topic. Subsequent debate has focused on fatherhood as a resource for men and as a source of a new kind of enjoyment, and has emphasized the significance of fathers as role models for (boy) children (Rantalaiho, 2003). Occasionally, however, men are warned against broadening their sphere too much, against becoming mothers or too much like women. Some men criticize the fact that women express new challenges to men but on the other hand do not allow them the space to do things in their own way. It is nevertheless obvious that there have been changes in the status of men and fathers. In the 1950s the father may have been the breadwinner and the highest court of appeal, but nowadays the breadwinning duties are shared by the spouses, and younger fathers especially share the responsibility of parenthood and caring (Hoikkala, 1998; Aalto, 2002).

Nevertheless, year after year time-use surveys confirm that the majority of domestic tasks fall on women in spite of their full-time jobs. According to a recent survey, the spouses spend an average of 45 hours on domestic tasks, of which the men's share is only 38%. Domestic duties are most evenly divided when the woman has a job and the man is unemployed. The men who manage the smallest share of domestic tasks are the ones with a full-time day job and a spouse in shift work. Moreover, the tasks are divided according to gender so that the women are mainly responsible for the care of clothing, cleaning, cooking, and childcare, while the men chiefly concentrate on traditional men's chores such as repairs, building jobs, vehicle maintenance, and outdoor tasks. When spending time with the children, men tend to focus on activities, such as playing games and sports (Pääkkönen & Niemi, 2002, pp. 34–38). It is interesting to note, however, that domestic tasks take up less time in Finland than in any other country included in the time-use surveys. In fact, one may draw the conclusion that cutting down on domestic tasks has been a way of adapting to full-time jobs. Finnish family life and daily routines have adapted to a rationalization of homes and home life (Julkunen, 1999, p. 95).

5. MARITAL RELATIONSHIPS

The nature of marital relationships has changed from earlier times. The old ideas of the sanctity of matrimony, which used to be upheld by such means as the shunning of unmarried mothers and children born out of wedlock, or the thought that men are the speaking partners in a marriage collective, have had to give way to the new ideas, practices, and challenges of today (Nätkin, 2003). The ending of an unsatisfactory marriage is easy in principle, but people are criticized for not being able to assume the responsibility required by marriage. The fact that many different kinds of unions have become culturally acceptable poses a challenge to the special status of marriage. The increased prevalence of cohabiting relationships and divorces, as well as the possibility of registering partnerships between same-sex couples, has created a situation where marriage is not the only adult relationship based on affection and approved by society. Relationships based on love or

parenthood are no longer dependent on the marriage institution. As a consequence, there is uncertainty about the actual significance of the marriage institution as a whole (Veijola & Jokinen, 2001).

As an official institution, marriage has lost some of its definition. One can still claim that marriage continues to have a symbolic significance. Rather than to the actual union, marriage is used to refer to situations where lovers begin to live *as if married.* Modern forms of marriage are no threat to the symbolic status of marriage, for a stable cohabiting relationship bears little moral or social difference from marriage. Nor are divorces a threat to the symbolic marriage (Jallinoja, 2000; Veijola & Jokinen, 2001). Indeed, as postdivorce parenthood has received more attention, a concept called the postmarital marriage has been created (Beck & Beck-Gernsheim, 1995, p. 147; Kuronen, 2003).

Marriage is most essentially determined by love, which also brings it under threat. Marriage may be regarded as a turning point in the lives of two adults who love each other. The relationship is made stable, daily routines step into the love affair, and the relationship is marked by the social and cultural norms related to marriage. Marriage unites, but it also organizes women, men, adults, and children. Marriage has an organizing effect on social life, sexuality, working life, and property. Marriage is a part of life even for people who are not married, have no intention of getting married, or cannot find a suitable partner. The daily routines and practices resulting from marriage change people's conceptions of passionate love and pose new challenges to their life as a couple (Jallinoja, 2000; Veijola & Jokinen, 2001).

In 1990 Mirja Tolkki-Nikkonen studied the factors that keep Finnish married couples together after the relationship has become stabilized and the daily routines of life are a reality. She crystallized her results into three cementing factors: the intimate relationship, the family relationship, and the circumstances. When intimacy was the cementing factor, it was described as close and confidential. When the family relationship explained the fact that the couple had stayed together, it meant that children and the family entity were important. When the stability of the marriage was explained through circumstances, the couple were committed to the marriage institution, were accustomed to their life, and feared loneliness or the lack of options (Tolkki-Nikkonen, 1990). Kaarina Määttä (2000) recently completed an analogous study; she explains stable marriages through an acceptance of differences and changes in the other, the ability to please the other, commitment, valuing of the self, talking, resolving conflicts, and receiving a response to one's expectations (Määttä, 2000).

The question of the relationship between the genders is one of the principal questions related to marriage, both for good and evil, and it is manifested in the domains of love, sexuality, domestic tasks and division of responsibility, childcare, housing arrangements, and earning and using money. As an example, studies concerning the internal finances of a family bring to light the gender differences made possible by the daily practices in marriage: The women may overlook their own consumption needs for the good of the family, while the men invest in their personal interests. As a result, the union that in formal terms is the same for both spouses may appear as two different ones in the light of the spouses' internal experiences: the woman's marriage and the man's marriage (Repo, 2002). These observations are embarrassing because public policy is so strongly committed to equality. Over time, the diverging modes of action based on masculine and feminine cultures may be on a collision course and gradually lead to an unbridgeable gap. The high divorce rates are often

explained by the fact that women demand more of men. However, women's demands are perhaps only concerned with the opportunities that men already possess (Veijola & Jokinen, 2001, p. 31).

Soile Veijola and Eeva Jokinen (2001) examine the Finnish marriage particularly from the gender point of view and state that the traditional identity models of spouse, wife, or husband have become outdated. The availability of models suitable for modern society, especially for the interplay and intimate togetherness of the spouses, is scant. There is a lively debate even on such things as the new fatherhood, but no debate on the new husband. Building on Luce Irigaray's ideas, Veijola and Jokinen call for a new ethical gender difference, a speculative dialogue and a respectful space for the other in marriages: "So far, we are not accustomed to encountering a manhood whose relationship to womanhood would allow an intensification of the strength and essential characteristics of both, so that they could create a space and locality for the freedom and difference of the other gender" (Veijola & Jokinen, 2001, p. 220).

6. FAMILY STRESSES AND VIOLENCE

The factors that form the framework of the daily lives of families with children have become harsher in the 1990s. Recently, the most vociferous debate has addressed the *high demands of working life* as a stress factor eroding family life. The fathers and mothers of small children generally have full-time jobs, and they go out to work more often and for longer hours than other types of households. Similarly, the employment rates of single parents are fairly high. The large volume of work is not always explained by a greater need for money, for some of the parents receive no compensation for overtime. The increase in working hours is also linked to the more demanding character of modern working life (Bardy et al., 2001, pp. 48–51). The greater prevalence of knowledge work has blurred the definition of working hours and the workplace, since knowledge work is often done at home. Many working parents view their employment as precarious. The changed conditions of working life absorb the energy of working parents and erode the energy and time otherwise available to children and the rest of family life. In conflict situations, it would appear that the family is the factor most frequently sacrificed by working parents of young children. The hectic pace of life erodes the sustained effort and peace required for the parents' task of bringing up the children (Bardy et al., 2001, p. 54; Kivimäki, 2003, pp. 186–187, 191–192).

It is only in recent years that there has been more debate on issues related to a better reconciliation of work and family life (Kivimäki, 2003, p. 186). The debate has focused on the issues important to families with children and two parents. Less serious attention has so far been directed to issues of other types of families, even though for single parents, for instance, the reconciling of work and family is very different from that of families with two breadwinners (Kröger & Zechner, 2001). Correspondingly, the needs of families with small children are different from the needs of families approaching retirement (Kivimäki, 2003, p. 190).

The *tightening of financial conditions* has been another stress factor eroding family life in recent years. The financial status of families and families with children, especially single-parent families, weakened during the 1990s due to the negative effect of the deep economic recession (Jähi, 2000; Hiilamo, 2002). The unprecedented economic boom following the depression exacerbated the income differentials. During the strong economic growth in the late 1990s, the income levels developed most favorably in households with income-generating property. In contrast, almost one-quarter of all families with children were classified as belonging to the lowest income quintile in 2000. The share of children living in families below the poverty line has risen to 12%. The dependence on social security of the families with the lowest income has increased. Unemployment continues to be a difficult issue for many families with children. The economic recession following on the heels of the strong burst of economic growth has, however, brought about a freezing or cutting back of many income transfers designed to benefit families with children, so that coping with finances is even more uncertain than before. Housing expenses, which are at their highest when the children are small, have also increased for families with children (Bardy et al., 2001). At the same time, basic services that are important to families with children have become scarcer, and the number of families needing such services as child protection has increased. A decreasing number of workers are employed in these services, and they often experience fatigue due to overburdening. It has been observed, with justification, that families with children have ended up paying for the recent developments in society (Bardy et al., 2001).

The third set of important stress factors in family life are various psychosocial problem situations, such as divorce crises followed by eventual custody and access conflicts, mental health problems of both children and adults, alcohol and drug problems of adults and young people, and violence in intimate relationships occurring in homes. In Finland, unlike, for instance, the other Nordic countries, violence in intimate relationships has up to now been predominantly thematized as domestic violence, classified as a relationship and interaction disorder. It is only recently, essentially after women's studies became more active in this field, that the concept of family violence and the attendant neutral factor, the approach that does not recognize victims and the gendered power dynamics, have begun to be dismantled. At the same time, there has been more sensitivity toward the characteristics specific to women and men in violence in intimate relationships. The particular angles of children (Forsberg, 2002; see also www.norfa.no) and elderly people (Perttu, 1995) on violence in intimate relationships have begun to receive attention. Violence in intimate relationships is often, although not necessarily, linked to alcohol or drugs (Nyqvist, 2001).

Violence in intimate relationships is one of the largest obstacles to improving women's position and gender equality. According to a nationwide survey, 22% of women living in an intimate relationship had encountered or been threatened with physical or sexual violence by their spouse, and 9% of them had experienced this within the past year. In addition to physical injuries and pain, women often suffer from serious psychological difficulties (Heiskanen & Piispa, 1998). The protection of women's corporeal rights, such as protection from sexual harassment and violence, has been poorly implemented in Finland (Julkunen, 1999, p. 82). It is only quite recently that there has been more understanding of the gender-based nature of violence and its links to masculinity and use of power as a cultural characteristic. Judging by the women's experience, violence can be manifested, on the one hand, as emotional coolness, subjugation, liaisons with other women, and rejection, or, on the other hand, as jealously, controlling of the woman on many different levels, and threats. Women generally experience feelings of guilt due to violence. Men's experiences are dominated by what has caused the violence, such as women's actions. It is rare for them to experience guilt and to assume responsibility for their behavior (Nyqvist, 2001, pp. 78–152).

Even though violence is regarded as nondesirable behavior, in certain situations it is idolized as manly. It may be considered a setback for gender equality that a culture of violence is becoming increasingly widespread in the world of girls and women. Violent behavior by girls was not tolerated or approved in earlier times. Instead of open or physical violence, women's culture has developed forms of indirect and psychological violence. The development toward equality appears to be leading to a situation where girls are, on the one hand, encouraged to express their aggressions and disappointments more openly, while, on the other hand, there is more approval of violence on the grounds that it is also permitted to men and boys (Jokinen, 2003).

7. DIVORCE, SEPARATION, AND REMARRIAGE

Divorce rates in Finland are the highest in the European Union. Finland shares first place with Sweden. Of all marriages undertaken, about 50% are expected to lead to divorce. Nevertheless, if one examines marriages undertaken in the period 1949–1993, almost one-quarter of them had led to divorce by 1994. If people keep up the increasingly widespread practice of divorce, it may be predicted that about one-half of the marriages entered into during the 1990s will end up in divorce at some point. Thus, divorce rates would be high in this particular divorce cohort. If break-ups of cohabiting relationships were included in official statistics, divorcing would be even more prevalent in Finland. It is generally known that cohabiting relationships break up clearly more frequently than marriages. Two-thirds of the divorces are initiated by women. Childless marriages are statistically more likely to end up in divorce than marriages with children, and divorce is less frequent in families with more than one child. The children's ages also afford statistical protection against divorce, for the divorce rates go up as the children grow older (Jallinoja, 2000, p. 151; Määttä, 2002, p. 13).

The reform of divorce legislation in the 1980s contributed to the emergence of a new divorce culture. After the reform, implemented in 1988, a momentary peak was seen, but since then the trend has evened out. The basic principle of the reform was to enable the dissolution of marriages with reflection and discussion. The principle of the guilty party was abandoned, and the intention was to cause as little humiliation and stress to the parties as possible. No grounds are necessary for obtaining a divorce. Thus, divorce may be considered a private matter based on a mutual agreement of the parties. In many Western countries, the development of family legislation has conformed to the ideas of free choice and the skill possessed by individuals to negotiate the best possible solution, even in conflict situations (Nousiainen, 2001, pp. 15–18). One of the parties may seek divorce alone, or both spouses may formally appear as applicants. The application is followed by a 6-month period of reflection, after which a repeat application is needed for the court to grant the divorce. In the event of a divorce, family relationships are redefined. Decisions concerning the division of property and the custody arrangements and financial support of and access to the children are regulated by law. The broad principle behind the legislation is the belief that the spouses will agree on these issues in mutual negotiation. About 4% of divorces are extremely difficult and may drag on for years with complicated arguments and recourse to several different authorities and court appearances (Määttä, 2002, p. 37).

Concern over the increase in divorce has been expressed for two main reasons: the effect of divorce on children and the erosion of moral principles linked to the family and marriage institution. Researchers agree that the marriage institution has become weaker

at least in the legal sense, for alongside marriage, cohabiting has become an accepted form of union. Divorce is legally easier than before and the status of the children is not necessarily dependent on the parents' marital status (Gottberg, 1997). There has been less agreement on whether the development has eroded the significance of the family and the intimate relationship. Some researchers consider divorce and the custodial and responsibility arrangement set up after it, concerning the couple's children in particular, as a new kind of postmarital marriage, in which the marriage, the intimate relationship between the spouses, is transformed from a union based on love into a union mediated by the children. From this point of view, the significance of the family remains, and the significance of parenthood increases, which is the case also with unions that are dissociated from parenthood (Kuronen, 2003).

Shared children are a factor that maintains the contacts of the "divorced family" in Finnish society. According to statistics, parenthood after divorce is clearly gender-segregated. The majority of children remain with their mother; the younger they are, the greater the number who live with their mother (Kuronen, 2003, p. 108). The ideological and legal changes in postdivorce parenthood have particularly affected the meanings assigned to fatherhood and fathers' rights. The focus has moved from the biological father's former obligation to provide for the child to an emphasis on the emotional bond between father and child (Kuronen, 2003, p. 109). In this debate, motherhood has remained in the background as natural and a matter of course, even though in practice mothers seem to have acquired the new responsibility of upholding and maintaining the child's new relationship to the father.

Remarriage became more common from the 1970s onward, with the increase in divorce rates. The change is aptly illustrated by the fact that in 1970 only 6% of marriages were concluded by divorce, but in 1998 the corresponding figure was 31%. Remarriages of widowed spouses have stabilized at about 2% of all marriages concluded. The annual number of remarriages is about one-half the number of divorces. It is not possible to estimate the number of new cohabiting unions; a rough guideline on the prevalence of breakups of cohabiting relationships is given by the general assumption that their number is twice that of divorces annually (Ritala-Koskinen, 2001, pp. 15–16).

Statistics on stepfamilies, formed by a divorced parent with children and a new spouse, have only been available since the 1990s. This time lag has been explained by the societal-social climate, which was not prepared to compile statistics on stepfamilies until that point in time (Kurkela & Sauli, 1998, pp. 35–36). The statistical stepfamilies are formed on the basis of where the child lives, which is why they do not capture the families where the child only visits one of its parents. In 1999, the share of stepfamilies was 7.6% of all families with children (the number includes families of both married and cohabiting spouses). About 90% of stepfamilies are formed on the basis of a mother and her children, which means that the new member in the family is the new father (and eventual new children) (Ritala-Koskinen, 2001, pp. 14–16).

Aino Ritala-Koskinen (2001) has studied the family conceptions of children living in stepfamilies, and points out that in these days, children also negotiate and choose their family relationships individually within the tolerances available to children as dependent on adults. Children actively construct and regulate closeness to or distance from the parent's new partner, the partner's children, and stepgrandparents. Thus, as a subjective experience, the child's family may not be the same as, say, the mother's family, even though they may live under the same roof (Ritala-Koskinen, 2001).

8. KINSHIP, PROPERTY, AND INHERITANCE

On the one hand, it is possible to claim that kinship is not a very significant factor in determining the social position of a Finnish person. Basic material and social security and education are guaranteed by the welfare society in the form of an individual entitlement to social security, various social services, and a free and universally accessible education system. On the other hand, however, the social, cultural, and material capital linked to kinship ties may be assumed to be of significance to individuals and families. However, there is scant research data on the movements of capital via kinship.

In marriage the main rule is that a spouse's property remains in his or her possession. Each spouse also holds the rights to what he or she acquires during the marriage (Anttonen, Forsberg, & Huhtanen, 1995, p. 67). Inherited property accumulates in the groups of households that are already the most prosperous, and in the older age-groups. In 1990–1994, the share of households receiving inheritances and fairly large gifts of money was 19%. The majority consisted of households already affluent, and property transfers without remuneration mostly concerned 55 to 64-year-olds. According to studies, the considerable economic boom at the end of the 1990s also increased the prosperity of the most affluent, in particular as regards dwellings, stocks and shares, and investments in funds (Kotitalouksien varallisuus, 2000). The legal right to inheritance concerns first and foremost the children of the deceased, whether they were born in or out of wedlock. Adopted children are also regarded as primary heirs. As a general rule, the inheritance is divided equally among the children. The inheritance of a childless person goes either to the surviving marriage partner or a registered same-sex spouse or, in the absence of these, the parents of the deceased or, in the event that they are already dead, the siblings of the deceased. A cohabiter is not entitled to inherit from the deceased spouse unless a will has been drawn up. However, even with a will, the cohabiting spouse will be liable to an inheritance tax three times greater than in the case of a married spouse (Anttonen et al., 1995, p. 67).

Kinship ties subjectively experienced as important appear to focus mainly on the nuclear kin, or the relationships between parents, children, and their siblings. In contrast, more remote kin lose their significance for the lives of individuals and families. Nuclear kinship is primarily based on friendship, interaction, and shared leisure pursuits. Grandparents also serve as an important resource for their adult children in childcare and minor financial problems (Oinonen, 2000, pp. 182–183). In minor financial problems, a significant number of people rely on their close kin: parents and children. In contrast, significantly fewer individuals resort to the same people in major financial difficulties. In the face of a greater threat, the help of authorities is preferred (Jähi, 1999, p. 151).

One could claim that the significance of blood ties has increased due to certain developments concerning family relationships. Biological parenthood, and fatherhood in particular, has become more important with the greater emphasis on the rights of children (and men). In some senses, however, kinship is a matter of agreement. In the legal sense, children's ties to their biological kin are completely severed in such cases as adoption (only the so-called strong adoption model is recognized in Finland). In contrast, the maintenance of biological kinship ties is promoted in cases of divorce and the forming of stepfamilies. The weight of one's biological origins is also a matter of

conflict in the preparation of legislation on artificial fertilization. These conflicts are related to, among other things, whether the child should have the right of knowing about its origin or the sperm donor. The threats seen here concern the possible maintenance responsibility of the sperm donor and the child's eventual rights of inheriting the donor's property.

9. AGING AND DEATH

The population of Finland—in line with the general European trend—is aging rapidly. In 2000, one Finn in every seven was over 65 years of age. By 2030, it is expected that the share of the over-65s will be as high as one-quarter of the population (Helin, 2002, p. 37). In Finland, women's average life span is about 7 years longer than men's (although recently it has been noted that the gap between men and women is closing somewhat). Men's average life span is currently about 74 years and women's slightly under 82 years. As the male partner is generally a few years older than the female partner, women typically spend the last years of their lives alone. With increasing age, living with someone else becomes more frequent; this can be one's child, the child's family, other kin, or an acquaintance. Nevertheless, one-half of the over-80s live alone, and 15% of the over-85s live in institutions (Pääkkönen & Niemi, 2002, p. 66).

Research data on the family relationships of old people in Finland is not readily available. As an example, research data on the partnerships of the elderly is amazingly scant. On the basis of statistics, 71% of people at retirement age live with their spouse, and over one-half of the over-75s still do, while only one-seventh of the over-85s live with their spouse (Pääkkönen & Niemi, 2002, p. 66). Most commonly, discussions of elderly people focus on their needs for health- and nursing care, and on the burden that they constitute for the ever-decreasing group of economically active people. It must be noted, however, that grandparenthood has been the object of new interest in recent years.

With the imminent retirement of the postwar generations, the service system of geriatric care is facing great pressures. As the public economy is undergoing a financial crisis, there are continued attempts to cut back on cost-intensive institutional care and to increase community services and to support elderly people who still live in their own homes. By retirement age, one-half of the population lives in single-family houses, but after that, living in flats becomes more frequent. Most pensioner households manage their household duties without external help, despite chronic illness and injuries. It is interesting to note that the amount of household work undertaken by men increases at this stage. With increasing age, the need for external help goes up (Pääkkönen & Niemi, 2002, pp. 68–70). In many municipalities the provision of community services is still fairly one-sided, which means that families must assume a great deal of responsibility for caring for the elderly.

Even though grown-up children have no legal responsibility for the care of their aged parents, in practice the care for the increasing numbers of elderly people cannot be managed without the help of families. On the basis of a questionnaire directed in 1996 to the over-75s resident in nine municipalities, most elderly people received daily help from their children and grandchildren and their spouses (Lehto, 1997, p. 18). The moral obligation experienced by people to assist their aged parents is a separate issue altogether. According to studies on attitudes, Finns appear, on the one hand, to support strongly society's obligation to provide support and services, but, on the other hand, they appear also to feel a moral obligation to look after their parents, especially when they get older and are in need of assistance (Ritamies & Fågel, 1998, pp. 33–37). Similarly, the aged themselves express a preference for public services rather than assistance from the family, but people in general believe that the responsibility of close kin will increase in the future (Vaarama, Hakkarainen, & Laaksonen, 1999, pp. 49, 53). Regardless of geographical distance, it is also very common for grown-up children, especially daughters, to remain in telephone contact, weekly at least, with their aged parents—especially the mother (Ritamies & Fågel, 1998, pp. 54–55; Lammi-Taskula & Suhonen, 1999).

Aging people are not just a burden on society and the younger generations. As aging people nowadays live longer and remain healthier, they can also help the younger generations in many ways. According to studies on attitudes, children do not appear to feel that they are entitled to expect services, assistance, or resources from their aging parents. Instead, people most frequently think that aging persons are entitled to think about themselves and to concentrate on their own lives. Nevertheless, according to studies, the parents of middle-age adults with small children provide significant help in caring for the grandchildren, and this is also often the stage when the adult children's relationships to their parents improve (Ritamies & Fågel, 1998, pp. 38–39). According to the old-age barometer, two-fifths of the over-60s care for their grandchildren at least occasionally, and one-fifth does so once a month (Vaarama et al., 1999).

More children of today have living grandparents than their parents did, since people nowadays live longer. The new formations of families also increase the number of potential grandparents. As public services are decreased and the daily lives of families with children become increasingly hectic, a new niche opens up for grandparenthood. Grandparents can provide an unexpected amount of help in many ways that may affect a family with children (Eräsaari, 2002).

Even though grandparents come in many shapes and sizes and live at varying distances, the fact that a grandparent still goes out to work may limit social interaction with the children's families. The grandmothers studied by Eräsaari (2002) regarded their grandparenthood as a rich and multilevel experience. The essential elements were the observing of the miracle of birth and growth of the new generation, becoming a link in the long chain of generations, the possibility of regulating the length of time spent with the grandchildren, enjoyment and caring, and a new opportunity of mending one's previous actions as a mother (Eräsaari, 2002).

The older people become, the more generally they experience loneliness. This is not necessarily linked with living alone. According to one study, for example, elderly Finns living alone experienced loneliness less frequently than elderly Greeks living in integrated communities (Jylhä & Jokela, 1990). Similarly, studies on elderly Finns have found that those living with a partner may experience loneliness when encountering illness in themselves or in their partner. Elderly people living in service flats or institutions that are surrounded by other people still typically experience loneliness (Heikkinen, 1999).

10. FAMILY AND OTHER INSTITUTIONS

In Finland, the welfare state with its institutions is present in the daily lives of families in many ways. One could say that Finnish society is based on four essential, partly unwritten, contracts that have shaped the position and significance of families and guided social policy. The first is a solidarity contract, which means that public authorities assume responsibility for dependent people in need of assistance, and citizens participate in this by paying taxes. The second is a gender contract, a striving to safeguard equal opportunities for both genders to participate in working life and social activity. Third, society is based on the normal employment contract, which has meant that life is based on a permanent paid job. Fourth, there is the generation contract, which addresses certain expectations, responsibilities, and obligations between the generations and age-groups. The generation contract consists of three important phases: childhood, adulthood, and old age. In childhood, the care, nurturing, and education of the individual is realized by the parents and the public institutions, such as day-care centers, children's clinics, basic healthcare services, and the school. In adulthood, people are involved in giving birth to the new generation, in the task of raising the new generation, in working life, and in financing the activities of society, such as caring for the older generations, through taxation. In old age, people retire and transfer the responsibility for maintaining society to the younger generations (Kautto, 2002). This context has led to a certain idea of family. Children, old people, and those dependent on others have not been left solely to the responsibility of individuals and families. There is also an attempt to share the costs caused by children and to safeguard the rights of minors and to promote gender equality. The basic actor in society is the individual, not the family (Anttonen et al., 1995; Millar & Warman, 1996).

As we have approached the present, these contracts have faced new challenges with the increasing prevalence of market-driven ideas and modes of action that stress efficiency and competition in all fields of society. This is visible both in the parents' jobs and in the activity of institutions for children. The number of old people is increasing, the percentage holding jobs is decreasing, the traditional standard life cycle is no longer very likely, and the changes in family structure pose new questions as to the smooth flow of everyday life. One of the greatest challenges of social policy is the safeguarding of services and benefits for the older age-groups without overburdening the economically active population. Families with children are generally a part of the economically active population, but the political weight of families with children is assumed to lessen with the decrease in the number of children. Stable economy and a policy striving for economic growth are regarded as the keywords for success. Recently, however, a debate on other values, not just economic values, has been called for (Bardy et al., 2001).

Not much can be done to change demographics, but political decisions can be taken that affect the dependency ratio. Current topics for reflection include the questions of safeguarding economic growth, increasing the size and length of the working career of the economically active population, the issues related to pensions, and the ways of preparing for the increasing need for social and health services. Visions of the future are fuzzy, since it is very difficult to predict economic developments, unemployment and employment rates, the development of profitability, inflation, and interest rates. What is clear is that expenditure is increasing. There is a fear that the growing expenditure will cause conflicts between age-groups and interest groups. Some have started keeping "generation accounts," calculating winners and losers. However, there is an assumption that age, for instance, is not necessarily the factor that binds people together as a group. It is also possible that kinship or family relationships are ultimately more significant for solidarity. Researchers of the SOCCARE project, for instance, have studied childcare arrangements in Europe and have found that Finns very frequently resort to unofficial networks (Lone Parent Families, 2002, p. 109). This, however, does not award the same kind of universal security as that provided by the income transfers and services effected by the public sector. The social security potential afforded by the family to its members is sometimes also assumed to have weakened, for the traditional idea of adulthood as consisting of professional skills, a job, and setting up a family has been postponed to a later age and has become a less stable phenomenon. It has also been suggested that as families grow smaller and more diversified, single-parent families or households consisting of aged people living alone are "weaker" as family types and are in greater need of support and services from society. On the other hand, friendships and relationships to neighbors may form important sources of unofficial help alongside family relationships (Oinonen, 1999, p. 181).

The dissolution of families, smaller family size, and low birthrates have been seen as signs of such diverse phenomena as increasing harshness in working life and less favorable conditions of life, a change in basic values, a strengthening of individualization, a decrease in the appreciation of family life, and the outdatedness of family policy. Critical statements point out that social policy has not shown an appreciation of family life. Rather, it has contributed to the plurality of family models by facilitating divorces, promoting the early move from home of the young with the housing allowance system, weakening the contact between generations through legislation on the relationships of grown-up children and parents, and narrowing the presence of adults in the lives of children as a consequence of political decisions. However, it appears that there are no grounds for saying that the family is no longer significant. The majority of the population still lives in families, divorcées set up new families, and people of all ages consider family life to be one of the key values in their lives (Oinonen, 1999, p. 180).

REFERENCES

Aalto, I. (2002). Kotiin päin—kodin muuttuvat merkitykset miesten isyyskertomuksissa. *Naistutkimus, 15*(2), 30–42.

Anttonen, A. (2003). Lastenhoidon kaksi maailmaa. In H. Forsberg & R. Nätkin (Eds.), *Perhe murroksessa—kriittisen perhetutkimuksen jäljillä* (pp. 159–185). Helsinki: Gaudeamus.

Anttonen, A., Forsberg, H., & Huhtanen, R. (1995). Family obligations in Finland. In J. Millar & A. Warman (Eds.), *Defining family obligations in Europe* (pp. 65–86). Bath Social Policy Papers No. 23. Centre for the Analysis of Social Policy. Bath, UK: University of Bath.

Anttonen, A., & Sipilä, J. (2000). *Suomalaista sosiaalipolitiikkaa.* Tampere: Vastapaino.

Bardy, M., Salmi, M., & Heino, T. (2001). *Mikä lapsiamme uhkaa? Suuntaviivoja 2000-luvun lapsipoliittiseen keskusteluun.* Stakes, Raportteja 263. Helsinki: Stakes.

Beck, U., & Beck-Gernsheim, E. (1995). *The normal chaos of love.* Cambridge, UK: Polity Press.

Castells, M., & Himanen, P. (2002). *Information society and the welfare state: The Finnish model.* Oxford: Oxford University Press.

Eräsaari, L. (2002). Moderni mummo. *Gerontologia, 16*(1), 10–20.

Families 2001 (2002). *Population 2002: 10, Statistics Finland.* Helsinki: Statistic Centre.

Forsberg, H. (2002). Children's feedback on the helping practices of shelters. In *Gender and Violence in the Nordic Countries* (p. 545). Tema Nord: Nordiska Ministerrådet.

Forsberg, H., & Pösö, T. (2001). Virtuaaliyhteisöllisyys ja langaton kommunikaatio—uhka ja mahdollisuus lapsille. In M. Kangassalo & J. Suoranta (Eds.), *Lasten tietoyhteiskunta* (pp. 193–206). Tampere: University Press.

Gottberg, E. (1997). *Perhesuhteet ja lainsäädäntö.* Turun yliopiston oikeustieteellisen tiedekunnan julkaisuja. Yksityisoikeuden julkaisusarja A:93. Turku: Turun yliopisto.

Harinen, P. (1998). *Uusi nuoriso ja uusi perhe Janus.*, 6(4), 419–428.

Heikkinen, L. (1999). Millaista on olla vanha ja yksin? *Hyvinvointikatsaus, 4*, 16–17.

Heiskanen, M., & Piispa, M. (1998). *Usko, toivo, hakkaus: Kyselytutkimus miesten naisille tekemästä väkivallasta.* Helsinki: Tilastokeskus.

Helin, S. (2002). Palvelujärjestelmä iäkkään ihmisen voimavarojen tukijana. In E. Heikkinen & M. Marin (Eds.), *Vanhuuden voimavarat* (pp. 35–67). Helsinki: Tammi.

Hiilamo, H. (2002). *The rise and fall of Nordic family policy? Historical development and changes during the 1990s in Sweden and Finland.* Stakes, research report 125. Helsinki: Stakes.

Hoikkala, T. (1993). *Katoaako kasvatus, himmeneekö aikuisuus?* Helsinki: Gaudeamus.

Hoikkala, T. (1998). Isyys ja vanhemmuus. In E. Saksala (Ed.), *Muutoksen sosiologia* (pp. 75–83). Helsinki: Yle.

Jähi, R. (2000). Luokkaperheet. In R. Blom (Ed.), *Mikä Suomessa muuttui? Sosiologinen kuva 1990-luvusta* (pp. 123–163). Helsinki: Gaudeamus & Hanki ja Jää.

Jallinoja, R. (2000). *Perheen aika.* Helsinki: Otava.

Jokinen, A. (2003). *Sukupuolten sodasta tasa-arvoon.* Retrieved June 2003, from www.uta.fi/laitokset/naistutkimus/miestutkimus/tasa-arvo_artikkeli.htm.

Julkunen, R. (1999). Sukupuoli, työ, hyvinvointivaltio. In *Suomalainen nainen* [Women in Finland] (pp. 79–100). Helsinki: Otava.

Jylhä, M., & Jokela, J. (1990). Individual experiences as cultural—a crosscultural study on loneliness. *Aging Society, 10,* 295–315.

Kantola, A., & Kautto, M. (2002). *Hyvinvoinnin valinnat. Suomen malli 2000-luvulla.* Helsinki: Edita.

Kartovaara, L., & Sauli, H. (2000). *Suomalainen lapsi.* Väestö 2000: 7. Helsinki: Tilastokeskus.

Kautto, M. (2002). Ikääntyvä väestö. In A. Kantola & M. Kautto, *Hyvinvoinnin valinnat. Suomen malli 2000-luvulla* (pp. 46–67). Helsinki: Edita.

Kivimäki, R. (2003). Perhe tuli työelämään. In H. Forsberg & R. Nätkin (Eds.), *Perhe murroksessa—kriittisen perhetutkimuksen jäljillä* (pp. 186–201). Helsinki: Gaudeamus.

Kotitalouksien varallisuus. (2000). *Tulot ja kulutus 2000: 26.* Helsinki: Tilastokeskus.

Kröger, T., & Zechner, M. (2001). *Care arrangements in single parent families. National report: Finland. SOCCARE Project Report 2.1, European Comission 5th Framework Programme, Improving Human Potential and Socio-Economic Knowledge Base.* Retrieved June 2003 from www.uta.fi/laitokset/sospol/soccare/report2.1.pdf.

Kurkela, R., & Sauli, H. (1998). Tilastolliset luokitukset ja arki. In S. Paananen, A. Juntto, & H. Sauli (Eds.), *Faktajuttu. Tilastollisen sosiaalitutkimuksen käytännöt* (pp. 27–42). Tampere: Vastapaino.

Kuronen, M. (2003). Eronnut perhe? In H. Forsberg & R. Nätkin (Eds.), *Perhe murroksessa—kriittisen perhetutkimuksen jäljillä* (pp. 103–120). Helsinki: Gaudeamus.

Lammi-Taskula, J., & Suhonen, A. S. (1999). *Puolin ja toisin. Sukupolvien välinen auttaminen Työ ja perhe—kyselyaineiston ja haastattelujen valossa.* Työpapereita 1/1999. Helsinki: Stakes.

Lehto, J. (1997). *Mistä apu ikääntyneille? Tuloksia yhdeksän kunnan 75 vuotta täyttäneille tehdystä kyselystä.* Stakes, Aiheita 19. Helsinki: Stakes.

Lone Parent Families. (2002). *Work and social care. A qualitative comparision of care arrangements in Finland, Italy, Portugal, the UK and France 2002.* SOCCARE Project Report 2. Retrieved May 2003, from www.uta.fi/laitokset/sospol/soccare/report 2.PDF.

Millar, J., & Warman, A. (1996). *Family obligations in Europe.* London: Family Policy Studies Centre.

Määttä, K. (2000). *Kestävä parisuhde.* Helsinki: WSOY.

Määttä, K. (2002). *Avioeron tuska ja helpotus.* Helsinki: Tammi.

Nätkin, R. (2003). Monaiset perhemuodot ja lapsen hyvä. In H. Forsberg & R. Nätkin (Eds.), *Perhe murroksessa—kriittisen perhetutkimuksen jäljillä,* (pp. 16–38).Gaudeamus: Helsinki.

Nikander, T. (1992). *Naisen elämänkulku ja perheellistyminen.* Väestö 1992: 1. Helsinki: Tilastokeskus.

Nousiainen, K. (2001). Yksityinen ja julkinen—perhe ja markkinat. *Naistutkimus, 14*(4), 6–21.

Nyqvist, L. (2001). *Väkivaltainen parisuhde, asiakkuus ja muutos.* Ensi- ja turvakotien liiton julkaisu 28. Helsinki: Ensi-ja turvakotien liitto.

Oinonen, E. (1999). Perheet ja pärjääminen. In R. Blom (Ed.), *Mikä Suomessa muuttui? Sosiologinen kuva 1990-luvusta* (pp. 163–191). Helsinki: Gaudeamus & Hanki ja Jää.

Paajanen, P. (2002). *Saako haikara tulla käymään? Suomalaisten lastenhankinnan ihanteet ja todellisuus.* Perhebarometri 2002. Katsauksia E 14/2002. Helsinki: Väestöliitto, Väestöntutkimuslaitos.

Pääkkönen, H., & Niemi, I. (2002). *Suomalainen arki. Ajankäyttö vuosituhannen vaihteessa.* Kulttuuri ja viestintä 2002:2. Helsinki: Tilastokeskus.

Parisuhdetilasto [Partnership Statistics]. (2002). Retrieved June 3, 2003, from www.vaestorekisterikeskus.fi/Parisuhdetilasto 2002.htm.

Perttu, S. (1995). *Ikääntyviin kohdistuva perheväkivalta.* Palveluiden kehittäminen kunnan vanhustenhuollossa. Raportti perheväkivallan hoitokokeilusta Vantaalla. Stakes, Aiheita 32. Helsinki: Stakes.

Pylkkänen, A. (1999). Suomalainen tasa-arvo. In *Suomalainen nainen* [Women in Finland] (pp. 24–38). Helsinki: Otava.

Rantalaiho, M. (2003). Pohjoismaisen isyyspolitiikan isäkuva. In H. Forsberg & R. Nätkin (Eds.), *Perhe murroksessa—kriittisen perhetutkimuksen jäljillä* (pp. 202–229). Helsinki: Gaudeamus.

Repo, K. (2002). *Raha ei kasva puussa: Perheen rahatalous ja sen diskursiivinen todellisuus.* Tampereen yliopisto: Sosiaalipolitiikan lisensiaatintutkielma.

Reuna, V. (1997). *Perhebarometri.* Väestöntutkimuslaitos. Katsauksia E 3/1997. Helsinki: Väestöliitto, Väestöntutkimuslaitos.

Ritala-Koskinen, A. (2001). *Mikä on lapsen perhe? Tulkintoja uusperhesuhteista.* Väestöntutkimuslaitoksen julkaisusarja D 38. Helsinki: Väestöntutkimuslaitos, Väestöliitto.

Ritamies, M., & Fågel, S. (1998). *Aikuiset avunsaajina.* Väestöntutkimuslaitos, Väestöliitto D 33, 1998. Helsinki: Väestöliitto, Väestöntutkimuslaitos.

Strandell, H. (2001). Lasten työnteko—merkki lapsuuden murroksesta. In M. Törrönen (Ed.), *Lapsuuden hyvinvointi* (pp. 85–98). Helsinki: Pelastakaa Lapsetry.

Takala, P. (2002). Suomi Ruotsin jalanjäljissä—kehitys kohti ydinperheen jälkeistä aikaa. In *Perheasioita. Puhetta nykyperheestä* (pp. 8–25). Tampere: Tampereen hiippakunnan vuosikirja.

Tolkki-Nikkonen, M. (1990). *Parisuhde, perhesuhde, olosuhde: Mikä pitää avioliiton koossa 15 vuoden jälkeen?* Helsinki: Gaudeamus.

Vaarama, M., Hakkarainen, A., & Laaksonen, S. (1999). *Vanhusbarometri [1998].* Sosiaali- ja terveysministeriön selvityksiä 3. Helsinki: Sosiaali- ja terveysministeriö.

Väestörekisterikeskus. (2003). Retrieved June 1, 2004, from www.vaestorek isterikeskus.fi.

Väestötilastot [Population Statistics]. (2003). Retrieved from www.stat.fi/tk/tp/ tasku/taskus_vaesto.html.

Veijola, S., & Jokinen, E. (2001). *Voiko naista rakastaa? Avion ja eron karuselli.* Helsinki: WSOY.

Vikat, A. (2002). *Fertility in Finland in the 1980s and 1990s: Analysis of fertility trend by age and parity.* Yearbook of Population Research in Finland 38. (pp. 159–177). Helsinki: Population Research Centre.

Vuori, J. (2003). Äitiyden ainekset. In H. Forsberg & R. Nätkin (Eds.), *Perhe murroksessa—kriittisen perhetutkimuksen jäljillä* (pp. 39–63). Helsinki: Gaudeamus.

CHAPTER **13**

Families in Germany

THOMAS KLEIN

BERNHARD NAUCK

1. HISTORICAL BACKGROUND

Due to its location in the center of Europe, Germany has always been a country in which various influences have come together, and its institutions have always been culturally diverse. Shifting boundaries, because of various wars during the centuries, have led to quite different populations living in German society and have helped to shape its social structure. In addition, a considerable amount of migration occurred after World War II. After the Second World War alone, 12.5 million refugees of German nationality from Eastern Europe and from former German territories entered Germany. With about 3.6 million inhabitants moving from East to West Germany, one out of every four inhabitants of West Germany was a refugee or an expellee (Rudolph, 1996). At present, Germany consists of about 82 million inhabitants, of which some 7 million are foreigners and about 4 million are German repatriates from Eastern European countries (Roloff & Schwarz, 2002). These diverse influences and the vast amount of available empirical

research make it quite difficult to report coherently on the situation of families in Germany, leading to unavoidable overgeneralizations and oversimplifications.

Before Bismarck's nation-building in the late 19th century, Germany was a rather diverse agglomeration of relatively small and independent states with their own cultural and religious traditions and autonomous institutional structures. This leaves us with a rather scattered picture of "traditional" marriage regulations and restrictions, as well as diverse heritage rules. Thus, for example, traditions of primogeniture, ultimogeniture, and equal distribution of the heritage among all sons or even among all descendants can be found in close proximity. These have resulted in totally different patterns of land ownership and sizes of properties. However, the major divide may be seen between the (predominantly Lutheran Protestant) north and the (predominantly Roman Catholic) south. Generally speaking, the family patterns of Germany's northeast regions resemble much more those of Denmark and Sweden, while Germany's southwest region has strong similarities with families in Austria and Italy.

This cultural heterogeneity with regard to marriage and the family is still present due to three different factors: First, the nation-building of Germany took place rather late—as compared with most of the other major societies in Europe—with the foundation of a German state in 1871. The first common legal regulations of marriage and the family are contained in the *Bürgerliche Gesetzbuch* of 1900, with its prescription for the patriarchal bourgeois family. Second, Germany still has a strong federal structure, giving its member states a considerable amount of cultural autonomy, especially in the educational domain—thus preserving the cultural diversity. Third, Germany has undergone several disruptive events during the 20th century, including the two world wars, with enormous population movements due to the expulsion of population from the former eastern territories, the economic depression in the 1920s, and the assumption of power of the Nazi regime, and, lately, the split between the Federal Republic (FRG) and the German Democratic Republic (GDR) after World War II until the unification in 1989–1990. The disruptive events of the world wars, the economic depression, and—even more so—political unification, had massive influences on the population structure of Germany, such as strong periodic drops in fertility rates and resulting cohort sizes. The two world wars also led to strong differences among the cohorts with regard to mortality risks and resulted in massive cohort-specific losses in the age distribution of German society. Moreover, these disruptions, being accompanied by political and constitutional changes, also led to many discontinuities in the legal regulations, such as far-reaching differences between the social and family policies of both German states during the more than 40 years of separation, providing totally different incentives for the family formation process.

The incentives in the FRG were primarily targeted toward marriage, a division of labor between spouses, and giving additional benefits to economically secured families through tax deductions. The GDR favored a model of early, standardized marriages, giving generous marriage credits and providing housing for young couples and, for dual-earner families, providing full day care for children from a very early age almost until late adolescence.

However, regional disparities and changes have taken place within a specific cultural framework. The cultural framework to which Germany has adhered during the last 1,000 years is described as the "Western European Marriage Pattern" by J. Hajnal (1965). This is a unique combination of (1) an advanced age at marriage and (2) a high proportion of people never marrying at all. Both are the consequence of the institutionalization of neolocal household formation in the medieval society, based on estates. Strong marriage regulations and limitations enforced the rule that a new household could only be established if an existing household was dissolved or if the financial means are proven to justify adding a new entity to the social structure. The principle behind this regulation was that each marriage results in a new household and that each household should not contain more than one couple (Laslett, 1976). Neolocal household formation based on marriage makes the couple the primary unit of solidarity, and the household the primary unit of production and reproduction. Consequently, remarriages after separation or widowhood were, unlike most lineage-based kinship systems, very common even for widows, and served the principle of immediate, efficient recompletion of the household, and frequently resulted in marriages with marked age differences. Many households contained additional, nonrelated, unmarried members, such as maids and servants (*Gesinde*), waiting—sometimes lifelong—for a marriage opportunity (Mitterauer, 1992). The institution of

Gesinde served for households as a means to react flexibly to shifting labor demands in hiring additional household members; for the maids and servants, this provided a moratorium on the flexible length between childhood and full social recognition in adulthood, which was strongly related to marriage.

Accordingly, kinship has never been a major economic unit in the German context. Strong rules of exogamy in combination with cognatic (bilinear) descent reduce the control rights of the family of origin after marriage to a minimum. Lineage systems and arranged marriages have always been limited to some noble families, while, for the vast majority of the German society, marriage by consent between spouses was predominant and kinship systems in the form of individual kindred played a subordinate role. This quite effectively reduced nonmarital births to a relatively low level, thus resulting—in combination with late marriage age—in a marked fertility restriction. Variations in population size because of nutrition crises, wars, and epidemic diseases were responded to by elasticity in marriage age (Laslett, 1971), which resulted in cohort-specific variations in marriage age and the proportion of lifelong unmarrieds (Mitterauer, 1990; Mitterauer & Sieder, 1984).

This institutional framework was easily transformed during the period of industrialization to the modern, privatized nuclear family, since bilinear descent, marriage of consent, and neolocalism had laid the ground for the intimization of family life thereafter. This intimization was the result of the separation between production and reproduction, which reduced the household size to the family members, and thus led to a sharp boundary between private family life and the public sphere. This transformation was accompanied by the increasing importance of strong personal emotions in the spousal relationships as well as inter generationally. Accordingly, romantic love became

the most salient selection mechanism in the partner selection process, and, at least by the second half of the 20th century, the only legitimate reason for marriage and family formation. Strong intergenerational bonds have led to a situation in which practically all children grow up with at least one biological parent, whereas the numbers of children given away for adoption and those in children's homes have decreased to near zero.

In the following sections, emphasis will be on those processes related to marriage and the family that are specific to German contexts, whereas those phenomena that are more or less common to all societies within the Western European marriage pattern will be dealt with in less detail.

2. MATE SELECTION, COHABITATION, AND LIVING APART TOGETHER

As in many other affluent societies in the tradition of the Western European marriage pattern, the romantic love principle has increased marriage endogamy considerably. Since similarities in knowledge, values, tastes, and lifestyle enhance mutual understanding and strong emotional bonds, partners are increasingly selected according to these criteria. Additionally, opportunities for meeting possible partners are also increasingly selective according to these criteria, as many of the institutions adolescents are related to are stratified according to age and social class, such as schools, sports clubs, or places for leisure activities. In Germany this is even more the case than in other comparable societies, because Germany has a strongly segregated system of school tracks, according to which students perform their school careers separately already by the age of 10. Therefore, chances to meet potential partners of a different family background or of a different educational level are minimized. Results show accordingly that marriage homogamy according to education has increased steadily over time (Klein, 1998b). On the other hand, religion has lost its significance for partner selection completely, both with regard to marriages within different Christian confessions and between Christians and atheists or other religions (Klein, 2000; Klein & Wunder, 1996). With respect to age, the mean age difference between partners is about 3 years, and has been unchanged for at least five decades. Yet, along with the increasing age at first marriage, the variance of age differences has increased.

Due to the world wars, Germany faced severe losses especially in some cohorts of the male population, which had significant implications for marriage opportunities. This resulted in a considerable marriage squeeze to the disadvantage of the women of those cohorts (or some years younger, respectively). As a result of these period effects, in combination with a slightly imbalanced sex ratio on the marriage market, until the 1960s more women than men remained unmarried for their lifetime. From the 1970s onward, this imbalance has changed to its opposite. Due to a male sex ratio at birth of 105:100, which remains practically stable until the marriage age, and due to a fertility rate below replacement level—in combination with a relatively stable age difference between marriage partners of about 3 years—there is an oversupply of males, or a shortage of females, on the marriage market.

Accordingly, in recent decades, more males than females remain unmarried, with the men with the least resources, such as education and financial outlook, in the most unfavorable situation in this competitive game. This situation became even more critical within the last decades, since women in Germany do better in educational achievement than men, and since many of the best-educated women are increasingly reluctant to enter into the marriage market at all. In line with these developments on the marriage market are the changing proportions in binational marriages. While in the past women especially entered into binational marriages, in recent years German males increasingly marry foreign women. Between 1991 and 1999, binational marriages of German men increased more than 50%, while binational marriages of German women decreased slightly during the same period (Roloff & Schwarz, 2002).

Figure 13.1 shows the long-term development of weddings (foreigners included) per 1,000 inhabitants of Germany. The readiness to marry was especially high after the two world wars. This may be explained by the catch-up on marrying and, in addition to that, by the remarriage of war widows and of postwar divorced. Especially in the middle of the 1950s and the beginning of the 1960s, there was an increase of weddings in Germany, which is a parallel development to the increase in births. After that time, there is a downward trend in weddings, and only in the 1980s is there an occasional (but low) reincrease observable, which has its cause not only in the years of high birthrates, but also in the growing significance of marriages following divorce. After German unification, in East Germany there was a slump in weddings and in births. Beside the given explanations in connection with earlier birth cohorts, the drastic decline in weddings has its causes in the institutional and administrative/technical reorganization of East Germany, which produced delays.

Relating to the age-specific rate of first marriages, there are similar shifts in marriages over the life course, as was already seen with regard to the births of children. After a 25-year period (1950–1975) of decline in age at first marriage, the age at first marriage has increased continually since then. That is, the average age of men at first marriage

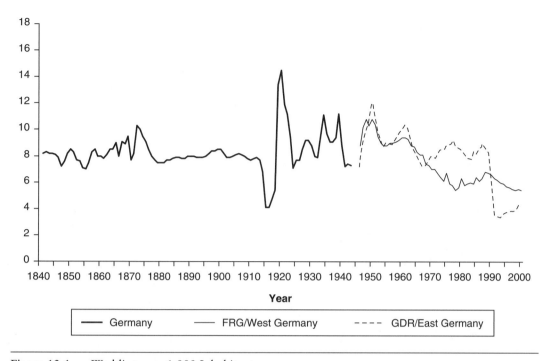

Figure 13.1   Weddings per 1,000 Inhabitants

SOURCE: Statistisches Bundesamt (2000) and Staatliche Zentralverwaltung für Statistik (1977).

was 28 years in 1950, 25.3 years in 1975, and 31.1 years in 1999 (former Federal territory).[1] For women, the average age is about 3 years lower. The development in the GDR shows a parallel tendency, but with a lower age at marriage: For men it was below 24 years in the 1970s, and for women it was below 22 years. In the 1990s, the age at marriage in East Germany converged toward that of West Germany.

The probability of ever marrying decreased continuously within the sequence of cohorts. The reduction started already with the cohort of 1940, and is more dramatic in the case of men. The share of lifelong singles in the 1960s was 28% for men and 19% for women (Engstler & Menning, 2003, p. 68).

First marriages and remarriages are distributed differently among men and women. Especially within the younger cohorts, a remarriage after divorce is more frequent in the case of women (Sommer, 1998, p. 233).

This means that many second marriages for women are first marriages for the men they marry.

In addition to formal marriage, other events, such as starting a union or founding a common household, are not only relevant for partnerships prior to marriage but also as an alternative to marriage. Figure 13.2 refers to 18- to 35-year-olds and describes the events of beginning a partnership. The figure differentiates between the forms of partnership, which are justified by the event. This figure shows again the declining number of marriages, this time among young adults. The values are, of course, a bit higher than those in Figure 13.1, which refers to all age-groups. Since the end of the 1970s, the decrease in readiness to marry corresponds with the increase in cohabitation, which happens now more frequently than marriage (compare Figure 13.2). The beginning of a (less solid) partnership occurs plainly more

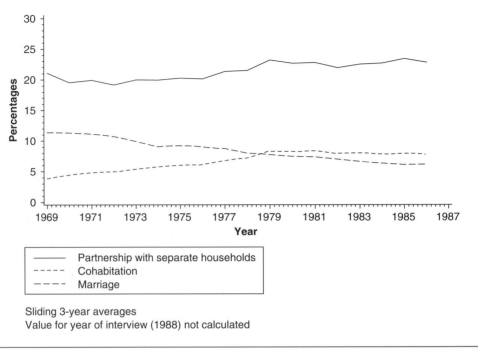

Sliding 3-year averages
Value for year of interview (1988) not calculated

Figure 13.2   Entry Into Different Forms of Partnership Among the 18- to 35-Year-Olds
(West Germany) (in Percentages)

SOURCE: Klein (1999c).

DATA: Familiensurvey 1988; author's calculations.

often: Every year, a good 20% of the 18- to 35-year-olds start a partnership without a common household. This tendency increased only slightly between the end of the 1960s and the end of the 1980s.

Figure 13.3 describes the spread of cohabitation in the life course, differentiated by birth years. Figure 13.3 makes it apparent that the delay in marrying, within the age category of 20 to 30, corresponds with an increase of cohabitation in West Germany (Klein, Lengerer, & Uzelac, 2002). From the mid-1930s, the increase of cohabitation is low within the sequence of cohorts in both parts of Germany. Consequently, cohabitation is still best seen as a phase before marriage rather than an alternative, at least in West Germany—which, we might add, is different from France, where cohabitation is more common.

The spread of partnerships without a common household is concentrated in the younger age-groups, in comparison to cohabitation (Klein, 1999c, p. 85). If you take a look at all forms of partnerships at the same time, as represented in Figure 13.4, astonishingly, the young adults show an increasing rate of commitment across the generations. Instead of an increasing tendency toward staying single, young adults show the opposite behavior. As a consequence, the middle age-groups show a far-reaching constant rate of commitment across the generations. It is true that marriage has lost some of its dominance, but companionship is not on the wane.

The change of living arrangements is often interpreted as being an expression of individualization and pluralization. While individualization is hardly true, pluralization of private living arrangements includes not

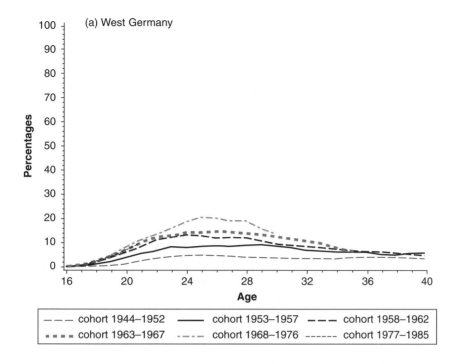

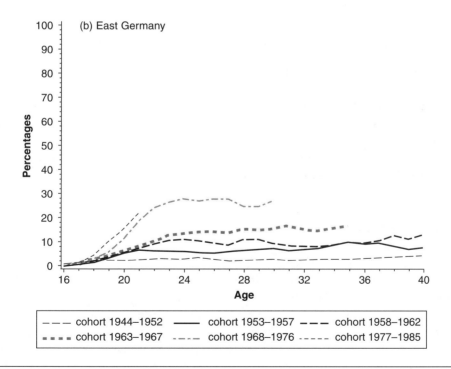

Figure 13.3   Cohabitions by Age and Cohort (in Percentages)

SOURCE: Klein (2003).
DATA: Familiensurvey (2000).

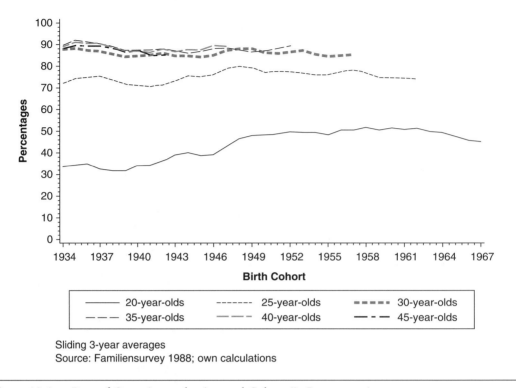

Sliding 3-year averages
Source: Familiensurvey 1988; own calculations

Figure 13.4   Rate of Commitment by Age and Cohort (in Percentages)
SOURCE: Klein (1999a).

just the increase of cohabitation, but also postdivorce cohabitation (Beck-Gernsheim, 1983, pp. 329, 333), and a slightly increasing tendency to remain single (Beck-Gernsheim, 1994, p. 131). With regard to other demographic changes, the connection between increasing numbers of divorces and the spread of cohabitation is often discussed. A rather obvious explanation for the phenomenon of an increasing divorce rate encouraging the spread of cohabitation is that second marriages are preceded by other forms of partnership, especially cohabitation. Moreover, the spread of cohabitation may be traced back to two developments: the increase of women's labor-force participation (especially in qualified jobs) and the general expansion of the educational system. The opportunity costs of a traditional marital division of labor are consistent with the better possibilities of gainful employment for women.

It is important to note that longer training and education periods, accompanied by low income and high occupational insecurity—also interpretable as insecurity about the relevant features of a potential partner—last until a higher age. In view of high unemployment and the spread of temporary employment, occupational insecurity may last longer than the training and education period. The prolongation of such insecurity supports the spread of cohabitation in a double sense: On the one hand, low income during the training period keeps investments in a partnership on a low level, but on the other hand, the delayed transition into a solid occupational career has a delaying effect on marriage (Oppenheimer, 1988, p. 565), since the longer biographical insecurity concerns the partner, too. Furthermore, the insecurity of mate selection, with respect to the partner's occupational success, explains an interest in the low separation costs of cohabitation. Both make it less attractive to marry in the educational phase of life. While delayed, the incentives to found a common household continue unchanged.

3. THE DEVELOPMENT OF FERTILITY IN GERMANY

Figure 13.5 shows the development of births since the 19th century in Germany. Changes in the size of population originated not only from the increase in population in the course of the demographic transformation but, above all, from territorial changes in the course of German history. Figure 13.5 relates the crude birthrate per 1,000 inhabitants. It is apparent from this figure that the birthrate of Germany was around 3.5 to 4 children at the beginning of the 20th century. Between 1900 and 1933 there was a continuous decline in the birthrate, which was interrupted by a near absence of births because of World War I. A short-term increase in births is limited to the time of the Third Reich, and again in the late 1950s and early 1960s, but between 1966 and 1973—a period of only 7 years—there was a new and drastic decrease in births.

Until the middle of the 1970s, the birthrate was nearly parallel in East and West Germany (see Figure 13.5), but since the mid-1970s, the former GDR government changed its population policy, for example, by giving advantages to larger families in respect to housing. As a consequence of this policy, there was an increase of births in the GDR (see Figure 13.5). But one cannot rule out the possibility that this was a short-term increase, which had its origin in a biographical encouragement to start a family, interpreted as an expression of a take away effect.

After 1990 there was a reduction in births in East Germany, which was even more dramatic than the decline in the 1960s in West Germany; in only 2 or 3 years, the birthrate decreased by 60%. Several factors have contributed to the birth decline after 1990 in East Germany (Klein, Niephaus, Diefenbach, & Kopp, 1996): (1) A change in the value of family was much discussed; (2) the family once held a high place in the socialistic system, because of being a place of retreat from the regimentation of public life (Höhn, Mammey, & Wendt, 1990, p. 148; Huinink, 1995, p. 39f.; Nauck, 1993); (3) it lost some of this significance because of the new gained

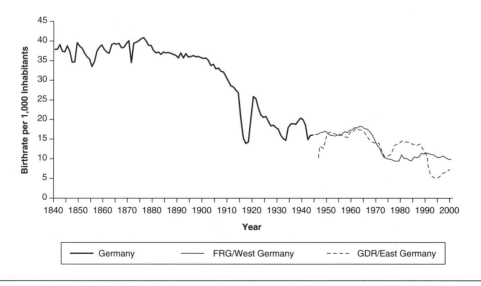

Figure 13.5   Development of Births in the Past 150 Years

SOURCE: Statistisches Bundesamt (2000) and Staatliche Zentralverwaltung für Statistik (1977).

liberty; and (4) the incentive structures changed as a result of changed institutional conditions after German unification (Kirner, Schulz, & Roloff, 1990; Schulz, Wagner, & Witte, 1993; Strohmeier & Schulze, 1995).

More dynamically, individual strategies to cope with changed circumstances are invoked to explain the slump in births (Schulz et al., 1993; Zapf & Mau, 1993). In other words, the delay in having children is interpreted as a rational reaction to the increased insecurity and uncertainty regarding the consequences of the generative behavior. Explanations that see the decline of births as "shock" and the "aggregate effect of individually experienced shocks" (Mau & Zapf, 1998; Zapf & Mau, 1993, p. 3) are oriented toward a more psychological context. Finally, the demographically caused age-structure effects are not unimportant as causes of decreasing births at the end of the 1960s, especially the selective migration to West Germany of many young people and their families (Dorbritz, 1992, p. 190; 1993, p. 413) and the decrease of cohort size.

The total fertility rate—that is, the number of children a woman is going to have in the course of her life—is actually 1.33 for Germany. The value has to be around 2 (in Western industrial societies about 2.1) to reproduce the population, because (1) the birthrate of boys is a bit higher than that of girls, and (2) not all descendants are going to survive until they are able to produce children. The net reproduction rate (NRR)—that is, the number of births of girls, adjusted to the mortality rate—is around 0.62. A value of exactly 1 is critical to continue current population size, while values that are below 1, as seen in the case of Germany, mean that the population is going to decline.

A problem in interpreting the described developments of fertility results from the calculation of period data from a calendar year. Calculation of the measured value concerned refers in that case not to the course of life of a specific cohort, but to all age-groups in a calendar year—a mixture of cohorts. Figure 13.6 shows how the age-specific numbers of births changed in the Federal Republic against the background of the birthrate bulge of the 1960s. The maximum number of births of women born in 1935 was reached at the age of 26. With the following cohorts, the maximum number of births-shifted little by little toward a younger age. Women born in 1945 had their highest single-year birthrate at the age of 22. Those born in 1950 have an even younger single-year birth rate high. But, the following cohorts delayed it more and more, and the number of births not only declined, but births were distributed more evenly through all age levels.

The implications of the changes in the timing of births and their consequences for German birth development become clear if the age-specific birthrates are represented by calendar time and not by age (Figure 13.7). The annual birthrate is the result of all[2] age-specific birthrates of the different cohorts within 1 calendar year. The predrawing (i.e., earlier timing) of births in the course of life implies that the following cohorts are going to realize high numbers of births in the same calendar year in which earlier cohorts are going to have their children. For instance, the peaks of the birthrates of the cohorts of 1935 and 1945, which are 10 years apart, have a gap of only 6 years (Figure 13.7). The increase of births between the middle of the 1950s and the middle of the 1960s exclusively goes back to this effect of compression, which is connected with the predrawing: Those cohorts that have a share in the predrawing and that are responsible for the increase in births are not going to have more children than those women who were born in 1935!

The baby boom is associated with the *Wirtschaftswunder*, which is the favorable economic development in the 1950s and 1960s of the last century, but it is not clear whether this is more likely a cohort effect or a historical (period) effect. In the shape of a cohort effect, the birth cohorts of the 1940s,

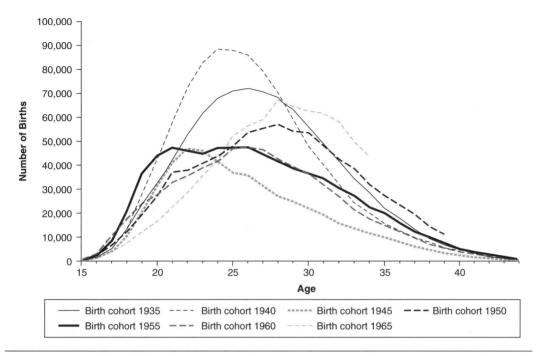

Figure 13.6 Age-Specific Birthrates by Age and Cohort

SOURCE: Statistisches Bundesamt (2000).

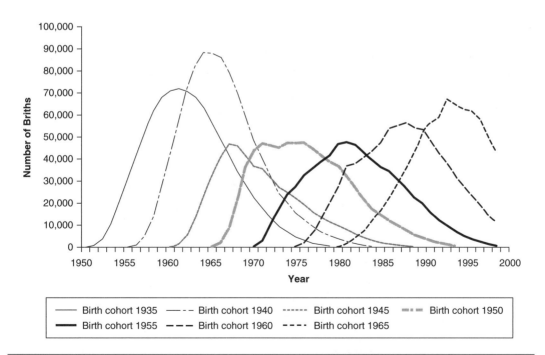

Figure 13.7 Development of Births in a Cross-Sectional and Longitudinal View

SOURCE: Statistisches Bundesamt (2000).

which were first socialized by material privation and afterward by the growing economic development, would have experienced a generational situation that would have been favorable for starting a family early. In addition to this, these cohorts are small and had experienced a favorable economic situation throughout their life (Easterlin, 1961, 1980). However, in favor of a period effect, all cohorts at the end of the 1950s and beginning of the 1960s, in their prevailing age, had higher fertility than other cohorts at the same age. The consequence for the birth cohorts of the 1930s is that the total fertility rate is bigger than that of older cohorts of the 20th century (Kopp, 2002, p. 38).

While the increase of births is accompanied by a predrawing of births, the decrease of births in the time between 1966 and 1973 has its cause in today's tendency to delay births until later in life. The delay leads to a decompression of birth frequencies from a calendar-time perspective. Taking the perspective of those cohorts, which have a share in the birth decrease, it is obvious that fertility

decreased, but not nearly so dramatically as calendar time would suggest. The total fertility rate decreased from 2.53 to 1.54 between 1966 and 1973, while the rate of cohort decreased from only 1.97 (cohort 1940) to 1.57 (cohort 1960) (Engstler, 1997, p. 88). Because of the cohort description, explanations for the birth decrease include, above all, the fact that there is a lengthening of biographical insecurity, first because of the expansion in education (Klein, 1989), and later on because of the start of working life, which became more and more difficult as a consequence of unemployment or because of limited-term employment.

Besides the total fertility rate of West Germany, Figure 13.8 also describes the accumulation of the parity-related birth-rate within the course of life. Here, those women born between 1940 and 1949 and those born between 1960 and 1969 are compared with each other. The figure shows a reduction in the readiness to start a family from 90% to 80%, or rather an increase of permanent childlessness to 20%.[3]

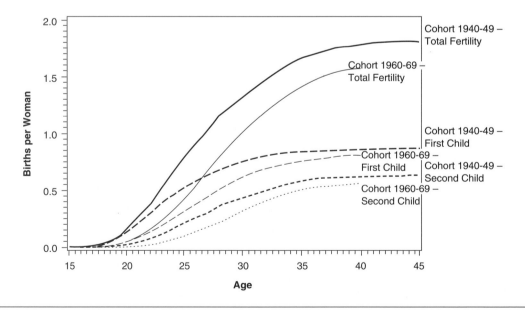

Figure 13.8 Development of Births by Parity

SOURCE: Author's own computations based on Familiensurvey 2000

Large numbers of children born to one mother, which was a historically widespread phenomenon, has become infrequent in today's living generations (Figure 13.8). It is finally worth mentioning that there are, in comparison to fewer than 800,000 births, more than 130,000 (induced) abortions per year, and it is assumed that this is only a minor portion of unintentional pregnancies.

Following the model of Leibenstein (1957, 1974), who distinguished between consumer, income, and insurance utility with regard to children, consumer utility in particular is decisive for Germany. In addition, a recent study by Nauck and Kohlmann (1999) refers to a social-normative dimension. The social-normative "value of children" implies that children are able to stabilize family relationships. In the context of the high divorce rate in Germany, the integrative function of common children is of special importance, especially the stabilizing effect on the partnership. A gender preference for children has more or less vanished (Brockmann, 2001; Hank & Kohler, 2003).

As in several other countries, fertility differs by women's level of education. The decrease of births that started in the mid-1960s in the Federal Republic—especially the increase of childlessness—may essentially be traced back to the expansion in education (Klein, 1989). Add to this that a longer education period leads to delays in starting a family (Blossfeld & Huinink, 1989; Galler, 1979). The educational effects, which are especially characteristic of West Germany, are connected with a lack of public childcare.

The described changes in generative behavior have several consequences for family and intergenerational relationships, for the socialization of the descendants, for the allocation of prosperity and poverty within the society, for the labor participation of women, and so on. With regard to family structure, the recent increase of childlessness in Germany is expected to have an effect on

social integration and on living conditions in the middle and higher age ranges. The missing family relationships are accompanied by further demands on the welfare state, and on the health- and nursing care system. The historic decrease of high numbers of children per family contributed additionally to the trimming down of family relationships. However, because of the far-reaching readiness to have a second or even third child after the first one, we do not expect the verticalization of family structures, which is a tendency in the United States and China (Bengston, Rosenthal, & Burton, 1990).

In addition, the timing of the birth of children within the life course is significant for intergenerational relationships. The described predrawing of starting a family, of the (women's) birth cohorts of 1940 and 1950, contributed (beside a longer life expectancy) to the extension of a common lifetime of family generations (Lauterbach, 1995). Starting a family early contributes also to an intensification of family relations, because of the fact that three or more generations live and experience one another at the same time. On the other hand, the delay in family formation in younger cohorts has a shortening effect on the durability of family relationships, which is hard to cushion by the extension of the relevant remaining lifetime.

Besides several other consequences of the development of births, the number of children and the interval between the generations has an influence on the economic situation of family members. From a historical perspective in Germany, child poverty has become a rare phenomenon, which has its cause in the smaller number of children. The interval between the generations gains a further significance because the requirements of children and the low income in younger years occur simultaneously. (For a critical discussion, see Klein, 1991 and Schwarz, 1980.) But the timing of having children and its effects on economic well-being has consequences not only for subsequent family generations, but also for that phase of life in which nursing and care for the elderly parents becomes necessary.

4. GENDER ROLES AND SOCIALIZATION

Cultural differences within Germany are especially revealed in the performance of gender roles. According to the different cultural traditions, egalitarianism is much more highly valued in the northeastern parts of Germany, with southwestern couples stressing gender differences. This is obvious in the division of labor between spouses: While the proportion of women who are housewives by choice is relatively high in southwestern Germany, East German women prefer a role model according to which both husband and wife are fully employed (and share the household chores accordingly). The preference for the housekeeping role is strongly related to the belief that staying at home is in the best interest of the children—at least during the preschool years, if not during their entire school career. Moreover, this division of labor is also related to the idea that gender-specific specialization may optimize the benefits of all family members. On the other hand, the northeastern idea of gender equality implies that it is to the benefit of all if both spouses are involved in all activities equally. These differences are revealed in several regionally differentiated family surveys: For East German women and men, the optimal situation is considered to be the wife reentering the labor market immediately, rather than when the kindergarten age childs reaches school age. Only 9% of the women and 10% of the men prefer that "one of them should stay at home" in the preschool years of the child. In West Germany, however, 63% of the male respondents and 56% of the females show preference for a parent at home (Dannenbeck, 1992; Gavranidou, 1993). These differences also show up in the context of international comparisons in the distribution of housework (Diefenbach, 2002): East German couples rank among the most equal with regard to the sharing of housework (in line with countries such as Canada and Sweden), while West Germany belongs to the societies in which the gendered division of labor in the household is strong (ranking next to Italy, Spain, and Japan).

These preferences for gender roles are not merely individual choices according to personal values, but are deeply rooted in responses to the general institutional structure of Germany. This institutional structure becomes, of course, continuously and politically legitimated through individual voting behavior related to those beliefs. Major features of this institutional structure are the educational system and the taxation system. The German taxation system privileges marriage more than parenthood. The major family-related financial transfer is that couples are taxed together, thus giving an incentive for a gender-related division of labor, as this decreases the relative share of taxes related to the joint income, whereas direct financial transfers related to parenthood or indirect transfers by tax deduction, respectively, are relatively unimportant. Accordingly, fully occupied couples, as well as single parents and low-income parents in general, profit least from this taxation system. Even more important are the specifics of the German educational system. Until now, the entire educational system from kindergarten to college level has been part time, implying that children are at home for the second half of the day. A major divide between East and West Germany is the availability of complementary child day care.

While East Germany has developed a full system of child day care that starts before kindergarten age, such institutions are practically unavailable in West Germany. Thus, even if mothers wanted to gain full-time employment, they would face severe restrictions on doing so. The demand for day care institutions increases slowly, as the relatively small proportion of such institutions in the private market indicates, which could be afforded only by more affluent couples. This low demand is to some extent related to the culturally based concept of "good mother-hood" (Schütze, 1986), but it also reflects the necessities of the German school system, which has some unique qualities. Its part-time organization is in favor of families with high cultural capital, as they can invest more efficiently in the school career than parents with a culturally disadvantaged background, such as lower-class families or migrant families, because the former are more able to supervise the extensive homework of their children and help them considerably. Additionally, the German school system is organized into different school tracks after the fourth grade. As mobility between school tracks is relatively low, the sorting-out process at this early age has strong implications for the social chances of children according to their family background. The later a sorting-out process starts, the higher the chances of children from disadvantaged families for upward mobility. According to the results of cross-national comparisons, Germany has the highest differences in school achievements between the social strata of the parents and the strongest relationship between the educational level of the mother and school achievement at the age of 15 (Deutsches PISA-Konsortium, 2001). This result is even more telling because of the fact that no fees for public education from the elementary level to university have to be paid, that private schools are very uncommon in Germany, that the entire educational career is related to state-controlled and -regulated institutions, and that there is practically no quality difference between schools or universities. Thus, the strong intergenerational transmission of social status through differential school success is mainly the effect of parental investments—not so much of money, as in many other comparable societies, but of time, energy, and social and cognitive support, typically provided by mothers.

5. MARRIAGE AND THE HOUSEHOLD CONTEXT

Changes and international differences in household composition and in the spread of private living arrangements are a result of demographic developments (especially the development of births) and of the changes in mate selection and partnership stability. Many sociological questions are only useful when referring to individuals, not to households: On the one hand, they concern persons who are deciding on matters such as founding or leaving a common household and especially on mate selection and separation. This is where theoretical explanations of structural changes of the household must start. On the other hand, they also concern persons who have to deal with the consequences of the household constellation and its changes, for example, poverty risk.

Figure 13.9 shows that living together with partner and children is often practiced by those in middle adulthood, while living together with only a partner is practiced by those in the latter half of life. Both curves of men are shifted to the right, because of the age difference between partners. In addition, men in their second half of life live with a partner more often than women. This difference has its cause in the surplus of women in the older ages, which goes back to the victims of World War II. The example shows that the age differentiation of a cross-sectional analysis, as is the case in Figure 13.9, should not be over-interpreted. The household context of future old people is expected to have a lower gender difference as the war generation dies out and as the present surplus of men in young- and middle-adulthood shifts toward higher ages.

In Figure 13.10 the respective share of singles and lone parents becomes obvious. In the 25 to 55 age-group, 1.5 to 2 times as

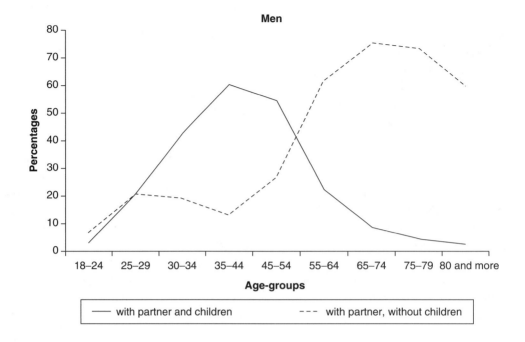

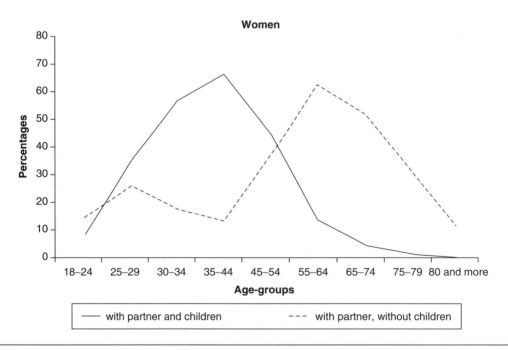

Figure 13.9   Living Together With Children and Partner (2000) (in Percentages)

SOURCE: Engstler & Menning (2003).

DATA: Statistisches Bundesamt (2000), Mikrozensus; authors' calculations.

many men than women are living alone. In higher age groups it is the other way around, which is explained by the surplus of women. The higher share of single men in young and middle adulthood corresponds with a virtual exclusion of men from the group of lone parents in the ages concerned. While this household form is hardly found among men, 10% of women between the ages of 35 and 44 are lone parents (compare Figure 13.10). Altogether, in 2000 1.77 million lone parents were living in Germany (Engstler & Menning, 2003, p. 40).[4] However, defining lone parents only with respect to the household context is misleading. Many "lone parents" have a steady partner who has his own household but slips into the role of a stepfather, and possibly participates in the educational task even more than many real fathers in a traditional family setting. According to Teubner's calculation (2002, p. 45), at least 245,000 out of the 1.77 million "lone parents" have such a partnership without a common household.[5]

In view of the increasing divorce rate and the simultaneously increasing chances of women marrying again, there is an increasing spread of stepfamilies. In 1999, 6% of families in West Germany and 11.5% of families in East Germany were stepfamilies with stepchildren under the age of 18 (Teubner, 2002, p. 40). As for children, 4.5% (West Germany) or 10.5% (East Germany) of children are stepchildren[6] living in stepfamilies (Teubner, 2002, p. 29). It is important to include not only stepfamilies but also cohabitors, because nearly one-half of all stepchildren in West Germany live with cohabiting adults. Besides,

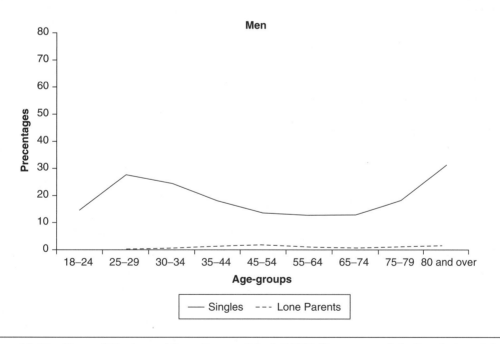

Figure 13.10 Share of Singles and Lone Parents (Men) (2000) (Percentage of the Population of the Same Age)

SOURCE: Engstler & Menning (2003).

DATA: Statistisches Bundesamt (2000), Mikrozensus; authors' calculations.

many "lone parents" have a steady partner. Considering those stepchildren in a wider but realistic sense, the share of stepchildren increases to 12.5% among all children (Teubner, 2002, p. 36). The majority—about 90%—live in a stepfather family, the rest in a stepmother or double stepfamilies, in which both partners are stepparents of one of the children. In stepfamilies there is the tendency to add at least one common child to the stepchildren shortly after the marriage (Klein & Eckhard, 2004).

Beside the family living conditions of children, the household context of the older part of the population is of interest. With growing age, the share of those who are not living in a private household but in an institution or shared household (such as old people's homes, nursing homes, etc.) increases. While only 1% of the 70- to 74-year-olds and about 3% of the 75- to 79-year-olds live in institutions, 12% of 80-year-olds and older do (Engstler & Menning, 2003, p. 29).[7] In a cross-sectional view, women are more or less twice as likely to live in an institution as men, which is due to women's higher life expectancy and the fact that women have a higher rate of entering those institutions, which may be explained by their frequency of being widowed, which, in turn, is caused by the age difference between mates and, again, women's higher life expectancy. In addition, 2.8% of the entire population aged 60 and over lives in an institution (Engstler & Menning, 2003, p. 29). This low share leads sometimes to the fallacy that the institutionalization risk in the course of life is rather low. An "appropriate" rate of 4% in the United States leads to the expression of the so-called 4% fallacy (Kastenbaum & Candy, 1973). The probability of ever living in such an institution in the course of one's life is, however, much higher (Kastenbaum & Candy, 1973). According to Klein and Salaske's calculations (Klein, 1994, 1996,

1998a; Klein & Salaske, 1994), the proportion of those spending at least some time in an institution is about 50% in West Germany.

The population that remains in private households often lives alone (see Figure 13.10). The differences between the age-groups are much higher for women than for men, but caution is advisable in interpreting longitudinally: The increase by age of those living alone is overlapped by cohort differences. You cannot really say that men—in comparison to women—should expect to spend their old age with a partner (Engstler & Menning, 2003, p. 31). This is still true for the current old population, but for future generations, we might assume (1) that men will no longer be decimated by war; (2) that the life expectancy of men is going to get closer to that of women; and (3) that the current surplus of men in younger and middle adulthood is going to shift toward older age-groups. All this should have the consequence that there are going to be more single men in advanced age in the future than there are today.

With regard to intergenerational relationships, it is important to note that two-thirds of all households consist of only one (family) generation, which are mainly couples without children and singles. Only one-third of all households consist of two generations, which consist of parents (or only mother or father) and children. Only 1% of all households in Germany consist of three or more generations, in which children, parents, and grandparents are living together (Engstler & Menning, 2003, p. 33).

As a consequence of reduced marriages, the variety of partner living arrangements increased in the last decades. At the same time, it is assumed that a great variety of today's living arrangements in Germany were also common in former centuries until the 20th century (Huinink & Wagner, 1998). Therefore, what we are seeing is a reincrease of heterogeneity under changed conditions. However, all empirical statements about pluralization are dependent on what kind of living arrangements are distinguished from one another, although the differentiation may be of little social relevance or sociological importance. For instance, the differentiation between marriage and cohabitation, which is the basis for the statement of pluralization, is less and less important.

Figure 13.11 shows the spread of living arrangements in partnerships among the population and their changes in calendar time. This figure refers to 18- to 30-year-olds, that is, those in young adulthood, the phase in which the living arrangements of partners develop and in which, now as ever, the life-partner—or at least a long-lasting partnership—is founded. Figure 13.11 shows clearly how the share of those persons living in cohabitation increased considerably in East and West Germany. While the share of 18- to 30-year-olds who are cohabiting was low in the 1970s, more than 10% in West Germany and nearly 20% in East Germany were cohabitors in the year 2000 in this age-group. In contrast, the share of those who are married has decreased. Taking a look at both developments, it becomes obvious that the decrease of marriages since the beginning of the 1990s is nearly the same as the increase in cohabitation. (For earlier periods, compare also Klein, 1999a.) Not until the late 1990s did the combination of married and cohabiting households decrease altogether among the younger adults (Schwarz, 2001, p. 24).

The share of those who are living in a more or less stable partnership of at least one year's duration and without a common household increased only moderately in West Germany (compare Figure 13.11). If you add all three living arrangements, it becomes obvious that the share of partnership commitment has remained nearly unchanged for a long period of time: About 60% of the 18- to 30-year-olds live in a more or less stable partnership with or without a common

household, and about 40% are single or have had partnerships of shorter duration. The rate of such commitment is, of course, age dependent: It amounts to only 55% in the case of 18- to 25-year-olds and is about 85% of 26- to 35-year-olds (Klein, 1999a, p. 479). Not until the end of the 1990s did a decreased rate of commitment begin to emerge, which is higher in the case of men than in women, due to a surplus of men in young adulthood. (For marriages and cohabitation, compare also Schwarz, 2001, p. 24.)

But we must record that the share of singles—persons without a steady partner— did not increase at all in the young population. An increasing tendency to have no ongoing relationship (Beck-Gernsheim, 1994, p. 131) is simply not found. On the one hand, to be single does not mean to have no relationship, and, on the other hand, the circumstance of living together with other adults in a common household—most of the time with one's parents—does not indicate that one lives in a steady partnership. The often-cited single-person household gives only limited information about the change of living arrangements. Indeed, while the spread of single households among young adults increased, the share of persons without a steady partner did not change. In addition, it becomes obvious that the living arrangements of partners in Germany are recorded incompletely by household, as mirrored in official statistics.

7. DIVORCE AND REMARRIAGE

Sociostructural analyses regarding the stability of partnerships refer in Germany, as in other countries, to divorce because of the data available. Although there is widespread cohabitation in other countries, and an increase in cohabitation in Germany, divorces are, as ever, a good indicator of the solidity of partnerships. But it must be taken into

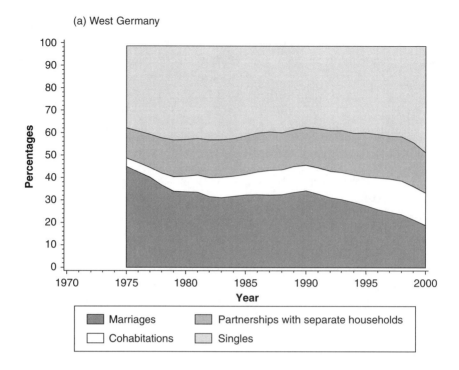

(a) West Germany

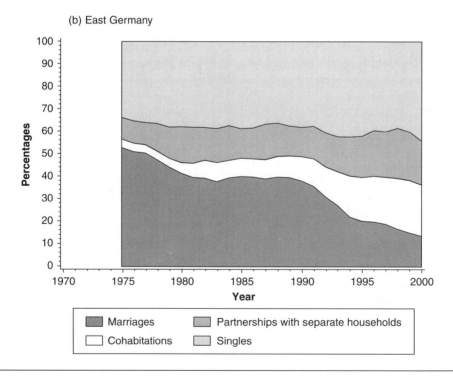

(b) East Germany

Figure 13.11 Partner Living Arrangements (Referring to Ages 18–35) (in Precentages)

SOURCE: Klein et al. (2002).

DATA: Familiensurvey (2000).

account that German marriages are still more often separated by the death of the partner than by divorce. Only one-third of marriages are terminated by divorce in Germany.

Figure 13.12 informs us about the long-term changes in divorces per 10,000 inhabitants. In Germany, as in other countries, the divorce rate increased considerably in the course of the 20th century. This tendency, which has now lasted more than 100 years, is only interrupted by three irregularities. Divorces were infrequent during World War I, but were even more frequent than usual afterward. The increase of the divorce rate after World War II was even more drastic. Besides the difficulty of finding a partner during the war, the marriage market, which was unbalanced because of the war, was also responsible for this development. A third decrease of divorces was due to the altering of divorce regulations in the 1970s. During the division of Germany, divorces were

relatively more frequent in the GDR than in the Federal Republic of Germany, but after German unification, the divorce rate of the newly formed German state decreased again. Similar factors as in the cases of decreased rates of birth and marriage are responsible for this development (see previous discussions).

For the marriage cohort of 1955 in West Germany, the total divorce rate after 25 years of marriage was 12%; for the marriage cohort of 1970, it is already 24.5% (Schwarz, 2001, p. 25). The rate is even higher in the case of younger cohorts. The total rate of remarriages after divorce in 1994 in West Germany was 65% for women and 58% for men—a decreasing trend (Dorbritz & Gärtner, 1995, p. 350). This corresponds both with the increase of other living arrangements (which is also true for initial marriages) and the increase of age at divorce (which is caused in part by the increasing age at first marriage). It is

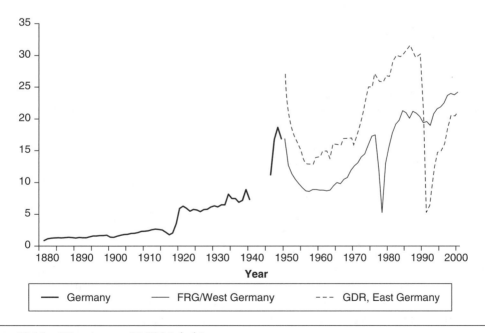

Figure 13.12   Divorces per 10,000 Inhabitants

SOURCE: Statistisches Bundesamt (2000); Emmerling (1999) Staatliche Zentralverwaltung für Statistik (1977); Statistisches Amt der DDR (1990).

recorded that the rate of remarriages of men, which was higher in the 1950s and 1960s (as a response to the changed imbalance of the marriage market), is now lower. Also, the rate of remarriages at the end of the 1980s was higher in the GDR than in the Federal Republic of Germany, but decreased drastically in East Germany after the German unification. Furthermore, the rate of remarriage decreases after divorce among older people and among women even more than men (Braun & Proebsting, 1986, p. 110). This is caused partly by the fact that imbalances in the marriage market in middle and higher ages are unfavorable for women.

Remarriage after being widowed is more rare than after divorce because of the higher age and because of the surplus of women in the older population. The age-specific remarriage rates of divorced or widowed men have a similar level, while those of divorced women are much higher than those of widowed women (Braun & Proebsting, 1986, p. 110).

8 & 9. INTERGENERATIONAL RELATIONS, AGING, AND DEATH

The age at which children are born influences the generational distance and also the socialization of the coming generation. (In regard to this discussion, see also Lauterbach & Klein, 2003.) The generational distance informs how emotionally distant and estranged the family generations are (Mannheim, 1964). Generational distance is due to two demographic developments: the change in the family-founding age and the number of children. A high age at family foundation increases the generational distance. At a given age of family foundation, the same is true for a high number of children.

In Germany the predrawing of the first child until the mid-1960s, together with the continuous reduction in higher numbers of children, has contributed to a narrow

generational distance for the respective cohorts. For the younger cohorts, however, the tendency has changed toward an increase in the generational gap.

With respect to aging and death, two topics are relevant. First, the common lifetime of family generations has increased considerably due to the narrowing gap between family members as well as to an extended life expectancy. Since the mid-1960s generation, however, the further increase of life expectancy is counterbalanced by the postponement of family foundation.

Simultaneously, it becomes obvious that it is more likely for a child to have living grandparents at birth. While during the first half of the 20th century children rarely had the opportunity to know their grandparents, their common lifetimes have increased. Table 13.1 shows the generational structure from the children's point of view. It is evident from Table 13.1 that at birth approximately 90% of children have at least one living grandfather. This is somewhat lower for the 1961–1966 cohort because of World War II mortality.

At birth, almost all children have at least one living grandmother (Table 13.1). With increasing age of the children, living grandparents become less frequent, of course. Yet, at age 10, seven out of 10 children still have at least one living grandfather and eight or nine out of 10 have one living grandmother. The sex-specific mortality and the higher marriage age of men become apparent with the increasing age of children (Lauterbach & Klein, 2003).

A second aspect of aging refers to household living conditions. Compared with other EU nations, the share of old people (65 and above) living alone is rather high (37.5%) in Germany (Engstler & Menning, 2003, p. 62), and only 1% of all households comprise three or more generations.

A special aspect of household living conditions deals with institutionalization in old age versus living alone or with relatives.

Table 13.1   Share of Children With Living Grandparents by Age (West Germany)

| Age of the child | Grandfather | | | Grandmother | | |
| | *Year of Birth of the Child* | | | | | |
	1941–1946	*1961–1966*	*1981–1986*	*1941–1946*	*1961–1966*	*1981–1986*
At birth	90.9	86.1	91.1	91.8	97.1	99.3
5 years	82.0	80.8	89.3	89.6	94.6	98.8
10 years	68.6	71.4		81.5	91.3	
15 years	53.7	62.6		74.2	84.3	
20 years	46.2	47.9		64.6	75.6	
25 years	35.0	39.8		54.3	67.1	
30 years	23.1			36.7		

SOURCE: Lauterbach & Klein (2003).

In Germany, institutionalization in old age is expensive and, apart from this, most elderly prefer to stay independent and live at home as long as possible. While cross-sectional analysis (as in other countries) finds about 4% to 5% of the population aged 65 and over living in an institution, longitudinal studies (Klein, 1994, 1996, 1998a) find a much higher percentage of the population reaching the age of 65 who become institutionalized at some time before death. In fact, lifetime institutionalization is experienced by more than 40% of the male population reaching age 65, and the figure for women is about 70%. Due to the greater life expectancy of women (as well as widowhood), the probability of women experiencing institutionalization is considerably higher than for men. Interestingly enough, the sex difference of institutionalization rates observed widely is almost entirely due to women reaching higher ages and to the fact that women experience widowhood more often than men.

As opposed to the sex impact, the age impact could not be ascribed to other variables. Even if declining health and an increasing number of widows are controlled for, the institutionalization rate increases by at least 40% with every additional year of age. Perhaps a slight overinterpretation would be that only mortality prevents individuals from institutionalization. One could argue that an increasing life expectancy in future generations will contribute to an increase in institutionalizations. However, life expectancy at the age of 65 has not increased as much as life expectancy at birth, due to control of children's diseases. Moreover, it is still undecided whether or not active life expectancy is also increasing (e.g., Klein, 1999b).

Concerning other determinants of institutionalization, the ratios of experiencing institutionalization individually are given by Table 13.2. Additionally, Table 13.2 reports on the average age of institutionalization.

Table 13.2   The Impact of Selected Determinants of the Institutionalization Rate on Lifetime
Probability and on the Average Age of Institutionalization of Men (West Germany)

	Lifetime Ratio of Institutionalization (%)	Average Age of Institutionalization (Years)
Men together	42.3	79.7
Health status:		
without chronic disease	39.5	80.1
with chronic disease	45.3	79.2
Marital status:		
Married	40.0	80.2
Single	61.8	75.6
Divorced	57.5	76.5
Widowed	49.7	78.2
Distance to public transport:		
less than 10 minutes	36.7	80.9
10–20 minutes	43.6	79.4
more than 20 minutes	50.6	78.0
not within walking distance	57.6	76.5

SOURCE: Klein (1996).

Chronic diseases account for almost 6% of institutionalizations and for almost 1 year of acceleration in institutionalization. Interestingly, the impact of social factors such as marital status and distance to public transport is even larger than the impact of chronic diseases. Walking distance to public transport, in particular, has a considerable impact on the rate of institutionalization, while the distance to single facilities is of minor importance.

FINAL REMARKS

The specifics of the German family, compared with families in other European societies, can be related to three different social processes: (1) Germany has shown an astonishingly long-lasting prevalence of the Western European marriage pattern, with its tradition of bilineal kinship, consensual marriage, neolocalism, and the nuclear family as the primary unit of solidarity—which was transformed easily during the process of industrialization into a privatized and highly emotional group with distinct boundaries. (2) Its location in the center of Europe, huge waves of immigration, and shifting boundaries of its territory brought about many diverse cultural influences and made the process of nation-building a long-lasting and conflict-filled one. This resulted not only in rather extreme demographic distortions but also in culturally different conceptions of gender roles and the allocation of rights and duties to family members in the respective regions. These differences are still reflected in diverging family policies, as advanced by the conservative (southern) versus social-democratic (northern) parties. However, in the long run, the conservative trait has always prevailed in German family policy. (3) The division of Germany into the GDR and FRG for four decades and the unification thereafter brought about extremely different living conditions for families and opposing family policies for two generations and, in conjunction with political unification again, extreme demographic distortions in the eastern part of the country.

Compared with European countries, the specific relationship between the traits of family life and the profile of family policy is remarkable (Kaufmann, 1997; Strohmeier & Huinink, 2003). In the European context, Germany is a unique case insofar as it *actively* supports a traditional *bourgeois* family model. Relating this issue loosely to the typology of welfare regimes of G. Esping-Andersen (1990), Germany's family policy is distinct from the Northern European social-democratic model with its strong support of

working mothers, the general support of educational achievement of children, and the vanishing importance of marriage. But it is also distinct from the liberal Anglo-Saxon model, with the latter's emphasis on family being a private matter, not targeted by any social policy, thus leaving the educational success of offspring to the (primarily economic) resources of the parents.

Finally, Germany is also distinct from the "traditional" Southern European model, with its strong emphasis on marriage and its presumption that social policy is subordinate to intergenerational bonds and duties. One of the unintended consequences of the relatively strong German social policy in actively supporting a traditional bourgeois family model is a polarization of the society into an increasing nonfamily sector (of lifelong childlessness, especially of women with education and a strong professional orientation) and a shrinking family sector, which itself remains traditional in the sense that it consists typically of a married couples with two or more children, whose mothers are predominantly not gainfully employed.

NOTES

1. Compare the statistical yearbook for the Federal Republic of Germany, different years (Staatliche Zentralverwaltung für Statistik, 1977, 1990).

2. It is true that Figure 13.7 is limited to cohorts in 5-year intervals for reasons of ease, but the annual birthrate results from all age-groups, including those that are among the 5-year intervals and not represented in Figure 13.7.

3. Other calculations show an even higher increase of childlessness.

4. Single parents are mothers who live with their children (under the age of 27), but not with a partner. In contrast to the numbers presented here, the Statistic Federal Office (Statistisches Bundesamt, 2000, p. 14) also includes those mothers who live in cohabitation.

5. Partnerships are in this case all relationships that have a duration of at least one year as well as all current partnerships (at the moment of interview), irrespective of the duration and irrespective of the marital status.

6. In several stepfamilies there are also common children, which are children of both partners (Klein & Eckhard, 2004).

7. This cross-sectional finding for the year 2000 describes thoroughly in which order of magnitude the increase by age takes place. The rate is essentially explained by the stationary need of care (Engstler & Menning, 2003, p. 30).

REFERENCES

Beck-Gernsheim, E. (1983). Vom "Dasein für andere" zum Anspruch auf ein Stück "eigenes Leben." Individualisierungsprozesse im weiblichen Lebenszusammenhang. *Soziale Welt, 34*(3), 307–340.

Beck-Gernsheim, E. (1994). Individualisierungstheorie: Veränderungen des Lebenslaufs in der Moderne. In H. Keupp (Ed.), *Zugänge zum Subjekt. Perspektiven einer reflexiven Sozialpsychologie* (pp. 125–146). Frankfurt: Suhrkamp.

Bengston, V. L., Rosenthal, C., & Burton, L. M. (1990). Families and aging: Diversity and heterogenity. In R. H. Binstock & L. K. George (Eds.), *Handbook of aging and social sciences* (Vol. 3, pp. 263–287). San Diego: Academic Press.

Blossfeld, H.-P., & Huinink, J. (1989). Die Verbesserung der Bildungs- und Berufschancen von Frauen und ihr Einfluß auf den Prozeß der Familienbildung. *Zeitschrift für Bevölkerungswissenschaft, 15*(4), 383–404.

Braun, W., & Proebsting, H. (1986). Heiratstafeln verwitweter Deutscher 1979/82 und geschiedener Deutscher 1980/83. *Wirtschaft und Statistik, 2,* 107–112.

Brockmann, H. (2001). Girls preferred? Changing patterns of gender preferences in the two German states. *European Journal of Sociology, 17,* 189–202.

Dannenbeck, C. (1992). Einstellungen zur Vereinbarkeit von Familie und Beruf. In H. Bertram (Ed.), *Die Familie in den neuen Bundesländern. Stabilität und Wandel in der gesellschaftlichen Umbruchsituation* (pp. 239–262). Opladen: Leske & Budrich.

Deutsches PISA-Konsortium. (Ed.). (2001). *PISA 2000. Basiskompetenzen von Schülerinnen und Schülern im internationalen Vergleich.* Opladen: Leske & Budrich.

Diefenbach, H. (2002). Gender ideologies, relative resources and the division of housework in intimate relationships: A test of Hyman Rodman's theory of resources in cultural context. *International Journal of Comparative Sociology, 43,* 45–64.

Dorbritz, J. (1992). Nuptialität, Fertilität und familiale Lebensformen in der sozialen Transformation—Übergang zu einer neuen Bevölkerungsweise in Ostdeutschland? *Zeitschrift für Bevölkerungswissenschaft, 18,* 167–196.

Dorbritz, J. (1993). Sozialer Systemwandel und die Folgen für die Familienbildung. *Berliner Journal für Soziologie, 3*(3), 355–368.

Dorbritz, J., & Gärtner, K. (1995). Bericht 1995 über die demographische Lage in Deutschland. *Zeitschrift für Bevölkerungswissenschaft, 20*(4), 339–448.

Easterlin, R. A. (1961). The American baby boom in historical perspective. *American Economic Review, 51,* 869–911.

Easterlin, R. A. (1980). *Birth and fortune: The impact of numbers on personal welfare.* New York: Basic Books.

Emmerling, D. (1999). Ehescheidungen 1998. *Wirtschaft und Statistik, 12,* 934–941.

Engstler, H. (1997). *Die Familie im Spiegel der amtlichen Statistik. Lebensformen, Familienstrukturen, wirtschaftliche Situation der Familien und familiendemographische Entwicklung in Deutschland.* Bonn: Bundesministerium für Familie Senioren Frauen und Jugend.

Engstler, H., & Menning, S. (2003). *Die Familie im Spiegel der amtlichen Statistik. Lebensformen, Familienstrukturen, wirtschaftliche Situation der Familien und familiendemographische Entwicklung in Deutschland.* Berlin: Bundesministerium für Familie, Senioren, Frauen und Jugend.

Esping-Andersen, G. (1990). *The three worlds of welfare capitalism.* Oxford, UK: Oxford University Press.

Galler, H. P. (1979). Schulische Bildung und Heiratsverhalten. *Zeitschrift für Bevölkerungswissenschaft, 5,* 199–213.

Gavranidou, M. (1993). Frauen wollen nicht nur das eine—Berufsorientierungen von Frauen. In B. Nauck (Ed.), *Lebensgestaltung von Frauen. Eine Regionalanalyse zur Integration von Familien- und Erwerbstätigkeit im Lebensverlauf* (pp. 87–117). Weinheim/München: Juventa.

Hajnal, J. (1965). European marriage patterns in perspective. In D. V. Glass & D. E. C. Eversley (Eds.), *Population in History* (pp. 101–143). Chicago: Aldine.

Hank, K., & Kohler, H.-P. (2003). Gender preferences for children revisited: New evidence from Germany. *Population, 58*(1), 133–143.

Höhn, C., Mammey, U., & Wendt, H. (1990). Bericht 1990 zur demographischen Lage: Trends in beiden Teilen Deutschlands und Ausländer in der Bundesrepublik Deutschland. *Zeitschrift für Bevölkerungswissenschaft, 16*(2), 135–205.

Huinink, J. (1995). Familienentwicklung und Haushaltsgründung in der DDR: Vom traditionellen Muster zur instrumentellen Lebensplanung? In B. Nauck, N. Schneider & A. Tölke (Eds.), *Familie und Lebensverlauf im gesellschaftlichen Umbruch* (pp. 39–55). Stuttgart: Enke.

Huinink, J., & Wagner, M. (1998). Individualisierung und Pluralisierung von Lebensformen. In J. Friedrichs (Ed.), *Die Individualisierungsthese* (pp. 85–106). Opladen: Leske & Budrich.

Kastenbaum, R., & Candy, S. E. (1973). The 4% fallacy: A methodological and empirical critique of extended care facility population statistics. *International Journal of Aging and Human Development, 4,* 15–21.

Kaufmann, F.-X. (1997). *Herausforderungen des Sozialstaates.* Frankfurt: Suhrkamp.

Kirner, E., Schulz, E., & Roloff, J. (1990). Vereintes Deutschland—Geteilte Frauengesellschaft? Erwerbsbeteiligung und Kinderzahl in beiden Teilen Deutschlands. *DIW-Wochenbericht, 41,* 575–582.

Klein, T. (1989). Bildungsexpansion und Geburtenrückgang—Eine kohortenbezogene Analyse zum Einfluß veränderter Bildungsbeteiligung auf die Geburt von Kindern im Lebensverlauf. *Kölner Zeitschrift für Soziologie und Sozialpsychologie, 41,* 483–503.

Klein, T. (1991). Zur ökonomischen Situation von Familien in Abhängigkeit von der Ehedauer. *Zeitschrift für Familienforschung, 3,* 5–20.

Klein, T. (1994). Der Heimeintritt im Alter. Neue Befunde für die Bundesrepublik Deutschland. *Sozialer Fortschritt, 43,* 44–50.

Klein, T. (1996). Determinants of institutionalization in old age. In R. Eisen & F. A. Sloan (Eds.), *Long-term care: Economic issues and policy solutions* (pp. 103–113). Boston: Kluwer.

Klein, T. (1998a). Der Heimeintritt alter Menschen und Chancen seiner Vermeidung. Ergebnisse einer Repräsentativerhebung in den Einrichtungen der stationären Altenhilfe. *Zeitschrift für Gerontologie und Geriatrie, 31*(6), 407–416.

Klein, T. (1998b). Entwicklung und Determinanten der bildungsbezogenen Partnerwahl. *Zeitschrift für Bevölkerungswissenschaft, 23*(2), 123–149.

Klein, T. (1999a). Pluralisierung versus Umstrukturierung am Beispiel partnerschaftlicher Lebensformen. *Kölner Zeitschrift für Soziologie und Sozialpsychologie, 51*, 469–490.

Klein, T. (1999b). Soziale Determinanten der aktiven Lebenserwartung. *Zeitschrift für Soziologie, 28*(6), 448–464.

Klein, T. (1999c). Verbreitung und Entwicklung Nichtehelicher Lebensgemeinschaften im Kontext des Wandels partnerschaftlicher Lebensformen. In T. Klein & W. Lauterbach (Eds.), *Nichteheliche Lebensgemeinschaften. Analysen zum Wandel partnerschaftlicher Lebensformen* (pp. 63–94). Opladen: Leske & Budrich.

Klein, T. (2000). Partnerwahl zwischen Deutschen und Ausländern. In Sachverständigenkommission 6. Familienbericht (Ed.), *Familien ausländischer Herkunft in Deutschland: Vol. 1. Empirische Beiträge zur Familienentwicklung und Akkulturation* (pp. 303–346). Opladen: Leske & Budrich.

Klein, T. (2003). Die Geburt von Kindern in paarbezogener Perspektive. *Zeitschrift für Soziologie*, im Druck.

Klein, T., & Eckhard, J. (2004). Fertilität in Stieffamilien. *Kölner Zeitschrift für Soziologie und Sozialpsychologie, 56*(1), 71–94.

Klein, T., Lengerer, A., & Uzelac, M. (2002). Partnerschaftliche Lebensformen im internationalen Vergleich. *Zeitschrift für Bevölkerungswissenschaft, 27*(3), 359–379.

Klein, T., Niephaus, Y., Diefenbach, H., & Kopp, J. (1996). Entwicklungsperspektiven von Elternschaft und ehelicher Stabilität in den fünf Neuen Bundesländern seit 1989. In W. Bien (Ed.), *Familie an der Schwelle zum neuen Jahrtausend. Wandel und Entwicklung familialer Lebensformen* (pp. 60–81). Opladen: Leske & Budrich.

Klein, T., & Salaske, I. (1994). Determinanten des Heimeintritts im Alter und Chancen seiner Vermeidung. Eine Längsschnittuntersuchung für die Bundesrepublik Deutschland. *Zeitschrift für Gerontologie, 27*, 442–455.

Klein, T., & Wunder, E. (1996). Regionale Disparitäten und Konfessionswechsel als Ursache konfessioneller Homogamie. *Kölner Zeitschrift für Soziologie und Sozialpsychologie, 48*(1), 96–125.

Kopp, J. (2002). *Geburtenentwicklung und Fertilitätsverhalten.* Konstanz: UVK Medien.

Laslett, P. (1971). *The world we have lost.* London: Methuen.

Laslett, P. (1976). Familie und Industrialisierung: eine "starke Theorie." In W. Conze (Ed.), *Sozialgeschichte der Familie in der Neuzeit Europas* (pp. 13–31). Stuttgart: E. Klett.

Lauterbach, W. (1995). Die gemeinsame Lebenszeit von Familiengenerationen. *Zeitschrift für Soziologie, 24*, 22–41.

Lauterbach, W., & Klein, T. (2003). The change of generational relations based on demographic developments: The case of Germany. *Journal of Comparative Family Studies.*

Leibenstein, H. (1957). *Economic backwardness and economic growth.* New York/London: Wiley.

Leibenstein, H. (1974). An interpretation of the economic theory of fertility: Promising path or blind alley? *Journal of Economic Literature, 12,* 457–479.

Mannheim, K. (1964). Das Problem der Generationen. In K. H. Wolff (Ed.), *Karl Mannheim. Wissenssoziologie* (pp. 509–565). Berlin: Luchterhand.

Mau, S., & Zapf, W. (1998). Zwischen Schock und Anpassung. *ISI, Informationsdienst Soziale Indikatoren, 20,* 1–4.

Mitterauer, M. (1990). *Historisch-Anthropologische Familienforschung. Fragestellungen und Zugangsweisen.* Wien/Köln: Böhlau.

Mitterauer, M. (1992). *Familie und Arbeitsteilung. Historisch-vergleichende Studien.* Wien/Köln: Böhlau.

Mitterauer, M., & Sieder, R. (1984). *Vom Patriarchat zur Partnerschaft.* München: Beck.

Nauck, B. (1993). Sozialstrukturelle Differenzierung der Lebensbedingungen von Kindern in West- und Ostdeutschland. In M. Markefka & B. Nauck (Eds.), *Handbuch der Kindheitsforschung* (pp. 143–163). Neuwied: Luchterhand.

Nauck, B., & Kohlmann, A. (1999). Values of children: Ein Forschungsprogramm zur Erklärung von generativem Verhalten und intergenerativen Beziehungen. In F. W. Busch, B. Nauck, & R. Nave-Herz (Eds.), *Aktuelle Forschungsfelder der Familienwissenschaft* (pp. 53–74). Würzburg: Ergon.

Oppenheimer, V. K. (1988). A theory of marriage timing. *American Journal of Sociology, 94,* 563–591.

Roloff, J., & Schwarz, K. (2002). Bericht 2001 über die demographische Lage in Deutschland mit dem Teil B "Sozio-ökonomische Strukturen der ausländischen Bevölkerung." *Zeitschrift für Bevölkerungswissenschaft, 27,* 3–68.

Rudolph, H. (1996). Die Dynamik der Einwanderung im Nichteinwanderungsland Deutschland. In H. Fassman & R. Münz (Eds.), *Migration in Europa. Historische Entwicklung, aktuelle Trends, politische Reaktionen* (pp. 161–181). Frankfurt/New York: Campus.

Schulz, E., Wagner, G., & Witte, J. C. (1993). *Gegenwärtiger Geburtenrückgang in Ostdeutschland läßt mittelfristig einen 'Babyboom' erwarten.* DIW-Diskussionspapier, 83.

Schütze, Y. (1986). *Die gute Mutter. Zur Geschichte des normativen Musters "Mutterliebe."* Bielefeld: Kleine.

Schwarz, K. (1980). Zur Einkommenslage junger Familien in der Bundesrepublik. *Zeitschrift für Bevölkerungswissenschaft, 6*(3/4), 317–334.

Schwarz, K. (2001). Bericht 2000 über die demographische Lage in Deutschland. *Zeitschrift für Bevölkerungswissenschaft, 26,* 3–54.

Sommer, B. (1998). Eheschließungen, Geburten und Sterbefälle 1996. *Wirtschaft und Statistik, 3,* 232–238.

Staatliche Zentralverwaltung für Statistik. (Ed.). (1977). *Statistisches Jahrbuch 1977 der Deutschen Demokratischen Republik* (Vol. 22). Berlin: Staatsverlag der DDR.

Statistisches Amt der DDR. (Ed.). (1990). *Statistisches Jahrbuch 1990 der Deutschen Demokratischen Republik* (Vol. 35). Berlin: Haufe.

Statistisches Bundesamt. (Ed.). (2000). *Fachserie 1: Haushalte und Familen, Reihe 3: Ergebnisse des Mikrozensus.* Stuttgart: Metzler-Poeschel.

Strohmeier, K. P., & Huinink, J. (2003). Germany. In J. J. Ponzetti (Ed.), *International encyclopedia of marriage and family* (2nd ed., pp. 735–743). New York: Macmillan.

Strohmeier, K. P., & Schulze, H.-J. (1995). Die Familienentwicklung der achtziger Jahre in Ost- und Westdeutschland im europäischen Kontext. In B. Nauck, N. F. Schneider, & A. Toelke (Eds.), *Familie und Lebensverlauf im gesellschaftlichen Umbruch* (pp. 26–38). Stuttgart: Enke.

Teubner, M. (2002). Wie viele Stieffamilien gibt es in Deutschland? In W. Bien, A. Hardt, & M. Teubner (Eds.), *Stieffamilien in Deutschland. Eltern und Kinder zwischen Normalität und Konflikt* (pp. 23–51). Opladen: Leske & Budrich.

Zapf, W., & Mau, S. (1993). Eine demographische Revolution in Ostdeutschland? *ISI, Informationsdienst Soziale Indikatoren, 10*, 1–5.

CHAPTER 14

Families in Hungary

OLGA TÓTH

PETER SOMLAI

1. PEOPLE AND NATION

Hungary lies in eastern Central Europe, a territory of 93,000 sq km, with a population of 10.15 million. Ethnic Hungarians make up 96.6% of the population. Other ethnic groups living in the country, including Germans, Slovaks, and Romanians, represent a low 3.4% of the population. At the same time, it is estimated that around 3 million ethnic Hungarians live in neighboring countries, which include Romania, Slovakia, Ukraine, and Austria. This is the result of the 1920 Treaty of Trianon marking the end of World War I, which reduced Hungary to 42% of its previous size.

The *Romas* are the largest ethnic minority in Hungary. They are estimated to make up 5% of 6% of the population. The Romas are overrepresented in most of the society's disadvantaged groups—such as those living below the poverty line or in poor housing conditions, the unemployed, the unskilled, and large families. Nevertheless, their recognition as an ethnic group is the subject of political debates (Havas, Kertesi, & Kemény, 1995).

Right up to the 1990s, Hungary was a sending country, that is, the number of persons emigrating from the country was greater than the number of immigrants to the country. Emigration was especially strong during and immediately after the 1956 revolution. Since the 1990s Hungary has become a receiving country. During the Romanian revolution of 1989–1990, the number of immigrants entering the country was between 33,000 and 37,000. By the end of the 1990s this number stabilized at an annual level of around 13,000 to 18,000. Ethnic Hungarian immigrants from Romania represent the greatest number, but immigrants and asylum- seekers from other Eastern European countries as well from Asia and Africa also appear. Even so, in the early 21st century Hungary is basically an ethnically homogeneous country.

We are grateful to the comments of László Cseh-Szombathy, who has taken time to go very carefully through our text.

After World War II, Hungary passed into the sphere of the Soviet Union. As a consequence, from 1949, similarly to the other countries of the region, the Communist Party ruled the country. Revolution broke out in 1956 and the insurgents demanded, among other things, free elections, the departure of Soviet troops, and a democratic system. The uprising was crushed by Soviet troops entering the country, and János Kádár became the general secretary of the reestablished Communist Party (Hungarian Socialist Workers' Party). Kádár's leadership began with reprisals, followed from the early 1960s by the gradual liberalization of the Communist regime, leading to what could be regarded as a political and social compromise. Democratic freedoms were lacking, but with full employment and free education, healthcare, and other social rights, the population experienced a slow and continuous growth in prosperity up to the end of the 1970s. An extensive "second economy" emerged. This comprised not only private tradesmen and retail traders but also the "supplementary activity" of state employees and members of cooperatives; some of these activities were tolerated and others were supported by the government. As a result, the constant shortages were eased and a "consumer society" developed within the frames of the socialist system. However, the price for all this was a highly exploitative way of life.

The socialist system collapsed in Hungary in 1989, and in 1990 free elections were held. The creation of democratic institutions and a liberal, constitutional state began. The social and economic changes of the past 15 years can be seen, on the one hand, in the big influx of foreign capital, the privatization of state enterprises, and the development of private businesses, and, on the other hand, in the emergence and persistence of unemployment, the growth of social inequalities, and poverty. In 2003 a referendum was held in which 84% of the population voted for the country's accession to the European Union, which took place on May 1, 2004.

2. PAIRING UP

In Hungarian society marriage and the family traditionally played an important role. Historically, the country has been characterized by the non-European marriage type according to the typology of John Hajnal (1965), that is, early marriage and a low proportion of persons who never marry.

Sociological and demographic surveys in the 1990s showed that on the level of values and attitudes, the family was more important for people than other aspects of life (career, self-fulfillment, leisure time, other relationships, etc.). This attitude was found not only among the married and people living in families, but also among those who lived alone. Largely positive meaning was attached to the concept of family, married people were generally considered to be happier than others, and the family was thought to be the most important (if not the only) sphere of solidarity. The concept of family was closely connected with marriage and child-raising. At the level of ideals, up to the 1990s people idealized the nuclear family of a married couple raising one or two children.

The generally positive evaluation of the family, and especially of marriage, is now changing. Real demographic behavior has drawn closer to the Western European model, and the process of transformation in family forms and patterns of cohabitation that began in the 1980s has continued since the change of political system. Already in the previous period the divorce and fertility behavior of Hungarian families corresponded to Western European trends, but in the last decade there have also been substantial changes in the area of marriage, cohabitation, and childbirth outside marriage.

Marriage

The number of marriages a year has now fallen to 43,000, which is one-half the average in 1948–1949, which was over 100,000. This decline is reflected not only in the absolute number of marriages. While there were 11.2 weddings per 1,000 inhabitants in the late 1940s, this rate was only 4.3 by 2001. In 1948–1949 the number of marriages was exceptionally high, due in part to marriages that had been postponed because of the war and to the re-forming of families divided by the war. This trend continued in the early 1950s, so the absolute number of marriages and the number of marriages for the population over 15 years remained very high (Table 14.1).

Important factors in this decline, besides the changes in family law (lowering of the age limit for marriage), were the changed political system and the resulting radical economic and social changes. Special mention

must be made here of the effect of social mobility and the transformation of the social structure, which went hand in hand with the possibility for rapid advancement for young people, the mass entry of women into employment, the high degree of geographical mobility, and the loosening of traditional social norms. Selection of a partner became much more free compared with the traditions of earlier decades; young people could choose from a much wider social and geographical circle. Nevertheless, at that time the significance of the family and marriage had not (yet) weakened. All these influences shaped the upswing in the number of marriages up to the mid-1950s.

After a relatively low point in the marriage rate in the second half of the 1950s, the number of marriages began to rise again from the 1960s, and there was another peak in marriages by the mid-1970s. It was then that the large cohorts born in the 1950s (during the ban on abortion)

Table 14.1 Main Indicators of Marriages (1948–2001)

Average for Year/Years	Number	Per 1,000 Inhabitants	Per 1,000 (Over 15 Years)	
			Men	Women
1948–1949	102,765	11.2	88.8	66.6
1950–1959	98,235	10.2	93.2	69.3
1960–1969	89,523	8.8	84.2	61.6
1970–1979	97,097	9.2	80.4	61.4
1980–1989	72,854	6.9	58.0	43.5
1990	66,405	6.4	47.4	35.9
1995	53,463	5.2	33.5	25.8
2001	43,583	4.3	24.4	18.9

SOURCE: *Történeti statisztikai idősorok* (1992) and *Demográfiai Évkönyvek* (1980–2001).

reached marriageable age. Demographic policy measures encouraging childbearing and the rising standard of living, in which some elements (particularly housing) were most accessible for married people, led to the early and large number of marriages. The gradual change in public opinion was also an important factor: In the 1970s sexual activity before marriage gained some social acceptance, but this was considered mainly within the frame of marriage. In this way, material interests, the prevailing ideology, and the norms of the parental family all encouraged young people to marry early and in large numbers (Tóth, 1994).

From the mid-1970s the trend in marriages turned and the number of marriages began to decline. As a consequence, since 1980 there has been a marriage deficit, meaning that more marriages are terminated each year than the number of new ones contracted. By 2001 there were only 24.4 marriages for every 1,000 men aged 15 years and over (compared with 80 in the 1970s), and 18.9 for every 1,000 women over 15 years (compared with 61.4 in the 1970s).

This trend in marriages and the low rate found in the 1990s can be explained as the combined effect of numerous factors. Perhaps the foremost of these is the change in the timing of marriage. In the 1970s men entered their first marriage on average at the age of 24 and women at the age of 21 years. Now the average age at first marriage has risen to 27.8 years for men and 25.2 years for women. This upward shift in the age of marriage is undoubtedly connected with the rise in the level of education among young people—particularly women. In 1990 there were 108,000 participants in higher education and in 2001 there were 350,000. Women make up 55% of the students. Another factor in the shift of first marriage to a later age is the mass unemployment among young people at the beginning of their careers. Because of the lack of perspective on creating an independent livelihood, young people remain in "child status" in the parental household.

Nonmarital Cohabitation

With the postponement of first marriages and the decline in the number of remarriages, society's attitude toward the various forms of cohabitation has changed. Research shows that while people may not necessarily favor cohabitation over marriage, from most points of view they regard the two-family forms as having the same value as marriage (Pongrácz & Spéder, 2001). This is especially true of those currently living in nonmarital cohabitation, but the opinion of married persons too has shifted in this direction. People feel that marriage is more suitable than cohabitation in two areas: bringing up children and winning the approval of parents and relatives.

Compared with the countries of Western Europe, the number and proportion of cohabiting partnerships within long-term relationships is still low in Hungary, but their number is steadily rising. The Census of 2001 found that nonmarital cohabitation represents 11% of all "marital-type" partnerships. This form of relationship is especially widespread in the young age-group. In 2001 71% of women aged 15 to 19 years living in a partnership were nonmarital cohabitors (in 1980 this proportion for women in the same age-group was 3%). The corresponding proportions for women aged 20 to 24 years were 39% in 2001 compared with only 1% in 1980 (Népszámlálás, 2001).

Those who opt for cohabitation rather than marriage can be classified in various groups on the basis of age, earlier marital status, and socioeconomic status. Widows are choosing cohabitation instead of remarriage for material reasons. Divorced women, especially if they are bringing up children, have very little chance of remarrying, and even entering a cohabiting partnership is difficult for them. Most women in their 30s living alone in Hungary are mothers raising a child alone (Utasi, 2002).

Young people choosing cohabitation as an alternative to marriage, or an independent status without a partnership, can also be classified into two main groups. One of these is the singles described in Western societies. They are the best-trained members of their age-group with the highest income. Some of them remain in their parents' household, living a half-adult, half-child post-adolescent way of life. Some have a separate apartment and postpone marriage or choose cohabitation, or have no long-term partnership. It is unquestionably a new phenomenon in Hungarian society that a substantial proportion of young people in their 20s and 30s are single, and within this, one-quarter of those in their 20s and one-fifth of those in their 30s do not have a steady partner. (In recent years growing interest has been shown in the singles phenomenon in the media and public discourse. The real size of this group in Hungarian society is small, but they have a big influence by providing a "model." The mass media devotes disproportionate attention to this model: these young people who "can't spare the time" for marriage or a partnership.)

In Hungary, as in earlier decades, the largest group of those living in cohabitation or without a long-term relationship consists of chronically unemployed young people with the lowest level of schooling, living in economically backward regions and small settlements. Men without an income from work and unable to enter employment do not marry, because the traditional family model is very strong in these circles. If a man does not have a steady job or regular income, he prefers the more informal cohabitation because he would not be able to support a family. It is interesting that public discourse tends to forget this group and

attributes the failure to marry simply to the individualization of young people with high earnings.

Nevertheless, as this example shows, despite the persistence of traditions, the *pluralization* of partnerships is well advanced in Hungary. The same applies to other areas and institutions of family life.

3. FERTILITY AND SOCIALIZATION

Parallel with the modernization of society, the rise in women's level of education, and their entry into employment, fertility has declined in Hungary (Table 14.2; Cseh-Szombathy, 1996). At the same time, it is a characteristic of Hungarian society that there are cyclical fluctuations in fertility, linked to the various demographic policy measures of the last 50 years (Kamarás, 2000).

Together with early marriage, early motherhood was also traditionally characteristic of Hungarian society. Although in the past decades families generally had fewer children than they had originally planned or would have regarded as ideal, only a very few chose to remain childless. In recent decades the two-child family model has been generally accepted. However, a fertility rate below the simple reproduction level emerged very early compared with other European countries. Fertility has been low in Hungary since the early 1960s.

In the 1990s, together with the postponement of marriages and the rising level of women's education, woman have started having children later in life. There has been a substantial decline in the fertility of women under 24 and a slight rise in that of women over 30. The average age of married women at the birth of their first child was 22.1 years in 1970, 23.3 years in 1990, and 25.4 years in 1999. The increase in the number of people living in nonmarital cohabitation has brought an exceptional

Table 14.2   Fertility Rates (1949–2001)

	Number of Live Births	Total Fertility Rate
1949	190,398	2.54
1960	146,461	2.02
1970	151,819	1.97
1980	148,673	1.92
1990	125,679	1.84
2001	97,047	1.31

SOURCE: *Demográfiai Évkönyvek* (1980–2001).

increase in the percentage of children born outside marriage (Pongrácz, 2002). This proportion was 13.1% in 1990 and 30% in 2000. The rate was especially high in the big cities, including Budapest. In addition, the phenomenon of consciously chosen childlessness also appeared: One out of every 10 women in their 20s expects to live without children.

Relations between parents and children in Hungary also follow the international trends that can be observed over a longer period of several decades. Among these, special mention must be made of the weakening of the authoritarian approach to child-raising and the strengthening of a permissive attitude to child-raising in families. While sincerity remained the value most preferred by parents between 1982 and 1997, by the end of the 1990s there was a decline in the choice of such traditional educational values as good behavior and obedience. Instead more emphasis was placed on modern values such as tolerance, respect of others, and a sense of responsibility.

The greatest shift toward modern values can be observed among parents with the highest level of schooling, while parents with a lower level of schooling continue to attach a high value to obedience in children. The wider spread of more modern educational principles was based on increased recognition of the values of children's world and the new, generational culture of young people and on 20th-century achievements in developmental and educational psychology and pedagogy. In other words, emphasis is on the recognition that the adult personality, character, and the shaping of relations can be traced back to childhood upbringing and the practice of early socialization. In keeping with this, there has been a change in the methods of reward and punishment used in the family and school, and this change has been accompanied by greater emphasis on the rights and autonomy of children.

At the same time we also find that working parents are not able to give their children sufficient time and emotional support. Children are more free, but they are left to their own devices. In addition, with the spread of television, the Internet, and modern mass culture, parents and teachers are less and less able to control what children know about the adult world (Somlai, 1999).

Hungarian middle-class families are very performance-oriented regarding their children. By the end of the 1990s, the Hungarian educational system became almost opaque in its complexity, and the possibility of switching from one type of school to another has been reduced. The different types of schools, and within them, individual schools, differ greatly in their educational norms and standards. As a result, middle-class parents feel that they must enroll their children in a timely fashion in what they consider to be the best schools and must push them to achieve a high performance there. Moreover, as they do not have confidence in many schools' standard of education, they have their children attend various regular private classes from an early age. As a result, the burden of study on children is very high, something that parents fundamentally approve, regarding it as an investment in the future.

Following the change of political system in 1989–1990, there was a sharp increase in income inequalities within Hungarian society. This is also reflected in the situation of children. Many children living with unemployed parents, single mothers, or several siblings, or growing up in regions of the country that are falling behind economically are sliding into the poverty category. For them the problem is not finding a school that offers the highest possible level of training but simply acquiring a schooling (Simonyi, 2002). The children of urban or rural poor parents with a typically low level of schooling occupy an important place in the division of labor within the family, since their earnings from casual work represent an important part of the family's budget. Their schooling is broken off prematurely or ends in learning a trade that enables them only to reproduce their parents' disadvantaged position on the labor market. Due to the lack of appropriate attention, their sociocultural disadvantages are not reduced by schooling.

The situation of the majority of children in Roma families is a special cause for concern. Their parents have a much higher than average rate of unemployment. It is very common among Romas living in rural areas for the family's sole source of cash income to be aid and benefits, and they have been the hardest hit by the inflated real value of family allowances since the change of political system. Roma children are overrepresented in diseases, school drop-out, commitment to state care, and juvenile detention, and they are greatly underrepresented in secondary school enrollment and in gaining vocational qualifications. There is strong prejudice against Romas in the general public, and even the state and church organizations distributing aid or dealing with family and child welfare are not exceptions.

4. GENDER ROLES

Similarly to the division of labor within the family, Hungarian families have a more traditional attitude to gender roles than those found in the countries of Western Europe. This is particularly striking in connection with women's employment. Women's mass entry into work outside the home began very early in Hungarian society, in the 1950s. "State feminism" (Neményi, 1996), that is, the introduction of female emancipation from above, tried to instill in society the view that employment is the only guarantee for full membership in society. The widespread entry of women into the labor market was not their own choice but the consequence of strong social pressure. By 1990 full employment had been reached for women too: The employment rate for the economically active female population rose to 75.5%, while the corresponding rate for men was 83.3%. In addition, the overwhelming majority of employed women worked full time.

This extensive change, which had a far-reaching impact on society, was quite compatible with the fact that women remained second-class employees. A good example of this is the institution of childcare allowance, introduced in 1967, or the childcare fee in 1973. By that time the demand for manpower in Hungary was declining, but the socialist system could not tolerate unemployment. Withdrawing part of the female labor force at least temporarily from the labor market seemed to be a suitable solution. Declaring childcare to be the exclusive task of the mother was unquestionably a step back toward the traditional division of labor between the genders, but it became a popular measure and caused women to suffer under the double burden of workplace and home. Most mothers of young children welcomed the childcare allowance and stayed at home for 3 to 6 years with one or two children. It was mainly women with the highest level of schooling who opted for an earlier return to work.

The attitude toward women's employment was thus marked by a duality. On the one hand, there was a great need for their earnings in the family, and the prevailing spirit of the time as well as official ideology pushed them toward employment. At the same time, traditional values and gender roles still persisted: The man was regarded as the family's breadwinner and the woman's task was to care for the household and the family.

Together with the restructuring of the economy, the change of political system also brought unemployment. The number of employed persons fell drastically in the 1990s. However, the female unemployment rate was lower throughout the 1990s than that of men, but by the end of the millennium the two rates were roughly the same again (6%–7% different).

A number of explanations can be found for the lower female unemployment. One is that the rapidly spreading unemployment in the early 1990s first affected the branches of the economy (such as heavy industry) employing mainly men. Parallel with this, the service sector began to grow, absorbing female labor. However, it is also a very important factor that a large group of women avoided unemployment by fleeing into early retirement and the status of housewife.

In 1990 only 4% of women of working age were housewives, compared with 14% in 1998. Women's unpaid housework makes a big contribution to the prosperity of families. This is especially important for families where women's potential earnings are close to the minimum wage. This means that for unskilled women with a low level of schooling, the status of housewife supplemented by casual work or the production of food for the family is more attractive and profitable than earning activity. It is not surprising that women with a lower level of schooling and living in regions that are falling behind economically adjust their attitude to realistic possibilities, and their approval of employment for women is low.

As a result, women's unemployment is substantially less than it was before the change of political system, and this has had the concomitant effect of a considerable improvement in qualifications and level of schooling of women on the labor market. Nevertheless, among women wishing to work, those above 45 years and young mothers who are often subject to hidden discrimination are at a disadvantage regardless of their qualifications. Young mothers also find it difficult to enter employment because the level of part-time employment remains very low in the Hungarian economy (around 5%), even though there might be a great demand for it.

5. MARITAL RELATIONSHIPS

In Hungarian families in the past, the division of labor within the family was rather uneven. Even during the period of full female employment, it was obvious that in most families the wife had to do the household work and care for the children. In fact, researchers still find traces of this (Table 14.3). Even women working full time feel that they have to be perfect housewives, they have to do all the household jobs, and they are the ones primarily responsible for the physical, mental, and educational development of their children. In close connection with this, women acknowledge with satisfaction even the slightest participation of men in housework and, by their own admission, do not really want more help. At the same time, gradual change can be observed in this area; this is clearly indicated by a comparison of the data from time-use surveys conducted in 1986–1987 and 1999–2000 (Életmód–időmérleg, 2002).

There was a substantial decline in the time spent on earning activity in the 15 years between the two studies. The principal cause is the appearance of unemployment. During the same period, there was hardly any decline in the time spent on housework, indicating the high value attached to the household economy. There was a small reduction in the time spent by women on household work,

while that spent by men increased slightly, thereby making the division of labor a little more even. It was mainly the time spent on traditional jobs (cleaning, ironing, repairs) that declined at the level of society, while, parallel with the appearance of the big shopping centers, the time women spent on shopping grew. It is encouraging to see that there has been a slight increase in free-time activities in families, such as the time spent playing with children and telling them stories.

Despite these changes, Hungarian families continue to be characterized by the traditional distribution of labor between the genders. This is clearly seen in the fact that on average men have 50 minutes per day more disposable time than women. Paradoxically, a shift toward a more even distribution of labor can be observed in two social groups: in young families and pensioners. Young fathers are increasingly participating in tasks previously regarded as the exclusive province of women, such as infant care, toilet training, nursing sick children, play, and learning at home. In some aging pensioner families, husbands are beginning to play a role in shopping, cleaning, and cooking, which were earlier regarded as women's tasks.

Table 14.3   Changes in the Use of Time by Men and Women for Selected Major Activities (1986/1987–1999/2000) (Minutes/Day)

	Men 1986/1987	*Women 1986/1987*	*Men 1999/2000*	*Women 1999/2000*
Time spent on earning activity	341	262	262	171
Time spent on study	22	19	34	33
Time spent on housework	86	261	94	240
Freely chosen activity	250	211	304	257

SOURCE: Életmód–időmérleg (2002).

In another important area of household relations, far more democratic practices and greater equality prevail in Hungarian families related to the use of money (Nagy, 1999). In the overwhelming majority of families, the husbands bring more income into the family. Exceptions to this are the poorest families where the husband is unemployed and the family's income consists mainly of social policy supports linked to the wife and children (childcare allowance, family allowance). The husband handles and disposes of the family income in only a tiny proportion of households. Interviewees report joint handling of money in around 60% of Hungarian families, in 30% of cases the wife handles the money, and the remaining 10% are divided between handling by the husband and in other ways.

It is of note that in two-thirds of Hungarian families, the adult members claim that there is a head of the family, and this is typically the man. At the same time, the existence of a family head does not influence either the distribution of labor within the family or the way in which money is handled. What we see here is for the most part the continued existence of a traditional concept now devoid of content.

6. FAMILY STRESS AND VIOLENCE

Up until the change of political system, the majority of families had two earners. In addition, everyone who could tried to earn extra income in the second economy, in a second job at night or on weekends, or by small-scale agricultural production (Szelényi, 1988). While this strengthened the importance of the immediate and wider family, the self-exploiting way of life also took its toll on people's physical and mental health. Although public opinion researchers regularly found that among the different areas of their life people were mostly satisfied with

their family life, a great deal of stress and tension nevertheless accumulated in families.

The change of political system brought a new situation: Hungarians, too, were obliged to make the acquaintance of unemployment and growing social inequalities. This in turn increased tensions within the family. One of the most frequent ways, means, and contexts for handling family conflicts is violence. We do not know whether there has been less or more violence within the family in Hungary in recent years, because it was only in the second half of the 1990s that researchers began to deal with this question. However, from that point on more and more research has been directed at violence against children and women, and some researchers have also drawn attention to men at risk.

Much public opinion in Hungary finds it difficult to accept that events occurring in the center of private life are of significance for public life and society and that the victims of violence in the home should be protected with legal sanctions. The greater part of society, for example, regards mild physical abuse of children as the parents' right and an accepted means of child-raising. An investigation conducted in a sample of adult women found that three-quarters of those interviewed regarded it as the parents' right to slap a child if the child "deserves" it (Tóth, 1999a). Many adults who do not otherwise practice it themselves agree with the use of a mild form of child abuse for disciplinary purposes.

Fewer than 1,000 reports a year are made in Hungary to the police regarding child abuse and around 250 persons are sentenced for endangering minors, but experts agree that the cases that come to light represent only the tip of the iceberg and that only the most brutal cases, sometimes ending in tragedy, are exposed. But, on the basis of self-confession, at least 12% to 13% of children are regularly abused or beaten badly at least once by a parent. The investigation found that the physical abuse of children is related on the one hand to the parents' high expectations regarding school, that is, a performance-oriented attitude. In other words, the parents, sensing the importance of scholastic qualifications and learning, try to squeeze the best performance out of children by abusing them physically. Together with this, many parents still expect obedience from children and try to impose this by beating them. In another sizable part of child beatings, the parents take out their own daily frustrations on the children.

Poor conflict management skills find expression not only in the abuse of children but also in violence between the spouses. The findings of an investigation in a nationally representative sample show that one in three adults come from a parental family where verbal or physical aggression between the parents is an everyday occurrence (Tóth, 1999a). This threat is present in one out of four of the present partnerships. The situation of divorced persons is especially problematic. Sixty-one percent of divorced women reported that they had been the victim of physical violence in their relationship. In some cases it was the violence that led to divorce, but in others violence appeared between the partners during the prolonged and stormy process of divorce.

Few studies conducted in Hungary have touched on the subject of the psychological and physical abuse of men within the family. A study covering the 22 to 26-year age-group (Tóth, in press) shows that a distinct group of young women were aggressive in the same way as men in their partnership. These young women typically come from families where they were abused as children or there was an abusive relationship between the parents. There is no investigation in Hungary at present dealing with the incidence of violence within the family against elderly or sick family members. However, it seems likely in view of the rather low level of tolerance and

conflict management that these forms of violence, too, are widespread.

Many legislators still think that violence in the home is the internal affair of families. Nevertheless, the social profession caring for victims strengthened in the 1990s, and civil organizations were also formed to take a stand against violence in the family. It was mainly in the wake of these changes that new acts were introduced in recent years to prevent family violence.

7. DIVORCE

An important factor shaping the family is the number of divorces, which has been very high in Hungary for decades. The number of divorces in Hungary rose rapidly after World War II. Already in 1949, more than 12,000 couples divorced, and this figure more than doubled by the 1980s. This peak divorce rate involved mainly marriages contracted at an early age in the 1970s and 1980s. At that time researchers found a striking ambivalence regarding the family: On the one hand, society, public opinion, and relatives still expected young couples to marry, while, on the other hand, it was accepted that a substantial percentage of marriages ended in divorce. With minor fluctuations, the number of divorces stabilized at around 24,000 a year in the 1990s, and this level was also found in the early 2000s. At the same time, the number of marriages fell with the result that the number of divorces per 1,000 marriages rose continuously, reaching 559.6 in 2001 (Table 14.4).

If the present divorce rates continue, 39% of the marriages contracted in the mid-1990s will end in divorce. Close to one-half of all divorces occur within the first 10 years of marriage, but the number of marriages of over 20 years that are dissolved is also increasing from year to year. In 2001 22% of all divorces involved marriages where the partners had been living together for

Table 14.4 Main Indicators of Divorce (1938–2000)

Year/Years	Number	Existing Marriages[a]	New Marriages[a]
1938	5,754	—	77.5
1949	12,556	5.8	116.5
1950–1959	14,032	5.8	144.0
1960–1969	19,474	7.4	217.3
1970–1979	25,671	8.3	265.3
1980–1989	27,940	10.3	384.4
1990	24,888	9.9	374.8
1995	24,857	10.5	464.9
2001	24,391	11.0	559.6

SOURCE: *Történeti statisztikai idősorok* (1992) and *Demográfiai Évkönyvek* (1980–2001).

a. Average divorces per 1,000.

more than 20 years. The same trend is reflected in the ages of the persons divorced. Among both men and women divorcing, the 40 to 49-year age-group is represented in the highest proportion, followed by women aged 25 to 29 years and men aged 30 to 34 years. There is a child in 80% of the marriages ending in divorce, and in 62% the child is a minor. As a result, the number of children growing up in one-parent families is increasing.

The rise in the number of divorces and the high level are related to the economic, social, and legal changes that have occurred in the country in recent decades. Women's entry into employment on a mass scale, social and geographical mobility, and the changes in the legal background of divorce have all had an influence in this direction. These changes are reinforced by the rise in the level of women's education, which changes their economic situation and labor market chances and shapes their attitude to traditional marriage.

In addition, it seems that some of the changes that began with the change of political system (mass unemployment, social loss of direction, livelihood difficulties, and, on the other hand, the possibility of becoming an entrepreneur and of becoming wealthy) have also weakened the stability of some marriages.

Together with social and economic causes, the high proportion of divorces is also related to the change in public opinion regarding partner relationships and institutions. Over the past decades, divorce not only became accepted but also became the best known and most widely preferred marital conflict-solving strategy (Tóth, 1999b). It is of note that it is mainly the middle-age and older age-groups that accept divorce as a conflict-solving strategy. In addition, women are more likely to hold this opinion than men. Opinions and attitudes are evolving in line with real behavior also, in that people no longer see any obstacle to divorce when marriage breaks down even if children are involved. Despite this, the institutional system dealing with the family within Hungarian society is not adequately equipped to ensure that divorces are handled in a civilized way. Divorces often last for years and are very stormy, especially when the partners are unable to agree on custody of the children.

An important negative consequence of divorce is that the divorced spouses and the children affected by the divorce have a chance of falling into the poverty group, either transitionally or permanently. This appears differently in the case of men and women. Among divorced women, mothers raising children alone are much more likely to become poor, while in the case of men, it is those who do not form a new relationship or who live in small towns and villages who face this risk. Around one-half of the homeless men, whose numbers have increased strikingly since the change of political system, become homeless because they find no solution for their housing problem after divorce. This clearly shows that today the Hungarian family basically

relies on two earners. If this setup is disrupted by divorce or unemployment, the family has a greatly increased chance of sliding into poverty. Divorce has an effect on the children involved over the longer term as well. A school sociology survey conducted recently in Hungary found that the children of divorced parents have lower grades and fewer of them enter general secondary school (the type of secondary school with the highest prestige), or in general go on to secondary schools giving a matriculation certificate.

Remarriage

One cause of the current lowering marriage rate is that the number of remarriages is falling. In Hungary up to the 1970s a substantial proportion of divorced persons and to a lesser extent widows remarried (Table 14.5). This was related to the fact that they attached a high value to marriage and the family, and also to the various social policy benefits, especially housing, that were accessible mainly for married persons. However, the

Table 14.5 Trend in Proportions of Marriages and Remarriages (1950–1994)[a]

Year/Years	Unmarried	Divorced	Widowed	Unmarried	Divorced	Widowed
1950–1959	92.5	272.3	45.1	114.8	114.8	10.9
1960–1969	81.8	211.8	33.8	105.7	94.1	6.2
1970–1979	83.0	128.9	22.6	115.6	70.8	4.3
1980–1989	62.0	73.3	14.6	91.0	46.8	3.0
1990	53.3	46.4	10.3	74.8	32.4	2.1
1995	37.1	33.0	7.5	49.9	22.4	1.6
2001	25.4	30.2	4.7	33.4	19.9	0.9

SOURCE: *Történeti statisztikai idősorok* (1992) and *Demográfiai Évkönyvek* (1980–2001).

a. Average per 1,000 (men and women) of corresponding marital status.

rate of remarriages has fallen drastically, to one-tenth of the previous level, among both divorcees and widows. Widows are one of the partners in only 2% of new marriages each year. This means there is a high chance that anyone who is widowed will not marry again. There are age and demographic reasons for this, as 79% of widows are over the age of 60 years. In the case of those widowed at a younger age, besides emotional reasons, social policy factors also play an important role: Persons entitled to a widow's pension lose that pension if they remarry. This is such a high material risk that people do not willingly take it, even though they may value marriage more highly than cohabitation.

In 20% of marriages formed in a year, one of the partners is divorced. Remarriage following divorce is more common among the young age-group. At the same time, it is of note that although men's chance and readiness for remarriage was slightly higher than that of women in 2000, the difference was very small compared with what it had been in earlier decades. In other words, divorced men, as well as divorced women, tend to prefer cohabitation rather than remarriage.

8 & 9. AGING AND KINSHIP

Hungary, like the other countries of Europe, has an aging society. According to the data of the 2001 Census, children aged 0 to 14 years represent 16.3% of the population, and those over 60, 20.6%. The extent of the imbalance between children and the elderly is growing. The aging of the population is manifested in the forms of both health status aging and social aging. In international comparison, the health status of the Hungarian population is very poor. This is quite clearly seen in the case of the elderly. One-half of those over 60 and two-thirds of those over 70 suffer a chronic illness that restricts their everyday life.

The mortality rates for the Hungarian population are extremely high. In 1999 life expectancy at birth for Hungarian men was 66.3 years, exactly the same as it was in 1970. Even in 1970 this rate was worse than that for most European countries. The Czech Republic, for example, which had a similar rate in 1970, reached 71.4 years by 1999. Women's life expectancy at birth is somewhat better than that of men, but it is also worse than the corresponding rate for other European countries (72.1 years in 1970, 75.1 years in 1999). Cardiovascular diseases stand out among the leading causes of death, mainly affecting men. Demographers analyzing Hungarian mortality speak of a change of epidemiological era and say that Hungary has dropped into the Third World as regards the life chances of individuals (Józan, 1996). The high mortality rates are closely related to the population's critical health status, alcoholism, smoking, and the stressful way of life. For decades per-capita consumption of alcohol has been very high in Hungary. Around 12% of the adult population are heavy drinkers and, based on the number of deaths due to liver cirrhosis, the number of alcoholics is estimated to be 500,000 to 600,000. The majority of alcoholics are men, but drinking is increasing considerably among women as well. The number of smokers is rising steadily and at present 35% of the population aged 15 to 64 years smoke. Within this, there is a slight decrease in the percentage of men smoking and an increase among women. The number of persons receiving psychiatric treatment has also been increasing from year to year since the change of political system. In the 1990s 130,000 psychiatric patients a year were recorded and their number is increasing by 20,000 a year. One-half of the patients are between 30 and 50 years, and one-quarter are elderly, from the over-60 group.

Due to the high mortality rate among middle-age men, widowed women make up a substantial part of the elderly population.

For women widowhood brings an increased risk of poverty. This is because employment had been widespread among today's elderly women, but they receive much lower pensions than men. Elderly women who have not earned entitlement to a pension in their own right are entitled to a widow's pension, which is much lower. Consequently, from the material point of view, elderly women living alone are among the losers of the change of political system. For emotional reasons, too, elderly women are in a very difficult situation. While one-half of the men over 80 live in marriage, only 7.5% of women of similar age have a spouse. Due to poverty, illness, and loneliness, the number of suicides among elderly women has increased in recent years despite the fact that the change of political system has brought an improvement in the suicide rate for the country as a whole.

Apart from the health aspect of aging, the phenomenon of social aging also causes problems. Following the change of political system, many people at risk of unemployment and close to retirement age escaped into retirement. In 1990 pensioners made up 24.3% of the population, and by 1997 this proportion was 30.7%. The substantial growth in the number of pensioners is caused by the growing number of early retirement and disability pensions awarded. At the same time, the escape into retirement only eased but did not end the financial problems, because the real value of pensions has not kept pace with inflation. This is a special problem for those who receive a disability pension and for those who have been in retirement for many years, or who live on a widow's pension.

Besides the financial problems, retirement also brings a weakening of the network of contacts. Time-use surveys show that people in general and especially elderly persons are spending less time on entertainment outside the home. In addition, very few people in Hungary (6% to 7%) are engaged in any kind of public activity or volunteer. Although some progress has been made in this respect in recent years, this proportion is still very low. This situation is in part related to the fact that the development of the nonprofit sphere and the spread of voluntary work is very slow in the country. The poor state of health of the elderly population and the attitude that does not approve of activity of this kind could also be factors. As a result, for many people in Hungarian society today, aging goes along with social exclusion and, especially for elderly women, loneliness.

The latter is eased by the relatively strong cohesion of the different generations of Hungarian families. Over the past decades in Hungarian society the role of kinship has been very important in passing on traditions, socialization, mutual help, and building up the social capital of individuals. In the socialist system, the shortage economy continuously created new possibilities for cooperation and mutual help among relatives and for forms of collective work (Sík & Tóth, 1998). Relatives (and fictive kin) continue to help each other in the market economy after the change of political system. Relations are still imbued with the spirit of equality and people regularly keep account of the balance of giving and receiving, and pay their "debts."

Research dealing with intergenerational transfers shows that three-fifths of Hungarian households provide and close to one-half (46.7%) receive some form of help (financial, work, or in kind) from other households (Spéder, 2002). Examined by age-group it is mainly young households (18–29 years and 30–39 years) that receive support in cash and kind from other households. In addition to the age-group in their 30s, it is mainly households over 70 years that receive much help from other households in the form of work. Those who provide the help are for the most part from the middle-age groups. Families with young children receive a larger share of all forms of support. It is worth noting that while one-third of old-age/ widow's pensioners receive some form of support from other households, close to two-thirds give some kind of support to others.

The supports appear mainly in vertical kinship relations, that is, between parents and children, while, compared to previous decades, the role of horizontal kinship support is declining. However, the supports are two-directional, that is, supporting parents and children simultaneously, in less than 4% of households. Middle-age families first help their parents and then when their children grow up, support them, too. In this way the "sandwich generation" phenomenon is spreading over time in Hungarian society.

REFERENCES

Cseh-Szombathy, L. (1996). The role of mental elements in demographic phenomena. In P. P. Tóth & E. Valkovics (Eds.), *Demography of contemporary Hungarian society* (pp. 246–264). Atlantic Studies on Society in Change, No. 85. Highland Lakes, NJ: Atlantic Research and Publications.

Demográfiai évkönyvek [Demographic yearbooks]. (1980–2001). Budapest: KSH.

Életmód–időmérleg. (2002). *A népesség időfelhasználása 1986/87-ben és 1999/2000-ben.* [Style of life–time budget. The use of time of the population during 1986/87 and 1999/2000]. Budapest: KSH.

Hajnal, J. (1965). European marriage patterns in perspective. In D. V. Glass & D. E. C. Eversley (Eds.), *Population in history* (pp. 101–143). London: Edward Arnold.

Havas, G., Kertesi, G., & Kemény, I. (1995). The statistics of deprivation. *The Hungarian Quarterly*, 36(138/Summer), 67–81.

Józan, P. (1996). Changes in mortality in Hungary between 1980 and 1994. In P.-P. Tóth & E. Valkovics (Eds.), *Demography of contemporary Hungarian society* (pp. 111–138). Atlantic Studies on Society in Change, No. 85. New York: Columbia University Press.

Kamarás, F. (2000). Termékenység, népesség-reprodukció [Fertility and reproduction of poplulation]. In T. Kolosi, I. G. Tóth, & G. Vukovich (Eds.), *Társadalmi riport* [Social report] (pp. 409–432). Budapest: TÁRKI.

Nagy, I. (1999). Családi pénzkezelési szokások a kilencvenes években [The use of money in families in the 1990s]. In I. Nagy, T. Pongrácz, & I. G. Tóth (Eds.), *Szerepváltozások* [Changes of roles] (pp. 74–97). Budapest: TÁRKI.

Neményi, M. (1996). Social construction of women's role in Hungary. *Replika, Special Issue*, 83–91.

Népszámlálás [Census] (Vol. 2). (2001). Budapest: KSH.

Pongrácz, T. (2002). *Birth out of wedlock*. Budapest: Demographic Research Institute, Hungarian Central Statistical Office.

Pongrácz, T., & Spéder, Z. (2001). Párkapcsolatok az ezredfordulón [Couple relations at the millenium]. In Z. Spéder (Ed.), *Demográfiai folyamatok és társadalmi környezet* [Population processes and social environment] (pp. 13–32). Budapest: KSH Népességtudományi Kutatóintézet.

Sík, E., & Tóth, I. J. (1998). Some elements of the hidden economy in Hungary today. In T. Kolosi, I. G. Tóth, & G. Vukovich (Eds.), *Social report* (pp. 100–122). Budapest: TÁRKI.

Simonyi, Á. (2002). Rural and urban families on the periphery of society. *Akadémia, 2,* 123–135.

Somlai, P. (1999). Diversities in socialization. In R. Richter & S. Supper (Eds.), *New qualities in the lifecourse* (pp. 63–71). Würzburg: Ergon Verlag.

Spéder, Z. (2002). Generációk és élethelyzetek: Háztartások közötti segítő kapcsolatok [Generations and conditions. Mutual help between households]. In Z. Spéder (Ed.), Demográfiai folyamatok és társadalmi környezet [Demographic processes and social environment] (pp. 96–107). Budapest: KSH Népességtudományi Kutatóintézet.

Szelényi, I. (1988). *Socialist entrepreneurs: Embourgeoisement in rural Hungary.* Madison: University of Wisconsin Press.

Történeti statisztikai idősorok, 1867–1992. I. kötet Népesség-népmozgalom [Time series in historical statistics, 1867–1992: Vol 1. Population]. (1992). Budapest: KSH.

Tóth, O. (1994). Sociological and historical aspects of entry into marriage. *Journal of Family History, 19*(4), 351–368.

Tóth, O. (1999a). *Erőszak a családban* [Violence in the family]. Társadalompolitikai füzetek 12. Budapest: TÁRKI.

Tóth, O. (1999b). Marriage, divorce and fertility in Hungary today: Tensions between facts and attitudes. In A. Pető & B. Rásky (Eds.), *Construction. Reconstruction. Women, family and politics in Central Europe* (pp. 127–146). Budapest: OSI, CEU.

Tóth, O. (2003). A családon belüli, partner elleni erőszak [Violence against the partner in families]. *Századvég.*

Utasi, Á. (2002). Fiatal, egyedülálló nők párkapcsolati esélye [Social chances of young single women]. In I. Nagy, T. Pongrácz, & I. G. Tóth (Eds.), *Szerepváltozások* [Changes of roles] (pp. 113–133). Budapest: TÁRKI.

CHAPTER 15

The Family in Portugal: Past and Present

FAUSTO AMARO

1. INTRODUCTION

Portugal is an old European country, independent since the 12th century and situated on the Atlantic coast of the Iberian Peninsula. The country is quite homogeneous, sociologically speaking, and includes the Madeira Island and the Azores, two regions inhabited by the Portuguese since the 15th century, when the islands were first discovered by navigators.

Portugal has a population of 10.3 million. Eighty-five percent of the population is concentrated along the coast. The two main cities, both located in coastal areas, are Lisbon and Porto, which are the two main centers of attraction for countryside populations. The Madeira and Azores islands constitute two politically autonomous areas, with about 4% of the population.

There are different kinds of settlements in Portugal: coastal versus countryside and north versus south of the Tagus River. Along the coast and north of the Tagus River there is a much larger population density, and settlement is more dispersed. The south is characterized by a smaller population density and it is more concentrated.

Politically, Portugal is a democratic state based on the rule of law and a member of the European Union since 1986. Although the country has an Atlantic coastline but not a Mediterranean one, it is sometimes considered part of the Southern European/Mediterranean culture. Nonetheless, Portuguese scholars have distinguished the Portugal of the south, with Mediterranean characteristics, from the Portugal of the north, with Atlantic characteristics (Ribeiro, 1963). The former was influenced by the Arab and Berber colonization that took place from the 8th to the 13th centuries, and the second by the European colonization of Celtic and German origin. In spite of these differences, the Portuguese anthropologist Jorge Dias (1961) defended the existence of a Portuguese culture that was relatively homogeneous, but with some particularities that are not always geographically related.

With regard to the family, the reference to Mediterranean culture has been made to highlight, above all, women's role in the family and the honor and shame pattern that was analyzed some decades ago by British anthropologists in the Mediterranean (Peristiany, 1965; Cutileiro, 1971).

From a statistical point of view, the family in Portugal is defined as

a group of persons living in the same dwelling and having a family relationship (*de jure* or *de facto*), who may occupy the whole of the dwelling or just part of it. Any independent person who, wholly or partially, occupies a dwelling may also be considered a family. Maids who live in the dwelling where they work also are considered part of the family. (Instituto Nacional de Estatística, 2002).

The average number of persons per family has been steadily decreasing since 1920. In 1920 it stood at 4.2, falling to 4.1 in 1930, 3.7 in 1960, and 3.4 in 1980. In 1991 it stood at 3.1, but in the last census taken in 2001, the figure was 2.8. This decline is due to lower birth and fertility rates. Between 1975 and 2000, the birthrate fell from 19.1 to 11.8, and the fertility rate, which stood at 3.1 in 1960 and at 2.5 in 1975, fell to 1.5 in 1999, one of its lowest figures ever.

2. PAIRING UP

The beginning of a romantic relationship that can lead to marriage depends on the couple's own free initiative. However, parents always try to influence their children's choices through rational approaches. In the rural areas, land ownership is still a factor influencing that decision. In urban areas, the upper classes make use of their children's marriage to create important alliances that can help maintain and develop family businesses. In these families, the mother is still the person who most attentively follows her children's dates and who, discreetly, tries to influence their partner selection (Lima, 2003). As a matter of fact, the mother has the important role of not only setting up special occasions for youths to meet, but also, acting as counselor, of trying to influence, in a positive or negative way, the choices that are made by the children.

As is shown in several surveys on family values (Almeida, 2003), family and marriage are still quite valued in Portugal, considering that the couple's romantic life is an important condition of happiness for 70% of the Portuguese over 18 years of age.

The Sexual Revolution

No longer than 30 years ago, students in elementary and secondary schools were still separated by gender, with both parents and teachers exercising a great deal of control over their youth's sexuality. Once the schools became mixed gender, and the number of years of compulsory schooling was increased to nine, a much broader socializing was allowed among teenagers without the parents' direct supervision. At home, the mother began to be less present, due to her participation in the labor force. These factors and the new ideas about sexuality altered the youth's sexual relationships deeply. At the beginning of the 1990s, a study conducted in the city of Lisbon showed that 80.0% of the men and 68.2% of the women between 21 and 24 years old had had sexual intercourse before the age of 20 (Amaro, Dantas, & Teles, 1995), but this behavior pattern coexists with the traditional vision that one has of the relationships between men and women.

In traditional society, a girl could not date without her parents' consent. This was true even in the largest urban centers, as well as within Portuguese communities in the United States (Cunha, 1997). Nowadays, a young woman no longer asks her parents for permission to date, but if the relationship lasts some time, she will introduce her boyfriend to her parents, the same being true of the boy and his parents. Sexual intercourse before marriage is also the norm, even when the idea of getting married is still absent.

Marriage

The next step is the engagement. It is generally in this stage that the woman's parents meet the boy's parents and go ahead with the formal wedding arrangements. These arrangements include, among other things, choosing the wedding dress, which, in spite of most brides not being a virgin, continues to be white—the symbol of virginity. The wedding party generally takes place in a restaurant. The wedding gift is a must. Not long ago, it was a tradition to give a gift of the same value that one had received. Nowadays, people have adopted a more practical way of organizing wedding gift lists.

A few days preceding the marriage, both the bride and the groom participate in bachelors' parties with friends. The parties can be separate, but many couples opt for joint parties. In these parties, special gifts are offered, but most are gags.

One of the characteristics that seems to be common in European Union member states is that people marry late, with men marrying later than women do. As shown in the Portuguese *Fertility and Family Survey* (Instituto Nacional de Estatística, 2001), in 1997, only 4% of the women interviewed in the 15 to 19 age-group were married. However, 24% of the women in the 45 to 49 age-group had married at the age of 15 to 19, and 73% were married before the age of 24 (Instituto Nacional de Estatística, 2001).

Between 1981 and 2001, the age difference in first marriages went up 2 years for women and 1.7 years for men, going from 23.3 to 25.3 and from 25.4 to 27.1, respectively.

Cohabitation

Although the formal marriage, which is usually ministered by the Catholic Church, is still the favorite form of marriage for engaged couples in cosmopolitan areas, the phenomenon of cohabitation is spreading. The main reasons can be economic, or the wish to know the partner better before marriage, or the wish to conclude some stage of their lives, such as completing education or getting into a new profession.

In Portugal, cohabitation rates were never very high. In 1991 couples that lived in cohabitation represented just 3.9% of the total. By 2001, they represented 6.9% of the couples living together. Therefore, the phenomenon of cohabitation is not very significant in Portugal compared with other European Union member states. Although cohabitation could mean a modern alternative to marriage, in Portugal it just seems with represent a transition period to marriage. Marriage usually happens when the couple finally resolve their financial situation, thus allowing them to buy a better home and giving them a chance to decide if they should or should not have their first child. This interpretation is in full accordance with the statistical data. In 2000 71.1% of couples with children had had their first child after getting married, while only 20.8% had their first child while cohabiting. In addition, the percentage of couples who were married when their second child was born was 89.5%, but only 9.5% for those who were cohabiting. Another interesting indicator is the number of marriages where both spouses shared the same dwelling by the time of their marriage. In 2001, that indicator represented 16.4% of the total marriages. We can, therefore, conclude that marriage will still continue to be the main institution characterizing most Portuguese families.

Family Types

Statistically, we can analyze the Portuguese family according to the following types: (1) couples with children (64.8% of the total couples); (2) one-person families (17.3% of the total families); (3) one-parent families (11.5% of the total family nuclei); and blended families (2.7% of the total couples with children). Couples with children, which represent two-thirds of the total couples, have an almost classic nuclear family structure, because in about 90% of the cases the household is just composed of the couple and its unmarried children. Under this statistical description, there is also the traditional extended family structure, with lots of kinship relationships, including the ritual kinship that will be mentioned later in this chapter.

3. FERTILITY AND SOCIALIZATION

In the period 1930–1934, the average number of children per woman was 3.75; in the period 1958–1962, it lowered to 3.16, and to 2.21 by 1982 (Barata, 1985). By 1999 that number had lowered to 1.5. This continuous drop in fertility rates followed the trend in other EU countries, although in Portugal, as in other Southern European countries, the drop in fertility happened a little later than in the other countries of the European Union (Almeida, André, & Lalanda, 2002). The decrease in the number of children per woman occurred within all age-groups. The largest number of births was seen in the 25 to 29 age-group, the time in life when most marriages take place (Barata, 1985).

The number of children born out of wedlock has been equally subjected to variations over the years. It represented 11.6% in 1900, 11.8% in 1950, and 7.2% in 1975. It later increased to 9.2% in 1980, 14.7% in 1990, and 22.2% in 2000. However, the illegitimacy rate lowered in 2001 to 12.3%. It seems that the number of children out of wedlock is related, on one hand, to the number of couples living in cohabitation, and on the other, to the number of single mothers (Almeida et al., 2002).

The Portuguese survey on family and fertility shows that the pill is the most used form of birth control (60.6%). Condoms are next, at 14.4%, the IUD at 9.8%, and coitus interruptus at 7.0%. The percentage of condom use is larger among the youth, with 38.8% representing usage in the 15 to 19 age-group. The number goes down with the increase in age, being as low as 12.2% in the age-group of 45 to 49. This low use of condoms was also observed in studies on AIDS, which endures as a serious problem in Portugal (Amaro, Frazão, Pereira, & Teles, 2004).

Abortion is not legal in Portugal. It can only be practiced in very specific situations, and only under medical supervision. Even in these situations, therapeutic abortion is only allowed during the first 12 weeks of pregnancy. In the case of abortions to avoid the spreading of noncurable diseases or the birth of a damaged infant, however, therapeutic abortions are allowed up to 16 weeks of pregnancy.

Children's Socialization

With regard to children's socialization, the statistical data of 2001 showed that 91.3% of children up to the age of 4 lived with both parents. Another 7.5% lived only with their mother. In the first case, 73.7% of the women, and in the second 69%, had a job outside the home. This represents a great change in children's socialization, and is due to the accelerated process of industrialization that had begun in the second half of the 20th century. From 1960 to 2001, women's participation in the labor force rose from 15.9% to 45.1%.

In the traditional family, the child's socialization occurred within the family environment up to the child's age of 7, when the child started attending primary school. In the urban areas, children were under the care of their mothers or other relatives at home. In the rural areas, young children usually joined their parents or grandparents in agricultural duties. Education was quite strict, and the male and female roles in which the children were brought up were quite different. In rural areas, for example, the boy accompanied the father in his manual agricultural labor. There was the desire to transmit to the boy the roles that would later identify him with his father, so that later he could be the leader of the family, home, and land (Wall, 1988).

Girls were brought up to play domestic roles, which meant that there would always be someone to look after aging parents in the later stages of their lives. The whole socialization process was subjected to great discipline, but compensated with a system of incentives to make the hard life more bearable for children and youth alike. The concern to maintain the family house and land made the parents try to create the appropriate motivations for each son or daughter. The oldest would begin to help the father and, progressively, take charge of agricultural labor. The younger siblings could help their brother, try their luck in emigration, or join the army or the republican guard. The youngest was encouraged to follow the ecclesiastical path. Having a son become a priest was the supreme ambition of rural families, not only because the priest had social prestige, but also because he could bring the family closer to God and ensure that the parents would be looked after when they reached an advanced age. Apart from socialization within the family, both the school and the Church played an important part as agents in the socialization of youths aged 7 and up, starting with the primary school and at the catechism classes held to prepare them for first communion. Discipline was strict. Children's socialization in Portugal was based on respect for parents and teachers, the values and principles held by the Catholic Church, and patriotic fervor.

During the political regime of Salazar, which lasted about 40 years and was only overthrown with the democratic revolution of 1974, the motto of the educational system was translated into three words: God, homeland, and family. The use of physical punishment in children's education was fairly common in the primary school. Nowadays, physical punishment is not allowed, but an authoritarian structure remains. In a survey carried out in the 1980s, about 50% of the interviewees were of the opinion that parents were entitled to physically punish their children as long as it was done moderately (Amaro, 1986).

Parents' Expectations

And what do parents expect from their children? In a study on European values (Almeida, 2003) carried out at the end of the 20th century, 83% of the people surveyed considered unconditional love for their parents as the ideal for children's socialization, independent of personal characteristics of individuals. In contrast with the Portuguese results, the percentage in Sweden was just 44%.

With regard to the qualities that children should have, the same study indicated the following: to have "good manners" (77%), to be "hardworking" (69%), to be "responsible" (60%), and to be "obedient" (39%). Qualities such as imagination and independence are referred to less by the Portuguese population when contrasted with the answers obtained in other European countries, especially Sweden.

Therefore, the trend seems to be maintaining traditional values and respecting institutional integration and social conformity, both influenced by Catholic Church ethics, which are still prevalent in the country.

In topics on which the parents were not willing to speak freely, such as sexuality, the young were usually taught by the older children.

With women's participation in the work force, the social structure of children's socialization became more flexible, especially after the 1974 revolution, when Church power weakened. This situation forced both couples and single mothers to find alternative ways of bringing up their children while they were at work. These alternatives were mainly day-care nurseries or infant schools, even though relatives often were asked to get involved, especially grandparents. Therefore, children's socialization is still under mixed influences, with contents that are changing and complex.

4. GENDER ROLES

In the Portuguese traditional family, gender roles were firmly established. Men had very instrumental roles, especially in relation to activities outside the home. In the 1960s men still represented 83.9% of the labor force. Emigration to other countries also was mainly a male phenomenon (Barata, 1987).

Women's participation in the labor force began to change with the second stage of the country's industrialization during the 1960s (Neto, 1968, 1971, Barata, 1987, 1988), but it was accelerated with the 1974 revolution. This trend takes into account women's participation in the workforce, which in 2001 already represented 45.1% of the total labor force.

Two factors already mentioned (industrialization and the political revolution of 1974), together with emigration and improvement in women's education, seem to have been the main causes of social change in Portugal, with regard to both masculine and feminine roles (Neto & Amaro, 1978). Even so, an opinion survey carried out in the late 1980s by the Family Department of the Ministry of Social Affairs still showed that 28% of the population considered it more appropriate for women not to work outside the home (Direção-General da Família, 1988). This seems to suggest the importance of financial considerations within the family, since one more full-time wage added to the domestic budget makes a difference in family access to the type of consumer goods that characterize the middle class.

Women's Traditional Tasks

Women's traditional tasks, usually related to domestic work, have not disappeared. Women continue to be responsible for the house, the husband, and the children. In the aforementioned survey, the interviewees were still of the opinion that it was the mother who should supervise the children's school performance (64%), that she should have the responsibility to take the children to the doctor (81%), and that she should stay at home when the children are sick (94%). So, even though the family protection law allows leave for the father for reasons that concern his children's health, it is generally the mother who assumes that role.

It is the same when the man helps with domestic tasks. The traditional pattern still prevails, as the man is usually seen as helping the woman and not as carrying out a male role. It also happens that, many times, the woman makes the sacrifice of combining her job workload and house duties, as a way of maintaining the domestic power that is attributed to her by traditional society, despite the fact that she might like her husband's help in the house.

The cited study on values (Almeida, 2003) shows continuity in the traditional pattern of the relationship between maternity and children's upbringing. Therefore, in a nationwide sample, about two-thirds of the interviewees said they believed that women only fulfill themselves as mothers. In the same sample, however, 69% were of the opinion that the father was as good an educator as the mother, which shows that the traditional pattern may or may not be adequate for women.

Changing Direction

Gender roles show a tendency for change from traditional roles, especially in regard to the participation of women within the labor force and in regard to their sexual behavior. A woman's work outside the home is socially accepted, and she is expected to contribute financially to the family budget. However, women still find themselves less well represented in vocations that are traditionally for men. The most remarkable example is in the world of politics, where women's involvement can still be seen as meager. In the 2002 elections, for example, only 4.5% of mayors were women and only 22.2% of the members of parliament were women.

Sexual Behavior

With regard to sexual behavior, the traditional pattern demanded that a woman marry while still a virgin. This was of extreme importance to the man. The tradition required being married by the Church, with the wife wearing white as a symbol of her virginity. Consequently, the number of women marrying while still virgins was quite high. Surveys on sexual behavior reveal that within the older generation, ages 50 to 59, only 14.7% were sexually initiated before the age of 20, and most were initiated on their wedding night. The introduction of safer contraceptive methods, a higher age by the time of marriage, and a more liberal sexual education led to a new sexual behavior pattern, built on the expectation that most women would be sexually initiated before marriage. This behavior is acknowledged by 60% and 70% of older men and women, respectively. However, most parents prefer that their teenager have the first sexual encounter later.

Another aspect of the revolution concerns sexual initiative. Traditionally it was up to the man to carry out this initiative, and it still happens in most cases, but it seems that a change is beginning to take place. In a 1996 survey of college students, 11% of the women said they had taken the first step. These data are insufficient to establish a trend, since the survey only asked college students and not the population in general. It should be borne in mind that Portuguese society is still very traditional with regard to this matter.

5. MARITAL RELATIONSHIPS

If we consider the period from the 1930s to the late 1960s, we can see that almost every marriage was celebrated by the Catholic Church. In the same period, the majority of marriage contracts were celebrated under the general regimen of common property, which included property that was acquired both before and during the marriage. Since the 1960s the most common marriage contract separates property acquired during the marriage from property acquired before, so that only the property acquired during the marriage would be divided in the advent of a divorce. In 2001, 86.1% of marriage contracts were of the second model, which considers common property to be only that acquired during the marriage.

The influence of the Roman Catholic Church still prevails in Portuguese society, as the great majority of the population (92.9%) still consider themselves Catholic. Not surprisingly, most couples get married within the Church—62.5% in 2001. However, nuptial patterns are changing. People are getting married later and legal marriage is not the only way to a marital relationship—although it still is the most significant.

Most often the couple looks forward to living in their own place, but most try not to live too far from the woman's mother. This shows a trend for quasi-matrilocal residence. The main reason for this seems to be the need for support in domestic duties, and the need for a place to leave the children when they need to be looked after. The main problem for Portuguese women is where to leave the children in their first two preschool years while the women are at work.

Couples' relationships tend to be egalitarian, as the law prohibits sexual discrimination. However, there is still a tendency to see the man as the family head. According to the 2001 Census, the family head was recognized as a male in 91.9% of cases.

Questions such as the number of children to have, income, and family budget management are activities that are supposed to be dealt with jointly today, that is, a new sharing of family power. The same happens with decision-making issues that concern children's education, holiday planning, and other family matters of considerable importance.

Despite this trend toward joint decision-making and home duties, the home is still primarily a woman-driven enterprise, just as it was in traditional families. Until recently, the wife depended on her husband in many moments of her life. Even the law, which is a reflection of social values held in the past, did not allow women to carry out a number of jobs without the husband's consent, including trips taken abroad.

On an intimate level, the wife was supposed to have a passive attitude. On a social level, if her husband was not present, she was expected to take no part in any appointments where she would be left in the company of other men. Woman's fidelity was a must in the old days. Back in the days when the old Portuguese penal laws were in effect, if the husband caught his wife and lover in flagrant adultery, he could get away with murder.

Attitudes and behavior have changed, due to women's broader access to education, the changes in the social structure, the introduction of egalitarian legislation, and women's access to the professional environment, freeing her from traditional submissive roles and allowing them to gain economic autonomy and a more sociable lifestyle.

The 1994 survey on sexual behavior revealed that men were more sexually satisfied than women, more satisfied about their own sexual pleasure as well as their general sexual life. Of course, the percentages of sexual unfaithfulness were higher for men (Amaro, 1994). The most stated reasons for sexual infidelity differed between men and women. Most men stated that it was the wish for adventure that drove them to infidelity, while women gave considerably more importance to communication and connection.

Regional Differences

These differences vary according to the role that women play in the family's professional activities, especially in fishing and agricultural areas, and occur in the north and central coastal regions. Studies carried out in these areas (Moreira, 1987; Cole, 1994; Brogger & Gilmore, 1997; Brettell, 1991, Gilmore, 2002; O'Neil, 1984) show that families are centered on the mother figure, as she is the one to be referred to in all family business decision making. Men have more moderated powers in these families concerning their working activities. However, female influence and power within the couple is not visible in the public sphere, where men dominate.

6. FAMILY VIOLENCE

Child Maltreatment

Family violence in Portugal was only brought to academic attention during the 1980s. Among the various forms of family violence, child abuse and neglect have been the main subjects of research in this area. They are also subjects of huge impact in the realm of public opinion.

The first nationwide research on child maltreatment was published in 1986. A prevalence rate of maltreated children was estimated, therefore, as being on the order of 19 per 10,000 families for psychological abuse. Physical abuse was on the order of 13 per 10,000 families, and child neglect was on the order of 30 per 10,000. Maltreatment and child neglect cases were mostly found within the lower classes. The largest percentage of maltreatment was seen in children between the ages of 6 and 14 who were born into a large family. The aggressors were the father or mother in most of the cases. The characteristics of the aggressors were, usually, low levels of education, unemployment, alcoholism, and an aggressive personality.

With regard to sexual abuse, the children's ages were essentially between 9 and 14 and their abusers were family members or individuals who were very close to the family and quite frequently around (Amaro, 1986; 1989).

Child maltreatment became a political issue by the end of the 1980s, and it was the parliament itself that financed a study that was published in 2001 (Almeida, André, & Almeida, 2001). Again, this study brought to light the aggressors' characteristics: alcoholism, drug addiction, and physical and mental handicaps. Popular awareness of these cases led public opinion to see them as situations of increasing seriousness. Some authors believe, however, that this phenomenon has not been increasing proportionately in Portugal (Miguel, 1999). The apparent increase in the number of cases could possibly be explained by the numerous new studies undertaken; these studies revealed realities that had been hidden until then. Legislation has been promulgated, and support and child abuse prevention structures developed; local commissions for infancy support and protection is of utmost importance today.

Spouse Violence

The concept of domestic violence is sometimes perceived as a synonym for men exercising violence over women (Mullender, 1996). As happened with child abuse, violence toward women was a phenomenon that caught researchers' attention for the first time during the late 1980s, but for cultural reasons the researchers in this area faced more difficulties than those studying child abuse. According to traditional family values, men were considered the authority figures; therefore, the use of violence toward women was tolerated. On a 1982 nationwide survey, 16% of the interviewees said that men could hit women in certain circumstances, and 2% stated that men could hit women no matter what the circumstances were (Costa, 2002).

Traditionally, women were supposed to be docile and submissive in all family life spheres, including the sexual. Thus, if a woman became a victim of family violence, she would hide the fact from other family members and friends and not complain to the authorities. Along with the feeling of shame, two other main factors contributed to this silence. One was the negative impact the situation would have on the children, both emotionally and financially, bearing in mind the father's role as the family earner. The other had to do with the negative impact that the situation would have on the family's social status within the community. Hence, women's hardship was magnified by their lack of financial independence.

Changes in mentalities and economic autonomy led to a change in women's behavior in which this kind of situation was no longer tolerated. However, it is presumed that there are still many cases concealed by victims and not reported to the authorities, because wives are still concerned about possible reprisals, or else they fear losing the affection of the man they married and who is the father of their children. The current situation is, therefore, obscure. Nevertheless, the Associação Portuguesa de Apoio à Vítima (APAV), a nongovernmental organization for victim support, registered in Portugal during 2002 a total of 18,418 cases of domestic violence (1.8 per 1,000 inhabitants), of which 95.5% were cases of violence against females, both children and adults. Since the violence against children represented about 8.5%, we can conclude that most of the family violence occurred against adult women. Of these women, 51.6% were married, with 53.5% of these living in nuclear families. The main types of violence were physical mistreatment (29.3%) and emotional abuse (28.1%). Victims came from all social strata and were in the 26 to 45 age-group. Regarding the aggressors, their main characteristic was excessive consumption of alcoholic beverages (71.5%).

Like the problems of child abuse, domestic violence is a subject of great concern for the Portuguese authorities. The Equality and Women's Rights Commission was developed and a nationwide plan against domestic violence created, with these main objectives in mind: information, sensitization, prevention, training, legislation, victim protection and social integration, research, evaluation, and concern for migrants.

7. MARITAL DISSOLUTION AND REMARRIAGE

Divorce

Since the birth of Portugal in the 12th century and up to the introduction of the Code of Civil Law in 1867, families could only be formed with an indissoluble Catholic marriage. Civil marriages were only introduced in 1867, setting down the foundations for the family's secularization, which was further developed with the introduction of divorce in 1910. Reactions from the Catholic Church led to the establishment of the 1940 Concordat between the Portuguese State and the Vatican, under which divorce was banned from Catholic marriages. The divorce laws were changed again in 1975, with an amendment to the Concordat giving couples married by the Catholic Church the right of divorce. Because of the difficulties raised by Portuguese law, divorce remained at a low level during most of the 20th century.

From 1975 onward, not only was divorce a right for those married outside the Church, but also for those married within, as the whole process of divorce and separation became simpler. Divorce based on mutual consent was reintroduced, along with a whole set of bureaucratic simplifications.

It was due to the introduction of these new rules, and also to the increase of nonreligious marriages, that divorce rates were rising by the end of 1975. In 1975 the raw divorce rate was of 0.15 per 1,000 persons in the population, going up almost every year since then, and reaching 1.1 per 1,000 in 1991, and 1.8 per 1,000 in 2001. In the total population, about 1.9% were divorced in 2001 and 0.7% were separated.

The duration of marriages that end in divorce can vary as well. In 2001 divorces occurred in the first 4 years of marriage in 18.3% of the cases and after 20 years in 26.5% of the cases. The other 55% broke up in 5 to 19 years. The reasons for divorcing do not seem to be connected to marriage duration. The divorce rate in Portugal has been explained by the increase in life expectancy, women's economic autonomy, and the level of satisfaction in the marriage, especially sexual satisfaction. These same reasons have been noted in other Western developed countries (Delgado, 1996; Shorter, 1975).

Many authors have rejected the argument that divorces are connected to the decreasing relevance of marriage and the family, due to the fact that many of those who are divorced get married again. This is what we also see happening in Portugal. In 2001, for example, 35.6% of all widowers and divorced men remarried within a year, as did 25.8% of all women in those same categories. About one-half of the widows (51.6%) were under 50, and 56.5% of the divorced people were under 40. Most widows and divorcées remarried men in the same age-group or older, with the exception of widows over 64 and divorcées over 69, who remarried younger men.

Widowhood

The decision to remarry is less frequent for widows. Despite the fact that widowhood represents only 6.6% of the entire population, that figure is still more than three times the percentage of divorces. Of all men and women married during 2001, only 1% were widows and 1.7% widowers.

8. KINSHIP

Kinship is an important element for defining relationships not only in the traditional extended family but also in the nuclear family. The Portuguese traditional system was patrilineal. Inheritance of name and property benefited the male line. In the nobility, an institution named *morgado* (majorat), which lasted until 1863, was in practice since the 13th century. The majorat was there to keep family properties from being divided upon the death of the family leader. The oldest son inherited it all. If there were no sons in the family, then a daughter could inherit it all, but the male's line was restored when there was a new male descendant. In the 19th century, the tradition of the majorat was also allowed within bourgeois families (Castro, 1966).

The current succession law is different. It is based on preferential classes of succession of family property as follows: (1) husband/wife and descendants; (2) husband/wife and ascendants; (3) brothers/sisters and their descendants; (4) other collateral kin up to the 4th order; (5) the state.

Especially since the political revolution of 1974, Portugal's legislation is not sexually discriminatory, that is, it is impossible to consider it a patrilineal or a matrilineal system. However, sociologically there are still two kinds of families in Portugal, one focused more on the father figure (patrifocal) and another on the mother (matrifocal). In the patrifocal kind, the father represents the authority and is the guardian of the family's honor. His concern with the future makes him want to have sons to carry on his properties and businesses. This type of attitude is mostly found in the upper classes, where maintaining family properties is a major concern. In these families, preference is still given to the oldest son. Because of the current egalitarian laws, families resort to donations and wills to make sure that the oldest son inherits what is necessary to ensure the family's continuity (Lima, 2003).

We can observe the same behavior among traditional farmers in the northern parts of Portugal. The choice can fall on either the oldest son or one of his brothers, as long as they are competent and willing to work the land successfully and provide the much needed affection and care when their parents reach an advanced age. The other sons can always join their brother or, alternatively, follow different paths with their parents' support. The parents look for their sons' consent, but in case of conflict, the chosen son may stay with his parents as a farm manager. When the time comes to proceed with the allotment, following the norms of the Code of Civil Law, he can negotiate and come to an agreement with his brothers to restore the family heritage (Wall, 1998). In lower-class families, the allotment of family assets is egalitarian, with an effort toward maintaining the parents' home as a symbolic landmark (Pina-Cabral, 1995).

Kinship Definitions

Portuguese kinship definitions are quite descriptive, as there is a word (for both genders) for designating kinship and affinity in each generation. For parents and grandparents, there are diminutives, with the appropriate degree of formality for each.

The word defining kinship is used in communication in the vocative form, with the person's name either following it or not, For instance, *Avó!* (Grandmother) or *Avô* (Grandfather) + first name and *Tio* (Uncle) + first name. The father-in-law and the mother-in-law cases pose special problems in communication when a Portuguese wishes to address one of them. Usually her or his attention is drawn first, and then verbal communication is engaged, for instance *olhe!* (look!). Sometimes, especially in urban environments, *mom/dad* or *Sr./Sra. (Mr./Mrs.)* + first name are used. This is a sign of the difficulty in establishing a relationship between son-in-law/mother-in-law and daughter-in-law/father-in-law. The most formal treatment is between parents and sons, whether or not they treat each other as *you* or by a more ceremonious expression, or simply as *dad*, *mom*, *mommy*, or *daddy*.

Ritual Kinship

Apart from kinship relations, there is also ritual kinship, which is also found in other Mediterranean cultures, and which is based on four different kinds of relationships: (1) between the godfather and the godson; (2) between the parents and their son's godfather; (3) between the husband's and wife's parents; and (4) between persons of the same region.

The godfather has a very significant role in the Portuguese family. He has the obligation to take the place of the child's parents if they fail the child for any reason. Also, the godfather is his godson's protector, with the responsibility of providing him help and advice in the course of his life. The godfather can help his godson financially if he so needs, and can also help him find a job when he reaches the appropriate age. Therefore, the godfather and the child's parents are mutually helpful.

There are two ways for choosing the godfather in Portugal. He is chosen from the same social class. This behavior predominates in rural areas where there are small independent farmers. In areas where there are fewer independent farmers and a larger number of wage workers, there seems to be a tendency to choose someone of a higher class as the godfather. Here the family gains from the different kinds of help that can be given, such as having the security of maintaining their jobs and being helped out in times of crisis. The godson and his parents have the responsibility of helping the godfather in his various needs and being loyal to him, politically and otherwise. This relationship is very important for the working classes and the poorest, for it is the only way of gaining access to the mechanisms of power. In urban areas, the godfather is usually chosen from a circle of friends, or even from a group of relatives, such as brothers and grandparents, making their bonds even more powerful and strong.

There are several ways of establishing the affiliation between godfathers and godsons. The most important one is through baptism, a Catholic religious ceremony that usually takes place a few weeks after the child's birth. The bond between godson and godfather is of great respect and loyalty. Another way of achieving that is through chrismation, a Catholic Church sacrament of confirmation of baptism that usually takes place before adolescence. However, chrismation is a ceremony that is less frequently used than baptism. The third way is through marriage. The bond between a person and the godfather is similar to the one achieved through baptism, but not as strong. The fourth way for this affiliation is asking someone (generally someone powerful) to be the godfather. For instance, the senior-year student may choose a professor to take that role, or, as in some companies, a protector may call his protégé *grandson*. In these cases, there isn't any kind of kinship relationship between the parents and the godfather.

Between the husband's parents and the wife's, a bond of *compadre* (godfather in relation to the godchild's parents) is also established. Bonds, almost as strong as the ones between family members, are also established outside the family circle. These are bonds based on sympathy and mutual help between people born in the same village, an attitude of solidarity that can be found not only in the place of origin but also in other Portuguese cities, and in the migration focal points in other countries.

9. AGING AND DEATH

In 2001 those over 65 represented 16.4% of the total population in Portugal, with only 16.0% of the population being under 15. These figures place Portugal among the aging European countries, with the rate of aging going up. The life expectancy of men and women is 73.5 and 80.3 years, respectively, showing a higher number of women in the advanced age-group. In fact, according to the 2001 census, there were 718 men for each 1,000 women over 65. These differences are larger at more advanced ages. The sex ratio in the age-group of 80 to 89 is 566, but it goes down to 376 in the 90 to 99 group. In the group over 99 years, the sex ratio is 192. In terms of marital status in 2001, 80.0% of men and 42.9% of women over 65 were married. Also in 2001, 13.9% of men were widowers and 42.9% of women were widows. This disparity is due to the fact that men in that age-group usually married younger women and that men have a shorter life expectancy than women. The death of a wife or husband always requires a great deal of adaptation and the ability to face widowhood, a period in life when some remarry. But, as was mentioned in the dissolution and remarriage section, the number of weddings in the group of widows and widowers over 65 is very low, especially in the rural areas. In these areas widows adopt a much more reserved lifestyle and generally never remarry.

The main problems faced by families in their retirement are economic. Solidarity and their sons' support are still of vital importance, especially in widowhood. In rural areas the widower or widow is taken to the home of his or her married offspring—one after the other—living the tradition of dividing the year among those who could have them. The father or mother could also be taken in by the son who had inherited the family home and became the family leader with the added commitment of taking good care of his parents. However, urban growth, with its shortage of space and women working out of their homes, leads to an ever more frequent choice of retirement homes as an alternative, especially when health problems and functional limitations occur.

The cult of the deceased person is still very strong. The widow frequently visits the cemetery where her late husband rests, as it is the relatives' responsibility, and especially the widow's, to keep the grave clean, tidy, and adorned with flowers. Visits to the cemetery are, therefore, a frequent chore for widows, as it would be socially censurable for them not to do so.

The death of a relative is always a reason for bringing all the family members together, even those who live very far away from the place where the deceased had lived. Some arrive at the funeral's eve, while others show up only at the funeral. At the funeral, it is absolutely expected to find the whole family present.

10. FAMILY AND OTHER INSTITUTIONS

Family and Economy

In Portugal the relationship between family and economy has been following the trends in the industrialized world. However, some peculiar aspects of Portuguese society deserve to be mentioned. Historically, the 40 years of Salazar's dictatorship are important, because of the ideology centered on the preservation of rural traditions. A late and slow industrialization set Portugal way behind the economic growth of other European countries. Low wages and low professional qualifications may, in part, explain the high number of women working out of their homes, since two full-time wages are vital for the family's financial balance.

The number of family businesses is fairly high. The activity in these family businesses is sometimes accompanied by a job in the industry or services general market. This seems to have a negative effect on the family's quality of life, especially in the relationships between parents and children, due to the work overload on both wife and husband. However, a family business contributes in a positive way to the strong bonds between the involved family members, broadening the family's solidarity.

In 1995 about one-third of the country's large corporations rated on the stock exchange were owned by a small number of families, with family members running the business themselves ("Portuguese Business," 1995). These families face, however, two kinds of problems: First, they must face the industry's competitors and their highly professional management standards; second, they must guarantee their own continuity, finding ways of keeping their real and symbolic property away from division and disagreement that might be originated by the leader's death and subsequent allotment between heirs.

To tackle the first problem, families turn to the members who are best suited and qualified for running their business. The second situation is dealt with through matrimonial alliances and with the choice of the main heir. As we have already mentioned, succession laws do not help the family's interests, because the law's allotment system is based on the equality of rights between the heirs.

Just as in the rural homes of the northern countryside (Wall, 1998), families who run large companies try to pass their properties to the chosen heir by means of a will or donation. While studying some of the most influential families of the Portuguese economy, Lima (2003) found that there is a constant concern to keep the family business within the family through the application of the aforementioned strategies. Therefore, there is great concern in the selectiveness of weddings among the families that own the largest Portuguese companies. The weddings should only take place within their restricted group of families, leading to an alliance policy by means of marriage (Lima, 2003).

Family and the Catholic Church

The Roman Catholic Church has an intimate relationship with the family, as the Church influences much of life. From the moment the Pope officially acknowledged Portugal as an independent nation in 1179, the Church has never been kept away from its decisive influence on the family as an institution. Even Salazar's political regime was largely inspired by the social philosophy of the Church. The Church's influence was very significant and prevailed on issues such as divorce, contraception, abortion, and children's religious education. Its influence was significant not only because of its proclaimed values but also because of the influence and pressure that the Church could exert on the government to obtain the most suitable legislation for its objectives.

With the country's democratization, a process of laicization and resecularization was initiated, reducing the relevance of the Church. However, its influence has proven to be deep in questions that concern the family, namely, issues such as contraception and abortion. The current trend is toward an increasing laicization of Portuguese society with a decrease in Church influence over family life. Even so, it is predictable that the Church will remain an important institution in Portuguese society in the areas of politics and children and youths' education.

11. SPECIAL TOPICS

Ethnicity

From an ethnic and linguistic point of view, Portugal is a fairly homogeneous country. Almost all Portuguese people speak standard Portuguese, almost everyone is Roman Catholic, and most of the Portuguese people relate to Portuguese culture. Some regional differences do exist but are not based on ethnic differences. The northern parts are more conservative and Catholic-oriented than the southern parts. People from other countries represent only 2% of the total population, mainly citizens of other European countries and citizens of African countries. The largest group (100,000) is of African origin, mainly from Angola, Cape Verde, and Guinea, three former Portuguese colonies.

Apart from these immigrants, there is a small group of Gypsies, a minority group that is still part of the country's tradition. The Gypsy culture has not changed relative to Portuguese society. The Gypsies have kept their own identity, remaining a seminomadic group living off trade. In fact, the Gypsy family has changed little over the years. It is still guided by its ancient traditions. Women marry young. There is an absolute respect for the woman's virginity before marriage. The husband can even reject her if she is not a virgin. Fidelity is mandatory for every wife and they are prohibited to marry anyone who is not a Gypsy. These rules are followed, and breaking them can cause strong social disapproval and sanctions from every corner of the community, some of them quite violent.

Future Directions and Trends

Demographic studies are largely represented in the Portuguese literature on the family. Indicators such as family size, birthrate, age at marriage, divorce rate, cohabitation, and so on show a trend similar to what is seen in Western industrialized countries. Attitudes and behavior related to family life are also changing in the same direction as shown in the cosmopolitan areas. However, the changes seem to be less significant in Portugal due to the influence of the Catholic Church and the traditional culture.

A new phenomenon influencing the Portuguese family structure is immigration, mainly immigration from Africa, with its different demographic patterns and different family values. Because the majority of Portuguese married women have full-time jobs out of the home, unskilled female immigrants are getting jobs in childcare facilities and Portuguese households. This fact will probably have an impact on child-rearing practices in those places, but what will then be the influence of these immigrant women in the socialization process?

Other issues that will need the attention of family sociologists include the following: (1) the values and expectations of parents in the socialization process; (2) the integration process of immigrants' children into Portuguese culture and society; (3) marital relationships within blended families; (4) family stresses that reflect behavior other than violence; (5) kinship relationships; (6) values and attitudes toward marriage and family; (7) power inside the family; and (8) pubic family policies.

REFERENCES

Almeida, A. N. (2003). Família, conjugalidade e procriação: Valores e papéis [Family, pairing up, and procreation: Values and roles]. In J. Vala, M. Cabral, & A. Ramos (Eds.), *Valores sociais: Mudanças e contrastes em Portugal e na Europa* [Social values: Changes and contrasts in Portugal and in Europe] (pp. 47–93). Lisbon: Imprensa de Ciências Sociais.

Almeida, A. N., André, I. M., & Almeida, H. N. (2001). *Famílias e maus tratos às crianças em Portugal* [Families and child maltreatment in Portugal]. Lisbon: Assembleia da República.

Almeida, A. N., André, I. M., & Lalanda, P. (2002). Novos padrões e outros cenários para a fecundidade em Portugal [New patterns and other scenarios for the fecundity in Portugal]. *Análise Social, 37*(163), 371–409.

Amaro, F. (1986). *Crianças maltratadas, negligenciadas ou praticando a mendicidade* [Child abuse and neglect and children practicing mendicancy]. Lisbon: Centro de Estudos Judiciários.

Amaro, F. (1989). Sociocultural aspects of child abuse and neglect in Portugal. In M. J. B. Marques, J. C. A. da Côrte, G. N. M. P. dos Santos, & I. C. R. Lencastre (Eds.), *Public health and protection of the population* (pp. 115–117). Amsterdam: Elsevier Science Publishers.

Amaro, F. (1994). *Opiniões, atitudes e comportamento sexual da população portuguesa* [Opinions, attitudes, and sexual behavior of the Portuguese population]. Lisbon: Comissão Nacional de Luta Contra a SIDA.

Amaro, F., Dantas, A. M., & Teles, L. C. (1995). Sexual behavior in the city of Lisbon. *International Journal of STD & AIDS, 6*, 35–41.

Amaro, F., Frazão, C., Pereira, M. E., & Teles, L. (2004). HIV/AIDS risk perception, attitudes and sexual behaviour in Portugal. *International Journal of STD and AIDS, 15*(1), 56–60.

Barata, O. S. (1985). *Natalidade e política social em Portugal* [Birthrate and social policy in Portugal]. Lisbon: ISCSP.

Barata, O. S. (1987). Mudança demográfica e estrutura social em Portugal [Demographic change and social structure in Portugal]. *Lisboa, 15*(3–4), 5–48.

Barata, O. S. (1988). *Dinâmica populacional e dinâmica social em Portugal* [Population and social dynamics in Portugal]. Paper presented at the First International Meeting of Joaquim Nabuco Foundation: Population in the Portuguese-Speaking World, Recife, Brazil.

Brettell, C. B. (1991). *Homens que partem, mulheres que esperam* [Men who migrate, women who wait]. Lisbon: Dom Quixote.

Brettell, C. B. (2002). Gendered lives. *Current Anthropology, 43*, 45–61.

Brogger, J., & Gilmore, D. D. (1997). The matrifocal family in Iberia: Spain and Portugal compared. *Ethnology, 36*(1), 13–30.

Castro, A. (1966). Morgado. In J. Serrão (Ed.), *Dicionário de história de Portugal* [Dictionary of Portuguese history]. Porto: Livraria Figueirinhas.

Cole, S. (1994). *Mulheres da Praia: O trabalho e a vida numa comunidade costeira portuguesa* [Women of the Praia: Work and lives in a Portuguese coastal community]. Lisbon: Dom Quixote.

Costa, D. G. (2002). *Percepção social da mulher vítima de violência conjugal* [Social perception of women who are victims of domestic violence]. Unpublished master's thesis, Technical University of Lisbon, ISCSP, Lisbon, Portugal.

Cunha, P. D. (1997). *Entre dois mundos: Vida quotidiana de famílias portuguesas na América* [Between two worlds: Daily life of Portuguese families in America]. Lisbon: Secretariado Coordenador dos Programas de Educação Multicultural do Ministério da Educação.

Cutileiro, J. (1971). *A Portuguese rural society.* Oxford: Clarendon Press.

Delgado, P. (1996). *Divórcio e separação em Portugal* [Divorce and separation in Portugal]. Lisbon: Editorial Estampa.

Dias, J. (1961). *Ensaios etnológicos* [Ethnological essays]. Lisbon: JIU.

Direção-General da Família. (1988). *Alguns dados sobre o quotidiano das famílias portuguesas* [Some data on the daily life of Portuguese families]. Lisbon: Author.

Instituto Nacional de Estatística. (2001). *Inquérito à fecundidade e família* [Fertility and family survey]. Lisbon: Author.

Instituto Nacional de Estatística. (2002). *Estatísticas demográficas* [Demographic statistics]. Lisbon: Author.

Lima, M. A. P. (2003). *Grandes famílias, grandes empresas* [Great families, great companies]. Lisbon: Dom Quixote.

Miguel, J. P. (1999). Epidemiologia do stress e da violência na criança e no jovem [Epidemiology of stress and violence in childhood and youth]. In João Gomes-Pedro (Ed.), *Stress and violence in childhood and youth* (pp. 235–247). Lisbon: Departamento de Educação Médica e Clínica Universitária de Pediatria da Faculdade de Medicina de Lisboa.

Moreira, C. D. (1987). *Populações marítimas em Portugal* [Fishing communities in Portugal]. Lisbon: ISCSP.

Mullender, A. (1996). *Rethinking domestic violence.* London: Routledge.

Neto, J. P. (1968). Social evolution in Portugal, since 1945. In R. S. Sayers (Ed.), *Portugal and Brazil in transition.* Minneapolis: University of Minnesota Press.

Neto, J. P. (1971). *A família e a sociedade portuguesa perante a industrialização* [The family and the Portuguese society facing industrialization]. Paper presented at the 24th Portuguese-Spanish Congress for the Progress of Sciences, Lisbon, Portugal.

Neto, J. P., & Amaro, F. (1978). *Social change in Portugal reconsidered—The case of the Lisbon area after 1974.* Paper presented at the Ninth World Congress of Socioloy, Uppsala, Sweden.

O'Neil, B. J. (1984). *Proprietários, lavradores e jornaleiros* [Social hierarchy in a northern Portuguese hamlet, 1870–1978]. Lisbon: Dom Quixote.

Peristiany, J. G. (1965). *Honour and shame.* London: George Weiddenfeld & Nicolson.

Pina-Cabral, J. (1995). Au Portugal: Reconstruire sa généalogie, garder la maison [In Portugal: To discover its genealogy, to keep the house]. In M. Gullestad & M. Segalen (Eds.), *La famille en Europe* (pp. 93–113). Paris: La Découverte.

Portuguese business: Family values. (1995, June 3). *The Economist.* London, p. 60.

Ribeiro, O. (1963). *Portugal, o Mediterrâneo e o Atlântico* [Portugal, the Mediterranean and the Atlantic]. Lisbon: Sá da Costa.

Shorter, E. (1975). *The making of the modern family.* New York: Basic Books.

Wall, K. (1988). Residência e sucessão na família camponesa do Baixo Minho [Residence and succession in the peasant family of Low Minho]. *Sociologia—Problemas e práticas, 5,* 39–60.

Wall, K. (1998). *Famílias no campo* [Families in the countryside]. Lisbon: Dom Quixote.

CHAPTER 16

Scandinavian Families

Jan Trost

Irene Levin

1. INTRODUCTION

Denmark, Norway, and Sweden are the three Scandinavian countries. Sometimes people include Iceland and Finland as Scandinavian countries, but that is in confusion with the term *Nordic countries*. All three countries are kingdoms, and over the centuries they have occupied each other or been in more or less voluntary unions. Sometimes they have been at war with each other and exchanged land in peace processes. Previous to Christianity the entire area practiced the Asa religion, which featured many female and male gods. Christianity came officially at about 1000 C.E., but it did not fully take hold until the 15th century (Carlsson, 1965, 1972). During the 16th century, the Lutheran version of Protestantism was introduced. As happened with Christianity, the kings decided on behalf of the people that that form of religion would be practiced. Today these churches are predominant, but many other varieties of religion exist. It is only a slight exaggeration to say that the Scandinavian countries are to a high extent secularized.

Today Denmark has a population of about 5.4 million, Norway has a population of about 4.6 million, and Sweden has a population of about 9 million. Population density is fairly low in Denmark, with about 125 inhabitants per sq km. In Norway and Sweden density is very low—12 inhabitants per sq km in Norway and 21 inhabitants per sq km in Sweden, in contrast to Belgium with 337 and Israel with 318 inhabitants per sq km. Traditionally all three Scandinavian countries have been fairly homogeneous, but during the last half of the 20th century, immigration has increased—first with immigration from Europe because of a shortage of labor and later with immigration of refugees from more distant areas.

All three Scandinavian countries are what are called welfare societies. This does not mean that people are on welfare, but that the state takes responsibility for its citizens and other inhabitants. This responsibility is financed by relatively high taxes—income taxes, a value-added tax (VAT), and other taxes. The responsibility taken by the state can be exemplified by the fact that all elderly people receive a state pension, that single parents are financially subsidized depending on their financial situation, that the state pays for a year of parental leave during a child's first year, and that disabled children and adults receive free medical and physical support of various kinds. Society takes a collective responsibility. Some say that the welfare state has become a new patriarch—that it both supports and controls the inhabitants, as fathers/husbands in the past were supposed to support their wives and children (Boje & Leira, 2000; Wærnes, 2002).

In the northern parts of Norway and Sweden a minority group called Saami (previously called Lapps) still engages in their traditional work of reindeer breeding. There are approximately 40,000 Saami in Norway and about one-half that in Sweden. They have by tradition the right to let their deer live freely, but their rights are more and more limited. The Saami fight for their rights and have their own parliament, but with very limited power. They also do what they can to keep their language alive.

2. PAIRING UP

The traditional courtship system of these three countries has been fairly similar to the rest of the Western world. However, contrary to the American tradition, *dating* has never existed as a term or as a concept. About one-third of established couples met at school or at work, another one-third were introduced by family or friends, and the last one-third met at dining and dancing establishments or at bars (Trost, 1993).

Engagement periods shorter than a year are very unusual and many couples are in the state of being engaged to be married for years. If one would ask a newly engaged person in Scandinavia about when the two would marry, an empty face would usually show that the question was absurd; they had decided *to* marry but not *when* to marry.

This tradition of engagements separated from marriage would not be found on the European continent; there they could answer the question. In Scandinavia, only the King's or Queen's children would be able to answer such a question.

This tradition seems to follow from the ancient *nattfrieri,* or night courtship, which existed in rural areas during the 18th and 19th centuries. At that time a young man would visit a young woman in the evening and stay overnight, but the system did not allow him to go under the blanket. If she liked him and he her, he could be welcome the next week. This way many young men and many young women met each other and became couples. The rule not to climb under the blanket was, of course, not always obeyed—which caused some premarital pregnancies (Carlsson, 1965, 1972).

During the 19th century and earlier, children born to a mother who was engaged to be married to the father of the child were registered as born within marriage, which shows that these long engagements were part of a social system.

Sometimes it was said that children born out of wedlock were just illegal, but in social reality there were four kinds of children—one kind where the child was born to a married woman and thus fully legal; another where the child was almost legal, born to a mother engaged to be married to the father of the child; a third where the child was almost illegal, having been born to a single mother and the father was known and accepted the child as his; and a fourth kind where the child was considered fully illegal, having been born to a single mother and an unknown father (Trost, 1993; Taussi-Sjöberg, 1988).

As will be discussed in a later section, at the same time that marriage rates declined very rapidly in Scandinavia, nonmarital cohabitation became common and was rapidly accepted in Scandinavia more rapidly than elsewhere. With the tradition of long engagements, so-called premarital sex was not only tolerated but readily accepted. Finland followed closely after Scandinavia in accepting nonmarital cohabitation.

3. FERTILITY AND SOCIALIZATION

Fertility

In the mid-1930s birth rates in Scandinavian countries declined sharply, to a historically low rate that alarmed some scholars and others active in public debate. Social democrats Alva and Gunnar Myrdal envisioned a welfare society based on social engineering. Among other issues that concerned them were the low birthrates. They argued for child support for all mothers of children younger than 16 years, paid for by the government and given to all, independent of financial status (Myrdal & Myrdal, 1934). (A considerably rewritten English version of their book was published in 1941.) The Myrdals also suggested housing subsidies for the poor. Aspiring for better and healthier citizens, they also argued for abortions and sterilization for the poor and for those with what were believed at the time to be inheritable illnesses of various kinds. (During this era, eugenics was not only popular but also politically correct.)

As in all Western countries, the fertility rate in Scandinavian countries declined considerably during the period after World War II. Demographers talk about the total fertility rate (TFR), which when stable at about 2.1 means that the population will remain constant in the long run (not considering emigration and immigration). If the TFR is higher for a long period of time, the population will increase in size. When it is lower, the population will decrease.

As in other Western countries, the median age at which Scandinavian women give birth has increased considerably. Half a century ago the median age of women at first birth

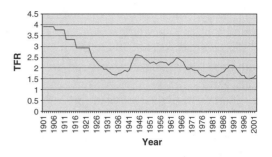

Figure 16.1   Total Fertility Rank in Sweden

was about 21.5 years. Now the age of women at first birth is about 28.5 years.

As can be seen in Figure 16.1, the TFR has gone up and down in Sweden but has never except just momentarily climbed to 2.1. The other Scandinavian countries are fairly similar in this respect. During recent decades, the TFR in Scandinavia has varied between 1.5 and 2.2.

Half a century ago women had more children than they may have wanted, but nowadays with efficient non-coitus-related contraceptives, almost no women have more children than they want, and quite a few will have fewer than they want. In Scandinavia the wished-for number of children among women in fertile ages has been fairly constant over the years at an average of approximately 2.3 to 2.4. Few women want children when they are not in a steady relationship with a man and few want children when their marriage is faltering—the old and traditional idea of saving the marital relationship with the birth of a child has become obsolete (Trost, 1990b, 1993).

In the beginning of the 1980s, many demographers and many politicians were concerned about low birthrates. The amount of governmental child support was increased considerably to encourage women to have more children. The fertility rate increased but would have done so in any case, according to some calculations (Trost, 1990a; Kälvemark, 1980).

With the high number of divorces and separations, many women will face a series of time periods when they are in no relationship or in a new and not yet steady relationship. With more women postponing a wish for children until they are older, the probability for sterility is higher—for the woman as well as for the man. All this taken together means that the TFR will never reach a stable and high level of fertility, except during very short periods as can be seen in the case of Sweden in 1990–1991. Thus, society has to plan for a decreasing population unless the low fertility rates are compensated for by immigration. However, the fertility rate of the immigrants rapidly adjusts to Scandinavian conditions, which can be seen with Sweden as an example in Figure 16.2. The diagram shows that the immigrant fertility rate is slightly higher than the nonimmigrant rate and that it follows the same pattern. At least this has been the case until the present time.

Socialization

Many of those who have seen Ingmar Bergman movies might believe that the tradition of spanking or physically abusing children as a means to socialize them into good citizens is old and strong in Scandinavia. Such a picture is very misleading. "Spare the rod and spoil the child" has never been an ideal in Scandinavia, as it has been in some other parts of the world and still is in some places.

Generally, in all of Scandinavia the socialization process in homes and at day-care centers is very liberal and democratic. Corporal punishment by teachers was abandoned long ago, and the practice by parents has been prohibited for decades. The Scandinavian ideology says that children, as well as parents and other adults, are human beings with rights. Sweden was first in the world to introduce an antispanking law, in 1979, and the other Scandinavian countries soon followed. This law was passed by the

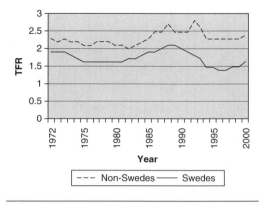

Figure 16.2   TFR in Sweden by Citizenship

Swedish Parliament almost unanimously, and it forbids parents (as well as anyone else) to physically or mentally abuse or spank children. Previously only serious abuse or spanking was illegal.

Warren DeLey (1986) compared American and Swedish university/college students' experience of parents' spanking them and also their attitude toward parents spanking their children. The results showed that of the Americans, 90% had been spanked, but only 60% of the Swedes had been spanked. Similarly, 60% of the Americans indicated that parents should spank their children, while only 20% of the Swedes agreed. These figures are shown to demonstrate the difference in cultural background and opinions about spanking. (The sample in the United States consisted of students in the social sciences, while the sample in Sweden consisted of students in business administration, which might indicate that the American students in the sample were relatively less conservative than the Swedish ones.)

Socialization in the form of education in Scandinavian countries includes a compulsory 9 years of primary education and high school, which is encouraged and free—there are no fees, and textbooks and other educational materials are free. Furthermore, the students at high schools will, when above

18 years of age, receive a small amount of support money from the local government.

Higher education at universities and colleges is also free of charge. All students can after application receive study support and also a loan from the government. The amount received is enough for housing, books, clothes, and food. Parents are not expected to pay anything for their children's studies at universities or colleges. The loans for education may be paid off over the person's active life, up to approximately age 65.

At the beginning of the 20th century, very few women were housewives—exaggerating slightly, one can say that they existed only among upper-class and upper-middle-class households. But subsequently, more and more of the wives became housewives and the system changed so that a husband was able to care for his wife and their children. This means that the children, at least technically, had a mother at home when they were small and when they came home from school.

In the 1960s, however, something happened. Both politicians and employers realized that there was a pool of potential workers in the homes. Thus, it would not be necessary to import foreign workers. The parliaments decided accordingly. With Sweden as an example, those housewives who wanted to go out to the labor market could be subsidized for going to schools and colleges for an education to prepare for work in offices, libraries, or factories, to mention just a few examples. The government supported the extra costs regardless of the husbands' income. Furthermore, the small system of day-care homes for preschool children was heavily extended to cover all preschool children at a low cost. Previously only single parents and poor parents could have their children in day care—others had to find other solutions when both parents were gainfully employed.

Very rapidly housewives disappeared as a social institution and could be found only among relatively elderly couples. Now it is very hard to find any young housewives in the Scandinavian countries. However, quite a few women—especially among those with younger children—work only half time. It could be argued that women are gainfully employed full time or less while men are gainfully employed full time or more.

Furthermore, the leave of absence after childbirth is comparatively long. The ideology says that it is better for the child's upbringing to have a parent at home than for the child under 1 year of age or so to be in day care. When the child is older, the day-care system is supposed to be better for the child, since it will meet other children and also adults other than the parents.

Somewhat simplified, parents have the right to a leave of absence for one of them for 1 year after childbirth. During that period, the one staying at home with the child will receive about 75% to 85% of her or his regular income. To receive all this time as a leave of absence, the father has to take at least 1 month off. In reality the mother of the child takes most of the time off. Thus, one could say that some of the system with housewives is still there: Women/mothers are those most responsible for taking care of children and the home.

In all three countries, day care is supported by local governments. However, there are varieties in the numbers of spaces for preschool children. In Sweden all local governments have to make sure that there is day care for as many children as needed by their parents. In most cases, one of the parents stays at home during the child's first year, while later almost all children are in organized day care. In Denmark the situation is similar, but more of the children stay in day care during the first year of their life.

Norway has a special arrangement with less access to day care. There society provides cash-for-care payments to those parents who stay at home to take care of their own preschool children. This system was introduced in 1998, and is heavily criticized. The philosophy among some politicians is that it is better for the child to stay at home with a parent than to be in day care. Thus, there is also a shortage of organized day care in Norway, with quite a few parents who want to work but have to stay at home to take care of their child. Criticism of the system is partly based on gender issues to the effect that the system forces mothers to interrupt their careers. Another criticism is based on the idea that children need to be together with other children when growing up and not isolated with their mothers (Ellingsæter, 2003).

4. GENDER ISSUES

As will be mentioned subsequently, there are many gender issues in the official debates in the Scandinavian countries. Active work for gender equality and later gender equity started in the middle of the 19th century and continued, with some breaks, until the mid-1950s, when feminists began actively debating the social order. In the 1960s, as elsewhere in the Western world, gender issues were discussed intensively. Housewives were more and more seen as old-fashioned, and party politics and labor politics went hand in hand, resulting in housewives going out of the home and into schools and the labor market. It could be said that women ended up with two jobs: to be gainfully employed and to take care of the home (Kvande & Rasmussen, 1992).

At the beginning of the 1980s, the prime minister in Norway, Gro Harlem Brundtland, decided that at least 40% of the members of her government had to be women. Later this idea spread to local, regional, and central governments in all three countries. The Swedish Government announced in 2003 that all stock companies needed to increase the number of women on their boards, or a law would be passed to formally require them to do so. Very soon the idea of a ratio of 40% to 60% became more and more accepted. However, reality did not follow ideology, which means that it took a long time before at least 40% of members of local, regional, and state parliaments were women. Men are still most common among decision makers in politics, as well as in industries and other companies.

Registration at universities and colleges shows more females than males, and they also obtain the lower degrees quicker and with better results than males, but at higher levels, males are more common. It will be a while yet before women hold a 40% distribution as professors. For example, in Norway only 15% of full professors are women; the relative numbers are increasing, but very slowly.

In all three Scandinavian countries, gender research has been rather extensive. Originally, *gender* studies really meant *women's* studies. However, during recent decades, male research has also been popular. Male research uses the male perspective as the analytical tool, as the women's research used the female. Nowadays, in female as well as in male gender studies, gender is not only used as a variable, but as a meaning-making analytical category (e.g., Dahle, 1990, 1991; Haavind, 1987; Hydén, 1994; Magnusson, 2000; Morgan, 1992, 1996; Søndergaard, 1996).

5. MARRIAGE, COHABITATION, AND LAT RELATIONSHIPS

The marriage rate increased during the 20th century until the mid-1960s, as illustrated in Figure 16.3, which shows the situation in Sweden where the marriage rate began decreasing rapidly in 1966. The other Scandinavian countries followed, with some delay and at a somewhat slower pace. At first Scandinavians didn't realize what was

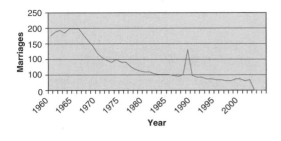

Figure 16.3   Marriages in Sweden per 1,000
Single Women

happening, but after some years they saw that nonmarital cohabitation had arrived in a renewed form.[1]

In the traditional pattern, a couple going steady would after some time become engaged to be married, and they would marry a year or later thereafter. Compared with many other cultures, as mentioned previously, Scandinavian engagements lasted a long time. When the couple eventually married, there were four elements normatively and closely connected, as in most other Western countries: the marital ceremony, the moving in together in a common home, the start of having sex together, and the birth of a child in about a year (Trost, 1990b, 1993).

Typical for Scandinavia was that the normative value of the third element was ideal and certainly not behavioral. Almost all couples had sex together during the relatively long engagement periods. This can be illustrated by the fact that in Sweden, for example, in the middle of the 20th century about 10% of the couples marrying already had a child, and that at least one-third of the brides were pregnant when they married. Some of these marriages were forced marriages, but more commonly the marriage was preponed (as opposed to postponed) or the couple was less concerned about contraceptive means since they in any case would marry soon.

In Scandinavia as elsewhere in Western Europe, neo-Marxism became prominent around 1970 and the neo-Marxists strongly

criticized society for registering people who married—without their consent to be registered—stating that marriage was a combination of Christianity and capitalism. That marriage existed and still exists without Christianity evidently did not matter for the activists. Others claimed that the nuclear family should be abandoned and replaced by a new form of extended family constituted of several couples with children. This sort of family would be protective and good especially for the children, since if one of the parents would disappear, there would be plenty of adults to take care of the child or children. Furthermore, in the public debate, the nuclear family was said to be protected by the capitalists since all these small households needed a vacuum cleaner each, a refrigerator each, and other facilities that easily would be enough for more persons than the small modern nuclear family.

With this as a background and with the introduction in the 1960s of the Pill and the intrauterine device (IUD), changes should not have been surprising. As a replacement for marriage came nonmarital cohabitation,[2] and the changes occurred more rapidly in Sweden than in any other country in the Western world. In the beginning, those who began cohabitation were those in opposition to existing traditions and norms; they actively chose not to marry and could be labeled deviants, since they broke the normative system. Very soon, however, there were followers who were not against the societal norms. They just started living together, not as a protest but because they loved each other and were now suddenly, historically, allowed to live together openly without having married.

After about a 10-year period in Sweden and a somewhat longer period in the other Scandinavian countries, cohabitation had become a social institution alongside or parallel to marriage. Many looked on cohabitation as a prestage to marriage and many looked on it as a trial period to see if the couple was compatible. These views were mainly views from outside and were not common among those cohabiting themselves (Trost, 1980). It is true, however, that many of the partners in these dyads believed that in the long run, if a couple stayed together, they should marry or be married. These two terms—*to marry* and *to be married*—can be seen as synonymous, but they are not. To marry is the relatively short process of changing from a marital status of single to a marital status of married; previously a *rite de passage*, now turned into a confirmation rite. To be married is the state after the marriage, a state that lasts until the couple divorces or one of the two dies.

The two terms *to marry* and *to be married* should not be mixed. In today's society the act of marrying is a mere rite with no real significance, and has no real meaning for most couples afterward. To be married is seen by some as more serious than just cohabiting. Furthermore, the wedding nowadays means a party for the marrying couple and their friends—contrary to the traditional wedding, which was organized by the bride's parents to celebrate with their friends that their daughter was going to change marital status.

For many decades, almost all those who eventually married had been cohabiting for some period prior to marrying. It has been almost impossible to find couples in the Scandinavian countries who moved in together only when they married. The old tradition with the four elements mentioned previously, which were closely connected to each other, has fully disappeared. At least officially these four elements were connected timewise in the traditional system, meaning the system we had prior to the mid-1960s.

To highlight the differences between the previous and the present systems and how the normative connection between the four elements has dissolved, we will use the following real example. Maria and Andreas met at a New Years party. They fell in love and she went home with him and more or less stayed there. After a while they could be said to be a cohabiting couple, that is, officially a couple. Later they decided to marry on a certain day in 1996, a day of importance for them. By this time, they had been cohabiting for 5 years. Together with her father she started planning for the wedding, but some months before it was to happen she told her father that there would be no marriage. He automatically asked if the two had quarreled and had decided to dissolve the relationship. Her answer was on the contrary and that they still loved each other.

What had happened was that she, without planning, had gotten pregnant. She did not want to marry when pregnant since she wanted to be able to freely dance and also drink and smoke at her own marriage. Therefore, the wedding was postponed for 2 years. They married 2 years later, in 1998, with their little daughter running around in church and at the big wedding party where many friends and some relatives were invited. The four parents were permitted to pay for the wedding and the party.

Within the previous system, her pregnancy would have meant that they would have been forced to marry as soon as possible to hide the pregnancy as much as possible. But with the present system, she acted to the contrary.

Most of the cohabiting couples are not against marriage. It is just that they moved in together because they wanted to live together, just the two of them. Since the traditional norms about the connection between the four elements mentioned previously have disappeared in Swedish society, there is no demand for marrying to have sex, to live together, or to have children together. At the same time, however, most of these couples have the perspective that in the long run, if they stay together as a couple, they should marry and be married.

As we know, to achieve the status of married, one has to go through the marriage ritual—meaning a very short process of change from one marital status to another. If many of these cohabiting couples have the idea that sometime in the future they will marry, the cue for starting a decision-making process to marry is evidently not connected to living together, having sex, or having a child. The cues can be of various sorts and they very often have no connection whatsoever to the ritual of marrying or to the state of being married.

On one hand, many cohabiting couples and individuals have the idea that in the long run they should be married, and thus marry sometime. On the other hand, there is the fact that there are no evident cues for when to marry. Previously the main cues were that they had gotten good jobs (at least the man had), that they had found an apartment (most couples live in rented apartments or co-ops), or that the woman was pregnant (there were very few forced marriages, but as already mentioned, the timing of the marriage may have been sped up a bit). Now these cues do not exist.

With the traditional system, marriage meant a change not only in formal marital status but also in many other respects, for example, living together and having sex without any issues of clandestine behavior. With the current system, the marriage ceremony or ritual has no effect other than formal ones.

On September 1, 1989, Denmark was the first country in the Western world to introduce laws about partnership colloquially called same-gender marriages. The laws clearly state that same-gender couples cannot be officially married, the two cannot be parents to the same child, and they cannot adopt a child. (Just as this book went to print, however, the laws changed: Now the same-gender couples can adopt a child together.) Otherwise, the laws apply as if the two were married. The same laws were passed in Norway in 1993 and in Sweden in 1994.

Another change has also become evident: A marriage is an occasion for a big party. Previously, the parents of the bride (and sometimes also the parents of the groom) not only paid for the wedding including a big dinner party but also decided who should be invited. Regularly those invited were first of all relatives and friends of the parents. Second were friends of the bride and the groom, if space and finances allowed. Now, the bride and the groom invite some close relatives and a lot of their own friends. The parents might negotiate to have some more relatives invited and some of their friends. When the bride and the groom have cohabited for a long time or otherwise might have a good financial situation of their own, they usually pay for the ceremony and for the dinner party. Frequently the parents have no or almost no say about who should be invited or what food will be served, and so on, but they might very well be allowed to pay for the feast.

1989?

As seen in Figure 16.3, the marriage rate in Sweden suddenly started to increase in Sweden for a short time. The number of marriages formed during the 5-year period of 1987 to 1991 was equally distributed, if we disregard December 1989. The monthly variation is very similar for the years before and after 1989. There is a tendency in these years for very few marriages during the beginning of the year and during the end of the year and peaks in May, June, and July. These peaks are connected to the Swedish tradition of marrying when spring has arrived, meaning in May, and also the tradition of marrying at Whitsuntide, which regularly occurs in May or June. Another Swedish tradition is to marry at Midsummer time, which is around June 24.

There was a small increase in the number of marriages in November 1989. Extrapolating from previous years, and also from later years, the number of marriages would have been around 2,000 in November 1989 but the actual total was 4,000. With the same sort of extrapolation, one could have expected about 2,000 marriages in December 1989. But in reality there were 64,000!

How should this be understood? Traditionally widows could have a widow's pension. This idea of a widow's pension builds on a society with a full-scale male economy, meaning that women are not in the labor force. With today's situation, where housewives are almost nonexistent (and certainly they are not a social institution any longer) and almost as many women as men are gainfully employed, a widow's pension seemed inaccurate. Therefore, the Swedish Parliament decided to change the law and abolished the widow's pension. So that the changes would not be too dramatic, it was decided that some parts of the old law would remain for a while.

Thus, parliament decided that any woman who was married by January 1, 1990, and had minor children both by the deadline and at the time of her husband's death would receive a reduced pension if her husband died. This would only be applicable, however, if the income of the wife was remarkably lower than that of the husband at the time of his death. Furthermore, the widow's pension is in any case very small. This construction of the law combined with, for example, the very high divorce rates, meant that this law would affect very few women.

What happened was that one of the branches of one of the labor unions in one of the counties or districts of Sweden wrote to its members a short letter informing them about the changes in the law and suggesting that those members who were cohabiting and who might qualify under the law might consider marrying before January 1, 1990.

What probably happened in the first round was that people threw away the letter, as is usually the case with such mail.

The letter from the union to its members was, however, noticed by a local journalist, who wrote about it. Some journalists in the national media noticed the article. Broadcast as well as press media published information about the new law, and more particularly, they claimed that large numbers of couples had already contacted the courts as well as the parish offices to make a reservation for a wedding. The reports claimed that there were long lines at courts and churches for couples that wanted to marry, when this was not yet true. Here we have a very remarkable and classical example of a self-fulfilling prophecy. What was not really true became true only because it was claimed to be true.

Thus, one could say that the law caused the marriage boom. But another interpretation is that the boom was caused by the mass media coverage and exaggerations. However, there is a third and complementary way of looking at the marriage boom of Sweden in 1989, a more sociological one. Not all of those who married at the end of 1989 were even affected by the new law. They were fairly representative of cohabiting couples. Quite a few were couples that would never be covered by the special law. Some did not have any children, some had children but not of minor age, some had an income distribution and prospects for the future income distribution that would make the law not applicable. What happened in December 1989 was really just a bandwagon effect. When some persons noticed what was said in the mass media, and when they also noticed that friends were marrying, they themselves decided to marry.

It would clearly be wrong to postulate that marriage suddenly became popular again. If that had been the case, the rates for 1990 and 1991 would not have been as low as and even lower than the rates in previous years. For example, the first-marriage rate (calculated as the number of first marriages per 1,000 never-married women 20 to 44 years old) in 1988 was 51.6, in 1989 was 132.4, in 1990 was 47.5, and in 1995 had decreased to 34.0.

What happened was that about 65,000 couples, who otherwise might have married later, married earlier. Of course, some of them would never have married since their cohabitation would have been dissolved by separation or by death.

To understand this change we have to think about what we know about the cohabiting couples. As mentioned previously, when cohabitation became widespread in the mid-1960s, those who took up cohabitation did so in opposition to society and its traditions and norms and in opposition to marriage. But, after a very few years, when cohabitation had become a social institution alongside marriage, those who formed cohabitational units were certainly not in opposition to society or to marriage.

An example will illustrate. A couple that had been cohabiting for more than 20 years had two children, neither a minor. The woman's mother lived far away and planned to visit the daughter and her cohabitant over Yule (or Christmas) of 1989. The mother was old and in bad physical condition and the woman felt that this would be the last time her mother could visit her, the cohabitant, and their children. Therefore she wanted to make the Yule visit a very special event for the mother. They discussed having some kind of extra festivities, and with the fuss in the mass media about all the marriages they came to the conclusion that a wedding ceremony and a wedding party would be a good gift for the mother. They also knew that the mother would appreciate her daughter changing her status into that of a married woman. So the couple married. (The mother recovered, so in that sense the marital ceremony and the party were wasted; some years later the two divorced.)

The changes in the marriage rate at the end of 1989 clearly show that cohabiting couples constitute a pool for potential marriages and what is needed is some kind of a cue for couples to eventually marry. This also clearly suggests that it is not reasonable to claim that cohabitation is an alternative to marriage. For something to be an alternative, it has to be an alternative to something that is the main road. Marriage was the main road but it is not the main road anymore in the Scandinavian countries. It is easy to argue for the social institution of marriage as a model, since it is in our minds as such, with sort of a model monopoly. At the same time, however, it is reasonable to see both marriage and cohabitation as social institutions and thus as two varieties of dyadic structure where neither has the monopoly.

LAT Relationships

Recently a third phenomenon has appeared: living apart together (LAT) relationships. They were first noted in the Netherlands by the Dutch journalist Michel Berkiel (1978), who also coined the term *LAT relatie*. This means that two persons form a couple living under marriage-like conditions, but they do not share the same home—they visit each other more or less regularly and more or less frequently. To be counted as living in a LAT relationship, they not only live separately but also define themselves as a steady couple and are so defined also by their social group.

There are very few estimates about how many of these couples there are, but in Sweden we have collected data since 1993. At that time, 2% to 3% of the population aged 18 to 74 were living in LAT relationships. The last measurement was in 2001, when we found that at least 5% of the same population (about 300,000 persons or 150,000 couples) was living in LAT relationships. In Norway the relative numbers seem to be about one-half of Sweden's (Levin & Trost, 2003). If LAT relationships were as common in the United States as in Sweden, the number of persons in LAT relationships would amount to approximately 7 or 8 million.

For comparison, a study in Germany from the Munich area shows that there are fewer couples in LAT relationships than in Sweden but more than in Norway (Schneider, 1996). Caradec (1996) found that in Paris about 6% of the adult population was in a LAT relationship. Thus, LAT relationships are not a typically Scandinavian phenomenon, but are most recognized there.

There are two somewhat different kinds of LAT relationships: those who do not live together because of one or another ground or reason and those who could live together but who do not want to do so (at least one of them does not).

Some of these couples live far from each other, some even in different countries, but they should not be mistaken for commuting married couples, who live in the same home and one of them, for example, stays in a small apartment during weekdays. Many of the LAT couples living far from each other plan to move in together when one or both have retired. (Whether they do so when retirement comes is another issue.)

Some of the LAT couples are divorced or separated persons with minor children at home, children from previous relationships, and live close to each other and do not want to move in together for the children's sake. They do not want to move in together and form a stepfamily household or home, but wait until the children are more grown up before they move in together.

Some are old-age couples, typically widowed. They want to remain a couple but do not want to move in together, for example, for the simple reason that to move all household goods would be too complicated. And questions such as "which of the furniture and other things should be brought to the other home?" can be difficult to address and resolve. Furthermore, for many of these people, moving far away from children and grandchildren would not be comprehensible. For some others, to move from a known neighborhood with acquaintances and friends would be like pulling up the plant with the root. There are also couples where at least one does not want to live together with the other for the reason that he or she does not want to make the same mistake twice. The mistake may have been a previous hurtful and complicated divorce. In these cases, the person sees living together as more technically binding than not living together. The dissolution of the marriage, therefore, is also seen as connected to the housing arrangements and not only to the emotional loss.

Some of the LAT couples are married but have moved apart to save the relationship—if they would have remained in the same home, too many quarrels and too much irritation would have made the relationship deteriorate. Thus, they separate to maintain the relationship (for some, such a separation might turn out to be the first step toward a calm divorce).

All this means that we nowadays in some countries have three parallel social institutions: married couples living together, nonmarital cohabiting couples, and LAT relationships. Had the four normative elements[3] not disappeared as a normative social system as a result of the introduction of nonmarital cohabitation, the LAT relationships would not have been possible as a social institution—only as a rare deviant phenomenon. Some might see these developments as socially and morally disturbing; others might see the changes as signs of increased responsibility and disappearance of unnecessary and disturbing bonds. Social changes such as those we have seen during the last half-century occur in democratic societies. With our perspective, two of these three social institutions are not alternatives to one of them—they are alternatives to each other, or more correctly, they are variations of same- or opposite-gender coupling.

6 & 7. DIVORCE, SEPARATION, REMARRIAGE, AND STRESSES

At the beginning of the 20th century, divorces were very unusual. But with the decreased mortality rate during the 19th century more and more of a demand came for easier divorce laws. Lifelong marriages did not fit social reality when the mortality rate decreased. The idea of lifelong marriages was seen as reasonable when mortality rates were high but became more and more unrealistic with low mortality rates. Demands for more liberalization of society and private lives also became demands for more liberal and permitting divorce laws. Thus, new and easier divorce laws came about in the 1910s and 1920s.

After fault divorce laws came no-fault divorce laws, first in Sweden in 1916 and then in the other two Scandinavian countries. The no-fault laws gave the couple the possibility to first get some kind of legal separation, which after a year's afterthought could lead to a final divorce. These legal separations were not the same as those found in Catholic countries, since the Scandinavian ones were just a step to a divorce if the two did not change their minds about their marriage and divorce. The Scandinavian legal separations were not *a mensa et toro,* to table and bed.

As can be seen in Figure 16.4 with Sweden as an example, the divorce rate increased until the mid-1950s, when there was a stable period. Then came the turmoil of the 1960s, with demands for even easier divorce laws—not only attacks on the institution of marriage—and also increasing divorce rates. During the 1970s the divorce laws were reformed again, making them even more liberal. Divorce laws now are fully no fault, with either party having the right to a legal divorce without any arguments or

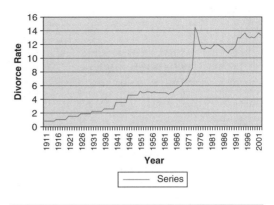

Figure 16.4   Divorce Rate in Sweden

explanations. However, if the couple has minor children, they will have a forced reconsideration period of 6 months, after which they are granted an immediate divorce if one or both so wishes. Joint custody came into being at about the same time. With that and the simplified legal system, the need for lawyers has almost disappeared except for very affluent persons. Battles about money and about custody are now much rarer then they were previously.

The radical increase in divorce rates in the mid-1970s, which can be seen in Figure 16.4, is mainly due to the fact that suddenly divorce procedures took much less time than previously. The last decades of divorce rates are, however, of almost no importance in the Scandinavian countries. As mentioned previously, nonmarital cohabitation began in the middle and at the end of the 1970s and soon became a social institution alongside or parallel to traditional marriage. This, in turn, means that we know almost nothing about separation rates for cohabiting couples.

According to our perspective, however, the separation rate for cohabitation is not comparable to the divorce rate among married couples. One has to take into consideration that nowadays no (or almost no) couples marry without having cohabited for a relatively long period of time. This means that almost all who divorce have cohabited with each other before marrying, while practically none of those cohabiting couples who separate have been married to each other. Therefore, to compare separation among cohabiting couples with divorces for those who are married is to compare two noncomparable entities.

Most of those who remarry or start a recohabitation do so based on a divorce or separation, while previously the remarriage was based on a dissolution caused by the death of a spouse (Sundt, 1855; Levin, 1994). Similarly, remarriage rates are no longer of any value, since many of those who separate from a cohabiting relationship just start to cohabit again, as do those who divorce from marriage. As mentioned previously, some of those who are living in a LAT relationship have been living together as a married or cohabiting couple and separate to save the relationship.

This means that a person at around age 20 will very likely start to cohabit and then after some years either separate or marry. After another period of time, the person who married will probably divorce and start a new relationship, either a cohabiting or a LAT relationship. This means that relationships will not be as stable as tradition has classified marriage (despite many divorces); many relationships will end in dissolution different from death. Furthermore, there will be only a few stable relationships that fully qualify as "stable over a long time." The turnover of relationships will also be combined with a turnover in forms of relationship.

When it comes to children whose parents have divorced, they will be children of divorce the rest of their life, which is different from the adult who will not be divorced when he or she remarries. However, divorce for the child is a different phenomenon immediately after one of the parents has moved out of the household, compared with later in the child's life. It is confusing, since the term *divorce* is used in both cases when the concept (phenomenon) is very different (Levin, 2001).

8. KINSHIP

A statement to the effect that kinship is of no importance in the Scandinavian countries is somewhat exaggerated, but not by much. There are no laws regulating any kinship connections. When laws mention terms such as *family* and *child*, the reference is to minor children and their parent(s). Though in everyday life relatives can be of importance, kinship is not important as a system. People might have close connections to grandparents and to aunts, uncles, cousins, and others usually connected to the term *kin*.

Some people confuse the terms *kin* and *family*. For some *family* means kin, for some *family* means the household, and for some *family* means those who are important to them. In this respect, *family* can seem to be very similar to network or to friendship (Trost & Levin, 1998; Levin & Trost, 1992). Usually there is a combination of household, kin, and sometimes friends that constitute family. Kin and family are not totally identical, but are overlapping.

An important sign of kinship is often in modern times the family name, or more correctly, a common surname of those living together. In the middle of the 19th century, only noble people and the upper classes had family names, which means that when a couple married, the wife took the surname of the husband. Around the start of the 20th century, laws were instituted to the effect that all couples marrying had to use the same name and the children also had the same surname as the parents. One could thus speak about family names.

In the middle of the 20th century, however, there were demands for change and the name laws were changed so that when marrying the couple has to decide what surname or surnames they will have. When a child is born, the parents have to not only decide what first names but also what surname the child will have, the mother's or the father's.

When the couple is not married, the child automatically will be given the mother's surname if the parents do not otherwise decide (Trost, 1991).

In Norway the Caspberg Children's Law was passed by the parliament in 1915. This gave the notmarried mother the right to give the child the father's surname. More important was that this law also gave children full inheritance rights from the father regardless of the marital situation of the parents; thus illegitimate children would be their fathers' heirs. The same law was passed as late as 1970 in Sweden.

9. AGING AND DEATH

Historically, the Scandinavians have cared for their elderly in various ways. One method has been the establishment of poverty houses, small houses where handicapped and elderly poor were placed. The local municipality paid for their housing and for some food and clothing. Since this was a local concern, the quality varied considerably; mainly the quality was very low and the poor barely survived. Another way of caring for the elderly was common among peasants and farmers. The system meant that when a child took over the farm, he also built a small house for his parents (if both were alive) and they were secured a certain amount of grain and firewood. The elderly could also cultivate a small lot around their little house.

In more modern times, all municipalities are required to make sure that there are service houses for those who need them. The quality of these are very good and the elderly who stay there pay only a small amount of the real cost, and usually they pay relative to their financial status and incomes.

All above 65 years of age are covered by a compulsory pension system, which guarantees them enough for survival (but not more). All those who have been gainfully employed will receive another pension, the amount of which depends on the number of years employed and the annual income during those years. Many also have private pensions. For all Scandinavians, regardless of age and financial status, healthcare is almost free; when a certain amount is paid during a 12-month period, the rest for that period is free. All care is subsidized based on the taxation system.

During the last two centuries, the mortality rate has decreased at all ages. With a historically very low birthrate, this means that the population pyramid does not at all look like a pyramid. About 200 years ago the sex ratio (the number of men relative to the number of women in each age-group) showed a surplus of males younger than age 15 and a surplus of females older than 15, but by the 1960s it had changed to more females than males at all ages. And, as in all Western countries, the numbers of elderly are increasing sharply.

Scandinavian countries are characterized by high taxes and many services to both individuals and families. The liberal/socialist approach to policy means that these countries are substantially different from many Western countries in lifestyle.

NOTES

1. Here we use the term *renewed* because nonmarital cohabitation had existed previously, demonstrated by, for example, Sundt (1855), but at that time only among the poor. See also Trost (1980).

2. From now on we will use the simple term *cohabitation* for nonmarital cohabitation.

3. The marriage ceremony, moving in together, having sex together, and expecting a child within about a year.

REFERENCES

Boje, T. P., & Leira, A. (2000). *Gender, welfare state and the market: Towards a new division of labour.* London: Routledge.

Caradec, V. (1996). Les forms de la vie conjugale des "jeunes" couple "ages." *Population, 51*, 897–928.

Carlsson, L. (1965). *Jag giver Dig min dotter,* åttonde vol. Lund: Rättshistoriskt bibliotek.

Carlsson, L. (1972). *Jag giver Dig min dotter,* II, tolfte vol. Lund: Rättshistoriskt bibliotek.

Dahle, R. (1990). *Arbejdsdeling—makt—identitet,* unpublished.

Dahle, R. (1991). Rom i fars hus. *Nytt om kvinneforskning, 5*, 82–93.

DeLey, W. (1986). Physical punishment of children: Sweden and the USA. *Journal of Comparative Family Studies, 19*, 419–431.

Ellingsæter, A. L. (2003). The complexity of family policy: The case of Norway. *European Societies, 5*, 419–443.

Haavind, H. (1987). *Liten og stor.* Oslo: Universitetsforlaget.

Hydén, M. (1994). *Woman battering as marital act: The construction of a violent marriage.* Oslo: Scandinavian University Press.

Kvande, E., & Rasmussen, B. (1992). Fra kvinner og ledelse til kjønn og organisasjoner, LOS-notat, No. 3.

Kälvemark, A.-S. (1980). *More children of better quality? Aspects on Swedish population policy in the 1930's.* Stockholm: Almqvist & Wiksell.

Levin, I. (1994). *Stefamilien—variasjon og mangfold.* Oslo: Aventura forlag.

Levin, I. (2001). Barns perspektiv på skilsmisse—ett eller flere fenomen? In K. Moxnes, H. Kaul, I. Kvaran, and I. Levin (Eds.), *Skilsmissens mange ansikter* (pp. 47–62). Kristiansand: Högskoleforlaget.

Levin, I., & Trost, J. (1992). Understanding the concept of family. *Family Relations, 41*, 348–351.

Levin, I., & Trost, J. (1999). Living apart together. *Community, Work & Family, 3*, 279–294.

Levin, I., & Trost, J. (2003). *Særbo—ett par, to hjem.* Oslo: N W Damm & Søn.

Magnusson, E. (2000). Stora pojkar gråter inte. *Forskning och framsteg, 35*, 38–42.

Morgan, D. (1992). *Discovering men.* London: Rutledge.

Morgan, D. (1996). *Family connections: An introduction to family studies.* Cambridge, UK: Polity Press.

Myrdal, A., & Myrdal, G. (1934). *Kris i befolkningsfrågan.* Stockholm: Bonniers förlag.

Myrdal, A., & Myrdal, G. (1941). *Nation and family: The Swedish experiment in democratic population policies.* New York and London: Harper and Brothers.

Schneider, N. (1996). Partnerschaften mit getrennten Haushalten in den neuen und alten Bundesländern. In W. Bien (Ed.), *Familie and der Schwelle zum neuen Jahrtausend* (pp. 88-97). Opladen: Leske & Budrich.

Søndergaard, D.-M. (1996). *Tegnet på kroppen. Køn: Koder og konstruktioner blant unge voksne i Akademia.* København: Museum Tusculanums Forlag.

Sundt, E. (1855) [1975]. *Om giftermål i Norge.* Oslo: Gyldendal Norsk Forlag.

Taussi-Sjöberg, M. (1988). *Skiljas.* Falkenberg: Författarförlaget.

Trost, J. (1980). *Unmarried cohabitation.* Västerås: International Library.

Trost, J. (1990a). Fertility and the process of decision making. *Family Reports, 16,* 1–55.

Trost, J. (1990b). On becoming a family. *Family Reports, 18,* 1–38.

Trost, J. (1991). What's in a surname? *Family Reports, 19,* 1–24.

Trost, J. (1993). *Familjen i Sverige.* Stockholm: Liber.

Trost, J., & Levin, I. (1998). Concepts of social networks and families. In S. C. Ziehl (Ed.), *Multicultural diversity and families* (pp. 305–331). Grahamstown, South Africa: Rhodes University.

Wærnes, K. (2002). Familien og helsetjenesten: Den senmoderne Velferdsstat. In B. S. Brinchmann (Ed.), *Bære hverandres byrder* (pp. 17–30). Bergen: Fagbokforlaget.

CHAPTER 17

Families in Turkey

Bernhard Nauck

Daniela Klaus

1 & 10. THE INSTITUTIONAL CONSTITUTION OF THE FAMILY IN TURKEY

The genesis of the forms of family life in today's Turkey can be traced back to three essential cultural factors in history. The first and, until modern times, the most influential factor is that the population of the territory of the Turkish state has been a segmented, rural peasant society. This peasant society has, however, always coexisted with a variety of minorities, especially in the urban areas and along the coast, specializing in specific income resources (e.g., trading, fishing, military service), or—like some Kurdish tribes in Eastern Turkey—living as nomadic shepherds because of ecological circumstances. A second influential factor, which is not always systematically separated from the latter, is Islam. It has to be considered that several schools of belief have coexisted in the territory of what is now Turkey, each with its own normative guidelines for marriage and family. Further, the other religious minorities (especially

Greek Orthodox Christians and Jews) lived according to their own legal regulations (including family regulations) during the Ottoman empire, being exempted from Islamic legal traditions. Finally, the foundation of the Turkish Republic in 1923 not only established a secular state according to the principles of Western democracies (including the right to vote for women, compulsory secular schooling, and the prohibition of religious schools), but also introduced a new civil code that was basically an adaptation of the Swiss legal system and accordingly regulated marriage and family issues.

The new civil code abolished religious jurisdiction and Islamic family law, after which marriage was seen as a civil contract between the two future partners or their representatives. Under Islamic law the husband was allowed not only to marry up to four women but also to purchase as many female slaves as he wanted. Further, he was allowed to cast off a wife. With the new civil code, the legal age of marriage was increased to 18 years for men and 17 years for women (in 1938 it was reduced again to 17 and

15 years, respectively, for men and women), and the consent of the marriage partners was made a requirement for marriage. Only civil marriage ceremonies and legal forms of divorce are officially acknowledged. One-sided disownment of the wife by the husband and polygamy were made illegal, and women were granted property and inheritance rights (Abadan-Unat, 1987; Karasan-Dirks, 1986). These influential factors did not supersede each other, but have retained their impact on marriage and the family simultaneously, which has led to a variety of coexisting family types with sometimes antagonistic norms in contemporary Turkey.

The persistence (or even the predominance) of components of a peasant culture in the Turkish family structure is related to the fact that peasant culture has existed in the territory of Turkey for an exceptionally long period of time. The peasant family culture thus provided all preconditions for the development of evolutionary stable family structures. "The seemingly different structural characteristics of the Near Eastern family should therefore be attributed to the heritage of an exceptionally long pre-industrial history of social development" (Ortayli, 1985, p. 104). In addition, the notoriously weak state has contributed considerably to the antagonistic coexistence of different family types, as the state has never been able to enforce its universalistic legal principles throughout its entire territory.

Besides the comprehensive changes in law, Turkey experienced rapid developments in its economy. Mainly since the 1950s, a more liberal economy furthered industrialization. Urged by state intervention, the capitalist production spread out. As one result, a radical change in the distribution of working places over different sectors took place. While in 1960 the majority of all working places were found in agriculture (75%) and only about 8% in industry and a further 17% in the service sector, the corresponding distribution in 1997 changed: 42% (agriculture), 23% (industry), and 34% (service) (State Institute of Statistics, 2001, p. 162). Due to large regional disparities, industrialization, modernization, and the allocation of workplaces, a huge migration began, which is still continuing. The nationwide migration took place mainly from the east to the west and into the cities.

There is a considerable international migration as well, supported by the government to ameliorate the enormous population explosion. Today about 3 million Turks live abroad (Ünalan, 2000, p. 2). The national emigration has resulted in a decrease in the rural population within the last century, and as a result the majority of the population of Turkey now lives in urban agglomerations: Whereas in 1927 about 76% of the total population of about 14 million Turks was rural, in 2000 the share has declined to 35% of the total population of 68 million (State Institute of Statistics, 2003, pp. 45f.).

Additionally, this massive growth of cities has to be considered in regard to higher birthrates in rural areas. The ongoing rural–urban migration has resulted in the situation that about one-half of the urban population in Turkey are rural immigrants (Kagitçibasi & Sunar, 1997). Due to insufficient accommodation facilities in the cities, so-called *gecekondus* are the most visible outcome. Gecekondus are houses established within one night on public property in the urban metropolises, in which many rural–urban migrants live. Amnesties by the state occur on a regular basis (and are thus highly anticipated by the inhabitants) and transform this practice (based on a customary law in agrarian areas to acquire new land) into the legal ownership of real estate.

As rural migrants in urban metropolises normally maintain strong social ties to their regions of origin, the migration process has only partially resulted in an urbanization of the family lifestyle. Moreover, it has primarily led to a confrontation and to an increased visibility of the differences between the previously segmented and regionally separated population groups. This has contributed to an increase in social tensions, while intermarriages between the respective population groups remain at a very low level.

Due to continuing population growth, the urban labor market faces the problem of a growing labor force accompanied by a stagnation of the economy since the recession of the middle 1980s. Competition in the labor market increases, and women in particular are disadvantaged, since they are less educated than their male counterparts (Ergöcmen, 1997, pp. 86f.; Özbay, 1985a, pp. 128f.); Most women retire to their homes. Nevertheless, low-income families (mainly gecekondu-families) are dependent on the female's income (Özbay, 1985a, p. 133; Sönmez, 1996). If women are working, they are frequently restricted to the informal sector, which implies unqualified jobs, bad working conditions, poor salary, and exclusion from social insurance (Ecevit, 1988; Kazgan, 1985, pp. 88f.; Özbay, 1991; Moghadam, 1996). In agrarian areas women are mostly affected by the reduction of agrarian working places, because they used to work in this sector mainly as unpaid family workers.

Looking at the education system, similar developments can be observed. In general, the availability of education has increased and participation has improved markedly, especially in primary education. With the founding of the Turkish Republic, compulsory schooling was introduced (Ergöcmen, 1997, p. 85; Tansel, 1998, p. 2), which resulted in a dramatic decrease in illiteracy rates. But again, discrepancies by region and sex continue to exist: In 1935 the illiteracy rate for females 6 years and older was 90% compared with 70% among males. Both rates have decreased but are still to the disadvantage of

females, with 28% compared with 11% of males in 1990 (State Institute of Statistics, 1993, p. 13).

Considering the enrollment rates for primary and higher education, many dropouts occur for both sexes on every level, though women are more affected. Besides the sex inequalities, the participation in cities is higher than in rural areas: In 1999 about 82% of children aged between 6 and 14 years old attended school in cities compared with 74% in rural areas (State Institute of Statistics, 2000a).

Altogether, the women in rural parts of Eastern Turkey have gained least from modernization. However, the female descendants of the middle and upper classes have experienced the strongest gains in educational degrees in the urban metropolises. Finally, spending for education is very low. In 1990 its share of the gross national product amounted to 3% (Tansel & Kazemi, 1995). For more detailed information concerning determinants of school attendance, see Tansel (1998).

Family and kinship are closely linked with the provision of social protection. Turkey is far from being a welfare state: In 1995 only about 7% of the gross domestic product was spent for social affairs (Organization of Economic Cooperation and Development [OECD]: Social Expenditure Database). Social security is largely provided by the family. However, nowadays three state-owned insurance institutions exist that mainly cover old-age pensions, but also health insurance: The Government Employees Retirement Fund, which dates back to 1949, is limited to the public sector. Later, the Social Security Institution (SSK) included all kinds of urban, white-collar workers, and Bag-Kur additionally covers all self-employees and workers in agriculture. But the coverage as well as the efficiency is poor. It can be assumed that even in the case of entitlement, the real pensions are very low and not sufficient to cover livelihood.

These institutional conditions are the background for the presentation and interpretation of selected empirical results about Turkish family structures and their social change during the process of modernization.

2 & 5. PARTNER SELECTION AND MARRYING

Two marriage regimes are present in Turkey, which differ in regard to whether they give priority to intergenerational or to conjugal relationships. This implies different conceptions of marriage with different logics about the family formation process (Nauck, 1997). The first one, the affinal marriage regime, is characterized by autonomous partner selection with a strong emphasis on the conjugal relationship within a bilineal kinship system, rather than the influence given to the respective families of origin. It results normally in a strong separation between the family of procreation and the family of origin. Accordingly, its inheritance rules favor primarily the surviving spouse and, in cases of conflict, the prime solidarity is with the members of the conjugal family. This form of marriage can be traced back historically and culturally to the urban societies of ancient Greece (Kaufmann, 1995). Typically, the affinal marriage regime is supposed to follow the following pattern: First, the human capital for family foundation has to be acquired in a qualification process. Then, the material prerequisites for a separate household (neolocal) have to be met, and then and only then may the family formation process start. The developmental logic of family formation thus is expected to follow consecutive steps: (1) (romantic) love, (2) economic security, (3) consensual marriage, and (4) children.

The focus of the descent marriage regime is on the exchange of goods and human capital within or between kinship systems. As a logical consequence, the family of origin has a strong influence over the partner selection process. Descent marriage provides a completely different logic of family formation: (1) arranged marriage, (2) children, (3) love in the spousal relationship intensifying over time, and then (4) due to children, economic security. Arranged marriages take place at an early age and in the absence of any economic independence, and they are explicitly unrelated to household foundation in form of patrilocal residence. Marriage as a personal matter of the two future partners is of little importance. Intergenerational solidarity and benefits are the center of interest. This is reflected by the inheritance rules, which favor primarily the children rather than the surviving widow. These characteristics can be traced back to pre-Islamic times. This type of marriage and household formation has strong parallels in the non-Islamic societies of the Balkans and of the northern rim of the Black Sea. This pattern is fundamentally different from the traditional Central European pattern of family formation (Anderson, 1980; Duben, 1985; Hajnal, 1965). Many of the custom law regulations of marriage and family from the rural traditions of what is now Turkey contradict codified Islamic law, especially regarding the payment of bridewealth to the woman's family of origin and regarding the exclusion of women from heritage (Ortayli, 1985).

Nowadays, arranged marriage still prevails. Authors' calculations using the Turkish Demographic and Health Surveys (TDHSs) 1993 and 1998 indicate about 52% of first-married women of the youngest birth cohort included (1979–1983) live in an arranged marriage, 40% live in a couple-initiated marriage, and about 8% escaped or were abducted. However, a shift from arranged to love marriage is visible. Looking at the oldest available birth cohort (1944–1948), the proportion of family-arranged marriages amounted to 78%. The affinal marriage regime is widely accepted among the younger and better-educated parts of the urban population, for whom the autonomous choice of marriage partner and marriage of consent is as self-evident as the legitimation principle of romantic love. The patrilineal marriage regime of descent is especially widespread in the rural population, in the Middle-, North, South-, and Eastern-Anatolian provinces, as well as among the less educated (migrant) in the urban metropolises.

To the extent that the marriage regime of descent is institutionalized, it is useful to refer to the marriage market in the literal sense, because goods are indeed exchanged—descendants over whom control rights exist. Within the patrilineal marriage regime of descent, marriages regulate the allocation of female labor between the communities of descent. One's own female descendants leave the household community during this marriage process (and become members of the community of descent of their husbands) and are successively substituted for by daughters-in-law. Two institutional regulations exist to balance the interests of the communities of descent (Levi-Strauss, 1984): the payment of bridewealth and reciprocal marriages between communities of descent, or marriages within one community of descent.

Payment of Bridewealth and Abduction

According to customary law, payments of bridewealth take place as transfers from the family of origin of the groom to the family of origin of the bride (*baslik*). This stands in contrast to codified Islamic law, according to which these payments become property of the bride and in case of the dissolution of the marriage are excluded from any inheritance (*mehr*). Bridewealth payments are a major component of marriage arrangements, which are frequently negotiated with the family of the bride by third parties (matchmakers) on the authority of the family of the groom. This arrangement helps to avoid losses of honor in those cases when negotiations break down. Probably stemming from the tradition of the nomadic tribes in Eastern Anatolia, there is, however, the institution of abduction, that is, the execution of marriage without the permit of the families of origin and without bridewealth payments. This does not always take place against the will of the bride, for example, if a possible marriage is in danger because of the amount of bridewealth the family of origin is asking for, or if the parents of the bride put a stop to marriage in general and her increasing age diminishes any further marriage chances, or in case of serious conflicts between the bride and her parents about the choice of the groom. (For further information, see Özgen, 1985.)

Endogamy and Reciprocal Marriage

High payments of bridewealth and the allocation of females create strong incentives for reciprocal marriages either between communities of descent, because of the flow-back of the invested means or within a community of descent, because in this case no outflow of means occurs. In fact, marriages among close relatives, especially between cousins (ideally in the form of cross-cousin marriages), are very common in Turkey. The primary marriage market is only extended to the entire village when a suitable candidate is lacking. Marriages outside this context are connected with status loss. Furthermore, such a regionally and social-structurally limited marriage market implies that search costs are rather low and the completeness of information about possible alternatives in this market is relatively high.

The total number and identity of potential marital matches become clear at very early stages for all of those involved. Such endogamous preference has the consequence, however, that the boundaries between the respective communities of descent become even sharper, and this implies extensive consequences for action. Contrary to the generalized exchange of descendants on a marriage market with strong rules of exogamy, the direct, reciprocal exchange within one community of descent means that obligations of loyalty only exist within one's own community of descent. As there are no mechanisms of social equilibration between communities of descent, many opportunities for distrust and conflict arise, often making for permanent qualities of relations between communities of descent. Particularism, nepotism, and patronage in the public sphere, blood feuds, and collective honor are thus closely related to these basic principles of social exchange.

Successful Matching and Hypergamy

Families in Turkey operate in the public sphere to a very high degree. Low exclusivity implies that the benefits of spouses are not marriage-specific or measured by the emotional quality of the relationship alone, but the benefits of marriage are also extramarital in nature and based on the social status of the husband and wife. Accordingly, the demand of women and their families of origin for men with more property, higher income, and (as a substitute) higher education is especially pronounced, as is the demand of men and their families of origin for young, nice-looking, well-educated women. These matches are considered to be successful marriages.

The clear ranking of the entire educational system (from preschool to university), together with the considerable amount of material investments of the families in the education of their offspring, contributes considerably to a situation where the partner selection process becomes an easily calculable affair. If it is mainly the status benefit that

dominates the partner selection process, then the achieved educational certificates are the most reliable clues for the future status of the spouse, besides the social status of his or her family of origin. Gender-specific status differentiation, however, opens numerous opportunities for hypergamy (marrying into a higher stratum) for young, attractive women from lower status groups.

High Marriage Rate and Low Age at First Marriage

If a large part of a population follows a descent marriage regime in conjunction with strong gender-specific status differentiation and low exclusivity of the family, consequences for the total marriage market are inevitable. Not only are the criteria of partner selection affected, but so are the marriage chances and the marriage process of those parts of Turkish society. Parental control interests in the communities of descent on the marriage of the sons and on the substitution of daughters-in-law for daughters contribute to a high marriage rate in Turkish society. And the higher the society's marriage rate, the higher the incentive for early marriage. The result is an early, highly standardized marriage process, which is driven by the search for partners for the sons, the substitution of daughters, and the descendants' own interest in a status-oriented, successful marriage.

Finally, the hypergamy of women with lower status also contributes to early marriage and its standardization. As hypergamy is probable only when the bride is young and physically attractive, it occurs in the form of early entry into the marriage market. Hypergamous women are thus a serious competitive threat for women of higher status, which also increases the pace of the marriage process. This explains the comparatively low average marriage age for even those Turkish women who follow the affinal marriage regime. It also explains why so many of these women conform to the standardized marriage process. The timing of this process is even shorter if the respective communities of descent rather than the spouses themselves perform partner selection by contractually securing the future marriage of their descendants. In doing so, a considerable part of the partner selection process is performed prematurely and these descendants are withdrawn from the marriage market by marital arrangements. The overall result is that the exit of female descendants from the community of descent is as early as possible, and, accordingly, women in Turkey are a scarce, highly valued good in a highly inflexible marriage market (Nauck, 2001a).

This structure of the marriage process is illustrated by the early age at marriage (Table 17.1). It can be assumed that these data provided by the registered statistics are overestimates. Religious ceremonies are considered by a large part of the population to be a legitimate alternative, that is, a substitute and not just a preliminary or subsequent addition to the ceremony at the registry office. In some cases, this form of marriage is associated with polygamy, which still enjoys a definite though vanishing frequency in some population groups. The most frequent reason for the preference of religious marriages (habitualized-traditional behavior aside) is, however, that it allows the families of origin to get around the minimal age requirement and significantly increase their influence over the marriage arrangements. A variety of state practices (campaigns try to force couples to legalize their relationships by postregistering their marriages) and of others involved (including adoption by the biological father, and at times a complicated series of donations within the kinship system) aim to harmonize the *de jure* and *de facto* situations of religious marriages. This happens, of course, after the minimal age of marriage is reached.

Whereas the register data in Table 17.1 (column 2) indicate only minor changes in the mean age at first marriage within the observed period of 70 years, survival analyses based on survey data (column 4) point out more changes in marital behavior. At the age of 20, only 28% of the females are still unmarried in the birth cohort 1948–1952. The respective share within the birth cohort 1978–1982 rises to 66%. In conclusion, the changing course of the survival function within the younger birth cohorts may not only indicate a postponement of first marriage but also a small (but increasing) part of women who can be expected to stay unmarried their entire life.

3. FERTILITY

Consistent with the change in marital behavior, fertility has changed as well, since extramarital births hardly exist in Turkey. According to the TDHS, only about 1% of women gave birth out of wedlock in 1998 (authors' calculations). As illustrated in Table 17.1, the total fertility rate in Turkey decreased steadily within the last decades starting with 6.2 in 1960; 40 years later it was 2.5—only a little over the reproduction level of the population. Besides the enormous decrease in fertility, considerable differences exist not only between urban (2.8) and rural (4.0) areas but also between the regions: Whereas the fertility is highest in the eastern part of Turkey (5.7), it falls continuously as one moves west, where it is lowest at 2.6 (State Institute of Statistics, 2002).

Looking at the proportions of women who did not give birth to at least one child by the age of 20, enormous changes in the birth cohorts can be seen (Table 17.1, column 5). These differences disappear in the higher parities, which suggests that when the decision for marriage—and thus for the first child—is made, subsequent children are born

Table 17.1   Indices Related to Marriage and Fertility

Year	Age of Women at First Marriage	TFR	Proportion of Women at the Age of 20 . . . by Birth Cohort[e]			Birth Cohort
			Unmarried	Childless	First Child Born but No Second One	
1930	19.5[a]	—				
1935	19.7[a]	—				
1940	19.9[a]	—				
1945	20.1[a]	—				
1950	19.7[a]	—				
1955	18.1[a]	—				
1960	19.2[a]	6.2[d]				
1965	19.6[a]	5.8[d]				
1970	19.9[b]	5.7[d]	28	48	73	1948–1952
1975	20.1[b]	5.1[d]	24	43	71	1953–1957
1980	20.7[b]	4.4[d]	32	49	71	1958–1962
1985	21.5[b]	3.6[d]	42	56	77	1963–1967
1990	22.0[b]	3.0[d]	43	59	78	1968–1972
1995	—	2.6[d]	49	63	72	1973–1977
2000	22.0[c]	2.5[d]	66	75	75	1978–1982

SOURCES:

a. Council of Europe (2000).
b. Council of Europe (1995).
c. State Institute of Statistics: Marriage and Divorce Statistic Series and Census of Population.
d. Council of Europe (2001).
e. Authors' calculations based on Turkish Demographic and Health Survey (1998).

quickly, even among younger women. The survival functions for the several parities demonstrate that the youngest birth cohorts do not start giving birth first but show the strongest dropouts from the age of approximately 17. Also, subsequent birth intervals are shorter for the younger birth cohorts. This may indicate a trend in the consolidation of the process of family foundation as well as family expansion—provided the decision was made on behalf of marriage. At present it is difficult to say if overall decreasing fertility can be traced to an emerging group of permanent childless women or the absence of births of higher parities (which refers to more than three children).

High Value of Children

Children in Turkey are highly valued for several reasons. First, the economic-utilitarian consequences of having children are important. Mainly in agrarian regions, children are seen as a source of manpower, contributing to family income by (early) work due to several possibilities of using unqualified child labor, for example, working in the fields or helping in the family-owned business. In addition, because of the lack of an adequate insurance system, children are an essential source of security against the risks of life such as unemployment, illness, and old age. In addition, children offer emotional support and social esteem, and they raise parents' status. Especially giving birth to a boy raises women's status, which in traditional settings is the only chance to improve her subordinate position within the family. The value of children has far-reaching implications for parenting behavior. Since any additional child increases economic-utilitarian benefits, it is rational to have many children—assuming that the initial investment costs are affordable. It is because the unit cost of children decreases by their number that the economic-utilitarian ratio becomes more favorable with each additional child. On the contrary, the social-emotional benefit cannot be accumulated in the same way. One or two children can provide as much emotional satisfaction as four or more children.

Sex Preference

Parental preference for male descendants is pronounced in Turkey. In the value of

children (VOC) study (Kagitçibasi, 1982a), 75% of Turkish mothers and 93% of Turkish fathers preferred male descendants. This investigation also indicated that sex preference is mainly related to the higher instrumentality of boys for both mothers and fathers in their work contribution and their potential insurance benefits. This is because the male descendants remain in the patrilineal household, whereas daughters leave at marriage. In addition, the social esteem in the community of descent is increased with having given birth to a son. This benefit seems to be more salient for fathers than for mothers. Smaller, new studies from urban metropolises in Turkey find a much smaller preference for sons in the case of mothers (Ataca & Sunar, 1999), while the preference for male descendants seems to be stable and high in the case of fathers throughout all population groups. (See also Basaran, 1985.)

Determinants for Fertility

Structural background is also very important for the value (potential) parents attribute to children, and therefore for the generative behavior. The costs and benefits of having children are mainly influenced by the opportunity structure of the social-ecological context of the family. The economic value especially depends heavily on the context. With modernization, working opportunities for children have decreased, since there has been a reduction of unqualified working places, and child labor has been forbidden by law. Further, with the introduction of compulsory education up to 8 years, the costs of bringing up (many) children have increased—including suitable clothing, textbooks, and fare for traveling. Simultaneously, the time children (need to) spend in school cannot be used for working. However, due to the lack of a sufficient institution, it can be assumed that children's contribution to parents' old age insurance is still of high value.

The influence on generative behavior of changes in the contextual conditions and in parental expectations about children has been extensively studied in the framework of the VOC studies (Kagitçibasi, 1982a, 1982b, 1982c; Nauck, 1997, 2001a). Despite comprehensive change in the opportunity structure, a reference to the importance and continuity of utility expectations in children in Turkey is provided by a comparison of the VOC study from 1975 with results of the smaller replication of 1992 in Istanbul. The results indicate the extent of economic-utilitarian expectations of Turkish parents in regard to their children in both 1975 and 1992. A value change in the expectation of parents toward their children can hardly be estimated for Turkey as a whole during this observational period. Moreover, there seems to be a tendency to subject daughters more often to these economic-utilitarian expectations. This adjustment of expectations toward daughters and sons on a very high level seems to indicate a mobilization even of female descendants for utilitarian expectations during the modernization process.

In addition to the respective opportunity structures in the regional context, individual options play a decisive role, and these are related to the cognition and motivation of the actors. Women's education is the crucial indicator variable here. In regard to the situation of Turkish women, it can be assumed that a minimum level of education (primary school) is a necessary precondition for the choice not to have many children to secure household production and old-age security. A maximum level of education (tertiary school degree) leads, however, for a Turkish woman to a situation where her own contribution to household production shifts. Educated women produce more immaterial goods, as material goods are regularly acquired under market conditions, namely as (poorly paid) services of low-status members of the same sex. It is likely that the availability of cheap services is a major precondition explaining why in Turkey—unlike in affluent welfare societies—there is no correlation between the educational level of women and their marriage rate.

One consequence of increasing options is, however, that the opportunity costs of decisions increase. Opportunity costs of choices are to be considered only if alternatives are actually available, but not if life courses are the chains of circumstantial pressures, the lack of alternatives, and deference to destiny, as is often the case among the extremely poor. Therefore, economic-utilitarian benefit expectations depend fundamentally on the individual alternatives of (potential) parents. The economic-utilitarian benefit expectation will decrease when (1) alternatives to children's help in the household increase (e.g., through mechanization and rationalization of household tasks); (2) more substitutes for child labor are available in the economy (e.g., the schooling and training of its parents); and (3) more direct contributions of children to their parents' old-age security are made unnecessary (e.g., by pension schemes on the state level). At the same time, social-emotional utility expectations become more salient in fertility decisions.

Socialization

The institutional constitution of the family in Turkey and the related value of children for their parents implies their existential dependence on the functioning of intergenerational relationships across the entire life course (but mainly in old age). This explains the embedded socialization processes in the family, parents' everyday theories about upbringing and education, child-rearing practices, and goals. Parents control the socialization process in a way that makes lifelong loyalty of the child and its engagement with its parents highly probable. Among the qualities that parents wish most for their children, obedience was mentioned most frequently (60%), while independence and self-esteem (18%) were named least frequently (Kagitçibasi, 1982a). A study by Imamoglu (1987) demonstrates that these educational goals vary with the social status of the parents in the expected direction: Urban, upper-class families show higher preferences for independence and self-esteem, while most mothers from the middle and the lower socioeconomic strata emphasize obedience, loyalty, and gratefulness.

Several comparative studies have illustrated that the educational style of Turkish parents is especially characterized by protective behavior ("overprotectiveness" in the perspective of more individualistic cultures) in the early years, and by a comparably high authoritative control in late childhood and adolescence (Kagitçibasi, 1982a, 1984, 1996; Kagitçibasi, Sunar, & Bekman, 1988; Nauck, 1989b). As the age of the child increases, the parent–child relationship changes. The respect for the authority of fathers increases and leads to a marked distance. Turkish fathers often see their role in establishing and reinforcing strict behavioral rules for the children by means of a detached authority. Adult children are expected to continue showing respect toward their father and to consult him when important decisions are to be made. Outbursts of anger in his presence are not tolerated. Therefore, mothers take over the role of mediator in the relationship of fathers to their older children (Kiray, 1976, 1985a). If a child confides in one of his parents, most probably it will be the mother. She will also speak in favor of the child in a case of conflict with the father. At the same time, the mother passes on the wishes of the father, his instructions, and even his punishments. Mothers express their affection in most cases very openly. This happens either physically with kisses and hugging or with words, and the children are encouraged to return these signs of love and affection (Kagitçibasi et al., 1988). Although children are not expected to show anger and rage toward mothers, it is not as rigidly forbidden as toward fathers (Kagitçibasi & Sunar, 1997, p. 156).

The persistence of the emotional interdependence of generations even when economic interdependence decreases (Kagitçibasi, 1996) constitutes the context of gender-specific socialization and explains some of the differences in gender attributes between Turkey and Western societies. Attributes such as obedience, reliability, loyalty, and consideration of other family members are taught to daughters and sons in the same way and to the same extent. Therefore, sons learn also some expressive behavioral patterns that are viewed in Western societies to be feminine. Fathers, for example, regularly care in a touchy way for the physical needs of toddlers and young children and play with them extensively (Kagitçibasi & Sunar, 1997, p. 155). However, since patrilineal descent implies that female descendants leave the community of descent through marriage, permanent expectations of loyalty differ for male and female descendants, as do control interests and parental investment strategies. While the investment strategies and loyalty expectations encompass the entire life span of male descendants, they are limited to the life span until marriage in the case of females, and control interests in the case of females are focused on marriage. The maintenance of family honor is the most important aspect in girls' education, which implies control, dependence, and low self-determination, whereas families do their best to educate their sons, since the former are dependent on the latter's financial assistance. However, especially among the urban population, the sex-related socialization is less pronounced: Girls raised in urban environments have a greater chance to be better educated and to be reared to greater autonomy and self-esteem than in rural areas. Kiray (1985b, p. 87) states, "It seems that the most significant change is observed in the socialization of girls who seem to be acquiring increasingly more extrovert personality characteristics."

4 & 5. GENDER ROLES AND MARITAL RELATIONSHIPS

The patrilineal descent regime in Turkey produces an advanced hierarchical structure in which the patriarch is authoritarian and entitled to make all decisions. It implies a strong status differentiation in favor of both older people and male descendants. The relationship between spouses is signified by the subsidiary position of women. Gender inequalities are extensively studied topics. Numerous papers depict the improving but still unequal female participation in education and employment. Some of these studies find an increasing status of women based on their gaining economic independence, due to higher education and more comprehensive participation in the paid labor market (Ecevit, 1988; Erman, 2001; Kagitçibasi, 1982c; Kandiyoti, 1977, 1982, 1988, 1991; Kiray, 1976; Kuyas, 1982; Özbay, 1985a, 1985b, 1988, 1991). Concerning women's intrafamily position, Kagitçibasi formulates that "male decision making in the family is widespread, communication and role sharing between spouses is limited, indicating well differentiated and non-overlapping sex roles" (1982c, p. 12).

Several studies explicitly deal with (changing) sex roles, decision-making arrangements, intrafamily division of labor, and communication (Ataca & Sunar, 1999; Basaran, 1985; Bolak, 1988, 1997; Ergöcmen, 1997; Erman, 2001; Fox, 1973; Imamoglu & Yasak, 1997; Kagitçibasi, 1985; Özbay, 1991; Olson, 1982; Olson-Prather, 1976). According to the classical assumptions about decision and task allocation derived from resource theory (Blood & Wolfe, 1960; Nauck, 1989a), the power of each spouse should increase with individual resources. These hypotheses were supported by studies done in modern societies but were challenged relatively early by empirical results from Yugoslavia (Buric & Zecevic, 1967), Greece (Safilios-Rothschild, 1967), and Turkey (Fox, 1973, 1975; Immamoglu & Yasak, 1997; Olson-Prather, 1976). Contrary to initial assumptions, the decision-making power of husbands in these countries decreased unexpectedly with educational level. This has considerably contributed to the reformulation of the theory as "resource theory in cultural context" (Rodman, 1972), which emphasizes the consideration of the cultural system. Under fully patriarchal conditions, clear gender norms exist within a society and therefore the location of power is quite independent of individual resources. Thus, for Turkey it can be assumed that the prevailing patriarchy fixes the authority of the husband independent of his resources. And, indeed, Kandiyoti emphasizes the significance of "social institutions and practices which are implicated in the creation and reproduction of gender hierarchies" (1988, p. 315). She states, "the male role seems to have been least affected by change, bolstered as it is by socialization practices, ideology and structural reports" (1982, p. 117). Also, if the wife is employed in a high position, a nursemaid or housekeeper is employed to perform family/household labor without involving the husband. Kandiyoti refers to a "considerable intergenerational continuity of socialization in the domestic/nurturant role by women" (1982, p. 116).

However, there are signs of trends toward a more egalitarian marital relationship. Besides the nonexistent or even negative relationship between males' resources and the balance of power (Fox, 1973; Imamoglu & Yasak, 1997), the wife in Turkish families is not a silent partner. Moreover, female resources have more impact on the balance of power than those of the husband:

> We found that for each of the four resources [education, urban residence, father's education, father's occupational status] the wife's characteristics made a greater impact than the husband's. Thus, when husband and wife are compared in terms of the same resource, the amount of the resource that the wife brings to the marriage plays a larger role in determining their power structure than the amount of that resource contributed by the husband. (Fox, 1973, p. 728)

This finding was replicated later for Turkish migrant families in Germany (Nauck, 1985) and matches with Rodman's (1972) predictions for modified patriarchal societies: A husband's power decreases as his resources increase, but a positive correlation exists between wife's resources and her power.

Within patriarchy, gender-specific status differentiation is related to the division of labor: The same tasks in the household economy cannot be transferred at will either to male or female descendants. Male descendants seldom undertake tasks that are supposed to be for female members of the household. At the same time, descendants of lower status are more flexible in doing an array of tasks (Schiffauer, 1987). Studies indicate a change that refers primarily to the decreasing influence of older family members (the patriarchs) in household affairs. Also, a new arrangement in the allocation of tasks between spouses has emerged, and joint decision making has increased (Özbay, 1991). Presumably, this is a matter of a two-step change: First, decision-making power is taken over by the husband from the old patriarch because of changes in the household economy during the urbanization process and the resulting increased structural identity of household and family.

In a second step, there emerges an increasingly syncratic-cooperative style of decision making and task allocation, depending on women's increased resources arising from higher education and gainful employment, and the resulting increased acceptance of the affinal marriage regime (Ataca & Sunar, 1999). Summarizing, the main determinants of an increasing female intrafamilial status, joint decision making, and a more cooperative division of labor within the household are higher education of the wife (beyond primary school) and participation in the labor market and urban residence. Wives' employment and the derived income seems to create a basis for negotiations in which changing attitudes and expectations occur. However, another crucial factor might be the husband's acknowledging the wife's contribution to the household income (Bolak, 1988, 1997).

Sex Segregation and Communication

The traditional family is not only characterized by strong differentiated and stratified sex roles but also by sex segregation and a low communication between the spouses. Olson (1982) attempted to summarize the specifics of the relationship between spouses in Turkish marriages with the thesis of the "duofocal family structure." Combining results from empirical social research and ethnographic casework, and based on theories of social networks, she came to the conclusion that the modernization process of families in Turkey cannot conclusively be described as a shift from traditional-patriarchal toward nuclear conjugal families, that is, an "egalitarian relationship, characterized by a high degree of communication and companionship between spouses and by joint decision-making" (Olson, 1982, pp. 33f.). She illustrates, moreover, that husbands and wives especially in modernized contexts maintain markedly separated social networks.

These extrafamilial networks themselves are relatively close-knit and mainly consist of same-sex friends, members of the family of origin, and member of one's own community of descent. Referring to Bott (1957, p. 92), Olson states, "a Turkish marriage tends to be more nearly the juxtaposition of two networks than the uniting of two individuals, because, as was true of the couples in Bott's study, the 'marriage is superimposed on these pre-existing relations'" (1982, p. 52). This separation of networks corresponds with the comparably low importance of marriage as compared with preexisting intergenerational relationships. This results in a situation in which social relationships with members of the opposite sex typically only include members of the family of origin. In the case of a husband, for example, his own sisters and especially his own mother are central:

> [I]t is likely that the most intimate cross-sex relationship he will ever have is the one he has with his mother both as a young boy and as an adult—a relationship which will probably be more intense and more important in several ways than the one he will develop with his wife. (Olson, 1982, p. 50)

This strong sex segregation can also be found in Turkish migrant families in Germany, where personal relationships to male persons outside the kinship system are practically nonexistent for women (Nauck & Kohlmann, 1999).

6. FAMILY STRESSES AND VIOLENCE

Violence within the family is an extremely sensitive topic, and therefore most of what literature exists deals with violence between the spouses (Arikan, 1987, 1993; Rittersberger-Tilic & Kalaycioglu, 1999; Üsür, 1993; Yüksel, 1991). In general, intrafamilial violence can be divided into violence between spouses and toward children.

Violence between spouses is mostly violence against the wife, which is not surprising in a male-dominated society such as Turkey. Men seek to demonstrate their power over wives. It is used to represent their higher status within the family and their control of the home. In addition, especially within the rapid and immense change in recent decades in Turkey, women and children started to question their traditional subordinate role. Moreover, males find it difficult to fulfill their role as breadwinner, due to rising unemployment and low salaries. All these are potential causes of quarreling, in which the wife often functions as a kind of buffer between father and son. However, the wives tend to justify or legitimize their husbands' violence on the basis of an acceptable cause. The authors' analyses, based on the Turkish Demographic and Health Survey 1998, show that about 35% of the women asked tolerated the husband's right to beat her if she quarrels with him. The next three accepted reasons for beating the wife are wife's neglect of child care (25%), talking to another man (24%), and money spent needlessly (23%). Another 17% of the women accept violence if the wife refuses intercourse and another 7% if the wife burns the food. In addition, the wife excuses her husband's violence due to his "quick-temper, alcohol and gambling habits and swearing" (Rittersberger-Tilic & Kalaycioglu, 1999, p. 236). The acceptance of violent acts within the marriage is more distributed in Central, East, and South Anatolia, and in rural areas. It is less tolerated within the better educated and well-off parts of population, as well as within the ethnic group of Turks compared with Kurds and Arabs. The Alevi orientation of Islam rejects violence against women more than Sunni Muslims do. Further, there is also quite a strong relationship between the acceptance of violence within the marriage and the marriage system. As expected, in the descent marriage regime violence is more accepted. Interestingly, only little modification occurs over time, and Rittersberger-Tilic and Kalaycioglu conclude, "women were themselves actively contributing to the reproduction of domestic violence that could hurt themselves and their children in the long run" (1999, p. 236).

Against the background of the Turkish patriarchal structure and high parental expectations for children, coercive acts of violence toward children are often considered a legitimate way to discipline them:

> For a majority of respondents the children were kept responsible for initiating violent acts; for example, if children were disobedient, naughty, and so on, they "deserved a good slapping or beating." The majority accepted violence towards children as undesired but necessary, as a "right of the parents" referring to its educational function. (Rittersberger-Tilic & Kalaycioglu, 1999, p. 234)

According to the most important educational goals, disobedience, disrespect, bad habits, lying, cheating, and protest are the prevalent causes for violence (Rittersberger-Tilic & Kalaycioglu, 1999, p. 234). Especially in lower-class families, the most frequent form of disciplining children is physical punishment or another form of "power maintenance," while putting shame on them is the second most frequent technique. Arguing and induction (making the child conscious for the consequences of its actions) are seldom observed (Kagitçibasi et al., 1988). The techniques of disciplining in the urban middle class are quite distinct. Here, physical punishment is the least preferred method, but shaming is quite common. The technique of isolation, which is frequently observed in individualized societies, is practically absent in both Turkish working- and middle-class families (Kagitçibasi & Sunar, 1997, pp. 157f.).

7. DIVORCE, WIDOWHOOD, AND REMARRIAGE

During the Ottoman Empire the husband was authorized to "outcast" his wife. With the adoption of the Swiss Civil Code, a uniform divorce law was introduced in which the one-sided right of outcasting was replaced by a court decision based on the explicit declaration of both spouses. Therefore, divorce, especially initiated by the husband, is no longer an easy matter. Additionally, a legally acknowledged guilt has to be named. None but the following are reasons for a divorce: adultery, plot against life, crime or dishonorable life, desertion, mental disease, and incompatibility (Magnarella, 1981, p. 127). Regardless of a slightly increasing crude divorce rate from 0.2 in 1935 to 0.5 in 1998 (State Institute of Statistics 2001, p. 29), divorces hardly exist. Therefore only about 1% of the population 15 years and older have been divorced. As already mentioned, within the descent regime marriage means exchange of goods, human capital, and the allocation of labor force. The physical strength of the individual is needed and highly valued, especially in agrarian regions. Since the family economy depends on marriage as a production component supplying not only short- but long-term labor force by their offspring, the whole family (of origin) would be affected in case of divorce.

The authors' calculations, using register data (State Institute of Statistics, 2000b), extract "incompatibility" as the main reason for divorce (1999 = 94%). It can be assumed that a variety of (other) reasons is subsumed in this category, including infertility. Looking at divorces by the number of children demonstrates that many divorces take place in childless marriages (1999 = 45%). Therefore, infertility seems within the customary law as an accepted reason for divorce, though not a legal one.

Another factor causing the dissolution of marriage is the death of a spouse. Widowhood is more common than divorce. The majority of surviving partners are female, and due to increasing life expectancy, couples' children are mostly grown up and have established their own families. Thus, widows usually move to their children's home. In case of early widowhood, traditionally (and most common within the Kurdish part of the population) the so-called *levirate* is practiced—meaning the marriage of the widow to her husband's brother, sometimes as a second wife.

About remarriage only a little has been studied, since it hardly exists. Looking at register data offered by State Institute of Statistics (2000b), the share of marriages in which at least one partner is divorced amounted to 8% of all marriages in 1997, and only 2% in which at least one partner is widowed.

8. FAMILY STRUCTURES AND KINSHIP

As already mentioned, in Turkey every person's life is linked with some kind of family and kinship. Tekeli states,

> In Turkey, the family remained such a widespread and alternativeless institution that it continues to be the only valid form of love, reproduction and security even when it loses its economic function. Therefore, in Turkish society it has become impossible for people, and especially for women, to have an identity independent from that of the family. (1986, p. 191)

On the one hand, such primary relationships constitute most important and necessary resources: Intergenerational relations are often

the only possible way to safeguard against the risks of life. Kinship as a source of solidarity offers help not only in the case of emergency but also in everyday life, whereas the range is from delivery of information to emotional and practical support to financial assistance. But family and kin ties are also connected with obligations, responsibilities, and expectations.

Family Structures

A widespread assumption based on structural-functional logic (Goode, 1963; Parsons, 1943) is that as modernization proceeds the extended family system will be replaced by the isolated nuclear family. The application of this Western model to Turkish society in particular is questionable. In general, referring to cross-cultural and historical research, any necessary relationship between nuclear family type on the one hand and urbanization and industrialization on the other hand can be rejected. For instance, studies done by Laslett (1971; Laslett & Wall, 1972) give evidence that even in areas where industrial capitalism first emerged, such as northwestern Europe, nuclear families occurred before the industrial revolution. Data indicate that in Turkey the proportion of extended family households never dominated in any historical period. In fact, they never exceeded one-third of households during the last four centuries. A cross-sectional analysis using the first representative Turkish Family Survey of 1968 revealed that about 32% of the households were extended, and only 19% were "patriarchal extended"—meaning the patriarch with his wife plus their child(ren)'s family—mostly son's family—living in one household (Timur, 1978, p. 232). Within the following 30 years, the proportion of extended families fell to 21% (1998, Ünalan, 2000, p. 9). However, a more detailed observation of the life cycle demonstrates that more than one-half of young families live in the household of the groom shortly after marriage. Especially in rural areas, the extended family is a kind of ideal, but some years after marriage the extended structure dissolves, mainly due to economic reasons. The extended household lasts as long as the estate and wealth can offer adequate opportunities to provide for the family. Therefore, families with huge properties and estates tend to live in such an extended form—independently of urbanization, industrialization, and region (Timur, 1978, 1985). Thus, the time span in which families have complex, extended structures is limited, but nearly everyone lives in an extended family sometime during the life course.

Kinship

Several studies deal with urbanization and migration to cities and their effect on family structures and kin ties (Duben, 1982, Günes-Ayata, 1996; Kongar, 1972, 1976; Kuyas, 1982; Senyapli, 1981). Whereas Louis Wirth (1938) argued that family ties get lost in the urban environment, Gans (1962) assumed that family and kinship remain the most significant aspect of daily life even in the cities. For Turkey it can be seen that migrants develop extensive and intensive networks, most of them stemming from rural origin. Many migrants set up modern relations with colleagues or neighbors or within unions, parties, and religious groups. Because of chain migration (Erder, 1997), it is very likely that relatives are already in the city—or at least friends, former neighbors, or people from the same community or village. When arriving the migrants depend on relatives' assistance in finding a place to stay and employment. Especially for poor migrants living in *gecekondus*, it can be observed that the majority live very close to relatives. They do this not only to have better access to information, solidarity, and interaction, but also

for better social control related to female and young family members, and for preserving the traditional value system.

The woman is supposed to do the kin-work, because she is most dependent on the help and solidarity of female kin in doing daily chores. Second, her world is usually limited to the private sphere. When women begin to participate in public life (e.g., by employment), the relative weight of kin decreases due to the establishing of relations outside the home. Income, education, and employment are main factors determining the importance of kin. Günes-Ayata (1996) states that the kin relations of the educated middle-class in the cities are still important, but less so. She summarizes:

> In all social groups and classes, the dominant form of interaction is solidarity and networking between relatives [...] The sole basis of solidarity and social security for a migrant is his relatives and co-villagers. [...] Kinship will remain the chief base of solidarity, comfort and support for the individual, even in big cities. (1996, p. 105).

In the same way, Duben states after reviewing several empirical studies,

> Extended family and wider kinship relations are extremely important in both rural and urban areas in Turkey among all social classes, despite the huge percentage of nuclear family residence in both these cases. The significance of kin relations seems not to be fading with increased urbanization or industrialization. (1982, pp. 93f.)

Abadan-Unat (1987) declares a type of "functionally extended family," which means even if the families of descendants and parents do not live in the same household, mutual solidarity and assistance continue. Kiray states:

> Despite migration ... the family, in major Turkish cities, is still the social institution

which provides care for individual, which accomplishes adaptation through change and which serves, for everybody, as a milieu where the most frequent and intimate relations are maintained. (1985b, p. 89)

9. AGING AND DEATH

Aging

As already demonstrated, the functioning of intergenerational relationships across the life course is particularly important in later life stages. As the public social security system provides neither a sufficient pension scheme nor health insurance coverage that allows the continuation of a lifestyle approximately as high as during gainful employment, the living standard of the elderly depends on additional income sources. One typical source of revenue is the leasing out of real estate that was purchased during the phase of gainful employment or inherited. The higher the social status and the more urban and modern the social context is, the higher is the proportion of old-age security derived from property.

Other typical income sources are payments, goods, and services from one's children as soon as they come to an age where they enter the labor market or contribute to the family economy. The contributions of offspring play the most decisive role for the poorer population groups. The same system also provides insurance against life risks; for example, those medical costs that exceed the state-guaranteed basic medical service supply will be covered by the family of descent if necessary.

It is quite obvious that this cooperative system implies high transaction costs and often inflicts tensions in the family of descent. Not infrequently, especially in the poorer population groups that have many descendants, fathers will retire quite early from full active participation in the labor

force and consider it their right to rely on the solidarity of their sons and their families. This can happen at the end of their 30s because of the small age difference between generations and the early entry of sons into gainful employment. Therefore, the interdependence of parents and their children in Turkish families comprises not only stable emotional relationships throughout the entire life course but also economic interdependence. Typically, intergenerational dependence shifts over the life course such that at first the children are dependent on their parents, and then in later life stages the parents become dependent on their children. This is true of mothers especially, because of their longer life expectancy and because the benefits are provided in patrilineal descent by the sons.

The unbroken solidarity between generations thus also guarantees that old-age poverty is not to be observed in Turkey. The material situation in old age depends on the resources of the offspring. Old-age homes and nursing homes are practically unknown in Turkey. Even hospitals are organized in a way that only makes it possible for patients to be nursed and cared for by relatives. Indeed, there is a need for these family services, as the hospital personnel do not consider this service as a genuine part of their task—unless they are paid extra by the family, in cases where family members cannot or will not provide care services themselves.

Inheritance

In the traditional patrilineal extended family, the death of the patriarch means the dissolution of the extended family household. The sons typically inherit equal shares of the family property and become patriarchs of their own family. The widow of the former patriarch lives in the household of one of her sons, preferably with her oldest son (Duben, 1985; Schiffauer, 1987). Rules of inheritance proved to be stable until well into the 20th century, as they did not, until then, contribute to the scattering of land ownership, and thus were not associated with the increasing poverty of the rural population. This stable situation was favored by two factors: the availability of land and the low mean life expectancy. Land availability was a given, because property rights were based on customary law and related to cultivation: The family that cultivated a piece of land was its acknowledged owner.

As large pieces of uncultivated land existed around the villages, which could be taken into possession and cultivated, estates could be flexibly adapted to family size and the available workforce. This practice, however, is becoming less frequent. Nowadays, all types of heritage, varying from the oldest son as the single inheritor, to the equal distribution of family estates among all male descendants and the equal distribution without regard to the sex of the offspring, are evident in Turkey. Whereas before the Turkish Civil Code the female spouse had no right of inheritance, the standard inheritance rule now is that one-third of the inheritance goes to the surviving spouse, while two-thirds goes to the children (with equal shares). Customary law regulations exist that still emphasize (patrilineal) descent, though, even to the complete exclusion of female family members from the inheritance. (For a detailed discussion about widowhood and its effects on women's financial situation see Zevkliler, 1985, pp. 385ff.)

OUTLOOK

As in most transitional societies, social change is dramatic in Turkey. As all regions and all segments of the population are not changing at the same pace, there are large social disparities in Turkey relative to most affluent societies. This inevitably has massive consequences for family structures and intergenerational relationships. Rapid social change is a challenge for intergenerational relationships, as the respective birth cohorts of the 20th century have faced very different political, economic, and sociostructural conditions in their various life phases. Clearly, changes in the contextual conditions and in individual resources have only slightly eroded intergenerational relationships. Rather, they have led—insofar as subsistence, poverty, and material interdependence have been concerned—to restructuring without any loss of intensity and complexity, and without the substitution of alternative social relationships.

A visible expression of restructuring is the strongly decreased birthrates in the second half of the 20th century, accompanied by consistently high parental expectations. Together, these result in altered strategies of parental investment in child-rearing with a focus away from the quantity to the quality of offspring. This alteration in intergenerational relationships implies, for example, that Turks consider it not at all unusual for mothers to leave their husbands temporarily and move with their child to a university town to continue care during the child's studies.

Strong social disparities mean, at the same time, that several institutional constitutions of the family coexist, and that one can hardly speak about one Turkish family culture. As far as we can tell, the parallel existence of the affinal and the descent marriage regimes can be traced back at least to the 19th century—but it may reach back to the ancient world. It is thus questionable to relate the existence of the affinal marriage regime to the diffusion process of Western lifestyles in the course of the modernization process. It also would be too hasty to conclude from the ongoing modernization process that it will result in a dying out of the marriage regime of descent and in the victory of the affinal regime in the near future. It is rather to be assumed that the marriage regime of descent will develop along its own modernization path (Kagitçibasi, 1985; Nauck, 2001b). There is no evidence that the primacy of intergenerational relationships is not compatible with the requirements of modernity for the private lifestyle. Individualized civil law regulations of insurance against the life risks are not replacing the high reliability and commitment between generations and spouses.

It is, at least in Turkey, the case that trust in the marriage institution and the stability of intergenerational relationships is higher than the trust in any corporate welfare and insurance system. This is indicated, for example, by undiminished marriage rates and the early marriage age, as well as the very extensive influence of parents on the partner selection process and marriage plans. Therefore, it is rather improbable that changes of generative behavior and intergenerational relationships will take the same pathway in Turkey as in individualized societies that are based on the affinal marriage regime. No polarization into a family and a nonfamily sector is to be expected, but an increasing concentration of all family resources of time, money, care, and education in fewer and fewer offspring. Childlessness will also be an unwanted event.

REFERENCES

Abadan-Unat, N. (1987). Die Familie in der Türkei—Aspekte aus struktureller und juristischer Sicht. *Zeitschrift des Deutschen Orient-Institutes, 28*(1), 66–82.

Anderson, M. (1980). *Approaches to the history of the western family 1500–1900.* London: Macmillan.

Arikan, C. (1987). *Sosyal Hizmetler Acisindan Siddet ve Bir Türü Olarak Evililkte Kadina Yönelik Siddet* [Violence toward women in marriage]. Ankara: Hacettepe University, Sosyal Hizmetler Yüksek Okulu Dergisi.

Arikan, C. (1993). *Kadin ve Siddet* [Women and violence]. Ankara: Turkish State Ministry, General Directorate for Status and Problems of Women.

Ataca, B., & Sunar, D. (1999). Continuity and change in Turkish urban family life. *Psychology and Developing Societies, 11,* 77–90.

Basaran, F. (1985). Attitude changes related to sex roles in the family. In T. Erder (Ed.), *Family in Turkish society: Sociological and legal studies* (pp. 167–182). Ankara: MAYA.

Blood, R. O., & Wolfe, D. H. (1960). *Husbands and wives: The dynamics of married living.* New York: Free Press.

Bolak, H. C. (1988). Towards a conceptualization of marital power dynamics: Women breadwinners and working-class household in Turkey. In S. Tekeli (Ed.), *Women in modern Turkish society: A reader* (pp. 167–182). London: Zed Books Ltd.

Bolak, H. C. (1997). Marital power dynamics: Women providers and working-class households in Istanbul. In J. Gugler (Ed.), *Cities in the developing world: Issues, theory, and policy* (pp. 218–232). Oxford, UK: Oxford University Press.

Bott, E. (1957). *Family and social network.* London: Tavistock.

Buric, O., & Zecevic, A. (1967). Family authority, marital satisfaction, and the social network in Yugoslavia. *Journal of Marriage and the Family, 29,* 325–336.

Council of Europe. (1995). *Recent demographic developments in Europe.* Strasbourg: Author.

Council of Europe. (2001). *Demographic Yearbook 2001.* Retrieved April 2003, from http://www.coe.int/t/e/social_cohesion/population/demographic_year_book/2001_Edition/Turkey%202001.asp#.

Duben, A. (1982). The significance of family and kinship in urban Turkey. In C. Kagitçibasi (Ed.), *Sex roles, family, and community in Turkey* (pp. 73–100). Bloomington: Indiana University.

Duben, A. (1985). Nineteenth and twentieth century Ottoman-Turkish family and household structures. In T. Erder (Ed.), *Family in Turkish society: Sociological and legal studies* (pp. 105–126). Ankara: MAYA.

Ecevit, F. Y. (1988). The status and changing forms of women's labour in the urban economy. In S. Tekeli (Ed.), *Women in modern Turkish society: A reader* (pp. 81–88). London: Zed Books.

Erder, S. (1997). *Kentsel gerilim* [Urban tension]. Ankara: Ugur Mumcu Foundation.

Ergöcmen, B. A. (1997). Women's status and fertility in Turkey. In *Fertility trends, women's status and reproductive expectations in Turkey: Results of further analysis of the 1993 Turkish Demographic and Health Survey* (pp. 79–104). Ankara: Institute of Populations Studies.

Erman, T. (2001). Rural migrants and patriarchy in Turkish cities. *International Journal of Urban and Regional Research, 25*(1), 118–133.

Fox, G. L. (1973). Another look at the comparative resources model: Assessing the balance of power in Turkish marriages. *Journal of Marriage and the Family, 35,* 718–730.

Fox, G. L. (1975). Love match and arranged marriage in a modernizing nation: Mate selection in Ankara, Turkey. *Journal of Marriage and the Family, 37,* 180–193.

Gans, H. (1962). *The urban villagers group and class in the life of Italian Americans.* New York: Free Press of Glecoe.

Goode, W. J. (1963). *World revolution and family patterns.* New York: Free Press.

Günes-Ayata, A. (1996). Solidarity in urban Turkish family. In G. Rasuly-Paleczek (Ed.), *Turkish families in transition* (pp. 98–109). Frankfurt am Main: Peter Lang.

Hajnal, J. (1965). European marriage patterns in perspective. In D. V. Glass & D. E. C. Eversley (Eds.), *Population in history* (pp. 101–143). Chicago: Aldine.

Imamoglu, E. O. (1987). An interdependence model of human development. In C. Kagitçibasi (Ed.), *Growth and progress in cross-cultural psychology* (pp. 138–145). Lisse: Swets & Zeitlinger.

Imamoglu, E. O., & Yasak, Y. (1997). Dimensions of marital relationships as perceived by Turkish husbands and wives. *Genetic, Social and General Psychological Monographs, 123*(2), 211ff.

Kagitçibasi, C. (1982a). *The changing value of children in Turkey.* Honolulu, HI: East-West Center.

Kagitçibasi, C. (1982b). Old age security value of children: Cross-cultural socio-economic evidence. *Journal of Cross-Cultural Psychology, 13,* 29–42.

Kagitçibasi, C. (Ed.). (1982c). *Sex roles, family, and community in Turkey.* Bloomington: Indiana University Press.

Kagitçibasi, C. (1984). Socialization in traditional society: A challenge to psychology. *International Journal of Psychology, 19,* 145–157.

Kagitçibasi, C. (1985). Intra-family interaction and a model of family change. In T. Erder (Ed.), *Family in Turkish society* (pp. 149–165). Ankara: Turkish Social Science Association.

Kagitçibasi, C. (1996). *Family and human development across cultures: A view from the other side*. Mahwah, NJ: Erlbaum.

Kagitçibasi, C., & Sunar, D. (1997). Familie und Sozialisation in der Türkei. In B. Nauck & U. Schönpflug (Eds.), *Familien in verschiedenen Kulturen* (pp. 145–161). Stuttgart: Enke.

Kagitçibasi, C., Sunar, D., & Bekman, S. (1988). *Comprehensive preschool educational project: Final report*. Ottawa: International Development Research Center.

Kandiyoti, D. (1977). Sex roles and social change: A comparative appraisal of Turkey's woman. *Signs, 3*(1), 57–73.

Kandiyoti, D. (1982). Urban change and women's roles in Turkey: An overview and evaluation. In C. Kagitçibasi (Ed.), *Sex roles, family, & community in Turkey* (pp. 101–120). Bloomington: Indiana University Press.

Kandiyoti, D. (1988). Patterns of patriarchy: Notes for an analysis of male dominance in Turkish society. In S. Tekeli (Ed.), *Women in modern Turkish society: A reader* (pp. 306–319). London: Zed Books Ltd.

Kandiyoti, D. (1991). Patriarchalische Muster. Notizen zu einer Analyse der Männerherrschaft in der türkischen Familie. In A. Neusel, S. Tekeli, & M. Akkent (Eds.), *Aufstand im Haus der Frauen. Frauenforschung aus der Türkei* (pp. 315–329). Berlin: Orlanda Frauenverlag.

Karasan-Dirks, S. (1986). *Die türkische Familie zwischen gestern und heute*. Bremen: Übersee-Museum.

Kaufmann, F. X. (1995). *Zukunft der Familie im vereinten Deutschland. Gesellschaftliche und politische Bedingungen* (2nd ed.). München: Beck.

Kazgan, G. (1985). Sozio-ökonomischer Status der Frauen in der türkischen Wirtschaft. In N. Abadan-Unat (Ed.), *Die Frau in der türkischen Gesellschaft* (pp. 77–117). Frankfurt am Main: Dagyeli.

Kiray, M. B. (1976). The changing roles of mothers: Changing intra-family relations in a Turkish town. In J. Peristiany (Ed.), *Mediterranean family structures* (pp. 261–271). London: Cambridge University Press.

Kiray, M. B. (1985a). Frauen in kleinen Städten. In N. Abadan-Unat (Ed.), *Die Frau in der türkischen Gesellschaft* (pp. 306–327). Frankfurt: Dagyeli.

Kiray, M. B. (1985b). Metropolitan city and the changing family. In T. Erder (Ed.), *Family in Turkish society* (pp. 79–89). Ankara: MAYA.

Kongar, E. (1972). Izmir' de Kentsel Aile [The urban family in Izmir]. In *Türk Sosyal Bilimler Dernegi* (pp. 43–62). Ankara: Turkish Association for the Social Sciences.

Kongar, E. (1976). A survey of familial change in two Turkish gecekondu areas. In J. G. Peristiany (Ed.), *Mediterranean family structures* (pp. 205–218). London: Cambridge University Press.

Kuyas, N. (1982). Female labor power relations in urban Turkish family. In C. Kagitçibasi (Ed.), *Sex roles, family and community in Turkey* (pp. 53–68). Bloomington: Indiana University Press.

Laslett, P. (1971). *The world we have lost*. London: Rethen.

Laslett, P., & Wall, R. (Eds.). (1972). *Household and family in past time*. Cambridge, UK: Cambridge University Press.

Levi-Strauss, C. (1984). *Die elementaren Strukturen der Verwandtschaft*. Frankfurt: Suhrkamp.

Magnarella, P. J. (1981). *Tradition and change in a Turkish town*. Cambridge, MA: Schenkman.

Moghadam, V. M. (1996). Development strategies, state policies, and the status of women: A comparative assessment of Iran, Turkey and Tunisia. In V. M. Moghadam (Ed.), *Patriarchy and development*. Oxford, UK: Clarendon.

Nauck, B. (1985). "Heimliches Matriarchat" in Familien türkischer Arbeitsmigranten? Empirische Ergebnisse zu Veränderungen der Entscheidungsmacht und Aufgabenallokation. *Zeitschrift für Soziologie, 14*, 450–465.

Nauck, B. (1989a). Individualistische Erklärungsansätze in der Familienforschung: die rational-choice-Basis von Familienökonomie, Ressourcen- und Austauschtheorien. In R. Nave-Herz & M. Markefka (Eds.), *Handbuch der Familien- und Jugendforschung* (Vol. 1: *Familienforschung*) (pp. 45–61). Neuwied/Frankfurt: Luchterhand.

Nauck, B. (1989b). Intergenerational relationships in families from Turkey and Germany: An extension of the "Value of Children" approach to educational attitudes and socialization practices. *European Sociological Review, 5*, 251–274.

Nauck, B. (1997). Sozialer Wandel, Migration und Familienbildung bei türkischen Frauen. In B. Nauck & U. Schönpflug (Eds.), *Familien in verschiedenen Kulturen* (pp. 62–199). Stuttgart: Enke.

Nauck, B. (2001a). Generationenbeziehungen und Heiratsregimes—theoretische Überlegungen zur Struktur von Heiratsmärkten und Partnerwahlprozessen am Beispiel der Türkei und Deutschlands. In T. Klein (Ed.), *Partnerwahl und Heiratsmuster. Sozialstrukturelle Voraussetzungen der Liebe* (pp. 35–55). Opladen: Leske & Budrich.

Nauck, B. (2001b). Der Wert von Kindern für ihre Eltern. "Value of Children" als spezielle Handlungstheorie des generativen Verhaltens und von Generationenbeziehungen im interkulturellen Vergleich. *Kölner Zeitschrift für Soziologie und Sozialpsychologie, 53*, 407–435.

Nauck, B., & Kohlmann, A. (1999). Kinship as social capital: Network relationships in Turkish migrant families. In R. Richter & S. Supper (Eds.), *New qualities in the life course: Intercultural aspects* (pp. 199–218). Würzburg: Ergon.

Olson, E. A. (1982). Duofocal family structure and an alternative model of husband-wife relationship. In C. Kagitçibasi (Ed.), *Sex roles, family, and community in Turkey* (pp. 33–72). Bloomington: Indiana University Press.

Olson-Prather, E. (1976). Family planning and husband-wife relationships in Turkey. *Journal of Marriage and the Family, 38*, 379–385.

Organization of Economic Cooperation and Development (OECD) (2002). *Public social expenditure by main category as a percentage of GDP (1980–1998)*. Retrieved June 10, 2004, from www.oecd.org/LongAbstract/ 0,2546,en_2649_33933_2087076_119656_1_1_1,00.html.

Ortayli, I. (1985). The family in Ottoman society. In T. Erder (Ed.), *Family in Turkish society: Sociological and legal studies* (pp. 93–104). Ankara: MAYA.

Özbay, F. (1985a). Die Auswirkungen der Bildung auf die türkische Frau auf dem Land und in der Stadt. In N. Abadan-Unat (Ed.), *Die Frau in der türkischen Gesellschaft* (pp. 118–145). Frankfurt am Main: Dagyeli.

Özbay, F. (1985b). Transformation of the socio-economic structure and changing family functions in rural Turkey. In T. Erder (Ed.), *Family in Turkish society: Sociological and legal studies* (pp. 43–77). Ankara: MAYA.

Özbay, F. (1988). Changes in women's activities both inside and outside the home. In S. Tekeli (Ed.), *Women in modern Turkish society: A reader* (pp. 89–111). London: Zed Books.

Özbay, F. (1991). Der Wandel der Arbeitssituation der Frau im innerhäuslichen und außerhäuslichen Bereich in den letzten sechzig Jahren. In A. Neusel, S. Tekeli, & M. Akkent (Eds.), *Aufstand im Haus der Frauen. Frauenforschung aus der Türkei* (pp. 120–148). Berlin: Orlanda Frauenverlag.

Özgen, E. (1985). Early marriage, brideprice and abduction. In T. Erder (Ed.), *Family in Turkish society. Sociological and legal studies* (pp. 313–349). Ankara: MAYA.

Parsons, T. (1943). The kinship system in contemporary United States. *American Anthropologist, 45*, 22–38.

Rittersberger-Tilic, H., & Kalaycioglu, S. (1999). Legitimating and re-production of domestic violence in Turkish families. *Zeitschrift für Türkeistudien, 12*(2), 225–240.

Rodman, H. (1972). Marital power and the theory of resources in cultural context. *Journal of Comparative Family Studies, 3*, 50–69.

Safilios-Rothschild, C. (1967). A comparison of power structure and marital satisfaction in urban Greek and French families. *Journal of Marriage and the Family, 29*, 345–352.

Schiffauer, W. (1987). *Die Bauern von Subay*. Stuttgart: Klett-Cotta.

Senyapli, T. (1981). *Gecekondu*. Ankara: ODTÜ [Middle East Technical University].

Sönmez, M. (1996). *Istanbul'un iki yüzü: 1980'den 2000'edegisim* [The two faces of Istanbul: Transformation from 1980 to 2000]. Ankara: Arkadas.

State Institute of Statistics. (1993). *1990 Census of population*. Ankara: Printing Division.

State Institute of Statistics. (2000a). *Household and labor force survey 1999*. Ankara: Printing Division.

State Institute of Statistics. (2000b). *1999 Statistical yearbook of Turkey*. Ankara: Printing Division.

State Institute of Statistics. (2001). *Statistical indicators 1923–1998*. Ankara: Printing Division.

State Institute of Statistics. (2002). Retrieved June 10, 2004, from www.die.gov .tr/cin/statistics/1TemelDG.gif.

State Institute of Statistics. (2003). *Census of population: Social and economic characteristics of population*. Ankara: Printing Division.

Tansel, A. (1998). *Determinants of school attainment of boys and girls in Turkey*. Center Discussion Paper No. 789. New Haven, CT: Yale University, Economic Growth Center.

Tansel, A., & Kazemi, A. (1995). Equity in educational expenditures in the Middle East and North Africa. Economic Research Forum Working Paper No. 9628. Cairo: ERF.

Tekeli, S. (1986). The rise and change of the new women's movement: Emergence of the feminist movement in Turkey. In D. Dahlenup (Ed.), *The new women's movement, feminism and political power in Europe and the USA* (pp. 179–199). London: Sage Publications.

Timur, S. (1978). Determinants of family structure in Turkey. In J. Allmann (Ed.), *Women's status and fertility in the Muslim world* (pp. 227–242). New York: Praeger.

Timur, S. (1985). Charakteristika der Familienstruktur in der Türkei. In N. Abadan-Unat (Ed.), *Die Frau in der türkischen Gesellschaft* (pp. 56–76). Frankfurt am Main: Dagyeli.

Ünalan, T. (2000, November). *Changing family structure in Turkey, 1968–1998.* Paper presented at the Seminar on Age Structural Transformations and Policy Implications, Phuket, Thailand.

Üsür, S. (1993). *Kadina Yönelik Siddet* [Violence toward women]. Ankara: Turkish State Ministry, General Directorate for Status and Problems of Women.

Wirth, L. (1938). Urbanism as a way of life. *American Journal of Sociology,* 44, 3–24.

Yüksel, S. (1991). Toplumsal Psikoloji Acisindan Kadin ve Siddet [Women and violence from the perspective of social psychology]. *Halk Sagligi Bülteni* [Bulletin of Community Health], 2, 4.

Zevkliler, A. (1985). Dissolution of marriage and the estate of the women. In T. Erder (Ed.), *Family in Turkish society: Sociological and legal studies* (pp. 365ff.). Ankara: MAYA.

Part IV

LATIN AMERICA

CHAPTER 18

The Family in Argentina: Modernity, Economic Crisis, and Politics

Elizabeth Jelin

1. INTRODUCTION

The family is a social institution anchored in biologically based universal human needs: sexuality, reproduction, and daily subsistence (based on coresidence in households). Its members share a social space based on kinship relations, conjugality, and parental ties.[1] It is a social organization, a microcosm of relations of production, reproduction, and distribution, with a power structure and strong ideological and affective components. There are collective tasks and interests, but members have also their own interests, rooted in their own location within production and reproduction processes.

Family relations are the basic criteria for the formation of households and the performance of tasks linked to biological and social reproduction in everyday life. In the Western modern paradigm, ties within the family are expected to be based on affection and mutual care, yet they also involve instrumental, strategic, and interest-based considerations, both in short (everyday) life and in longer intergenerational perspectives.

As a social institution, the family involves the pattern of legitimized sexuality, marriage, conjugality, and fertility. It also involves issues of divorce and separation, as well as the intergenerational transmission of social and economic capital (inheritance). Formal rules embodied in law, and commonsense norms that often contradict the law, are at the same time a reflection of and a guide for social practices.

The family is never an isolated institution, but rather part and parcel of wider societal processes, including the productive and reproductive dimensions of societies, cultural patterns, and political systems. Households and family organizations are linked to the labor market and the organization of social networks; sociodemographic trends such as fertility rates, divorce rates, and processes of aging are part of wider social and cultural processes as well as subject to public policy; and as a basic societal institution, the family is enmeshed in issues of basic cultural values and in political processes.

Given the fact that census and survey information usually is based on households,

I thank Ana Rita Diaz Muñoz for her help throughout the preparation of this paper.

there is a tendency to identify the family with the household. In general, population statistics are based on household counts. It is easy to conflate the concept of the family with that of the household, taking data available for the latter as indicators of the former. For many purposes related to everyday life and the satisfaction of basic needs such as food and shelter, households are an appropriate unit of analysis. However, for analyzing the dynamics of family and kinship ties, especially at times of high divorce rates and of diversified migratory patterns, one has to put special emphasis on the lack of correspondence between households and families. Under such conditions, family responsibilities and obligations can be met by members who do not share a household. Love and care can be exchanged on a nondaily basis. And these are issues that will have to be raised to fully understand contemporary family trends.

Furthermore, an often neglected dimension of the theme involves the symbolic and ideological significance of the family. Beyond the institutional and practical aspects of family life, there are social values and ideology in images of "normal" or "natural" families. By "naturalizing" a certain type of family, other forms are stigmatized, and those who push for greater choice in living arrangements (or sexual orientation) can then be seen as abnormal, subversive, or the devil. In fact, although seldom taken as a research theme in itself, the belief system and the political presence of family and kinship bonds is a highly significant phenomenon of public life.

The Country and Its People

Argentina is a country in the southern part of South America. With a territory of close to 3 million sq km and a population of close to 37 million people, its territory is sparsely populated. Furthermore, its population is highly concentrated: One-third live in the area of Greater Buenos Aires, and another one-third in the rest of the Province of Buenos Aires (surrounding the capital city).

The country emerged as an independent state in the first half of the 19th century after two centuries of Spanish colonization. It had a very sparse indigenous population, which was decimated during the last part of the 19th century as part of a policy designed to "conquer the desert" and establish state sovereignty over the territory. The liberal ruling elites defined the country as an empty space, sponsoring European immigration from early on, following an ideology and an interpretive framework that contrasted "barbarism," that is, the indigenous peoples, and the "civilization" that the European immigrants were going to bring.

Fostering immigration from Europe, the population of the country increased considerably during the last part of the 19th century and the beginning of the 20th century. In 1869 (the date of the first national census) the population of the country was 1.7 million; by 1914 there were 7.8 million people. Thirty percent of the population was foreign-born, and the process of modernization was well under way: More than one-half of the population of the country lived in urban areas. Literacy rates had reached 65% of the adult population, and fertility rates were already declining (Torrado, 1993; Pantelides, 1989).

From the early optimism of the elites and their commitment to modernity and modernization (i.e., following the Western paradigm), the story of Argentina is not one of smooth and linear progress and development. Rather, the history of the 20th century is one of economic ups and downs, periods of social mobilization followed by military coups and dictatorships, an expansion of welfare-state provisions and progressive income redistribution, followed by processes of economic and social polarization.

The last decades of the 20th century were times of political turmoil and deep transformations of the social structure. Politically, deep and violent political conflict in the early

1970s led to a military coup and bloody repressive dictatorship in 1976. The transition to a democratically elected political regime in 1983 was coupled with neoliberal adjustment policies, downsizing state services, increasing foreign debt, and engaging in a policy of privatization of utilities and public services. At the turn of the 21st century, the country faces the highest rates of unemployment in its history, previously unknown degrees of economic and social polarization, deep economic recession, and high rates of impoverishment and poverty, which were expressed in a political crisis in December 2001, and in social protest and mobilization.

The family as a social institution cannot remain immune to and unaffected by these macro- and microprocesses. It is subject to the effects of long-term social and demographic trends, and to shorter-term economic and political events. State policies, in terms of employment and social services on the one hand, and political regimes—dictatorship and democratically elected governments—on the other, affect greatly the structural characteristics of families, as well as their meaning and value.

In the context of the deep difficulties and crisis situations that Argentina has experienced in recent years, the family has gained salience in social discourse as the basic unit of subsistence and reproduction. It is seen as an important resource for its members and as a refuge for those who live in conditions of social exclusion, insecurity, and violence, yet this centrality is not translated into an explicit consideration of its role and its diverse forms for public policy planning and implementation (CEPAL, 2001).

The Family in Public Life and Discourse

Argentina was colonized by Spain, introducing Catholicism as the basic normative parameter. Canonical principles were prevalent in colonial times, and only gradually did civil law and lay principles evolve (Cicerchia, 1994). In 1869, the state sanctioned a civil code, including legislation on several aspects of the family, yet many of its principles still followed Catholic norms. Furthermore, all through the 20th century, there were recurring conflicts regarding family norms between, on the one hand, the hierarchy of the Catholic Church and its civil allies, who were trying to maintain the Argentine legal system as close as possible to the views about the family sustained by the Church, and, on the other hand, progressive and liberal social actors who pushed for legal changes. The result has been a sharp discrepancy between social patterns of behavior and the legal framework. Legislation about separation, divorce, and the formation of new unions, provision of contraceptive devices and sexual education in public institutions, and the rights of mothers vis-à-vis their children, among other themes, were (and still are) subjects of public debate. In general, social change has taken place earlier and in a more widespread way than legal changes.

Civil marriage was introduced in 1888, yet the legal recognition of divorce had to wait another 100 years (1987). Patriarchal principles were clearly established in law: Women were subject to their husbands' decisions in many areas of life, and the father had legal rights over his children. *Patria potestad* only changed in 1985, allowing for shared paternal and maternal rights. Also, equality of rights between children of married couples and children born out of wedlock were only introduced at that time (1985). Finally, with the constitutional reform of 1994, international treaties became part of the constitutional text, thus recognizing the rights of children, the denunciation of all forms of discrimination against women, and the recognition of basic human rights.

Legal and policy changes in the last part of the 20th century have been significant, ranging from the recognition of rights of partners in consensual unions (health benefits, survivor pension rights, but not inheritance and other rights) to the introduction (in the city of Buenos Aires) of same-sex civil unions in 2003, in spite of considerable opposition.

2. PAIRING UP: CHANGES IN CONJUGALITY AND NUPTIALITY

One could anchor the process of family formation in the initial stage of pairing up. To a large extent, Argentina (especially the urban middle class) has followed modern Western patterns of dating and mate selection. The expectation is that young people select their partners freely, based on love. After a period of dating, marked by various social rituals, the couple eventually marries and has children. If this is the expectation, there are many ways in which the norm is broken, leading to alterations in the expected sequencing of events: early active sexuality leading to adolescent and even child pregnancies (often linked to incest and rape), cohabitation without legal marriage, limitations to the freedom of choice of partners, and silenced or hidden arrangements (homosexual couples, for instance). Obviously, there are social class and rural-urban differentials in these types of patterns: Consensual unions were historically prevalent among rural and low-income populations of the poorer areas of the country.

One should note that Argentina is a country where cultural differences are comparatively smaller than in other places: Indigenous populations have been decimated, and although they do exist and have legal recognition, their numbers are very small and have not maintained alternative family forms. Migration could also be a source of cultural diversity in family forms. Early migration to Argentina was of European origin, bringing with it the model of the nuclear family.[2] There has been a significant immigration from neighboring countries (Paraguay, Bolivia, Chile, Uruguay, Brazil, and more recently Perú) as well as a recent Korean influx. These populations, however, do not have strong alternative models of family formation, although some variants of the dominant model can be detected, for instance, different norms regarding dating, higher rates of cohabitation, and a younger age at first child in populations coming from the Andean highlands tradition.

To what extent do the different migratory groups intermarry? The issue of endogamy and exogamy has not been the object of systematic study in Argentina. Statistical data are not easily available and cover basically overseas rather than South American migrants. After analyzing whatever longitudinal data are available for immigrant groups, Torrado concludes that during the period of high overseas immigration (at the turn of the 20th century), immigrant populations tended to marry within the same nationality (and even within people from the same region or community of origin). This pattern was maintained in the second generation—not a melting pot but rather cultural pluralism. Only in the third generation is intermarriage a common pattern (Torrado, 2003; Otero, 1990).[3] As for social and residential homogamy, although there are no specific studies of these issues, available nonsystematic data indicate that people clearly tend to marry their likes, noticeably in terms of education (Torrado, 2003, p. 303).

One of the most important trends regarding family formation in the last decades is the clear increase in cohabitation and its expansion from backward rural areas to urban and middle-class populations. Cohabitation and consensual unions existed since early times as a popular practice, at times followed after some years by civil or religious marriage. This practice began to decline with the process of urbanization and modernization.

Cohabitation without formal marriage has grown in numbers during the last decades. It represented 7% of all unions in 1960, increasing to 18% in 1991 (Torrado, 2003, p. 268). There are two variants: consensual unions as an initial stage, to be followed by a legal union (mostly when children are born), and as an alternative to the legal bond. Stable consensual unions can be a chosen option, both in the case of the first union and more often in successive ones (the only form possible until the divorce law of 1987). While the incidence of consensual unions is highest in the poorest regions of the country (in 1991 they represented 32.5% of all unions in the northeastern region of the country), the figures for the city of Buenos Aires are impressive: 1.5% in 1960, 13.6% in 1991, and 21% in 2001.[4]

Lower marriage rates and higher cohabitation rates indicate that the major change has been in marriage as a formal institution. At the same time, there has been an increase in divorce rates.[5] This set of phenomena has been interpreted as an indication of the weakening of conjugal relations or of a crisis in the conjugal couple, yet the prevalence of couples as the preferred living arrangement has not decreased. In fact, when considering the quality of the bonds, decreased marriage rates and higher divorce rates can also be seen as indications of an increasing freedom to exit unsatisfying relationships and of a process leading to the constitution of new family forms.

Age at marriage is another significant dimension of family formation. Argentina shares the Western model of relatively late (and increasingly so) marriage. Among women, age at marriage in the city of Buenos Aires increased from 23 to 26 in the period 1900–1960, continuing its upward trend to reach 28.2 in 1995. Men's age at marriage grew much less, from 28.9 in 1900 to 31 in 1960, and from then on it declined slightly, reaching 29.5 in 1995 (Torrado, 2003).

Thus, there has been a very significant decline in the age at marriage differential by sex all through the 20th century: from almost 6 years in 1900 to slightly over 1 year in 1995.

The pattern of family formation, however, needs further attention, since age at marriage may hide or combine the first formation of a couple (which may be consensual) with the legal marriage ceremony. Also, cohort effects may be at play. Yet, an intercohort comparison of patterns of family formation in the city of Buenos Aires indicates clearly the trend toward postponing marriage. Women born in the 1960s have made the major break with their predecessors, and there is a clear increase of age at marriage since then. It is also clear that legal marriage is increasingly a second stage in the process of family formation, and cohabitation is becoming the most frequent first stage. Younger cohorts not only cohabit more frequently, but they also do it for longer periods of time. Yet, when combining both dimensions, the study shows that living arrangements do not give a full explanation of the increasing age at marriage. Each cohort shows an increasing age of family formation, be it via marriage or cohabitation (Binstock, 2003).

3. TRENDS IN FERTILITY, SEXUALITY, AND REPRODUCTIVE BEHAVIOR

The issues of reproductive rights and national policies linked to reproductive behavior merit some attention. The elites of the 19th century saw in European immigration the way to solve the population deficit of the country. This hegemonic perspective was to change in the 1930s, when immigration policies became much more restrictive while fertility rates were reaching their lowest point in Argentine history.[6] The new perspective was clearly pronatalist and called for active social policies fostering larger families. In the 1960s, while U.S.-sponsored policies for Latin America called for fertility control to slow down population growth in the region, Argentina was the exception: Both the Catholic and nationalist right (based on moral and geopolitical considerations) and the Left (based on anti-imperialist stands) opposed active policies of population control.

These policy debates—including also the link between population policy and development plans—had concrete effects on actual behavior. If up to the mid-1970s pronatalist policies operated through incentives (for instance, increased social benefits for large families) with little practical effect, in 1974 a presidential decree was introduced to control the marketing of contraceptive devices. At the same time, public health activities geared to fertility control were forbidden. This policy implied a clear social stratification effect: Those who could afford private medicine had access to specialized modern reproductive control knowledge and services; the others, that is, the poor, were left out of family planning public services.

During the 1980s, a new paradigm to interpret reproductive behavior took hold in many social groups in the country, although not necessarily among government officials and public policies. With the return to democratically elected government in 1983 and the opening of the public sphere to new social actors (such as the human rights and the feminist movements), the issue of reproductive health began to be interpreted in the framework of reproductive rights. Argentina ratified international treaties dealing with the rights of women, yet it aligned itself with the Vatican in international forums when issues of population control and reproductive rights were advanced (in the Cairo Population Conference and in the Beijing Women's Conference). Political confrontations regarding reproductive rights legislation and regarding the depenalization of abortion

(a widespread practice resulting from the inadequacy or even the failure of sexual education and reproductive health public services) are ongoing. In the midst of these unending disputes, the fate of women—of poor women—is left unattended.

Fertility rates have consistently been declining in the country. In fact, Argentina represents an exception in Latin America, because of its very early decline in fertility, beginning in the last decade of the 19th century.[7] This decline can be linked to the process of secularization of its population, which implied an early process of urbanization and an increase in educational levels for both men and women. The ideology of family progress through educational and occupational mobility took hold easily among European immigrants and native middle classes. In that paradigm, there was a widespread aspiration to regulate fertility to achieve a small family size. The interesting fact is that this early demographic transition began way before modern contraceptive devices were developed.

By the end of the overseas massive immigration period (1930) the country showed a dual population model: "modern" immigrants and urban middle classes on the one hand, traditional patterns of fertility (high nonregulated fertility) in the rest of the population. Internal rural to urban migration in the following years, coupled with vigorous economic growth and redistributive policies of the Peronist government (1946–1955) led to a decline in fertility differentials between urban middle and working classes (but a moderate baby boom in the second half of the 1940s). The total fertility rate was approximately 3.2 in 1947, a level that remained constant until 1980, to continue its slow descending trend afterward. It was 2.8 for the period 1990–1995. Estimates for 2000–2005 are 2.4 children per woman. Regional differentials are very large: While total fertility in the city of Buenos Aires for

2000–2005 is 1.47 children, the comparable figure for the province of Misiones is 3.34 (National Census, 2001; General Household Survey, 2003).

As mentioned previously, fertility decline took place in spite of (and even against) state population policies. In recent decades, when modern contraceptive techniques entered the market, state policies hindered the access of poorer women to information and use by not providing reproductive health services in public institutions. This implies that many women end up undergoing an abortion to interrupt unwanted pregnancies, performed in clandestine clinics. Although there are no reliable statistics, several studies show that abortion is a common practice (estimates vary between 335,000 and 500,000 abortions per year) (Ramos et al., 2001; Checa & Rosemberg, 1996).

Perhaps a snapshot of the prevalence of an ideal of a small family size can be provided by an in-depth longitudinal study of a small number of families carried out in the 1980s (Jelin & Feiloó, 1980; Ramos, 1984; Llovet, 1984). Ramos followed the reproductive history of several low-income women. The life stories indicate that in all cases when the women had a third child, the pregnancy was not planned, and the women considered abortion but "failed" to carry it to completion.[8]

Issues related to fertility behavior entered the public sphere of debate during the last two decades, since the return to democratic government in 1983. The demands raised by the feminist movement and the governmental commitment to comply with the action plans of various international conferences and treaties established the bases for the recognition of reproductive rights, providing legitimacy to initiatives for the definition of policies in this field.[9] The constitutional reform of 1994 incorporates international treaties into the Argentine constitution, generating a process of debate and mobilization around these issues. The process led to passing (at the national and provincial levels) various laws on reproductive health. If the implementation of the laws is still to be seen, at least they are reversing previous prohibitions[10] and are setting the stage for further progress. Yet, each move brings about the reaction of the Catholic Church and its allies, attempting systematically to limit or obstruct the application of the law.

Several studies have shown, and activists have denounced, the differential access to information and education concerning sexual and reproductive behavior, as well as to counseling and provision of contraceptives and to adequate medical services (Ramos et al., 2001).[11] As is well-known, there is a strong relationship between the social position of women and fertility rates. In terms of education, higher-educated women have significantly fewer children than less educated ones. Increase in the educational level of women affects the age of sexual initiation—the age at first union. It also delays the arrival of the first child, thereby broadening women's horizons and expectations outside family boundaries, and facilitating for them the information needed to decide when and how many children to have. In the transition toward new women's identities, the value of children and family life gradually drops from the central position it used to have, especially for highly educated women. Still, the values associated with marriage and motherhood are extremely strong in the country. As mentioned previously, Binstock and Cerrutti show that while in 1983 the proportion of people who considered that it is not necessary for a woman to have a child to feel fulfilled was 50%, it decreased to 44% in 1995. Higher education and not having children are the main determinants of not identifying women's fulfillment with motherhood (Binstock & Cerrutti, 2002).

Education is also very important at the other end of the social scale. Data regarding sexual initiation show that school attendance prevents young and unwanted sexual initiation. High school education helps in developing cognitive and interpersonal skills that foster preventive practices, allowing one to postpone sexual initiation and to evaluate the quality of a dating relationship. Also, school attendance is linked to the development of personal projects that are not anchored in traditional patterns of marriage and maternity (Geldstein & Pantelides, 2003).

In fact, adolescent and child fertility require special attention. Adolescent boys and girls tend to initiate their sexual life earlier than in previous decades, and this fact may have effects on their fertility. The possibility of dissociating sexual activity from childbearing is based on sexual education, the availability of contraceptives, and an active practice of prevention of pregnancy. These are not the usual practice in the country, and therefore there has not been a fertility decline in this age-group. Close to 15% of all births are to young mothers (below 20), a pattern of fertility that has not changed in the last decade. Motherhood of very young women (under 15, a high-risk situation both for the mother and the baby) represents 0.4% of all births. This pattern implies that the decline in fertility that the country experienced was mostly due to older women, and not to a decline in adolescent fertility (Ministerio de Salud y Acción Social, 1995).

Early motherhood, still quite high in the country, is a very risky medical and social condition. It involves higher rates of maternal and child mortality and morbidity. Since early childbirth is more common among poorer and less educated sectors, the experience of early motherhood incorporates the young mothers into the circle of intergenerational reproduction of poverty. Assuming child-rearing responsibilities narrows educational and occupational opportunities, thus compromising their own and their offspring's future.

Health services usually neglect the needs of the boys and girls in these age-groups. This involves not only the young themselves, but also those who can orient and help them in their decision-making process regarding sexual behavior—particularly parents and other family members. The type of family and household structure, as well as the sexual history of the mother, is important here. On the one hand, adolescents living in poor households with only one parent (the mother, most often) are more prone to have an early sexual initiation with no preventive behavior. Given the fact that public schools are not offering sexual education, it is up to parents and other family members who accompany the process of growing up to orient the young toward patterns of behavior that avoid risks of unwanted pregnancies, unsafe and illegal abortions, and sexually transmitted diseases. And this is clearly differentiated by social class. On the other hand, many studies have shown a strong relationship between the age when the mother had her first child and the age of the first pregnancy of her daughter (Geldstein & Pantelides, 2001).

There is a further important consideration, implying a significant social problem: children's sexual abuse and resulting pregnancies. Young 10- to 14-year-old girls' pregnancies are not, and should not be considered, indications of an early voluntary sexual initiation. There are clear indications that sexual initiation at very early ages is usually based on coercion, rape, and incestuous sexual molestation. Secrecy and "blaming the victim" are usual practices in these cases. There is little systematic research on the subject. A study that dealt with sexual initiation of adolescents in the city of Buenos Aires found that one-fourth of the women who began their sexual activity before age 15 reported being forced to do it. One-half of the women declared that they gave in to the will of the partner, but would have chosen other circumstances and a different timing.

Only one-fourth of the women declared that they entered their first sexual encounter voluntarily (Geldstein & Pantelides, 2003). Knowledge about this phenomenon and denunciation of the crimes involved should be a priority of any action program.

4. GENDER ROLES AND HOUSEHOLDS

In the prototype of the patriarchal nuclear family, gender division of labor is well entrenched: The father-husband-provider role of the adult male is coupled with the mother-housewife-caretaker role of the adult female. Children are taken care of, go to school, and eventually leave the household to establish their own families, at times maintaining living arrangements with the older generation in extended family households.

Argentine reality has always been very far from this model, and class differences have been significant since early on. In rural and urban working classes, women—especially the young and unmarried—have always been engaged in productive activities: domestic service, textile and garment workers, family helpers in farms, and so on. Urbanization and modernization implied a decline in the labor-force participation of women, and all along the 20th century there have been shifts in rates of participation and in the type of economic activities performed by women.

Furthermore, modernization and secularization in Argentina implied the establishment of free and mandatory lay public education, beginning in the 1870s. Although the spread of public schools throughout the country did not follow automatically and immediately the passage of the law, school attendance increased and illiteracy started to decline, among both men and women. By the 1930s there was practically no gender differential in illiteracy rates and in primary school enrollment. During the 1950s and 1960s women equaled men in secondary school attendance. By the 1990s, there were more women than men enrolled in higher education.

The picture is not one of total educational equality, however. Women have higher dropout rates at all levels of the educational system, and they are concentrated in certain gender-typed careers, although there is a trend toward wider choices and feminization of some professions (medicine, for example).

The link between educational attainment, labor-force participation, and family gender roles is a significant key to understanding the shifts in organization of everyday family life. Around 1950, participation rates of women reached their lowest point, but then began to grow again, slowly and steadily. For the country as a whole, 23% of adult (14 and over) women were in the labor force in 1947, 25% in 1970, and 27% in 1980, and the percentage increased significantly after that.[12] In the 1990s, with increasing unemployment and poverty for both men and women, participation rates of women continued to grow. As a result of neoliberal economic restructuring, unemployment, underemployment, and poverty affected about one-half of the population of the country, both men and women. Thus, the increase in the labor supply of women during the 1980s and 1990s does not reflect a reaction to new opportunities, but an adaptive behavior to cope with crisis.

Looking at the second half of the 20th century, the significant fact for the analysis of the family is that the increase in labor force participation of women did not involve only young, single, highly educated women, or a return to the labor force of older, mostly widowed or separated women. It also meant higher participation rates of married women, even those with small children, of all educational levels (Wainerman, 2003a). Two trends can be detected in these shifts. The increase in higher education of women had the effect of greater participation in the labor force of professional women, who tend to enter the labor force and continue working even after the process of family formation. The other trend is linked to the economic conjuncture and increase in unemployment and precariousness of job conditions. Under such circumstances of economic deterioration and crisis, women may become the sole or principal earner in poor households (Geldstein, 1999), or may enter the labor force to supplement the lost or decreased income of the primary worker(s).

The result of these trends is clear: The patriarchal nuclear family model with one male wage earner is dramatically altered, with an increase in two-earner households. Furthermore, given the increase in separation and divorce, many women are becoming the sole earner of their households.

The model of the male-provider nuclear family was undoubtedly the idealized urban family for most of the 20th century. School textbooks conveyed this naturalized image of family life, from the beginning of the 20th century up to the 1980s. Textbooks presented girls playing "mother" with their dolls, while boys played "jobs" with their trucks and tools; mothers cleaned and prepared food, while fathers worked and came back home in the evening. Only in the 1990s do textbooks incorporate other family models besides the breadwinner/homemaker nuclear one, such as women who work, and boys and girls sharing the same games (Wainerman & Heredia, 1991).

The reality of family and household responsibilities shifted considerably in the last two decades, however. Among households with female spouses aged 20 to 60 in the metropolitan area of Buenos Aires, the single male-provider household declined from 74.5% to 54.7% between 1980 and 2000, while two-provider households increased from 25.5% to 45.3%. This shift took place in households at all stages of family life, with or without small children, although it is more common among households with one coresident child than among those with more children and, as would be expected, it is more prevalent among higher educated women. Also, it is more common among the upper and lower socioeconomic strata than among the middle ones (Wainerman, 2003a).

In-depth analysis of two-earner households in the metropolitan area of Buenos Aires shows some interesting facts: In the period 1980–2000, the educational and income differentials between husband and wife in two-provider households have declined. Also, the difference in time devoted to work (whether full or part time) declined. These changes can be seen as evidence that women have been gaining in potential sources of power related to their cultural capital, their income, and the time contributed to economic maintenance of the household (Wainerman, 2003a, p. 94). However, as Wainerman's and other studies have shown, these shifts in gender-related work patterns have not been accompanied by significant shifts in the domestic realm: No major "domestic revolution" implying shared domestic responsibilities is in sight.[13]

Household Size and Composition

Trends in marriage patterns, fertility behavior, and material conditions affect the ways in which people live together, that is, the size and composition of households. The type of household is further affected by public policy regarding housing, insofar as housing shortages bring about doubling or extended household arrangements. Although census definitions of households have shifted over the years, it is clear that the average size of households in Argentina has been decreasing since the end of the 19th century. From close to six members in 1869, it decreased to 4.3 members in 1947. Since then, the decrease has continued slowly but steadily. In 1980 it was 3.86 persons per household, and 3.57 in 2001 (General Household Survey, 2003).

Household size is strongly and systematically associated with income level and urbanization. Urban households are smaller than rural households on average, and their size declines faster, implying that the rural-urban differential is increasing. Likewise, trend data indicate a growing income differential: Low-income households diminish their average size at a slower rate than high-income households, and some even increase their size.

The sharp contrasts in household size can be seen when comparing the city of Buenos Aires—capital of the country, with the highest income per capita—with an average of 2.7 persons per household in 2001, with a poor and much more rural province, Santiago del Estero, with an average of 4.49 members per household. In fact, for the whole country, poor households have on the average 0.8 more members than the rest (General Household Survey, 2003).

Table 18.1 presents data on average household size by income level in the metropolitan area of Buenos Aires.[14] The difference in average size is quite large: 2.5 members more in the average low-income household than in the highest one in 2003. While the average size of the lowest quintile increased 21% in the last 20 years, the households of the higher income groups decreased their average size by 16%.

At first sight, differences in household size may seem to be associated with fertility rates: Larger households involve families producing more children, but the issue is much more complex, insofar as understanding household size implies looking into household composition—not an easy matter. Normatively, households are made up of members related by kinship ties, although their composition changes according to family dynamics and the transitions in the life course of their members. At any specific point in time, household composition is the result of all the family-related processes that occurred in the past. Yet these processes are hidden and masked by the static way of collecting household data in surveys and census forms.

Household composition can be classified in the following way (adapted from Torrado, 2003):

Table 18.1 Average Household Size by Income Level Metropolitan Area of Buenos Aires, 1980–2003

Year	Average No. of Members	Income Level[a]	
		Quintile 1	*Quintile 5*
1980[a]	3.31	4.04	2.84
1990[a]	3.29	4.33	2.37
2003[b]	3.31	4.89	2.36

SOURCE: General Household Survey (2003).

a. October.
b. May.

I. Single person
II. Conjugal household
   A. Nuclear household
      1. Couple with no children
      2. Lone parent with children
      3. Couple with children
   B. Extended (nuclear plus other relatives)
   C. Composed (nuclear or extended plus nonkin members)
III. Nonconjugal nuclear composition (kin-based or not)

This static classification hides histories of divorce, new conjugal couples, and non-coresidential parenthood. It also assumes that coresidential patterns involve strong links of shared domesticity, budgets, and responsibilities, but this is increasingly called into question, as adult family responsibilities extend to kin that do not live together—both of the older and the younger generations.

The incidence of single-person households is on the increase in the country. In the period 1980–2001, the rate of single-person households grew from 10% to 15% (General Household Survey, 2003). Single-person households are more prevalent in highly urbanized and relatively more developed areas, as well as in higher income groups. In the city of Buenos Aires, this category of household represented 15.6% in 1980, and grew to 22.4% of households in 1991. In 2001 single-person households represented 26.2% of the households of the city. This increase reflects in part the aging process, the differential life expectancy of men and women, and the gender difference (among younger people) in socially accepted living arrangements. While in 1947 83% of single persons living alone in Argentina were men, in 1991 the comparable percentage was 45% (Torrado, 2003, p. 437). Young men living alone was a common feature of immigration during the first half of the 20th century. By 1947 60% of men living alone were under 45, and their percentage decreased to 18% in 1991. It is older women who make up the largest change in single-person households: In 1991 46% of single-person households were women over 45.

The increase in the number of single-person households in urban areas reflects in part the process of aging of the population, and will probably continue to increase. It also reflects other incipient cultural and social trends: a growing dissociation between leaving the parental household and establishing a conjugal union on the part of the young and increasing divorce rates, which mean that one of the partners (mostly the male) establishes a new household by himself. Traditionally in urban areas the young left the parental home when marrying or starting a consensual union; nowadays the young look for their autonomy independently from the process of family formation. This trend is incipient and affects only upper income sectors, given the costs involved in living alone. It is still more prevalent among young men than among young women.[15]

Extended three-generation households have been the ideal type of the patriarchal family based on intergenerational transmission of power and wealth. It was also the way in which elderly widows and widowers were taken care of by their children. Nevertheless, in spite of the continuing aging process of Argentina,[16] the proportion of extended households represented about 20% of households in the last decades.

The most common living arrangement is the nuclear household. Within the category of nuclear households, there has been a slight increase in the proportion of "incomplete nuclear" households, which in most cases consist of a woman and her children (84% of the "lone parent with children" category in 2001 are women). The incidence of this type of household has grown more significant among economically disadvantaged sectors, as Table 18.2 shows for the metropolitan area of Buenos Aires. Its existence tends to compound other difficulties these social

Table 18.2   Types of Household, Argentina (1991/2001)

Types of Household	1991	2001
Single-person	13.3	15.0
Conjugal	85.5	84.2
• Nuclear	64.1	63.2
• Couple with no children	12.8	12.2
• Lone parent with children	8.9	10.2
• Couple with children	42.3	40.8
• Extended (nuclear plus other relatives)	19.3	19.6
• Composed (nuclear or extended plus nonkin members)	2.2	1.4
Nonconjugal nuclear composition (kin-based or not)	1.1	0.8

SOURCE: National Census (1991, 2001).

groups face. If women are the only financial and effective pillars in their families, and do not have any further assistance (income supplementation, childcare and school support, among others), they have to carry a double (or even triple) responsibility: being in charge of economic support, domestic activities, and the emotional care of their children. This is a situation that involves an excessive load for the woman and often exposes her and her children to high risk.

Usually, census and survey data provide information about female-headed households, and there is an implicit assumption on the part of those who analyze this information that they correspond to "incomplete nuclear" ones, but it is important to realize that, in line with the overdue revision of the category *head of household* (Arriagada, 2001), female heads can be in all categories of households, and not only among the single-parent incomplete nuclear one. The incidence of female-headed households has increased in the country over time: 14.1% in 1947, 19.2% in 1980, and 27.7% in 2001 (INDEC, 1991, 2001).

Female-headed household exist in all social strata, reflecting, however, different social processes. Increased education for women, increased labor-force participation, and increased divorce and separation rates during the second half of the 20th century are clearly linked to this relatively new pattern of household composition, but the conditions are different for different social strata. For the higher income sectors, it is a result of higher divorce rates and the process of aging (older women living alone). However, the effects of macroeconomic policies and the provision of social services are felt by lower income groups: regressive income distribution policies since the 1976 dictatorship. Neoliberal adjustment policies in the 1980s and especially during the 1990s implied increased unemployment and underemployment of working-class males, a decline in job security for all, and a crisis in the provision of social services. The strain on households is unmistakable, leading to increased numbers of women who work to support their children. In fact, as Geldstein (1994) shows, the number of poor women who have become the main provider for their households is larger than the number of female heads of households.

There are many households with unemployed males where women are the providers but not recognized as heads. Among the poorest or indigent sectors of the population (where the proportion is the highest), female-headed households are an indication of the feminization of poverty. Given the pattern of gender discrimination in the labor force and the domestic burden on women, the double/triple responsibility of poor women is both socially nonviable and morally incorrect. Public policies have not sufficiently addressed this issue, and the longer-term negative effect on the women and their children of this pattern of living together has not been recognized.

As a counterpoint to the increase in female-headed households, one type of household that is growing very fast, having started from almost zero in statistical terms, is single-parent male-headed households (2.9% of households in the country in 2001). Fathers who raise their children is a new phenomenon, linked to transformations in masculinity. In this case, however, they tend to be middle- and upper-income households, and thus there can be household help and the risks referred to previously are not visible. Longer-term effects of children being raised in different types of households have not been analyzed yet.

Furthermore, with the rising instability of conjugal unions and patterns of remarriage and formation of new unions, there is a large increase in reassembled households—those made up of a (new) couple and children from previous unions. Current statistical data-gathering techniques, however, are not prepared to sort out different types of family processes in household formation. They capture synchronic data, not the history of family formation behind it, and thus they appear under the complete nuclear or extended categories. Such households—and the family links that are created by the new

unions—are still not framed within clear legal doctrine, and the relationships they produce among their members (beyond the traditional image of the steprelative) have not yet been typified legally, or in terms of social norms and habits.

Finally, although only a small percentage of the population, the increasing display of choice of sexual orientation implies the slow emergence and recognition of same-sex couples, with or without children, in a new same-sex nuclear family form.[17] The government of the city of Buenos Aires recognized in 2003 the civil union of homosexual couples, recognizing rights and mutual obligations.

There is a clear interclass difference in the prevalence of one or another form of household, especially in the case of single-person and extended households. Single-person households are a choice for the upper strata and are almost nonviable among the poorest sectors of society. Extended and composed households, that is, living arrangements that extend beyond the nuclear family to include three generations or other kin members, are more frequent among the poorest strata, as shown in Table 18.3.

6 & 7. STRESSES, DIVORCE, AND SEPARATION

Increase in divorce and separation has been well-documented in Argentina. The proportion of people (aged 14 and older) found to be separated or divorced in each of the censuses grew from 0.6% in 1960 to 3.9% in 1991 and 4.8% in 2001. As mentioned previously, divorce was legalized only in 1986. People moved to divorce (and then remarry) to legalize their actual marital situation, but then it leveled off. In the city of Buenos Aires during the 1990s, there were about 3.4 divorces for each 10 marriages (Gobierno de Buenos Aires, 2000).

Table 18.3 Types of Urban Households by Level of Household Income (Metropolitan Area of Buenos Aires, 1980–2003)

Year	Quintile	Total	Single Person	Couple (With Children/No Children)	Lone Parent With Children	Extended/ Composed
1980[a]	1 (20% poorest)	100.0	3.6	70.4	7.3	18.7
	5 (20% richest)	100.0	15.3	63.1	7.5	14.1
1990[a]	1 (20% poorest)	100.0	2.4	72.4	6.8	18.7
	5 (20% richest)	100.0	25.3	57.0	10.4	14.1
2003[b]	1 (20% poorest)	100.0	5.3	53.5	13.6	18.4
	5 (20% richest)	100.0	28.8	52.0	11.4	7.8

SOURCE: General Household Survey (2003).

a. October.
b. May.

The increase in divorce rates and separations should be examined in the light of complex sociocultural processes linked to individuation. The spread of modern values of personal autonomy, free choice of a partner based on romantic love, and the growing social expectation of being able to act on one's wishes and feelings—all these have their counterpart in the freedom to sever ties when there is no more love, when the costs of maintaining a conflictful relationship exceed those of severing the conjugal bond. Up until recent decades, separation carried a strong social stigma for women, who were blamed for the failure of their marriages. Married status and motherhood were the natural condition of decent women. Nowadays changes in the cultural models that govern conjugal relationships toward greater gender equity involve greater freedom to choose. Furthermore, increasing financial autonomy through their incorporation into the labor market provides women with the possibility of choosing to exit unsatisfying (and at times even violent) marriages.

How are these changes perceived and evaluated by the population? How do they affect views about the family? A recent study analyzing data of two waves of the World Value Survey (1983, 1995) containing information about people's family values and measures of attitudes toward marriage, childrearing, divorce, and abortion in Argentina (the sample covered the urbanized central portion of the country) are illustrative. Between 1983 and 1995, there has been a significant increase in the approval of divorce, going from 4.3 to 5.5 on a 1-to-10 scale. There is a high endorsement of the institution of marriage in general, and its benefits for children in particular. In fact, Argentineans have become more persuaded about the validity of the institution of marriage. There has also been a significant increase in the approval of women wanting to have and raise a child without a stable partner, going from 26% to 60%, and a wider acceptance of abortion (from 2.6 to 3.2 on a 1-to-10 scale). The majority still think—many more strongly than before—that marriage is not an outdated institution, that children are better off when raised by both parents, and that women need to have children to be fulfilled (Binstock & Cerrutti, 2002).

Furthermore, the patterns of attitudinal change have not been the same among men and women. The authors find that

women have led a trend of increased emphasis on individual freedom and tolerance in the family arena. Men seem to have accompanied more slowly this increase and they have also strengthened their conformity with a set of long-established values, such as marriage and traditional gender roles.

Thus, they conclude that

as women are changing their roles outside and within the family, men might feel threatened by their relative lack of power (inside and outside of marriage), responding to that by expressing a desire for family patterns of the past that provided men with greater status. (Binstock & Cerrutti, 2002, p. 19)

11. SPECIAL TOPIC: THE FAMILY IN THE POLITICS OF MEMORY

Family ties and the image of the family have in contemporary Argentina a very special and unique place since the military dictatorship and state terrorism (1976–1983), its violations of human rights, and the politics of the human rights movement. The factual story of the link between family ties and human rights is perhaps well-known in the international human rights community, but much less so in the international community of research on the family.

In the midst of deep political conflict and widespread political violence, a military coup took place in Argentina in March 1976. The military government defined itself as the savior of the nation, bringing back peace and order where chaos and subversion were destroying "natural" Argentine values and

institutions.[18] To recapture these values, it was mandatory to protect the nation, the family, and the people from the dangers of subversion. The military were to lead a "Process of National Reorganization," calling "fathers, mothers and healthy children of the country" to "take care of your homes. Keep your security. Do not accept generously the ideas implanted in the young minds by international subversive experts. . . . The security and peace of the people are to be built inside homes and schools" (La Nación, June 19, 1976, quoted by Filc, 1997).

The military who took power in Argentina in 1976 used (and abused) reference to the family. The family, as the "basic cell" of society, and the nation, understood as a "grand family," are part of an image that was read in different and even contradictory ways, but they went much further than metaphor and discourse; they intervened violently in the privacy and intimacy of family life in Argentina.

The reference to the traditional family was paramount in the framing of the military coup. First, it defined society as an organism constituted by cells (families). In this way, it linked social structure to its biological origin, naturalizing family roles and values. There was only one way, the "natural" way, in which Argentine society could be organized. Thus, the military developed a massive campaign to consolidate family unity, justified because of the place of the family in the natural social order. Furthermore, family ties were defined as "undissolvable," and the rights of parents over their children as "unalienable." Since the metaphor of the family was used for the nation as a whole, the Father-State had unalienable rights over the moral and physical fate of its citizens. The image of the nation as the "Grand Argentine Family" implied that only the "good" children-citizens were truly Argentine, while official discourse represented citizens as immature children needing a strong father.

In such discourse, paternal authority was paramount. Sons and daughters were expected to follow the moral duties of obedience. There was no room for citizens with rights, for human beings with personal autonomy. In that "natural" rather than social or cultural world, the danger of evil or of illness comes always from the outside—some extraneous body that invades and infects. And to reestablish the natural equilibrium, it becomes necessary to surgically intervene, to extract and destroy the infected social tissues. The military regime thus becomes the protective father who will take upon himself the arduous responsibility of cleaning and protecting his family, helped by other "minor" parents, in charge of controlling and disciplining rebellious adolescents. State-sponsored advertisements on TV would ask, "Do you know where your child is now?"—urging parents to reproduce *ad infinitum* the policing and controlling that the military were carrying out.

The image of the family as the "cell" of the nation implied that parents had to protect the family-cell from outside penetration, since a virus or infection that invades a single cell can expand itself through contagion into the whole body. Children and youth represented the weak boundaries of the national-family body, and by contact with the outside, then could bring the infection into the social body. The only way to defend the nation, then, was to confront the enemy at the point of entry: the link between the young and their families. At this point, if the Father-State is to protect the nation, it has to look inside the family. In that way, the distinction between public life and private family disappears.

The defense of the traditional patriarchal family was a clear and explicit policy of the government (Filc, 1997), but, at the same time, the military implemented a systematic policy of clandestine repression that directly affected thousands of families. The policy included massive kidnappings of people from their own homes, to then be tortured and *disappeared*, as the basic policy to handle political conflict and to wipe out the existing armed political groups (Calveiro, 1998). Young children were also kidnapped with their parents, and pregnant young women were kept alive until giving birth. With changed identities, the children were appropriated by military personnel and others linked to their ranks. Estimates of disappearances vary, with figures of up to 30,000; estimates of surviving kidnapped children with false identities reach 500 (of which about 80 cases have been solved).

In 1976 relatives of detained and disappeared persons organized themselves in the Familiares de Detenidos y Desaparecidos por Razones Políticas (Relatives of Detained and Disappeared for Political Reasons). April 1977 marked the initial meetings of what later became the emblem of the human rights movement, the Madres de Plaza de Mayo (Mothers of Plaza de Mayo). In November of that same year, the Asociación de Abuelas de Plaza de Mayo (Association of Grandmothers of Plaza de Mayo) was created.

Why should the denunciation and demands of the human rights movement be couched in kinship terms? In the political context of dictatorship, repression, and censorship, political organizations and labor unions were suspended. The use that the dictatorial discourse made of the family as the natural unit of social organization had its mirror image in part of the human rights movement—the denunciation and protest of relatives was, in fact, the only one that could be voiced. After all, it was a mother searching for her child. . . .

Dictatorship signaled parents with the final responsibility to prevent their children from becoming subversives. When parents of disappeared people approached the government asking about the fate of their children, the answer was an accusation: They did not know what their children were doing because they were not exerting adequate parental authority; if young people became "subversives," it was because of deficiencies in their upbringing.

Thus, the paradox in the Argentine military regime of 1976–1983 (with similarities to the other military regimes of the Southern Cone at that time) was that the language and the image of the family were the central metaphor of the military government, but also the central image of the discourse and practices of the human rights movement. What they were denouncing were crimes against the family, projecting at the same time an image of the "good child" and of "normal" family life. The paradigmatic image is that of the Mother, symbolized by the Madres de Plaza de Mayo, with their diapers-headscarves, the mother who leaves her "natural" private realm of family life to invade the public sphere in search of her kidnapped-disappeared child. In parallel with the figure of Antigone in Greek tragedy, the Mother challenges the powerful, expressing family mandates linked to caring and protecting. Relatives, Mothers, and Grandmothers in the 1970s, H.I.J.O.S (Children of the Disappeared) 20 years later, and Hermanos (Siblings) afterward are the organizations that keep active their demands for truth, justice, and memory. What is significant here is that they enter the public sphere not as metaphors or symbolic images of family ties, but grounded in actual kin relations.

Both sides talked about families, about close links, although with different orientations. For one, the family was control and authority, covered up in terms of protection against threats and evil. For others, the private and personalized family tie justified and motivated public action, with the purpose of subverting the image of the "bad family" that the military wanted to convey regarding the families of the victims. The disappeared and the imprisoned were presented by their relatives as exemplary children, good students, and members of families living in

harmony, in sum, as ideal or "normal." In addition, the family loss acted to push private ties and feelings into the public sphere, breaking drastically the boundaries between private life and the public realm.

This public emergence of family ties in political life is significant beyond its own presence. It implies a reconceptualization of the relationship between private and public life. In the image that the human rights movement conveys to society, the family link to the victim is the basic justification and legitimacy for action. For the justice system, it is actually the only one. Only relatives are considered "affected" in the demands for reparation—personalized and individualized. However, this public and political familism has some weaknesses in terms of its political and cultural impact. The Mothers may have generalized their maternity, with the slogan that all the disappeared are the children of all the Mothers, but at the same time, and as an effect of this understanding of the notion of the family, a distance is created in public mobilization between those who are the carriers of "truth"—of personal and private suffering—and those who mobilize politically for the same cause but presumably with other motives, which are not seen as equally transparent and legitimate. It is as if in the public realm of debate, participation is not equal but stratified according to the public exposure of the family tie—a process that may paradoxically imply new conflicts and tensions in the process of democratization and in the promotion of equality.

The Search of the Abuelas: DNA Testing and Recovered Identities

As indicated previously, the Argentine case of political repression is unique in more than one way. The military kidnapped and "disappeared" thousands of people. In many cases, children were kidnapped with their parents. In other cases, young pregnant women were also abducted. At times, abducted children were returned to their relatives, often their grandparents, but not always. This led to a double search on the part of relatives of the kidnapped: searching for the young adults and at the same time searching for the children. The Abuelas de Plaza de Mayo began their organization and the elaboration of their strategy when, in late 1977, several women realized (meeting each other in unending visits to police stations, governmental offices, churches, and other organizations) that each case was not unique, that besides their missing children, there were also grandchildren to look for. At the same time, rumors started that in clandestine detention centers, pregnant women were kept alive until delivery to then disappear, while their newborn babies were taken away.

What followed was the realization that these children were becoming "war trophies," appropriated and illegally adopted by the kidnappers themselves or given away to others—mostly people related to the repressive apparatus. When it became clear that not all abducted children were killed, and that many were living with changed identities, the Grandmothers moved in several directions: looking for hints about where they could be and looking for international support to prepare for the hoped-for situation where an abducted child could recover his or her identity. For that, the international scientific community advanced thorough DNA testing techniques: It was necessary to elaborate genetic tests based on second- or third-degree kinship, since biological parents had disappeared, and tests had to be made on grandparents, uncles, and aunts. Immediately after the transition to a constitutional government in 1983, moves were made to establish a National Genetic Bank, where relatives of disappeared children could leave their genetic material for eventual future tests. In 1992 the National Committee of the Right to Identity was established, creating the National Genetic

Bank. As of 2003, 75 kidnapped children had recovered their legal identity.[19]

After 25 years, the abducted children and those born in captivity are now young adults in their 20s. Thus, the constant campaigns of *Abuelas* are geared to young people. There are publicity campaigns, including one with the message, "If you have doubts about your identity, contact the *Abuelas*." Each case is full of tension, full of emotion, and full of ethical and moral dilemmas. Let us illustrate this with a case that was in the news in 2003.

A young 27-year-old man raised by a family as their biological son began to have doubts about his biological identity (as many adolescents do). "I was always looking for a physical resemblance with my parents, since I am physically very different from them. I never found a convincing answer, and thus my hunches grew" (*Página 12* [*Buenos Aires*], May 10, 2003). In conversations with his fiancée, he finally decided to approach CONADI. After genetic testing, it was confirmed that he was the son of disappeared parents, and his biological identity was established. The day he received the official information, conveyed by the justice system, his reaction was, "Now I will be ready to have my own children." In 1976 a military officer appropriated the baby when his mother was killed. The military officer promised to give away the child to a colleague. When the friend decided that he did not want the child, the officer gave him away to the woman who worked for his family as a domestic helper. The child was raised normally in this working-class family. Thus, in this case—differently from many others—the recovery of identity did not entail a major conflict with the "parents," since they were not the perpetrators.[20]

Identity restitution is a complex legal, psychological, scientific, and social intervention. The justice system is, at the end, the final arbiter in charge of solving the conflicts and tensions involved. There are at least two parts to each case: the crime of kidnapping and changing identity committed by the military (or others), and the issue of personal identity of the child/young adult. Involved are also the claims of the family of the disappeared and their right to truth, and of society as a whole in maintaining the public interest in truth and justice. In a very controversial case in 2003, the Supreme Court ruled that a young woman, the kidnapped daughter of disappeared parents, had the right *not* to submit herself to DNA testing to determine her biological identity. The crime of the appropriators (the "parents" who raised her) is being prosecuted, but the young woman does not give her consent to the blood test, justifying this stand by the fact that it may damage the defense of her "father." She affirms that she will submit to the test by her own free will, when the case against her "father" is closed. The societal reaction—voiced by relatives of the disappeared and by the human rights movement—was, as expected, very critical of the Supreme Court decision.[21]

The social and cultural impact of the issue of restitution of identity is quite significant, although yet difficult to gauge. There is clearly widespread societal support for the *Abuelas* and for the restitution of identity. The Genetic Bank and DNA testing are seen as the proper means to proceed. This process involves a belief that the final test of truth lies in DNA testing, in genetics, in biology, and in blood. Undoubtedly, this has been a major development, and the Argentine society welcomes it.

However, there is here a paradox. This biologization of proof comes at a time when there are also major developments in assisted reproductive techniques, which imply stressing blood (or genetic) belonging, but parenthood and family are cultural and social ties. How will society and law systems deal with the tensions between these two normative clues? Undoubtedly, Argentine society—perhaps even world society—faces the need to deal with the ethical issues in the application of reproductive technologies, norms regarding adoption, and the right of children to know their lineage or filiations (introduced in the international convention on the rights of children), and advances in medicine that stress genetic dispositions, among other issues. Because of the cultural and political significance of the recuperation of stolen identity that Argentina has been facing during the last 25 years, it may be a crucial case to see how the issue of the link between biology and culture in the family is being approached.

NOTES

1. The conceptual framework behind the ideas presented in this paper is to be found in Jelin (1998).

2. Figures for 1991 indicate a rate of 36%, but because of changes in measurement techniques, figures are not totally comparable (Wainerman, 2003a, p. 60).

3. A study of a border area between Argentina and Brazil (Grimson, 2003) traced marriage patterns between two adjoining cities (Paso de los Libres in Argentina and Uruguayana in Brazil). Intermarriage was higher in the second decade of the 20th century, and then it began to decline consistently. Also, it shows that it is Brazilian women who marry Argentine males, rather than the opposite.

4. An indicator in the same direction is the sustained increase in "extra-marital" births: In 1990 37% of births were to parents not legally married; the percentage increased to 58% in 2000 (Estadísticas Vitales, Información Básica 1990, serie 4, No. 34; Estadísticas Vitales, Información Básica 2000, Serie 5, No. 44, Ministerio de Salud).

5. Changes in legislation undoubtedly affect statistical information. Only in 1986 did divorce (and the legal capacity to remarry) become legal in Argentina. Before the law, *de facto* separations and new conjugal bonds did not involve marriage but rather consensual unions. The law was followed by 5 years in which there was a boom in divorces and a sharp increase of marriage rates, involving mostly the legalization of *de facto* conditions.

6. The concern about low fertility, especially among modern middle classes, was acute among nationalist Catholic intellectuals in the 1930s and 1940s. They saw the threat coming from the future burden of an aging population and the fear of a loss of the supremacy of the white population. The remedy would come through higher fertility among the "more fortunate" sections of the population, and through a regulated social policy geared to population growth among the poorer sectors of society. Torrado (2003, pp. 144–153) provides a lucid presentation of these arguments.

7. In 1895 the rate was seven children per woman; in 1914 it declined to 5.3, reaching 3.2 in 1947 and leveling off at that rate until 1980 (Torrado, 2003).

8. The reasons women gave for having that child range from realizing the pregnancy too late for an abortion to fears of dying and leaving orphaned children. Actually, maternal death due to induced abortion is extremely high in the country. In 1993 it was estimated that 29% of maternal deaths in the country were due to complications from induced abortions (Ministerio de Salud y Acción Social, 1995).

9. The International Conference of Population and Development (Cairo, 1994) recognized and incorporated sexual and reproductive rights in the international agenda. The IV International Conference on Women (Beijing, 1995) extended the proposals to guarantee these rights.

10. These prohibitions affected provision of reproductive health services in public health institutions, which cover approximately 90% of the population of the country. Only the top 10% of the population by income relies on private medicine.

11. Argentina has not participated in international fertility surveys. Neither has the government promoted or carried out national surveys dealing with reproductive behavior, thus the sparsity of systematic information on the subject.

12. Figures for 1991 indicate a rate of 36%, but because of changes in measurement techniques, figures are not totally comparable (Wainerman, 2003a, p. 60).

13. Furthermore, studies based on separate interviews of men and women indicate that men tend to report more shared responsibilities in household tasks than women, mostly through "overestimating" their own participation. Women tend to report more often their sole responsibility and even loneliness in their domestic chores (Wainerman, 2003b).

14. The metropolitan area of Buenos Aires includes the city of Buenos Aires and surrounding districts. Its population of about 12 million people represents 32% of the total population of the country.

15. Among the young, single-person households are mostly of single men; in adulthood, divorced men prevail; among the older ones, it is widowed women (Torrado, 2003).

16. The Argentine population is, in comparative terms, relatively aged. In 2001 9.9% of the country's population was 65 and over, reaching 17.2% of the population of the city of Buenos Aires.

17. As an indicator of changes toward the recognition of homosexual couples, recent court decisions regarding child tenure and visiting rights recognized that maternal or paternal homosexual living arrangements are not an impediment for child tenure, since they do not constitute a moral danger or risk

(*Página 12* [Buenos Aires], July 23, 2002 and August 26, 2003). That such situations require judicial intervention (and that judges not always accept homosexuality as normal) is a clear indication of the long way to go in such matters.

18. The Argentine military coup and military government was not an isolated phenomenon in the region. Brazil was governed by a military dictatorship since 1964, Uruguay and Chile had their military coups in 1973, and Paraguay and Bolivia also experienced dictatorship and military coups. In the early 1970s, armed guerrilla movements existed in the region. It was also a time of heightened Cold War tensions and of the prevalence of the Doctrine of National Security.

19. www.abuelas.org.ar.

20. Only a couple of months after the identity recovery, a new dramatic event took place. The forensic anthropology team was working on a common grave in the Cemetery of San Vicente in the city of Córdoba, where many bodies of disappeared persons had been found. DNA testing allowed the identification of the body of Horacio Pietragalla, Horacio Jr.'s father, and he recovered the remains of his biological father (*Página 12* [Buenos Aires], August 28, 2003).

21. In another recent case, a young man found out while surfing the Internet that he was the son of a disappeared person and that his "father" was a perpetrator.

REFERENCES

Arriagada, I. (2001). *Familias Latinoamericanas, diagnóstico y políticas públicas en los inicios del nuevo siglo*. Serie Políticas Sociales No. 57. Santiago: Naciones Unidas, División de Desarrollo Social, CEPAL-ECLAC.

Binstock, G. P. (2003, November). *Transformaciones en la formación de la familia: Evidencias de la Encuesta Anual de Hogares de la Ciudad de Buenos Aires*. Paper presented at the VII Jornadas Argentinas de Estudios de Población, Tucumán.

Binstock, G. P., & Cerrutti, M. (2002, May). *Changing attitudes towards the family in Argentina, 1980–1995*. Paper presented at the Annual Meeting of the Population Association of America, Atlanta.

Calveiro, P. (1998). *Poder y desaparición. Los campos de concentración en Argentina*. Buenos Aires: Colihue.

CEPAL. (2001). *Panorama social de América Latina 2000–2001*. Santiago: Author.

Checa, S., & Rosemberg. M. (1996). *Aborto hospitalizado. Una cuestión de derechos reproductivos, un problema de salud pública*. Buenos Aires: El Cielo por Asalto.

Cicerchia, R. (1994). Familia: La historia de una idea. Los desórdenes domésticos de la plebe urbana porteña, Buenos Aires, 1776–1850. In C. Wainerman (Ed.), *Vivir en familia*. Buenos Aires: UNICEF-Losada.

Filc, J. (1997). *Entre el parentesco y la política. Familia y dictadura, 1976–1983*. Buenos Aires: Biblos.

Geldstein, R. (1994). Familias con liderazgo femenino en sectores populares de Buenos Aires. In C. Wainerman (Ed.), *Vivir en familia*. Buenos Aires: UNICEF/Losada.

Geldstein, R. (1999). *Los roles de género en la crisis: Mujeres como principal sostén económicodel hogar*. Cuaderno del Cenep, número 50. Buenos Aires: CENEP.

Geldstein, R., & Pantelides, E. A. (2001). Riesgo reproductivo en la adolescencia. Desigualdad y asimetría de género. *Cuadernos de UNICEF 8*. Buenos Aires: UNICEF.

Geldstein, R., & Pantelides, E. A. (2003). Coerción, consentimiento y deseo en la "primera vez." In S. Checa (Ed.), *Genero, Sexualidad y Derechos Reproductivos.* Buenos Aires: Editorial Paidós.

General Household Survey (Encuesta Permanente de Hogares). (2003, May). INDEC (Instituto National de Estadística y Censos).

Gobierno de Buenos Aires Secretaria de Hacienda y Finanzas, Dirección General de Estadística y Censos. (2000). *Anuario Estadístico de la Ciudad Autónoma de Buenos Aires 2000.*

Grimson, A. (2003). *La nación en sus límites. Contrabandistas y exiliados en la frontera Argentina-Brasil.* Buenos Aires: Gedisa.

Jelin, E. (1998). *Pan y afectos. La transformación de las familias.* Buenos Aires: Fondo de Cultura Económica.

Jelin, E., & Feijoó, M. C. (1980). *Trabajo y familia en el ciclo de vida femenino: el caso de los sectores populares de Buenos Aires.* Buenos Aires: Estudios Cedes.

Llovet, J. J. (1984). *Servicios de salud y sectores populares. Los años del Proceso.* Buenos Aires: Estudios Cedes.

Ministerio de Salud y Acción Social (1995). *Estadisticas vitals. Información básica 1990.* Buenos Aires: Author.

National Census (*Censo Nacional de Población y Vivienda).* (1991, 2001). INDEC (Instituto National de Estadística y Censos).

Otero, H. (1990). Una visión crítica de la endogamia: Reflexiones a partir de una reconstrucción de familias francesas (Tandil, 1850–1914). *Estudios Migratorios Latinoamericanos, 5*(15–16), 343–378.

Página 12. (23/7/2002, 26/8/2003, 28/8/2003, 10/5/2003). Buenos Aires: Argentina.

Pantelides, A. (1989). *La fecundidad argentina desde mediados del siglo XX.* In *Cuaderno del CENEP,* número 41, Buenos Aires: CENEP.

Ramos, S. (1984). *Las relaciones de parentesco y de ayuda mutua en los sectores populares urbanos.* Buenos Aires: Estudios Cedes.

Ramos, S., et al. (2001). *Los médicos frente a la anticoncepción y el aborto, ¿una transición ideológica?* Buenos Aires: CEDES.

Torrado, S. (1993). *Procreación en Argentina. Hechos e ideas.* Buenos Aires: Ediciones de la Flor.

Torrado, S. (2003). *Historia de la familia en la Argentina moderna (1870–2000).* Buenos Aires: Ediciones de la Flor.

Wainerman, C. (2003a). La reestructuración de las fronteras de género. In C. Wainerman (Ed.), *Familia, trabajo y género. Un mundo de nuevas relaciones.* Buenos Aires: UNICEF—Fondo de Cultura Económica.

Wainerman, C. (2003b). Padres y maridos. Los varones en la familia. In C. Wainerman (Ed.), *Familia, trabajo y género. Un mundo de nuevas relaciones.* Buenos Aires: UNICEF—Fondo de Cultura Económica.

Wainerman, C., & Heredia, M. (1991). *¿Mamá amasa la masa? Cien años de los libros de lectura de la escuela primaria.* Buenos Aires: Universidad de Belgrano.

World Value Survey. (1983, 1995). Information retrieved from http://www.worldvaluesurvey.org/.

CHAPTER 19

Families in Cuba: From Colonialism to Revolution

ANNE R. ROSCHELLE

MAURA I. TORO-MORN

ELISA FACIO

1 & 10. CUBA AND CUBANS: HISTORY AND POLITICS

Government, Demographics, and History

Cuba is an archipelago made up of more than 1,600 keys and small islands. The two most important islands in the archipelago are Cuba itself and the Isle of Youth, known until 1978 as the Isle of Pines. The Cuban archipelago is located very close to the Tropic of Cancer in the Caribbean Sea at the entrance to the Gulf of Mexico. The countries closest to Cuba are Haiti and the Dominican Republic 77 km to the east, Jamaica 140 km to the south, the United States 180 km to the north, and Mexico 210 km to the west. The entire archipelago extends over an area of approximately 111,000 sq km. The main island of Cuba is 1,200 km long and ranges from 32 km in width at the narrowest point to 190 km at its widest (Navarro, 2000).

In fact, Cuba is the largest island in the Caribbean (Buckman, 2003). The country is divided into 14 provinces and 169 municipalities (Navarro, 2000).

In 2002 Cuba reported a population of 11 million inhabitants. Seventy percent of the population lives in urban centers, and 30% in rural areas. Its capital city, Havana, has an estimated population of 2.4 million inhabitants (Buckman, 2002). Havana is also the center of political, scientific, and administrative life in Cuba. The demographic density of Cuba is 99 inhabitants per sq km, and there are 10 cities whose population exceeds 10,000 (Navarro, 2000). The official language of the country is Spanish, and its main religion is Catholicism, a vestige of Spanish colonialism. Many Cubans also practice Santeria—an African-based religion, introduced during the era of slavery. However, religion was discouraged by Castro's revolutionary government and is therefore not as central to Cuban life as it is to other Latin American countries.

Although Cuba is considered to be a developing country, a number of demographic measures place it alongside many industrialized countries in the world. For example, Cuba ranks among the most educated nations in the world, with a literacy rate of 96%. There is one teacher for every 42 inhabitants, and 500,000 university-trained professionals. Life expectancy hovers around 74 years for males and 79 years for females. At the turn of the 21st century, the fertility rate was 12 births per 1,000, while the death rate was 7.35 deaths per 1,000. The infant mortality rate hovered around 7.27 per 1,000 live births. Like many industrialized countries, the fecundity rates of Cuban women have dropped significantly to 1.44 children per woman, and the population is graying with 10% of the population over 65 years of age. Cuba is one of the most racially diverse countries in the hemisphere. Approximately 66% of Cubans are white, 12% are of African descent, 21.9% are multiracial, and 0.1% are of Asian descent (Navarro, 2000).

Cuban Families Under Colonial Rule

Spanish Colonial Rule

The colonization of Cuba by Spain was a significant event that shaped the culture and major social institutions of the country. Columbus arrived at the coast of Cuba on October 27, 1492. However, Cuba remained virtually ignored until 1510 when Diego Velázquez arrived on the southern coast of Cuba's easternmost region, and the occupation began in earnest. The Spanish conquistadors under Velázquez were particularly brutal to the indigenous population, so unlike other regions of South and Central America, the Indians had very little impact on the formation of Cuban culture. The original inhabitants of the island of Cuba were the Tainos, Siboneyes or Ciboneyes, and Guanajatabeyes. These indigenous people were quickly wiped out by the exceedingly violent Spanish conquest, disease, and the loss of their socioeconomic way of life. Since the original inhabitants of the island had not advanced beyond the Stone Age, there is no written record of their culture. As a result there is very little knowledge of Taino, Siboneye, or Guanajatabeye family life. We do know that the Tainos are descendants of the Aruacos of South America, originating from the basin of the Orinoco river in Venezuela. Less is known about the origins of the Siboneyes or Guanajatabeyes. These two groups were less developed than the Tainos, who carved and polished stone, cultivated the land, and generally had a higher level of social organization than the other two groups. Evidence suggests that the Tainos worked the land collectively and equally distributed the products of their labor. The Tainos produced only what they consumed and rarely traded with other communities. Evidence also suggests that when the Spanish arrived, the Tainos were undergoing some changes in their lifestyles. They were moving from a matriarchal to a patriarchal family structure and their social system was becoming more hierarchical. However, the Spanish conquest prevented further development of Taino culture, and 40 years after the conquest the indigenous population had essentially disappeared, with only a few thousand remaining (Navarro, 2000).

As the Indian population decreased, the Spaniards needed to find an alternative labor source. They began importing slaves from Africa in the early 16th century. Slave labor increased throughout the century, during which time slaves worked in mines, on sugar plantations, and on tobacco farms. Throughout the 17th century differences between classes and social groups increased, and slavery became more brutal. Several slave revolts took place and many slaves tried to escape. Maroons and *palenques* (maroon settlements) increased, and in 1727 over 300 slaves revolted at the Quiebra Hacha sugar mill. This revolt was followed by the uprising of the El Cobre mine workers in 1731. Perhaps the most important rebellion occurred in 1812. Under the leadership of José Antonio Aponte, the rebellion was intended to unite black slaves and to form a revolution that would abolish slavery. The revolution failed and Aponte and his main collaborators were hung (Navarro, 2000).

Spanish and British Colonial Rule

For a brief period Spanish domination of Cuba was challenged. In 1740 British Admiral Vernon sailed to the southern coast of Cuba and landed in Guantánamo and began an advance on Santiago de Cuba. However, after 5 months of attacks by Creoles (descendants of Spaniards born in Cuba), the British retreated. In June 1762 another British squadron landed at Havana Bay, attacked the city, and took control. The British occupied the western part of Cuba while the rest of the country remained under Spanish colonial rule. The most significant result of the British conquest was the end of the Spanish monopoly on commerce (Navarro, 2000). Prior to 1762 the Cuban market had been closed to foreigners, although there was a significant amount of smuggling (Thomas, 1993). Cuba began trading with other countries, particularly the United States and England. British domination over Havana lasted 12 months, during which time the exportation of sugar, tobacco, and other goods multiplied. Spanish domination was reestablished in July 1763, but the commercial monopolies ended and trade opened up (Navarro, 2000). One of the most profound impacts of the British occupation of Cuba was the increase in slave labor. During the yearlong occupation, 4,000 slaves were sold in Cuba, approximately one-eighth of the number of slaves already on the island (Thomas, 1993).

Although trade was now open, not everyone in Cuba benefited equally. The slave trade continued to expand (Thomas, 1993), and the emergence of different classes began to increase. There was a new class of rich slave-owners who possessed sugar plantations, large amounts of land, and farm animals. Plantation owners, slave traders, and import merchants formed an extremely powerful cartel (Navarro, 2000). Throughout the 1770s Cuba was exporting over 10,000 tons of sugar; by the 1790s it rose to 30,000 tons. The number of plantations growing sugar increased from about 100 to about 500, and the land used for sugarcane had increased from 10,000 acres to almost 200,000 acres (Thomas, 1993). There were also small landowners, artisans, and professionals who were much less affluent and often had difficulty obtaining the necessary resources needed to work. In addition, the black slave population had grown substantially. There was conflict between Creole plantation owners and Spanish merchants who were charging landowners exorbitant interest rates and making huge profits (Navarro, 2000). These class differences significantly affected family life. Slave women were forced to work long hours on the plantations and frequently performed the same tasks as men. Women were more likely than men to perform domestic chores for slave owners but only men rose to supervisory positions in sugar production. Childcare was primarily the domain of slave women who had to work with their children in tow. Men were often sold separately from their families, so black women did not develop a tradition of dependency on men (Safa, 1995). The wives of rich plantation owners and merchants led a bourgeois existence with servants to care for their children and to do the bulk of the household labor. As a result, privileged white women were highly dependent on their husbands and servants (Navarro, 2000).

These class differences bred resentment and led to a variety of reform movements within Cuba. By the mid-1860s a strong anticolonial sentiment swept the nation. In 1868 the fight for independence began with the onslaught of the Ten Years' War. Freed slaves, intellectuals, radical Cuban plantation owners, and people from a variety of social classes supported the revolution. Ultimately, the colonial government squashed the revolution and the war ended (Navarro, 2000), but it contributed to the development of a national conscience in which a collective identity became more firmly entrenched (Aguilar, 1993). By 1868 the pattern of how Cuba would look in the future was established. The population was slightly over one-half Spanish origin and slightly under one-half black or mulatto, with a small population of Chinese, Anglo-Saxon, and French (Thomas, 1993). The independence movement united people from these different racial-ethnic and class backgrounds and was the motivating force behind the abolition of slavery. After a series of laws weakening slavery, it was completely abolished in 1886.

During this period U.S. investment in Cuba increased, and by 1895 U.S. investments reached $50 million. Although Cuba remained a colony of Spain, the influence of the United States was becoming increasingly significant (Navarro, 2000). A growing independence movement was sweeping the nation, and in February 1895 the second war of independence began. The war ended in 1898 with Cuba defeating Spain (Trento, 2000). This coincided with the end of the Spanish American war, in which the Spanish were defeated by the United States. The Paris Treaty was signed by the United States and Spain on January 10, 1898, signaling the end of the war and ending Spanish occupation of Cuba, Puerto Rico, and the Philippines (Aguilar, 1993; Navarro, 2000). The United States prevented Cuban representatives from taking part in peace talks and from signing the Paris Treaty, effectively beginning the U.S. occupation of Cuba. During the struggle against Spain, the Cuban people created new "revolutionary traditions" that promoted equality for all Cubans. Cross-racial mobilization and the emergence of a nationalist ideology that imagined political independence and egalitarian principles underlay the new republic. A desire for racial-ethnic and class equality coexisted with a new sense of "Cubanness" (de la Fuente, 2001).

U.S. Colonial Rule

Cuba was considered to be a vital economic, political, and military testing ground for the United States. In the first 6 months, occupation forces eliminated the independence movement's three representative bodies, fostering U.S. political and economic domination in Cuba. In 1898, before officially taking over Cuba, the U.S. government cut tariffs on U.S. goods exported to Cuba but refused to do the same for Cuban exports to the United States. In addition, it was required that all government payments be made in U.S. dollars. United States businesses flooded Cuba, and the United States gained control of the sugar, mining, and tobacco industries. By 1902 U.S. companies controlled 80% of ore exports and a large percentage of the cigar and cigarette factories. In addition, the U.S. government refused to provide credit to small- and medium-sized agricultural industries, effectively forcing them into bankruptcy. Many landowners were evicted by U.S. citizens and companies. Similarly, the growth of large U.S. estates in Cuba also increased and by 1905 nearly 10% of Cuba's total land belonged to U.S. citizens. During the occupation the U.S. government did improve health conditions and created a compulsory education system for children ages 4 to 16 (Navarro, 2000). As a result, the education of Cuban women increased gradually during the 20th century.

In 1899 the literacy rate for women over 10 was 42%, although in some rural areas it was much lower, particularly among black women. In fact, during this period the majority of rural Afro-Cuban women were not educated beyond the third grade (Smith & Padula, 1996).

Cubans from different social classes who resented U.S. imperialist policies formed popular resistance movements. Subsequently the U.S. War Secretary was forced to announce that municipal elections would be held, that a constituent assembly would be set up, and that, following general elections, the government would be handed over to the Cubans. The first Municipal and Constituent Assembly elections were held in 1900 and proindependence candidates were overwhelmingly elected. The assembly drew up and passed the first constitution, which included some democratic reforms, although it denied women the right to vote. Despite significant democratic reforms, the U.S. government did not give Cuba its independence (Navarro, 2000). In fact, in 1901 the Platt Amendment, which undermined Cuba's sovereignty, was added to the Cuban constitution. The Platt Amendment gave the United States the right to intervene in Cuban affairs. The island's government could not confer special privileges to other nations, could not assume new debt, was denied treaty-making authority, and required that all the laws originating with the occupying government be recognized. Most important, it gave Washington the right to intercede militarily to protect the life, property, and rights of citizens. Although many members of the assembly opposed the amendment and provided several counter-proposals to protect Cuba's sovereignty, the United States refused to negotiate and said if Cuba did not sign the amendment, the United States would not remove occupation troops from the island (Aguilar, 1993; Navarro, 2000; Trento, 2000). On May 28, 1901, by a vote of 14 to 15, the convention adopted the proposed appendix to the Cuban constitution (Aguilar, 1993).

Essentially, the U.S. government retained control over Cuba without having to annex it. The first president of Cuba was elected in December 1901. Tomás Estrada Palma was favored by the U.S. government over General Bartolomé Masó, because Masó vehemently opposed the Platt Amendment and any U.S. intervention in Cuba. Although Masó had popular support, he withdrew his candidacy because of U.S. manipulation of the elections, and Estrada Palma was elected on May 20, 1902. Estrada Palma's cabinet did not include one revolutionary member or anyone who had been imprisoned during the war of independence (Navarro, 2000).

Between 1901 and 1959 the United States government exerted considerable power over Cuba. During Cuba's first republic (1902–1933), the U.S. government controlled key economic activities such as sugar and nickel production. United States investors had enormous impact over governmental and social policies in Cuba. The desire for an egalitarian Cuba was also undermined by Conservative control of the political machinery. Conservatives undermined Afro-Cubans' chances of being represented in government. In fact, the proportion of blacks in Congress declined after 1912 when Conservatives came to power and began the racist repression against the Independent Party of Color (de la Fuente, 2001). Over the first half of the 20th century, there were 10 different presidents, four of whom served two terms. Throughout the century the United States dominated Cuban politics and there were numerous struggles for independence. Several of the administrations were racked with corruption and some presidents welcomed the influence of U.S. investors.

Integral to the development of Cuban society and family relations was the production of sugar. During the administration of President Menocal (1913–1921), sugar production rose—primarily as a result of World War I. Due to the war, crops in Europe were devastated, increasing the demand for sugar from Cuba. In addition, the mining of manganese and iron increased. Revenues for Cuba skyrocketed and Cuba was extremely prosperous. This economic boom became known as the Dance of the Millions, although it primarily benefited sugar magnates, bankers, and other elites (Navarro, 2000, p. 93). In addition, because the cane production system was based on extensive planting instead of intensive cultivation, large tracts of land were necessary. As profits rose, plantation owners acquired more land. As a result *colonos* (planters who sold their sugar to mills) became disenfranchised and hacienda owners imported cheap labor from Haiti and Jamaica, exacerbating racial tension and undercutting wages (Aguilar, 1993).

In addition to controlling a large share of productive land, foreign sugar investors also promoted the importation of contract labor or *braceros*. By the mid-1920s foreign investors owned 15% to 20% of the national territory. U.S. investors benefited the most from this process, and between 1899 and 1905 approximately 13,000 U.S. corporations and individual investors obtained about 60% of all rural land in Cuba, particularly in the Oriente province (de la Fuente, 2001). The concentration of U.S. wealth was particularly harmful to Afro-Cubans, who in 1899 controlled 25% of the total number of farms in Cuba as owners or renters—43% in Oriente province. Prior to the loss of their land Afro-Cubans in Oriente province controlled 48% of the land used for rice production, 59% for coffee, 61% for cocoa, and 61% for malanga (de la Fuente, 2001). Between 1899 and 1931 Afro-Cubans lost control of 50% of their land, and by 1931 controlled only 8.5% of the country's farmland. According to de la Fuente (2001), this represented "the proletarianization of the

Afro-Cuban peasantry" (p. 106). In addition, employment opportunities for wage work were restricted for Afro-Cubans. They were given the most labor-intensive, lowest-paying jobs. In addition, the industrial and administrative jobs associated with sugar production were reserved for white, mostly foreign workers. These racial barriers in sugar manufacturing persisted until the end of the republic in 1959 (de la Fuente, 2001). As a result, a large number of Afro-Cubans migrated to cities in search of work. Throughout this period families struggled to survive. Reliance on a male breadwinner was impossible, particularly for impoverished families. Nonetheless, traditional notions of *machismo* (the belief in men's sexual prowess and their primacy over women) endured.

Stimulated by the increase in sugar export, manufacturing, and trade, employment opportunities increased in urban centers. Between 1907 and 1919 alone, 62,923 new jobs were created in manufacturing in urban centers. Manufacturing jobs in cement, paper, shoe, soap, perfume, liquor, and clothing industries were created. Jobs within the public sector also increased at record rates. However, as in the rural areas, blacks and women were given the lowest-paying jobs in the least-skilled labor markets. The Great Depression stimulated further movement to the cities and contributed to the collapse of the sugar market (de la Fuente, 2001). The collapse of the sugar industry was devastating for Cubans, particularly on the *colono* system, which had been expanding during the 19th century, creating a rural middle class. Approximately 18,000 *colonos* lost their land and a majority of rural Cubans became almost totally dependent on the will of the sugar mill owners (Aguilar, 1993). All Cubans suffered as a result, but racial and gender discrimination in the labor market contributed to severe stratification and higher rates of poverty among Afro-Cubans and women in both rural and urban areas. Inner-city poverty became rampant and class differences became even more pronounced. Black families had higher rates of illiteracy, infant mortality, illness, and inadequate housing.

As a result of this crisis, President Machado began to diversify agriculture, regulate the sugar industry, create public works jobs, and construct a central highway from Havana to Santiago. He eradicated corruption in the government and created thousands of jobs in his first 2 years in office. However, with no opposition, Machado ultimately used the political machinery to fuel his personal ambition and began steps toward a dictatorship. In 1927 a pro-Machado Constitutional Assembly extended the presidential term to 6 years and invited Machado to accept a new term in office. Then, in 1928 Congress passed an Emergency Law prohibiting presidential nominations by any other parties than the Liberal, Conservative, and Popular parties, who had all nominated Machado. The unconstitutionality of the process notwithstanding, Machado was reelected. The reelection of the increasingly repressive Machado fomented social dissent, and the worsening economic conditions intensified political confrontation in Cuba (Aguilar, 1993; L. A. Perez, 1993).

As new opposition leaders emerged and protest movements increased, Machado was forced to resign. He was replaced by Carlos M. Cespedes, who was swiftly ousted by the Student Directory (an activist student group) and a group of soldiers who, while protesting against inadequate military housing and low pay, found themselves in a state of mutiny and ultimately in a rebellion against the government. On September 5, 1928, a provisional revolutionary government was proclaimed, and the establishment of a new democracy that recognized the sovereignty of Cuba was proclaimed (L. A. Perez, 1993). The government was essentially composed of radical students who, facing opposition, proclaimed Ramón Grau San Martín, a university professor, president. Fear of social upheaval prompted the new government to raise Fulgencio Batista to the rank of Colonel and appoint him as the new army chief. Former officers were arrested as deserters and Batista completely reorganized the army, strengthening his own power within the military (L. A. Perez, 1993).

As interim president, Grau Martín gave women the right to vote. Women were responsible for electing seven female representatives to the congress and fought for protective legislation. One major result was the 1934 law requiring employers to provide maternity leave for 12 weeks. In addition, factories and institutions employing more than 50 women were required to provide on-site nurseries for children under 2 years of age. Unfortunately, the new legislation did not include domestic workers, who composed one-fourth of the female workforce, nor did it include agricultural workers. In addition, to avoid the expense of providing childcare, some factories simply refused to hire women, while other employers ignored the new law (Smith & Padula, 1996). The exclusion of domestic and agricultural labor from the legislation systematically disenfranchised Afro-Cubans and other members of the poorer and less-educated segments of the population. Although lasting only 4 months, this revolutionary government reflected the growing tensions that began in Cuba during the 1920s and the desire to break free of U.S. dominance (Navarro, 2000), as well as the beginning of Batista's ascension to power.

The turmoil of 1930–1934 created nationalistic social and political forces that signaled a new era of political radicalism and created new political parties dedicated to Cuba's independence that dominated Cuba for the next 25 years (Aguilar, 1993). During the second republic (1933–1958), North American interests continued to shape internal policies. However, from 1940 to 1952, Cuba experienced an era of democratic reform. Batista was elected president in 1940, and he helped implement a new constitution that incorporated feminist reforms and included a section guaranteeing the rights of children born out of formal wedlock. In addition, the new constitution included an equal rights article to protect women in the labor market (Smith & Padula, 1996). Nonetheless, many Cubans opposed continuing U.S. hegemony in Cuba, and as a result radical social movement organizations were founded. Social movement organizations advocated a free and sovereign constituent assembly, racial equality, and freedom from U.S. dominance (Navarro, 2000). The national disillusionment that began in the 1920s and continued unabated in the 1930s blossomed and found expression in university reform and artistic and literary expression that focused on anti-imperialism, nationalism, and social justice (L. A. Perez, 1993). These events paved the way for a variety of strikes, political activism, and increased resistance to U.S. hegemony on the island over the next 20 years.

Unfortunately, by the mid-1940s—after years of strikes, oppressive tactics on the part of various presidents, corruption, and the use of violence and terror in party politics—there were leadership struggles in many of the political parties and in social movement organizations. After a significant power struggle, Batista staged a military coup on March 10, 1952, and returned to power. Sites of potential protest demonstrations against the coup were watched by the military. The university and opposition presses were closed. Union and Communist party headquarters were occupied, and many activists were arrested. "The effects of nearly a decade of graft, corruption and scandal at all levels of government paved the way for the return of military rule in 1952" (L. A. Perez, 1993, p. 83). The Batista dictatorship immediately abolished the 1940 constitution. It imposed

constitutional statutes that gave legal backing to all of Batista's despotic acts. Constitutional guarantees and the right to strike were suspended. Batista dissolved the congress and replaced it with a consultative council, made up primarily of bankers, landowners, traditional politicians, and rich businessmen. The dictatorship forbade political rallies, postponed general elections, and began a wave of detention, kidnapping, and incarceration of citizens. Mass arrests and acts of violence were commonplace. Batista also courted U.S. economic intervention on the island. As a result, U.S. investments in Cuba increased from $713 million in 1951 to $1 billion by 1958 (Navarro, 1998).

The Cuban Revolution

A variety of student groups, labor organizations, and political parties began organizing against the Batista dictatorship. On July 26, 1953, Fidel Castro and 131 of his fellow revolutionaries assaulted the Moncada barracks in Santiago de Cuba, the capital of Oriente province. Moncada was the country's second largest military base, with approximately 1,000 troops. However, facing defeat, Castro ordered a retreat. Immediately after the assault, a wave of even more brutal repression swept the country, unleashing one of the most repressive and violent periods in Cuban history. All constitutional guarantees were suspended, newspapers were shut down, and media censorship was enforced. Rebels who were captured were savagely tortured and eventually killed. Fidel Castro stood trial and was condemned to 15 years in prison. The July 26 attack triggered a period of armed struggle that did not end until the overthrow of Batista (Navarro, 1998).

In May 1955 Fidel Castro and other imprisoned revolutionaries were given amnesty and released from prison (Trento, 2000). On the boat from the Isle of Pines to the mainland, the 26th of July movement was founded. Members of the movement were under constant surveillance from the government. In July 1955 Fidel fled to Mexico and met with his brother Raúl. While in Mexico, Fidel wrote the 26th of July Movement Manifesto #1, in which he advocated armed insurrection. Castro envisioned this insurrection not just against the Batista dictatorship but against the previous 50 years of neocolonial rule (Navarro, 1998). In September Fidel met Ernesto (Che) Guevara, an Argentinean physician who was also a revolutionary. Che became committed to the movement. In 1956 Castro organized another uprising in Santiago to coincide with his return from Mexico on November 30 aboard the small yacht *Granma*, but the revolt was crushed and the *Granma* survivors had to retreat to the southeastern mountain range. Castro and his revolutionary forces began attacking guard posts and liberating territory in rural areas. The expanding struggle in the countryside gained support from urban underground groups. Mounting Batista opposition was occurring even within the ranks of the military. In 1958 the 26th of July Movement began a war against property and production facilities across the island to isolate Batista from the support of foreign economic elites. In February, the guerrilla leadership announced that they planned attacks on sugar mills, tobacco factories, public utilities, oil refineries, and railroads. In March they destroyed 2 million tons of sugar. Throughout most of 1958, Cuba was on the verge of revolution. Batista responded by launching an offensive against the guerrilla leadership and their revolutionary forces in the Sierra Maestra. An estimated 12,000 troops descended on the Sierra Maestra. By the end of the summer, the army ceased fighting and many soldiers deserted. In late summer the guerrillas launched a counteroffensive, and on New Years Eve 1958, Batista fled Cuba.

In January 1959 the old regime collapsed and the revolutionary government came to power (L. A. Perez, 1993).

Cuba's Sovereign Revolutionary Government

The Constitution of the Republic, in effect since 1976, establishes Cuba as a socialist state. The constitution is the legal base on which the country's economic, political, social, and cultural organization is built. It guarantees equal rights for all Cubans regardless of race, sex, beliefs, and so on. In addition, it allows for the full expression of religious beliefs and the practice of any cult, as long as it does not violate the law. However, in reality, strong expressions of religiosity are discouraged and many religious rituals occur in secret. The constitution also provides for the preservation of Cuba as an independent and sovereign nation (Navarro, 2000).

The People's Power system is made up of municipal and provincial assemblies, and a national assembly, or parliament, which is the highest body of power in Cuba. The parliament is entrusted with overseeing the work of both the state and the government apparatus (Navarro, 2000). Cuba has been a pioneer in Latin America and the Caribbean in promoting gender equity through political participation. Women make up 27.6% of parliamentary representation in Cuba (it is only 14% in the United States). In fact, Cuba's female parliamentary representation ranks among the top 15 countries in the world, although it has yet to reach 30%, the amount assumed necessary for true equality (Chant, 2003; Hernandez-Truyol, 2004).

In Cuba all men and women over 16 years of age have the right to vote. The only exceptions are for people with a mental disability or who are incarcerated. All state branches, including the executive and judiciary, are elected and periodically renewed. Delegates to the municipal and provincial assemblies, as well as deputies to the National Assembly, are also periodically elected by universal, direct, and secret vote. A candidate must capture more than 50% of the valid votes cast to be elected, and elected officials can be recalled at any time if a majority of their constituency deem it necessary (Navarro, 2000).

The administration of justice in Cuba is under the auspices of the Supreme Court, the National Assembly, and the Council of State. The Council of State acts in place of the National Assembly when it is not in session, and represents the Cuban state. The Council of Ministers, or Cabinet, is the highest executive and administrative body making up the government of the Republic (Navarro, 2000).

In spite of progressive reforms, women did not receive total equality during the first 20 years of the revolution. By condemning racial but not gender discrimination, the constitution of 1976 relegated women to a secondary status. In addition, the constitution allowed women's workforce participation to be restricted to protect their reproductive capacity. However, in 1992 Cuba ratified a new constitution that stated that discrimination based on "race, skin color, sex, national origin, religious belief, and any other affront to human dignity is proscribed and sanctioned by law" (Smith & Padula, 1996, p. 46). In addition, the new constitution guaranteed that "men and women have equal rights in the economic, political, cultural, and social realms and in the family" (Smith & Padula, 1996, p. 46). Even with these important feminist reforms and tremendous gains in social, economic, and political power, women in Cuba have still not achieved complete parity with men.

The Special Period

Before moving on to a discussion of the Cuban family it is essential to provide a brief discussion of the current economic crisis that exists in Cuba. The Special Period (*Periódo Especial*) refers to the economic crisis that began in the early 1990s after the collapse of the Soviet Union and the tightening of the U.S. economic blockade. Once the Soviet Union embraced capitalism, Cuba lost a significant trading partner with which to exchange products, food, and medicine. Subsequently, in the early 1990s Cuba lost 85% of its foreign trade and experienced a 51% decline in foreign exchange earnings. In addition to a loss in foreign trade, there was also a decline in Cuba's gross domestic product, nonsugar-related production, and oil importation. Furthermore, sugar, nickel, and petroleum exports fell precipitously. As a result of the U.S. blockade and discontinuing trade with the former Soviet Union and other Eastern Block countries, food consumption in Cuba also declined considerably. The lack of food and the loss of petroleum products exacerbated problems of malnutrition. Cubans experienced substantial weight loss and their diet was severely limited (Campbell, 1999). In addition, many components of the social safety net began to unravel. Declining access to day care, medicine, clothing, food, and skilled labor was difficult on families, especially women, who were primarily responsible for childcare and housework.

2. PAIRING UP IN CUBA

There is very little research documenting the mating relations and pairing up practices of Cubans. However, historians have theorized that mating patterns have been shaped by strong cultural and religious traditions dating back to Spanish colonial rule. For example, members of the upper class insisted that their children marry in the Church, observe all the duties of marriage, and, most important, marry equally influential families. Members of the upper class were also expected to have large families so that the children of the ruling elite would maintain their power and extend family traditions intergenerationally. Marriage patterns among landless peasants were also affected by strict religious and cultural norms imposed by the colonizing power. Peasants had large families, and marriage at an early age was common. Peasants were tied to the land of plantation owners, and their servitude was passed from one generation to the next (Gonzalez, 1994).

Throughout the 19th century, inter-racial marriage was highly restricted in Cuba. Inter-racial marriage required both parental consent and approval from civil authorities. According to Safa (1995), state control of intermarriage represented the movement of patriarchal domination of women away from individual men to the state. However, in 1881 (1 year after the abolition of slavery) the regulations against inter-racial marriage were lifted. The abolition of intermarriage reflected the realities of a growing population of freed blacks and the necessity of racial integration in the fight for Cuban independence. Many inter-racial couples married legally, but a majority were consensual unions. Consensual marriage was more common among Afro-Cuban women than among women of Spanish descent. Consensual unions weakened women's dependence on a male breadwinner, because they often had greater economic responsibility for children than legally married women. As a result of women's greater economic independence from men, consensual unions were more likely to dissolve than legal marriages (Safa, 1995). Subsequently, Afro-Cuban women were less dependent on men than women of Spanish descent.

Inter-racial unions continue to be a controversial issue in Cuba. Given Cuba's racial heterogeneity one would expect inter-racial mating and dating to be commonly accepted, but research conducted by Nadine

Fernandez (1996) suggests that entrenched racial ideologies of black inferiority introduced in Cuba during Spanish and U.S. colonialism persist. Racist beliefs about black inferiority and racial purity continue to shape mating practices in contemporary Cuba. Even though the Cuban government attempted to eradicate racism by abolishing racial segregation in public places, by eliminating workplace discrimination, and by incorporating Afro-Cubans into the educational system, racism still exists. Although darker-skinned Cubans have made impressive socioeconomic gains, evidence suggests that they are still over-represented in the lowest positions of the social structure.

Although it is difficult to assess the exact number of inter-racial couples in Cuba (Fernandez, 1996), population census data indicate that the vast majority of marriages are racially endogamous. For example, 1981 census data illustrated that 93% of white, 70% of black, and 68.7% of mulatto household heads married someone of the same race (Safa, 1995). Although inter-racial friendships are common and widely accepted by family and peer groups, inter-racial romance and marriage are not. Many inter-racial couples feel caught between the ideology of equality endorsed by the Revolution and the lingering racism espoused by parents and grandparents (Fernandez, 1996).

Marriage and consensual unions in contemporary Cuba must be understood within the context of the socialist revolution. The newly created revolutionary state affirmed the role of the family as the cornerstone of society and sought to protect its social role. Within a year of its rise to power, the government instituted a program called Operation Family, which legalized consensual unions and reduced the fees and paperwork required to get married. As a result, people rushed to legalize their marriages. One estimate suggests that within the first 4 years of Operation Family, 106,063 couples were married (L. Perez, 1980). Despite this initial marriage boom, consensual unions increased after Castro's rise to power and the percentage of legal marriages declined (Safa, 1995; Smith & Padula, 1996).

After the Revolution consensual unions continued to be a major characteristic of family life and were formally sanctioned by the passage of the Family Code of 1975. This law was an attempt by the revolutionary government to legislate social reproduction, to protect women and children, and to foster gender equity in the family. The Family Code acknowledged the prevalence of consensual unions and in Article 18 recognized them "as binding legally as formalized marriages" (Stone, 1981, p. 182).

Consensual unions are currently the most common form of intimate partner relationship. Between 1981 and 1987 the percentage of consensual unions increased from 23.1% to 28.4% among women 15 to 49. In 1987, 28.7% of Cuban women between the ages of 15 and 49 were in consensual unions, compared with 34.7% for legally married women (Catasús Cervera, 1992; Safa, 1995). Currently, fewer than three in five couples in Cuba legally marry (Chant, 2003; Lumsden, 1996). National data indicate that women in consensual relationships have lower levels of education, show lower levels of labor-force participation, and are more likely to be employed in the secondary labor market than legally married women (Safa, 1995).

In addition, the age of first union and first pregnancy has declined despite increases in educational and occupational attainment among women. In a study of textile workers, Safa (1995) found that nearly two-thirds of the women sampled had their first child under the age of 20, and 28.6% of them had more than one intimate partner. National-level data illustrate that between 1981 and 1987 the average age for first unions in Cuba declined from 19.7 to 18.4 among women

between the ages of 15 and 49 (Safa, 1995). Given that Cuban women have among the highest literacy rates in the world and have made tremendous inroads in public life, it is surprising to find that they are having children so young. In most parts of the world, increased education and labor-force participation is usually associated with delayed childbirth.

3. FERTILITY AND TEENAGE PREGNANCY

Cuba has the lowest fertility rate of all Latin American countries and has rates comparable to many advanced industrialized nations (Safa, 1995). High labor-force participation rates, high levels of educational attainment, free access to birth control, and the legalization of abortion have led to these low rates of fertility among Cuban women. According to Fleites-Lear (1999), after an initial baby boom in the 1960s, there was a decline in fertility. For example, in 1975, 1988, and 1994, the total fertility rates among Cuban women were 2.74, 1.88, and 1.5, respectively. Between 1995 and 2000 the fertility rate stabilized around 1.6. This rate is the lowest in Latin America, is below replacement levels (Chant, 2003; Safa, 1995), and represents an annual population growth of approximately 10 per 1,000 people (Fleites-Lear, 1999).

Cuba also has among the highest rates of contraceptive use in Latin America and the Caribbean. Between 1990 and 1999 it is estimated that 82% of married (legally or not) couples used some form of birth control. Unlike most other Latin American countries, men in Cuba seem to have accepted women's desires to use birth control and to have fewer children. This phenomenon could be attributed to the availability of reproductive resources and legal support women have had under the revolutionary government (Chant, 2003). In addition, the influence of the Catholic church on Cuban life was significantly reduced after the Revolution, and the Church does not have the same influence in Cuba that it does in most of Latin America. For example, the Roman Catholic Church has not been able to restrict or prevent national family planning programs, contraceptive use, or abortion in Cuba, as it has done throughout Latin America (Chant, 2003). Finally, children learn about contraception at an early age devoid of stigmatization. Subsequently, birth control is widely available, widely accepted, and widely used.

Although Cuba has one of the lowest rates of fertility in the world, teenage pregnancy and single motherhood are increasing. In a study of female workers where contraception and abortion were widely available, 50% of the sample had their first child before the age of 20 (Chant, 2003; Safa, 1995). In fact, research shows that despite the availability of contraception and abortion, many single mothers do not plan their pregnancies. For example, one study of 200 single mothers found that 48% of them wanted an abortion but never obtained one. The rise in teenage pregnancy has resulted in a concomitant rise in single motherhood. Between 1973 and 1988, 39% of all children born in Cuba were born to single mothers. By 1989 the percentage had increased to 61.2%. In 1987 a nationwide survey found that 27% of women with children had no ongoing relationship with the father of their child. In addition, 72% of the single mothers surveyed were under the age of 25, and 38% were under the age of 20. As in other countries, teenage single motherhood limits women's educational, occupational, and social opportunities (Safa, 1995).

Further exacerbating the difficulties associated with single motherhood is the fact that many Cuban fathers do not help raise their children, provide child support, or even see their children. In 1989, for example, 85.5%

of fathers of children born out of wedlock acknowledged their offspring, but many did not help to raise or support them. In one study of single mothers, researchers found that 59% of fathers were not paying child support. Another study of 108 single mothers in the late 1980s found that 85% of the fathers were either completely or partially estranged from their children, 59% of the men did not provide any child support, and 31% paid only sporadically. In the same study researchers found that 56% of the mothers did not know where the father lived, and 66% did not know where they worked. Because of the lack of information on the men's whereabouts, single teenage mothers had great difficulty in obtaining child support. Although the Family Code stipulates that men are legally responsible for all children regardless of whether or not a formal marriage took place, it does not include any provisions for securing payment of child support (Smith & Padula, 1996). Because of the prevalence of multigenerational households, a guarantee of minimum foodstuffs, access to childcare, and universal healthcare, single mothers in Cuba are free from the grinding poverty and homelessness that plague their counterparts in Latin America and other Third World countries.

4. GENDER ROLES

Historically, gender roles in Cuba have been rooted in traditional ideology found throughout Latin America and the Caribbean. Family scholars have traced the origins of such traditional beliefs to Spanish colonization and to the influence of the Catholic Church (Gonzalez, 1994). Although the impact of Catholicism was not uniform throughout Latin America and the Caribbean, it is clear that religious conquest played a significant role in the development of sexuality and gender ideology. The ideologies of *marianismo* (the idealization of chastity and motherhood) and *machismo* have been linked to religious beliefs that men are naturally suited to be the providers and protectors of the family, while women are inherently suited to be the nurturers. These essentialist beliefs have been used for centuries to foster women's subordination to men (Chant, 2003) and glorify their roles as wives and mothers. In prerevolutionary Cuba, *marianismo* and *machismo* served as the archetypes of appropriate sexual behavior. A double standard existed that encouraged men to explore their sexuality, yet required women to remain virgins until marriage. *Machismo* gave men the right to be sexually promiscuous while simultaneously compelling women to repress their sexuality. Women were expected to remain faithful to their husbands, but men were rarely held to the same standard (Gonzalez, 1994). According to Gonzalez, "often the acceptance of the *machismo* complex resulted in the exaggeration of the idealized qualities of maleness and manhood, such as hyper-sexuality, infidelity, physical strength, arrogance, alcohol abuse, and verbal abuse" (1994, p. 208). These gender distinctions also existed in the public sphere and were traditionally expressed in the distinction between *casa* (home, the domain of women, and *calle* (street, the domain of men (Safa, 1995). Subsequently, these traditional gender roles shaped women's work experiences. For example, in prerevolutionary Cuba most married women did not work outside the home, and one-fourth of working women were employed as domestics (Safa, 1995).

Although 20th-century Cuban women defied traditional gender roles by joining the revolutionary struggle, the Revolution was slow to address gender inequality in Cuban society. Although Fidel Castro made some statements about women's equality prior to the declaration of socialism, the "woman question" was never part of the revolutionary struggle. It was with the creation of the Federation of Cuban Women (FMC) on August 23, 1960, that the "woman question" was first addressed. The FMC was created to bring women into the revolutionary process. In 1961 the FMC launched a massive literacy campaign in which 70,000 volunteers traveled throughout the country teaching people to read and write. In addition, they raised over $1 million for day care in 1963 and developed a national day-care system (Smith & Padula, 1996). Members of the FMC organized militias and Committees for the Defense of the Revolution (CDRs) throughout the country. Because the FMC was an organization made up of and led entirely by women, individuals who had never participated in public life felt comfortable in its ranks (Stone, 1981). The FMC also provided a place where women could discuss gender inequality and advocate for social change. As a result of the FMC's social movement activity, women obtained the right to an education, a job, paid maternity leave, childcare, and abortion on demand. In addition, the FMC was instrumental in eliminating prostitution and ending such degrading customs as sexist advertising and beauty contests. In 1989 the FMC had nearly 3.4 million members (Lutjens, 1995).

One of the most significant struggles facing the FMC was raising consciousness about the importance of incorporating women into the labor market. Women's workforce participation was encouraged by the Cuban leadership, but the motivation was not solely driven by the needs of the Revolution. The revolutionary government acknowledged that women's oppression stemmed from their being confined to the home, isolated from broader social life, and economically dependent on their husbands. An important first step toward the integration of women into the workforce was the voluntary labor that women carried out throughout the 1960s. By 1968 a new stage of incorporating women into the labor force began with the initiation of an FMC campaign designed to bring 100,000 women into full-time work each year. During this campaign, stereotypes about the kinds of jobs women were capable of doing were subverted. Women became doctors, engineers, lawyers, university professors, and technicians. Women also began to work in sugar mills, factories, and in other light industries (Jennissen & Lundy, 2001; Smith & Padula, 1996).

Over time it became clear that the goal of increasing the number of women workers was not being met. In her report to the Second Congress of the FMC in 1974, Vilma Espín attributed the reasons for women's declining labor-force participation to a lack of social services, inadequate safety and hygiene at work sites, and a lack of understanding of women's social and familial roles. Most important, the FMC denounced the unequal division of labor in the home and traditional notions of patriarchy that marginalized and overburdened women. As a result, the 1975 Family Code was introduced to replace pre-revolutionary laws on marriage, divorce, adoption, and alimony. The most controversial aspects of the Family Code stipulated that women should be equal in marriage and that men should share in housework and childcare. This section of the code also stated that both partners should have an equal right to pursue an education and a job. Furthermore, the code stipulated that partners should cooperate with each other to make education and employment possible.[1]

> Article 28: Both partners have the right to practice their profession or skill and they have the duty of helping each other and cooperating in order to make this possible and to study and improve their knowledge. However, they must always see to it that home life is organized in such a way that these activities are coordinated with their fulfillment of the obligations of this code. (Code of Ministers, 1975, as cited in Stone, 1981, pp. 183–184)

Although the country's leadership put its authority behind the code, many Cuban men vehemently objected. Nonetheless, the Family Code was passed by an overwhelming majority of the population and became law on International Women's Day, March 8, 1975 (Jennissen & Lundy, 2001; Smith & Padula, 1996). Despite the elimination of much gender inequity in Cuba and the rejection of the old *casa/calle* distinction, the radicalization of traditional gender roles has remained elusive. While it is true that Cuban families became more egalitarian after the passage of the Family Code, research indicates that a significant imbalance in men's and women's work in the home tenaciously persists (Chant, 2003; Safa, 1995; Toro-Morn, Roschelle, & Facio, 2002). Cuban feminist scholars refer to this problem as "the unfinished revolution."

5. MARITAL RELATIONSHIPS

Despite the great strides Cuban women made in the aftermath of the Revolution, scholars have documented the persistence of gender inequality in both the home and the workplace (Safa, 1995; Smith & Padula, 1996). Given the long history of race, class, and gender inequality that existed under colonial and neocolonial rule and pervasive notions of *machismo,* it is not surprising that gender inequality still exists. Despite legislative attempts to promote gender equity in the family, it is unreasonable to expect 400 years of patriarchal domination to be eradicated in 45 short years. Still, The Family Code was a genuine effort by the revolutionary government to promote equality within families. The Family Code stipulates that marriage is an equitable partnership in which childcare and the division of household labor should be shared. Despite the passage of this radical legislation, Cuban women and men continue to negotiate the gender division of labor within the home. Struggles over housework and childcare have been exacerbated by the current economic crisis.

Our research on Cuban families reveals that men and women have different views on whether or not gender equity exists in the home. The men we interviewed often articulated that there is gender equality in their families and that they share equally in domestic labor. Most of the Cuban women we interviewed vehemently disagreed, providing copious examples of how they performed the bulk of housework and childcare. Women indicated that men still define the household as primarily a women's domain and that *machismo* is still very prevalent. Women asserted that although equality exists in the law, it does not exist in reality. In our research it became clear that men absolutely do not participate equally in domestic labor, and, in fact, many women do all the housework and are totally responsible for the family domain (Toro-Morn et al., 2002).

Implicit in the research are profound contradictions about how Cuban men perceive their participation in the gender division of household labor. Although most women do the majority of household work, men often claim to be sharing equally, even as they call their labor "help." In Cuba, as in other industrial and developing countries, there has not been a paradigm shift in the way men perceive their household responsibilities in the family (Toro-Morn et al., 2002). In rural areas women still have complete responsibility for childcare and housework, limiting their participation in activities other than paid work and household labor (Rosendahl, 1997). Men continue to see themselves as "helpers" rather than equal partners.

Men's ability to avoid contributing equally to the household division of labor is facilitated by the presence of female extended-family members (Toro-Morn et al., 2002). Safa, who conducted research in Cuba prior to the Special Period, has observed that

[T]he high percentage of three-generation households reinforces traditional patterns of authority and domestic labor. Additional women in the extended family may provide working mothers with important assistance in childcare and other household tasks, but they discourage men from taking more responsibility. (1995, p. 163)

Safa (1995) also found that women relied on the state to provide childcare services rather than requiring more from their husbands. Our research suggests that during the Special Period, working women no longer expect the state to provide familial resources, such as childcare, but rather turn to their partners to provide both material and emotional support. Unfortunately, many men simply refuse to provide that support (Toro-Morn et al., 2002).

As a result of the severe housing shortages during the Special Period, and the increase in teenage pregnancy, two- and three-generation households have become even more common. The severe shortages of food, medicine, and other household supplies have made the presence of extended family members even more critical to the survival of the family. Extended families have higher incomes because of the large number of wage earners and the availability of free childcare. However, these families also tend to be more patriarchal, with a high degree of authority among the older generation and a more traditional sexual division of labor (Safa, 1995). It is rare to find a family that does not rely on the help of older women. Oftentimes it is retired grandmothers, fictive kin, and unemployed neighbors who provided childcare, collect rationed goods, and purchase resources in the dollar stores when families have U.S. dollars (Toro-Morn et al., 2002). In addition to elderly parents providing family members with desperately needed childcare and housework, they also receive benefits from living with family members. Elderly people residing with family members are well taken care of as they age. Furthermore, socialized medicine means that the elderly have universal access to healthcare.

Unfortunately, the presence of several women in a home decreases the pressure on men to share in household labor. In working-class families men do not share in household tasks nor do women put much pressure on them to participate. In middle-class families in which women are legally married, highly educated, highly skilled, and gainfully employed, more egalitarian patterns of childcare and housework can be found (Safa, 1995). Despite the state's attempt to legislate equality in the home through the Family Code, gender inequity continues to persist. This gender inequity has been exacerbated during the Special Period, because women can no longer rely on the state for help, and men often refuse to participate in childcare and housework. Many women in Cuba expressed anger and frustration at their partners' resistance and refusal to share in the day-to-day activities of the household (Safa, 1995; Toro-Morn et al., 2002). Clearly, Cuban women continue to look forward to the gender revolution in the household division of labor.

6. FAMILY STRESSES AND VIOLENCE

Research on highly controversial topics in Cuba can be very difficult. Cuban scholars are restricted in their critique of the Cuban state by the realities of a nondemocratic regime. As Smith and Padula point out, "Cuban social scientists and historians have resisted writing about the post-1959 period because it is simply too politically sensitive" (1996, p. viii). Even in the late 1980s, when a growing body of work on gender, sexuality, and social relations emerged from the island's universities and research centers, many topics could simply not be discussed. One such topic that has been virtually unexplored is domestic violence. In fact, during the first 20 years of the revolutionary government, there was a denial that domestic violence even existed. Cuban officials vehemently denied that Cuban women were victims of domestic violence, and there were no shelters for battered women. In addition, there were no media stories about child abuse, incest, or intimate partner violence. Domestic violence and rape were portrayed as problems associated with capitalism. In addition, neither domestic violence nor rape were included in Cuban crime statistics. The existence of domestic violence was not even publicly recognized until 1992, when a journalist wrote an article discussing the problem of intimate partner violence and the reticence of government officials to admit its existence. Nevertheless, as late as 1993, members of the FMC publicly announced that domestic violence was not a problem in Cuba and discussions of it were merely a reflection of North Americans projecting their own shortcomings onto Cuban society (Smith & Padula, 1996). Public denials of the existence of domestic violence in Cuba have led to an absence of research and knowledge about the seriousness and extent of the problem.

One area of family stress that is documented both by the Cuban state and by scholars is the difficult housing conditions under which families are forced to live. When the Revolution came to power, housing conditions were deplorable. Rents were exceedingly high, evictions were common, and electricity and toilets were scarce. Castro announced that the new government would ameliorate these "wretched conditions" (Smith & Padula, 1996, p. 149). Immediately after taking office, Castro cut rents, lowered electricity rates, and limited evictions. The state became the nation's landlord and rents did not exceed 10% of a family's income. Over time renters were able to buy their homes, which was particularly helpful to the poor who previously could not own a home.

Large homes that belonged to the bourgeoisie prior to the Revolution were seized and turned into schools and office buildings. In the 1960s large housing projects in urban areas were built and concrete floors were poured in many *bohios* (peasant huts) in rural areas. Yet in the late 1960, 40% of homes were overcrowded and many families lived in four-generation households. Although the revolutionary government built 500,000 housing units between 1959 and 1988, there was still a shortage. Individual families began to build their own homes during this period and built approximately 1 million housing units (Smith & Padula, 1996). Castro provided building materials to families and communities, and between 1981 and 1983 private families constructed almost four times as many homes as the government. In addition to overcrowding, houses were also becoming more dilapidated. In 1980 it was estimated that 30,625 domiciles in Havana were propped up with scaffolding to prevent them from falling down (Smith & Padula, 1996).

The widespread crowding and dangerous conditions were particularly stressful for young newly married couples. Many newlyweds could not find apartments and had to live with parents or in-laws. Some Cubans added *barbacoas* (sleeping lofts) to their apartments, while others built extra rooms on rooftops and porches and in garages (Smith & Padula, 1996). Divorced couples also suffered from housing shortages. Divorced couples who were unable to find alternative housing were forced to remain together under the same roof. Some divorced couples who could not find separate housing divided their living quarters with sheets (Smith & Padula, 1996). Inadequate housing also created problems for gay male[2] couples, many of whom had not come out to their families and were forced to meet in secret. However, because of the primacy of family in Cuba, some young men did live in their parents' homes with their same-sex partners. For these couples, the core of their self-identity was not based on their sexuality but rather on their family and *barrio* (neighborhood) relationships. As long as homosexual family members didn't discuss the details of their intimate relationships, and didn't come out in the formal sense, they were sometimes accepted by their families and neighbors (Lumsden, 1996).

Severe housing shortages have led to the development of *posadas* (love hotels), in which couples rent rooms by the hour. However, these trysting establishments are only available to heterosexual couples. Homosexuals who have not come out to their families must resort to elaborate schemes to have sex in their homes, and many consider it *falta de respeto* (disrespectful) to do so. Subsequently, gay couples must find other ways of expressing their sexuality in a country that has been notoriously oppressive toward homosexuality (Lumsden, 1996). The revolutionary government defined homosexuality as an abhorrent vestige of capitalism, and although homosexuality was decriminalized in 1979, homophobia is still rampant in Cuba. This state-sponsored homophobia and the pressure on gay men to be discreet means that there are very few openly gay men living together (Chant, 2003; Lumsden, 1996).

Despite all the attempts to provide Cuban families with sufficient housing, the National Housing Institute determined that for construction to keep pace with need, Cuba would have to build 1 million new houses in the year 2000 (Smith & Padula, 1996). In 2004 that goal has not been met, and families continue to struggle with overcrowding, lack of privacy, and increased stress as a result of the dire housing situation.

7. DIVORCE, SEPARATION, AND REMARRIAGE

Overcrowded housing, consensual unions, and the stresses of the Special Period have contributed to high rates of divorce in Cuba. In addition, the revolutionary government made getting a divorce easier with the passage of the 1975 Family Code. In 1918 the first divorce laws were passed that prescribed the terms of property settlement, accorded women child support and alimony, and gave women authority over the children. Changes in family law in 1930 and 1934 made both partners financially responsible for family maintenance. The period of abandonment necessary for a divorce was decreased from 5 years to 6 months. However, the awarding of custody was based on parental income, which marginalized middle-class women, many of whom did not work, and working-class women and women of color, who were systematically paid less then men (Smith & Padula, 1996). With the passage of the Family Code, no-fault divorce became codified. As stated in Articles 53 through 56, either party has the right to end the marriage. Except in special cases, custody would be awarded to the mother, but both parents remained responsible for the physical and emotional care of the children. Regardless of gender, the unemployed spouse would be awarded alimony for 6 to 12 months. Long-term alimony would only be awarded in the case of severe illness, disability, age, or legitimate barriers to employment (Smith & Padula, 1996; Stone, 1981). In the case of divorce or the dissolution of a consensual union, property is divided equally between the two parties. This joint property stipulation prevents women from being overly dependent on men and relying on their willingness to provide material goods to the family (Chant, 2003).

Prior to the Revolution, divorce was not commonplace in Cuba. In 1958 there was one divorce for every 11 marriages. In 1988, 43 out of every 100 marriages ended in divorce, and in 1991 one out of every 2.3 marriages ended in divorce. In 1981, 59% of women over age 14 lived with a husband or partner, while 12% were divorced or separated. During this period, 8.9% of the adult population was classified as divorced or separated, twice the figure for 1970. Cuba currently has one of the highest divorce rates in the world, particularly among younger couples (Safa, 1995; Smith & Padula, 1996). As a result of the Family Code, divorce laws in Cuba are among the most progressive in Latin America and the Caribbean. Subsequently, Cuban women are financially less dependent on their ex-spouses and are not at the mercy of their goodwill (Chant, 2003).

High divorce rates, early pregnancy, and consensual unions are the primary reasons for the formation of female-headed households in Cuba, which increased from 14% in 1953 to 28.1% in 1981. In her research, Safa (1995) found female-headed households were more common among women who had their first child prior to age 20 (57%) compared with married women who had their first child after age 20 (42.1%). In addition, she found that 56% of black women in the sample were female household heads, compared with about 30% of white and mulatto women. One reason for high rates of marital dissolution and female-headed households may be the greater economic independence of Cuban women, most of whom are in the paid labor market. In addition, the prevalence of multi-generational households and access to health- and childcare make women less dependent on men to help raise children. In addition, women who head their own households are given preferential employment opportunities. Unlike other Caribbean nations, such as Puerto Rico or the Dominican Republic, marital instability is not a result of high rates of male unemployment (Safa, 1995).

11. SPECIAL TOPICS: MIGRATION AND CUBAN FAMILIES

The study of Cuban migration to the United States has captured the attention of social scientists across a broad range of disciplines. Today an impressive body of work exists that documents the different waves of migration (Masud-Piloto, 1996; Portes, Clark, & Bach, 1977; Pedraza-Bailey, 1985; L. Perez, 1985), the political predicament of Cuban refugees (Masud-Piloto, 1996; Nackerud, Springer, & Larrison, 1999), and their much celebrated assimilation story (L. Perez, 1994). Yet, the story that captured the public imagination and illustrated the predicament of Cuban families in the United States happened on Thanksgiving Day 1999, when a little boy named Elian Gonzalez was found clinging to an inner tube off the Florida coast. In this section, we use the Elian Gonzalez story to contextualize the connections that exist between Cuban families in the United States and in Cuba. The story of Elian can best be summarized as an international custody case that magnified the problems of U.S. foreign policy toward Cuba, the current economic crisis facing Cuban families, and the migration saga of families across generations.

A Family Saga: The Elian Gonzalez Story

Elian Gonzales was one of three survivors on a raft that left Cuba with 11 people on board. His mother, Elizabeth Brotons, and her boyfriend, Lazaro Rafael Munero, perished on the ill-fated trip. After being treated at a local Miami hospital, Elian was turned over to his distant uncle Lazaro Cardenas. Mr. Cardenas, a Cuban refugee, lives in Little Havana with his daughter Marisleysis. Little Havana has been home to generations of political exiles going back to the first wave of Cuban immigrants that came to the United States in the aftermath of the Revolution. The case of Elian Gonzalez captured the world's attention and brought to the forefront the struggles and problems of Cuban families on both sides of the Straits of Florida.

Elian's parents were divorced but they remained close as they shared custody of their son. When his father, Juan Miguel Gonzalez,

learned that Elizabeth and Lazaro had fled Cuba with Elian and that Elian had survived, he immediately tried to have Elian returned to Cuba. The little boy quickly became a celebrity in the Cuban-American community and a symbol of the evils of communism. Elian's arrival fueled intense anti-Castro sentiment among many Cuban exiles, particularly in South Florida. The Cardenas family demanded that the boy be granted political asylum and be allowed to stay with them. The Cardenas family took Elian's case to the U.S. courts for legal support.

Newspaper and television reports quickly capitalized on the story and within weeks mass demonstrations and political protests broke out in Miami. In December, Elian's sixth birthday celebration became a worldwide media event. He was shown going to Disney World, playing with toy guns, and was surrounded by family members. For the Miami relatives and the people who gathered in Little Havana, Elian became a political symbol used to discredit the communist government of Fidel Castro. Local politicians visited him and publicly welcomed him into the country. The Republican-controlled Congress proposed granting him U.S. citizenship so that he would not be deported to Cuba. Elected officials suggested giving Juan Miguel resident alien status so he could come to the United States to live with his son. On the other side of the ocean, Castro's government also capitalized on the plight of the Cardenas family as mass demonstrations were organized in Havana.

In keeping with U.S. and international law, the Immigration and Naturalization Service (INS) ruled that the child must be returned to his father, the legal custodian of the child. After many legal court battles, the U.S. government granted a visa to Juan Miguel so that he could be reunited with his son. After his arrival in the United States, Juan Miguel had to wait several months to see Elian and take him back to Cuba, because the Miami relatives refused to turn over the child. On April 22, 2000, INS agents stormed the residence of the Cardenas family in Miami and seized the little boy by force. Legal battles ensued for several months until June 28, 2000, when father and son returned to Cuba, to be welcomed as heroes.

At first glance, the saga of the little boy who was rescued on Thanksgiving Day seemed to be an international custody dispute between families that had been separated by political forces beyond their control. In actuality, this was a story of a transnational family conflict in the era of global politics. On the Miami side of the straits were Elian's relatives representing the refugee community, who have been separated from their families for decades. In addition to the physical separation, there was a symbolic one anchored in passionate anti-Castro sentiments. On the Cuban side of the straits, the story is of an economically disenfranchised mother who risked everything to provide a better life for her family. The thread weaving these two narratives together was the story of a divorced father simply wishing to regain custody of his son. Underlying the media images of this custody battle was the strength of Cuban families and the persistence of *familism* (the values, attitudes, and beliefs that are associated with the extended family) that continue to characterize Cuban families in both locales. The images of Juan Miguel Gonzalez's struggle to reunite with his son challenged long-held stereotypes and prejudices about the role of Latino men, in general, and Cuban men, in particular, as absent and uncaring fathers. Indeed, the Gonzalez saga is a story about the resiliency of family values across transnational fields. It is a story that shows the flexibility of the family as an institution that mediates broad societal changes while at the same time resists social change.

Cuban Families in the United States

After fleeing the Revolution, the first wave of Cuban refugees to the United States found themselves in the typical immigrant predicament that characterized post-World War II migration. Highly educated elite men could not transfer their degrees and credentials to the U.S. workforce. Lack of professional contacts and language barriers further hampered their ability to assume the traditional breadwinner role. While some men could not find work, others took jobs that were below their educational and professional training. Consequently, their wives were forced to enter the labor market to help support their families. In fact, recent research on Cuban immigrants in the United States has linked their economic success to family organization. Using census data, L. Perez (1994) found that Cubans have proportionately more workers in the labor market per family than the Latino/a and general U.S. populations and higher rates of female labor-force participation.

Although the majority of women were not employed outside the home prior to the Revolution, as émigrés they were forced to seek employment for economic survival. Gonzalez argues that "the ability of these women to bring money into the household gave them a new basis for power and respect in the family" (1994, p. 209). However, social scientists warn us not to interpret the high incidence of labor-force participation among Cuban women in the United States as an indication of gender equality. In fact, research shows that high rates of female workforce participation often coexist with fairly traditional gender roles (Suarez, 1998). Many men simply refused to accept the reality of women's employment and were unwilling to contribute to the household labor (L. Perez, 1994). In addition, women's growing sense of independence was often met with staunch resistance from their husbands and led to marital instability. In

1980, 5.2% of Cuban-Americans aged 15 and older reported being divorced; by 1990 the percentage increased to 8.3 (Suarez, 1998). Women's double burden of employment and domestic labor often creates the structural conditions that are associated with marital conflict and ultimately divorce.

As in other Latino/a immigrant communities, researchers have also found marked generational conflicts between parents and second- and third-generation U.S.-born Cuban youth. L. Perez (1994) observed that one aspect of intergenerational tension is the conflict over dependence and independence. In Cuba cultural norms encourage the dependence of children on their parents even into adulthood, whereas in the United States cultural norms favor independence. Nevertheless, researchers have found that biculturality has helped reduce intergenerational conflict among Cuban families. "Parents learn how to remain loyal to their ethnic background while becoming skilled in interacting with their youngsters' Americanized values and behaviors, and vice versa" (Szapocznick & Hernandez, 1988, p. 168, as quoted in L. Perez, 1994, p. 108).

Marriage patterns are another indicator of the emerging cultural influences on Cuban-American families. Elizabeth Arias (2001) found that marital behavior among Cuban-American families is similar to the majority of the U.S. population. She found that the likelihood of interethnic marriages increases with an increase in socioeconomic status. According to Arias (2001) the probability of a U.S.-born Cuban male with 5 or more years of university education marrying an Anglo female is (.62), compared with the probability of him marrying a Cuban woman (.25) or someone of another ethnicity (.13). Interestingly, second-generation males with only a high school education are more likely to marry an Anglo than a Cuban-origin woman, suggesting that nativity has an effect beyond that of socioeconomic status.

The Elian Gonzalez story shows that an important characteristic of American-Cuban families is their relationship to family members who are still living in Cuba and the strong ties between them. Studies of such transnational family ties have yielded interesting results. Eckstein and Barberia (2002) interviewed two cohorts of émigrés in Florida and in New Jersey. The first wave of émigrés, who left Cuba between 1959 and 1979, were political refugees who articulated the strongest sentiments against Fidel Castro. The second wave of émigrés (known as *Marielitos*) left Cuba after 1980, for economic, not political reasons. It has been well documented that first-wave émigrés were Cuban elites who were either officials in the Batista government, upper-class businessmen, or highly educated professionals. On their arrival in the United States, the first-wave émigrés were defined as "victims of communism" and offered a wide range of local, state, and federal aid to help with the process of adaptation. They also qualified for benefits only available to U.S. citizens, such as Medicare. *Marielitos*, on the other hand, have been generally stigmatized as "undesirables," because they include darker-skinned and less well off Cubans. In fact, even members of their own ethnic enclaves have snubbed and segregated them.

For many years, first-wave émigrés opposed travel to Cuba. In fact, for them travel to Cuba was not an option because of government restrictions in both the United States and in Cuba. The U.S. embargo prohibited travel to Cuba and the Cuban government prohibited visits by most exiles who had rejected the regime. In the 1990s restrictions against travel to Cuba were eased. The Cuban government eliminated a visitor quota, and it allowed Cuban-Americans to stay with their island relatives for up to 3 weeks per trip. As a result, "Cuban American travel increased from approximately 7,000 to over 140,000, with an estimated minimum of 100,000 emigres visiting annually between 1996 and 1999" (Eckstein & Barberia, 2002, p. 807).

Interestingly, Eckstein and Barberia (2002) report that most of the people visiting the island are second-wave émigrés. They suggest that the shift in motivation for immigration helps explain the differences in travel and continued family connections with the island. While first-wave émigrés left for political reasons, second-wave and more recent émigrés came to the United States in search of economic opportunities and to help the families they left behind.

Nostalgia and reestablishment of roots is now driving first-wave émigrés back to Cuba. Second- and third-generation children of émigrés are also visiting the island. For first-wave émigrés and their children, traveling to Cuba can be difficult and somewhat traumatic, although Eckstein and Barberia report that "bonds are fast to form in a culture where blood ties are strong" (2002, p. 809). Generational differences are evident among the experiences of Cuban-American visitors to the island. First-wave émigrés often return to the United States feeling validated by their decision to leave and their disdain for the government. For second- and third-generation Cuban-Americans, their visits are often transforming and very positive. *Marielitos* and post-1990 émigrés are more likely to travel whenever they can, even though they are less financially secure than first-wave émigrés. In addition, they are much less critical of family members who have chosen to remain on the island:

> Those of us who left after Mariel understand the intentions of the Revolution—to improve the living conditions for the working class in Cuba—and to recognize the achievements in health and education. We are more tolerant and respectful of Cubans who choose to remain on the island. Unlike older exiles, we know and understand the conditions under which our families struggle to survive, because we lived them ourselves. We do not feel it appropriate to demand that our families and friends in Cuba make sacrifices (that is, live without dollars) or take action (against the government) that we were unwilling to make. (Eckstein & Barberia, 2002, p. 835)

Indeed, the remittances (U.S. dollars) that émigrés bring (and send) to Cuba have become an important form of extra currency for families throughout the class spectrum. The Cuban government has also benefited from such economic transfers. In an attempt to capitalize on the flow of U.S. currency, the government created state-owned and -controlled dollar stores, where Cubans can buy food and other products not available in government-run stores. One unintended macroeconomic effect of remittances and travel to Cuba is the undermining of Cuba's socialist economy. In addition, family visits to Cuba are creating new transnational social and cultural ties previously beyond reach (Eckstein & Barberia, 2002).

CONCLUSION AND FUTURE DIRECTIONS

In this chapter, we provided a historical overview of the development of Cuban families under Spanish and U.S. colonial rule. Historical accounts place the origins of important family cultural norms and practices in the context of colonization of the island. Indeed, as a result of its colonization by Spain and the United States, social class and race have differentiated Cuban family life for centuries. Our analysis of Cuban families would not be complete if we did not address the effects of the Cuban Revolution on family structure. Clearly, a major goal of the Cuban Revolution was to promote race, class, and gender equality in the family and larger society. The Family Code represented a legislative attempt to eradicate patriarchy in the home and encourage the equitable division of housework. In addition, we documented how the Special Period has affected Cuban families and has (re)gendered the division of household labor. At the turn of the 21st century, the Cuban family is once again at a crossroad. As a result of the fall of the Soviet Union, increased foreign investment on the island, and increased international trade, Cuba has moved from a strictly socialist economy to a more market-driven economy. Throughout the scholarly and exile communities, people are wondering what Cuba will look like in the remaining years of Castro's regime and how his death will affect Cuban families and the larger social order. Our research indicates that most Cuban families fear the loss of their social safety net and are hoping for European-style social democracy, not unbridled U.S. capitalism.

NOTES

1. Article 24: Marriage is established with equal rights and duties for both partners.

Article 25: Partners must live together, be loyal, considerate, respectful and mutually helpful to each other. The rights and duties that this Code establishes for partners will remain in effect as long as the marriage is not legally terminated, even if partners do not live together for any well-founded reason.

Article 26: Both partners must care for the family they have created and must cooperate with the other in the education, upbringing, and guidance of the children according to the principles of socialist morality. They must participate, to the extent of their capacity or possibilities, in the running of the home, and cooperate so that it will develop in the best possible way.

Article 27: The partners must help meet the needs of the family that has been created with their marriage, each according to his or her ability and financial status. However, if one of them only contributes by working at home and caring for the children, the other partner must contribute to this support alone, without prejudice to his duty of cooperating in the aforementioned work and care.

2. In comparison with the literature on gay men in Latin America, there is very little written on lesbians. The absence of literature on lesbians is linked to assumptions about female sexual passivity and to *machismo*. Because sexuality is seen as being centered on penetration, and women are believed to be less important than men, lesbians are often defined as devoid of sexuality and are rendered invisible. In addition, because of the repression against gays and lesbians in Cuba, there has been less social movement activity than there has been among lesbians in other parts of Latin America (Chant, 2003).

REFERENCES

Aguilar, L. E. (1993). Cuba, c. 1860–c. 1930. In L. Bethell (Ed.), *Cuba: A short history* (pp. 21–55). Cambridge, UK: University of Cambridge Press.

Arias, E. (2001). Change in nuptiality patterns among Cuban Americans: Evidence of cultural and structural assimilation? *International Migration Review*, 35(2), 525–556.

Buckman, R. T. (2002). *Latin America 2002* (World Today series). Harpers Ferry, VA: Stryker-Post.

Campbell, A. (1999). The Cuban economy has turned the corner: The question now is where is it going? *Global Development Studies, 1*(3-4), 150–192.

Catasús Cervera, S. (1992). La nupcialidad de la década de los ochenta en Cuba. In Centro de Estudios Demográfias (Ed.), *La demográfia Cubana ante el quinto centenario* (pp. 30–42). Havana, Cuba: Editorial de Ciencias Sociales.

Chant, S., with Craske, N. (2003). *Gender in Latin America.* New Brunswick, NJ: Rutgers University Press.

de la Fuente, A. (2001). *A nation for all: Race, inequality, and politics in twentieth-century Cuba.* Chapel Hill, NC: University of North Carolina Press.

Eckstein, S., & Barberia, L. (2002). Grounding immigrant generations in history: Cuban Americans and their transnational ties. *International Migration Review, 36*(3), 799–837.

Fernandez, N. (1996). The color of love: Young interracial couples in Cuba. *Latin American Perspectives, 23*(1), 99–117.

Fleites-Lear, M. (1999). Women, family, and the Cuban revolution: A personal and socio-political analysis. *Global Development Studies, 1*(3-4), 31–56.

Gonzalez, J., Jr. (1994). *Racial and ethnic families in America.* Dubuque, IA: Kendall/Hunt Publishing.

Hernandez-Truyol, B. (2004). *Out in left field: The challenges of good governance in Cuba.* Symposium conducted at the meeting of the University of Iowa Center for International Finance & Development, College of Law, and International Programs, Iowa City, IA.

Jennissen, T., & Lundy, C. (2001). Women in Cuba and the move to a private market economy. *Women's Studies International Forum, 24*(2), 181–198.

Lumsden, I. (1996). *Machos, maricones, and gays: Cuba and homosexuality.* Philadelphia, PA: Temple University Press.

Lutjens, S. L. (1995). Reading between the lines: Women, the state, and rectification in Cuba. *Latin American Perspectives, 85*(22), 100–124.

Masud-Piloto, F. (1996). *From welcomed exiles to illegal immigrants: Cuban migration to the U.S., 1959–1995.* Lanham, Maryland: Rowman and Littlefield.

Nackerud, L., Springer, A., & Larrison, C. (1999). The end of the Cuban contradiction in U.S. refugee policy. *International Migration Review, 33* (1), 176–192.

Navarro, J. C. (1998). *History of Cuba: The challenges of the yoke and the star.* Havana, Cuba Si-Mar S.A.

Pedraza-Bailey, S. (1985). *Political and economic migrants in America: Cubans and Mexicans.* Austin: University of Texas Press.

Perez, L. (1980). The family in Cuba. In M. Singh Das & C. J. Jesser (Eds.), *The family in Latin America* (pp. 235–269). New Delhi: Vikas Publishing House.

Perez, L. (1985). The Cuban population of the United States: The results of the 1980 U.S. census of population. *Cuban Studies, 15*(2), 1–18.

Perez, L. (1994). Cuban families in the United States. In R. Taylor (Ed.), *Minority families in the United States: A multicultural perspective* (pp. 95–112). Englewood Cliffs, NJ: Prentice Hall.

Perez, L. A., Jr. (1993). Cuba, c. 1930–1959. In L. Bethell (Ed.), *Cuba: A short history* (pp. 57-93). Cambridge, UK: University of Oxford Press.

Portes, A., Clark, J. M., & Bach, R. L. (1977). The new wave: A statistical profile of recent Cuban exiles to the United States. *Cuban Studies/Estudios Cubanos*, 1–32.

Rosendahl, M. (1997). *Inside the revolution: Everyday life in socialist Cuba*. Ithaca, NY: Cornell University Press.

Safa, H. I. (1995). *The myth of the male breadwinner: Women and industrialization in the Caribbean*. Boulder, CO: Westview Press.

Smith, L. M., & Padula, A. (1996). *Sex and revolution: Women in socialist Cuba*. New York: Oxford University Press.

Stone, E. (1981). *Women and the Cuban revolution: Speeches & documents by Fidel Castro, Vilma Espin & others*. New York: Pathfinder.

Suarez, Z. (1998). Cuban American families. In C. H. Mindel, R. Haberstein, & R. Wright Jr. (Eds.), *Ethnic families in America: Patterns and variations* (pp. 172–198). Englewood Cliffs, NJ: Prentice Hall.

Thomas, H. (1993). Cuba, c. 1750–c. 1860. In L. Bethell (Ed.), *Cuba: A short history* (pp. 1-20). Cambridge, UK: University Cambridge Press.

Toro-Morn, M. I., Roschelle, A. R., & Facio, E. (2002). Gender, work, and family in Cuba: The challenges of the special period. *Journal of Developing Societies*, *18*(2–3), 32–58.

Trento, A. (2000). *Castro and Cuba: From revolution to the present*. New York: Interlink Books.

CHAPTER 20

The Family in Puerto Rico: Colonialism, Industrialization, and Migration

Maura I. Toro-Morn

1. PUERTO RICO AND PUERTO RICANS

Government, Demographics, and History

Of all the countries in Latin America and the Caribbean, Puerto Rico has the most peculiar status (Duany, 2002). In 1493 Puerto Rico was colonized by Spain and remained in its control until the Spanish-American War in 1898, making it one of the countries with the longest Hispanic influence in the hemisphere. On July 25, 1898, Puerto Rico was invaded by U.S. troops and taken under U.S. control. Over 100 years of U.S. influence has meant "an intense penetration of American capital, commodities, laws, and customs, unequaled in other Latin American countries" (Duany, 2002, p. 1). Puerto Rican national identity is, nevertheless, as strong as many independent countries in the region. Anthropologist Jorge Duany has observed that

> at the beginning of the twenty-first century, Puerto Rico presents the apparent paradox of a stateless nation that has not assimilated

into the American mainstream. After more than one hundred years of U.S. colonialism, the Island remains a Spanish-speaking Afro-Hispanic-Caribbean nation. (2002, p. 1)

Due to the U.S. influence, the government of Puerto Rico resembles that of a state of the union. For example, every 4 years Puerto Ricans elect a governor, 28 senators, and 51 members of the house of representatives (Gonzalez, 2000). Further, Puerto Ricans elect a nonvoting member to the U.S. House of Representatives. Transportation, immigration, foreign trade, and other areas of government are controlled by the U.S. government. The complexities of the colonial status can be further observed in that Puerto Ricans contribute to Social Security and serve in the U.S. military, but do not vote for the U.S. president and do not pay federal taxes (Gonzalez, 2000). Federal government programs apply to Puerto Rico, but levels of assistance are lower than those provided to the people living in the 50 states (Mather, 2003). For example, "in 1999, the average monthly payment to families through the Temporary

Assistance for Needy Families (TANF) program was $101 in Puerto Rico, compared with $454 in New York—the state where Puerto Ricans are most highly concentrated" (Mather, 2003, p. 1).

According to the U.S. Census of Population, there were 4 million Puerto Ricans living on the island in 2002, but if one adds the 3.4 million Puerto Ricans living in the 50 states and the District of Columbia, the population of Puerto Ricans is over 7 million. Mather (2003, p. 1) observes that with over 1,100 people per square mile, the population density of the island is similar to New Jersey, the most densely populated state. As of 2002, the fertility rate is 2 children born per woman, and the average family size is 3.5 people. Infant mortality is about 10 deaths per 1,000 live births, while the average life expectancy at birth is approximately 76.7 years. Puerto Rico has a relatively low literacy rate of 89% for the entire population, compared with other Caribbean countries, such as Cuba, which holds a 96% literacy rate. Income levels in Puerto Rico fall behind those in the United States. Mather (2003, p. 2) reports that in 1999, the median household income in Puerto Rico was $14,412, compared with West Virginia's—the lowest state in the union—of $29,696. New Jersey had the highest median household income with $55,146. The median household income for Latinos living in New Jersey ($39,609) was 2.5 times that of those in Puerto Rico (Mather, 2003).

Many aspects of Puerto Rican culture are derived from its early Spanish influence. The majority of Puerto Ricans practice Roman Catholicism, while the remaining follow Protestantism and various other religions. Spanish and English are the languages spoken on the island (CIA World FactBook, 2002).

Puerto Rican Families Under Two Colonial Regimes

The colonization of Puerto Rico first by Spain and then by the United States had a profound impact on the history and formation of Puerto Rican families. Before Spain invaded Puerto Rico in 1493, the island was home to the Taino Indians. We know very little about Taino Indian culture and family structure. Tainos lived in villages called *yucayeques*. Historians have established that Taino culture was characterized by a matrilineal family structure, that is, power and influence was transmitted through the mother's side of the family (Tovar, 1972). We also know that indigenous women had access to the highest political position in Taino society as *caciques*, tribal leaders (Acosta-Belen, 1986). Further, their religious culture included both male and female gods. The Tainos were an agricultural society; thus, given what we know about primitive agricultural societies, a gender division of labor assigned both men and women important tasks in the production and reproduction of food, shelter, and clothing. Within a few years of the Spanish invasion, the Taino population had been virtually wiped out by wars and disease. Thus, their influence on the formation of cultural family patterns was minimal, but their influence on Puerto Rican culture is still felt. For example, indigenous words blend with the Spanish language, giving Puerto Rican Spanish a unique flavor.

To meet labor shortages in the colonies, Spaniards transported African slaves to Puerto Rico from the mid-1500s until 1873, when slavery was officially abolished in Puerto Rico, thus making Puerto Rico, like Cuba, a multiracial society from its origins. But, it is the migration of Spanish men and women, an important part of the process of empire building, that shaped the culture, history, and family practices in enduring ways (Toro-Morn, forthcoming).

Spanish Colonialism

Traditional accounts of the Spanish colonization of the Americas tend to describe the movement and settlement in the Spanish colonies as mostly a man's job. Feminist historians have challenged this narrow and androcentric view of colonialism (Toro-Morn, forthcoming). The migration and settlement of the colonies was a task that required the energy, skills, and work of both men and women of different races and nationalities. It required the subjugation of indigenous people who were forced into labor, Africans who were transported to the colonies by force, and Spanish men and women who not only represented the Spanish empire but also helped manage and administer the colonies. In the 16th century, Spanish cultural notions determined that leaving home and family was expected of men, although that did not mean that women were completely sedentary. Gendered cultural notions determined that women moved to prearranged destinations where they got married, or migrated with husbands and fathers. The discovery of the New World simply expanded the terrain for the migration of European men and women (Toro-Morn, forthcoming).

Here it is important to point out that Spain, as well as other colonial powers, encouraged and supported the migration of women. For example, the Spanish government sought to maintain the migration of Spanish women to the new colonies by requiring that ships leaving for the New World had to include at least 10% women. Indeed, the migration of Spanish women from different class sectors must be seen within the larger context of the changing needs of the empire. Although Spanish colonial policies did not condone marriages and consensual unions between indigenous women and Spanish men, the migration of Spanish women encouraged the development of a domestic ideology more in keeping with colonial interests. As part of the colonial entourage, Spanish women assumed the traditional female roles expected of Iberian society. They became mothers, wives, and homemakers, and contributed to the education and acculturation of the first *criollo* class, the next generation of landowners. Their productive and reproductive labor was very important to fostering the needs of the empire (Toro-Morn, forthcoming). It is common historical knowledge that in the absence of Spanish women, men took indigenous and slave women as concubines. Juan Gonzalez Jr. writes that

> most Spanish men lived in *union libre* (free union) with their mistresses and most of these children were recognized by their fathers and were raised in a bi-cultural environment. As they matured they were integrated into Spanish society and were recognized as a mix-blood or mestizo population. (1998, p. 228)

The Spanish colonial legacy shaped family values and culture in profound ways. According to Puerto Rican feminist Edna Acosta-Belen (1986, p. 3), the Spanish colonial empire was a patriarchal, paternalistic, and military-oriented society that demanded the complete subordination of women. Across social classes, women were socialized to be "obedient daughters, faithful wives, and devoted mothers" (Acosta-Belen, 1986, p. 3). These cultural values were enforced by law. For example, the Spanish Civil Code gave absolute power to the husband as head of the family and administrator of family property. The code also gave the father authority over children. There were also elaborate laws that regulated inheritance, marriage, adultery, and even widowhood. Clearly, most of these laws limited the rights of women. As a colony of Spain, the Catholic Church was an important institution that influenced family life in strong ways. These social norms guided family life for several centuries.

Within the first decades of colonization, Spain had mined the riches of Puerto Rico and converted the colony into a supplier of agricultural goods, mostly coffee and sugar, for European markets. By the 19th century, Puerto Rico had a small but very wealthy and influential upper class, known as *hacendados*, a very small middle class, and a huge mass of working poor and poor families, *jornaleros*, who worked the land for a living. The hacendado families, descendants of Spanish colonizers, created a family culture of strong religious and cultural traditions with strong connections to Spain. The Puerto Rican practice of using two family names as surnames, which is still prevalent today, originated in the marriage practices of hacendado families for whom marriage was the union of prominent families and the maintenance of social status (Fitzpatrick, 1987). Across social classes, the family has always been central to the lives of Puerto Ricans, yet research that examines and documents its structure, values, and historical changes is limited (Roschelle, 1997).

U.S. Colonialism

The Americans that came to Puerto Rico in 1898 knew little about Puerto Rico's history and culture. They found a sparsely populated island with a very small urban population and a highly dispersed rural population (Ramirez de Arellano & Seipp, 1983). At the time of the U.S. occupation, the population of the country was reported to be about 900,000 persons. Landless agricultural workers lived close to each other in the coastal areas, or scattered through the mountainous interior, inaccessible by roads. Social class and racial differences were a source of confusion for the occupying empire. As a multiracial society, the lack of overt racial segregation between racial groups mystified (and continues to mystify) Americans, who are accustomed to a dichotomous racial world. Similarly, the marked social class differences found in the population at the time of the invasion perplexed Americans. According to Annette Ramirez de Arellano and Conrad Seipp,

> [m]ost Americans viewed the conditions that they encountered in Puerto Rico as appalling. The people were seen as dirty, ignorant, and lazy. There was a general lack of sanitation, and most families relied upon contaminated sources of water supply. Health hazards were acute, as the commanders of the American army of occupation quickly discovered. After six months in Puerto Rico nearly one-fourth of the troops were ineffective owing to syphilis, gonorrhea, and cancroids. (1983, p. 7)

The maternal death rate and infant mortality rate were very high: One in four newborns died within the first year of life. Tuberculosis, malnutrition, and anemia were devastating diseases to families. The condition of the family also generated social commentary. The role of the father as the head of the family and the subordination of women continued to characterize families across social classes. Most families were not consummated in marriage; consensual union was the most common family arrangement for over one-half of all Puerto Rican families (Ramirez de Arellano & Seipp, 1983).

Consequently, the Americanization of the island entailed not only a change in the socioeconomic systems of production to fit the needs of the new empire, but equally important, changing cultural practices and institutions more in keeping with American values and beliefs. For example, in the 1920s health reform, in particular the treatment of venereal diseases, was pursued with passion and determination. The government mobilized 15,000 troops to the San Juan area and ordered them to arrest every known prostitute. Over 1,000 women were incarcerated without benefit of trial. Protestant religious groups carried out many of the social reforms of the Americanization program. They operated hospitals, schools, and community organizations. As a result, a significant proportion of the Puerto Rican population abandoned Catholicism and converted to the various Protestant denominations with representatives on the island.

The first major economic change occurred in the first part of the 20th century as Puerto Rico became integrated into the economic system of the new colonial power. The political economy of the island underwent dramatic changes. In other words, the hacienda social structure was replaced by a sugar-plantation economy, more in keeping with the needs of the new colonial power. According to the History Task Force (1979, p. 94), "U.S. companies established control over all aspects of the Island's economy, including transport, communications, finance, agriculture, and small-scale manufacturing." A legal apparatus of laws and decrees of the military government that ruled the island from 1898 to 1900 made all of these changes possible. These changes also entailed converting the Puerto Rican labor force into a rural proletariat (History Task Force, 1979). Again, Rivera captures the historical changes under way: "The traditional classes of nineteenth-century Puerto Rico, immersed in a culture of deference generated by the hacienda social structure, were broken up and aggressive struggle replaced deference and paternalism" (1986, p. 33).

The development of a sugar-based plantation economy had the most profound effect on Puerto Rican families across all social classes. Hacendado families found themselves near extinction by social and economic policies that expropriated them of land and political power (Toro-Morn, 2001). Many landowning families lost their land and moved to the cities. Daughters in these families were encouraged to pursue education and professional work, leading to the rise of a small class of professional women. Most women went into the teaching profession, radically altering the gender composition of teaching. In 1899, 70% of teachers on the island were men. By 1930 75% of teachers were women.

Further, the economic changes imposed by the new colonial power accelerated the incorporation of poor and working-class women into salaried work (Azize, 1987; Acevedo, 1993; Ortiz, 1996; Toro-Morn, 2001). Poor and working-class women became integrated into a sex-segregated labor market that closely related to the needs of U.S. colonial capitalism (Ortiz, 1996). During the first three decades of the 20th century, women worked stripping tobacco, needleworking at home, and making straw hats, work that can be seen as an extension of their reproductive roles in the home. In the tobacco industry, for example, women worked as leaf strippers, sorters, and packers, work that took excruciatingly long hours, was poorly paid, and was done under dangerous conditions. Needlework was also very exploitative, and wages never rose above survival (Ortiz, 1996). Rivera (1986, p. 37) observes that U.S. colonialism opened the spectrum of employment opportunities for women, while at the same time it increased their exploitation as workers. In fact, this is the context that propelled women's involvement in the labor movement. Working-class women "rejected views of feminine fragility, moral superiority, and passivity that were attributed to women by other social classes" (Rivera, 1986, p. 37).

Historians have documented how both needle and tobacco women workers organized labor unions and participated in labor strikes to challenge women's inequality and exploitation as both women and workers. For example, when New Deal legislation threatened to wipe out the home needlework industry because it allegedly did not adhere to U.S. standards, needlewomen workers challenged island trade unions and fought for their right to do homework in the context of their social role as homemakers (Boris, 1996). Home needleworkers, according to Boris (1996, p. 48), defended their work as the only means by which they could provide their families with food. In other words, it was precisely their roles as breadwinners that women workers used to demand higher wages and better working conditions. In the end, New Deal legislation upgraded standards for needlewomen workers on paper, but it failed them by not honoring their desire to hold onto the home as their workplace.

Another important consequence of the rise of a capitalist-based sugarcane plantation economy was the displacement of families through massive migrations internally, regionally, and internationally. At the turn of the 20th century, Puerto Ricans began to move internally from the mountainous (coffee-growing) inland areas to the coastal sugarcane-growing municipalities, and to the growing urban site of tobacco and other small manufacturing industries (History Task Force, 1979). When internal employment proved limited, Puerto Rican men, in particular, were recruited to do agricultural work in Hawaii, Cuba, and Santo Domingo. Eventually, Puerto Rican men and women were propelled to migrate to the United States, in particular East Coast industrial centers, to meet acute labor shortages due to World War I (History Task Force, 1979).

These migrations were shaped by family dynamics and at the same time affected family life in many ways. Men were recruited as immigrant labor throughout the hemisphere due to the transitional nature of work and traditional gender notions about women's proper place in the family. In addition, lessons from the turbulent past of forced labor, peonage, and indentured labor history in the United States made employers view voluntary contracted workers as more rational and humanistic, and an efficient way to meet labor needs. In fact, U.S. labor needs in the hemisphere demanded the movement of Latin American and Caribbean male immigrant workers to build the Panama Canal and work in the sugar fields of Cuba, the coffee plantations in Brazil, and the banana plantations in Costa Rica and Nicaragua (Toro-Morn, forthcoming).

These changes implemented as a result of U.S. economic policies created widespread poverty and destitution among the poor and working-class Puerto Ricans, thus driving men to take on work as contracted immigrant workers. At the beginning of the 20th century, Caribbean islands, such as Puerto Rico, became islands of women and children left behind due to male migration. Women survived by trying to find wage work in their rural villages or by moving to urban centers to work as domestics. Further, due to the precarious conditions in most labor camps and the lack of communication facilities, many men found it difficult to maintain constant communication with their families and send remittances home (Toro-Morn, forthcoming).

Eventually, Puerto Rican women joined men in the process of migration leading to the formation of Puerto Rican communities in the United States (Sanchez-Korrol, 1983). Like their husbands, Puerto Rican women left the island motivated by economic need. Life in the early barrios of New York City was hard for both men and women.

Social scientists in both Puerto Rico and the United States agree that within the first three decades under U.S. control, political and economic changes had created social dislocations, widespread poverty, and destitution, problems that affected the well-being of working-class and poor families. These problems became even more marked in Puerto Rico in the Great Depression years. The standard of living worsened for families across the social spectrum, in particular the working class. Wages of sugarcane workers, the largest sector of the working class, fell from 90 cents per day to 50 cents in 1931–1932 (Dietz, 1986). Ironically, while wages decreased dramatically, the number of hours worked increased. For example, in 1933 tobacco workers, among the lowest-paid workers in the economy, worked an average of 29.5 hours per week and earned an average of $1.27 per week. Workers across different sectors of the economy revolted against employers. At this time, the Nationalist Party helped to mobilize Puerto Rican discontent against U.S. colonialism. Economist James Dietz writes that

> [t]he coming of the Great Depression simply made manifest the severity of the conditions that debilitated the island economy: it did not create or invent them. The problem that confronted the colonial administrators in Washington and San Juan was how to transform the colonial development model and improve its functioning in such a way as to preserve the colonial relation. (1986, p. 136)

Operation Bootstrap and the changes in the colonial status of the island that took place in the 1950s helped to accomplish such changes, a topic that will be discussed later in the chapter.

2. PAIRING UP IN PUERTO RICO

There is very little research that examines the mate selection and pairing up practices of Puerto Ricans on the island and abroad. Thus, the topic is indeed a fertile area of study for future social scientists. Historically, we know that Spanish colonial authorities were more tolerant of sexual unions and relations between Spaniard, indigenous, and slave populations. Indeed, racial mixing and pairing up between Spaniards, Indians, and slaves led to the racial diversity that exists today in Puerto Rico and most Latin American and Caribbean countries. In fact, although racism has always been a problem in Puerto Rico, dating, marriages, and coupling has not been affected by the severe racial restrictions that have existed in the United States. Underlying these early pairing-up practices between racial groups, tacitly endorsed by the Spanish colonial power, was the notion that racial mixing for the most part did not subvert the class structure. In other words, for the colonial elite, marriage was a way to secure inheritance and the maintenance of power, and frequently children of such mixed unions were raised and socialized to become part of the elite landholding *criollo* class.

The most recent historical family research about pairing up focuses on a group that has frequently been ignored in Puerto Rican family studies, namely, slave families (Stark, 1996). David Stark (1996), who researched parish registers in Arecibo, Caguas, Coamo, San German, and Yauco, shows that most slaves who married selected their spouses from a marriage pool limited to other slaves belonging to the same owner or to the owner's immediate family and relatives. This was a process that was enforced by 18th-century slave marriage laws in Puerto Rico. He observed that 18th-century slave family life was very stable. Both married and unmarried mothers displayed healthy and regular reproductive behavior. Although there were some variations in the towns studied and between married and unmarried women, Stark found that the spacing of children for married slave mothers was less than 36 months, similar to European (German) women and other slave black women in the British West Indies. He concludes that these marriage and birthing strategies could be seen as an attempt to create a space of their own and as a retreat from the brutalities of slavery.

Until recently, most Puerto Ricans tended to live in consensual unions (Ramirez de Arellano & Seipp, 1983; Gonzalez, 1998; Canabal, 1990). A consensual union has been defined as "a relatively stable union of a man and a woman who have never gone through a religious or civil marriage ceremony" (Fitzpatrick, 1987). Usually, men and women in consensual unions live together for many years and have children who are officially recognized by the father. Fitzpatrick (1987, p. 75) writes that this type of marriage is observed more among working-class and poor Puerto Ricans. He adds that most Puerto Ricans do not perceive this form of union as immoral. In fact, consensual unions are guided by traditional gender role expectations. Fitzpatrick writes,

> [t]hese people recognize that a man needs a woman and a woman needs a man, and they begin to live together and bring up the children resulting from their union or from other unions. They judge the moral quality of the union in terms of their relationship to each other. He is a good man if he works to support the woman and children, treats them respectfully, and does not abandon them. She is a good woman if she keeps his house, cooks his meals, takes care of his clothes, and raises children properly. (1987, pp. 75–76)

In 1899 consensual unions represented 34.7% of all unions in Puerto Rico (Fitzpatrick, 1987). By 1950 the number of consensual unions in Puerto Rico had declined to 25%. By 1980, 5% of all existing unions in Puerto Rico were consensual.

Among mainland Puerto Ricans, however, Nancy Landale and Katherine Fennelly (1992) found an increase in consensual unions. Further, they found that mainland Puerto Rican women in informal unions are a very heterogeneous group, as they include women who are in long-term committed relationships and unions of short duration, but most women in consensual relations are mothers and their experiences tend to be similar to married women. Finally, the most innovative aspect of their research is that respondents were allowed to define in their own terms the meaning of cohabitation. Landale and Fennelley (1992, p. 278) found that the vast majority of women in informal unions regarded their relationships as a form of marriage.

3. FERTILITY ISSUES

The fertility of Puerto Rican women has been a topic of concern for social scientists, policy analysts, and government officials. In fact, overpopulation and the high fertility rates of Puerto Rico were perceived by the occupying U.S. forces to be the most serious social problem affecting Puerto Rico (Ramirez de Arellano & Seipp, 1983). The Puerto Rican government agreed with such analysis and since the 1930s has supported birth-control programs (Gonzalez, 1998). For a good part of the 20th century, and most notably in the 1940s and 1950s, concerns about population growth and fertility were "intertwined with issues that had at their base the political, economic, social, and cultural relationship between Puerto Rico and the United States" (Ramirez de Arellano & Seipp, 1983, p. 14). In 1950 the fertility rate in Puerto Rico was 5.2 births per woman.

In the 1940s Puerto Rico had become a laboratory for demographers and other social scientists interested in understanding population growth. With the aid of the office of Social Science Research at the University of Puerto Rico, a wave of studies were published at the time that sought to understand the social and cultural conditions affecting fertility. (See, e.g., Ramirez de Arellano and Seipp, 1983, for a more detailed discussion.) For example, one group of researchers found that low-income Puerto Ricans had higher fertility rates. They also found that a high proportion of Catholics favored small families and did not object to the use of contraceptives. At the same time, corporate manufacturers of the Pill and other technological fixes focused their attention on Puerto Rico as a potential experimental site. Indeed, with the aide of researchers and public officials, the contraceptive pill was first introduced in Puerto Rico and tried on small groups of women in Rio Piedras. Other trials took place in Humacao.

While oral contraception was being evaluated, the search for alternative methods continued (Ramirez de Arellano & Seipp, 1983). For example, a vaginal foam cream was also tested in Puerto Rico. The Puerto Rican Family Planning Association agreed to help its manufacturers to conduct a study to examine the effectiveness of the product. In one of the worst slums of San Juan, the Family Planning Association distributed the foam to 222 women of childbearing age, and 69% agreed to use it. The results of the test satisfied its manufacturers. The pregnancy rate, which was 80 per 100 women, decreased to 29 per 100 women during the time the method was used. Eventually, Emko, as the foam was known in Puerto Rico, was distributed throughout the entire island, but results were not that impressive. Between 1959 and 1962, the birth rate went from 32.3 to 31.3 per 1,000 inhabitants (Ramirez de Arellano & Seipp, 1983, p. 130). At the same time, a local hospital began to provide sterilization through cauterization (Ramirez de Arellano & Seipp, 1983). *La operacion* (the operation), as it became known among women, slowly became the most used method of contraception in Puerto Rico. Ramirez de Arellano and Seipp report that the policy of the Presbyterian Hospital, the first hospital to provide these services, was to "approve the operation if the woman had three living children" (1983, p. 137), but some hospitals didn't even secure informed consent of their patients. Very quickly, the intimate taboo subject of birth control and reproduction became a culturally and morally neutral topic when framed by the medical language of *la operacion*. Last, abortion became a much more controversial form of birth control in Puerto Rico, with very few advocates and public defenders. By 1970 the fertility rate had fallen to 2.3 births per woman, and by 2000 it had dropped to 1.9 births per woman. These declines in the fertility rates have been linked to the use of oral contraceptives, but sterilization continues to be the most used method of contraception. The most recent reproductive health data continue to show that among married women, contraceptive use is high,

and that sterilization is still the most popular method of birth control (Remez, 1999). One of the most interesting findings is that education matters in the methods women used for contraception. While 61% of women with 6 or fewer years of education have been sterilized, for women with some college education, the proportion drops to 37% (Remez, 1999).

For Puerto Rican women, these experiments and government policies coincided with a significant shift in their traditional roles as women: large-scale entrance into the service and industrial sectors of the economy due to the changes introduced by Operation Bootstrap. As wage earners, they too became "more conscious of the economic implications of having additional children, thus increasing their motivation to use contraception" (Ramirez de Arellano & Seipp, 1983, p. 142). In the 1950s and 1960s, the most popular phrase that women used to describe the end of their reproductive life (most likely sterilization) was "cerrar la fabrica" (close down the factory), ironically equating childbearing with the production process.

4 & 5. GENDER ROLES, MARRIAGE, AND SOCIALIZATION

There seems to be a consensus among social scientists in both Puerto Rico and the United States that historically the Puerto Rican family tended to maintain traditional norms with respect to gender roles. As Melba Sanchez-Ayendez states, "from early childhood, individuals are socialized to a double standard about gender and an interaction pattern of male dominance" (1998, p. 204). Strict gender-role socialization means, among other things, that men are expected to exercise the authority in the family and that women play a subordinate role. However, we know that historically men and women of all social classes have worked around and negotiated with these norms. For example, although upper-class families tended to be the most vigilant with respect to social norms about women's behavior, most women of the hacendado class were educated and played an important role in the social life of the country. Further, there is evidence to suggest that women of the hacendado class were part of political movements such as advocating the rights of poor women to education (Acosta-Belen, 1986).

Similarly, for poor and working-class Puerto Ricans, there has always been a tension between endorsing traditional family values (i.e., the husband as the main breadwinner and the wife as a stay-at-home mom) and the reality of family life. Under Spanish colonialism, strict limitations were put in place to shape the employment practices of both men and women workers. Sociologist Marcia Rivera (1986) points out that for many centuries under Spanish colonization, the Puerto Rican economy was organized on the basis of independent farmers producing for family consumption. In other words, the family was both a production and consumption unit. In this subsistence agriculture, although the work was gendered—that is, there were male- and female-specific tasks—the work of both partners was central to the working of the family. It was with the introduction of commercial cultivation of sugar and coffee that we begin to see the incorporation of women into salaried labor (Rivera, 1986). In fact, the Spanish government enacted several measures to force landless peasants into becoming laborers. For example, the Reglamento de Jornaleros enforced the obligation to work and established penalties if it was violated. Rivera (1986) observed that, ironically, women were excluded from paid agricultural work and segregated into mostly domestic service, as cooks, seamstresses, and laundresses on the haciendas. This is the socioeconomic context in which extended families and kin relations become important

family practices. Historically, for rural and working-class families, the kin network has been a source of strength and support.

In the 1950s, under the auspices of the U.S. government and transnational U.S.-owned corporations, Puerto Rico underwent yet another major change in the political economy of the island that continued to shape family dynamics. Operation Bootstrap (Operacion Manos a la Obra) was a government program intended not only to attract capital and jobs to the island to improve the general well-being of Puerto Ricans but, more important, to position Puerto Rico within the global age of export production. The government granted incentives to private investors, such as tax exemptions, and subsidized factory space to lure capital to the island. In the 1960s Puerto Rico became the showcase of the Caribbean, tempting other countries in the hemisphere to follow on Puerto Rico's example and endorse a free-enterprise form of capitalism. The problem is that while Puerto Rico experienced high levels of economic growth, economists also noted that high levels of unemployment persisted on the island, which they sought to address by encouraging migration to the United States.

Although Operation Bootstrap was designed to improve the employment opportunities of men, the kinds of industry attracted to the island (i.e., export-oriented manufacturing) resulted in a strong demand for women workers (Rios, 1990; Safa, 1995). In the 1950s a survey of Puerto Rican industrial workers established that 79% of the women surveyed found their first job in a factory (Rios, 1995, p. 133). Women, such as Esmeralda Santiago's mother, felt compelled to take on outside employment to provide for their families, especially when husbands were negligent, but culturally women still encountered stigma and disapproval. In the following quote, Santiago captures her mother's experiences with factory employment:

Mami was one of the first mothers in Macun to have a job outside the home. The barrio looked at us with new eyes. Gone was the bland acceptance of people minding their own business, replaced by a visible, angry resentment that became gossip, and taunts and name-calling in the school yard. . . . Papi seemed to have the same opinion about Mami's job as the neighbors. (Santiago, 1994, p. 122)

According to Rios "the disproportionate presence of women in Puerto Rico's manufacturing sector is not an aberration or a chance occurrence but an inherent feature of a developing strategy that has been part of the World War II restructuring of the world economy" (1993, p. 98). More than one-half of all the jobs created between 1960 and 1980 went to women. Luz del Alba Acevedo (1990) states that younger, more-educated Puerto Rican women workers went into better paying white-collar jobs in the government, while older, less-educated women went into the declining manufacturing industries and low-paying jobs. While the industrialization program incorporated women as workers, the surplus labor (i.e., mostly men) was absorbed into the U.S. labor market via migration.

Helen Safa's (1995) groundbreaking research has furthered our understanding of the impact of women's employment on the family, in particular the gender division of labor and gender relations between men and women. In her early work she documented that women's industrial employment did not alter the gender division of labor and that men were reluctant to accept women's work outside the home (Safa, 1980). More recently, she found that some things had changed, but others stayed the same for Puerto Rican women workers (Safa, 1995). For example, she found that men were more likely to accept women's work outside the home, and did not consider it a threat to their authority, because they realized that it was impossible to live on a single wage (Safa, 1995, p. 86). She also found, however, that with respect to the gender division of labor, women workers continued to be responsible for housework, childcare, and most of the reproductive work in their families. Pérez-Herranz, who has also found similar results, suggests that "maintaining this traditional ideology in modern Puerto Rico has provided these women with much-needed space in which to experience greater gratification and more control over their lives" (1996, p. 155). Safa (1995) adds that the patriarchal gender ideologies found in labor unions, the government, and political parties also contribute to maintain women's subordination. This problem has also been found among white-collar workers. (See, e.g., Casey, 1996.)

Although women's work has contributed to the well-being of their families, rising costs of living and declining wages have made the economic situation of Puerto Rican working families precarious. Declining employment forced families to find ways to make money to provide for the family in areas outside the formal sector. Many unemployed people sought income in what is known as "the informal sector," including subsistence production, bartering, occupying land, illegal activities such as crime or drug dealing, and producing goods and services for sale to others (Amott & Matthaei, 1991). Another result of low wages and high costs of living was the dependency on federal welfare programs for survival, particularly on food stamps. Amott and Matthaei (1991) state that food stamps became a means of existing for the majority of Puerto Ricans.

The most recent research about gender-role socialization in Puerto Rico continues to support the idea that Puerto Ricans are for the most part a very traditional culture. For example, Izcoa (1985) documented how

Puerto Rican adolescents (13–14 years of age) valued the qualities of being courteous, good natured, and honest, qualities that connected to the Puerto Rican core value of respect. Research with Puerto Rican mothers showed similar results. For example, Harwood, Miller, and Lucca-Irizarry (1995) found that Puerto Rican mothers valued acquiring proper demeanor (defined as being polite, kind, and respectful) and becoming a person of integrity (defined as being responsible, honest, and hardworking). More recently, Gibbons, Brusi-Figueroa, and Fisher (1997) conducted research with adolescents in Puerto Rico to investigate their views of the ideal man and ideal woman. They, too, found that the values of interpersonal respect and integrity—core Puerto Rican values—were present among the sample of adolescents they studied in Puerto Rico. Puerto Rican adolescents were also shown to be fairly traditional about gender roles. Gibbons et al. (1997) asked respondents to draw their ideal woman and ideal man. In their drawings, the ideal woman was more likely to be drawn working than the ideal man. Further, when asked about the type of work she was doing, 49% of the respondents depicted her doing housework.

Researchers have also observed that endorsement of traditional values varies by socioeconomic status (Ortiz-Archilla, 1992). For example, Harwood et al. (1995) showed that working-class mothers in Puerto Rico endorsed traditional values in the socialization of their children more than middle-class mothers. Sheila Ortiz-Archilla (1992, p. 163), in discussing research conducted by Vazquez-Rodriguez (1979) affirms that social class also mattered in childrearing practices. According to Ortiz-Archilla,

> better educated mothers preferred the didactic verbal style to discipline both for control of aggression and for handling modesty. Among families with lower

educational levels, lower status occupations, and lower socioeconomic status, mothers tended to use the authoritarian physical style to handle discipline, modesty, cleanliness, sex, and to control aggression. (1992, p. 164)

6 & 7. DIVORCE AND STRESSES

The legalization of divorce was another issue that radically changed family life in the 1950s and 1960s. United States officials thought it necessary to "bring the island out of an inert, disordered state of nature and into a civilized way of life" by regulating marriage and divorce (Suarez-Findlay, 1999). Historically, as stated earlier, most men and women were merely joined through consensual unions, not marriage.

Once divorce was made a viable option for women, the demand began to flow into the courts (Munoz-Vazquez, 1986). Petitions illustrated the struggles over gender power relations that permeated familial life. There is still very little research about the history of divorce in Puerto Rico and how it is used by both men and women. Psychologist Mayra Munoz-Vazquez conducted interviews with Puerto Rican women about their role expectations in marriage. She found that "middle class women had achieved slightly more power in their marriages than lower-class women" (1986, p. 119). She also found that across social classes women are still far from reaching an egalitarian relationship with their partners, but that middle-class women were more likely to subscribe to egalitarian norms of relationships and negotiate with their husbands the terms of their contributions to housework, among other issues. She also found that as women struggle to achieve a more egalitarian position in marriage, they are willing to divorce instead of staying in a relationship of subordination and powerlessness. In fact, the statistics about divorce in Puerto Rico bear this out. In 1975 nearly 40% of all marriages in Puerto Rico ended in divorce (Munoz-Vazquez, 1980). In 1977 Puerto Rico achieved the peculiar reputation of having the highest rates of divorce, next to the United States. In the 1990s, nearly 44% of Puerto Rican marriages ended in divorce. Munoz-Vazquez reports that the reasons women tend to divorce men relate to domestic violence and abusive husbands. Other reasons pushing Puerto Rican women to divorce were alcoholism and infidelity. The reality of family life in Puerto Rico is that although women have gained civil rights related to politics, work, and marriage, many patriarchal privileges remain in place, leaving the husband much power and gender relations in the family fairly unchanged (Findlay, 1999).

More recently, Maria Canabal (1990) sought to address the socioeconomic determinants of marital dissolution in Puerto Rico and its connections to the rise of female-headed families. In an attempt to overcome the limitations from previous studies of divorce in Puerto Rico that tended to focus on a small sample of informants, she turned to the Puerto Rican Fertility and Family Planning Assessment (PRFFPA) survey, designed by the U.S Centers for Disease Control and administered by the University of Puerto Rico School of Public Health and the Puerto Rican Department of Health. The survey included a total of 4,500 households and 3,175 women aged 15 to 49. She found the following: (1) The longer a couple stays married, the lower the probability of dissolution; (2) the presence of children, in particular less than 6 years of age, deters people from getting a divorce; (3) increased educational levels of women contribute to the stability of marriage; (4) changes in the employment status of women can also affect marriage stability. Canabal (1990) identified four groups as "dissolution-prone," that

is, couples for whom the potential of dissolution is high; include couples in metropolitan areas, young couples, couples with financial problems, and those in consensual marriages. But she suggested that marriage counseling services could help mitigate marital dissolution.

Family Stress: Poverty

The high rates of poverty found among Puerto Rican families in both Puerto Rico and the United States has preoccupied social scientists for decades. In fact, the classic, yet controversial, account of Puerto Rican family life, *La Vida: A Puerto Rican Family in the Culture of Poverty—San Juan and New York* (1965), by the well-known anthropologist Oscar Lewis, places Puerto Rican families at the center of one of the most important scholarly debates to date. Although Lewis (1965, p. xiii) set out to provide an account that captured the voices of people who were rarely heard—the marginalized poor—his ethnographic study heralded the "culture of poverty" thesis, thereby marking Puerto Rican families as pathological, deficient, and forever doomed to poverty. Lewis defined the culture of poverty as "both an adaptation and a reaction of the poor to their marginal position in a class-stratified, highly individualistic, capitalistic society." It is a way of life that "[o]nce it comes into existence it tends to perpetuate itself from generation to generation" (1965, p. xliv).

Lewis studied the Rios family, which consisted of five households: "a mother and two married daughters and a married son and daughter in New York City" (1965, p. xxiv). Fernanda Fuentes was the black matriarch of the family, and she and her husband, Cristobal Rios, a light-skinned Puerto Rican, were residents of a slum in San Juan that Lewis called La Esmeralda. Lewis describes the Rios family as reflecting "many of the characteristics of the subculture of poverty" (1965, p. xxv). He adds,

> In the Rios family, uncontrolled rage, aggression, violence and even bloodshed are not uncommon; their extreme impulsivity affects the whole tenor of their lives. There is an overwhelming preoccupation with sex, the most frequent cause of quarrels. Sex is used to satisfy a great variety of needs—for children, for pleasure, for money, for revenge, for love, to express *machismo* (manliness), and to compensate for all the emptiness in their lives. Even family unity, one of the most sacred values in this family-oriented culture—is sometimes threatened by the danger of seduction by stepfathers. . . . (1965, p. xxvi)

The women in the Rios family were depicted as demanding, aggressive, and more violence-prone than men. Oscar Lewis (1965) argued that their inability to accept the traditional submissive role of women created tensions and problems in their marital relations. He added, "their behavior is caused by a deep ambivalence about their role as women, by their occupational history and by their experience as heads of matrifocal households, a common occurrence in the culture of poverty" (1965, p. xxvi). The Rios family became classified as a "multi-problem family," deemed unstable, disorganized, and pathological, tenacious cultural patterns that spanned over four generations. These problems also surfaced in New York, where Lewis followed the Rios family and studied other migrant families.

In the 1960s the culture of poverty thesis was embraced by social policy makers, politicians, academics across many disciplines, and a wider public who began to perceive Puerto Rican immigrants as a "problem people" (Perez, 2001). Whalen captures the situation in the following passage: "[T]hese perceptions of Puerto Ricans' cultural deficiencies—dependency,

lack of a work ethic, defective families—were extended to the Puerto Rican community. The assumption was that Puerto Ricans lacked community and lacked willingness or the ability to improve their communities" (2001, p. 203).

The culture of poverty thesis has been subject to debate and critique for decades. For example, Anne Roschelle (1997, p. 13) thinks it is contradictory to argue that the family is pathological because of its extreme patriarchal structure, while at the same time presenting women as more aggressive and powerful than men. Further, the culture of poverty thesis is also problematic because of its emphasis on negative attributes that then become inherent qualities of Puerto Rican families.

As a new generation of Puerto Rican writers and scholars became part of the academic establishment, an alternative body of literature developed to challenge the negative depictions of Puerto Rican families and to provide alternative accounts for the problems facing families in the United States and Puerto Rico. Felix Padilla's (1987) ethnographic study of Puerto Rican families in Chicago is an example of such new scholarship. Similarly, Carmen Whalen's work about Puerto Ricans in Philadelphia describes how city agencies bought into the culture of poverty thesis and presented assimilation as the solution to the problems facing Puerto Rican families. Whalen (2001) stresses how Puerto Ricans created institutions of their own and turned to churches and extended family for assistance as their life chances in the city declined. According to Whalen, "despite deteriorating conditions, migrants continued their struggles to provide for themselves and their families, to instill a work ethic in their children, and to provide with an education" (2001, p. 230).

More recently, the persistent problem of poverty among minority families has been (re)defined as a problem of the underclass. The concept of the underclass was coined by sociologist William Julius Wilson to explain the problems of African-American poverty in the inner city. In a radical departure from traditional explanations of poverty that tend to focus on the individual, Wilson (1987) placed the persistence of poverty as a result of economic structuring, the changes in the U.S. economy that led to a loss of jobs and a shift to a postindustrial economy. He also added a new dimension to discussions of poverty, namely, the impact of neighborhood factors, such as the migration of middle-class black families from the inner city. The flight of middle- and working-class families led to a "concentration effect." Poor people in the inner city became isolated from the mainstream and were more likely to engage in "underclass behavior."

Very quickly, policy analysts and conservative politicians hijacked the concept to further a political agenda that placed explanations of poverty on the individual. For example, the behavior of black males became connected to the rise of the underclass. Journalist Nicholas Lehman labeled Puerto Ricans "the other underclass," and suddenly Puerto Rican poverty was again linked to the behavior and cultural practices of a people (Whalen, 2001). Leman reintroduced the issue of family dissolution and the lack of a work ethic as explanations for the rise of Puerto Rican poverty and its new form, the underclass. His analysis also recycled the culture of poverty thesis: "The statistics show Puerto Ricans to be more severely afflicted than Mexican-Americans by what might be called the secondary effects of poverty, such as family breakups, and not trying to find employment—which work to ensure that poverty will continue beyond one generation" (Leman, 1991, as quoted in Whalen, 2001, p. 239). Scholars who studied Latino poverty were intrigued by Wilson's hypothesis and eagerly tested its application to explanations of poverty among Latino groups. (See Moore and Pinderhughes, 1993 for a sample of this work.)

The consensus seems to be that economic restructuring has also shaped Latino poverty, but other factors, such as the migration of middle-class families, do not appear to apply to Latinos, including Puerto Ricans. For example, the Puerto Rican community of Sunset Park, Brooklyn, has experienced economic restructuring, loss of jobs, instability, crime problems, and concentrated pockets of poor families, but there are important cultural differences that invalidate the underclass theory for this community of Puerto Ricans (Sullivan, 1993). Perhaps the most important critique of the underclass model as applied to Latinos, including Puerto Ricans, is that it does not account for important cultural and historical differences prevalent across these immigrant communities. Clearly, more research is needed to further the study of Latino poverty, in particular, Puerto Rican poverty and its effects on the family.

Puerto Rican poverty is indeed one of the most serious problems affecting Puerto Rican families both on the island and in mainland communities. In particular, a manifestation of family poverty that continues to worry social scientists and policymakers is the number of female-headed families that live below the poverty level. In fact, the most recent report sponsored by the Annie E. Casey Foundation, a national organization that tracks the status of children in the United States, called attention to the increasing number of children living in single-parent families. According to Mark Mather (2003), the author of the report, in 1999 more than one-half of the children in Puerto Rico lived in families with incomes below the poverty level. Child poverty was the highest in Puerto Rico's rural areas. In 1999, 70% of Puerto Rico's rural children were living in poverty. Mather (2003) connects the high rates of rural child poverty to the lack of jobs. In 2000 one in four adults in rural areas was unemployed (25%). Unemployment in the central cities (16%) and suburbs (21%) was considerably lower. The municipality with the largest concentration of child poverty was Vieques (81%), the site of the most recent conflict with the U.S. government over the Navy military practices. The rural municipalities of Mariaco (77%), Las Marias (76%), and Adjuntas, Guanica, and Orocovis (75% each) also reported high child poverty rates. The municipalities with the lowest child poverty rates were Trujillo Alto (40%), Guaynabo (42%), Ceiba (43%), Bayamon and Toa Alta (44% each), and Carolina (45%). Although census reports at the turn of the 21st century show some declines in the rates described previously, Mather (2003) concluded that children in Puerto Rico are at a serious disadvantage compared with children living in the United States. Teenagers are also a group at risk. One out of every seven teenagers aged 16 to 19 drops out of school. These vulnerable young Puerto Ricans have joined the ranks of the unemployed and underemployed to make a living. Crime and drugs are also a very serious problem for the youth in Puerto Rico.

11. SPECIAL TOPICS: MIGRATION AND PUERTO RICO

The migrant Puerto Rican family has been the focus of numerous research studies in the United States. (See, e.g., Carrasquillo, 1994, Roschelle, 1997, Rogler Cooney, 1984, Sanchez-Ayendez, 1998, Sanchez-Korrol, 1983, Toro-Morn, 1995, and Whalen, 1998, 2001.) As pointed out earlier in this chapter, Puerto Rican families have migrated to the United States and other parts of the hemisphere since the beginning of the 20th century. Historically, New York has always had the largest Puerto Rican community in the

United States. In the 1950s more than 400,000 Puerto Ricans left the island for familiar places, such as New York, and to new places in need of cheap labor, such as Chicago. According to the U.S. Census of Population, in the 1990s New York accounted for 40% of the U.S. Puerto Rican population (Sanchez-Ayendez, 1998, p. 208). Sizable communities of Puerto Ricans can also be found in New Jersey, Florida, Massachusetts, Illinois, and California.

According to Sanchez-Ayendez (1998, p. 208), the demographic profile of Puerto Rican families in the U.S is as follows:

- Fifty-six percent of Puerto Rican families are married couples.
- Thirty-seven percent are female-headed families, with no husband present.
- Nine percent are headed by a male, with no wife present.

Although Latinas are known for their higher fertility rates compared with white and black women, the fertility rates of Puerto Rican women have been declining. Yet, one aspect of Puerto Rican women's fertility that tends to worry social scientists is the high numbers of births among teenagers. In 1991, 22% of births among Puerto Rican women were to teenage mothers (Sanchez-Ayendez, 1998). Another issue that has concerned social analysts is the large number of female-headed households with no husband present that live below the poverty level.

Gender plays an important role in the migration and reconstruction of family life in the U.S.-Puerto Rican communities (Alicea, 1997; Toro-Morn, 1995). Researchers have documented that domestic gender relations play a very important role in the process of migration. For example, Toro-Morn's (1995) study suggests that class and gender differences shaped the migration and family experiences of Puerto Ricans moving to

Chicago. She found that working-class women talked about migration as a family project. For working-class and poor families, migration took place in stages: Husbands moved first, secured employment and housing arrangements, and then sent for the rest of the family. Even though women had been able to secure employment in Puerto Rico, many left their jobs to be with their husbands and keep the family together. Working-class women struggled over the decision to leave Puerto Rico, but in the end it was their family obligations and responsibilities that compelled them to move to Chicago. In contrast, for educated and professional women, moving was a joint family project (Toro-Morn, 1995). Toro-Morn found that middle-class and professional women were less encumbered by familial relations of authority as they shared in the decision making, were less dependent on other family members to make the move, and had professional agendas of their own. But regardless of their migration experience, both working-class and middle-class women had to contend with the problem of balancing family and work responsibilities.

In Chicago Toro-Morn (1995) found that among working-class families, gender relations and the gender division of labor underwent some changes, but it still contained a great deal of the traditionalism characteristic of families on the island. For example, she found that working-class husbands resisted the idea of their wives entering the labor force. In fact, men took on a double shift so that wives could stay home, take care of the children, and maintain a traditional home life. Although most working-class married women gave in to their husband's wishes and stayed at home, some women resisted. Toro-Morn (1995) describes the experiences of an immigrant woman, Rita, whose husband did not want her to work. Since the family needed the money, she took on employment in a factory without telling her husband.

Eventually, she told her husband, and upon his request she stopped working. In the following passage she describe how she was able to work without her husband's knowledge:

> [S]ince he left to work very early I found someone to take care of my smallest child, and the others went to school. My work hours where from 9:00 to 3:30 so by the time my husband got home I had everything done. I had the house clean, the children were cleaned and had eaten, and I was all put together. My husband did not like when I was not put together. (Toro-Morn, 1995, p. 721)

With the money she earned she was able to buy a sewing machine and continue to contribute to her family's income by sewing clothes for her children and for neighborhood families.

The reality of life in Chicago, however, required the income contributions of working wives, so eventually some working husbands adjusted to the idea of their wife's employment. Toro-Morn (1995) found that regardless of their employment status, working-class women continued to bear the burden of the second shift, that is, the work that is done primarily at home, such as housework and childcare. Toro-Morn (1995) found that one way working mothers dealt with their competing responsibilities was by socializing daughters to household responsibilities very early and leaving them to care for younger brothers and sisters. For example, when Claudia, a Puerto Rican immigrant daughter, reached 9 years of age, "she acquired household responsibilities. She was given keys to the apartment, and after school she was expected to clean the kitchen, pick up around the house, and start dinner" (Toro-Morn, 1995, p. 722). In some cases, working mothers brought over other women relatives to help them care for children. These childcare practices have also been documented in the early Puerto Rican colonies of New York (Sanchez-Korrol, 1983).

For educated and professional women, the situation was considerably different. Professional and educated women placed their career goals alongside their family responsibilities (Toro-Morn, 1995, p. 723). Husbands supported their wife's career and were a little more receptive to their experiences as working mothers. But when husbands resisted, they found a way to negotiate their work and family responsibilities.

Zayas and Palleja (1988) point out that regardless of all the changes the Puerto Rican family has undergone while on the mainland, they have sustained important values such as *familism*. Rogler and Cooney (1984) described familism as "a traditional modality in Puerto Rican culture" that supports family integrity and gives shape and direction to the conduct among members. This concept gives emphasis to both the nuclear and extended family. Rogler and Cooney (1984, p. 69) observed that although Puerto Rican immigrants were exposed to a very different culture in the United States, "they continued to retain much of their Puerto Rican culture." Their children, however, represent a different story. Rogler and Cooney found that second-generation Puerto Ricans raised in New York differed from their parents in significant ways. They found that second-generation Puerto Ricans "appeared to be significantly less committed than the parents to values associated with traditional Puerto Rican culture" (1984, p. 76). For example, they found marked differences in spousal relationships between the parent (immigrant) generation and second-generation couples.

More recently, Toro-Morn and Alicea (2003) conducted interviews with second- and third-generation Puerto Ricans in Chicago, and they found that Puerto Rican parents worked hard to reconstruct a family life in Chicago in keeping with traditional Puerto Rican cultural norms and expected their children to conform to traditional gender roles and values. Puerto Rican parents worked hard to build home life as a space where children were socialized into traditional Puerto Rican ways of living. Like Puerto Rican parents in New York, parents in Chicago subscribed to the traditional gender division of labor where men function as providers and women are relegated to caretakers of the home and children. Toro-Morn and Alicea (2003) found that such socialization led to conflicts between parents and children. For example, Toro-Morn and Alicea (2003) report that daughters admired their mothers' struggle to juggle work and family responsibilities, but resented their parents overprotectiveness and gender expectations concerning their sexuality. Similarly, sons worked hard to reconcile the conflicts, ambiguities, and tensions of their masculine identities.

Toro-Morn and Alicea (2003) argue that parental expectations, conflicts, and contradictions are rooted in the disadvantaged position that Puerto Ricans confront in both the United States and Puerto Rico. In other words,

> Puerto Rican women encourage their daughters to be good housewives and teach them that the household is their domain, but the reality is that they themselves had to work outside the household. Puerto Rican parents encourage their daughters to fulfill traditional gender expectations as a way to define a cultural space that is pure and pristine and that challenges inferior definitions of their race, but they also encourage their daughters to pursue an education. (Toro-Morn & Alicea, 2003)

In fact, in Chicago daughters resented their parents' overprotectiveness and found many ways to resist and challenge traditional family expectations. For example, some daughters challenged directly the authority of their parents by eloping or getting married. Others subverted traditionalism by using education as a way to leave home. Puerto Rican parents believed in the value of education for social mobility and consequently supported their children's educational efforts, even if it meant that they would be away from home. Toro-Morn and Alicea concluded that as parents socialized children in the values and beliefs of Puerto Rican culture, they inadvertently presented Puerto Rican culture as fixed in time and space. The second- and third-generation Puerto Ricans they interviewed struggled with such views because it meant their submission and conformity to rules and codes of behavior that many saw as oppressive. Instead, they saw themselves as active agents in the process of (re)creating Puerto Rican culture, and they wanted to decide which aspects of their culture to take and which to reject. Nevertheless, some second- and third-generation Puerto Ricans tended to fall into a dualistic way of thinking with respect to perceiving U.S. society as being more egalitarian than their homeland and U.S. Puerto Rican communities. Toro-Morn and Alicea called this "the distortions of the borderlands" (2003) because it fails to see the exploitation and subordination that their parents and other family members encountered as workers and as immigrants.

The plight of Puerto Rican migrant families in the United States in the second half of the 20th century was shaped by the shift from an industrial to a postindustrial economy, racial discrimination, and changing government policies (Whalen, 2001). The loss of manufacturing jobs and growth of the service economy spelled disaster for working-class and poor Puerto Rican families across the United States. Carmen Whalen's (2001) ethnographic study of the Puerto Rican community in Philadelphia describes how Puerto Ricans became displaced labor

migrants and slowly filled the ranks of the urban poor.

Across cities in the United States, Puerto Rican men and women workers were found in declining sectors of the economy, such as manufacturing. Thus, economic restructuring spelled disaster for mainland families. Puerto Rican women workers were most affected by economic restructuring (Colon-Warren, 1996). Single women raising children alone quickly swelled the ranks of families living below the poverty level. Puerto Rican female-headed households in the United States shot up from 27% to 40% between the years of 1970 and 1980, and stayed steady at 42% since 1990 (Colon-Warren, 1998). This is much higher than the 18% for the total population during the same period (Colon-Warren, 1998). Colon-Warren (1998) found that there is a complex relationship between poverty and the frequency of female-headed households. Economic hardship and the scarcity of male jobs may cause marital instability, thus leading to the phenomenon of female-headed families. It might be that poverty is the cause of marital instability and increasing female heads of family, not that female heads cause women and families to fall into poverty. Female-headed households are finding living conditions straining, because these families are more likely to be without wage earners (Colon-Warren, 1998).

CONCLUSIONS: FUTURE DIRECTIONS AND TRENDS

The study of the family in Puerto Rico, one of the last remaining colonies in the world, offers students of the family a case in point to understanding how global political processes shape the family as an institution. Here we have seen how two empires implemented social, economic, and political policies, which in turn had profound implications for the family as an institution. This chapter supports the claims of family scholars around the world that diversity in family patterns is related to macrosocial forces (Chow & Berheide, 1994). In Puerto Rico's case, the colonization of the island by Spain and then the United States influenced family life in unique ways. For example, family values found today can be traced back to the Spanish influence. But we need to know more about family life in Puerto Rico during the three centuries that Spain colonized the island. In particular, future historians could help us document more thoroughly family life in the different stages of the Spanish colonization of the island. Further, future scholars of the family in Puerto Rico need to be more attentive to variations in family life across social classes and racial groups.

By contrast, the well-established body of work that has studied the impact of the U.S. colonization of Puerto Rico has yielded important insights with respect to the family. We know that the U.S. colonization sharpened the social class differences that already existed in Puerto Rico and introduced new ones (Dietz, 1986; History Task Force, 1979; Meléndez & Meléndez, 1993). The changes in the political economy of the island introduced by the new colonial power brought havoc to Puerto Rican families across social classes. For example, the colonization accelerated the entrance of women into the labor force and introduced migration as a survival strategy for poor and working-class families. Those two issues alone are at the heart of many of the social problems confronting families in both the United States and Puerto Rico at the turn of the 21st century.

In keeping with recent scholarship in the field of family studies, our chapter documents how historically a traditional gender-role ideology and division of labor continues to shape women's subordination within the family. Globally, feminists contend that the family is a patriarchal institution that helps perpetuate gender inequality. Puerto Rico is a case in point. Although Puerto Rican families have always relied on the reproductive work of women, the entrance of women into salaried work, a trend that continues today, has placed Puerto Rican women in a double bind. Puerto Rican women, like other women around the world, continue to confront the double burden of not only working for pay but also being responsible for the work in the home. As we have documented in this chapter, gender roles and the gender division of labor have been resistant to change in Puerto Rican families across the social spectrum both on the island and in mainland communities. Indeed, an important issue facing Puerto Rican working women is their ability to be able to negotiate with their partners, husbands, and families the gender division of labor. It remains to be seen whether the income contributions of working Puerto Rican women will translate into more influence in the decisions that affect family life, a change that has been documented in other countries.

As we have seen in this chapter, historically family life has varied by social class, but we need to know more about family life across the entire social class spectrum. Studies of poor families abound, but we do not know much about middle-class families, a social class that grew in the aftermath of the development program implemented in Puerto Rico in the 1950s. From a sociopsychological perspective, we need to know more about the mating choices of educated Puerto Rican men and women and perceptions of love and marriage, among other issues. Further, it would be interesting to learn more about how Puerto Rican men and women (re)construct their feminine and masculine ideals and how these play themselves out in the realm of the family. Do these differ by social class or race?

The shift from an industrial to a postindustrial economic base in the United States and Puerto Rico has been disastrous for poor and working-class families. The poor and working-class Puerto Rican families that migrated to the United States in the aftermath of Operation Bootstrap encountered a share of discrimination in the job market, schooling, and political arenas, thus making their assimilation into American culture nearly impossible. For them the family was a safe haven to escape the exploitation and oppression encountered in mainstream society. The family offered members support, stability, and security, but a more balanced view of the family requires that we move beyond the functionalist approach that has always characterized studies of the family.

The immigrant Puerto Rican family in the United States was also a site of conflict between parents, who wanted to uphold traditional values and idealized notions of Puerto Rican culture, and their children. Second- and third-generation Puerto Ricans struggled with traditional notions of femininity and masculinity. Now second- and third-generation Puerto Ricans are raising families of their own, but there is very little research available that documents their journeys into parenthood. We also need more work comparing the experiences of second- and third-generation educated and professional Puerto Ricans in the United States with their equivalents in Puerto Rico.

In the same vein, while social scientists and policy makers have made poor Puerto Rican families, in particular, female-headed households, the embodiment of pathos, misery, and social problems, we have yet to turn the page in this body of research and begin to explore how these families could also be a site for resisting racial and social class oppression. In closing, for sociologists and other social scientists, the study of Puerto Rican families is indeed a fertile ground to pursue new and innovative approaches to studying the family as a changing and complex institution.

REFERENCES

Acevedo, L. A. (1990). Industrialization and employment: Changes in the patterns of women's work in Puerto Rico. *World Development, 18*(2), 231–255.

Acevedo, L. A. (1993). Género, trabajo asalariado y desarrollo industrial en Puerto Rico: La división sexual del trabajo en la manufactura. In M. C. Baerga (Ed.), *Género y trabajo: La industria de la aguja en Puerto Rico y el Caribe* (pp. 161–212). Rio Piedras, Puerto Rico: University of Puerto Rico Press.

Acosta-Belen, E. (1986). *The Puerto Rican woman: Perspectives on culture, history, and society*. New York: Praeger.

Alicea, M. (1997). "A Chambered Nautilus": The contradictory nature of Puerto Rican women's role in the social construction of a transnational community. *Gender and Society, 11*(5), 597–626.

Amott, T., & Matthaei, J. A. (1991). *Race, gender, and work: A multicultural economic history of women in the United States*. Boston: South End Press.

Azize, Y. (1987). *La mujer en Puerto Rico: Ensayos de investigación*. Rio Piedras, Puerto Rico: Editorial Cultural.

Boris, E. (1996). Needlewomen under the New Deal in Puerto Rico, 1920–1945. In A. Ortiz (Ed.), *Puerto Rican women and work: Bridges in transnational labor* (pp. 33–54). Philadelphia: Temple University Press.

Canabal, M. (1990). An economic approach to marital dissolution in Puerto Rico. *Journal of Marriage and the Family, 52*(May), 515–530.

Carrasquillo, H. (1994). The Puerto Rican family. In R. L. Taylor (Ed.), *Minority families in the United States: A multicultural perspective* (pp. 82–94). Englewood Cliffs, NJ: Prentice Hall.

Casey, G. J. (1996). New tappings on the keys: Changes in work and gender roles for women clerical workers in Puerto Rico. In A. Ortiz (Ed.), *Puerto Rican women and work: Bridges in transnational labor* (pp. 209–233). Philadelphia: Temple University Press.

Chow, E. N.-L., & Berheide, C. W. (1994). *Women, the family and policy: A global perspective.* Albany: State University of New York Press.

CIA World Factbook, 2002. Available online from: www.odci.gov/cia/publications/factbook/index.html. Retrieved October 11, 2004.

Colon-Warren, A. (1996). The impact of job losses on Puerto Rican women in the Middle Atlantic region. In A. Ortiz (Ed.), *Puerto Rican women and work: Bridges in transnational labor* (pp. 105–138). Philadelphia: Temple University Press.

Colon-Warren, A. (1998). The feminization of poverty among women in Puerto Rico and Puerto Rican women in the Middle Atlantic region of the United States. *The Brown Journal of World Affairs, 5*(2), 262–282.

Dietz, J. L. (1986). *Economic history of Puerto Rico: Institutional change and capitalist development.* Princeton, NJ: Princeton University Press.

Duany, J. (2002). *The Puerto Rican nation on the move: Identities on the island and in the United States.* Chapel Hill: University of North Carolina Press.

Findlay, E. (1999). *Imposing decency: The politics of sexuality and race in Puerto Rico, 1870–1920.* Durham, NC: Duke University.

Fitzpatrick, J. P. (1987). *Puerto Rican Americans: The meaning of migration to the mainland.* Englewood Cliffs, NJ: Prentice-Hall.

Gibbons, J. L., Brusi-Figueroa, R., & Fisher, S. (1997). Gender-related ideals of Puerto Rican adolescents: Gender and school context. *Journal of Early Adolescense 17*(4), 349–370.

Gonzalez, J. L., Jr. (1998). *Racial and ethnic families in America* (2nd ed.). Dubuque, IA: Kendall/Hunt Publishing.

Hardwood R. L., Miller, J. G., & Lucca-Irizarry, N. (1995). *Culture and attachment: Perceptions of the child in context.* New York: Guilford.

Harwood, R. L., Schoelmrich, A., Ventura-Cook, E., Schulze, P. A., & Wilson, S. P. (1996). Culture and class influences on Anglo and Puerto Rican mothers' beliefs regarding long-term socialization goals and child behavior. *Child Development, 67*(5), 2446–2461.

History Task Force. (1979). *Labor migration under Capitalism: The Puerto Rican experience.* New York: Monthly Review Press.

Izcoa, A. E. (1985). Estudio Comparativo de la imagen propia de adolescents puertoriquenos: Immigrantes y no-migrantes. *Homines, 9,* 57–71.

Landale, N. S., & Fennelly, K. (1992). Informal unions among mainland Puerto Ricans: Cohabitation or an alternative to legal marriage? *Journal of Marriage and the Family, 54*(May), 269–280.

Leman, N. (1991, December). The other underclass. *Atlantic Monthly, 268*(6), 96–110.

Lewis, O. (1965). *La vida: A Puerto Rican family in the culture of poverty—San Juan and New York.* New York: Random House.

Mather, M. (2003). *Children in Puerto Rico: Results from the 2000 census.* Baltimore, MD: Annie E. Casey Foundation and the Population Reference Bureau.

Meléndez, E., & Meléndez, E. (1993). *Colonial dilemma: Critical perspectives on contemporary Puerto Rico*. Boston: South End Press.

Moore, J., & Pinderhughes, R. (1993). *In the barrios: Latinos and the underclass debate*. New York: Russell Sage Foundation.

Munoz-Vazquez, M. (1980). Matrimonio y divorcio en Puerto Rico. In E. Acosta-Belen (Ed.), *La mujer en la sociedad Puertoriquena* (pp. 110–119). Rio Piedras, Puerto Rico: Ediciones Huracan.

Munoz-Vazquez, M. (1986). The effects of role expectations on the marital status of urban Puerto Rican women. In E. Acosta-Belen (Ed.), *The Puerto Rican woman: Perspectives on culture, history and society* (pp. 211–235). New York: Praeger.

Ortiz, A. (1996). *Puerto Rican women and work: Bridges in transnational labor*. Philadelphia: Temple University Press.

Ortiz, A. (1998). Puerto Rican women workers in the twentieth century: A historical appraisal of the literature. In F. Matos-Rodríguez & L. C. Delgado (Eds.), *Puerto Rican women's history: New perspectives* (pp. 55–81). Armonk, NY: M. E. Sharpe.

Ortiz-Archilla, S. (1992). Families in Puerto Rico: An analysis of the socialization process from a macro-structural perspective. In J. L. Roopnarine & D. B. Carter (Eds.), *Parent child socialization in diverse cultures: Advances in applied developmental psychology, vol. 5.* (pp. 159–171). Norwood, NJ: Ablex.

Padilla, F. (1987). *Puerto Ricans Chicago*. Indiana: University of Notre Dame Press.

Perez, G. (2001). An upbeat West Side story: Puerto Ricans and postwar racial politics in Chicago. *Centro: Journal of the Center for Puerto Rican Studies, 13*(2), 46–71.

Pérez-Herranz, C. (1996). Our two full-time jobs: Women garment workers balance factory and domestic demands in Puerto Rico. In A. Ortiz (Ed.), *Puerto Rican women and work: Bridges in transnational labor* (pp. 139–160). Philadelphia: Temple University Press.

Ramirez de Arellano, A., & Seipp, C. (1983). *Colonialism, Catholicism, and contraception: A history of birth control in Puerto Rico*. Chapel Hill: University of North Carolina Press.

Remez, L. 1999. Puerto Rico-contraceptive use is high, sterilization is the most popular method. *Family Planning Perspectives 31*(1), 47-48.

Rios, P. (1990). Export-oriented industrialization and the demand for female labor: Puerto Rican women in the manufacturing sector. *Gender and Society, 4*(5), 321–337.

Rios, P. (1993). Export-oriented industrialization and the demand for female labor: Puerto Rican women in the manufacturing sector, 1952–1980. In E. Meléndez & E. Meléndez (Eds.), *Colonial dilemma: Critical perspectives on contemporary Puerto Rico*. Boston: South End Press.

Rios, P. (1995). *Women in the Latin American development process*. Philadelphia: Temple University Press.

Rivera, M. (1986). The development of capitalism in Puerto Rico and the incorporation of women into the labor force. In E. Acosta-Belen (Ed.), *The Puerto Rican woman: Perspectives on culture, history and society* (pp. 30–45). New York: Praeger.

Rogler, L. H., & Cooney, R. S. (1984). *Puerto Rican families in New York City: Intergenerational processes* (Monograph No. 11). New York: Hispanic Research Center, Fordham University.

Roschelle, A. R. (1997). *No more kin: Exploring race, class, and gender in family networks.* Thousand Oaks, CA: Sage Publications.

Safa, H. (1980). Class consciousness among working-class women in Latin America: Puerto Rico. In J. Nash & H. I. Safa (Eds.), *Sex and class in Latin America* (pp. 69–85). South Hadley, MA: Bergin and Garvey Publishers.

Safa, H. (1995). *The myth of the male breadwinner: Women and industrialization in the Caribbean.* Boulder, CO: Westview Press.

Sanchez-Ayendez, M. (1998). The Puerto Rican family. In C. H. Mindel, R. W. Habenstein, & R. Wright Jr. (Eds.), *Ethnic families in America: Patterns and variations,* (pp. 199–222). New Jersey: Prentice Hall.

Sanchez-Korrol, V. (1983). *From colonia to community: The history of Puerto Ricans in New York City, 1917–1948.* Westport, CT: Greenwood Press.

Santiago, E. (1993). *When I was Puerto Rican.* New York: Vintage Books.

Stark, D. M. (1996). Discovering the invisible Puerto Rican slave family: Demographic evidence from the eighteenth century. *Journal of Family History, 21,* 395–418.

Suarez-Findlay, E. (1999). *Imposing decency: The politics of sexuality and race in Puerto Rico, 1870–1920.* Durham, NC: Duke University Press.

Sullivan, M. L. (1993). Puerto Ricans in Sunset Park, Brooklyn: Poverty amidst ethnic and economic diversity. In J. Moore & R. Pinderhughes (Eds.), *In the barrios: Latinos and the underclass debate* (pp. 1–25). New York: Russell Sage Foundation.

Toro-Morn, M. I. (1995). Gender, class, family, and migration: Puerto Rican women in Chicago. *Gender and Society, 9*(6), 706–723.

Toro-Morn, M. I. (2001). "Yo era muy arriesgada": A historical overview of the work experiences of Puerto Rican women in Chicago. *Centro: Journal of the Center for Puerto Rican Studies, 8*(2), 25–43.

Toro-Morn, M. I. (forthcoming). *A gendered view of global migrations.* Unpublished book manuscript.

Toro-Morn, M. I., & Alicea, M. (2003). Gendered geographies of home: Mapping second and third generation Puerto Ricans' sense of home. In P. Hondagneu-Sotelo (Ed.), *Gender and U.S. immigration: Contemporary trends* (pp. 194–214). Berkeley: University of California Press.

Tovar, F. R. (1972). *La mujer Puertoriquena: Su vida y evolucion a traves de la historia.* New York: Plus Ultra Educational.

Vazquez-Rodriguez, J. L. (1979). *Study of child rearing practices, parent information and child development outcomes in Puerto Rico* (Vols. 1 & 2). Hato Rey, Puerto Rico: Health and Social Studies, Inc.

Whalen, C. (1998). Labor migrants or submissive wives: Competing narratives of Puerto Rican women in the post-World War II era. In F. Matos Rodríguez & L. C. Delgado (Eds.), *Puerto Rican women's history: New perspectives* (pp. 206–226). Armonk, NY: M. E. Sharpe.

Whalen, C. (2001). *From Puerto Rico to Philadelphia: Puerto Rican workers and post-war economies.* Philadelphia: Temple University Press.

Wilson, W. J. (1987). *The truly disadvantaged: The inner city, the underclass, and public policy.* Chicago: University of Chicago Press.

Zayas, L., & Palleja, J. (1988). Puerto Rican familism: Considerations for family therapy. *Family Relations, 5*(37), 260–264.

Part V

THE MIDDLE EAST

CHAPTER 21

Families in Iran: The Contemporary Situation

Taghi Azadarmaki

1. INTRODUCTION

Prologue: Changes

During the recent century Iranian families have faced major changes compared with past centuries. Increase in age at marriage, increase in rate of divorce, reduction in the size of family, freedom in choosing a spouse, prevention of selecting a second wife for men, the right of a wife to present a divorce petition, more participation of women in politics due to the importance of individual votes in the elections, and the possibility for women to be educated and to undertake modern jobs are among the major changes in Iranian families.

Throughout history, the family has been an important structure in Iranian society, along with religion and politics. Despite the institutional development in Iran, these three institutions have formed the central structures and social relationships in Iran. People in families have the duties of reproduction and raising children, in addition to taking care of and supporting adults and maintaining cultural and religious heritages. In the course of cultural, social, and political modernization

of the country, Iranian families have been undergoing basic changes. The changes in families in Iran are reflected in routine life. At the same time, they have been focused on by psychologists, pedagogical scholars and researchers, historians, and sociologists of family, as well.

Studies on the Iranian family coincided with the establishment of the Studies and Social Research Institute at the Faculty of Social Science of Tehran University in 1958, and since then, they have continued in a regular academic form for more than four decades. Paying attention to family in Iran in an academic form led to the establishment of the Family Sociology Research Section, the Research Center in family studies discipline, and the publication of many papers, articles, and books in this area. Now there are students enrolled in the family studies bachelor's and master's degree courses in four universities, and more than 200 students in different educational degrees are studying and researching in this area.

The present chapter gives a short account of the family situation in Iran in historical terms and focuses on the characteristics and changes in it. In studying changes in families in Iran, we plan to discuss whether the changes made in the family are implications of some collapse or not, and, as part of this, generational relationships in the family are discussed.

THE HISTORY OF FAMILY IN IRAN

Both in historical and social respects, family is one of the most essential and effective social institutions in Iran. The survival of Iranian society without family is unthinkable. In other words, in defining Iranian society one must consider the family institution. It is for this reason that the Iranian family should be studied historically and contemporarily.

Family history in Iran could be discussed and followed in three general stages. The first stage is ancient Iran, the second is family in the Islamic era from the 7th century to the second half of the 18th century, and the third is the new stage that starts with the rise of the Qajar dynasty and continues to modern times. Despite similarities in all three stages, Iranian families have faced major changes. We will give a short description of the situation of family in these three stages.

Ancient Iran

In this era, matrimonial life was the core of family life, and many efforts were taken to save and maintain it. This is written in *Avesta*, the religious book of the Zoroastrians: "The rank of a married man is higher than a man without wife." Worshiping ancestors in ancient Iran was another reason for family formation, since by marriage and the birth of children who could inherit, the ancestors could be defended (Mazaheri, 1994, p. 12).

According to the teachings of Zoroaster's religion and the social realities of ancient Iran, the Iranian man could marry one woman. However, the nobleman, due to his financial abilities, was allowed to marry two women (Mazaheri, 1994, p. 156).

The main form of family in ancient Iran was an expanded family. The members of an expanded family consisted of a few families in one place, except for the girls who had left the family and had moved to their spouse's house. The expanded family lived under the supervision of the head of family. In the Sassanid era, marriage age was 15 for girls and 20 for boys (Fathi, 1985).

In this historical stage, there were five types of marriage in families: monogamy, polygamy, borrowing marriage, marrying two women, and marrying the next of kin. Marriage of a woman and a few men was called the commune marriage (polyandry). This type of marriage has been found rarely and few records are found. Nevertheless, polygamy means marrying more than one woman. Mazaheri has pointed out evidence in his discussion on commune marriage, but much of his discussion involves assumptions and guesses more than reality. He believed Mazdak and his followers supported commune marriage (Mazaheri, 1994, p. 162).

The borrowing marriage, marrying two women, and marrying immediate relatives have more importance in identifying the situation of family in this period than monogamy and polygamy. Despite the social means for marrying more than one woman, only nobles who had financial abilities were able to do so (Mazaheri, 1994, p. 151). There were two types of women in the houses of the noblemen in the Sassanid era: women with first rank who were called "Lord wife" and women with second rank who were called "maids." The difference between the rank of these two women in their husbands' houses depended on their class. The wife in first rank had the same class as the man, while the second rank women had a lower class status. For this reason, these women were mostly the servants of the first wife.

The lord woman used to receive daily alimony and at the same time she would have the same share of the man's bequeath as the man's sons after the husband's death. In turn, girls who were not married took one-half of their brothers' and mother's share of inheritance. Like their mother, the children of the second wife had no share in the inheritance, unless the father allocated them a share.

The borrowing or lending marriage was more common in the middle class. The noble class didn't use this marriage, in which the wife would be borrowed from another man for a limited time. There were two main reasons for this: the wife with an incurable disease was one of those reasons. Since the ill wife could not take care of children, the borrowed wife would undertake this duty. The second reason went back to the time when a wife had died, and the man needed a woman to take care of his children. The new husband or substitute had to take good care of the borrowed woman and sustain her and pay for her other needs. Those children who were born during a borrowed marriage would belong to the main husband, not the substitute one.

The third type of marriage was marrying with immediate relatives. Mazaheri believed that despite finding this type of marriage in ancient Iran once in a while, it was vanishing during the Sassanid era (Mazaheri, 1994, p. 143). The main reason for marrying an immediate relative was to maintain the purity of family blood and its nobility, and was among the class privileges of the noble class, since noble Iranians put high importance on the superiority of race and married an immediate relative to prevent any racial and class mingling (Ejazi, 1997, p. 77).

Family During the Islamic Era

In Islamic thought, family formation through marriage is of high importance to continue the generations, and for education and social and emotional integrity. For this reason, marriage and healthy relationship inside the family are very important among the Muslims of Iranian society. This can be found in the *Holy Koran* and other religious texts attributed to the Prophet of Islam and his followers. In particular, in the Nessa (Woman) verse, the importance of family, status of women and men, and their relationships are taught. Especially in verse 21 of Nessa, the importance of family is the focus. For this reason, during the Islamic era in Iran, family has been called a necessity for reproduction, for raising a Muslim individual and transferring cultural heritage, and establishing a balanced society. Khajeh Nassireddin Toosi, a scholar and religious jurisprudence thinker in the 14th century, states in his *Naseri Ethic*: "despite the fact that sexual needs act as the first step for family formation, it is affection that causes its sustainability" (1985, p. 12).

The family in the Islamic era changed from family in ancient Iran thus: (1) Women gained ownership rights, and (2) borrowing marriage and marrying the immediate relative were abolished. In turn, polygamy and temporary marriage with special conditions of financial means and approval of social conventions (which are most important) were approved.

Family in Contemporary Iran

Before facing modernity, the traditional and expanded families were the dominant ones. Since the second half of the 19th century, which coincides with the rule of Nasereddin Shah of Qajar, who was a ruler of the Khajar dynasty, family in Iran faced major changes. The changes resulted from the trips of noble families to foreign countries, the arrival of foreigners in Iran, and involvement with them. The first change was shown in the marriage of girls and boys, since the court women found new interests in selecting their husbands after acquaintance with the families and women in foreign families and, as a result, had more of a role in selecting their husbands.

By the development of the Constitutional Revolution in 1909, more changes were observed in the families, since, at that time, urban women took part in the Constitutional Revolution. Also, women's societies gained political participation. The changes found new structure during the First and Second Pahlavi periods, and helped to end the conventional and traditional stages. The Civil Status Registration Office, the legal and civil institutes for families, and the divorce court are all the results of efforts made in this period. On the other hand, development of new organizations, such as social security and modern education, took away part of the duty to raise and support children. Thus, family was not the only institution that had responsibilities for these (Mehdi, 1975, p. 58; Azadarmaki, 2000, p. 24). In subsequent years, Iranian society was exposed to major transformations. Changes in the marriage age of girls and boys, women's dress, marriage portion, education provisions for girls and women, limiting men in remarriage, and right to divorce—with special conditions such as remarriage of the man or financial problems and deviations in men—were recognized for women.

Collapse or Change in Family

Since the first encounter of family with modernity in Iran, a question has been asked: Has the Iranian family changed? If yes, has this encounter led to its collapse?

To answer these questions, there are two totally different and contradictory views. Some see these changes as the collapse and degradation of family, and another group sees the family surviving despite changes in it. Philosophers who argued for abolishing the family included Marx and Engels in the 19th century. They believed in transferring family functions such as raising children, supporting the old, and socializing people to other institutions such as schools, government, nursery schools, and "old houses." They did not believe in the need for the survival of family. In their criticism of male-dominated society, some contemporary feminist groups have called for the abolishment of the family as the only solution to save women from a patriarchal society.

Cooper is one of those who argues for the collapse of family. He has discussed this in his book *The Death of the Family* (1970). He believes that family prevents improvement of the self and ignores the individual freedom necessary for the personality to flourish. As people internalize their family's values, each member of the family incorporates a part of the other members, and the consequence of this for most people is the death (or underdevelopment) of the self (Haralamlos & Heald, 1980, p. 338).

Furthermore, Marx, Engels, feminists, and Cooper think of the family's death as positive. In Iran many events—such as lack of intention to form a family, increase in marriage age, sexual relations outside marriage, living together without marriage, increase in the divorce rate, and some women choosing to have children without marriage—that are considered signs of the collapse of the family have been occurring in large cities such as Tehran.

Opposite to the aforementioned view, there are several other sociological approaches—such as functionalism, evolutionism, and structuralism—that see the family as both changing and surviving. Some forms of structural functionalism, such as those of Durkheim, Talcott Parsons, and Merton, claim that families change as the needs of people and society change. In other words, the changes in family are simply changes, not signs of collapse (Haralamlos & Heald 1980, p. 325).

This second view sees family as a global phenomenon. The family continues to respond to the most essential human and social needs such as reproduction, raising children, and supporting its members. Thus, it will never collapse. Mehdi says, "Family is a phenomena that according to growth is under constant transformation in each moment and benefits from structuralization, disstructuralization and restructuralization processes. Any view of family must be a dynamic and dialectic perspective" (Mehdi, 1975, p. 64).

2. PAIRING UP

Spouse Selection Range

There was much less immigration and population movement in the past, and parents used to select spouses for their children, often from the geographic area where they were born or were living. However, the young people of the next generation have had marriage options from a larger area.

If you look at the third generation, however, people are born in migration cities, such as Tehran, and many of them select their spouses from the boys or girls they see in their block, on the way to work, at work, in schools, or in public places—essentially making their own choices.

In fact, both the first generation to live in the place where they were born and the third generation mostly married people form their own cities. However, the first group did this with parental interference, while the third mostly selected spouses themselves.

These differences are not quite as dramatic as the foregoing discussion makes them seem. According to the results of research (Azadarmaki, 2000), 88% of the first generation married local people, while more than 58% of the second generation and 69% of the third generation did.

In the first and second generations, marrying relatives occurred more on the father's side than the mother's; however, by the third generation, it was the opposite—that is, marriages with relatives on the mother's side occurred almost 1.3 times more often than on the father's (Azadarmaki, 2000, p. 13). If we accept that one of the criteria in selecting a spouse is acceptance by the other side and his or her family, an increase in marrying relatives on the mother's side can be taken as acceptance of the mother's views and intentions and improvement in her decision-making role.

As we see in Table 21.1, more than 40% of first-generation men married their wives without interference of others. Since more than 21% of first-generation men married more than once, the specifications of the last marriage (men or women) have also been registered. For this group, the specifications for their second to tenth marriages included more independence and more options than their first marriages—even in legal terms.[1] Most husbands of the first-generation women were familiar with their wives and married them with little interference of others, and this is also true of the third generation.

The second form of acquaintance among the three generations is their kinship and the previous relationship between spouses. Marrying relatives in the first and second generations was done mostly because of parents' willingness, and the regulations and traditions. The existence of beliefs, such as "cousins are married in the sky," and the giving of priority to marriage inside kinship networks to maintain blood purity and to save money, property, and inheritance were the motives for in-group or family marriages. But in the third generation, marriages between close relatives show a decrease, compared with the first and second generations. Despite the existence of traditions, one of the effective factors leading to an increase in non-kin marriage could be the publication

Table 21.1 Frequency of Three Generations of Individuals Marrying People From Their Own City

Description	First Generation		Second Generation		Third Generation	
	Frequency	Percentage	Frequency	Percentage	Frequency	Percentage
Local place (same city or village)	670	88.0	221	58.5	401	69.0
Different cities or villages in a province	37	4.8	58	15.3	36	6.2
Different cities or villages in two different provinces with different languages	4	1.0	27	7.1	38	6.5
Different cities or villages of two provinces with same language	29	5.2	66	17.5	96	16.5
Foreigner	6	0.7	2	0.5	4	0.7
Other	2	0.3	4	1.1	6	1.1
Total	761	100.0	378	100.0	581	100.0

SOURCE: Azadarmaki (2000).

of dangerous genetic consequences of marrying close kin, that is, an improvement in scientific public knowledge.

One might accept that the network of kin is still the strongest and most suitable grounds for acquaintance, but this has not lessened the change. In the past, the perspective of kinship and family relations was mostly an ideological view; however, social, economic, and other changes external to the family have resulted in an increasing valuing of relationship quality.

For three generations, the role of family friends, neighbors, parents, and brothers or sisters in introducing two families has continued to be crucial. However, parents had a greater role in selecting spouses for the first

generation than for the later generations. This is also true of the role of others, such as brothers and uncles. Their role has decreased in the third generation. It is only in the most recent (third) generation that the boy's or girl's preference in selecting a spouse has become more important than the parents'.

There are several similarities in the generations in different areas that could be outlined as follows. The first and second generations were concerned with dowry and the bath ceremonies, while the third generation gave more attention to the day-after-marriage party, marriage ceremony, and childbirth bath ceremony.

There are major similarities between the generations in the marriage ceremony (marriage registry, how to select a spouse, firstborn infant's presents, marriage portion, naming the child), which reveals the unity of the generations on the importance of family and social traditions, because if the society were facing a social collapse, this should have been manifested in changes in such rituals and ceremonies. If we want to observe whether the old traditions have been uprooted, marriage ceremonies would serve as a good measure and test (de Tocqueville, 1856, p. 164).

Changes in the Number of Wives

In ancient times, particularly during the Sassanid era, there was a kind of endogamy; however, it was not common except among the higher classes and nobles. With the arrival of Islam, with its emphasis on religious exogamy, this practice disappeared entirely (Mehdi, 1975, p. 15). In general, marriage in the Iranian family is now exogamous.

Polygamy in Iran is restricted to polygyny (a man marrying more than one woman), and this is still practiced. No evidence has been found of polyandry in Iran, even from the settlement of the Aryans in the Iranian Plateau (Ezzazi, 1997; Amani, 2001).

Although Islam has allowed men to marry up to four women at the same time and to have unlimited numbers of temporary wives, *monogamy has been more common in Iran than having more than two wives.* In public opinion, *sighe* (temporary marriage) is an undesirable act, and it is usually done in secret (Mehdi, 1975, pp. 16–17).

Despite the theoretical means for and religious approval of having more than one wife, the social reality of Iran is monogamy. In the past, wealthy people had the option of having more than one wife; however, nowadays polygamy faces various restrictions. In particular, an increase in the knowledge and education of women, more social participation of women in the society, passing restrictive laws that limit this option for

a man by requiring the consent of the present wife, and the activity of women and organizations for defending women's rights are among the main factors strengthening the monogamy base.

The degree of polygamy practiced among Iranian men during the last six decades can be calculated based on calculation of the number of married women and married men. In census figures, polygamy has always been present in Iranian society. In the first census after the Islamic Revolution, the degree of polygamy reached its height. However, by 1996 the number had reduced to a point that it revealed society's disapproval. Nevertheless, poverty and economic pressures in some families force some daughters to marry an already married man who can give them financial support. The figures in Table 21.2 give an estimate of polygamy.

These figures show a diminishing process in polygamy in Iran. The number of men with two or more wives has declined in recent years. Men with more than one wife are mostly from the first and second generation, not the third.

Change in Marriage Age

According to historical texts and travel accounts, marriage age in Iran was low, especially among the nobles during the Qajar period. Nasereddin Shah's sister, who was the wife of his prime minister, Amir Kabir, married when she was 12 years old and he was a middle-age man. Also, Nasereddin Shah's daughter, Tajolsaltaneh, married when she was only 8 (Ezzazi, 1997, p. 55). The emphasis in Islam on marriage was an important factor in low marriage age.

According to results published by the Iranian Census Center, the number of those marrying between 15 and 19 years old has decreased. During the 40-year period of 1956 to 1996, it went from 6.3% to 2.6% for men, and more important, from 41% to

Table 21.2   Number of Wives per 1,000 Husbands

Census Year	Number of Wives
1956	1,011
1966	1,010
1976	1,013
1986	1,022
1996	1,007

SOURCE: Amani (2001, p. 42).

17.9% for women. Like most developing countries, marriage is common in Iran, and in the census of 1996, the number of never-married people was only 1.6% for women (Mirzaei et al., 1999, p. 59).

The age at first marriage for women has increased from 18.7 in 1966 to 22.5 in 1996. However, the average age of first marriage for men went down from 1956 to 1986, but by 1991 it showed a significant increase. The census of 1996 shows that this is still continuing. In the statistics of 1996, the marriage age was 25.6 for men and 22.5 for women. Education has been one of the main factors increasing the average marriage age for girls.

The results of the research carried out in the city of Tehran show different marriage ages in the three generations. Among the men of the first generation, 27.2% married when they were 16 to 20 years old, with 40% of second-generation men marrying then, and the rest later. This percentage rose again in the third generation (along with, of course, the age at marriage). Among the women of the first generation, 48.3% had married between 11 and 15, and 32.7% between 16 and 20. This means that over 80% of that generation married before age 20. Among women, the percentage of marriages before 15 years old decreased in the next two generations, while marrying in the years 16 to 20 and 21 to 25 increased gradually.

After studying and comparing the marriage age of three generations, the men and women in our study were asked the most suitable age for marriage, for both men and women. Among the men subjects, those who believed 15 to 19 years old to be a suitable age to marry were almost all born in a village. Two-thirds of the male subjects who believed 25 to 29 years old to be the most suitable age to marry were born in the city.

3. FERTILITY AND SOCIALIZATION

Size of Family

Iran's population has increased in the last century and a half from 7,654,000 in 1861 to 60,055,488 in 1996. Large families were observed in Iran in the past; however, based on the census and statistics of the recent four decades, we observe an interesting change. There has been a decrease in both very large and very small households between 1966 and 1996. As you can see in Table 21.3, there are fewer one-person families and families of six or more person now than previously. Thus, the numbers of three- and four-person

Table 21.3   Percentages of Household Types

Year	One Person	Two Persons	Three Persons	Four Persons	Five Persons	Six Persons	Seven Persons	Eight or More Persons
1966	5.5	11.6	13.5	15.2	15.4	13.9	10.6	14.3
1976	5.6	11.4	13.2	15.2	15.2	13.9	10.8	14.7
1986	4.5	10.6	12.2	16.2	15.2	13.2	10.6	16.5
1996	4.4	11.3	16.0	18.4	16.0	12.7	9.7	11.6

SOURCE: Iranian Data Base. Iranian Census (1969–1996).

families increased considerably between 1966 and 1996.

Importance of Children

Family in Iran is still the "warm center" for raising children. When asked the question, "Does the child's happiness depend on having a family with parents?," 81.4% said yes.

However, this answer does not indicate that Iranians are necessarily satisfied with the *number* of children they have. We asked our respondents how many children they preferred, and more than one-half indicated that they preferred two children (58.3%).

In fact, almost 88% preferred one, two, or three children. When compared with the actual numbers in Table 21.3, it is apparent that many families have more than they would have wished for. Table 21.4 shows the data for how many children respondents would prefer to have.

Emotional Load

In its past form, the family had many functions, such as sexual, economic, educational, cultural, and interactive, while in its present form economic, social, and cultural changes have limited its functions. However, the Iranian family is still the center of emotional support for its members. Parents and children have emotional relationships with each other and have strong attachments. By emotional relationships we mean sustained and continuous interactions and feelings that continue between the parents and children until their death and are not reduced by the lapse of time or local separation.

This attachment and link is found both in traditional families and in families in large cities such as Tehran. The father is expected to support his children until the end of his life. Although his support is economic only until a certain age, it does not lose its emotional aspect. In Western societies, the child's leaving the family could be taken as the end of the parents' domination of the child both economically and socially; however, in Iran the child, even after marriage and having children, still maintains a special emotional link with his parents' family. Kindness, emotional support, love, self-sacrifice, and generosity to family members are some of the main characteristics considered for the family institution in Iran.

The conjugal family in Iran has strong ties with the larger family network, which compensates for any shortages or deficits,

Table 21.4   The Preferred Number of Children

Preferred Number	Number of Respondents	Percentage
0	91	3.6
1	367	14.5
2	1,474	58.3
3	380	15
4	110	4.3
5	34	1.3
6+	26	1.0

SOURCE: Azadarmaki (2002).

Table 21.5   Supportive Processes Between Parents and Children

The Way of Support	Preparing Housing	Financial Aids	Take Care	Solving Family Problems	No Support
Children helping parents	13.8	18.7	27.2	14.9	54.3
Parents helping children	40.2	48.8	41.3	29.5	22.7

SOURCE: Azadarmaki (2002, p. 202).

particularly emotionally. This emotional load in Iranian families is much greater than in Western families. These characteristics are the result of the social environment seen in Iran—a spirit resembling Durkheim's mechanical solidarity both inside and outside families (Mehdi, 1975, pp. 39–42).

Emotional relations between the generations are related to financial supports. Hence, the first generation try to support the second and third generation financially, while the third generation tries to help the first generation be happy, and takes care of them. The results of the relations between the generations are shown in Table 21.5.

4 & 5. MARRIAGE RELATIONSHIPS, FAMILY, AND GENDER

The Transitional Situation

The change in families is from the expanded or extended family to the nuclear one. In the processes of modernization, urbanism, increasing numbers of educated people, and women's employment, families have moved toward the nuclear, which is now found in both the cities and villages.

The nuclear family in Iran is different from families in the Western countries, since this type—which I prefer to call the "spouse family"—has links with the kin network. These nuclear families in Iran maintain strong, complex links with relative networks. As the research of Pole Viellie and Katebi show, this attachment is both emotional and economic, but is also a cultural one (Mehdi, 1975, pp. 2–3).

Individuals in the spouse family in Iran are situated in a network of kin, which compensates for any individual shortcomings. This supportive and emotional load is large in the Iranian families (Ladier-Fouladi, 1997, p. 199).

The relatives and kin are a group of people who have joined or are linked to each other by blood or marriage, and have socioeconomic and emotional relationships. These networks follow traditional social and financial obligations and responsibilities. Intermarriage is one of their main characteristics (Behnam, 1971, p. 47). It is for this reason that despite the development of the nuclear family in Iranian society, important relationships among people and families include the kin network.

In a study carried out by the author and his colleagues in Tehran in 1999, the ties of the nuclear family and the relatives network are seen. Although most who are younger than 29 years old were born in Tehran and live there, in many respects, particularly in selecting a spouse, they follow the family patterns of past generations. Most of the stated criteria such as being from the same family, city, and block are still important standards in selecting their spouses (Azadarmaki, 2000).

Women's Education

According to the population and housing census of 1996, women constituted 49.2% of Iran's population, of whom 61% were in urban regions, 35.6% were in rural regions, and less than 4% were nonsettled. In terms of education, 81.7% of urban women and 61% of rural women were literate, and the average of women's literacy in the country was 74.2%.

In the first university admission examinations after the Cultural Revolution in 1983, of 312,000 people who participated in the examinations, 131,427 were female and 181,258 were male. The statistics show that the women's situation was still not equal to men's in terms of academic level. While 42% of those who took the exam were female, only 32% of those admitted were female. From 1983 to 1992, almost no improvement was seen in the number of female participants; however, during that decade there was a slight decrease in the gender difference in admissions. By the year 2000, that is, 8 years later, the situation changed drastically, and the percentage of women's admissions became higher than those for men.

From 1983 to 1989 there were limitations on the admission of women to some disciplines. However, gradually during 1989 to 1995, most subjects, except mathematics and technical departments, admitted more women than men. In fields such as agricultural engineering, agricultural improvement and education, soil science, horticulture, agronomy, plant reform, and forestry, more than 70% of the admitted students were females.

For the first time, in 1998 the number of female college students (52%) exceeded the number of males, and it reached 61.4% in 2001. In that year, more than 59.7% of those registered for university entrance examinations were girls—a 2% increase in female registration rate from the previous year.

With respect to the higher percentage of girls passing the entrance examinations in the year 2000, the admissions were almost 60% females (Table 21.6). And for the fist time, the total number of girls in the Iranian state universities exceeded the number of boys.

Table 21.6 Number of Candidates and Admissions in Entrance Exams in 2000 per Gender

	Total	Female	Male
Exam candidates	1,459,000	818,000	640,000
Admitted	152,000	91,000	61,000
Percentage	100	59.8	40.2

SOURCE: Higher Education Statistics in 2000–2001.

As for university faculties, in 1998, 18.4% of faculty members were women and 81.6% were men. So, even though university enrollment of females has increased substantially, university faculties are still primarily men.

Changing our focus of attention to when, in their lifetimes, women held jobs, we will compare the older (or first) generation with the second and third. Table 21.7 shows the difference in women's employment timing in the three generations. Most women of the first generation worked with their husbands on farms and in workshops, and only a few women of this generation worked in the city. Those employed in the cities in this generation were employed in occupations such as unskilled and semiskilled labor in jobs such as rice farms, shoe making, carpet weaving, cooking, and maids in houses, and some were working as low-rank employees in offices and civil departments and in jobs such as dressmaking and makeup.

Most of these women started their jobs after marriage and going to their husband's house, while some worked as carpet weavers before marriage but did not continue it after marriage. The motive for working for most women in the first generation was their financial need, and only a very few liked to work outside the home or gained status from their work.

By the third generation women were working before or after marriage, or both. The idea of working after widowhood and before a second marriage had virtually disappeared.

Although family members such as spouses, children, and parents work for the survival of the family, their positions have changed with respect to the new social and cultural conditions of the Iranian and global society. Thus, women have acquired knowledge and techniques to improve their social and cultural positions. As a result, women are earning income by taking jobs in the educational, administrative, and service along with—and in some instances sectors in competition with—men, performing jobs that belonged to men in the past. This occupational displacement is a part of the social and cultural displacement of men and women in society.

7. DIVORCE

The Family Protection Law, passed in 1967, contained 24 articles. Articles 1–7 introduced the nonreligious marriage and divorce registry. Article 8 stipulated that divorce should be performed only through filing a petition to the Family Protection Court. These courts were obliged to make compromises between the spouses, and if they failed, the divorce would be registered if a certificate of incompatibility had been issued. Article 9 recognized the custody of children upon the agreement of the parties. This law also gave women permission to divorce, if it was

Table 21.7   Women's Employment Timing for Three Generations

Occupation Time	First Generation		Second Generation		Third Generation	
	Frequency	*Percentage*	*Frequency*	*Percentage*	*Frequency*	*Percentage*
Before marriage	3	15.0	12	33.3	24	24.7
After marriage	7	35.0	8	22.2	26	26.8
Both before and after marriage	5	25.0	10	27.8	44	45.4
Before and after marriage until birth of child	—	—	—	—	3	3.1
As widow and before second marriage	5	25.0	60	16.7	—	—
Total	20	100.0	36	100.0	97	100.0

SOURCE: Azadarmaki (2000).

proved that the husband had married without the permission of his present wife.

In 1973 the bar association of women criticized the Family Protection Law for giving permission to men to marry again, and keeping women from filing a divorce request if their husband contracted a contagious and harmful disease. The women's organization of Iran announced that they had asked for the establishment of a special committee for necessary reforms in the Family Protection Law. In 1973 the law was reformed. The Family Protection Law had 28 articles then, including one that stated that the minimum marriage age was 20 for men and 18 years for women. The same law emphasized the prohibition of a second wife, despite the wife's permission.

An increase in the rate of divorce in both the cities and villages is one of the signs of change in the Iranian family. Divorce is more frequent in cities than villages. Of every 100 divorce incidents across Iran during 1963 and 1964, 27 were in Tehran, even though

Tehran has only 10% of Iran's population. More than 27,000 divorce incidents were registered in the first 6 months of 1964. Table 21.8 shows the urban and rural divorce statistics for 1986–2001.

According to a publication released through the family courts during February 1968, of the 1,443 cases of divorce petitions registered in 13 branches of the court, 712 cases were initiated by men and 731 by women. This statistic shows that divorces are not initiated less often by women.

The statistics show that for men, divorce is more frequent in the 21 to 40 age-group. Seventy-three percent of men who divorce do so during that period.

Almost one-half of the divorce petitions to the courts lead to reconciliation instead of divorce. Among 2,000 requests for divorce sent to the courts for investigation, almost 1,000 requests lead to compromise, and an incompatibility (divorce) certificate is issued for the rest.

Table 21.8 Urban and Rural Divorce Statistics (1986–2001)

Year	Urban	Rural	Total
1986	29,379	5,832	35,211
1991	33,210	6,226	39,436
1992	28,289	5,694	33,983
1993	25,469	38,43	29,312
1994	28,385	4,321	32, 706
1995	30,277	4,461	34, 738
1996	32,697	2,120	34,717
1997	36,459	5,357	41,816
1998	37,626	4,765	42,391
1999	44,503	5,679	50,182
2000	47,936	5,861	53,797
2001	55,005	6,008	61,013

SOURCE: Web Site of Civil Status Registration Office. www.nocrir.com.

In 1968, there were 9,552 divorces, compared with 39,000 marriages; that is, one for each four new marriages. In 1971 and 1973, the ratio was closer to three divorces for every 10 new marriages.

Number of Marriages

Change in the number of marriages is a factor that shows change in Iranian families. This does not refer to multiple wives, but to remarriages. About 88% of each gender had been married more than once in the civil registration and Ministry of Health and Medical Education statistics. The frequency of marriage is shown in Table 21.9.

This study showed that 7.9% of men had two wives and 3.5% had three wives (in succession) (Amani, 2001, p. 43). Table 21.10 shows the number of (re)marriages in each of the three generations.

The main cause of remarriages among the first-generation men and women was the death of their spouse, though divorce is a second cause. However, divorce is now the most common cause for remarriage.

8. KINSHIP: THE GENERATION LINKS IN THE FAMILY

Paternal Families to Maternal Families

The Iranian family is mostly defined by paternal status. The paternal family has meant that Iranian history is seen as male

Table 21.9 Number of Marriages for Men and Women (by Percentage)

Number of Marriages	Women (%)	Men (%)
1	87.9	88.6
2	3.9	7.9
3 or more	8.2	3.5
Total	100.0	100.0

Table 21.10 Number of (Re)Marriages for Three Generations

	First Generation		Second Generation		Third Generation	
	Men	Women	Men	Women	Men	Women
1	79.0	93.8	91.9	95.0	98.5	98.3
2	16.0	5.8	8.1	5.0	1.5	1.7
3	2.8	0.4	—	—	—	—
4–10	2.2	—	—	—	—	—
Total	100.0	100.0	100.0	100.0	100.0	100.0

history (Barahani, 1972, p. 8). Although family in Iran is transitional, from a traditional structure to a modern one, the paternal family attitude still dominates the family. For this reason, it is best to label the Iranian family as a limited paternal family—still under the father's dominance.

Kinship in the past was mostly unilineal, not omnilineal, though signs of bilateralism can be found. Due to its unilateral (and unilineal) character, the family has been patrilineal, patronymic, and patrilocal—bringing the wife and children into the father's family. In this type of family, children take the name of their father (Sarukhani, 1991, p. 17).

Each of four generations of Iranian families has its own definite characteristics and functions. To clarify the function of each generation in families, see Table 21.11.

As the table shows, the first (oldest) generation gives emotional and moral support to the family, the second generation provides house management and financial facilities for the family, the third generation transfers cultural heritage (through socializing the children) and innovates and revises in-home culture, and the fourth generation shows compatibility with social and cultural conditions through internalizing culture and society.

Despite differences in the generations, intergenerational relations also help to implement gradual change in the Iranian family, without its collapse. The four generations maintain a supplementary relationship while maintaining their independence. The two processes that affect the generations are as follows:

Table 21.11   Family Functions of Different Generations

Age-Group	Generation	Generation Functions
+55	First	Emotions, wishes, and emotional support of other generations
30–54	Second	House management, economic support of first, third, and fourth generation
15–29	Third	Transfer of cultural heritage and innovation in family
1–14	Fourth	Compatibility with social and cultural conditions by accepting the culture

1. To internalize culture through transfer of culture via first and second generations.

2. The arrival process of new social and cultural elements with respect to the third and fourth generations' abilities.

Thus, the intergenerational relationship acts as a link and interaction between the generations. The first generation is an old one, the second generation is a middle-age one with the ability to transfer the experiences, culture, and civilization heritage to the third generation, which is made up of young adults, and the fourth generation, which is made up of children and teenagers. In this manner, there will be no generational interruption.

The third and fourth generations have the ability to transfer the new generative experiences within the family. Therefore, the third and fourth generations are not marginal, protesting, or passive generations while being exposed to the ancient culture and heritage or while being exposed to change. The same dual conditions have been transferred to the third and fourth generations. However, these two generations are more likely to implement cultural changes. In other words, if the generations were fully independent with no relationship, there would have been the possibility of social collapse or disjuncture, but despite generational differences, the intergenerational relationship makes the flow of culture and change relatively smooth.

We have attempted to show the generational continuity and change at the same time. The elements of a family such as wife, husband, parents, children, grandparents, and other associated members are the components of intergenerational relationships. Parents are the main family members in intergenerational links.

Men's Occupations by Generation

Among the first-generation men, traditional jobs such as shop keeping, limited trading, agriculture, cattle breeding, horticulture, and technical jobs such as carpentry, forging, and copper works are common. These activities are mainly based on having at least some limited financial capital.

There has been a slight decrease in the number of employees in these occupations among the second and third generations, though they are the most popular ones in the third generation, as in the first generation.

This is one similarity between the first and third generations. The unskilled laborers and small-time jobs (such as peddlers, vendors, office servants, teahouse workers, farm laborers, bakery workers, tanners, public bath servants, and coppersmiths) are substantially fewer, but are still the second most frequent jobs done by the first generation.

The retired civil employees are the third job group in the first generation. Among the second generation, the retired and those who work in governmental offices are the most common job group for men. To explain this, one may point out the expansion of the economic functions of the government after land reform and the increase in oil prices and the revenue of the country during the 1960s and 1970s, which enabled the government to expand its number of employees. The civil employees need no financial capital for their job and work by relying on the education and training courses they have taken.

In comparison with the second generation, the number of employees who need initial capital increased in the third generation. In turn, the number of civil employees in this generation has decreased.

It is not possible for those young people who have spent most of their time in education centers to collect even limited capital for starting a business; this is usually possible only through the help of parents or others. This is a give-and-take process in the family that shows the continuity of the supportive function of family for the younger members.

Despite some similarities in leisure time, there are major differences among the three generations. The third and fourth generations (younger) mostly pass leisure time by watching TV, traveling with friends, and going to the cinema and parks, while parents mostly prefer to be with their family and relatives or to travel to holy cities or their hometown.

10. FAMILY AND RELIGION

Compared with the importance of religion, the family is very important. In terms of an international survey in Iran, family and religion are two main social institutions. In a 2002 survey, 97.5% of Iranians saw family as important, and 92.5% saw religion that way. However, only 85% of the Tehran respondents saw religion as very important—an indication, as has been found in other studies, that urban life does affect religion.

SUMMARY

In summary, the Iranian family is undergoing a major change in terms of increase in marriage age and increase in the number of divorces and remarriages. Many of the third generation are born in Tehran, and know themselves as Tehrani, while the second and first generations are mostly from small towns and farms. The number of the educated people in comparison with the illiterate is higher in the third generation than the second and first generations, if elementary and secondary school education are counted. There are differences in generations in terms of occupation model. The second generation is more likely to have worked in the civil service than either the preceding or following generation. With the lapse of time, Iranian families face "generation" issues. The old, middle-age, and young generations of each family have their own characteristics. Despite such generation differences, though, the people of each generation are linked with the others through family and religious ceremonies, rituals, and traditions. This link has emotional, social, and economic consequences. For leisure time or selecting a wife, the first generation is different from the others. Although all three generations have commonalities in passing leisure time, such as visiting elders, pilgrimages, watching TV, and family relations, the out-of-home recreation and being in family is more important for the third generation. Also, the third generation is much more likely to make their own choices in pairing, rather than having partners determined by parents and kin.

NOTE

1. As an example, according to the law, a girl is not allowed to marry unless she has her father's permission (verbally or through an instrument in writing); however, this condition is not present for next marriages.

REFERENCES

Amani, M. (1970). *Shape and transformation of family in Iran.* Tehran: The Population Section of the Institute for Social Studies, University of Tehran.

Amani, M. (2001). An outlook to forty years of demographic transformation of marriage in Iran (1956–1996). *Social Science Journal, 17*(Spring/Summer), 33–46.

Azadarmaki, T. (2000). *Studying cultural-social changes in the Tehrani families in three generations.* Tehran: Social Studies and Research Institute, Tehran University.

Azadarmaki , T. (2002). *Sociology theories* (2nd ed.). Tehran, Iran: Soroush Publication.

Barahani, R. (1972). *Male history, factors of cultural dispersion in Iran.* Unpublished essay.

Behnam, J. (1971). *Structures of family and relatives in Iran.* Tehran: Kharazmi Publication.

Cooper, D. G. (1970). *The death of the family.* New York: Pantheon Books.

de Tocqueville, A. (1856). *L'Ancien régime et la révolution.* Paris: Michel Lévy Frères. Octavo, XXI.

Ejazi, S. (1997). *Sociology of family.* Tehran: Roshangaran and Motaleate Zanan.

Engels, F. (1978). *Origin of family, private ownership and government in light of Lewis Morgan's studies* (2nd ed.). (K. Parsa Trans.). Tehran: Jami Publisher.

Ezzazi, S. (1997). *Sociology of family with emphasis on the role, structure and function of family in contemporary time.* Tehran: Rohangaran and Women Studies Publication.

Fathi, A. K. (1985). Social integration in the traditional urban Iranian family. In A. Fathi (Ed.), *Social, economic and political studies of the Middle East: Vol. 38. Women and the family in Iran* (pp. 151–157). Leiden, The Netherlands: E. J. Brill.

Haralamlos, M., & Heald, R. M. (1980). *Sociology themes and perspectives.* Oxford, UK: Oxford University.

Ladier-Fouladi, M. (1997). The fertility transition in Iran. *Population: An English Selection, 9,* 191–214.

Mazaheri, A. A. (1994). *Pre-Islam family in Iran.* (A. Tavakol Trans.). Tehran: Nashre Ghatreh Publisher.

Mehdi, A. A. (1975). *Sociology of Iranian families.* Tehran: Payam Publication.

Mirzaei, M. Mohammad, Habibillah, Zanjani, & Mohmodi. (1999). *Population, development and reproduction development.* Theran: Boshra Publisher.

Sarukhani, B. (1991). *Introduction to sociology of family* (1st ed.). Tehran: Soroush Publication.

Toosi, K. N. (1985). *Akhlaghe naseri* (3rd ed.). (M. Minovi & A. Haydari Eds.). Tehran: Kharazmi Publishing.

CHAPTER 22

Families in Israel

RUTH KATZ

YOAV LAVEE

Is there a pattern, a form, or a structure of family that can be identified as uniquely Israeli? In what way is this "Israeli family" different from any other family in a similarly modernized, industrialized society? If there is a unique form of Israeli family, is it equally shared by all Israelis, or is it the dominant pattern among some sectors of the population and not among others?

(Shamgar-Handelman, 1996, p. 388)

This chapter provides a look at families in Israel. Following Shamgar-Handelman (1996) we contend that there is no single, distinct, unique "Israeli family," but rather there is a diversity of family patterns and lifestyles.

Israel is characterized by a vast diversity in family patterns, manifested by a plethora of family values, attitudes toward gender roles, and choices of lifestyles. Clear differences exist between Jewish and Arab families. Among Jewish families, large differences exist between ultraorthodox and secular families as well as between families of various countries of origin. Among Arab families, marked differences can be found between urban and rural families of different religious affiliations (Muslims, Christians, Druze, and others). Among both Jews and Arabs, there are families with strong traditional values and lifestyles, while others are characterized by more liberal views and practices. Thus, family patterns and norms do not pertain equally to all families. Indeed, there is a wide diversity of norms, customs, and family lifestyles, both between and within groups.

1. ISRAELI SOCIETY: AN OVERVIEW

Israel is a small country (20,770 sq km), located in the Middle East. It is flanked by

This chapter is a revised and updated version of Katz and Lavee (in press).

the Mediterranean Sea on the west, Jordan and Syria on the east, Lebanon on the north, and Egypt on the south. The population is about 6.5 million, of which about 78% are Jewish and the rest are non-Jewish, primarily Arabs (Central Bureau of Statistics, 2002).

Israel is also a young and dynamic country. Its population has always been characterized by a rapid rate of increase, and the demographic composition of the Jewish population has been changing continually as a consequence of many large waves of immigrants. In 1948, when the State of Israel was established, the population was 873,000. Over the last 50 years, there has been a six-fold increase in the population. Immigrants have arrived from almost every corner of the globe, bringing with them a wide variety of cultures, lifestyles, and family patterns. Two large influxes occurred shortly after Israeli independence was declared: Holocaust survivors from Europe and Jews from Islamic countries (mainly North Africa, Iraq, Syria, and Yemen). The 1950s saw a relatively large wave of immigrants arrive from Europe and North Africa, whereas the 1960s were characterized by immigration from the affluent West (the United States, Canada, and the United Kingdom), and the 1970s and 1980s by immigration from the USSR. In the 1990s, there was massive immigration (about 700,000) from the former Soviet Union. Jews from Ethiopia (about 56,000) have immigrated in two waves: first in the mid-1980s and again in the early 1990s.

The Jewish majority today is composed of two main ethnic clusters: "Orientals" or *Sepharadim* (Spanish), who themselves or their ancestors originated from the Near East, North Africa, Yemen, Ethiopia, the Balkans, Iran, Iraq, India, and the Muslim republics of the former Soviet Union; and *Ashkenazim,* whose origin is in American or European continents. At present, 33.5% of the Jewish population are Asian-African born or children of Asian-African origin; 40% are European-American born or children of American-European origin; and 26.5% were born in Israel to Israeli-born parents (Central Bureau of Statistics, 2002). The Arab population itself is composed of several religious groups: Muslims (75%), Christians (16%), and Druze and others (9%).

This portrayal of the population highlights its pluralistic nature: a mix of Jews and Arabs; different ethnic/religious groups within each of these sectors; different levels of religiosity, ranging from secular to ultra-orthodox among both Jews and Arabs; a variety of countries of origin, traditions, and heritage; and a mix of new immigrants and veteran Israelis.

Despite this diversity, the predominant form of the family in Israel is the traditional nuclear family. The overwhelming majority of couples have children (2.7, on average), and the majority (about 75%) remain married for the entire life cycle. The average size of a household is 3.79. About 62% of the households are composed of couples with their children, and another 20% consist of couples without children (including couples in the empty-nest stage of their family life cycle). Only 10% of the households are composed of a single parent and her or his children. Nearly all families live in separate households but remain in close contact with their extended family.

2. PAIRING UP

Dating and Mate Selection

For most Israeli Jews, dating begins during adolescence within peer social groups such as high school, youth movements, and higher education institutions. Military service is one of the main avenues of acquaintance, as service is compulsory for men (3 years) and for women (18–24 months) starting at age 18. After a period of acquaintance that is usually brief, young people introduce their intended spouses to parents and friends. Shared entertainment, meals in the family setting, and, at times, staying overnight in the home of the boyfriend or girlfriend's parents are normative.

Two other patterns of mate selection are also common, albeit in a much smaller proportion: arranged marriages within the ultraorthodox population and semiarranged marriages among Arabs. Within the ultraorthodox community, dating is not accepted. The bride's purity is of the utmost importance, and the family is interested in their daughter's marriage at the earliest age permissible (17 years). Men, too, are expected to marry at an early age, because marriage is the only permissible avenue for a sexual outlet. Marriages are arranged by the parents, often with the assistance of traditional "matchmakers," persons known in the community for their ability and success in arranging suitable matches between unmarried men and women. The couple meets only a few times before marriage, and only in the presence of their family. Usually, the couple accepts the parents' selection, although they may have veto power (Safir, 1991).

In Arab society, the process of selecting a marital partner is determined by key members of both families, even though the tradition of arranged marriages is rapidly disappearing (Haj-Yahia, 1995). Traditionally, the groom's parents selected an appropriate bride for their son and proposed a "marriage transaction" to the bride's parents. Only after parents on both sides agreed to the match would their sons and daughters be informed about what had been done. Today this tradition remains only a framework for mate selection, and parents rarely force their children to marry a partner against their will (Avitzur, 1987). Many young men and women choose their own mates, although dating is not "public." Free encounters between unmarried men and women in the village are not accepted and are actually prohibited in certain locations, but many couples know each other before they marry and meet outside of the village or away from their home environment. When they decide to marry, the groom's parents are expected to speak to the prospective bride's parents "to ask for her hand." As soon as both partners receive the consent of their families, they announce their engagement. The tradition, therefore, is upheld in some respects but not in others. Arab women today still cannot marry without the consent of their parents and even the consent of brothers and other relatives.

Cohabitation

Cohabitation as a prelude to formal marriage is widespread among young Jewish couples, especially the secular and more educated. It is rare among less-educated Jewish couples, and is not practiced among orthodox Jews or Arabs. In a recent survey of a representative sample of 2,000 Jewish respondents, 26% reported having lived with their present marital spouse before marriage, and 19% reported that they had lived together with a partner whom they did not end up marrying (Katz, 2001).

Nearly 63% of Jewish Israelis believe that "it is better for a couple who plan to get married to live together first," and more than 60% approve of cohabitation even if the couple does not plan to get married (Steier, Oren, Elias, & Lewin-Epstein, 1998). However, cohabitation is not perceived as an alternative to formal marriage. In most cases, couples formalize their relationship after several years, especially when they wish to have children.

Marriage

Marriage in Israel is almost universal and has not changed much over time. Among all population groups, men and women alike, less than 3% have never been married by the time they are 50 years old (Central Bureau of Statistics, 2002). However, the average age at marriage is rising, and there are indications that the marriage rate is expected to decline.

The large majority of people have a favorable attitude toward marriage. Apparently, having children is one of the major motivating factors for marriage. Results from a study with a representative sample of 1,159 people (Steier et al., 1998) show that nearly 50% of the respondents believe that the major purpose of marriage today is to have children, and 73% believe that people who want to have children should get married. However, less than 50% believe that married people are happier than their unmarried counterparts. Only a small percentage of people (11.2%), both men and women, young and old alike, believe that it is better to have an unsatisfactory marriage than to not be married at all.

Despite defining themselves as secular, most young couples in Israel accept the set of religious laws and rules and enter into formal (religious) marriages. Only a small minority of Jewish men and women (about 4%) prefer a legal nonreligious marital contract. Because Jewish marriages can only be held through the religious legal system (*rabbanut*), marriages in civil courts are usually held in neighboring countries (primarily Cyprus). An even smaller minority of couples choose to forfeit formal marriage and remain in cohabitation as a permanent lifestyle.

In all sectors of society, the wedding ceremony is usually conducted in large halls, with anywhere from a few hundred to 1,000 or more guests invited, including family, friends, neighbors, and coworkers of both sides. Aside from a relatively brief religious wedding ceremony conducted in the hall itself, the wedding involves catered food, music and dancing, and sometimes also professional performers. Whereas in the past household gifts such as small appliances, linens, kitchen goods, and so forth were the norm, nowadays it is more common for guests to bring money gifts to help defray the wedding costs and to assist the young couple in starting their new life together.

There are various wedding traditions followed by several ethnic groups, primarily of North African and Asian origin, such as the Henna, and other religious ceremonies, such as the Mikveh and groom's Sabbath, practiced by orthodox Jews and by many secular couples as well. The Mikveh is a religious purification ritual, in which the bride is immersed in water prior to the wedding to symbolize her purity and virginity. Following the Mikveh, on the night immediately preceding the wedding ceremony, is the Henna ceremony, a ritual in which the bride's hair, feet, and hands are dyed by red dried leaves to protect against the evil eye. The groom's Sabbath is a religious service that takes place in the synagogue on the Sabbath preceding or following the wedding (depending on one's cultural origin) with the male members of the family, followed by a reception at the groom's family house.

Arab weddings often involve several large parties. The bride's family may hold a large celebration several days before the wedding for the bride to formally part from her female relatives and friends, as she usually joins the groom in his family home after marriage. In addition, the groom's family has a party to welcome the bride into her new family. At a rural wedding celebration, the whole community is often invited. Traditionally, all celebrations, including the reception, meals, and dancing, are held separately for men and women.

3. FERTILITY AND SOCIALIZATION

In 2001 the total fertility for an average Israeli woman was 2.89. However, the birth pattern is not uniform among all groups in

Israel. It is significantly higher among Muslims (4.71 children) and Druze (3.02) than among Jewish and Christian-Arab women (2.59 and 2.46, respectively). In the Jewish population itself, the fertility rate is considerably higher among ultraorthodox women and lowest among secular and highly educated women of Ashkenazi origin. In the Arab population, birth patterns are most significantly shaped by education and other indicators of traditionalism (Peritz & Baras, 1992). It is worthy of note that these birthrates are higher than those in other developed countries. In the United States, for example, the fertility rate is 2.07 children per woman (Central Intelligence Agency, 1998), and in Europe it ranges between 1.2 children per woman in Italy to 1.9 in Ireland (Eurostat, 1997).

The Place and Role of Children

Israel is a "child-oriented" society. Married couples are expected to have children, and a childless couple is not considered a family. Nearly 60% of Israelis believe that childless people have an "empty life," and more than 80% believe that "the greatest joy in life is to follow children's growing up" (Steier et al., 1998). On average Israelis desire more children (3.48) and have more children (2.7) than people in other industrialized countries. Children are highly valued not only by their parents, who usually give their needs top priority, but also by society as a whole. The welfare of children is considered a collective responsibility.

The attitude of Israeli society toward its children is manifested in the policy that all women receive a birth allowance and families receive a monthly children's allowance and tax deductions depending on the number of children in the family. There are special discounts for large families for public childcare and for summer camps, as well as for municipal taxes (Safir, 1991). The Health Ministry provides mother and child health clinics all over the country, in which free pre- and postnatal care is provided to all mothers and their children up to the age of 3 (Rosenthal, 1994).

As the marriage rate is relatively high and the divorce rate is relatively low, the probability of children growing up in a dual-parent family is high. Ninety percent of children aged 0 to 17 live with their biological or adoptive parents, and an additional 5% live in a reconstituted family that also functions as a dual-parent family. More than 50% of children live in the same household with one or two other children. Only 14.4% of children are the only child in their household, while 33% of children live with three or more siblings (Central Bureau of Statistics, 2002). Thus, most children grow up in households that include other children as well.

The emphasis on children has not prevented women from seeking employment outside the home. The basic assumption of Israeli women from all population categories, including the ultraorthodox, is that family and outside work can be combined. Thus, employment of mothers with young children is a rather common phenomenon in Israel. In the 1990s, about 54% of mothers whose youngest child was under the age of 1, and 67% of mothers with children under the age of 15, were employed (Katz, 1997).

Combining family and job roles is made easier by government policies and by the availability of public and private services. To facilitate the participation of mothers of young children in the labor market, legislation was passed in 1955 granting maternity leave, which enables working mothers to receive their salary while staying home for 12 weeks following delivery. The National Insurance Institute pays for maternity leave and also provides each family with a special grant on the birth of a child. The policy has evolved over the years so that today working mothers can take an additional 9 months of unpaid leave without losing their job. Recently, the law providing for a fully paid 3-month maternity leave was changed to *parental* leave to include the father. We do not yet know how many fathers use this right, to what extent employers are willing to grant it, or the ability of the authorities to enforce it.

Although these policies encourage at-home care by the mother for up to 12 months, the strong family orientation has never led to a "motherhood cult" that assigns the care of infants and toddlers exclusively to the mother (Azmon & Izraeli, 1993). Day care centers that provide full-day care for babies and toddlers from the age of 3 months are widespread (about 1,000) throughout the country. Most of these childcare facilities are run by women's organizations and are subsidized by the Ministry of Labor and Welfare, making them affordable to low-income families and single mothers. Private daycare centers, as well as centers run by local authorities, are also available. In addition, large companies and academic institutions often provide on-site day care facilities for working parents. There is generally a positive attitude among parents in Israel toward the use of day care and preschool services, which are commonly believed to enhance rather than impair the child's intellectual, emotional, and social development (Azmon & Izraeli, 1993). A few Israeli scholars, however, challenge this belief, arguing that while early childcare centers may enhance intellectual and interpersonal capacities, they pay little attention to the emotional dimensions of the children's development (Sagi & Koren-Karie, 1993).

Among Arab families, unlike many Jewish Israeli families, it is very rare to find babies who are left with caregivers, babysitters, or other strangers (Haj-Yahia, 1995). Members of the extended family often help parents fulfill the basic tasks of disciplining and taking care of children. In these families, the role of the father (and other males in the family) is to control and discipline, while the role of the mother (and other females in the family) is to nurture and support the children.

Parenting Practices

Although each parent develops his or her own parenting style based on past experiences, beliefs about parenting also exist within a cultural context. Parents often have an ideal image of the "adaptive adult" that guides them in socializing their children (Roer-Strier, 1996). In a multicultural society such as Israel, which is marked by immigration, parenting practices are tied to individual perceptions of family heritage, customs, and norms of behavior relative to the host society. Using a metaphor from the animal world, Roer-Strier (1996) presents three different parenting styles—the "cuckoos," who entrust their children to socializing agents, such as boarding schools or kibbutzim; the "kangaroos," who see themselves as their children's chief socializing agents and tend to raise their children according to the traditions followed in their native culture; and the "chameleons," who adopt bicultural practices by encouraging the child to behave like others outside of the home but to behave at home according to the parents' culture of origin.

Children in Israel remain a central focus of concern for their parents for a longer period of time than in most industrialized countries. When sons and daughters begin compulsory military service at 18, parenting often becomes even more intense than previously (Azmon & Izraeli, 1993). At the age when most young people fulfill their developmental task of separation and individuation, Israeli soldiers are becoming closer to their parents (especially to the mother). Three years after completing military service, two-thirds of these young adults are still living at home and are economically dependent on their parents (Mayseless, 1991, 1993).

4. GENDER ROLES

Two contradictory sets of ideological systems coexist in Israel: an egalitarian ideology, which minimizes gender differences, and a traditional ideology, which assigns different sets of rights and obligations to men and women (Azmon & Izraeli, 1993; Raday, 1991). Thus, while the country as a whole has adopted an egalitarian ideology, with an egalitarian educational system and opportunities open to men and women alike, a notable portion of the population is still within, or just one generation away from, its traditional origins. Family laws are also marked by duality: The legal status of women is determined simultaneously by some of the most modern legal approaches as well as by one of the most ancient legal systems in the world (Raday, 1991). Women's rights for equal opportunity are explicitly recognized in the legal system and in the Declaration of Independence. At the same time, the ancient Jewish law, which serves as the legal authority in matters of marriage and divorce, imposes a different legal status on men and women.

Educational opportunities are largely equal for men and women. The median number of years of schooling is 12.3 for men and women alike (Central Bureau of Statistics, 2002). A significant increase in educational level has taken place among Arab women in the past decade: from a median of 7.5 years of schooling in the 1980s to 11.0 years in 2001. In the past two decades, the number of women in higher education has doubled, while the number of men has remained constant. By 2001, 38.9% of women and 38.2% of men had postsecondary education.

Similar progress is also evident in the increased proportion of women's participation in the labor force, which has increased steadily from 22 to 25% in the 1950s and 1960s to 48% in 2000. These rates, however, are not equally distributed among all ethnic groups. Among Muslim women, only 13% participate in the labor force, compared with one-third of Christian and Druze women and more than 50% of Jewish women. Although women with young children constitute the largest portion of working women (71% of them are in the labor force), labor force participation of women increases with the age of the youngest child and decreases with the number of children in the family.

The progress in gender equality is not reflected in the type of occupations, organizational status, or incomes of men and women. Despite some changes in the past two decades, the labor market is still segregated, with women most frequently employed in education, health, and welfare services, while occupying only one-fifth of managerial positions. Additionally, many women work part time— much more frequently than men (30% and 9%, respectively)—and their average income per hour is only 80% of men's.

A few steps have been taken by policymakers to promote women's participation in the labor force and to further the equality of women in employment and in pay. Among them are the legislative efforts to provide protection to working mothers, such as maternity leave, the Equal Opportunity in Employment Law (1981), and the Equal Opportunity Law (1988). These laws have made discrimination on the basis of either sex or family status illegal in job advertising, hiring, training, promotion, and firing. However, since these laws are difficult to enforce and do not include affirmative action, gender segregation persists (Raday, 1991). Likewise, the Equal Pay Law (1964) provided that an employer is required to pay female employees a wage equal to that of male employees in the same workplace for work that is essentially equal. In reality, however, the law has not succeeded in achieving a redistribution of wages between the sexes.

5. MARITAL RELATIONSHIPS

Marital Satisfaction

What are the most important components of marital satisfaction? Both husbands and wives tend to associate healthy marital relationships with a sense of bonding, caring, and feeling of unity and companionship, followed by mutual understanding, respect, and trust between the partners (Lavee, 1997). Additional ingredients of marital satisfaction mentioned by respondents were satisfactory sexual relationship, communication, and compatibility (that is, similar mentality, worldview, and character, as well as mutual leisure and social interests).

Similar ingredients of marital satisfaction were found in a study of long-term marriages (Sharlin, 1996). Sharlin found the most frequent motives for staying together were love and appreciation of closeness and comfort with each other, enjoyment of one's lifestyle and reluctance to change it, a belief that marriage is a partnership for life, and the perceptions that "we complement each other in spite of occasional tensions" and that "our shared experiences have drawn us closer together." At the same time, many long-term couples stay together for other reasons. When asked about crucial motives for staying together during marital crises, social conventions (e.g., "marriage is a partnership for life") and responsibility for children were just as frequently mentioned "marriage keepers" as love.

In general people tend to express satisfaction with their marital quality. In a study of 1,504 Jewish men and women aged 18 and over (Shaked, 1994), 74% of the men and 61% of the women reported being very satisfied with their marital relationships. Only 7% of men and women reported being distressed. The respondents also reported a fairly high satisfaction with their sex life (67% and 72% of the men and women, respectively, being very satisfied).

At the same time, more women than men (14% and 7%, respectively) expressed a marked dissatisfaction with their sex life. Educational level was associated with sexual satisfaction for women (more dissatisfaction among women with low education), but not for men (Shaked, 1994).

There is little data on marriage values among Arab couples. A comparative study of various ethnic/religious groups in Israel (Lavee, 1995) has shown that marital satisfaction varies positively with the degree of traditionalism: The more traditional the community, the higher the perceived quality of the relationship. Thus, Druze couples, who hold the most traditional family values and lifestyle, report the highest level of marital quality, followed by Muslims, Christian Arabs, and Jews. The differences among these groups remained even after controlling for educational level, economic situation, level of religiosity, and number of children. Furthermore, Katz, Lavee, and Azaiza (1998) found that among Arab couples, marital satisfaction was highest among rural Muslims and lowest among women in a mixed Arab-Jewish urban community.

Division of Labor and Power Distribution

Attitudes toward marital division of labor range from the most egalitarian to the traditional. In a recent poll, 54% of the respondents expressed egalitarian values, whereas 39% of the men and 29% of the women surveyed expressed more traditional values (Gross, 1999). As expected, egalitarian values are found to be more prevalent among the younger generation and among the more educated than among older and less educated couples.

To what extent is gender equality *actually* maintained within families? One way of answering this question is by examining the overall burden—labor force and family work combined—on husbands and wives. Generally speaking, the household division of labor has not changed in parallel with the massive entrance of mothers into the labor force, and has remained largely traditional. The strong emphasis on maintaining family ties, on having two or more children, and on caring for elderly parents results in differential loads for women and men. Women are normatively responsible for the functioning of the household, for childcare, and for maintaining ties with kin. Husbands do not significantly share the additional burden arising from their wives' employment. The number of hours they devote to home and children is about the same, whether or not their wives are employed. Husbands, in general, invest most of their time—much more than their spouses—in their jobs (Katz, 1989). However, when the wife's income is equal to or greater than that of her husband, the division of labor in the family is more egalitarian and both tend to attribute as much importance to the career success of their spouses as to their own (Izraeli, 1994).

Interestingly the segregated division of labor and the additional burden incurred on women are not necessarily perceived by them as unfair. Lavee and Katz (2002) found that gender role ideology is an important moderating factor between household division of labor and perceived fairness and marital satisfaction. In particular, perceived fairness in the division of labor and the level of marital satisfaction were highest among couples with the most segregated role division (Muslim Arabs) and lowest among families with a more egalitarian role division (Jews and Christian Arabs).

In addition to division of labor, gender differences are reflected in the decision-making process of husbands and wives. Wives are more dominant in family decisions regarding childcare and education as well as family leisure, whereas men are more dominant in decisions regarding family finances,

car purchase, and both spouses' jobs. Other major household purchases, such as furniture and appliances, most commonly are made by joint decisions. A wife's personal resources (e.g., education, income, and occupational prestige) have a considerable impact on her share in marital decisions, while the husband's resources have very little impact (Katz & Peres, 1993).

In the Arab family, the status of women has always been lower than that of men. Arab women are expected to be dependent on their husbands and to satisfy their needs. The status of women is especially lower in the public sphere, and decisions at the community level are primarily a male domain. In the private sphere, however, the status of women is much stronger, reflecting a gap between the patriarchal ideology and the actual power of women in the family (Al-Haj, 1989). The influence and role of women in decision making is increasing, particularly among younger couples, and husbands tend to consult their wives about almost everything (Haj-Yahia, 1995). It is still unclear as to whether recent changes in women's status and power in the family are due to sociocultural and sociopolitical developments or whether they are a consequence of women's increasing personal resources, such as education and contribution to family income (Al-Haj, 1989; Haj-Yahia, 1995).

6. FAMILY STRESSES

For the most part, Israeli families face life challenges similar to those faced by families in other industrialized countries: normative, developmental transitions, as well as nonnormative life events; chronic stressors and economic strains; daily hassles due to conflicting demands of workplace and home; and strains and stresses of family relationships, including intergenerational conflicts, marital crises, divorce, and violence. There are, however, certain sources of stress unique to Israel. Most notable are stresses and strains inflicted by the Israeli-Arab conflict—repeated wars, terrorist acts, and other security-related issues. In addition, stresses for immigrant families may be viewed as characteristic of Israeli society because these families constitute a large proportion of the society.

Wars, Terrorism, and Security-Related Stress

Israel (and before it, Palestine) has lived in a state of war with its neighboring countries for over 100 years. Wars, terrorist acts, and security threats are at the core of Israel's existential reality. In its 50 years of existence, Israel has fought seven wars and suffered a ceaseless chain of hostilities, including repeated shelling of border settlements and numerous terrorist activities inside the country. The armed conflict between Israel and its neighboring Arab countries has resulted in thousands of military and civilian casualties. The percentage of Israeli families who have suffered injury or loss, or who have close relatives or personal friends who have experienced this suffering approaches 100% (Milgram, 1993).

In discussing Israeli families' coping with the stress of war and security threats, it is difficult—and perhaps unwise—to distinguish between the stress and coping of individuals, families, and the community. Due to the small size of the country and the high degree of identification with the victims—whether a terrorist attack or border shelling—the fallout from events in any part of the country unleashes nationwide empathy (Good & Ben-David, 1995). At the same time, family coping cannot be understood without viewing the management of stress by the community organized to provide support and intervention to the victims and their families (Ayalon, 1993).

Since the establishment of the State of Israel in 1948, more than 19,000 soldiers have lost their lives. There are currently more than 18,000 bereaved families. Needless to say, the loss of a spouse, a father, a sibling, or a son has a major effect on the life course of all family members, especially on parents. Research on bereaved parents has shown that a heightened level of bereavement responses is demonstrated beyond the number of years normally expected (Rubin, 1993, 1996). In fact, Rubin and his colleagues (Rubin, Malkinson, & Witztum, 1999) suggest that terms such as *coping, adaptation,* and *resolution* are inadequate for describing the experience of the majority of bereaved parents.

Combat stress reaction (CSR) and post-traumatic stress disorder (PTSD) have long-lasting effects on the army veteran's life and his family (Solomon, 1993). CSR casualties report more problems in social, family, sexual, and work functioning. In addition, secondary post-traumatic symptoms leading to severe marital distress have been found among wives of CSR veterans (Waysman, Mikulincer, Solomon, & Weisenberg, 1993).

Shelling targeted against border communities, particularly in northern Israel, has been an ongoing source of stress for families over the past 30 years. Most of the research on this population has focused on children's reactions and has shown that children's coping is highly influenced by the community's response. The social cohesiveness of the community was found to moderate children's anxiety (Ziv & Israeli, 1973; Zuckerman-Bareli, 1979) and to provide ground rules for acceptable behavior during crisis situations.

The Gulf War provided a unique opportunity for examining family coping under stress. During a 5-week period (January–February 1991), the civilian population, throughout the country, was exposed to missile attacks with potential chemical weapons and families were repeatedly confined to hermetically sealed rooms. In research on the entire family as a coping unit (Ben-David &

Lavee, 1992; Lavee & Ben-David, 1993), four types of families were identified based on the level of stress, roles, and interaction styles: (1) *anxious families,* characterized by high level of stress, low or no role distribution, and negative interaction style; (2) *cautious families,* with a high level of stress, clear role allocation, and positive interaction among members; (3) *confident families,* typified by a relatively low stress level, clear role allocation, and little interpersonal interaction with a positive overall family atmosphere; and (4) *indifferent families,* characterized by a low stress level, no role allocation, and little interaction among family members.

More recent geopolitical developments in the Middle East, namely the peace process between Israel and the Palestinians (1993–2000) and the armed Palestinian *intifada* (uprising) that erupted in September 2000 have given rise to new sources of stress for families, both Jews and Arabs alike (Ben-David & Lavee, 1996; Lavee, Ben-David, & Azaiza, 1997; Lev, 1998; Shamai & Lev, 1999). A new wave of violent terrorist attacks on civilians has been occurring in a variety of urban settings, such as buses, discotheques, restaurants, and open-air markets, killing more than 400 civilians and injuring thousands of others.

Support for families is provided by social workers and psychologists in hospitals, social welfare agencies, and schools, as well as by the National Insurance Institute. Information centers for families are opened in hospitals a few minutes after casualties arrive following a terrorist attack. These information centers, staffed by specially trained personnel, give telephone and face-to-face information as well as initial support for family members. This is followed by more intensive support provided by family professionals who arrive at the hospital shortly after the attack. They assist families of the deceased, escort family members of the injured to see their loved ones, attend to each family's special needs, and coordinate all contacts between families and hospital staff.

Long-term care and support is provided by the National Insurance Institute to injured and disabled persons, as well as to the dependents and bereaved families of terrorist attack victims. They receive medical care, vocational training, financial aid, and rehabilitation allowances, in addition to counseling and treatment from social services. Psychological treatment is also given to trauma victims who were present at the scene and witnessed the atrocities. At the same time, school psychologists, educational counselors, and trained teachers offer support to schoolchildren, who are encouraged to discuss their fears and concerns.

Immigration and Immigrant Families

As was noted earlier in this chapter, Israel has been shaped by massive waves of immigration from all corners of the globe. More than 700,000 immigrants arrived from the former Soviet Union in the last decade alone, and about 56,000 immigrants came from Ethiopia in the mid-1980s and early 1990s. Although immigration is not unique to Israel, its proportions require family professionals to attend to the wide range of difficulties faced by immigrant families.

Immigration poses major stress for the families involved in a number of ways: movement from one geographical location to another, often requiring changes in climate and lifestyle; disengagement from a familiar network of social relations, with the disruption of long-standing ties and the accompanying sense of loneliness, isolation, and lack of support; and the need to abandon old norms and values and adopt new ones (Levenbach & Lewak, 1995; Shuval, 1993).

Research on immigrant children, adolescents, adults, and the elderly, primarily those who have immigrated in the past decade from the former Soviet Union and Ethiopia, indicated that they suffer heightened psychological distress for a long period of time following migration. The most significant stressors are material-related, followed by stressors relating to culture, information, and health (Ritsner, Modai, & Ponizovsky, 2000). Compared with their Israeli-born counterparts, immigrant adolescents express less satisfaction with their lives (Mirsky, Baron-Draiman, & Peri, 2002), which is associated with their perceived pressure to assimilate with the host society (Roccas, Horenczyk, & Schwartz, 2000). For the elderly, adjustment and psychological well-being are associated primarily with expressive difficulties and cultural differences (Ron, 2001).

To ease material and economic difficulties, many immigrants choose to live in multi-generational households (70% of the elderly immigrants from the former Soviet Union). Katz and Lowenstein (1999), who have studied two adult generations in shared households, found that the best adjustment was reported by married older immigrants who received formal support. Past and current intergenerational solidarity and, to some extent, current family functioning affect adjustment among the older generation but hardly affect the younger generation.

Immigration often affects interpersonal relationships in the family—between marital partners as well as between parents and children. Differences between family members in their willingness to immigrate and differences in their rate of absorption sometimes intensify interpersonal conflicts. New work conditions and living arrangements create shifts in patterns of closeness-distance regulation and changes in patterns of conflict resolution (Ben-David & Lavee, 1994). Additionally, migration often results in changes in family structure and a shift in the balance of power, both between spouses and between generations (Sharlin &

Elshanskaya, 1997). For example, a father who traditionally wielded the power in the family may find himself stripped of his accustomed role, and role reversal may occur as children become "socializing agents" and mediators in their parents' relations with authorities.

7. DIVORCE AND REMARRIAGE

In the past three decades, the crude rate of divorce (per 1,000 population) increased from 0.9 and 0.5 for Jews and Muslims, respectively, in the 1970s to 1.8 and 1.2 in the mid-1990s. The difference between Jews and Muslims is best reflected in the divorce/marriage ratio, which indicates the number of divorces per number of marriages in a given year. In 1995 the divorce/marriage ratio for Jewish couples was 32%, whereas for Muslims it was 11%. Interestingly, the crude divorce rate and divorce/marriage ratio for Muslims in the mid-1990s resembles those of the Jewish population in Israel in 1970 (Central Bureau of Statistics, 2002). These figures point to a slow decline in marital stability, especially since the mid-1980s (Katz & Peres, 1995). However, the divorce rate is still significantly lower than it is in most industrialized countries. In the United States, for instance, the divorce rate in 1996 was 4.3 (National Center for Health Statistics, 1998).

In a follow-up study of the entire cohort of marriages in 1964, less than 15% have divorced in a 20-year period (DellaPergola, 1993). However, a comparison of couples who have been married in different years shows a steady increase in the divorce rate. The Jewish population is significantly more prone to divorce than the Arabs, and among Jewish couples, those of European-American origin divorce more than those of Asian-African origin (Peres & Katz, 1991).

The majority of people (nearly 63%) believe that divorce is the best solution for couples who are unable to resolve their conflicts, and only a minority believe that couples should stay together even if they don't get along (Steier et al., 1998). This attitude toward divorce, however, depends on whether the couple has children. Whereas only about 8% believe that conflictual couples should stay together when they don't have children, more than 26% believe that when there are children involved, the parents should stay together even if they don't get along. In regard to these beliefs, more conservative values are held by men than by women, and by older persons (age 56 or over) than by the young (age 35 or less) (Steier et al., 1998).

Divorce Law and Customs

One of the unique features of marriage and divorce in Israel is the religious legal system that regulates marital and family status. Since the passage of the Marital Status Law (1953), all matters of marriage and divorce have been delegated to the religious courts of the various communities—rabbinical courts for Jews, Sharia courts for Muslims, and corresponding institutions for adherents of other religions, including Christians and Druze. The law also makes divorce harder to obtain, especially for women, since the husband signs a writ of divorce (the *Get*) and the wife is the one who receives it. It is harder to force a husband to sign the writ than to force the wife to accept it. In response to pressures brought by women's organizations, a double system of courts has been established. All issues of property division and child custody may be adjudicated in either a civil court or a rabbinical court, but the writ of divorce remains solely under the authority of the religious court. To prevent the possibility of adjudication of a given case in two courts simultaneously, the law states that whenever one spouse brings suit against the other in a given legal system, all proceedings must continue in that system. Since the civil courts are generally viewed as more favorable to women and the rabbinical courts more favorable to men, it is in each spouse's interest to be the first to file suit in the court of his or her preference. (For more details about the laws and the duality of the legal system, see Rosen-Zvi, (1990) and Sharshevski, 1993.)

The Muslim courts also contend with a dual legal system composed of religious law and unofficial custom. Divorce in Muslim law can be effected in any of three ways (Al-Karnawi & Graham, 1998; Cohen & Savaya, 1997). The first is for the husband to declare the irrevocable *talaq* three times in the presence of two witnesses, after which the process is completed in a religious court. This option is not legitimate in Israeli law and is not commonly practiced. The second is when husband and wife both agree to the divorce and the woman returns the bride-price (*Mohar*) his family paid for her. The third is for either the husband or the wife to file a court suit for divorce.

Remarriage

With the rise of the divorce rate, Israel, like other modern societies, has witnessed an increase in second marriages—from 7,830 couples in the 1970s to 13,314 in the late 1990s. About 13% of all marriages in 1999 were couples in which either the groom or the bride, or both, were divorced, compared with 8% in the 1970s (Central Bureau of Statistics, 2002). Divorced or widowed men are twice as likely to remarry as are women. In 2000 the most prevalent pattern of remarriage (38.5%) was between divorced men and never-married women, followed by couples in which both spouses previously divorced (32.2%). In contrast, only 20% of remarriages were between divorced women and never-married men. Remarriages of widowed men composed about 6% of all remarriages, and those of widowed women were 4% of those who remarried in 2000.

Analyzing data on the stability of different patterns of marriage, Katz and Peres (1995) found that the divorce rates are higher among second marriages than first marriages. Are there certain patterns of remarriage (i.e., combination of groom's and bride's previous marital status) that are more prone to divorce following remarriage? Katz and Peres postulated that marriages of previously divorced people would be most at risk for divorce. Surprisingly, they found that marriages between widows and never-married men were the least stable. They explained the instability of such a pairing on the basis of mutual adjustment problems due to different life experiences.

8 & 9. KINSHIP AND AGING

Relative to other modern societies, Israel is still a young society. Only about 10% of its population are aged 65 or more, compared with 16% to 18% in European countries. However, the total population has been growing older in the past five decades: In 1948 only 4% of the population was 65 years of age or older. Furthermore, about 40% of the Israeli elderly population is over 75 years of age, an eightfold increase since 1948. Three factors play a major role in the aging of Israeli society: a decline in the fertility rate, an increase in life expectancy (which is among the highest in the world), and an influx of elderly immigrants. Most notably, the age structure of the newcomers from the former Soviet Union during the 1990s is marked by their older age, contributing significantly to growth in the elderly population (Brodsky, 1998).

The composition of the elderly population also differs by sociocultural groups. While Jews comprise 80% of the population, their share in the elderly population is about 94%. Of those, only 6% are Israeli-born, and the rest immigrated from Europe and America (70%) or from Asian-African countries (24%) (Brodsky, 1998). Among Arabs and recent immigrant Jews (primarily from the former Soviet Union), the elderly are noted for a higher disability rate than those of the veteran Jewish population (22%, 14%, and 8%, respectively) (Beer, 1996). Since these two groups (Arabs and new immigrants) are also more economically disadvantaged, they are unable to purchase the services they need and are therefore forced to rely primarily on their families for assistance.

The elders have a major significance in both the Jewish and Arab traditions. This is reflected in the role of the elderly in family life as well as in the filial responsibility of families and communities toward their aged. In Judaism the duty of filial responsibility is expressed in the fifth commandment "Honor thy father and thy mother." The great majority of elderly people in Israel live in close proximity to at least one of their children, and contact is maintained on a daily basis, either in person or by phone. The healthy aged are usually highly involved in the lives of their offspring (children and grandchildren), have Sabbath meals together, are an important source of support and assistance to their adult children, and are considered an integral part of the family. For example, many grandparents care for their grandchildren while the parents are working or on vacation. They also provide financial and other tangible support, such as preparing meals and shopping. As they grow older and frailer, elderly people are commonly cared for by their children. People believe that good and supportive family relations greatly influence the quality of life of the aged. The overwhelming majority of children of the elderly wish to keep their aging parents at home, caring for them themselves. As a result, more than 95% of the healthy elderly and 76% of the disabled elderly continue to live at home (Brodsky, 1998).

In Arab society, the elders are of major importance as the leaders, the carriers of tradition, and the source of wisdom and respect for the family and community. Even though some changes have taken place in Arab society in Israel with respect to governance and political control, the extended family is still the basic social unit responsible for the care and support of aged family members. Consequently, the informal support network in the Arab sector is quite active and extensive: Sixty-eight percent of elderly Arabs live with their family (compared with 18% of the Jewish elderly), most of them with their children (Brodsky, 1998).

Until recently, there were no nursing homes for the elderly in the Arab sector in Israel. However, recent changes, primarily the rise in young Arab women's participation in the labor force, have forced families of disabled elderly to seek formal support provided by the state (Azaiza & Brodsky, 1998). For example, following the Community Long-Term Care Insurance Law (1988), 11% of the Arab elderly today receive such services. Azaiza and Brodsky (1998) express the fear that formal services may harm the existing delicate intergenerational fabric and suggest that newly developed services for the Arab elderly must find a balance between the familial and the public care systems.

Multigenerational living arrangements, in which the elderly continue to live with their family of procreation, are also common among new immigrants from the former Soviet Union, albeit for a different reason. It is estimated that two-thirds of these elderly immigrants live with their families (Strosberg & Naon, 1997). In a recent study (Katz & Lowenstein, 1999), the main reasons cited by older-generation immigrants (age 65 or more) for establishing shared households with children and grandchildren were economic constraints, housing shortages, the need for mutual help, and familiarity with this type of living arrangement. The study also revealed that this type of living arrangement, as well as intergenerational solidarity and family functioning, were important factors favoring adjustment to their new country.

Thus, it appears that the extent of informal support to the elderly in Israel depends on each individual's family status, living arrangements, and proximity to family members, as well as children's values and beliefs regarding who is responsible for elderly care. Many families expect to keep elderly relatives at home, caring for them themselves. During the past decade, a fair number of formal services have been established to complement the informal support system, with the aim of balancing public and family resources. These service systems are challenged by the need to adapt to the patterns of care and expectations of Israel's varied ethnic and cultural groups (Katz, Lowenstein, Prilutzky, & Mellhausen-Hassoen, 2003).

11. SPECIAL TOPICS: THE FAMILY IN THE KIBBUTZ

Perhaps nothing is as uniquely Israeli as the kibbutz. This type of settlement also has been unique in terms of family roles and functions. We therefore conclude this chapter with a discussion of the family in the kibbutz.

The first kibbutz was founded in 1909 and others were created in the following years. The early kibbutzim were relatively small collectives (*kvutzot*) that gradually evolved into the larger and more extended communities. By the late 20th century, there were more than 200 kibbutzim in Israel, having a total population of more than 100,000.

The early pioneers of the kibbutz movement wished to create a collective society that strived to achieve personal independence under conditions of perfect equality. They sought to discourage individualism, abolish gender inequality, and bring up a new type of person who would be socialized to live communal life. Within this collectivist ideology, the family was viewed as a competing force of influence that might reduce identification with the collective (Talmon, 1972). The kibbutz community was regarded a "collective parent" that is committed to satisfying the needs of each and every child without the mediation of the family (Aviezer, Sagi, & van Ijzendoorn, 2000).

The kibbutz family has attracted much attention on the part of social scientists in the past 50 years (Beit-Hallahmi, 1981; Ben-Rafael & Weitman, 1984). In the early days, kibbutz ideology and practices were described as antifamilistic (Talmon, 1972): the absence of formal weddings; the discouraging of spouses from spending their free time together; the rejection of symbols of family ties; and the delegation of childcare to the collective. Communal child-rearing was seen as a major task for the whole commune.

The kibbutz family has given up its economic production and consumption functions as well as most of its socialization function. Family functions such as food preparation, laundry, childcare, and socialization were accorded to the collective. Families did not commonly have meals together, as adults ate in the communal dining room and children had their meals in children's houses. However, the founders' philosophy did not abolish the family altogether (Talmon, 1972). The family did exist in a psychological sense: It provided physical and emotional intimacy and an exclusive subunit separate from the larger group.

Up until the 1950s, collective sleeping for children away from their parents constitutes the most distinctive characteristic of kibbutz child-rearing practices. Children spent most of their time, ate their meals, bathed, and slept at night in much the same way as they would in family homes. Family time was spent in the parents' dwelling in designated hours and children returned to the children's

house for their night sleep (Aviezer et al., 2002).

The 1950s and 1960s were marked by a change in the balance between the collective and family life (Irvine, 1966). The kibbutz has become a family-oriented society and the family has regained more socialization roles (Palgi, 1991). Mother-child interaction during infancy was encouraged and there was a growing campaign in favor of family-based sleeping arrangements. In the 1970s and 1980s, the family has become dominant in kibbutz life. Familistic trends were supported by growing economic prosperity, which enabled improved family housing, and by weakened ideological identification of young members (Lavi, 1990). The family has regained functions in the areas of consumption and socialization and an increasing number of kibbutzim changed to home sleeping.

More recently, a privatization process has "normalized" the kibbutz family, turning it into a "regular" household that is responsible for most of its own functions and services (Palgi, 1997). The family-based sleeping arrangement has become the norm. The communal dining hall has ceased to be the only place where meals are prepared and consumed, and families eat together, away from the rest of the commune. Thus, the kibbutz upbringing, which began with a sense of distrust in parental capabilities, evolved into crediting the family with the primary authority over the care of children (Aviezer et al., 2002).

Over the years, the extended family has become an important component of the kibbutz community, with several generations and several separate household units within the community maintaining daily contact. The kibbutz has become not just a community of families, but a community of extended families as well. This has been the final victory of the family over the historical antifamilistic ideology (Beit-Hallahmi, 1981).

SUMMARY AND CONCLUSIONS

Israel is a small country marked by cultural diversity. This country, shaped by massive waves of immigration from more than 70 countries around the world, as well as by a mix of Jewish and Arab populations, is characterized by many languages, traditional family patterns alongside modern lifestyles, the influence of Western culture together with Middle-Eastern heritage, and values and practices ranging from highly orthodox religious ones to secular ones.

Despite this diversity there has been some convergence in the lifestyles of different subgroups during the past five decades—between Jews and Arabs, among Jews of different origins, and among Arabs of different religious affiliations. This convergence is evident in the narrowing gap in marriage and fertility rates, gender preferences, parenting attitudes and practices, women's status in society and in the family, distribution of power, and household division of labor. Within the Jewish population, a large proportion of interethnic marriages and integration in the educational system and in military service have eroded much of the difference between groups. Arab and Jewish families also have become more similar in terms of family structure and lifestyle patterns as a consequence of the increasing educational level of Arab men and women, greater participation of women in the labor force, and frequent contact between Arabs and Jews. The resulting portrait of Israeli families depicts a slow process of convergence while maintaining a diversity of family patterns.

Analysis of changes in marriage and family patterns over the past five decades shows that families have become more similar to their counterparts in other Western industrialized countries. People are marrying later in life, the acceptance of cohabitation is increasing, families are becoming smaller due to a decline in the average number of children, and the divorce rate is rising, especially among younger cohorts. On the other hand, the family in Israel is stronger and more stable than in other industrialized nations. Families have, on average, more children, a significantly lower divorce rate, more traditional gender roles, and a largely traditional cultural heritage in family lifestyle.

REFERENCES

Al-Haj, M. (1989). Social research on family lifestyles among Arabs in Israel. *Journal of Comparative Family Studies, 20,* 175–195.

Al-Karnawi, A., & Graham, J. R. (1998). Divorce among Muslim Arab women in Israel. *Journal of Divorce and Remarriage, 29,* 103–119.

Aviezer, O., Sagi, A., & van Ijzendoorn, M. (2002). Balancing the family and the collective in raising children: Why communal sleeping in kibbutzim was predestined to end. *Family Process, 41,* 435–454.

Avitzur, M. (1987). The Arab family: Tradition and change (in Hebrew). In H. Ganot (Ed.), *The family in Israel* (pp. 99–115). Jerusalem: Council of Schools of Social Work in Israel.

Ayalon, O. (1993). Posttraumatic stress recovery of terrorist survivors. In J. P. Wilson & B. Raphael (Eds.), *International handbook of traumatic stress syndromes* (pp. 855–866). New York: Plenum Press.

Azaiza, F., & Brodsky, J. (1998). Changes in the Arab society in Israel and development of services for the Arab elderly during the past decade (in Hebrew). In G. Friedman & J. Brodsky (Eds.), *Aging in the Mediterranean and the*

Middle East (pp. 117–127). Jerusalem: JDC-Brookdale Institute of Gerontology and Human Development.

Azmon, Y., & Izraeli, D. N. (1993). Introduction: Women in Israel—sociological overview. In Y. Azmon & D. N. Izraeli (Eds.), *Women in Israel* (pp. 1–21). New Brunswick, NJ: Transaction Publishers.

Beer, S. (1996). *Estimates of the needs for services for the elderly in Israel by geographic region, 1994–2005* (in Hebrew). Jerusalem: JDC-Brookdale Institute of Gerontology and Human Development.

Beit-Hallahmi, B. (1981). The kibbutz family: Revival and survival. *Journal of Family Issues, 2,* 259–274.

Ben-David, A., & Lavee, Y. (1992). Families in the sealed room: Interaction patterns of Israeli families during SCUD missile attacks. *Family Process, 31,* 35–44.

Ben-David, A., & Lavee, Y. (1994). Migration and marital distress: The case of Soviet immigrants. *Journal of Divorce and Remarriage, 21,* 133–146.

Ben-David, A., & Lavee, Y. (1996). Between war and peace: Interactional patterns of couples under prolonged uncertainty. *American Journal of Family Therapy, 24,* 343–357.

Ben-Rafael, E., & Weitman, S. (1984). The reconstruction of the family in the kibbutz. *European Journal of Sociology, 21,* 1–27.

Brodsky, J. (1998). The elderly in Israel (in Hebrew). In G. Friedman & J. Brodsky (Eds.), *Aging in the Mediterranean and the Middle East* (pp. 67–80). Jerusalem: JDC-Brookdale Institute of Gerontology and Human Development.

Central Bureau of Statistics. (2002). *Statistical Abstracts of Israel.* Jerusalem: Author.

Central Intelligence Agency. (1998). *The world factbook.* Washington, DC: Author.

Cohen, O., & Savaya, R. (1997). "Broken glass": The divorced woman in Moslem Arab society in Israel. *Family Process, 36,* 225–245.

DellaPergola, S. (1993). Demographic changes in the state of Israel in the early nineties (in Hebrew). In Y. Koff (Ed.), *Allocation of resources to social services 1992–1993* (pp. 63–108). Jerusalem: Center for the Study of Social Policy in Israel.

Eurostat. (1997). *Demographic statistics 1997.* Luxembourg: Author.

Good, I. J., & Ben-David, A. (1995). Family therapy in Israel: A review of therapy done under unusual circumstances. *Contemporary Family Therapy, 17,* 353–366.

Gross, Y. (1999, March 1). Survey: 54% of the population stands for equality between spouses (in Hebrew). *Maariv,* p. 24.

Haj-Yahia, M. M. (1995). Toward culturally sensitive intervention with Arab families in Israel. *Contemporary Family Therapy, 17,* 429–447.

Irvine, E. E. (1966). Children in kibbutzim: Thirteen years after. *Journal of Child Psychology and Psychiatry, 7,* 167–178.

Izraeli, D. N. (1994). Money matters: Spousal incomes and family/work relations among physician couples in Israel. *Sociological Quarterly, 35,* 69–84.

Katz, R. (1989). Strain and enrichment in the role of employed mothers in Israel. *Marriage and Family Review, 14,* 203–218.

Katz, R. (1997). Employed mothers and their families: The Israeli experience. In J. Frankel (Ed.), *Families of employed mothers—An international perspective* (pp. 99–121). New York: Gerald Publishing, Inc.

Katz, R. (2001). Effects of migration, ethnicity and religiosity on cohabitation. *Journal of Comparative Family Studies, 32,* 587–599.

Katz, R., & Lavee, Y. (in press). The family in Israel: Between tradition and modernity. *Marriage & Family Review, 34.*

Katz, R., Lavee, Y., & Azaiza, F. (1998). Family patterns in Israeli Arab communities: Division of labor and marital quality. In S. C. Ziehl (Ed.), *Multi-cultural diversity and families.* Grahamstown, South Africa: Rhodes University.

Katz, R., & Lowenstein, A. (1999). Adjustment of older Soviet immigrant parents and their adult children residing in shared households: An intergenerational comparison. *Family Relations, 48,* 43–50.

Katz, R., Lowenstein, A., Prilutzky, D., & Mellhausen-Hassoen, D. (2003). Imtergenerational solidarity. In A. Lowenstein & J. Ogg (Eds.), *OASIS: Old age and autonomy—The role of service systems and intergenerational family solidarity* (pp. 165–192). Haifa: Haifa University, Center for Research and Study of Aging.

Katz, R., & Peres, Y. (1993). Is resource theory equally applicable to wives and husbands? In Y. Azmon & D. N. Izraeli (Eds.), *Women in Israel* (pp. 25–34). New Brunswick, NJ: Transaction Publishers.

Katz, R., & Peres, Y. (1995). Marital Crisis and therapy in their social context. *Contemporary Family Therapy, 17,* 395–412.

Lavee, Y. (1995, May). *Marital quality: Comparison of Jews and Arabs in Israel.* Paper presented at the Committee on Family Research Seminar of the International Sociological Association, Jerusalem.

Lavee, Y. (1997). The components of healthy marriages: Perceptions of Israeli social workers and their clients. *Journal of Family Social Work, 2,* 1–14.

Lavee, Y., & Ben-David, A. (1993). Families under war: Stresses and strains of Israeli families during the Gulf War. *Journal of Traumatic Stress, 6,* 239–254.

Lavee, Y., Ben-David, A., & Azaiza, F. (1997). Israeli and Palestinian families in the peace process: Sources of stress and response patterns. *Family Process, 36,* 247–263.

Lavee, Y., & Katz, R. (2002). Division of labor, perceived fairness, and marital quality: The moderating effect of gender ideology. *Journal of Marriage and Family, 64,* 24–39.

Lavi, Z. (1990). Transition from communal to family sleeping arrangement of children in kibbutzim: Causes and outcomes. In Z. Lavi (Ed.), *Kibbutz members study kibbutz children* (pp. 51–55). Westport, CT: Greenwood Press.

Lev, R. (1998). Coping with the stress associated with forced relocation in the Golan Heights, Israel. *Journal of Applied Behavioral Science, 34,* 143–160.

Levenbach, D., & Lewak, B. (1995). Immigration: Going home or going to pieces. *Contemporary Family Therapy, 17,* 379–394.

Mayseless, O. (1991). *Youth released from the IDF: Social and vocational coping* (Research Report) (in Hebrew). Zikhron Yaakov, Israel: Israeli Institute for Military Studies.

Mayseless, O. (1993). Military service as a central factor in the Israeli experience (in Hebrew). *Skira Hodshit, 8–9,* 3–19.

Milgram, N. (1993). War-related trauma and victimization: Principles of traumatic stress prevention in Israel. In J. P. Wilson & B. Raphael (Eds.), *International handbook of traumatic stress syndromes* (pp. 811–820). New York: Plenum Press.

Mirsky, J., Baron-Draiman, Y., & Peri, K. (2002). Social support and psychological distress among young immigrants from the former Soviet Union in Israel. *International Social Work, 45,* 83–97.

National Center for Health Statistics. (1998). Births, marriages, divorces and deaths for 1997. *Monthly vital statistics report* (Vol. 46, No. 12). Hyattsville, MD: NCHS.

Palgi, M. (1991). Motherhood in the kibbutz. In B. Swirski & M. P. Safir (Eds.), *Calling the equality bluff: Women in Israel* (pp. 261–267). New York: Pergamon.

Palgi, M. (1997). Women in the changing world of the kibbutz. *Women in Judaism: A Multidisciplinary Journal, 1*, 1–9.

Peres, Y., & Katz, R. (1991). The family in Israel: Change and continuity (in Hebrew). In L. Shamgar-Handelman & R. Bar-Yosef (Eds.), *Families in Israel* (pp. 9–32). Jerusalem: Academon.

Peritz, E., & Baras, M. (Eds.). (1992). *Studies in the fertility of Israel.* Jerusalem: The Hebrew University, Institute of Contemporary Jewry.

Raday, F. (1991). Women in the Israeli law. In B. Zwirski & M. P. Safir (Eds.), *Calling the equality bluff: Women in Israel* (pp. 178–187). New York: Pergamon Press.

Ritsner, M., Modai, I., & Ponizovsky, A. (2000). The stress-support patterns and psychological distress of immigrants. *Stress Medicine, 16*, 139–147.

Roccas, S., Horenczyk, G., & Schwartz, S. H. (2000). Acculturation discrepancies and well-being: The moderating role of conformity. *European Journal of Social Psychology, 30*, 323–334.

Roer-Strier, D. (1996). Coping strategies of immigrant parents: Directions for family therapy. *Family Process, 35*, 363–376.

Ron, P. (2001). The process of acculturation in Israel among elderly immigrants from the former Soviet Union. *Illness, Crisis and Loss, 9*, 357–368.

Rosenthal, M. K. (1994). *An ecological approach to the study of child care: Family day care in Israel.* Hillsdale, NJ: Lawrence Erlbaum Associates.

Rosen-Zvi, A. (1990). *Family law in Israel* (in Hebrew). Jerusalem: Papyrus Publishers.

Rubin, S. (1993). The death of a child is forever: The life course impact of child loss. In M. S. Stroebe, W. Stroebe, & R. O. Hansson (Eds.), *Handbook of bereavement: Theory, research and intervention* (pp. 285–299). Cambridge, UK: Cambridge University Press.

Rubin, S. (1996). The wounded family: Bereaved parents and the impact of adult child loss. In D. Klass, P. Silverman, & S. Nickman (Eds.), *Continuing bonds: Understanding the resolution of grief* (pp. 217–232). Washington, DC: Taylor and Francis.

Rubin, S., Malkinson, R., & Witztum, E. (1999). The pervasive impact of war-related loss and bereavement in Israel. *International Journal of Group Tensions, 28*(1/2), 137–153.

Safir, M. P. (1991). Religion, tradition and public policy give family first priority. In B. Zwirski & M. P. Safir (Eds.), *Calling the equality bluff: Women in Israel* (pp. 57–65). New York: Pergamon Press.

Sagi, A., & Koren-Karie, N. (1993). Israel. In M. Cochran (Ed.), *International handbook of social care policies and programs.* Westport, CT: Greenwood Press.

Shaked, A. (1994). *Sex in blue and white: A survey of sexual behaviors in Israel* (in Hebrew). Tel Aviv: Motive-Dvir Katzman.

Shamai, M., & Lev, R. (1999). Marital quality among couples living under the threat of forced relocation: The case of families in the Golan Heights. *Journal of Marital and Family Therapy, 25*, 237–252.

Shamgar-Handelman, L. (1996). Family sociology in a small academic community: Family research and theory in Israel. *Marriage & Family Review, 23*, 377–416.

Sharlin, S. A. (1996). Long-term successful marriages in Israel. *Contemporary Family Therapy, 18,* 225–242.

Sharlin, S., & Elshanskaya, I. (1997). Parental attitudes of Soviets in Israel to the immigration process and their impact on parental stress and tensions. In S. Dreman (Ed.), *The family on the threshold of the 21st century: Trends and implications* (pp. 229–244). London: Erlbaum.

Sharshevski, B. (1993). *Family law* (in Hebrew). Jerusalem: Mass Publishers.

Shuval, J. T. (1993). Migration and stress. In L. Goldberger & S. Breznitz (Eds.), *Handbook of stress: Theoretical and clinical aspects* (2nd ed., pp. 641–657). New York: The Free Press.

Solomon, Z. (1993). Immediate and long-term effects of traumatic combat stress among Israeli veterans of the Lebanon war. In J. P. Wilson & B. Raphael (Eds.), *International handbook of traumatic stress syndromes* (pp. 321–332). New York: Plenum Press.

Steier, H., Oren, A., Elias, N., & Lewin-Epstein, N. (1998). *Gender roles, family, and women's participation in the labor force: Attitudes of veteran Israelis and newcomers in a comparative perspective—Research report* (in Hebrew). Tel Aviv: The Institute for Social Research.

Strosberg, N., & Naon, D. (1997). The absorption of elderly immigrants from the former Soviet Union: Selected findings regarding housing, social integration, and health (in Hebrew). *Gerontology, 79,* 5–15.

Talmon, Y. (1972). *Family and community in the kibbutz.* Cambridge, MA: Harvard University Press.

Waysman, M., Mikulincer, M., Solomon, Z., & Weisenberg, M. (1993). Secondary traumatization among wives of posttraumatic combat veterans: A family typology. *Journal of Family Psychology, 7,* 104–118.

Ziv, A., & Israeli, R. (1973). Effects of bombardment on the manifest anxiety levels of children living in the kibbutz. *Journal of Consulting and Clinical Psychology, 40,* 287–291.

Zuckerman-Bareli, C. (1979). Effects of border tension on residents of an Israeli town. *Journal of Human Stress, 5,* 29–40.

CHAPTER 23

Kuwait's Families

Fahad Al Naser

1. KUWAIT: AN INTRODUCTION

Description of Kuwait

The State of Kuwait is located at the northwest corner of the Arabian Gulf. The total population is a little more than 2 million (Table 23.1). Kuwait was founded as a state under the rule of the Sabah clan in 1760. Kuwait's constitution declared that it is an independent Arab country, adopting a democratic system. The Kuwaiti government provides a comprehensive welfare system for all its citizens, which includes free education (university included), free health services, social services, jobs for every Kuwaiti who seeks employment, practically free housing for low-income Kuwaitis, subsidized water, electricity, telephone services, gas, transportation, and basic nutritional foods—without levying any form of taxes on income, state, property, inheritance, or even sales. Kuwait does not fit easily into the traditional concept of either developed or underdeveloped economies. Its economy mainly depends on oil and foreign investments. At the same time, Kuwait has signs of having a well-developed economy because of the high per capita income, one of the highest saving rates, a strong annual growth rate, and a consistent healthy balance of payments (Social Development Office, 1997, pp. 137–165).

Depending on oil revenues, Kuwait's infrastructure has accelerated the transformation process. Government expenditure on the development of Kuwait has been the principal mechanism facilitating this transformation, made possible by the country's steadily increasing gross domestic product (GDP). The production of oil and gas accounted for 41% of GDP and 91% of export earnings in 1996. An important and largely untapped source of government revenue is income from its substantial financial investments abroad.

The dawn of August 2, 1990, witnessed the invasion of this nation. Their achievements were left as ashes as a result. The 7 months of occupation affected every aspect of life for the people and for the country as a whole. Oil wells were set ablaze, and basics such as food, water, shelter, electricity, and medical facilities were affected. There was mass looting of both private and government properties. Though Kuwait has come a long way as a modern society, the sudden invasion checked its progress, at least temporarily.

Table 23.1   Estimated Midyear Population by Nationality and Gender (1995–2001)

Year	Kuwaiti			Non-Kuwaiti			Total Population		
	Females	Males	Total	Females	Males	Total	Females	Males	Total
1995	350,013	344,595	694,608	355,011	752,178	1,107,189	705,024	1,096,773	1,801,797
1996	363,628	357,023	720,651	388,051	785,660	1,173,711	751,679	1,142,683	1,894,362
1997	377,921	369,172	747,093	406,597	825,999	1,232,596	784,518	1,195,171	1,979,689
1998	394,000	382,383	776,383	406,329	844,391	1,250,720	800,329	1,226,774	2,027,103
1999	407,600	396,345	803,945	420,773	882,477	1,303,250	828,373	1,278,822	2,107,195
2000	420,831	410,850	831,681	435,880	922,107	1,357,987	856,711	1,332,957	2,189,668
2001	435,139	424,819	859,958	451,877	963,145	1,415,022	887,016	1,387,964	2,274,980

SOURCE: Ministry of Planning

NOTE: Table does not include Kuwaitis residing permanently abroad.

508

Geographical Setting

The State of Kuwait lies between 28° and 30° north latitude, and between 46° and 48° east longitude. To the north and west, Kuwait shares a border with Iraq; to the south and to the southeast, with Saudi Arabia. To the east, Kuwait has a coastline of about 290 km on the Arabian Gulf. The total area of Kuwait is 17,818 sq km. The Kuwaiti land is desert, and greenery is scarce. The climate is hot in summer, with seasonal dusty winds, and somewhat cold in winter.

Population

The main concern regarding the population in Kuwait, per the 1985/1986–1989/1990 Plan, was to reduce the expatriate labor force and consequently reduce the non-Kuwaiti population.

Table 23.1 shows the development of the population in Kuwait from 1957 to 1999. It indicates the number of Kuwaitis compared with non-Kuwaitis. To augment the low population and labor force of Kuwaiti nationals, policies relating to fertility and mortality were designed to maximize the growth rate. The objective was to achieve a balance between nationals and expatriates, and to guarantee that nationals compose at least one-half of the population by the year 2000. To achieve this objective, specific strategies had to be implemented, which included increased stress on health services and a reduction of infant mortality and mortality from traffic accidents. High fertility was encouraged through early marriage and various programs such as a monthly allowance for children, by reducing infertility among spouses, by maintaining a reasonable gap between children to improve health for mothers and children, and by providing housing plans suitable for large families. After the liberation of Kuwait from the Iraqi occupation in 1991, changes

became apparent in the Kuwaiti population structure. Kuwaitis composed a larger portion of the population, either because expatriates opted to leave the country due to the crisis or were not called back to rejoin duty—in some cases because certain nationalities who had opposed Kuwait during the Gulf war were not invited back. Even now, the general policy of restricting the appointment of additional expatriates is being implemented in the government sector. The total population was more than 2 million in 2001, as shown in Table 23.1.

Table 23.2 shows the development of the population from 1970 to 1999 based on age-groups. It proves that the age-groups of 20 to 35 years represent a large segment within the Kuwaiti population.

Political System

Kuwait was founded as a state under the rule of the Sabah clan in 1760. In January 1899 a treaty between Kuwait and Great Britain was signed. Under this agreement, Great Britain granted Kuwait protection against any external threat to its independence and sovereignty. According to the treaty, Kuwait's foreign relations were handled through the British Foreign Office. In 1904 the British Political Agency was established in Kuwait. This was the only foreign government agency in Kuwait until an American consulate was opened shortly after World War II (Ismael, 1982, p. 40).

On June 18, 1961, during the regime of Sheikh Abdullah Al Salem Al Sabah, an agreement was signed between Kuwait and Great Britain, stressing the sovereignty of Kuwait as a state facilitating the requirement of a welfare state. Kuwait has since joined the Arab League, the United Nations, and other international organizations.

The first cabinet consisting of 14 members was formed in 1962. A council of seven has

Table 23.2   Percentage of Kuwaitis According to Gender and Age-Group

Age	1970			1980			1988			1999		
	Male	Female	%	Male	Female	%	Male	Female	%	Male	Female	%
0–4	19.4	22.8	19.5	19.7	18.8	19.3	14.9	14.4	14.6	16.1	15.0	15.6
5–9	17.4	17.4	17.4	16.6	16.0	16.3	13.9	13.1	13.7	14.9	14.0	14.4
10–14	13.5	12.8	13.2	13.8	13.5	13.6	13.4	12.2	12.8	12.9	12.4	12.7
15–19	9.5	10.6	10.0	10.7	10.9	10.8	13.4	13.5	13.4	10.9	10.5	10.7
20–24	7.8	8.4	8.1	8.4	9.3	8.9	11.5	10.9	11.2	9.2	8.9	9.0
25–29	6.8	7.8	7.3	6.8	7.7	7.3	7.8	7.8	7.8	8.0	7.9	7.9
30–34	5.7	5.2	5.4	4.8	5.7	5.3	5.0	6.1	5.5	6.9	7.1	7.0
35–39	5.0	4.6	4.8	4.3	4.7	4.4	3.6	6.0	4.8	5.6	6.0	5.8
40–44	3.7	2.9	3.3	4.0	3.6	3.7	3.2	4.1	3.6	4.1	5.0	4.6
45–49	3.0	2.4	2.7	3.0	2.6	2.8	3.7	4.0	3.8	3.1	3.9	3.5
50–54	2.6	2.5	2.7	2.5	2.1	2.3	3.0	2.8	2.9	2.1	3.0	2.5
55–59	1.4	1.2	1.1	1.6	1.5	1.6	2.2	1.7	2.0	1.9	2.2	2.1
60+	4.2	4.5	4.4	3.8	3.6	3.7	4.4	3.2	3.9	4.3	4.1	4.2
	100	100	100	100	100	100	100	100	100	100	100	100

since succeeded it. Kuwait's constitution declared that Kuwait was an independent Arab country, adopting a democratic system, and derived its power from the nation, the source of authority. The ruling system did not stress complete separation of authorities but cooperation among them. H.H. the Amir is the head of state, the National Assembly is the executive authority that is directed by the Amir, and the cabinet directs the legislative authority. The constitution makes clear that the number of ministers must not exceed one-third of the number of National Assembly members. Accordingly, the Council of Ministers should not nominate more than 16 members in each legislative term, as the National Assembly consists of 50 elected members. Those members are elected by direct secret ballot. The appointed ministers become members of the assembly as a result of the post they hold (Ministry of Information, 1995, pp. 77–94).

Social Welfare System

The Kuwaiti government skillfully utilizes its huge oil revenues and invests them to provide a comprehensive welfare system for all its citizens. This encompasses all facets of life, including free education (university included), medical services, and so on. The best part of this cradle-to-grave welfare system is that all these services are provided without levying any form of taxes. The Kuwaiti Constitution Articles 10, 11, and 13 guarantee social security, medical care, education, and the opportunity to work (Ministry of Information, 1995, p. 81).

The Kuwaiti government has stepped up the fight to eradicate illiteracy. The government places a high priority on education, which is compulsory for all children from the ages of 6 to 14 years. However, there is still illiteracy among the Kuwaiti population. The government's fight against illiteracy

has yielded remarkable results. While the percentage was 44.6% in 1975, it was reduced to 36.4% in 1980, and 23.2% of the total population in 1988. An Amiri Decree issued in 1981 urged all Kuwaitis to join centers for eradication of illiteracy, and the government offered KD 50 (about £100) as a reward for those who passed literacy exams (Al Ghazali, 1992, pp. 18–38). In addition to the basic services, the government provides a fraction of the cost through subsidies for utilities such as electricity and water, since modern housing and increase in the cost of living continue to raise demands for these services. Other subsidies, including basic foods such as milk, rice, sugar, and bread, have been provided since 1975.

Economy

Kuwait is a country of small size, whose geographic location has affected its environment and its economic activities. The desert and sea have also played a part in shaping its economic structure. It has a number of indicators of an underdeveloped economy, such as reliance on a single resource (oil), a short supply of technical skills and labor of its own, and a heavy dependence on the import of capital and consumer goods. At the same time, Kuwait has indicators that are associated with a developed economy, as noted earlier.

During the pre-oil era, Kuwait's basic lack of resources and its geographical location forced its population to depend on the sea as its major source of livelihood and trade. Pearl diving and boat building, for example, flourished in the Gulf area. The favorable geographical location of Kuwait helped the population to become some of the foremost seafaring traders in the Gulf region.

After the discovery of oil, Kuwait's infrastructure accelerated the transformation process. Government expenditure on the development of Kuwait has been the principal mechanism facilitating this transformation, made possible by the country's steadily increasing gross domestic production (GDP). The production of oil and gas accounted for 41% of GDP and 91% of export earnings in 1996 (Ministry of Planning, 1998, pp. 228–234). These were vulnerable to the fluctuation of the international oil market. The agricultural and fisheries sectors were insignificant because of limited natural resources, and although strenuous attempts were made to diversify the domestic economy by building up the industrial and financial services sectors, these have been only partly successful.

Before the outbreak of the Gulf War, Kuwaiti merchants had a thriving export trade with both Iraq and Iran, but in recent years this has been reduced considerably. An important and largely untapped source of government revenue is income from its substantial financial investments abroad (Ministry of Planning, 1995, pp. 228–232). Since 1981, the nationalized oil industry has pursued aggressive downstream investment overseas, together with a program of increased domestic refining and petrochemical capacity. After the Iraqi occupation, this overseas downstream network was the only element of the Kuwaiti economy that continued to operate.

Family Structure

Family patterns have always been an indicator of change. However, Kuwait, with its recent economic growth, has witnessed these patterns changing continuously and rapidly. The reasons for these changes are many and will be discussed further.

Universally, there are two kinds of family forms: nuclear (urbanized) and extended (tribal/traditional). Kuwait is no exception. After the discovery of oil and the consequent rise in the standard of living, development of

education, and the rise in the economy, some Kuwaiti families that had followed the extended form of living began to follow the nuclear form of living. Some newly married couples separated from their parents and the joint structure and started living in their own separate apartment. One would call the Kuwaiti family structure a new form of family that has evolved and is known as the transitional form. It has the nuclear family structure, yet it behaves like the extended family. It is important to shed light on the different family forms existing in Kuwait and the new transitional pattern that is fast becoming popular and to further discuss the reasons and causes for the changes and compare all the three kinds of family forms to increase public awareness of families in Kuwait.

The economic, social, and political changes taking place in Kuwaiti society during the last four decades can be attributed to many historical, cultural, and socioeconomic factors. The discovery of oil played a significant role in accelerating the process of socioeconomic development. After a long period as a country with a primitive and orthodox society, Kuwait found itself suddenly expanding and developing in a relatively short time.

In recent years the spread of education has been tremendous. Citizens have been encouraged to go abroad for further studies. And this contact with the West and East has led to a radical change affecting not only the material aspects, but also the norms and values of the society as a whole. It has been asserted by some sociologists that, with the development of an industrial economy and the creation and growth of cities, the family structure of a society changes toward an isolated nuclear family. This has been an issue of major discussion and argument in family sociology for the last 40 years.

The term *family structure* refers to the size of the family and the generation unit. The husband and wife, with or without children, would constitute a nuclear family, whereas a husband, wife, and their married offspring who live with them would constitute an extended family.

Nuclear Family Structure

The nuclear family structure is usually found in an industrialized society. It consists of a husband, wife, and their children (two generations only). This style is well-known and common in urban societies. It is small in size, individualistic, and based on relative freedom and a democratic atmosphere.

Extended Family Structure

The structure of the extended family is larger in size, consisting of two or three generations (husband, wife, their married children, and grandchildren), and is common in rural and tribal societies and less developed countries. Authority in the family rests with the elders, and they characteristically behave in a conservative manner and encourage group attitudes—and the selection of mates is based on social status and is the responsibility of the elders. The differences between the nuclear family type and the extended family type are illustrated briefly in Table 23.3.

In identifying the distinctions of the modern family from the larger kinship structure, sociologists define the history of family as the decline of the large, extended, patriarchal unit. The proponents of the notion that family structure of a society changes toward an isolated nuclear structure have been somewhat ambivalent.

Some studies have been conducted that seem to predict that with the influence of industrialization and urbanization, the family will decline from a large structure to a smaller one, from an extended family to a conjugal or nuclear type. One such study was completed by Parsons (1943), and, cross-cultural study was conducted by Goode (1963).

Parsons talked about the isolation of the urban middle-class family. He concluded his argument by stating that in various ways society is oriented to values particularly appropriate to the younger age-groups so that there is a tendency for older people to be left out.

Goode, in his cross-cultural study, pointed out that

> wherever the economic system expands through industrialization, family patterns change, extended kinship ties weaken, lineage patterns dissolve and a trend towards some form of the conjugal system generally begins to appear. That is, the nuclear family becomes a more independent kinship unit. (1963, pp. 7–10)

He found throughout the world a tendency for the industrialization process to be accompanied by a move toward what he calls the "conjugal type of family." This form appears to be most suitable for an industrialized society because of its ability to adapt easily to the economy and mode of production, for in such a society physical movement from one locality to another is necessary, and class mobility is more flexible.

Goode supported his thesis with evidence from various societies. For instance, he cited the example of India, where change has been taking place in the face of relatively little industrialization in the total family-kin structure.

It is important to note that both studies argue that urbanization and industrialization affect the family structure in certain ways, such as erosion of older family patterns, a decline in household size, and breakdown of extended kinship ties within the family.

Coming back to the family structure in the Arab Peninsula Region, many traditional societies, large or extended-family structure, have existed alongside nuclear family patterns. In fact, it is more likely that the society that has just one pattern of family will stand out distinctly, because the coexistence of a

Table 23.3   Differences Between the Nuclear and Extended Family Types

#	Nuclear Family	Extended Family
1	Small in size (number of family members)	Larger in size (number of family members)
2	Two or fewer generations	More than two generations
3	Democratic authority between husband and wife	Authority held by the elders, usually the grandfather
4	Common in industrialized and urbanized societies	Prevalent in rural, tribal societies and some less-developed countries
5	Mate selection based on individual characteristics and premarital relations	Mate selection based on social and tribal status by the elders
6	More expenditures and high standard of living	Based on sharing between different nuclear families
7	Socialization based on help from others (some institutions)	Different socialization, either of the grandparents substituting when the father is not around
8	Less control on the behavior of children	More control on the behavior of children
9	Weak kinship system	Strong kinship system
10	Individual activities	Group activities
11	More flexible toward changes	Rejects changes
12	High divorce rate	Low divorce rate

variety of family patterns is the rule rather than the exception.

Another historical phenomenon of family structure observed is that the extended families divide into small nuclear families for a generation or so and later these nuclear families reunite to form new extended families. Another aspect of the variation is that the size of the nuclear family is not always small, nor the extended always large. Sometimes a large nuclear family (having 12 unmarried children) may outnumber the size of a small extended family. This is not an uncommon phenomenon in Kuwait or Saudi Arabia. Most studies of the family structure

in Arabian societies conclude that the general pattern of family structure is the extended family (Patai, 1962; Berger, 1962).

Contrary to this conclusion, a study by Al Thakeb found that the majority of the households in a random survey sample were nuclear or conjugal. He noted that "our findings clearly demonstrate that even if the economic and demographic conditions are very favorable in a country like Kuwait, the traditional extended family is still a minority" (1974, p. 248). He further concluded that his findings have necessitated rejection of the earlier assumptions of such studies. This is not surprising, since the majority of writers in the past used little or no data. The nuclear family, whether or not it is a statistical majority, is considered the ideal type by the majority.

2. MARRIAGE/PAIRING UP

Kuwait is an Islamic country. Its laws and social institutions are governed by Islamic law (Shariah jurisprudence) like other Middle Eastern Arab societies. Islam sanctions marriage not only as a social but also as a sacred contract. Sexual contact outside marriage is prohibited and thereby punishable. Indeed, Islam regards marriage as one of the most basic cohesive bonds of society. According to Islamic teachings, the only condition spouses must satisfy is that they profess Islam or one of the other Semitic religions (Judaism or Christianity). Considerations of class, color, and race are repugnant to the Islamic moral code. Yet, members of different tribal groups seldom, if ever, intermarry, and marriage between individuals professing Islam but belonging to different races or nationalities is rare.

Although social change has been taking place in Kuwait for the last three decades, people are still under kin pressure, and the country's traditional method of mate selection still exists. There have been breakthroughs, but only on the individual level and against family rules, sometimes with social punishment (ostracism) and restrictions. This indicates that the society is in a stage between tradition and modernization, a transitional stage in which traditional and modern values exist together, and an individual may follow either, depending on his or her exposure to change in family and other social institutions.

At one time in Kuwait, a man's wife was from his extended family, a parallel cousin, or, in the case of Bedouins, from the same clan or tribe. In the case of urbanized groups, a mate not from the man's extended family came from a family having similar socioeconomic status. This concept is slowly changing.

Kuwaitis have a very strong tendency to marry homogamously in terms of religion, sect, nationality, and caste, although the numbers of those marrying across these lines have increased in the past 10 years, especially among people of higher socioeconomic status who have a university education and high-status job.

Mate Selection

In most Middle Eastern societies, mate selection operates within rather carefully defined limits. The State of Kuwait is no exception. A Kuwaiti youth, for instance, is expected to marry someone who shares his or her own religion, caste, nationality, age, and socioeconomic status. This practice is referred to as *assortative mating* and *homogamy*.

In view of the strong influence of the factors listed previously, and the current counter-tendency toward heterogamy, the potential for a revolutionary change in the marital habits of Kuwaitis does exist. People challenging the traditional homogamous norms and customs assert both the right and the desirability of marriage between persons of different groups. Persons who practice heterogamy are indulging in behavior that deviates from well-established norms and values of marriage. Furthermore, when Kuwaiti men marry non-Kuwaiti women, many Kuwaiti women are left without a mate and, therefore, as victims of the negative social status that traditional Kuwaiti norms assign to spinsters. When Kuwaiti women marry non-Kuwaiti men, political problems for the government can arise, such as civil rights, political participation, employment, and rights of citizenship.

Marriage is a basic social institution. However, like any social institution, it is a product of socioeconomic circumstances and situations. Social values and norms have a great role in determining mate selection, and they influence not only who one will marry, but also when. Things that were once taboo in Kuwait, such as women working outside the home, higher education for members of both genders, and intercultural contact leading to befriending people from different cultures, are now becoming acceptable. Family structure has also changed. Fathers were normally harsh, authoritative powers who determined their family's norms and values and passed them on to their sons and daughters; now they exhibit more flexibility and permit other members of the family, such as mothers and sons, to share this authority. Basically, the following *three* kinds of mate selection are practiced in Kuwait.

Familial Mate Selection

Familial mate selection, which was predominant in Kuwaiti society until recent times, is a type of arranged marriage that still exists. This involves the right and duty of the parents or elders in the family to choose a partner for their son or daughter. The prospective bride or bridegroom is not involved in the process of mate selection. His or her opinion is not in any way sought in this matter. The family plays the role of the agent of marriage, that is, in choosing the marriage partner for the eligible person. There is no chance for love or relations before marriage. The social basis of mate selection, such as tribal or family background, is important and scrutinized very carefully. The elderly males of the family have the say in this type of mate selection.

Individual Mate Selection

In individual mate selection, the choice is based on physical and personal characteristics. This provides room for premarital relations. This extreme, existing in the West and other modernized states, involves the forthrightness of the prospective bride or bridegroom to choose his or her own partner. They meet and decide on their own to tie the proverbial "knot." Their families are later involved, but have little say regarding the selection. It is not a very common type of mate selection in Kuwait, because the elders are not consulted while the choice is made. Due to the high number of Kuwaiti males going abroad to study, this is becoming a wider circle, because they tend to marry when abroad.

FAMIND

The third type of mate selection is the transitional one, which is a combination of the family and the individual system (FAMIND). This type is becoming more and more apparent in societies that are undergoing social change and are in the process of transition from a traditional to a more urbanized society. In this type of selection, the elders of the family are involved, but only after the individual has made his choice. There is scope, not wide, though, for premarital relations. After the families are informed, the elderly females will visit the potential bride's family, and only if they like what they see will they involve the elderly males of the family, who will then take the initiative. Thus, ultimately, the family selection is made, but according to the individual's choice. It should be noted that this process is not encouraged in Kuwait and other Middle Eastern states. However, due to the social changes taking place in the Middle East, which we discussed earlier, this approach to choosing a marriage partner is becoming more accepted.

This situation, therefore, where the individual chooses a partner and then informs his or her parents about the choice, with the elders taking the matter from there, is on the increase. The potential bride and bridegroom do not involve themselves directly, but they do choose their own life partner. The parents, on the other hand, do not make the choice, but they do make the proposal. This kind of mate selection is being seen often nowadays in societies that used to follow the kin method of mate selection, due to the influence of the West, newer ideas, higher education, and so on.

For many Kuwaitis, the circle of marriage choices has become progressively wider. Socioeconomic changes have made it impossible to continue the traditional "parallel cousin marriage" custom. The first step in widening the circle was to permit marriage with people from families in one's neighborhood who are from the same religion and sect. Next came neighboring communities with similar cultural and ethnic backgrounds. The widening of the range from which marital partners may be chosen is accompanied by a change in who does the selecting: The individual makes the selection. Increase in educational and employment opportunities have gradually changed many of the society's traditional social values and norms, and this has an impact on the process of mate selection. Individual tastes and characteristics are increasingly replacing family concerns in the choice of marital partners.

Factors Affecting Mate Selection

In many cultures, education, caste, religion, race, nationality, age, and other cultural factors play a significant role in the choice of a mate. Even in the most industrialized societies, these factors have not been entirely eliminated when choosing a marriage partner.

Age

According to Table 23.4, 15- to 24-year-old females has always shown the highest percentage of marriages. Females still marry at an early age. For males, although the highest percentage of marriages takes place in the 15- to 24-year-olds age-group, this represents only slightly more than 50% of marriage cases. For females, the 25- to 34-year-old age-group has increased from 11.8% of marriages in 1975 to 19.5% in 1999 because some pursue higher studies.

In an empirical study on immigration and social isolation in Kuwaiti society by Al-Gardawi (1984), the majority of the sample (63%) supported early marriage as ideal. This concept is still common in Kuwait and other Islamic societies, because it is one of the attitudes encouraged by Islam. Analysis proves that social change has affected the age of marriage. In this study, three groups were studied: Kuwaiti men marrying Kuwaiti women, Kuwaiti men marrying non-Kuwaiti women, and Kuwait women marrying non-Kuwaiti men. The mean age at marriage differs for the three groups from the period 1974 to 1995. In 1974 the mean age of marriage for men was 28.2 years, in 1984 it was 27.9 years, and in 1995 it was 26.2. For women, on the other hand, there was a slight increase from 22.2 years in 1974 to 22.4 in 1984, and then a decrease to 22 years in 1995.

A decrease in the mean age was observed after the Gulf War, which could be due to men wanting to feel more secure. The mean age of Kuwaiti women marrying Kuwaiti men also increased from 20.2 years in 1974 to 22.0 years in 1984, and later decreased to 21.6 in 1995. More women are achieving a greater level of education before marrying. In addition, as individuals have increasing choice not only about whom to marry but also about when, they are choosing to marry later. Another reason for the increase in age at marriage is that parental expectations and duties have changed. At one time, it was the parental responsibility to arrange the marriages of their children. They wanted to discharge this responsibility as early as possible to be certain their children were well settled. Two factors have changed this situation:

Table 23.4   Distribution of Kuwaiti Marriages According to Age and Gender

Year	Gender	Age-Groups												
		15–24		25–34		35–44		45 and Above		Not Stated		Total	
		N	%	N	%	N	%	N	%	N	%	N	%
1975	Male	1,684	46.3	1,401	38.5	264	7.3	154	4.2	135	3.7	3,638	100
	Female	2,995	82.3	428	11.8	61	1.7	22	0.6	132	3.6	3,638	100
1980	Male	3,149	52.6	2,229	37.2	351	5.9	240	4.0	18	0.3	5,987	100
	Female	4,970	83.0	866	14.5	102	1.7	32	0.5	17	—	5,987	100
1985	Male	3,057	54.0	2,130	37.7	320	5.7	146	2.6	2	0.1	5,655	100
	Female	4,512	79.8	968	17.1	144	2.5	27	0.5	4	0.1	5,655	100
1989	Male	3,091	51.6	2,276	38.0	307	5.1	309	5.2	8	0.1	5,991	100
	Female	4,676	78.1	1,021	17.0	152	2.5	137	2.3	5	—	5,991	100
1995	Male	3,275	54.6	2,226	37.1	332	5.5	168	2.8	—	—	6,001	100
	Female	4,676	77.9	1,101	18.3	178	3.0	46	0.8	—	—	6,001	100
1999	Male	3,091	50.4	2,510	40.9	387	6.3	149	2.4	—	—	6,137	100
	Female	4,688	76.4	1,199	19.5	222	3.6	28	0.5	—	—	6,137	100

SOURCE: Ministry of Planning (1999).

First, as we have noted, young people have more say in the choice of a partner. Second, since life expectancy has increased, perhaps the need for parents to arrange marriages of their children early has lessened (Korson & Sabzwari, 1985).

Burchinal, in his work on young (early) marriage in 1960, predicted that rates of young marriages would decline. This has proven to be true. In his opinion, the increased value placed on higher education would have an impact on young marriages. "Increased school and post-high school attendance should be associated with a reduction in young marriage rates" (p. 7).

Since there is a relationship between age at marriage and education, it is expected that we will see a relationship between socio-economic status and age at marriage as well. This researcher asserted that the higher one's socioeconomic status, the later he or she will marry. Conversely, the lower one's socio-economic status, the younger his or her age will be at marriage, particularly among women.

One reason for delaying marriage, especially for males, is a need to achieve vocational stability, thereby assuring the bride's family of the welfare of their daughter.

For other groups in the study, namely Kuwaiti men marrying non-Kuwaiti women, the mean age of marriage for men decreased from 35.8 years in 1974 to 30.0 years in 1984, and still further in 1995 to 27.2. For women it decreased from 23.8 years in 1974 to 22.7 years in 1984. This indicates a change that is not obvious from the data presented here. Formerly, older men who, for various reasons, had been unable to marry Kuwaiti women, went to less wealthy neighboring countries to obtain a wife/wives. But with increasing social freedom, younger Kuwaiti men have made contact with non-Kuwaiti women, and subsequently have taken the bold step of choosing a wife based on personal characteristics and relationships.

For the last group, non-Kuwaiti husbands who marry Kuwaiti wives, the mean age at marriage has again decreased for husbands. For non-Kuwaiti husbands, it has decreased from 29.2 years in 1974 to 27.5 years in 1984. For wives, it decreased from 25.7 years in 1974 to 22.6 in 1984, and later an increase was observed to 24.0 in 1995. An explanation for this could be that, in the past, Kuwaiti women married non-Kuwaiti men only as a last resort. Now marriage is based more on personal choice and relationships. As the society has changed and women have more contact with others in educational institutions and in the workplace, they are more likely to meet and marry non-Kuwaitis as a choice and not as a last resort.

Additionally, influencing the age of marriage, especially for Kuwaiti marriages, is the relative economic independence of children from family authority. A young man must be financially independent of his family to marry. Therefore, he finishes school and gets a job before deciding whom to marry and when. Since a young man has to cover the marriage expenses (bride-price, wedding ceremony, honeymoon, etc.), he delays it until he can afford it.

The mean age differences between spouses for all groups combined decreased from 6.0 years in 1974, to 5.5 years in 1984, to 4.0 years in 1995. Also, when each group was examined separately, the mean age difference decreased. For marriages between Kuwaiti husbands and Kuwaiti wives, it decreased from 5.2 years in 1974 to 4.2 in 1984 and 3.1 in 1995. For marriages between Kuwaiti husbands and non-Kuwaiti wives, it dramatically decreased from 12 years in 1974 to 7.3 years in 1984.

Notice that the age gap between spouses is getting relatively smaller. The only increase in age difference since 1974 was among Kuwaiti men who married non-Kuwaiti women, and that is because younger Kuwaiti women have been marrying non-Kuwaiti men. In addition, husbands are still older than their wives, a typical phenomenon in a patriarchal society where males are heads of families. Another reason is that males must accumulate sufficient resources to pay the amount of dowry (*mahr*) required for marriage. Also, the necessity for the man being older than his wife may be because he has always been the primary provider for the family. The additional years enable him to complete his education and obtain successful work experience. The reasons for a man marrying a much younger woman are less obvious. Apparently, the beauty of eligible young girls is an added factor.

Some Western researchers consider age differences of 3 years or younger to be homogamous, and those of more than 3 years as different degrees of heterogamy. However, with the increased intensive social change and urbanization going on in Kuwait, including the spread of college education and the increase in the number of women working outside the home, it is expected that spouses will be closer in age and that age-homogamous marriages will be on the rise in the future.

This researcher had predicted that the age of marriage would decrease for both husbands and wives on the assumption that young people are turning more toward religion. Islamic doctrine encourages marriage as soon as an individual is able to do so and prohibits premarital sexual relations. Incidentally, coeducation is also prohibited, since it encourages cross-cultural contact and a wider circle of relationships.

Nationality

As mentioned earlier, social change has led to contact with other cultures both because Kuwaiti people are increasingly able to travel to other societies, such as Europe and America, and because opportunities in the labor market attract people of many different nationalities to Kuwait. Those who are eligible to travel are exposed to more non-Arabs than their counterparts who stay at home. The more Westernization they experience, the more likely they are to marry people from non-Arab countries. Although we see an increase in this tendency from 1974 to 1984 and 1995, it is not statistically significant. The level of education was also not generally significant in marriage between Kuwaitis and other nationalities, except in the case of Kuwaiti men marrying non-Arab women.

Al-Naser's (1986) study indicated that Kuwaiti men/non-Arab women marriages increased from 10% in 1974 to 10.3% in 1986, and that when Kuwaiti men marry other nationalities, the first choice is a wife from an Arab country (90% in 1974; 89.7% in 1984). In addition, men without college degrees married women of different nationalities more often than the men with college degrees (51.6% to 43.1%) (Al-Naser, 1986).

It is interesting to note that the number of Kuwaiti women marrying non-Kuwaiti men has increased over the years, more than the number of Kuwaiti men marrying non-Kuwaiti women. This might be explained by the fact that Kuwaiti women have only recently been involved in interactions with non-Kuwaiti men in Kuwait or abroad.

The statistics of 1995 show 63% of marriages between Kuwaiti men and Kuwaiti women, 11% between Kuwaiti men and non-Kuwaiti women, and 6.3% between non-Kuwaiti men and Kuwaiti women. The remaining 19.7% can be attributed to the marriages between non-Kuwaiti men and non-Kuwaiti women.

One common opinion is that Kuwaiti men marry women of other nationalities for financial reasons. First, the male dowry or *mahr* that Kuwaiti men are supposed to pay when marrying Kuwaiti women is very high. The amount varies depending on family status, but the lowest expected is usually around US$7,000. In 1974 the *mahr* was estimated to be between US$2,500 and US$3,000, and now in recent years is about US$15,000. Furthermore, the *mahr* is only part of the expenditure that a groom has to bear. Furniture, sets of gold jewelry, and the marriage ceremony expenses are a man's responsibility as well, bringing the cost of marriage to US$20,000 to U$25,000. In spite of the fact that when Kuwaiti men marry non-Kuwaiti women they are not entitled to the approximate US$13,000 financial assistance from the government, the phenomenon of Kuwaiti men marrying non-Kuwaiti women is increasing.

Since Kuwait has a very high standard of living, these costs are high. For a young man, even a college graduate, these costs might cause him to delay marriage until his financial situation is stable, or they could cause him to look outside his society. In many of the countries neighboring Kuwait, the standard of living is lower and there is no costly bride dowry or marriage expense. In countries such as Egypt or Iraq, many girls look forward to helping their families financially by accepting marriage with Kuwaiti husbands. They will even accept husbands who might have more than one wife or where there is a considerable age difference.

In this researcher's opinion, many dependent variables affect marrying across nationalities. These include educational level, occupational level, previous marital status, and age. The cost of marriage to a Kuwaiti wife may well motivate some lower-class men to marry across nationalities, but among those of higher classes, such marriages are probably based on individual selection. Al-Gardawi's study indicated that 22.9% of the Kuwaitis sampled would be willing to marry heterogamously with non-Kuwaitis, but this represents attitude, not behavior.

Mixed marriages in Kuwait may occur for the following reasons: the easy contact of Kuwaitis with other nationals, cultures, and civilizations; the higher job opportunity for non-Kuwaitis, especially young unmarried males; and the high prices of *mahr* and the marriage expenses. These are some of the factors that have caused the increase in Kuwaiti males marrying non-Kuwaiti females.

Table 23.5 shows an increase in the number of heterogamous marriages between 1975 and 1999 from 564 to 1,728. The percentages of all marriages increased from 15.5 to 28.1. (Table 23.6). Historically, Kuwaitis have shown a relative flexibility toward other cultures.

The study concluded that social change has weakened social relationships and that both Kuwaitis and non-Kuwaitis in Kuwait prefer to have relationships with their own national groups because of their customs, socioeconomic status, place of residence, and other such factors.

Marriage Ceremonies

There has been considerable change in the marriage ceremony. In the past the ceremony was very simple. It involved a small get-together at the residence of the bride. Segregation of the genders was observed. The dress style was very traditional, including a veil for the bride and a simple *bisht* (a cover made of fine material to be worn over the customary *disdasha*) for the groom. Music was incorporated into these social events. The singer was accompanied by one or two musical instruments to make the occasion more lively. The guests were mostly close family relatives and friends. Gifts offered by the guests mostly consisted of household items, appliances, furniture, clothes, and so on. After the party, the bride and groom were left to start their new life in their home. The concept of a honeymoon was alien to them.

Wedding parties of the recent past and the present are very different from the one described previously. Lavish parties are thrown at famous five-star hotels or at wedding halls built specially for these events. Segregation of the genders is still observed, but to a lesser extent. The bride is ushered

Table 23.5   Heterogamous Marriages

Year	Kuwaiti Males and Non-Kuwaiti Females		Kuwaiti Females and Non-Kuwaiti Males		Total	
	N	%	N	%	N	%
1975	451	80	113	20	564	100
1980	713	68.2	333	31.8	1,046	100
1985	882	61.1	562	38.9	1,444	100
1989	1,297	67.9	612	32.1	1,909	100
1995	1,081	64.2	602	35.8	1,683	100
1999	1,108	64.1	620	35.9	1,728	100

SOURCE: Ministry of Justice (1999).

Table 23.6   Heterogamous Marriages

Year	Total Marriages	Heterogamous Marriages	%
1975	3,638	564	15.5
1980	5,987	1,046	17.5
1985	5,655	1,444	25.5
1989	5,991	1,909	31.8
1995	6,001	1,683	28
1999	6,137	1,728	28.1

SOURCE: Ministry of Justice (1999).

into the hall with great pomp and show. Confetti is thrown at the bride, gas balloons and small pigeons are let loose, guns are shot in the air to herald the entrance, and so on.

The dress style has changed since the 1970s. The bridal dress is made of the finest materials, either tailored or bought ready-made from boutiques stocking famous designer labels.

Expenses are not spared. The groom's *bisht* is made of the finest cloth lined with embroidery of the best kind. Guests include relatives (close and distant), friends, colleagues, and even relatives from abroad.

The buffet includes intercontinental and continental dishes. The variety in main courses and desserts, salads, and drinks is enormous. Nowadays financial gifts are common. This gives the newly married couple a chance to do with it whatever they choose. After the party, the couple either stays back at the hotel for a few days and thus starts a new life, or else they go to their new house, and most often leave right away for their honeymoon trip to observe the world through each other's eyes.

3. FERTILITY AND MORTALITY

Fertility and mortality are not uniform across populations but vary according to certain biological, socioeconomic, environmental, and demographic factors. There is no standard classification according to which the various determinants may be categorized. It is important to remember that death and disease are caused by a multitude of factors, each of which may exert influence in different settings. In the case of Kuwait, the determinants of infant mortality consist of various factors including socioeconomic status, healthcare services, demographic risk factors of the mother, and such. During the past two decades, Kuwait has made vast improvements in infant mortality, and the reasons may include improvements in water and sanitary conditions, deliveries at hospital rather than at home, nutrition, immunization coverage, and education and awareness. Subsequently, life expectancy has been rising.

Table 23.7 the shows the development of the crude birthrate and general fertility rate for Kuwaitis and non-Kuwaitis between 1975 and 1999. These statistics indicate that the society (Kuwaitis and non-Kuwaitis included) is opting for a lower fertility rate. A major reason for this change could be the urbanization and modernization process in this changing society.

Table 23.8 shows the crude and infant mortality rate and life expectancy at birth of the world in comparison to Kuwait.

4 & 5. GENDER/MARRIAGE: EDUCATION AND OCCUPATION

It is expected in a strongly patriarchal society such as Kuwait that men will be more educated than their wives, although change has been taking place. This society still regards men as superior, although we are seeing an increasing number of marriages between people of the same educational level.

High income and education appear to be positively related to heterogamous marriage; that is, the higher one's education and income, the more likely one is to marry outside of traditional rules. The present analysis supports this assumption, since it appears that people with higher education and income often work together, as do those with lower education and income, thereby offering them opportunities to interact.

Occupation is influenced by education. The higher the social class, the greater the degree of occupational propinquity, a link that can be explained by the importance attached to educational similarity in the higher social classes.

The results of the author's research suggest a number of basic propositions or theoretical interpretations. First, the data suggest that highly educated people marry "out" more often than people with less education. We can assume, therefore, that with higher education comes increased contact with other ethnic/racial groups, bringing an increased likelihood of out-marriages. It can be postulated that Kuwaitis who attain college degrees come into greater contact with non-Kuwaitis and non-Arabs than do people who do not attain college degrees, thus increasing their chances of intermarriage. The higher the educational level and occupation and the higher a person's socioeconomic status, the greater is the possibility that cross-cultural interaction will go beyond job-related friendships and lead to marriage.

Table 23.7 Crude Birthrate and General Fertility Rate: Kuwaitis and Non-Kuwaitis per 1,000

Year	Kuwaitis		Non-Kuwaitis		Total	
	Crude Birthrate	General Fertility Rate	Crude Birthrate	General Fertility Rate	Crude Birthrate	General Fertility Rate
1975	51.2	237.5	36	182.4	—	—
1976	50.6	232.4	36.6	186.6	43	208.9
1977	48.5	222.4	35.2	183.1	41.2	202
1978	47.4	217	33.6	178.1	39.6	196.6
1979	46.4	212	30.7	166.3	37.4	187.7
1980	47.3	211	30.2	156	37.3	180.9
1981	47.3	211.1	28.6	147.3	36.3	175.9
1982	47.3	210.8	28.6	146.4	36.2	175
1983	47.1	210.4	27.5	140.5	35.5	171.2
1984	46.9	209.5	26.4	133.9	34.7	166.8
1985	45.7	199.9	23.1	102.5	32.2	141.8
1986	44.5	194.8	20.5	90.5	30.1	132.2
1987	39	—	23.5	—	27.7	—
1988	39.8	—	22.4	97.3	27.1	—
1989	39.2	—	21	—	25.9	—

524

Table 23.7 (Continued)

Year	Kuwaitis		Non-Kuwaitis		Total	
	Crude Birthrate	General Fertility Rate	Crude Birthrate	General Fertility Rate	Crude Birthrate	General Fertility Rate
1990[a]	—	—	—	—	—	—
1991[a]	—	—	—	—	—	—
1992	37.7	163.6	14	—	24.5	—
1993	38.4	166.3	15.3	—	25.6	—
1994	37.8	163.3	14.2	—	24	—
1995	37.6	162.7	15.1	—	24.4	—
1996	36.8	159.2	17.5	—	25.4	—
1997	35.3	152.7	15.6	—	23.7	—
1998	33.3	135.3	12.5	45.7	20.4	—
1999	—	128.8	—	—	—	—

SOURCE: Ministry of Planning (1999).

a. No data due to invasion by Iraq.

Table 23.8   Crude Death and Infant Mortality Rates and Life Expectancy at Birth per 100

Area	Crude Death Rate	Infant Mortality	Life Expectancy at Birth
World	9	58	66
More developed	10	8	75
Less developed	9	64	63
Africa	15	91	52
Asia	8	57	65
Asia excluding China	8	66	63
China	7	31	71
North America	8	7	76
Latin America	7	36	69
Europe	11	10	73
Russia	14	17	67
Oceania	7	28	73
Kuwait	2	10	72

SOURCE: PRB (1989).

Male university degree holders and those with higher-status jobs marry across religion and across nationalities, including marriage with non-Arabs. They also marry across tribal or caste lines, but surprisingly, college graduates and men with high-status jobs do not marry across sect any more often than others. As explained earlier, this might be because the strength of sectarian divisions in the society has been enhanced by the Iranian revolution (Khomeinism) and the Islamic revival in the area.

Marrying at the same occupational level did not become significant until 1974, perhaps because there were not many women in the labor force until that time, and those women who were in the labor force were concentrated in jobs that are generally considered gender specific, such as teaching and nursing. In the future, one can expect to see a greater tendency toward husband and wife having the same occupational level.

Educational level may have important implications for a woman who extends her formal education, particularly beyond the undergraduate degree. Advanced education and increased age place her in a marriage market in which the number of available males who both are older than she and have as much or more education than she has is very limited. The pool is further limited by the fact that men are permitted to marry "down," both in age and education, so that the older, more educated woman faces competition from younger and less-educated women for available unmarried men.

In a study of 300 Kuwaiti and non-Kuwaiti families, Al-Gardawi (1984) found that 33% of the Kuwaiti men supported the idea of their wives working outside the home, while 41% of non-Kuwaiti men did so. For the most part, the difference is economic. The Kuwaiti family does not need the woman's salary as much as the non-Kuwaiti family does. In the same study, 80% of the people interviewed supported the concept of women (in general) working outside the home. The difference of opinion relates to the fact that Kuwaiti men are still conservative when it comes to the idea of their own wives or close family members working outside the home, although they have more liberal general ideas.

Table 23.9 shows that the number of marriages has increased from 3,638 in 1975 to 6,137 in 1999, that is, by 68.6% in 25 years due to the increase in the total population. The number of marriages among the illiterate has been decreasing since 1975, due to the decrease in illiteracy. Thus, 29.9% of males and 49.3% of females marrying were illiterate, decreasing to 8.2% in 1985 among males and 19.7% of females, until it reached 1.5% for males in 1985 and 19.7% for females.

These results strongly indicate that Kuwaiti society is in the middle of a transitional process in terms of female education and occupation.

6 & 7. DIVORCE AND VIOLENCE

Divorce in its general meaning is termination of marriage between a man and a woman. However, it is also considered the only way to put an end to problems and dissatisfaction between two spouses. Some people take divorce as a personal misfortune or bad luck. In all cases divorce indicates tension and destruction of connections and relationships that existed at one time between two families

through a marriage of their son or daughter. Divorce usually triggers negative psychological effects on the family members, particularly the mother and children (Al-Rashidi & Al-Khulaifi, 1997, p. 539).

The extent of these functions depends primarily on the traditions, culture, and economic status of the society. Problems and malfunctions arise that may lead to dissolution of the family. Again, it must be noted that there are several factors that contribute to the disintegration of any family. When two people separate or divorce, it is not likely that it is due to any single factor.

Developing countries are observing an increase in divorce rates. This situation could develop behavioral abnormalities in the future that would be deleterious to whole societies.

Kuwait is no different. Divorce, which once was a rare phenomenon in Kuwait, now occurs in nearly one-third of all marriages. The divorce rate is on the increase, noticeably so since the disastrous Iraqi invasion (Al-Rashidi, 1997). According to statistics published by the Ministry of Justice, the divorce rate among Kuwaitis reached 37% in 1996 (Ministry of Justice, 1996). Table 23.10 shows an increase in divorce from 1991 to 1994 in Kuwait, in comparison with other Arab societies.

Since Kuwait is an Islamic society, the Shariah (Islamic law) is implemented to control social life, divorce being no exception. Moreover, the divorce procedure in Islam is such as to encourage reconciliation where possible. After divorce the woman should wait three monthly cycles during which her husband remains responsible for her welfare and maintenance. He is not permitted to drive her out of the house during this period. She will be advised not to leave the house of the divorcing husband to enhance the chances of reconciliation, as well as to protect her right of sustenance during the 3-month waiting period.

The main purpose of this waiting period is to clarify whether the divorced wife is or is

Table 23.9 Distribution of Kuwaiti Marriages According to Education and Gender

Year	Gender	Illiterate/ Read and Write		Elementary/ Intermediate		High School/ College		University and Higher		Not Stated		Total	
		N	%	N	%	N	%	N	%	N	%	N	%
1975	Male	1,087	29.9	1,594	43.8	660	18.1	129	3.6	168	4.6	3,638	100
	Female	1,794	49.3	1,105	30.4	537	14.7	39	1.1	163	4.5	3,638	100
1980	Male	1,420	23.7	2,838	47.5	1,306	21.8	404	6.7	19	0.3	5,987	100
	Female	2,339	39.1	2,118	35.4	1,209	20.2	301	5.0	20	0.3	5,987	100
1985	Male	464	8.2	2,955	52.2	1,667	29.5	563	10.0	6	0.1	5,655	100
	Female	1,117	19.7	2,639	46.7	1,563	27.6	331	5.9	5	0.1	5,655	100
1989	Male	327	5.5	2,889	48.2	2,003	23.4	761	12.7	11	0.2	5,991	100
	Female	624	10.4	2,785	46.5	2,054	34.3	519	8.7	9	0.1	5,991	100
1995	Male	89	1.5	2,823	47.0	2,261	37.7	807	13.5	21	0.3	6,001	100
	Female	163	2.7	2,503	41.7	2,725	45.4	599	10.0	11	0.2	6,001	100
1999	Male	47	0.8	2,657	43.3	2,351	38.3	1,046	17.0	36	0.6	6,137	100
	Female	84	1.4	1,861	30.3	3,028	49.3	1,141	18.6	23	0.4	6,137	100

SOURCE: Ministry of Planning (1999).

Table 23.10 Divorce Statistics

Number				Country	Rate (%)			
1991	*1992*	*1993*	*1994*		*1991*	*1992*	*1993*	*1994*
—	78,490	77,571	89,938	Egypt	—	1.41	1.37	1.55
661	574	636	663	Bahrain	1.30	1.11	1.18	1.19
5,363	5,513	6,092	6,251	Jordan	1.21	2.96	2.69	—
1,768	2,709	2,594	—	Kuwait	0.85	1.90	1.77	—
9,078	9,127	10,343	10,343	Syria	0.72	0.70	0.77	0.75
—	—	416	432	Qatar	—	0.78	0.77	0.87
—	—	—	2,121	UAE	—	—	—	1.14

SOURCE: Ministry of Justice (1999).

not expecting a child. Its second use is as a cooling-off period during which the relatives and other members of the family or the community may try to help toward a reconciliation and better understanding between the partners. The Qur'an says, "And if you fear a breach between the two, then appoint a judge from his people and a judge from her people; if they both desire agreement, Allah will effect harmony between them, surely Allah is Knowing, Aware." (4:35). If they are reconciled, they may resume the marriage relations at any time within the waiting period, whereupon the divorce is automatically revoked. If further trouble arises and divorce is pronounced a second time, the same procedure is followed. Only if the matter reaches a third divorce does it become irrevocable. The wife is then to leave the house and is free after three monthly cycles to marry another man if she wishes. The first husband is not then permitted to remarry her unless she has in the meantime married another man and been divorced in the same legal manner. This procedure is the normal one followed if the husband is the one seeking divorce, or if the divorce is by mutual consent. If the wife seeks divorce against the wishes of the husband, she may take her case to the court and obtain a divorce.

In Islamic society there is a misconception on the issue of divorce. If the husband utters *Talak,* or divorce, three times in the same breath, it is considered an irrevocable divorce, and there is no chance of reconciliation between the couple. Under this strict view, which is not supported by many classical and modern Islamic scholars, many families are broken and the women and children are mostly affected. According to the view supported by many modern Islamic scholars, three or more utterances of divorce at a time are regarded as only one *Talak* (divorce). But, according to all scholars, to utter such number of *divorce* at a time is not encouraged in Islam and the person who pursues this undesirable system will be considered sinful. If it is held to be irrevocable and the divorce final, then the option offered by Allah to take back one's wife within 90 days is frustrated. In consequence, the rate of the dissolution of marriage increases and, as a matter of course, more women and children become helpless.

Some people raise the question regarding the right of a wife to pronounce divorce in Islam, and there are many misunderstandings in our society centering on this issue. In Islam, women are deprived in no respect, and any question of injustice or antiwoman bias is inconceivable. In Islam the wife is fully entitled to initiate or pronounce divorce, though the procedure is different from that of her husband. If the husband is missing for a certain period of time, suffers from a fatal, incurable disease, is sexually impotent, or in some other circumstances, the wife is given every right to initiate divorce. Moreover, if she suffers unhappiness, misery, or incompatibility with her husband, then she can do it with the intervention of a court. There is another system of dissolution of marriage by the woman that is called *Khula*, through which a wife can get separation from her husband by returning the marital gift or part of it. It isnot necessary that she should have a definite ground for pursuing *Khula*. Thus, both the husband and the wife can initiate divorce in Islam, though the procedures are different.

The husband seems to be given the right to practice divorce arbitrarily, but this is not really so. In pursuing divorce, the husband encounters financial disadvantages as he married his wife by giving her *mahr* (marital gift), and he is bound to give it to his wife at the time of dissolution of marriage if it is unpaid yet. Moreover, he will have to pay *mahr* for the second time if he wants to get married again. Dr. Jamal A. Badawi, a prominent Islamic scholar, says:

> Although both husband and wife suffer as a result of a divorce (psychologically for instance), a man has the additional burden of a heavy responsibility. He loses the marriage gift, the wife is entitled to maintenance whilst in the waiting period (which

can be as little as three months or as much as nine months); she is entitled to child maintenance if young children are in her custody; according to some jurists she would also be entitled to a consolation maintenance for a year, etc. The fact that a husband has so much to lose financially if he divorces his wife acts as a natural deterrent from abusing his right of divorce. If Muslim women had such a right, however, there would be no such check on them because they do not have financial responsibilities towards their husbands.

It does not mean, however, that Islam does not give the wife the right to break the marital bond if she wants to. It only checks the abusing of such a right.

Discussing the conditions under which a wife can unilaterally divorce her husband without seeking the court's approval, Dr. Jamal A. Badawi points to two situations: "1) Delegated Repudiation, where at the time of marriage or afterwards, the husband transferred his unilateral right of divorce to his wife; and 2) Conditional Repudiation, where at the time of the signing of the marriage contract, the wife stipulated certain conditions to her husband, the breach of which would result in a divorce."

The grounds on which a wife can seek divorce from her husband in the courts are as follows:

- Inability or refusal of the husband to maintain his wife. (Even if she happens to be rich, it is still the full responsibility of the husband to maintain her.)
- Abuse/mistreatment (which includes beating and swearing, cursing, and attempting to force her to do wrong).
- Impotence of her husband (in recognition of the wife's legitimate instinctive needs).
- Imprisonment of the husband.
- Deception or concealment of important information at the time of the marriage.
- Incurable, repulsive disease in the husband or insanity.

- Extended absence or desertion by the husband: If his whereabouts are known, he is given the chance to return to his wife before the divorce takes effect; if his whereabouts are unknown, a 6-month or 1-year waiting period is placed on the wife. If the husband fails to return, the wife is divorced from him.

There are two methods of divorce by mutual consent:

1. *Mubarra,* where husband and wife agree to release each other from the marriage vows—they also agree on the financial and other conditions for the release.

2. Self-redemption (*Khula*), where, if the wife is unhappy with the conduct of her husband and has genuine grievances that she fears will cause her to fall into error if she continues in the marriage, then she obtains separation by returning her husband's marriage gift in return for the dissolution of the marriage. Conditions that should be observed when using the *Khula* method of divorce are as follows: There must be a genuine reason for seeking divorce; dissolution may be imposed on the husband if he refuses to let his wife go; no husband may pressure his wife into asking for *Khula* so that he can regain the marriage gift; and this form of dissolution can take place at any time.

Thus, the lack of an unconditional unilateral right of divorce does not prevent a wife from seeking divorce from her husband, if she has good reasons for it, in any of the ways described previously. It is true that in most cases rural wives are deprived of the right to divorce (and also of many other social, political, and religious rights). It is because of the failure of governments in Muslim countries and their leaders to educate them and inform them of their rights. The system of *Khula Talak* is not as cumbersome as some people of inadequate knowledge about Islam assume. It is a procedure

about which people should be better informed.

Research has shown that in Kuwait, a high rate of divorce is becoming apparent. Table 23.11 shows an increase in divorce between Kuwaitis since 1975 for the different age-groups. While we cannot relate this increase to population and marriage number, we can relate it to different reasons. Many studies emphasize social change in general, but they have not gone into why this happened (Gloom et al., 1975). Some Western studies emphasize the change of family structure from extended to nuclear, which changed the nature of the relation between individuals and society. There are many potential reasons for the high divorce rate in Kuwait: Mate selection has changed from social and familial to a more individual basis with more individual-based characteristics; the financial independence of women has affected the divorce rates; the average size of families is smaller; and there is a higher rate of nationally heterogamous marriages.

Table 23.11 shows a high divorce rate for the 15 to 24 age-group for females (1995: 46.3%), but it is lower for females in the 35 to 44 age-group—an indication that the family is more stable at this age for women. The highest divorce rate for males is at 25 to 34 years—many of whom are divorcing women between ages 15 and 24.

In some other societies, it is very easy to break the bond of marriage, and there is no check against the abuse of the practice of divorce. In fact, the consequences of both over-restriction and overliberalization are harmful. In the case of overrestriction, that is, keeping an unsuccessful marriage intact, there occurs a permanently bitter and hostile relation between the husband and wife. In the case of overliberalization, the family as an institution disintegrates and the society as a whole suffers. In contrast to these extremes, Islam takes a moderate view

Table 23.11 Divorce According to Age and Gender

Year	Gender	Age-Groups										Total	
		15–24		25–34		35–44		45 and Over		N & %		Total	
		N	%	N	%	N	%	N	%	N	%	Total	%
1975	Male	192	17.6	376	34.6	248	22.8	270	24.8	2	0.2	1,088	100
	Female	610	56.1	287	26.4	119	10.9	71	6.5	1	0.1	1,088	100
1980	Male	342	22.9	576	38.5	310	20.8	260	17.4	6	0.4	1,494	100
	Female	750	50.2	499	33.4	165	11.0	74	5.0	6	0.4	1,494	100
1985	Male	393	23.5	739	44.2	280	16.7	242	14.5	19	1.1	1,673	100
	Female	774	46.3	553	33.0	235	14.1	91	5.4	20	1.2	1,673	100
1989	Male	405	24.2	773	46.3	220	13.2	263	15.7	10	0.6	1,671	100
	Female	783	46.8	596	35.7	185	11.1	95	5.7	12	0.7	1,671	100
1995	Male	478	25.7	862	46.3	264	14.2	258	13.8	—	—	1,862	100
	Female	862	46.3	657	35.3	224	12.0	119	6.4	—	—	1,862	100
1999	Male	447	22.2	980	48.6	352	17.5	235	11.7	—	—	2,014	100
	Female	900	44.7	745	37.0	244	12.1	125	6.2	—	—	2,014	100

SOURCE: Ministry of Planning (1999).

on divorce. To remove the misery of an unsuccessful marriage, Islam supports divorce as the final resort only to liberate both spouses from the bitterness of the relationship, and in Islam divorce can only be pursued when all other avenues have been taken to reconcile the couple, but have come to no avail.

The law of Islam does not, therefore, compel unhappy couples to stay together, but its procedures help them find a basis on which they can be reconciled with each other. If reconciliation is impossible the law does not impose any unnecessary delay or obstacle in the way of either partner's remarriage.

One may observe that modern developments in marriage law in Great Britain and other Western countries are tending toward the Islamic pattern, albeit unconsciously in many ways, stressing guidance and counseling before divorce, privacy of divorce proceedings, and speeding up of the process of divorce once it has been established that the marriage has irretrievably broken down.

In nationally heterogamous marriages in 1975–1999, divorces are frequent. The rate of divorce of Kuwaiti males from non-Kuwaiti wives is especially high. For the year 1999, the total number of nationally heterogamous divorces was 785. Such heterogamous divorces represented 38.97% of the total divorce rate in 1999—more than one-third of all divorces.

8. KINSHIP STRUCTURE IN A CHANGING SOCIETY

Even where the nuclear family structure exists, people are involved in extended traditional families. Married offspring may live in the vicinity of the parents' or in-laws' residences, deriving the benefits of daily visits, shared meals, communication, and emotional support. In Kuwait, this structure is common. Some areas are characterized by large families who have the same last name. They might not live together under the same roof but reside in the same town. Prothro and Lutfy (1974) referred to this pattern of family structure as the social/psychological pattern of extended family in their book entitled *Changing Family Patterns in the Arab East*. Family members gather together in moments of crisis, festive occasions, births, marriages, serious illnesses, deaths, other misfortunes, and important events, such as running for elections. For all practical purposes, members act as part of an extended family. The callers at the central meeting place include not only friends but also cousins, uncles, aunts, and other traceable relatives who may not live within a shared household.

Marrying relatives is another reason for the existence of extended families. The preference for this is still very much evident. A substantial minority of wives interviewed had lived with the husband's parents for several years, and a majority still lived in the same town or city as the in-laws. In addition, a majority of wives reported daily or weekly visits to their parents and in-laws. Prothro and Lutfy further concluded that the ties of the extended family remain strong for those living in the conjugal type of household.

The family structure in Kuwait, however, is in transition. It is not the isolated nuclear family structure nor is it the extended family structure. Although many Kuwaiti families do have a nuclear structure, they behave as extended families. The characteristics of the Kuwaiti family include the following: (1) the family is large in size; (2) there are strong relations with kinship lines; (3) the nuclear family usually resides next to the home of the elders; (4) many related families live next to each other; (5) they share the same business; and (6) mate selection is based on the joint decision of the individual and elders.

One would anticipate that the conjugal family will become increasingly dominant, yet the extended family pattern won't disappear. Industrialization alone does not lead to a change in the family structure. A combination of factors such as the political system, changes in value, and socioeconomic pressures will have to act in concert to bring about a significant change in the currently observable structure.

CONCLUSIONS

The entire Arab Middle Eastern world is going through rapid social change, which is affecting every aspect of social life with globalization and easy communication. No society can exclude itself. Family structure has been changing from an extended traditional or transitional one to a nuclear one, which characterizes the family household as a small family size. The marriage norms and patterns are also undergoing change. Individual mate selection is increasing, although the familial opinions are considered. Marriage ceremonies are more elaborate and modern. Divorce rates are higher due to many reasons, such as women becoming more independent financially. Individual mate choice makes it easier to dissolve a marriage. Endogamous marriages are decreasing, and heterogamous marriages are on the increase—which is also a reason for the higher rate of divorce. Divorce is not stigmatized as it was in the past. For all these reasons—including modernization, urbanization, and influence of the West—we see the tendency toward the buildup of nuclear families, individual mate selection, and a high divorce rate.

REFERENCES

Al Ati, H. A. (1977). *The family structure in Islam.* Baltimore, MD: American Trust Publications.

Al-Gardawi, A. R. A. (1984). *Al-hajra wa alozla alijtemayia fi al-mojtma al-Kuwaiti* [Immigration and social isolation in Kuwaiti society]. Kuwait: Al-Robian.

Al Ghazali, S. M. (1992). *Kuwait's fourth fence* (Vol. 3). Kuwait: Al Shamey.

Al-Naser, F. (1986). *Socio-cultural dimensions of homogamous and heterogamous marriages in Kuwait.* Unpublished doctoral dissertation, East Lansing: Michigan State University.

Al-Rashidi, B. (1997). *War and society: PTSD studies on Kuwait society.* Kuwait City, State of Kuwait: Amiri Diwan.

Al-Rashidi, B., & Al-Khulaifi, I. (1997). *Psychology of family life.* Kuwait City, State of Kuwait: That Al Salaseel Printing Press.

Al Thakeb, F. (1974). *The Kuwait family, today & yesterday.* Unpublished doctoral dissertation, Ohio State University, Columbus, OH.

Berger, M. (1962). *The Arab world today.* Garden City, NY: Doubleday.

Burchinal, L. G. (1960). Research on young marriages: Implications for family life education. *Family Life Co-ordinator,* (September–December), 7–17.

Goode, W. I. (1963). *World revolution and family patterns.* New York: The Free Press.

Ismael, F. (1982). *Social change in Kuwaiti society.* Unpublished masters' thesis, Alexandria University, Alexandria, Egypt.

Korson, H. J., & Sabzwari, M. A. (1985). Age and social status at marriage, Karadu, Pakistan, 1961–66 and 1980: A comparative study. *Journal of Comparative Family Studies, 15*(2), 257–279.

Ministry of Information. (1995). *Annual statistical book.* Kuwait City: State of Kuwait.

Ministry of Justice. (1999). *Marriage and divorce statistics.* Kuwait City, State of Kuwait: Author.

Ministry of Planning. (1995). *A statistical package.* Kuwait City: State of Kuwait.

Ministry of Planning. (1998). *A statistical package.* Kuwait City: State of Kuwait.

Ministry of Planning. (1999). *Annual statistical book.* Kuwait City: State of Kuwait.

Parsons, T. (1943). The kinship system of the contemporary United States. *American Anthropologist, 45,* 22–38.

Patai, R. (1962). *Golden river to golden road: Society, culture and change in the Middle East.* Philadelphia: University of Pennsylvania Press.

Prothro, E. T., & Lufty, N. D. (1974). *Changing family patterns in the Arab East.* Beirut: American University of Beirut.

Social Development Office. (1997). *Value system in Kuwaiti society.* Kuwait City, State of Kuwait: Amiri Diwan.

Part VI

NORTH AMERICA

CHAPTER 24

Families in Canada

CAROL D. H. HARVEY

1. DESCRIPTION OF CANADA AND CANADIANS

Geography, Government, and Families

Canada is the second largest country in the world, covering more than four time zones, an area in which one could put both the continental United States and Australia and have room left. Canada stretches from sea to sea to sea (Atlantic Ocean on the east, Arctic Ocean on the north, and Pacific Ocean on the west). Its southern border with the United States is the longest undefended border in the world. With large cities in the south, over 90% of Canadians live in urban areas within 100 km of the United States. Canada is rich in natural resources and industries using high technology, and it has a literate population. It has been designated as one of the top countries in the world in which to live on the Human Development Index of social indicators by the United Nations.

Canada is a bilingual and multicultural society (Baker, 2001). By official policy (adopted in 1980) Canada promotes cultural retention and language diversity (see

Multiculturalism Act, 1985). Canada is officially bilingual: English and French.

Settlement by Europeans began 500 years ago with a Norse settlement in Newfoundland, Aux-au-Meadows. White Europeans brought a tradition of English common law to "upper Canada," south of the St. Lawrence River, while French laws, customs, and Roman Catholic religion became dominant in "lower Canada," north of the St. Lawrence. The Province of Quebec, which has one-fourth of the Canadian population, is still culturally and linguistically unique within the country. European domination of aboriginal peoples (Inuit in the extreme north, natives and the French/native Metís across the south) resulted in a colonial legacy that has current ramifications and challenges (Mandell & Momirov, 2000).

Canada has slightly fewer than 30 million inhabitants (Statistics Canada, 2004b). In terms of composition of the society, most are of British, French, or European descent (over 90% in 2001). Aboriginal populations composed 3.3% of Canadians; Asians or Africans made up 1.3%; and others were the remaining 5% in 2001 (Statistics Canada,

The author would like to thank Douglas A. Brownridge for his comments on this chapter.

2004a). The official definition of *family* used by the census, which is conducted every 5 years, includes married couples with or without offspring, common-law couples with or without children, and lone parents with at least one unmarried offspring coresident (McDaniel & Tepperman, 2002). In the 1996 Census, 71.9% of Canadians lived in families and 28.1% were in "other" households, largely persons living alone. Within families, married couples made up 73.7%, while 11.7% were cohabiting couples, and 14.5% were one-parent families (Gee, 2000, p. 83). People living alone were 9.1% of the population, while 3.5% lived with nonrelatives, and 1.6% live in collective dwellings (Vanier Institute, 2000). The majority of Canadians living alone are elderly women.

Canada is governed by a constitutional monarchy and is part of the British Commonwealth. At the national level, Parliament is headed by a prime minister and has an elected House of Commons and a selected senate. The country is divided into 10 provinces and three territories, each of which has its own government, beneath the federal one. Cities and rural municipalities are a third level of government. Many of the laws affecting families are formulated at the provincial level, including healthcare, education, and marriage, resulting in variation across the country. Some family law, for example, governing divorce, is formulated at the national level and applies to all Canadians. Canada can be characterized as a liberal welfare state, similar to Australia and New Zealand, in which families are supported only when their own resources have been depleted and when they can demonstrate that fact through means testing (Baker, 2001).

Background: Aboriginal Peoples

Canada was settled prior to European contact, with Inuit peoples living in the far north and various native groups in the south. Archeologists have found projectile points, used to hunt big animals, as evidence that people have lived in Canada for 20,000 years (Steckley, 1997). Aboriginal groups include Indians (defined by the Federal Government, a definition that has changed over time), Inuit in the far north, and Metís. Aboriginals, divided into 10 groups, according to Steckley, speak over 50 languages.

European contact changed the way of life of the original people drastically. The vast agricultural lands of the inland south and the coastal waters of the east and west were taken over by Europeans, and the official colonial policies were designed to destroy aboriginal culture and assimilate people into the Euro-Canadian system (Fiske & Johnny, 2003). Although many groups were given treaty rights, these so-called First Nations are still fighting through the courts to get land settlements and fishing rights promised them in the 1700s and 1800s. Early Europeans took native "wives," whose role was to make homes and serve their European "husbands." The Metís are descended from the many French trappers and others who took native wives. Many of these men later abandoned the women and children, importing "proper" European wives (Das Gupta, 2000).

Not only did the colonial powers deny movement to native peoples and resettle them on reserves, but they also required native children to attend residential schools. In the residential schools, often run by Anglican or Catholic churches, natives were denied the right to speak their own language, practice their own religion, or wear their own clothes. Forced by the Royal Canadian Mounted Police from their homes, they saw their families very little. Many reported they lost their cultural identity (Lawrenchuk & Harvey, 2000). Inability to have parent role models left many unable to perform parenting themselves (Lawrenchuk, Harvey, & Berkowitz, 2000). Current programs, such as Aboriginal Head Start, are designed to help aboriginal parents learn parenting skills.

Aboriginal families are poorer than other Canadians. They have lower educational attainment, higher birth rates, and higher rates of single-parent families (Statistics Canada, 2003). Although just over 3% of the current population of Canada, in some provinces (Saskatchewan and Manitoba, particularly) native families represent a higher percentage. Gaining entry into the dominant culture via establishing native businesses and improving native educational attainment is on the political agenda of native groups (Margaret Swan, Southern Chief, Manitoba, personal communication, September 2002).

Rita Joe (1996) discusses the poverty and racial discrimination she experienced growing up on Canada's east coast as a Mi'kmaq. Orphaned at a young age, Joe enrolled herself in a residential school, and she later married Frank Joe and had a large family. She took care of her family and wrote poetry and songs, eventually earning an honorary doctor of laws from Dalhousie University and the Order of Canada (Joe, 1996). Her journey was long and arduous, helped by her optimism and belief in others.

Bearing in mind that aboriginal Canadians compose a small percentage of the total population and none of the dominant political or social structure, it is the dominant white population, largely British and French descendants of original settlers as well as later immigrants, that is considered through most of the chapter. The last section considers immigrant, refugee, and nonwhite families.

2. PAIRING UP IN CANADA

Prior to pairing up many Canadians go on dates to movies, sporting events, dinner, concerts, or parties. Dating has the functions of socializing young people into adult roles, providing entertainment, bestowing prestige if the date has high status in the group, and serving as part of courtship (Ward, 1994). Sexual intercourse may be part of dating,

and it is more likely if the female partner is sexually experienced (Ward, 1994).

Many Canadians live together without marrying. For some, living together is done before marriage (and usually before children are born); for others, living together by common law is a replacement for marriage. The province of Quebec provides for a legal document that protects partners of consensual unions (Brownridge, 2002), and the rate of nonmarried unions in Quebec is now about 30% (Brownridge, forthcoming). The legal recognition of common-law couples varies by province (Eichler, 1997), but the proportion of common-law unions has risen from 3.8% in 1981 to 6.9% in 1991 (McDaniel & Tepperman, 2002) to 11.7% in 1996 (Gee, 2000). Legalization of common-law unions provides an alternative to marriage, and its presence means that many couples marry later now than in earlier decades (Gee, 2000). Wu (2000) uses Canadian General Social Survey data to report that 41% of adults from Quebec had cohabited, while 23% of other Canadians had done so (p. 76). Rates of cohabitation are higher among people who are "employed, less-educated (women), non-students, have no religious orientation, Canadian-born, and Quebecers" (Wu, 2000, p. 81).

Over 90% of Canadians eventually marry. The median age at first marriage is 29 for men and 27 for women (Eshelman & Wilson, 1998). Most Canadians suggest they marry for "love," selecting their own partners. People commonly meet through social contacts at work, school, sports, or religious groups. Less common alternatives include personal advertisements in newspapers (Sev'er, 1990) or on the Internet. Arranged marriage is also practiced; the arranged marriage alternative is more likely among immigrants from the Middle East, India, and Asia (McDaniel & Tepperman, 2002).

Canadians select marital partners according to the homogamy principle: Couples are similar in age, propinquity, education, and social class (Eshelman & Wilson, 1998). Partners are also similar in ethnic origins, with immigrants from countries such as China, India, and Japan having the highest endogamy rates (Eshelman & Wilson, 1998).

Marriage in Canada involves getting a license from the province or territory in which the couple resides, having the marriage solemnized by a religious authority or a civil marriage commissioner, and getting the marriage registered with the local political jurisdiction (Nett, 1988). Wedding ceremonies are often elaborate, with parents from some cultural groups saving money for a daughter's wedding from the time of her birth.

Until 2003 marriage was a legal union between a man and a woman and involved the expectation of sexual interaction, common domicile, and procreation of children. In 2003 courts in three provinces (Quebec, British Columbia, and Ontario) ruled that same-sex unions must also be legalized under marriage laws ("Gay Marriage Is Legalized," 2003). The courts reasoned that confining marriage to heterosexual unions was discriminatory, and thus same-sex couples must have the same rights and benefits as heterosexual couples. Previous rulings gave same-sex couples the right to inherit from one another and provide one another pension benefits, and to be protected under the law from discrimination based on sexual orientation. The federal government is deciding how to change the law to reflect court rulings, and legislation has been proposed to define marriage as "between two persons." If that is passed, Canada would become the third country in the world to recognize same-sex marriage under civil law ("Gay Marriage Is Legalized," 2003).

3. FERTILITY AND SOCIALIZATION OF CHILDREN

Childbirth

Childbirth timing and numbers have been characterized by the phrase, "Not so soon, not so many" (Ondercin-Bourne, 1997). Fertility has taken a downward trend in Canada since World War II, similar to other industrialized countries. In 1996, based on 1,000 women, lifetime fertility was estimated to be 1,620 (Gee, 2000). Factors influencing lower fertility include urbanization, increase in the paid employment and education of women, decrease in religious participation, and improvements in contraception (Gee, 2000). Social class influences fertility timing in Canada, with more-privileged women having children later than less-privileged ones (Gee, 2000). Quebec provided fertility incentives starting in 1988, measures that have largely been ineffective in raising fertility (Krull, 2003).

Since couples are marrying later and postponing the birth of the first child, infertility rates in Canada have been rising. An estimate of couples unable to have children is 23%, although some of those may eventually have children. Only 5% of Canadian women say that they do not want children. Couples who are voluntarily childless tend to be better educated, earn more, and have less gender role stereotyping in their relationship (McDaniel & Tepperman, 2002).

New reproductive technologies are used by some infertile couples determined to have children, at great expense to the couples, since treatment for infertility is not covered by social medical insurance. Difficulty in conceiving and subsequent involvement in assisted reproductive technology has given rise to Internet chat rooms devoted to supporting participants in the process. Research (Wingert, 2003) shows social support by and for women to be high in the Internet chat rooms, while at the same time the medical information exchanged is not regulated and can be highly inaccurate.

Contraception is known and widely practiced in Canada. Sterilization is also used; one study in the 1980s showed that one-half of couples were sterilized (McDaniel & Tepperman, 2002). The number of children born to teenage mothers has been declining in Canada, largely due to availability of contraception and abortion. Abortion is regulated only by medical practice standards in Canada, rather than by law.

By 1991, 27% of Canadian babies were born to unmarried women (Eshelman & Wilson, 1998), not all to teen mothers, which suggests planning for pregnancy by common-law partners. However, in 1993–1994, 8.7% of children were born to Canadian women who did not live with the child's father (McDaniel & Tepperman, 2002).

Socialization of children is considered a family responsibility in Canada; however, state support for child-rearing is provided in all provinces with the regulation of child-care centers and public support for child-care for poor families. In Quebec a new piece of legislation provides universal access to childcare for a low fee (Krull, 2003). State support is also available to parents employed full time with up to a year of parental leave paid at the rate of employment insurance.

While parents are at work, 17% of two-parent families and 36% of one-parent families had preschool children in licensed childcare (Lero & Brockman, 1993). Thirty-two percent of two-parent families look after their own preschoolers in their homes although no one-parent families do so. The percentage of preschooler care by a relative or unregulated caregiver is 18% for two-parent and 31% for one-parent families (Lero & Brockman, 1993).

Children who grow up in poverty in Canada are numerous (1 in 5 in 1994, as estimated by Ross, Scott, & Kelly, 1996). Poverty in Canada is associated with higher rates of maternal and child morbidity and mortality (Harman, 2000), as well as higher rates of child malnutrition, chronic illness, low academic achievement, and living in unsafe housing. Poverty is associated with ethnic origin, with aboriginal peoples the poorest (Harman, 2000). Poverty among

single-parent mothers is particularly a problem in Canada, with 60% of female-headed households with children spending more than 57% of their income on food, clothing, and shelter (Harman, 2000, pp. 190–191). Providing housing for these families that is safe, secure, adequate, and appropriate is needed (Spector & Klodawsky, 1993). According to results from the 1994 National Longitudinal Study of Children and Youth, hunger is also a problem for youth. Results show 1.2% of families in Canada are hungry, with single-parent families, those on social assistance, and off-reserve aboriginals at the highest risk (McIntyre, Connor, & Warren, 2000).

Children in Canada are likely to grow up in dual-earner families. Couples in which both partners were in the workforce made up 61.3% of households in 1997; only 21.4% were single-earner families (Lero, 2003). A sizable proportion of husband-wife couples has no earners (17.4%); in most of those, the man is retired. Canadian parents work to provide economic necessities, and even with both partners working, families with children are particularly vulnerable to economic hardship (Lero, 2003).

An increase in single-parent families has happened in Canada over the past few decades, with 14.5% of all families headed by single parents, according to the 1996 Census. Some have estimated that as many as one-third of all mothers will be single at some point in the life of their children (Lynn, 2003). According to the Vanier Institute on the Family, rates of single parenting, attendant rates of poverty, and lower educational attainment levels are higher among aboriginal families (Lynn, 2003). In Quebec equal numbers of children are born to married and unmarried parents (Lynn, 2003). Rates of single parenting are also higher among families where the mother has a disability (Blackford & Israelite, 2003).

Children may experience some of their formative years in a stepfamily. Statistics

Canada identifies stepfamilies as 10% of all couples with children in 1995 and 12% in 2001 (Statistics Canada, 2002). These families tend to have more residential fluidity, a large extended kin network, and a greater number of multiple roles than other families (Church, 2003).

Child Socialization

Child socialization is more a responsibility of mothers than fathers. Indeed research points to the fact that both sons and daughters feel closer to their mothers than their fathers (Eichler, 1997). Mothers have taken on more responsibility for economic contributions to their families without a decrease in time spent in household work and childcare (Duncan, 2000). Lesbian mothers in Canada tend to be more egalitarian than heterosexual mothers, and they socialize their children to be so too (Epstein, 2003).

Child socialization in families with two fathers is characterized in a self–case study by Miller (2003). He suggests his family emphasizes the following values: "brazenness, perversity, flexibility, courage, pride, esprit, and queerness" (pp. 104–118).

Children are expected to behave; parents tend to value corporal punishment for child misbehavior (Durrant, 1995). There is political pressure at the national level to outlaw corporal punishment of children at home and at school, but such changes have not yet been incorporated into the Canadian Criminal Code, which currently allows parents and teachers to use "reasonable force" to control children.

Multigenerational families are rare in Canada. Gee and Mitchell (2003) cite 1996 Census data as having only 208,000 such families but also note that the increase is nearly 40% over the decade from 1986 to 1996. More than one-half of multigenerational families have a single parent in the middle generation, suggesting that divorce is a common reason generations move into the same household. In addition, values show that Asian immigrants also favor multigenerational families (Gee & Mitchell, 2003).

4. GENDER ROLES

Immigrants to Canada from Europe in the 18th century were mainly fishers and farmers, and a patriarchal family system was the norm, in both the English and French communities (Mandell & Momirov, 2000). As industrialization occurred in the 19th century, single women moved to cities to engage in industrial wage work. After marriage, most worked at home (Mandell & Momirov, 2000). As a wage-labor economy emerged in the 20th century, women of the lower class turned to kin for social support, while middle-class families began to glorify privacy and sentimental love in families. Thus a "cult of domesticity" was born (Mandell & Momirov, 2000, p. 37). By the end of the 19th century, child labor laws came into effect, and children were valued for their emotional contributions rather than economic ones. Many immigrant men from other parts of the world (Japan, China, and India, for example) were restricted from bringing families with them to Canada, and they often sent wages home to their families. Also, black women from the Caribbean and Africa worked as domestics, often without being allowed to bring their families to Canada. Even as late as the 1940s, Chinese women were not allowed to work as teachers or nurses, which forced them to work in family-owned businesses (Mandell & Momirov, 2000).

During labor shortages of World War II, Canadian married women began to work for wages outside the home. Increases in female labor-force participation have occurred in every decade since the war, to the point that the majority of married women, even those with infants, are now in the labor force. Some have called their labor-force participation a "double ghetto" of poorly paid wage labor coupled with high amounts of unpaid home labor (Armstrong & Armstrong, cited in Harman, 2000).

Controversy over gender role ideology exists in Canada. On the one hand, feminists and reformists argue that patriarchy and its attendant ideology define and oppress women to the detriment of society (Andrushko, 2003). On the other hand, traditionalists want to "protect" families by encouraging women to accept their "rightful" place. The trend toward equality in men's and women's labor-force participation and family responsibilities has an effect of encouraging adult independence and participation in child-rearing (Beaujot, 2000). For couples with egalitarian roles, the birth of a child is likely to produce a shift to more traditional roles (Fox, cited in Cheal, 2002).

Women tend to work at a job and at home in Canada (Duncan, 2000), much like their Northern European counterparts (Ghysels, 2000). The result is a feeling of being "time crunched," a situation particularly felt by parents of young children, especially mothers (Duncan, 2000). Household work is primarily the task of women in Canada. Women in Canada report less time for leisure activities than men, with family leisure activities reported as being "television viewing, hobbies, sports (perhaps more frequently spectator than active), and reading" (Horna, 1989, p. 303). Gender role socialization of children continues to be primarily along traditional lines. Getting Canadian families to the point of a "genderless society" is thus a long way off (Eichler, 1997).

Social policy over time has moved from a male-breadwinner family model to a more egalitarian one, that is, "gradually integrated labor market policy with income support programs" (Baker, 2001, p. 226). Unfortunately, dividing the work of men and women into separate realms, the so-called dual-labor market, still exists, with the result being that women earn less than men. They also have more home responsibilities, with the result that "women, and especially mothers with young children, can be disadvantaged in an already tight job market" (p. 226).

5. MARITAL RELATIONSHIPS: MARRIAGE AND SAME-SEX PARTNERS

Marriage tends to be satisfactory to a large number of Canadians. For example, research by Clearwater and Harvey (1988), using a Manitoba low-income sample of couples, found marital satisfaction high particularly among couples who were satisfied with each other's communication and financial management. Satisfaction with sexual interaction is also important to Canadian couples (Nett, 1988).

Similar to couples in the United States, Canadian couples have been found to experience a decrease in marital satisfaction with the birth of the first child (Cowan & Cowan, 1995). There is a subsequent increase in marital satisfaction when the last child leaves home.

Legal protection for same-sex couples began in 1969 in Canada when Prime Minister Trudeau declared that "the state has no business in the bedrooms of the nation" (Miller, 2003). Discrimination on the basis of sexual orientation is prohibited under the 1982 Charter of Rights and Freedoms, and by 2003 three provincial courts had ruled the definition of marriage should not include the "one man, one woman" words in it ("Gay Marriage Is Legalized," 2003). Despite legal protection, discriminatory practices continue against families with two fathers or two mothers (Epstein, 2003; Miller, 2003). How those practices affect couple relationships needs more scientific investigation.

6. FAMILY STRESSES AND VIOLENCE

Stress in Canadian families is related to lack of time to complete household and work tasks (Duncan, 2000), financial pressures (Harman, 2000), sexual difficulties (Nett, 1988), communication problems (Ambert, 2000), racial discrimination and prejudice (Das Gupta, 2000), and multiple roles in stepfamilies (Church, 2003), to name a few. Families in which a member has a disability also experience stress in managing daily activities (Edelson, 2000), as do families where care for a frail member is needed. For example, the stress on families with a member with Alzheimer's Disease is considerable (Wuest, Noerager, & Irwin, 2001). Stressors are even greater if a member has a stigmatized illness such as AIDS; indeed, a family may be unwilling or unable to care for an HIV/AIDS patient, giving rise to the creation of a family of fictive kin (King & Salter, 2002; Wong-Wylie, Doherty-Poirier, & Kieren, 1999). Stress is also created in families where an addiction is present, causing disruption in ability to work and interact, as well as an increase in the likelihood of violence (Wenger & McKechnie, 2002). Not only are people affected by alcohol or drug addiction, but also with the spread of state-sponsored gambling in recent years; problem gambling is also increasing and causing stress on families (Berry, Fraehlich, & Toderian, 2002).

Violence is also present in Canadian families, creating stress and other long-term effects for members. Keeping in mind that Brownridge and Halli (1999) distinguish between prevalence and incidence, the 1993 Canadian Violence Against Women Survey showed that almost one in three women "experienced violence from an intimate partner" (Duffy & Momirov, 2000, p. 292). Interestingly, Brownridge and Halli's (2001) research using the same nationally representative sample of Canadian women shows that women who cohabit are more likely to experience partner violence than other women. Additionally, rates of violence against women vary by province (Brownridge, 2002). Ristock (2002) shows that lesbian partners in violent relationships receive little of the services available to other Canadian women who are victims of violence.

In addition to violence between partners, children in Canada are subject to a variety of difficulties. Not only is there a large number of children in poor families (1 in 5 by some estimates) who face uncertain futures, but children are also at risk for neglect or maltreatment (Durrant, 1995). Parents may also be too controlling, resulting in anxious or withdrawn children (Mills, Nazar, & Farrell, 2002).

7. DIVORCE, SEPARATION, REMARRIAGE, AND WIDOWHOOD

Divorce rates in Canada are about one-half of the rates in the United States (Ambert, 2000). The rate in 1995 was 2.6 per 1,000 persons (Eshelman & Wilson, 1998). The percentage of couples that divorce within 10 years of marriage has risen from 11% in 1978 to 18% in 1994 (Statistics Canada, cited by Vanier Institute, 2000). Furthermore, a third of all marriages are undertaken by couples in which at least one partner has been married previously.

Canadians are governed by federal divorce laws, which were loosened in 1988 and again in 2002. Current law permits divorce by mutual consent (the so-called no-fault law), and most couples file for divorce on the basis of irreconcilable differences. Property after divorce tends to be divided equally between spouses, as is responsibility for children. The assumption of the courts generally is that "each spouse can attain economic independence and contribute financially to the upkeep of their children"

(Chunn, 2000, p. 236). The recent changes in law are related to child custody, in which parental responsibility is now stressed, following a long-term legal interest in protecting the best interests of the child (Eichler, 1997). Couples are more prone to divorce if they were teens when married, were pregnant at the time of marriage, have low income or education, come from dissimilar backgrounds, or have one partner with a previous marriage (Boyd, cited in Nett, 1988; Gaudry & Harvey, 1992). Separation is generally brief, related to the fact that living separately for a year will convince a court of irreconcilable differences for a divorce to be granted.

Effects of divorce on Canadian children have been investigated. Since mothers generally are awarded custody of their children, and women earn less than men, most children suffer from poverty upon divorce, coupled with moving to a different place, often changing schools in the process (Harman, 2000). In fact, "the proportion of children entering a low-income situation jumped almost five times" after a parent's divorce, compared with the rate of entry into poverty for other reasons (Cheal, 2002, p. 43).

Remarriage rates of divorced persons are relatively high in Canada, suggesting that people who get tired of a particular spouse have not rejected the institution of marriage. The most recent trends for women include somewhat lower remarriage rates than for men (Ambert, 2000).

If stepfamilies are created by remarriage, then boundary ambiguity (not knowing who is in and who is out of the family) is likely to occur, at least in the early stages of the remarriage (Boss, 2002). Such ambiguity is stressful for stepfamilies (Eshelman & Wilson, 1998), and the relationships are extremely complex (Eichler, 1997). Indeed Eichler identifies eight different types of father roles that are possible, as well as the myriad of roles of mothers, grandparents, and other kin. She suggests fathers can be biological or not, socially responsible for children or not, and the only father figure in the child's life or not (Eichler, 1997). Besides the confusion over roles and responsibilities, stepfamilies also have to work out residence, visitations to the noncustodial parent and his or her kin, and money.

Most marriages in Canada are dissolved by the death of one partner. Since Canadians are long-lived, many marriages are intact over a period of 50 years or more. The surviving spouse is generally a woman, since women marry men older than themselves, men die sooner, and men remarry if widowed (Martin Matthews, 2000). The age and gender-specific rates of widowhood show that the majority of women in Canada are widowed by the time they are 65, while the average man is widowed at age 80 (Martin Matthews, 2000). Widowhood for women increases chances of poverty, but it does not increase chances of low morale except if accompanied by poverty (Harvey, Barnes, & Greenwood, 1987). Widowhood for men may depress morale, but widowers who participate in household activities have higher morale than others (Harvey, Barnes, Greenwood, & Nyakabwa, 1987). Widowhood may be accompanied by changes in the self, with women expressing more independence (Martin Matthews, 2000).

8. KINSHIP, PROPERTY, AND INHERITANCE

For the dominant white culture in Canada, kinship is "mildly patrilineal" (McDaniel & Tepperman, 2002, p. 8), where women usually take their husband's surname upon marriage, live where husbands have work, and give children the husband's surname. Such actions are based on custom rather than law, except for the province of Quebec, which prohibits women from taking their husband's name (McDaniel & Tepperman, 2002). Women have influence in the kinship groups, often acting as kin-keepers (McDaniel & Tepperman, 2002), arranging family social activities, and maintaining contact with the extended family. The lack of importance of kinship is shown by the lack of specific words to distinguish between the wife's kin and the husband's; for example, *brother-in-law* can refer to the wife's brother, the wife's sister's husband, or the same people on the husband's side.

Property and inheritance laws vary by province in Canada, although some court decisions apply to the whole country. In a famous case heard by the Supreme Court of Canada in 1968, Alberta ranchers named Murdoch divorced. Although Irene Murdock did work on the farm for 25 years, she was given alimony but not one-half of the farm property, for, in the words of the court, she did "the work done by any ranch wife" (Chunn, 2000, p. 239).

In what Chunn (2000) calls the second wave of feminism, begun in the 1960s and continuing to the present, sexual discrimination and dependency have diminished and formal legal equality exists in family law. In general, "separate property rights exist so long as the marriage is intact, but if the relationship dissolves, all marital property is shared equally between the spouses" (Chunn, 2000, p. 236). Further, property is defined as "the usual things such as land, but also deferred-profit-sharing plans, pensions, and interests in estates or trusts" (p. 236). Reforms such as the introduction of parental leave, recognition of women's contributions to marriage (much wider than the interpretation in the Murdoch case), and recognition of property rights in the breakdown of same-sex relationships have contributed to the evolution of family law equality between the sexes.

Intergenerational transfer of income from parents to children has some consequences for offspring. Beaujot (2000) cites a 1998 study by Corak and Heisz that showed "income from assets playing a more significant positive role and income from unemployment insurance playing a negative role" (p. 291) on eventual educational attainment of children. Considering transfers across generations as a whole, therefore, "human capital plays the largest role." However, "financial capital and social capital are also important, while social transfers have a leveling effect" (p. 291).

9. AGING AND DEATH: RETIREMENT, INSTITUTIONAL LIVING, AND CAREGIVING IN FAMILIES

Canada's population is aging. The proportion of people over age 65 was 12% in 1996 and is expected to rise to 14% by 2011 (Martin Matthews, 2000, p. 325). This proportion varies by province, with Manitoba and Saskatchewan having more than 13% elderly, while Alberta has 9.9% and Yukon Territory has less than 5% (p. 325). Of those over 65, about one-third retired before that age.

Older families in Canada have the lowest income of all age-groups except the youngest families (Beaujot, 2000), although on average the income of older persons has risen slightly in recent decades due to the effect of increasing rates of transfer payments. Older people are more likely than younger ones to own their homes outright (Martin Matthews, 2000), and the Canadian Medicare system helps to keep expenses of frail health in older age down. Subsidized housing is also available for some elderly (Martin Matthews, 2000).

Family ties in later life in Canada revolve around spouses, offspring, grandchildren, and siblings. Over one-half of the older population is married; however, with increasing age there is a surplus of widows over widowers (Martin Matthews, 2000). Bearing in mind that couples that are married a long time are different from others and that there is social desirability in telling researchers how satisfied people are, marriages in old age in Canada are reported to be companionate and satisfactory (Connidis, 1994). Since women tend to live longer than men, at advanced ages it is generally wives caring for husbands, although men do expect to care for their wives if needed. Thus, most of the caregiving of frail elderly is done by the spouse (Martin Matthews, 2000). Remarriage by widowed persons is relatively rare among older Canadians, but those who do remarry tend to be males (Rosenthal & Gladstone, 1994).

Over 80% of Canada's elderly have offspring and 10% of the offspring are past 65 years of age themselves, suggesting diversity in families with elderly persons (Martin Matthews, 2000). Generational exchange is provided, with grandparents giving gifts, emotional support, childcare, financial assistance, and advice (Martin Matthews, 2000). Middle-age offspring, on the other hand, particularly daughters, provide emotional support, transportation, and instrumental help if needed, particularly when their mother is widowed. Contact between generations is frequent, with two-thirds of elderly parents visiting with a child weekly or more often, and one-half talk to an offspring every day or two on the telephone (Rosenthal & Gladstone, 1994).

Sibling ties in old age are "more sociable and less obligatory" than ties to spouse or offspring (Connidis, 1994, p. 201). Given that older Canadians are more likely to have a living sibling than a living spouse (over 80% of elderly have a living sibling), it is the case that the sibling relationship is the one of longest duration for most families and therefore has the most potential for support. However, Canadian research on sibling ties is sparse (Connidis, 1994; Martin Matthews, 2000).

Canadians typically become grandparents in midlife, and by old age their grandchildren are usually young adults (Martin Matthews, 2000). The extent to which grandparents are emotionally close to their grandchildren depends in part on geographical proximity (Connidis, cited in Ward, 1994). Contact between these generations is also frequent—once per month or more. Social support by grandparents is given in terms of providing gifts or babysitting, as well as acting as role models and keepers of family history (Rosenthal & Gladstone, 1994).

Caregiving to frail elderly can be stressful. Indeed, more stress is reported by middle-age offspring than by spouses (Morrison, 2001); contradictory findings are also found (Rosenthal & Gladstone, 1994). Women tend to feel filial obligation more than men in Canada, and much of the care work is done by them (Aronson, 1994).

Deaths in Canada generally occur in old age, in hospitals or personal care homes. Palliative care, directed toward comfort and care of dying persons, is available across Canada (Novak, 1993). Furthermore, Canadians can arrange advance directives, specifying the extent to which they want heroic medical intervention to prolong life (Hamel, Guse, Hawranik, & Bond, 2002).

10. FAMILIES AND OTHER SOCIAL INSTITUTIONS

Religion

Religion provides families with a way to perceive the unknown and unknowable and provides for social interaction and a value structure by which to organize family role behavior. Since church and state are officially separate in Canada, families are free to practice the religion of their choice. However, since Christianity is dominant, the state does provide legal holidays around Christian holy days. Researchers at the Vanier Institute of the Family, using Canada's

General Social Survey, 1995 Cycle 10, estimated that Roman Catholics make up 44.9% of Canada's population, Protestants 34.4%, no religion 15.3%, and other 5.6% (Vanier Institute, 2000).

Some religions are so intertwined with social customs and daily practices that they are considered to be religioethnic groups. Old Order Mennonites, for example, are Anabaptist Christians living in Ontario who have set themselves apart from the dominant society. Family practices of Old Order Mennonites are detailed by Peters (2001), who shows that dating is regulated and generally confined to group events, such as singing. Middle-age parents save money to help sons buy farms and prepare daughters to raise families; elders live in *daudy* houses, small homes on the farm of an offspring, and they are helped by family members.

Education

Canadians spend a lot of time in school, attending full time as children and young adults. Adults engage in various educational pursuits, generally on a part-time basis. Education is a provincial responsibility, so variations in school law and practice occur. Attendance is generally required for children, unless parents make special arrangements to provide homeschooling. The population is generally literate, although some immigrants may not be able to read English or French.

Social Welfare

Canadians are able to get transfer payments to assist them. Families who qualify may receive Employment Insurance (EI) when unemployed, Parental Leave for up to a year after the birth of a child at EI rates, or Canada or Quebec Pension after retirement. In addition, provincial or territorial assistance for low-income families, in the form of monetary transfers, tax credits, or supplements for specific expenses such as home repairs may be available. Quebec now offers all families with young children day care for a nominal fee—the only province to do so.

For families unable to care for their children, a child welfare system, controlled by the provinces, exists. Foster families are paid to care for these children, and in some cases adolescents may be placed in group homes.

Economy

Most Canadian heads of household spend the majority of their waking time at work. For married men under age 65, 48% of their time is spent at work, while 43% of married women's time is spent at work (Statistics Canada, Time Use Study of 1998, cited by the Vanier Institute, 2000).

Canadian families vary in their ability to accumulate net worth (difference between assets and liabilities). Using Statistics Canada's Survey of Financial Security, Sauvé (2003) shows that the "top ten percent of households control 45 percent of all the net worth . . . while the bottom 10 percent have no net worth at all (Highlights and Key Findings). More net worth is accumulated by those with university education, by homeowners, and by couples with two or more in the household headed by men. Debts, which are greater among young families, are most commonly home mortgages and credit card and installment debt. Assets typically include pension-related savings, homes, and motor vehicles. The families most likely to have the highest debt relative to assets are headed by single mothers. The largest amount of net worth is held by people over 65 years of age with assets primarily in pension funds and homes (Sauvé, 2003).

Unemployment is a problem for a significant number of families. Citing the 1996 Statistics Canada Survey of Consumer Finances, the Vanier Institute (2000) reports 32% of

Canadian families have at least one member out of work. The rate of unemployment varies by province, with the highest rates in the Atlantic region.

Not only does unemployment contribute to poverty in families, but wages are low for some workers. Indeed, 87% of female low-income single parents had earnings, but the amount was insufficient to get them above the poverty line (Vanier Institute, 2000).

Families do various things to balance demands of work with family life, particularly care of young children (Cheal, 2002). Strategies used include home-based work, work at nonstandard times of the day, work practice alteration, reduction of work hours, change of household division of labor, and use of childcare or homemaking services.

11. SPECIAL TOPIC: IMMIGRANT, REFUGEE, AND ETHNIC FAMILIES

In this section some special features of Canadian family life will be discussed. A large number of people from all over the world migrate to Canada on an ongoing basis, the result being that 17.4% of the population are immigrants (Statistics Canada, cited by the Vanier Institute, 2000). A discussion of the changes that immigrant and refugee families undergo is therefore in order. Canada allows immigration on the basis of need for specific skilled workers, for family reunification, and as refugees. In the case of immigration for work or to be reunited with family members, new Canadians come with some social supports available to them. In the case of refugees, Canada generally allows some housing, transfer payments, and language training for families during the first year of resettlement. The effect on families tends to be a honeymoon stage for the first year or so, followed by disillusionment, and finally some sort of integration into the society (Szekely, 1990).

Young children in immigrant families who do not speak English or French on arrival tend to acquire language rapidly and are thus thrust into the role of gatekeepers, sometimes upsetting previous role allocations (Copeland & Harvey, 1989).

Many immigrants face occupational deflection, particularly when credentials for professional persons such as physicians or engineers are not recognized in Canada. Women who immigrate in the family reunification class are in a dependent status, assumed to have primary responsibility for childcare (Das Gupta, 2000). Women's dependent status is further reinforced if they are abused in their families, as they risk deportation if they do not stay with their husbands (Das Gupta, 2000).

Selected European Immigrants

European immigration into Canada is generally allowed, although some European Jews were denied entry during World War II. In a study of Italian immigrants to Alberta, Fanella (1999) states that Italians are the fourth most numerous ethnic group in Canada (after English, French, and Germans). A large wave of Italian immigrants, mostly from the south of Italy, came to Canada after World War II. They, like other immigrants, tended to settle in ethnic enclaves. In Calgary, Alberta, for example, there are 10,000 people of Italian descent. Fanella notes their resettlement into Canada involved a process, like other ethnic groups, of "constantly defining and redefining themselves while in the process contributing to change in the society around them" (1999, p. 6). Coming to Calgary from southern Italy, these immigrants were poor and faced discrimination in their country of origin. They were greeted in Canada with stereotyped notions of crime and social disorganization within the community, despite research at the time (see Smith's 1957 report, cited in Fanella, 1999) that showed Italian crime rates to be lower than rates for immigrants from Scandinavia, the United States, or the United Kingdom (Fanella, 1999, p. 50). Italian immigrants met in churches, formed sports clubs such as the soccer one in Calgary, and started businesses. They tended to follow traditional gender roles, but women generally were able to work for wages outside the home, as families needed their financial contributions. Family was highly valued, and *onore* (honor) was emphasized. Children born to immigrants complained that "strict parental control prevented them from being as independent as they wished to be" (Fanella, 1999, p. 74). Marriage signified adult status, and offspring in their 20s were pressured to marry within the community. Even if offspring married non-Italians, they tended to marry within the Roman Catholic faith, and parents insisted that a lavish wedding be performed in church (Fanella, 1999, p. 78). Italio-Canadians were determined to avoid the poverty they felt in Italy, and over time they were successful in getting material goods. By now, successful integration into the dominant society means the demise of "little Italy" and effective community leadership (Fanella, 1999, p. 91).

Similar integration into Canadian life by Portuguese immigrants is described by Noivo (1999). Largely forced out of Portugal by poor economic conditions, families resettled in Canada, with a large wave coming in the 1950s. Women's roles as "helpers" were emphasized, with pressure on women to establish a good home and to contribute to the family income. Portuguese-Canadian women interviewed in Montreal by Noivo negotiated pressures by expanding "their capacity to absorb the multiple contradictions from added roles by distorting several social and political realities" (1999, p. 19), including disregarding or minimizing "the demands that their husbands and children place on them" (1999, p. 19). Like Italians, Portuguese immigrant offspring struggled to gain independence and to marry the people they chose.

Finnish immigration to Canada also peaked in the 1950s. Like the Italians and the Portuguese, Finns tended to settle in ethnic communities. They reproduced Finland in their home life, building Finnish-style bathhouses (*sauna*), participating in ethnic festivals, and establishing clubs where they could speak their own language (Heinonen & Harvey, 2001). By the third generation, Finns had intermarried with Canadians and largely felt no need for ethnic organizations, although many of this group visited the old country regularly and maintained the use of Finnish-style things in their homes.

Immigrants From Asia, India, and Africa

Chinese

In stark contrast to the immigration experiences of Europeans, who were largely able to integrate into Canadian society by the third generation, were the experiences of visible minorities. Often legislated to be allowed into Canada, men without their families came for specific work periods, and their temporary status was reflected in the term used: *sojourners* (Das Gupta, 2000). By 1923 the Chinese Exclusion Act prohibited Chinese immigration altogether, as the need for Chinese laborers to build railways and develop mines had waned. Men already in Canada could not bring their families from China until the act was repealed in 1947 (Guo, 1992). Experiences of early Chinese-Canadian women, therefore, tended to be ones of long separations of 40 years or more from their husbands, followed by immigration to Canada. Later generations of Chinese-Canadians faced discrimination, forcing many to work in family-owned businesses. Second-generation offspring reported, like Shirley Welsh did, working before school in the family restaurant in Saskatchewan, during school lunch break, and after school until midnight closing. "I didn't resent the fact that I was the only one in my family helping my parents. But I guess there was resentment when I worked so hard without any pay" (Guo, 2000, p. 147). Besides work, Chinese-Canadian offspring were expected to do very well in school. Marital endogamy was expected of early generations, but now intermarriage with the dominant society is practiced to some extent. Later Chinese immigrants, particularly from Hong Kong, were "middle class, highly educated, cosmopolitan, and able to speak English" (Das Gupta, 2000, p. 173). Some were "astronauts," maintaining homes in Canada and in Hong Kong.

South Asians

Like the Chinese, men from South Asia were also imported to do work in Canada, and they too were denied the opportunity to bring their families with them. By 1919 women were allowed to enter Canada, but only as wives (Das Gupta, 2000). In early stages of immigration, South Asians were not free to do as other citizens and live where they wished (Dhruvarajan, 1996). By 1967 immigration restrictions were lifted, and a point system that did not consider race was implemented. Since then South Asian immigration has been by professional and technical workers who have come with their families (Das Gupta, 2000). These immigrants tended to hold traditional roles for men and women, and marriages continued to be arranged by parents. Some South Asians continue arranged marriage practices today (Dhruvarajan, 1996).

Vietnamese

Vietnamese refugee immigration to Canada peaked in the early 1980s. Emphasizing a collectivist orientation and stressing the importance of family lineage, the Vietnamese tried to help the most employable persons

immigrate. The idea was for that person to settle in Canada and then sponsor other family members. If family members were missing or had died, substitute kin were arranged (Johnson, 2003). Using quantitative methods, Vietnamese immigrants to Vancouver were interviewed by Johnson and her colleagues. The third wave of interviews was conducted in 1991–1993 with 647 respondents who originally came as boat people between 1979 and 1981. Results of an investigation of financial beliefs and practices showed that family needs took precedence over individual ones. On the other hand, respondents were pragmatic and felt that low-income or elderly person transfer payments, available to all Canadians, were all right to accept (Johnson, 2003).

Japanese

Japanese immigrants to Canada in the early 1900s were far fewer than Chinese, due to an agreement with the Japanese government that restricted their exodus (Das Gupta, 2000). Among early workers, men who wanted to marry were unable to return to Japan to find brides and thus resorted to introductions by mail, the so-called picture brides. By the time of the Japanese attack on Pearl Harbor, Canadians, like Americans, were so anti-Japanese that they forced Japanese-Canadians from the Pacific Coast inland to relocation camps and seized their property. It was not until the 1990s that Canada officially apologized to the Japanese-Canadians for the treatment they received during the war. Intermarriage by *sansei* (second generation) is 59% (Das Gupta, 2000), and third-generation rates are even higher.

Blacks From Africa, the United States, and the Caribbean

Canadian blacks have come in different time periods, and from different places. Early immigration by blacks was as slaves. From "the late 1600's until the early 1800's, black slaves were held in Quebec, Nova Scotia, New Brunswick, and Ontario" (Calliste, 2003). After the American revolution of 1776, many British loyalists, including blacks, came to Canada. Blacks were freed by the British government, which controlled Canada at the time, and were promised land that they never received. Later, during the American Civil War (1865), blacks came to Canada, largely to Ontario, clandestinely in the "underground railroad," a perilous journey over land, to avoid slavery.

Black women who came from Africa and the Caribbean to Canada after World War II to work were channeled by immigration policy into jobs as domestics. Many were not allowed to bring their families with them. These women faced "low rates of pay, seasonal layoffs, and lack of trade unionization" (Mandell & Momirov, 2000, p. 40).

Racial discrimination and occupational deflection confronted black African immigrants who came in the 1980s (Nyakabwa & Harvey, 1990). Many were denied the opportunity to use their professional qualifications in Canada, necessitating retraining or working at a lower-status job, a practice that continues today. Some come as refugees from Eritrea, Sudan, and other countries, with some of these immigrants being professionals.

FUTURE DIRECTIONS AND TRENDS

In sum, certain trends in Canadian family life are likely to continue for the next 25 years. Families will continue to include a small number of people, late parenthood, and a rise in infertility. Children are likely to spend more time in single-parent households, generally residing with mothers. The number and proportion of elderly persons will continue to rise, with a corresponding increase in family groups with four or five generations.

Because of changes in law and social customs, there will be more divorces and more same-sex unions, including marriages. The gap in income between the rich and the poor is unlikely to disappear. Public pressure for support for families with young children is likely to increase, particularly if the results from Quebec's current policies are favorable. There will be pressure also for the size of transfer payments to increase, largely to reduce the numbers of children living in poverty, and governments and private companies will be asked to compensate families for care of frail members.

REFERENCES

Ambert, A. M. (2000). Children's role in the parent-child relationship: An interactive perspective on socialization. In N. Mandell & A. Duffy (Eds.), *Canadian families: Diversity, conflict, and change* (2nd ed., pp. 48–77). Toronto: Harcourt Brace Canada.

Andrushko, K. (2003). "Are we there yet?" The quest for gender equity in family analysis. *Canadian Home Economics Journal, 52,* 29–32.

Aronson, J. (1994). Women's sense of responsibility for the care of old people: "But who else is going to do it?" In V. Marshall & B. McPherson (Eds.), *Aging: Canadian perspectives* (pp. 175–194). Peterborough, ON: Broadview Press.

Baker, M. (2001). *Families: Labor and love.* Vancouver: UBC Press.

Beaujot, R. (2000). *Earning and caring in Canadian families.* Peterborough, ON: Broadview Press.

Berry, R. E., Fraehlich, C., & Toderian, S. (2002). *Northwestern Ontario women's experiences with gambling and problem gambling.* Report for the Ontario Problem Gambling Research Centre. Winnipeg: University of Manitoba.

Blackford, K. A., & Israelite, N. K. (2003). Families and parents with disabilities. In M. Lynn (Ed.), *Voices: Essays on Canadian families* (2nd ed., pp. 131–151). Scarborough, ON: Thomson Nelson.

Boss, P. (2002). *Family stress management: A contextual approach* (2nd ed.). Thousand Oaks, CA: Sage Publications.

Brownridge, D. A. (2002). Cultural variation in male partner violence against women: A comparison of Quebec with the rest of Canada. *Violence Against Women, 8,* 87–115.

Brownridge, D. A. (forthcoming). Understanding women's heightened risk of violence in common-law unions: Revisiting the selection and relationship hypothesis. *Violence Against Women.*

Brownridge, D. A., & Halli, S. S. (1999). Measuring family violence: The conceptualization and utilization of prevalence and incidence rates. *Journal of Family Violence, 14,* 333–350.

Brownridge, D. A., & Halli, S. S. (2001). *Explaining violence against women in Canada.* Lexington, MA: Lexington Books.

Calliste, A. (2003). Black families in Canada: Exploring interconnections of race, class and gender. In M. Lynn (Ed.), *Voices: Essays on Canadian families* (2nd ed., pp. 199–220). Toronto: Thomson Nelson.

Cheal, D. (2002). *Sociology of family life.* New York: Palgrave.

Chunn, D. E. (2000). "Politicizing the personal": Feminism, law, and public policy. In N. Mandell & A. Duffy (Eds.), *Canadian families: Diversity, conflict, and change* (pp. 225–259). Toronto: Harcourt Brace Canada.

Church, E. (2003). Kinship and step-families. In M. Lynn (Ed.), *Voices: Essays on Canadian families* (2nd ed., pp. 55–75). Scarborough, ON: Thomson Nelson.

Clearwater, E., & Harvey, C. D. H. (1988). Correlates of marital satisfaction in a Manitoba low income sample. *Journal of Consumer Studies and Home Economics, 12,* 183–197.

Connidis, I. A. (1994). Growing up and old together: Some observations on families in later life. In V. Marshall & B. McPherson (Eds.), *Aging: Canadian perspectives* (pp. 195–205). Toronto: Broadview Press.

Copeland, N. H., & Harvey, C. D. H. (1989). Refugee adaptation: The case of Southeast Asian adolescents and young adults in a Western Canadian city. *Canadian Home Economics Journal, 39,* 163–168.

Cowan, C. P., & Cowan, P. A. (1995). Interventions to ease the transition to parenthood: Why they are needed and what they can do. *Family Relations, 44,* 412–424.

Das Gupta, T. (2000). Families of native people, immigrants, and people of colour. In N. Mandell & A. Duffy (Eds.), *Canadian families: Diversity, conflict, and change* (pp. 146–187). Toronto: Harcourt Brace Canada.

Dhruvarajan, V. (1996). Hindu Indo-Canadian families. In M. Lynn (Ed.), *Voices: Essays on Canadian families* (pp. 301–328). Toronto: Nelson Canada.

Duffy, A., & Momirov, J. (2000). Family violence: Issues and advances at the end of the twentieth century. In N. Mandell & A. Duffy (Eds.), *Canadian families: Diversity, conflict, and change* (2nd ed., pp. 290–322). Toronto: Harcourt Brace Canada.

Duncan, K. A. (2000). Balancing employment and household work activities: The role of workplace location. In C. D. H. Harvey (Ed.), *Walking a tightrope: Meeting the challenges of work and family* (pp. 117–132). Aldershoot, UK: Ashgate.

Durrant, J. E. (1995). Culture, corporal punishment and child abuse. In K. Covell (Ed.), *Readings in child development* (pp. 28–48). Toronto: Nelson Canada.

Edelson, M. (2000). *My journey with Jake: A memoir of parenting and disability.* Toronto: Between the Lines.

Eichler, M. (1997). *Family shifts: Families, policies, and gender equality.* Don Mills, ON: Oxford University Press.

Epstein, R. (2003). Lesbian families. In M. Lynn (Ed.), *Voices: Essays on Canadian families* (2nd ed., pp. 76–102). Scarborough, ON: Thomson Nelson.

Eshelman, J. R., & Wilson, S. J. (1998). *The family* (2nd Canadian ed.). Scarborough, ON: Prentice-Hall Canada.

Fanella, A. (1999). *With heart and soul: Calgary's Italian community.* Calgary, AL: University of Calgary Press.

Fiske, J. A., & Johnny, R. (2003). The Lake Babine First Nation family: Yesterday and today. In M. Lynn (Ed.), *Voices: Essays on Canadian families* (2nd ed., pp. 181–198). Scarborough, ON: Thomson Nelson.

Gaudry, J. M., & Harvey, C. D. H. (1992). Adaptation of a family consumer decision model to the initiation of the divorce process. *Canadian Home Economics Journal, 42,* 138–145.

Gay marriage is legalized. (2003, June 11). *Globe and Mail,* p. 1.

Gee, E. M. (2000). Contemporary diversities. In N. Mandell & A. Duffy (Eds.), *Canadian families: Diversity, conflict, and change* (2nd ed., pp. 78–114). Toronto: Harcourt Brace Canada.

Gee, E. M., & Mitchell, B. A. (2003). One roof: Exploring multi-generational households in Canada. In M. Lynn (Ed.), *Voices: Essays on Canadian families* (2nd ed. pp. 291–311). Toronto: Nelson Canada.

Ghysels, J. (2000). Influence of family type on work in Denmark, Belgium and Spain. In C. D. H. Harvey (Ed.), *Walking a tightrope: Meeting the challenges of work and family* (pp. 43–68). Aldershot, UK: Ashgate.

Guo, J. (1992). *Voices of Chinese Canadian women. Toronto,* Canada: Women's Press.

Hamel, F. F., Guse, L. W., Hawranik, P. G., & Bond, J. B. (2002). Advance directives and community-dwelling older adults. *Western Journal of Nursing Research, 24,* 143–158.

Harman, L. D. (2000). Family poverty and economic struggles. In N. Mandell & A. Duffy (Eds.), *Canadian families: Diversity, conflict, and change* (2nd ed., pp. 188–224). Toronto: Harcourt Brace Canada.

Harvey, C. D. H., Barnes, G. E., & Greenwood, L. (1987). Correlates of morale among Canadian widowed persons. *Social Psychiatry, 22,* 65–72.

Harvey, C. D. H., Barnes, G. E., Greenwood, L., & Nyakabwa, R. K. (1987). Activities, religiosity, and morale of Canadian widowed persons. In H. Z. Lopata (Ed.), *Widows: Vol. 2, North America* (pp. 251–272). Durham: Duke University Press.

Heinonen, T., & Harvey, C. D. H. (2001). The social construction of home by Finnish immigrants in Winnipeg, Canada. *Journal of Finnish Studies, 5,* 41–48.

Horna, J. L. A. (1989). Family and leisure. In K. Ishwaran (Ed.), *Family and marriage: Cross cultural perspectives* (pp. 293–306). Toronto: Wall & Thompson.

Joe, R. (1996). *Song of Rita Joe: Autobiography of a Mi'kmaq poet*. Charlottetown, PEI: Ragweed Press.

Johnson, P. J. (2003). Financial responsibility for the family: The case of Southeast Asian refugees in Canada. *Journal of Family and Economic Issues, 24*, 121–142.

King, R., & Salter, S. M. (2002). The "family" context of HIV: A need for comprehensive health and social policies. *AIDS Care, 14*, 261–279.

Krull, C. D. (2003). Pronatalism, feminism, and family policy in Quebec. In M. Lynn (Ed.), *Voices: Essays on Canadian families* (2nd ed., pp. 245–265). Toronto: Nelson Canada.

Lawrenchuk, R., & Harvey, C. D. H. (2000). Parent participation in a Cree and Ojibway Head Start program. In J. Oakes, R. Riewe, S. Koolage, L. Simpson, & N. Schuster (Eds.), *Aboriginal health, identity and resources* (pp. 83–92). Winnipeg: Departments of Native Studies and Zoology and Faculty of Graduate Studies, University of Manitoba.

Lawrenchuk, R., Harvey, C. D. H., & Berkowitz, M. (2002). Parents and children together—The development of the Oshki-majahitowiin Head Start Program. *Early Childhood Matters, 95*, 24–29.

Lero, D. S. (2003). Dual-earner families. In M. Lynn (Ed.), *Voices: Essays on Canadian families* (2nd ed., pp. 6–31). Scarborough, ON: Thomson Nelson.

Lero, D. S., & Brockman, L. M. (1993). Single parent families in Canada: A closer look. In J. Hudson & B. Galaway (Eds.), *Single parent families: Perspectives on research and policy* (pp. 91–114). Toronto: Thompson Educational Publishing.

Lynn, M. (2003). Single-parent families. In M. Lynn (Ed.), *Voices: Essays on Canadian families* (2nd ed., pp. 32–54). Scarborough, ON: Thomson Nelson.

Mandell, N., & Momirov, J. (2000). Family histories. In N. Mandell & A. Duffy (Eds.), *Canadian families: Diversity, conflict, and change* (2nd ed., pp. 17–47). Toronto: Harcourt Brace Canada.

Martin Matthews, A. (2000). Change and diversity in aging families and inter-generational relations. In N. Mandell & A. Duffy (Eds.), *Canadian families: Diversity, conflict and change* (2nd ed., pp. 323–360). Toronto: Harcourt Brace.

McDaniel, S., & Tepperman, L. (2002). *Close Relations: An introduction to the sociology of families*. Toronto: Prentice Hall.

McIntyre, L., Connor, S. K., & Warren, J. (2000). Child hunger in Canada: Results of the 1994 National Longitudinal Survey of Children and Youth. *Canadian Medical Association Journal, 163*, 961–966.

Miller, J. (2003). Out family values. In M. Lynn (Ed.), *Voices: Essays on Canadian families* (2nd ed., pp. 103–130). Scarborough, ON: Thomson Nelson.

Mills, R. S. L., Nazar, J., & Farrell, K. M. (2002). Child and parent perceptions of hurtful messages. *Journal of Social and Personal Relationships, 19*, 731–754.

Morrison, L. C. D. (2001). *Understanding subjective family burden in elder care*. Unpublished master's thesis, University of Manitoba, Winnipeg, Manitoba, Canada.

Multiculturalism Act. (1985). Retrieved June 7, 2004, from http://lois.justice.gc.ca/en/c-18.7/.

Nett, E. (1988). *Canadian families: Past and Present*. Toronto: Butterworths.

Noivo, E. (1999). *Inside ethnic families: Three generations of Portuguese-Canadians*. Montreal: McGill–Queen's University Press.

Novak, M. (1993). *Aging and society: A Canadian perspective.* Toronto: Nelson Canada.

Nyakabwa, K., & Harvey, C. D. H. (1990). Adaptation to Canada: The case of black immigrant women. In V. Dhruvarajan (Ed.), *Women and well-being* (pp. 138–149). Kingston, ON: Queen's University Press.

Ondercin-Bourne, G. (1997). The myth of the traditional family: Diversity in Canadian families. In P. U. Angelini (Ed.), *Our society: Human diversity in Canada* (pp. 241–271). Toronto: ITP Nelson.

Peters, J. E. (2001). The Old Order Mennonites: Application of family life cycle stages. In C. D. H. Harvey (Ed.), *Maintaining our differences: Minority families in multicultural societies* (pp. 1–14). Aldershoot, UK: Ashgate.

Ristock, J. (2002). *No more secrets: Bearing witness to violence in lesbian relationships.* London: Routledge Press.

Rosenthal, C., & Gladstone, J. (1994). Family relationships and support in later life. In V. Marshall & B. McPherson (Eds.), *Aging: Canadian perspectives* (pp. 158–174). Peterborough, ON: Broadview Press.

Ross, D. P., Scott, K., & Kelly, M. (1996). *Child poverty: What are the consequences?* Ottawa: Canadian Council on Social Development.

Sauvé, R. (2003). *The dreams and the reality: Assets, debts and net worth of Canadian households.* Ottawa: Vanier Institute of the Family. Retrieved July 17, 2003, from www.vifamily.ca/library/wealth/wealth.html.

Sev'er, A. (1990). Mate selection patterns of men and women in personal advertisements. *Atlantis: A Women's Studies Journal, 15,* 70–76.

Spector, A. N., & Klodawsky, F. (1993). The housing needs of single parent families in Canada: A dilemma for the 1990s. In J. Hudson & B. Galaway (Eds.), *Single parent families: Perspectives on research and policy* (pp. 239–252). Toronto: Thompson Educational Publishing.

Statistics Canada. (2002). *Profile of Canadian families and households: Diversification continuing* (96F0030X1G2001 003). Ottawa: Author.

Statistics Canada. (2003). *Results of 2001 Census.* Retrieved June 17, 2003, from www.statcan.ca/english/Pgdb/dem039a.html.

Statistics Canada. (2004a). *Origins and visible minorities.* Retrieved June 18, 2004, from www.statcan.com/english/Pgdb/popula.htm>http://www.statcan.com/english/Pgdb/popula.htm.

Statistics Canada. (2004b). *Population of Canada.* Retrieved June 18, 2004, from www.statcan.ca/english/Pgdb/demo02.htm>http://www.statcan.ca/english/Pgdb/demo02.htm.

Steckley, J. (1997). Aboriginal peoples. In P. U. Angelini (Ed.), *Our society: Human diversity in Canada* (pp. 131–158). Toronto: ITP Nelson.

Szekely, E. A. (1990). Immigrant women and the problem of difference. In V. Dhruvarajan (Ed.), *Women and well-being* (pp. 125–137). Montreal: McGill–Queen's University Press.

Vanier Institute of the Family. (2000). Profiling Canada's families II. Ottawa: Vanier Institute. Retrieved June 18, 2004, from www.vifamily.ca/library/profiling2/profiling2.html>http://www.vifamily.ca/library/profiling2/profiling2.html.

Ward, M. (1994). *The family dynamic: A Canadian perspective.* Scarborough, ON: Nelson Canada.

Wenger, L., & McKechnie, B. (2002). *Fast facts on alcohol.* Winnipeg: Addictions Foundation of Manitoba.

Wingert, S. K. (2003). *Women's interaction on an on-line bulletin board for assisted reproductive technology users: A qualitative analysis.* Unpublished master's thesis, University of Manitoba, Winnipeg, Manitoba, Canada.

Women's Book Committee, Chinese Canadian National Council. (1992). *Jin Guo: Voices of Chinese Canadian women.* Toronto: Women's Press.

Wong-Wylie, G., Doherty-Poirier, M., & Kieren, D. (1999). Family structure and functions identified by persons living with HIV/AIDS. *Canadian Home Economics Journal, 49,* 91–96.

Wu, Z. (2000). *Cohabitation: An alternative form of family living.* Don Mills, ON: Oxford University Press.

Wuest, J., Noerager, P., & Irwin, G. W., Sr. (2001). Connected and disconnected support: The impact on the caregiving process in Alzheimer's Disease. *Health Care for Women International, 22,* 115–131.

CHAPTER 25

U.S. Families

BARBARA H. SETTLES

1. INTRODUCTION

American families are diverse in both structures and processes, with much opportunity for each to develop their own paradigms. As noted by Susser, "The concept of the United States itself has a history of shifting frontiers and contested boundaries" (2001, p. 4). From its formation, divisions arose with respect to cultural practices and beliefs. The concern for and protection of privacy by government and communities, and the society's dependence on individual family responsibility for its member's well-being, also allows much greater individual family and household variation and unique lifestyle. Several specific characteristics of American society are woven throughout all the descriptions of various family systems: definition of family, legal considerations, and cultural and historic influences. Because these are specifically intertwined, a brief overview is given before describing American families topically.

Definitions of Family

The *family* in the United States must first be seen as *families*. While there is a patina of similarity that is viewed worldwide as an American cultural interpretation of family, it is not true that American families either act or want to act in these stereotypical patterns. The variety and adaptability of family relationships is a particular strength of this family system (Settles, 1999, 2001c). The roots of this diversity are found in the many cultures represented by immigrants to the New World, the vast regional differences in climate, economy, and specific migrations, and the innovations and integrations of individual families and subcultural groups.

Definitions of family have several functions in the professional study of families, the design and implementation of programs and treatments, education and training of specialists in family studies, and the political and policy discourse and evaluation of the impact on families of different strategies. In

I would like to thank Xuewen Sheng for his assistance in revising the paper, Katie Esposito for library research, Tara Maloney for reading and correcting final drafts, and my husband, Robert A. (Andy) Settles, for Web searching, fact checking, and editing.

the broader society understandings of families are based on personal experiences, media portrayals, and institutional regulation. Theoretically, much attention has been given to the issue of definition in family studies in the United States, as well as internationally—especially in the last 15 years (Settles, Steinmetz, Peterson, & Sussman, 1999). Some aspects of the debate reach everyone in terms of social and economic support and recognition. Exploring a number of conceptual choices in proscribing what is meant by the term *family*, it is possible to leave out groups that are behaving as families or to include households who only share space, not family ties and support. "The fluid quality of the word *family* makes it especially useful for political propagandizing and as a residual variable in societal studies" (Settles, 1986, p. 161). If anything, this political discourse has become more intense in the United States, and the implications have become more critical to the health and well-being of individuals and families (Settles, 1999).

Definitions that are helpful to professionals may conflict with popular views. American families cannot be defined in a simplistic manner without doing damage to programs that propose to help and support families. Throughout the review of family topics in this chapter, one can see that almost every section confronts definitional issues. Among them are boundaries of family reunification in immigration, the open adoption movement, genetic testing of putative fathers for child support, gay and lesbian foster care and adoption, custody and partnership status, stepparent and grandparent scope in caring for children in their households, medical consent and decision making, surrogate and donor rights and responsibilities, and persons who are included in family therapy sessions or mandated interventions with families. How families are viewed both theoretically and in research shapes what advocates and policymakers use as a base for future options.

Legal Considerations in U.S. Families

States Have Legal Prominence

The states within the United States are the primary force in the legal regulation of family status, provision of interventions to assist or otherwise regulate families, and the administration of federal and state family support programs. Family programs may be further localized in their administration by city and rural county government entities, either for implementation or development (Rosen, 1999). Litigation is adversarial in civil and criminal courts, but some family and children's issues may be addressed in the family court system, which provides for differential treatment of children and the sealing of records from public scrutiny. A good lawyer is aware of potential differences in outcome, depending on which judge or court hears the case. Bench law in terms of judicial discretion is crucial in family legal matters. Three major exceptions to state control are as follows: (1) Supreme Court decisions, (2) Congressional legislation requiring states to develop uniform standards in areas such as child support, and (3) the National Conference of Commissioners model codes that shape state policies (Rosen, 1999). This legal complex of local, state, national, and international codes and enforcement creates confusion and controversy, but there is reluctance to give up local culture and needs (Settles, 1999).

National and State Confusion and Conflict in Family Policy

Many areas of family legal practice, that is, adoption, custody, legal requirements for marriage, guardianship of children, the disabled and frail elderly, parental rights, and inheritance illustrate the differences in state laws. However, family scholars have difficulty in finding out how family law and policies operate across states. Recently, a private non-governmental orgnaization (NGO), the Annie E. Casey Foundation, initiated with the National Research Council an analysis of federal resources for knowledge about child and family statistics. Then the foundation supplied the resources for states to track and publish important statistics about children and families (National Research Council, 1995). Areas of policy interest such as aging, caregiving, foster care and adoption, drug and substance abuse prevention, education, labor patterns, and disabilities care are served by government centers or clearing-houses that keep reports and local studies and make them available to scholars and policymakers. Many federal laws affect families or seek to bring some uniformity to a controversial family issue. National family policies influence the entire country primarily in the economic rights and responsibilities of family members and support for issues that are affected by relatively intranational mobil-ity. The absence of a federal family focus has historic roots in establishing individual opportunity and avoiding patronage based on family ties (Bogenschneider, 2002). Kamerman and Kahn (2001) believe that children especially have suffered from a lack of coordinated family policy and comprehen-sive programs that address children's needs. Their comparisons with European programs have been influential in the development of greater interest in family policy in academia in the United States.

Other Legal Issues Affecting Families

The overall balance in the United States between individual liberty and the common good is reflected in the controversies over family law (Henderson & Monroe, 2002). The expansion of personhood to include more individuals and to extend to women, young adults, and minorities legal and social rights has been a major movement over two centuries of national development (Settles, 1998). It has been necessary not only to change the constitution but to provide for means of enforcement through such mech-anisms as civil rights legislation and incentives for state compliance.

While in most institutional interventions that affect families the trends have been toward deinstitutionalization and smaller institutions in community settings, criminal justice has moved in the direction of greater institutionalization, with longer and often mandated sentences served at great distances from home communities (Settles, 1999). This trend has included both state and federal levels with approximately 1 in 37 adults in 2001 having been confined to prison at some time in his or her lifetime (DOJ, 2003). "If the 2001 rates were to continue indefinitely, a black male would have a 1 in 3 chance of going to prison during his lifetime, while a Hispanic male would have a 1 in 6 chance and a white male would have a 1 in 17 chance of going to prison (p. 1)." Prevalence rates are lower for women but have increased dramati-cally (six times greater than in 1970 for women and three times greater for men). Among black males, the rate of adults in 2001 who have ever served time in prison is 16.6%; groups of adults showing lower rates include black females (1.7%), Hispanic males (7.7%), Hispanic females (0.7%), white males (2.6%), and white females (0.3%) (Bonczar, 2003). The likelihood is that the prisoner is younger rather than older, and only one-third of the rise in general is due to an increase in overall population, with crime gun possession peaking at 18 or 19 years of age (Bonczar, 2003; DOT & DOJ, 1999). The enforcement against and definitions of drug and firearms-related crimes as felonies has broadened the numbers of people who are barred from voting and participating in many family support programs including housing. Many employment opportunities discourage or bar felons, and their earnings are often less

(Uggen & Manza, 2002; Western, 2002). This trend has created a large sector of households and families that have limited horizons.

Trends in the Regulation of Families

Recent federal laws affecting families have included (1) initiatives for child support enforcement across state lines, (2) refusal to accept broader definitions of marriage for federally funded governmental programs, (3) adoption regulations that forbid local authorities from blocking cross-cultural or -racial adoptions, (4) model programs for parent education in Head Start preschool programs and substance abuse programs, and (5) welfare reform, or TANF (Temporary Assistance for Needy Families), which presses adolescent mothers to live with parents or other relatives to receive services, and also requires programming to encourage marriage (Moen & Forest, 1999). When researchers wish to compare different states, they face many differences in operation and implementation of federal policies as well as different programs. Vlosky and Monroe (2002) report on the procedures and decisions they went through to tie down the standard dates for divorce law reforms. In some states a clear and simple transition appeared with the adoption of legislation that specified a change to "no fault." In others a more gradual set of amendments to grounds for divorce or length of separation was required, or interpretation of or even repeal and revision of the statutes, which made it uncertain as to when the transition became effective. Devolvement of family and welfare programs at the state and local level has been the hallmark of recent changes at the federal level. The states are strongly influenced from the federal level, especially when financially strong incentives such as child support are at risk (Braver, Cookston, & Cohen, 2002). Policymakers are often unfamiliar with family information in their own constituencies (Bogenschneider, 2002).

Cultural and Historic Influences on U.S. Families

U.S. families have had many innovative alternatives and historic social movements, and experimental and reform groups have been created for social change in the new society. In the early 19th century, there were new communities that featured new family roles and structures and forged different relationships between men and women. These groups introduced "new patterns of religious and social life" and forecast "radical social change, community formation and sex-role organization" in new ways (Foster, 1991, p. 13). More recently, small communal households were founded in the 1970s, perhaps as many as 45,000, and so-called open or multilateral families were started, with a few surviving today (Aidala & Zablocki, 1991; Macklin, 1980). The history of such groups as the Shakers, the Oneida Community, the Amish, and regional and social organizations, such as women's clubs, benevolence, missionary, evangelical, abolitionist, temperance, and labor movements, including family and gender alternatives, has considerable power in the rhetoric of family functioning and values today (Boylan, 2002; Foster, 1991). Some historic experiments and survivals such as the Oneida Community and the Shakers are known now mostly as landmarks and curiosities having tourist interest. In contrast, the Church of Jesus Christ of Latter-Day Saints, sometimes known as the Mormons, having adapted for statehood by dropping polygamy as a doctrine in 1890, has been a fast-growing organization since World War II (Foster, 1991) with strong conservative opinions on family life and gender roles. Their active missionary programs have led to both regional dominance in Utah and surrounding states and strong growth nationally and internationally. Other communities, such as the Hutterites, Old Order Amish, and the Mennonites, have maintained their communities. Kephart (1982) noted that there are at least 1,200 religious groups and over 100 ethnic groups in America. Some early ethnic and religious communities lasted less than a generation, while others have maintained themselves over time (Logan, Alba, & Zhang, 2002). Ethnic communities may become retirement homes for the elder generation or earlier arrivals. In addition, new waves of immigrants arrive in places such as south Philadelphia, where a long-time Italian neighborhood remains with a new influx of Southeast Asians and African-Americans (Young, 1995).

> The history of the migration may not be forgotten in both the enclave and the individual family situation. An oral history may evolve. The "exodus" story may develop to explain how we came, what we were promised, and how it was realized. All of the usual elements of myth and symbol have their place in this narrative. What was it like in the old place? What was it that was lost? What was it that was escaped? Who were the lost kin and what were they like and where are they now? The sense that a family has a story is greater than its current place in one of the continuities in family life, which give a sense of shared meaning and identity. (Settles, 1993, pp. 24–25)

Regional lifestyles and subcultures are numerous with accents, vocabularies, and preferences all their own; for example, Native Americans, Appalachian small farm and coal mining communities, New England mill and farm communities, down-east Maine forests, farms, and fishing, West coast sunshine and outdoor living, company towns, Chesapeake Bay, the Plains, and Mountain regional foci, to name only a few. Analyzing by region has been less frequent in family studies, but new methods of presenting data using models and mapping may allow more attention to be paid to this

element. For example, Hurtling, Grusky, and Van Rompaey (1997) examine migration among the states in terms of regional differences in holding power and migration patterns and demonstrate strong regional patterns. Attempting to put today's families in perspective is limited by myths about what earlier families were like. Many of the rituals we think of as traditional, such as the sit-down family meal, were of recent invention (Coontz, 2000). "There never existed in American society or in western Europe an era when co-residence of three generations in the same household was the dominant pattern" (Hareven, 2000, p. 303). While it is no doubt true that many families were larger in the 19th century, Hareven (2000, p. 12) makes the point that extra adults were often boarders and lodgers. Coontz (2000) suggests we must be especially careful of comparisons with the 1950s, since it was a single, historic, and temporary stage.

The two-party political system that dominates the representative government of the United States depends heavily on major contributors from the private sector and on the ability of organizations such as labor unions and religious conservatives and communities such as Hispanics and African-Americans to deliver voters for the party. The division across the country is not found equally at the state and local level, with some states being frequently in one or another's party camp. While at times the differences between these complex organizations seem quite modest in terms of family programs and policies, the Democrats are often willing to have programs and grants that are administered from the federal level directly for clients, and Republicans tend toward block grants to states with less specific guidelines. The few programs that target families, or regulations that affect family options, usually have some mix of these approaches and are often underfunded. There is no strong set of family advocates among the lobbyists that shapes the information and pressures on the legislative process. Age, religious, and disabilities organizations are found actively trying to shape the agenda. However, there are no organizations that lobby for families except religious conservatives who have a particular view of family programs and policies. The needs of some minority groups also affect how legislation handles family issues. Governmental action is a series of incremental changes still primarily directed at individuals (Moen & Forest, 1999).

Description of American Families and Households

Available Data and Analyses

Changes in family and household composition are normal transitions even when there is no marital disruption, according to Sweet and Bumpass (1987). They suggest that, while family relationships extend beyond household boundaries, households define "a set of primary relationships, a pool of resources and a number of people with whom those resources are shared" (p. 1). However, it is important to note that household data do not reflect the full complexity of family life or how families are defined by themselves, by those who would seek to represent them, or by professionals in the fields related to family studies in the United States (Gubrium & Holstein, 1990; Settles, 1986, 1999). Coontz notes, "The historical changes that have the biggest impact on family organization and values often emerge when incremental and quantitative changes suddenly produce something that is qualitatively new" (2000, p. 292). The challenge is to find appropriate ways of identifying comparable descriptions, even comparable groups, as they are historically constructed. The U.S. Census' primary purpose is for redistricting election units and other governmental applications; however, scholars using

the data have contributed new ideas about the complexity and trends in American families (U.S. Census Bureau, 2003).

Teachman, Tedrow, and Crowder (2000) note that one may want to look at the multiplicity of family types, but that census definitions and measures constrain the comparisons. The U.S. Census does not count families; they count households, a housing unit in which at least one person is living. "A family household has at least two members related by blood, marriage or adoption and one of whom is a householder" (Fields & Casper, 2001, p. 1). However, married couples and even unrelated couples are both equated with households, and common family relationships that extend beyond households are ignored. Controversies over what might be included have raged around each census (M. J. Anderson & Fienberg, 2001). In an interview after his retirement (Settles & Liprie, 1987), Paul Glick shared some of the controversies and concerns that he experienced, including having a minder placed in his office to follow what he was doing in changing forms of questions. Thus, the response patterns also make comparisons difficult. Other large sample surveys and panel studies have supplemented our understanding about families (Teachman, Polonko, & Scanzoni, 1999).

General Descriptors of American Families and Households

According to *U.S. Statistics in Brief* (2003), one can select few statistics to illustrate the situation for families at the turn of the 21st century. Roughly 285 million people live in the United States with approximately 104.7 million households and 72 million families, as defined in the census. About one-quarter of the households were one-person units, and the average number of persons per household was relatively unchanged from 1990 (2.63) to 2000 (2.62). Of the families, 34.6 million had children under 18 years of age. The United States was overwhelmingly rural in 1790 (94.9%) but has become mainly urban in 1990 (75.2%) and in 2000 (79%), with the tipping point coming between the 1910 and 1929 censuses (United States Summary, 1998). Geographically, the population is unevenly spread throughout the nation. The picture is a rim around the edges of the East and West Coasts and a similar northern edge around the Great Lakes and upper Midwest, with the addition of the urban areas in the South and Florida. The center of the country, the Great Plains and desert, have become less populated proportionately since they were settled. "Rural migration is nothing new," as the loss of farmers was well documented throughout the 20th century (Jurich, Collins, & Griffin, 1993, p. 78). Racial and ethnic diversity is also patterned, with cities and the East and West Coast and Southwest having more diversity (*Mapping Census 2000*, n.d.).

Housing and Households

Housing is dominated by owner occupancy in the United States, with 67.8 million of the 107 million occupied housing units reported in 2001. There were 10,424,540 unoccupied housing units reported in 2000. Most (60.3%) units in the occupied housing stock reported in 2000 are single detached homes, an additional 5.6% are attached single units, 17.7% are in small multidwelling structures, 8% are in units with 20 or more, and 7.8% are mobile homes, boats, vans, and so on. The housing stock is relatively new, with only 35% older than 1959 and 17% built in the last decade. Housing units are relatively large, with 94.2% having one or fewer occupants per room, with the median number of rooms per unit being 5.3. The median value of owner-occupied homes in 2000 was $119,600 with 40.3% valued at less than $100,000. The growth market of large and expensive homes is an important

characteristic, with 9.5% of houses valued at over $300,000. There were 313,759 homes (0.6%) valued at $1 million or more. There were 8,929,905 homes (7.7%) with nine or more rooms. The amount of equity householders have in their homes is affected by economic climate and opportunities. In low-interest situations, refinancing is popular and as the economic downturn affected people in the early 21st century, many families took out equity in refinancing and some used that funding for everyday expenses. Seventy percent of owner-occupied units had mortgages with a median payment of $1,088 per month. A good-sized population was living in units with major deficiencies: 670,986 (0.6%) without complete plumbing facilities; 715,535 (0.7%) without complete kitchen facilities; and 2,570,705 (2.4%) without telephone service. Rental housing is divided into many specialty markets. Only 10.4% of renters pay less than $300 per month, with a median rent of $602 in 2000. At the high end, 2.9 % pay more than $2,000 per month. Rental costs are extremely high for the poor, with 29.5% of renters paying 35% or more of their income for housing (*2000 Census Data Sampler*, 2003).

Housing and living arrangements for families and individuals reflect values, available incomes, housing policy, lifestyle choices, regional and rural-urban opportunities, and socioeconomic status. United States housing choices are based on idealization of rural life, seen in an attraction for the suburbs of cities. Having one's own separate house with a yard is almost a requirement for a family with young children (Hardill, 2002). These preferences are used in policy arguments, program development, and media interest. "Home ownership represents the largest investment decision most people will ever make and qualifying for homeownership requires accountability for previous financial decisions and practices" (Osteen & Auberle, 2002, p. 29). Housing policy has encouraged building owner-occupied home units: first, for the very wealthy by interest deductions; second, for the middle class by readily available insured mortgages and expanding the value of house mortgages to reflect both spouses' incomes; and third, in the latest round of federally financed housing projects for the poor, large apartment buildings have been torn down and replaced by detached and semidetached dwellings. There is a rhetoric of ownership even for the poor. Unemployment threatens families with loss of the house and frequently this results in moving in with kin or friends (Langman, 1987). The impact of instability of work on family is a major impetus to family disruption (Voydanoff, 1990). The ability to have an autonomous household is a measure of functioning for the marginally employed (Edin & Lein, 1997) and for the divorced or female-headed households (Orloff, 1993; Settles, 2001a, p. 629).

Homelessness attracts interest because, even in relatively good economic times, it is a problem. Two groups are particularly difficult to address:

1. Mothers with children who have already been in some informal housing option or doubling up and now need another alternative (Letiecq, Anderson, & Koblinsky, 1998). Mothers who have been in emergency shelters or transitional housing usually have smaller networks of support, which may be exacerbated by the rules and polices of those programs, which often cut off telephone privileges and contact with male relatives.

2. The formerly institutionalized mental or addiction patient who is often a male living on the street. Large numbers of the mentally ill live in unwelcoming and threatening environments, or if they live with their parents, with strain and stress (Cook & Wright, 1995).

Sometimes these groups overlap when mothers or adolescents have such problems, but they require specialized resources. Homeless youth and runaways are often unable to turn to family, either due to abusive home relationships or actually being pushed out of the house (Ennett, Bailey, & Federman, 1999). Even a few social ties can make a considerable difference for youth. Currently, most governmental assistance and nonprofit efforts are organized around service-intensive shelters instead of welfare hotels (Bogard, McConnell, Gerstel, & Schwartz, 1999). The wide diversity of homeless people challenges the design of programs to meet the different needs and the theories that underlie them (Pescosolido & Rubin, 2000). Emphasis on the homeless, as in need of treatment for a disability or mental health issue, distracts attention from the relevance of economic decline, underemployment, and the lack of affordable housing. Many governmental housing programs have long waiting lists and complex subsidy programs that require help to navigate.

Commuting and Transportation

Economic and community development from the founding of the United States has been a real estate "hustle" based on speculation and vast land availability. From the air, one can see lines and squares that are applied without much acceptance of land use priorities (Linklater, 2002). This template for surveying was central to the easy transfer and sale of land, and to locating land to be lived on and worked as part of claiming ownership. While 19th- and early-20th-century development included canals, main-line railroads, and light rail, in the 20th century these infrastructures were neglected and destroyed and intercity bus lines were diminished after the development of the interstate highway system and air service. A few large cities continue to have subways and reasonable bus service, but most families depend on driving to get to work and to purchase goods and services, and on school buses to take children to schools. Workers over the age of 16 (128,270,000) mostly commute by car alone (75.7%) with another 12.2% carpooling. Only 4.7% use public transportation, 2.9% walk, 1.2% use other means, and 3.3% work at home. The average travel to work is 25.5 minutes. Only in Washington, D.C. (33.2%) and New York (24.4%) do a significant number of workers use public transportation. In New York City over one-half (52.8%) use public transportation, with a 40-minute mean travel time. Of the 25 largest cities in the United States, only four other cities have more than one-quarter of workers using public transportation (Philadelphia, 25.4%; Chicago, 26.1%; San Francisco, 31.1%; Boston, 32.3%) (*2000 Census Data Sampler*, 2003). Families may have different and conflicting work schedules for spouses and other workers and devote much time to commuting. With suburban living, people often live at great distances from their work. Poor people from the city or very rural areas try to commute to new suburban jobs, and they may be at the mercy of old and undependable cars.

Internal Migration

The availability of land on the frontier and the lack of funds to pay soldiers in the Revolutionary War gave a boost to the movement of people within the states and on the frontier (Linklater, 2002). The opening of new lands and migration across the continent allowed individuals and nuclear families to relocate and recover from economic failures and worn-out agricultural farmlands. An American attitude has been the sense that one could always start over, that one's identity was fluid and open to change, and that anyone could become an American. In the latter part of the 20th century, trading up in real estate in midlife and changing living arrangements at or during retirement to

accommodate different needs occurred. In 2000, 45.9% of the population 5 years and older were living in a different residence than in 1995. One-half of these (24.9%) were living in the same county, while only 8.4% had moved to a different state (Berkner & Faber, 2003). While western expansion dominated the 19th century, in the early 20th century significant numbers of southerners, both black and white, moved north, resulting in rapid growth of northern cities. Often, however, white immigrants were attracted to cities with fewer African-Americans (Tolnay, Crowder, & Adelman, 2002). In the second half of the 20th century, a return migration to the South occurred following the improvement of civil rights, the relocation of many northern plants, improved highways and airline hubs, and the wide availability of air conditioning (Glick, 1993).

In the 2000 Census (Berkner & Faber, 2003) a comparison to 1995 of place of residence found 142,027,000 (54.1%) of those 5 years of age and older to still be in the same house and 112,852,000 (45.9%) in a different house. Most of these moves (65,435,000) (24.9%) were within the same area in the same county and the rest split between the same state (25,327,000), a different state (22,089,000), and 7,496,000 abroad in 1995. The picture in various states has many different dynamics. Large states provide many choices, and different regional economic opportunities attract migrants.

Immigration

"The United States is peopled almost entirely by migrants and their descendents" (Lieberson & Waters, 1988, p. 1). Even Native Americans are thought to be a migrant population from Asia, and in 1980 only 3% of Americans reported being partly indigenous: American Indian, Eskimo, Aleutian, and Hawaiian. The major role of religious, ethnic, and economic discrimination in bringing a wide array of families to America is the story of the country. Categories have undergone numerous changes, with religious and national groups disappearing into larger groups and excluded groups becoming accepted. The census has not regularly asked questions to reveal perceived ethnicity. There is overlap among the meaning of different phrases with, for example, the Scotch-Irish and English/British sometimes being separable and often fused in response patterns (Lieberson & Waters, 1988). Some ethnic groups account for more people than those in their native countries today. Because of a great deal of intermarriage, what ethnicity to acknowledge is a complex decision for each family. Fashion or opportunity influences which ethnicity is recognized and celebrated. Nagel (1995) examined the dramatic increase in people who identify as American Indian, which was not based on population growth but may be better described as a revision of identity, invention, and ethnic renewal built on political activism and new pride.

While there is interest in minority groups, it is important to recognize that *white* is still the dominant identification and European the most common origin, representing three-fourths of those immigrating to the United States between 1820 and 1979 (Lieberson & Waters, 1988). Different ethnic groups were attracted or sent to different parts of the country, and they became defined in terms of those regional and sectional subcultural themes. "Groups which are numerically small in national terms, but highly concentrated locally, can have political and social influence beyond what one would expect given a simple demographic count" (Lieberson & Waters, 1988, p. 54). Armenians are known for their small overall numbers with a well-organized presence in California and high-profile political impact. The settlement of refugee groups in specific towns and chain migration have led to concentrations that give special cultural features to smaller locales. Ethnicity and race are overlapping concepts with many contradictions in definition and impact. We resort to illustrations that lump categories; white, black (African-Americans and foreign-born blacks) and Hispanic (any Latin American origin, originally Mexican-American, usually Spanish speaking, begun in the 1970 census as a question) as categories for examining familial, educational, or other socioeconomic variables. There may be a note on Asian or Pacific Rim and American Indian as different but too few to analyze. [See discussion in Sweet & Bumpass, 1987.) With the 1980 census, the question on parents' place of birth was dropped, and with the 2000 census everyone was given the opportunity to check one or more than one racial/ethnic category from a long list (Glazer, 2001; Prewitt, 2002). Most checked one race (97.6%), while 2.4% checked two or more. Two races were checked by 2.26%, three by 0.145%, four by 0.0135%, five by 0.00307%, and six by 0.000292% or 823 persons (Jones & Smith, 2001). Harris and Sim (2002), analyzing youth data, suggest that fluidity of racial identity has a contextual element and is influenced by the questioning procedure and its context.

The U.S. Immigration and Naturalization Service estimates that 13.5 million foreign-born residents moved to the United States in the 1990s. Most (8.0 million) were in a legal status. The others were illegal, which brought the total of illegals to 7 million in 2000 in the United States (INS, 2003). Many illegal immigrants are encouraged by jobs in the farming sector and other low-wage jobs and can be exploited because of their undocumented status. While in earlier studies of immigration the concern was how immigrants became assimilated, acculturated, and integrated into the American society, many new immigrants are seen as maintaining ties to the home country and developing a transnational stance (Portes,

Haller, & Guarnizo, 2002). In their study of three Latin American groups, Colombian, Dominican, and Salvadoran, they found some support for transnational entrepreneurship based on such ties and providing bridges to keep such ties alive. Now reunions of family groups are common, as there are many communication and transportation routes of access across national borders.

Immigration into the United States is not evenly dispersed across all countries. In the last 6 years (1996–2002), 16.4% of legal immigrants have come from Mexico. Another 29.7% are from four countries combined: India, the People's Republic of China, the Philippines, and Vietnam. Likewise legal immigrants are not dispersed across all states. Two-thirds have chosen to settle in just six states (California, 25.5%; New York, 13.5%; Florida, 9.6%; Texas, 7.9%; New Jersey, 5.5%; and Illinois, 4.7%), the other one-third settled mostly in the Southwest and on the East Coast (BIC, 2002a; 2002b; 2002c, 2003).

Opportunities for Stability and Mobility

The changing global economic scene affects where people live. Beautiful places such as West Virginia (Schwarzweller, Brown, & Mangalam, 1971) and Wyoming have difficulty holding on to their youth due to few good jobs and career ladders. Industrial agriculture is a mature trend, but organic farming has some popularity in contrast to modernization in general. The family farm and the small town are critical to the American ideal way of life, but throughout the heartland and southern United States, small farms and communities are not thriving (Jurich et al., 1993). Without the income of wives and husbands working away from the farm, many more family farms would be lost. In addition, many of the extractive, durable goods, and heavy industries that once

gave good incomes to blue-collar workers have been downsized or eliminated from the economy. Younger, less-educated male workers have fewer opportunities for well-paid work and may in fact earn relatively less than their own fathers at the same points in their life course (Carlin, 1999; Levy & Michel, 1991).

2. PAIRING UP

Americans like to be a part of a couple. Of the population 15 years and older (221,148,671), 54.4% in 2000 were currently married and not separated, with 27% never married and the rest having been married but separated (*2000 Census Data Sampler*, 2003). The median age at first marriage went down for both men and women from a high in 1880 (men, 27; women, 23.5) to 1950 (men, 23.2; women, 20.8), and has now turned upward again (men, 26.8; women, 25.1) (Fields & Casper, 2001), but with less difference in age between husband and wife than previously (Haines, 1996; Sweet & Bumpass, 1987). Haines notes that where there were historically lower ages at marriage for blacks, now this has been reversed with higher ages for both African-American men and women. Goldstein and Kenney (2001) found that the likelihood for women to marry remains high and that being educated is now a plus for eventual marriage. Many spend some time in a cohabiting relationship; in 2000, 4.88 million opposite-sex couples were cohabiting (8.1% of total couples) and 594,000 same-sex couples were living together (1% of total couples), almost equally divided between males and females (Simmons & O'Connell, 2003). Cohabitation for many is a stage toward marriage. A question concerns whether a child living with his or her cohabiting parents should be seen, as policy often does, to be in a single-parent household (Seltzer, 2000). Middle-age and older adults are less frequently in cohabiting relationships, but the numbers are growing with those who are in the sunbelt being more likely to cohabit (Chevan, 1996). When the couple is elderly, other family or economic commitments may block marriage.

While Americans do not marry as young as in the middle of the 20th century, most will marry. Some will marry more than once, divorced men more frequently than divorced women. While there is a body of research on dating and courtship, it seems not to reflect current practice. Opportunity structures vary for potential marriage partners. Older never-married women are often less eligible for marriage, especially as older men choose younger women. Certain immigrant groups also have skewed sex ratios that promote either single status or intermarriage. Trends suggest that the lower rate of marriage for black women will continue. Between 1970 and 1990 the percentage of black women over 18 who were married decreased from 62% to 43%, and for young women under 35 the marriage rate decreased from 49% to 35% (Crowder & Tolnay, 2000). There are many reasons why black women do not find marriage easily available and are married fewer years if they do marry, including a shortage of marriageable black men (Taylor, 2002). High youthful mortality and incarceration rates, poor economic prospects, and the greater out-marriage of economically favored black grooms to nonblack brides shape the pool of possible relationships. The economic situation for African-American families entails a substantial risk of unemployment and earnings interruption, so class may play a part in understanding marriage differences (White & Rogers, 2000). When marriage cannot be taken for granted, other kinds of relationships and household arrangements emerge. The second Bush administration decided to put some support and energy into promoting marriage for those mother-headed households assisted by welfare and

specifically Temporary Assistance for Needy Families (TANF), but it is not easy to alter the structural and social dynamics of single parenthood and other nonmarital arrangements, especially as they are not well researched (E. A. Anderson, Braun, Oravecz, & Kohler, 2003).

Propinquity, especially in schooling and work, is a key factor in relationships, whatever one's ethnicity. Some limited use is made of new technologies (Merkle & Richardson, 2000) and commercial dating services, but most use peer introductions and casual contact in social and work situations. Families may vet the proposed mate, express approval or concern, or arouse the peer network to find possible candidates, but as marriage is delayed, the choice of partners is less and less a family matter (Sprecher & Felmlee, 1992). From a parent's point of view, as time goes by any marriage or long-term relationship may look promising.

Dual employment and job changes are a challenge. Commuter marriages to manage work commitments and opportunities in professional and semiprofessional occupations are becoming more frequent (E. A. Anderson & Spruill, 1993; Hardill, 2002). Displacement in working-class families more often causes the whole family to move to a new community. The concept of living apart together (LAT) that has been focused on in Europe is less visible to researchers and the public here (Seltzer, 2000; Trost, 1998).

One of the major shifts in couple relationships is the increasingly open acceptance of homosexual couples and their ability to continue kinship ties. Parents and siblings have been more supportive and accepting of long-term relationships as familial. While there is a huge controversy over the legal and normative basis of support, benefits and legal supports are increasingly being offered to same-sex couples. In some locales those opposed to such families have sought and obtained legal regulations opposing these changes (Stacey & Biblarz, 2001). Policies vary widely state by state and municipality by municipality. Public response to homosexuality includes a growing reluctance to restrict the civil liberties of homosexuals, but a slower change in terms of accepting the morality of the practice (Loftus, 2001). The interest in adopting and having children by modern technologies has blunted the attitude of parents that the homosexuality of an adult child may end the family trajectory to a future. Being a grandparent could become increasingly likely, whatever one's offspring's sexual orientation. "Ultimately, lesbian and gay couples and parents might come to be viewed as couples and parents like others . . ." (Patterson, 2000, p. 1065).

3. FERTILITY AND SOCIALIZATION OF CHILDREN

Fertility

Although the baby boom (1946–1964) resulted in an increase in fertility and produced a smaller ripple a generation later, generally family size has continued the downward trend (Hernandez, 1995). Americans see having children as satisfying and important, although they view it more as voluntary than as something one ought to do (Thornton & Young-DeMarco, 2001). The desired family size continues to be closer to two than one child, and certain subgroups have preferences for larger completed family size. While the birthrate per 1,000 had dropped from 1990 (at 16.7) to 14.7 in 2000 and 14.5 in 2001, the fertility rate for 2000 was 2.130, slightly higher than in 1990, which was 2.087 (U.S. Statistics in Brief, 2003). The ideal is to have two children, one boy and one girl, but having both of the same sex is not a strong push for another child, as it seemed to be in the last century (Pollard & Morgan, 2002). Unplanned pregnancies have

been reduced dramatically (Friedman, Hechter, & Kanazawa, 1999). Unwanted children do still affect family and individual lives, and result from a dynamic set of opinions over timing, context, and alternatives (Barber, Axinn, & Thornton, 1999). Although abortion is legal and usually available in urban areas, the ongoing political and social controversy and ambivalence make choosing to terminate a pregnancy difficult—especially for teenagers needing parental consent (Teachman et al., 1999). Most childbearing occurs in a committed relationship, and postponing childbirth leads to greater probability of childlessness (Heaton, Jacobson, & Holland, 1999). Black Americans are less likely to be postponers and have children significantly earlier (Taylor, 2002). Greater fertility tracks with immigration levels, especially for Hispanics, who tend to favor younger adults still in their fertile years (Prewitt, 2002). If immigration is reduced, the ratios of young to old decrease. Older couples may expect to have a child and may use fertility technologies or adopt a child, often internationally. The privileging of upper income and health-insured families in using reproductive technologies is an unsettled policy question (Moen & Forest, 1999).

The percentage of one-parent households with children under 18 has risen from 24% in 1990 to 27% in 2000 (U.S. Statistics in Brief, 2003). Separation, divorce, and widowhood account for most of these families. The rise in teens that have out-of-wedlock births is accompanied by a general drop in birthrates for this same age-group, as there are fewer-married teens having children (Elo, King, & Furstenberg, 1999). Most nonmarital births are to women in their 20s, many of whom are disadvantaged economically (Driscoll et al., 1999). The practice of having children in a cohabiting relationship is not so common as in Europe, although it has increased from 12% in the 1980s to 15% in the 1990s (Seltzer, 2000), and having children may be a reason to marry. Remarriage may also account for some of the slightly higher reproductive patterns of Americans, with about one-half of women giving birth to at least one child (Coleman, Ganong, & Fine, 2000).

Socialization of Children

The roles of parents and other adults in the lives of children vary with socioeconomic trends and housing arrangements. Although a short-term anomaly occurred in the baby boom after World War II, the long-term trends saw adults spending less of their lives with children in their homes (Goldscheider, Hogan, & Bures, 2001). Patterns of custody after divorce and remarriage give men less opportunity to live with their own children and greater opportunity to be involved with children of a new spouse. "From the perspective of children, families are increasingly likely to be in more than one household, with one biological parent, typically the father, living in a separate household" (Manning & Smock, 2000, p. 111).

Attachment of children to parents, especially mothers, has dominated the research on parenting over the last half-century. The works of Bowlby, Ainsworth, and others shaped attention toward parenting and suggested that the primal tie and foundation of family life was the mother/child dyad (Demo & Cox, 2000). This theme affected legal practice in placement of children in custody with the emphasis being on the "tender years doctrine," which awarded young children to their mothers (Rosen, 1999, p. 562). If there was a conflict, the "best interests of the child" concept, built on psychoanalytic concepts, usually focused on the mother. Mother–child interaction has long been central to programs such as childbirth education and early intervention. Parent education programs have focused on families with young children and youth thought to be at risk (Settles, Davis,

Grasse-Bachman, Janvier, & Rosas, 2000). Concern for parents' involvement in the education of their children, and in providing appropriate enrichment activities for their schoolchildren, has been a major issue in school reform in the early 21st century (Bowen & Bowen, 1998).

Previously, the view of fathers and stepfathers focused on paternity, material support, and some recreational or disciplinary interaction. The role of fathers in childhood socialization is still a puzzle, and the new attention to fatherhood in professional and political fields reflects changes in expectations for a nurturing father (Palkovitz, 2002a, 2002b). In new parents' expectations for each other, concern of fathers to provide for their families remains salient, with both parents also expecting high participation of fathers in support for their new family member, and wives expecting somewhat less help than fathers think they will give (Fox, Bruce, & Combs-Orme, 2000). Mothers may serve as gatekeepers to fathers' involvement with their children (Doherty, Kouneski, & Erickson, 1998). Early involvement with young children leads toward later involvement, as fathers develop a "taste for active child rearing" (Aldous, Mulligan, & Bjarnason, 1998, p. 818). Amato and Gilbreth (1999) reviewed a broad spectrum of studies on nonresident fathers and found that the content of visits was more important in good outcomes than simply frequency. King and Heard (1999) suggest that conflict and satisfaction with the mother may influence outcomes with children, although most children do well regardless of family type. In a qualitative study of single young men who were asked about their visions of and readiness for fatherhood, the themes were being a good provider, spending time with their children and being actively involved in their lives, and the importance of biological fatherhood (Marsiglio, Hutchinson, & Cohan, 2000).

The way children and adolescents spend their time, and how parents try to structure those choices, has been affected by the changing participation of parents in the workforce and the availability of alternatives for children's activities and supervision. Hofferth and Sandberg (2001) analyzed how children under 13 spent their time in a 1997 study, noting that American children of school age (6–12) spend 32 to 33 hours a week in school including travel time, with preschool children spending 12 hours a day. Day care adds from .5 to 1.75 hours to the school-age child's day. The free time children have is split between unstructured play (15 hours) and television watching (12 hours), with about 9 hours of structured activities such as sports, clubs, and lessons. Children whose mothers are employed spend less time watching television, more in day care, and less time in other activities including sleep and play. Family time and housework do not vary by parental work patterns, with the most frequent shared housework activity being shopping. Daly (2001) has noted, in his analysis of how families assess their time use, that feeling guilty or rushed has as much to do with the ideals of what family time should be like as what is actually done.

Although young and elementary-age children are expected to need parental inputs, adolescents also respond to parental inputs with their choices of behavior and attitudes. In a study of rural teenagers on health risk and lifestyle, adolescents appeared to model parents' risk behavior with boys following the fathers' and girls following mothers' patterns (Wickrama, Conger, Wallace, & Elder, 1999). Age at first intercourse has leveled off, but "the gap between the onset of sexual activity and marriage is huge compared with what it was in the 1950's" (Furstenberg, 2000, p. 899). Parents appear to monitor young teens' activities and relax older adolescents' rules, with black

parents being more restrictive (Furstenberg, Cook, Eccles, Elder, & Sameroff, 1999). Parenting is an essential influence, but it is not a simple set of practices and must be responsive to children's changing capacities and circumstances (Furstenberg et al., 1999, p. 214). The very real risks of adolescence and young adulthood in America are found in drug and substance abuse, including binge drinking; accidents, especially in driving; increased criminal prosecution and harsher sentences; health and decision-making issues such as pregnancy, venereal disease, nutrition, and anorexia; mental health; and suicide rates (Steinmetz, 1999). The dynamic quality of socialization across time and situations appears to be essential, and many parents find appropriate resources that suit their adolescent's needs.

Greater investment in each child, with fewer children being born at a later stage in the parents' life course, has changed the way fertility and socialization interact in America. Longer adolescence and greater sponsorship by parents in young adulthood are based in part on the changing economic situation, but also on changing dynamics of the parent–child relationship.

4. GENDER ROLES

Sexuality and Gender

While sexualization of everyday media and public activities is seen internationally as a major American social norm and cultural export, there is ambivalence in the American media and political discourse. There is extreme rejection of sex education and sexually oriented materials and what is seen as pornography by some influential religious and socially conservative groups, but in sharp contrast there is support for sexual education by many parents and family life and health educators across the life span

(Francoeur & Hendrixson, 1999; Powell & Cassidy, 2001).

The conceptual relationship between sexuality and gender in family life is often confused and misapplied, and terms have different meanings and measures (Francoeur & Hendrixson, 1999). The delineation of a conceptual difference between sexuality and gender has been a useful tool in sociology and feminist thought, as it has drawn attention to the socially constructed meaning of gender and how the content of gendered roles changes (L. Thompson & Walker, 1995). In marriage or cohabitation, including same-sex partnerships, there may well be a negotiated gendered relationship that does not follow stereotypes (Patterson, 2000). People say they do the activities that suit their skills and interests and, if this overlaps with the traditional gendered roles, claim it is by choice.

While a type of serial monogamy dominates the way people understand sexuality, enough of a double standard remains to excuse men from a full expectation of monogamous sexual commitment. Most Americans (70% to 80%) express complete disapproval of extramarital sexual activity and low rates of extramarital sex have been reported recently (4% in past year, cumulative rates at least once of 25% of married men and 15% of married women (Christopher & Sprecher, 2000). At least as far as the U.S. media are concerned, women are supposed to break off relationships with men who are known to be unfaithful or otherwise abusive. Privacy can protect secret behaviors, and when the behavior becomes public, action is expected (Fox, 1999).

Gender and Employment

The greater participation of women in the workplace has gender role implications. Earning an income gives more personal freedom in the family and provides identity and accomplishment that may improve self-esteem and efficacy for action in unhappy situations. Women's employment cushions men from the full impact of being a breadwinner. Sweeney suggests that contrary to Becker's earlier economic theory that posited a specialization of men in work and women in home roles as being conducive to marriage, today's marriage choices may be enhanced by women's work and prospects. This follows Oppenheimer's argument that the choice to marry is affected by affordability of a standard of living. Consumption patterns may alter the context of marriage formation (Sweeney, 2000, p. 134).

The movement of women into new fields of work appears liberating, until the continuing difference between men's and women's wages is examined. The earnings gap between men and women has not gone away, although it has continued to narrow, with women working more hours, and for the first time men's incomes have stagnated especially among the young adults (White & Rogers, 2000). Gains in economic status in the last decade were unequally distributed, with most increases going to the top 20% and declines being found in the lower two quintiles. Some of the difference may be attributable in the United States to women, with only one-third of the difference being explained by type of past job experience and seniority and with young women who have children having about a 7% additional penalty (Budig & England, 2001). While most women with children work outside the home, many religious and social groups do not support this trend (Haas, 1999).

Most poor families cannot cover their expenses from welfare programs alone. Many women work "off the books," receive help from boyfriends and relatives, and otherwise struggle to provide. Part of the political force to put welfare women to work in the last decade came from the realization that they were the only group not expected to support their family and forbidden to augment their government income with employment (Edin & Lein, 1997). Stay-at-home mothers today are now expected to justify their situation, often homeschooling the children and working from home to provide economic support (Barbour & Barbour, 1997).

Gender, Home, and Housework

In women's studies and family research, housework has been treated as a symbolic indicator of gender equity (Coltrane, 2000; Oakley, 1974; L. Thompson & Walker, 1995). The dynamics of assigning tasks and dividing responsibility and time spent in activities are of interest in terms of this line of research. In earlier work in home economics, housework was treated as work done at home and examined for how it might be altered or managed to be less physically and energy demanding (Settles, 1995; Vanek, 1974; Walker & Woods, 1976).

Knudsen-Martin and Mahoney point out that

> marital equality involves much more than the division of household labor. Much of the negotiations of gender roles and egalitarian values involves creating a myth of equality by avoiding confrontations and framing what exists as fair if not equal. Conscious and direct negotiation might allow issues to be addressed but avoidance of conflict also seems important to young couples beginning their marriages. (1998, p. 82)

Using housework to estimate gender role allocations must be seen in the context of the lack of personal services for households and childcare in the United States, with few Americans ever having regular help beyond a teenage babysitter or lawn service. Few families have household help outside of family members, though the house size has increased (Robinson & Milkie, 1998). Some help is provided by family and neighbors, especially for African-Americans and Hispanics, but finding alternative, quality, stable care is a challenge to working families (Perry-Jenkins, Repetti, & Crouter, 2000; Uttal, 1999). Women with more economic resources may buy services and employ immigrant or minority women to help them with home or other services (Coltrane, 2000). Cohabitants and same-sex couples are more likely to have egalitarian splits on household tasks than married couples (Patterson, 2000). Men are more likely to do childcare, transportation, and shopping tasks than formerly in all households—as well as knowing how to cook, clean, and do laundry. Their participation is related both to their own and their wife's gender ideology, with high egalitarian values contributing to men's higher participation (Greenstein, 1996). Much increase in men's proportion of household work comes from women cutting back rather than men increasing their efforts (Bird, 1999). Women take on work, advanced education, and outside activities only as long as they can manage the household so no one else is inconvenienced. Bird (1999) suggests that perceived inequity is more important than the amount and division of household work. For many women, attention to childcare—especially if under difficult economic circumstances—results in anger and depression (Ross & Van Willigen, 1996). Mothers from dual-earner families may do more childcare tasks as a way of feeling competent and being "a good mother" (Ehrenberg, Gearing-Small, Hunter, & Small, 2001). Ambivalence and concern about gendered roles is the current status of familial and societal situations. Women have few cultural norms to guide them regarding caregiving for both the young and the old, household work, negotiating reasonable working conditions and benefits, and gaining support from the men in their lives. Men are not so trapped in breadwinning, "the good provider" role, as their only route to family success, but well-paid employment is still strongly central to couple and gender relationships (Potuchek, 1997). While men's roles seem to have changed less as women's roles have become more complex, with some role overload, increasing egalitarianism seems to be occurring.

Changes in lifestyle, technologies, and leisure often add to the complexity of running households, but they occasionally reduce effort or produce products and services that ease demands on individuals. New products and services alter standards of home life. One reason the number of hours in household tasks is not always reduced by innovation is that the technology allows increase in other home practices. For example, cell phones and computers may enhance communication and monitoring of family members, but they also create an expectation of more contact and coordination.

5. MARITAL RELATIONSHIPS

There are probably more happy marriages than ever before, as happiness is now considered essential. Certainly the bar has been raised on what is a successful marital relationship and a family worth preserving. Most marriages last a long time compared the past, when marriages were often broken by early death or desertion. Married people are healthier and have lower mortality rates according to many American studies (Ross & Mirowsky, 2002). Mental health findings are similar, but how singleness, widowhood, divorce, never being married, and cohabitation affect well-being is less clear (Cotton, 1999). One can have several marriages that each equal in length a lifetime marriage in past times. Fifty-year marriages are routinely celebrated in the newspapers and by great-grandchildren, and once in a while these are

second or third marriages for one or both. Closer similarity of couple ages also encourages longer marriages.

A persistent finding in American family research is a downturn in marital satisfaction with childbearing that is not fully reversed until the children leave home (Twenge, Campbell, & Foster, 2003). This would seem to be counterintuitive for family stability, but it does suggest the need for the couple relationship to maintain content outside of the parental roles to be positive. Marital happiness is linked to parental satisfaction, with mothers more likely to report high satisfaction (Rogers & White, 1998). In their analysis, Rogers and White found that being married or remarried also tracked with satisfaction. Apparently, marital happiness and proneness to divorce changed little since the 1980s. Kiecolt (2003) used the 1973–1994 general social surveys to examine whether job satisfaction and satisfaction with family life had changed and found that satisfaction with family life gained over work satisfaction. Paul Amato, Johnson, Booth, and Rogers (2003) compared their research to an earlier study in 1980 using the same questions with a similar sample and response rates and found little change in marital quality. At the same time there were substantial changes for couples marrying at older ages, which were more likely to be in a second or other remarriage, to be Hispanics or other nonwhites, to be heterogamous dyads, to have cohabited prior to marriage, to be better educated, and to have more economic resources (Amato et al., 2003, p. 17). Generally there were changes toward gender equity, with more women employed and contributing greater income, men contributing more to housework, and both facing greater job demands and sharing decision making. Less traditional views of gender were noted earlier in the chapter, but there is also support for lifelong marriage and religious influence. The amount of marital interaction with shared activities was less frequent in the recent survey. Men seemed less pleased when they did an increased share of housework. Within dyads, the processes that perpetuate couple involvement are studied in smaller in-depth studies. In a study of 129 couples, differences in husbands' and wives' perceptions of marriage were related to their use of maintenance behaviors such as positive, open, affirming actions and shared activities and tasks, with wives having higher likelihood of these behaviors when both partners feel positive about the marriage (Weigal & Ballard-Reisch, 1999). Husbands were more focused on their own satisfaction. Handling conflict well contributes to long-term satisfaction and marital quality. Depression is related to dysfunctional conflict in both clinical and nonclinical depressive symptom groups, with more effect on wives' strategies (Marchand & Hock, 2000).

Retirement may strain a marriage: If a couple's careers are not on the same time frame, one may be disengaging while the other's situation is becoming more exciting. Spending time together may be wonderful, but it also may reveal conflicts and different assumptions. Couples also face hard times when there are health crises or economic issues to be addressed. An interesting finding is that women are less likely to hold onto a couple relationship if their own health is at risk, though they may care for their husbands even at risk to their own health (Price & Rose, 2000).

Couple relationships after divorce are shaped by parental responsibilities. Children create an impetus for a continued but redefined relationship. Women may complain about their former husbands still thinking a sexual relationship is possible. Men are concerned that their role is interpreted as mainly economic support. Being welcome to visit their children may depend on how up-to-date their child support checks are. Negative relationship issues often continue after divorce and may affect children's adjustment. The nonrandom nature of divorce conflates preexisting differences in children and the results of marital breakup (Furstenberg & Kiernan, 2001).

There is a wealth of family therapy literature that focuses on the processes of marital interaction, and quality is seen not just as a marital satisfaction score but rather as an ongoing process involving communication, emotional expression, developing a shared history, and adapting to the inevitable life course changes. The concept of protective factors that has been useful in looking for resilience in children under stress may be an appropriate way to look at marital quality as well.

6. FAMILY STRESSES AND VIOLENCE

The attention to violence, abuse, and underlying stressors in families must be recognized as a change in our understanding of families. Discipline of children, wives, and servants was once accepted in Western culture as including physical punishment (Straus & Gelles, 1986).

> Human beings have a high toleration for everyday violence and mayhem and a highly developed interest in the excitement and entertainment of violence. If you, yourself are in a position of safe viewing, you may tolerate real or fictional violence. In some respects we do not remember the past in terms of violence and risk any better than we do the perception of family and community in past times. (Settles, 1998, p. 271)

Recognition of domestic violence and child and elder abuse is relatively recent. Kemp's evidence of child battering presented in the *Journal of the American Medical Association* in 1962 (Gelles, 1980; J. M. Johnson, 1997) was popularized in the medical, social science, and specifically the family research communities concurrent with the feminist movement in the 1970s. As this caught media and legislative attention, it resulted in major changes in awareness, action, and public opinion. While family boundaries have been sacred, according to Coontz, "the pathologies of family life simply cannot allow concern for 'privacy' to override the need for protection of abused family members" (1989, p. 14).

Frequency and Attention to Violent Behavior

Reported abuse and neglect are much higher than in earlier eras (Gelles & Conte, 1990; Straus & Gelles, 1986), but these statistics may reflect either increased events or increased awareness and legal obligation to report. There is increasing attention to sexual abuse, including pedophilia and incest. The greater availability of shelters and the generally more serious way that domestic violence between spouses is treated have developed concurrently with a raised awareness of other family violence. Sexual assault and coercion by husbands has been recognized as abuse but is not sufficiently addressed by law or research (Christopher & Sprecher, 2000, p. 1007). The greater reporting of violence in poor and disadvantaged settings suggests greater difficulty in maintaining privacy and isolation, as well as the different resources the abuser can bring to bear in the adjudication process.

Lloyd (1991) has suggested that in courtship, notions of romance allow couples to confuse jealousy and violence with love and to engage in relationships that have violent content from the beginning. M. P. Johnson and Ferraro (2000) recommend that partner violence research and literature could benefit from clearer distinctions between violence and control issues. They note that the intimate physical terrorism that receives much attention in the press and service community is not the only type of violence that

should concern us. More attention should be paid to emotional abuse and neglect. M. P. Johnson and Ferraro (2000, p. 956) draw attention to the fact, in a study by Campbell, that many couple victims do take action to end abusive relationships or else to negotiate an end to the violence. In Campbell's study, at the end of 2.5 years, three-quarters of women were no longer in a violent relationship—43% having left and 32% having negotiated change. In the treatment of child abuse, some parents benefit from the linking of developmental information about children with new options for dealing with child resistance. In fact, multiservice programs are more likely than traditional therapeutic interventions to produce change. Likewise, men confronted with domestic violence charges may respond to treatment that helps them take responsibility for their own behavior, although there is debate about whether arrest is a useful strategy (Morris, 1994).

Physical Punishment of Children

While most of the Western world has abandoned corporal punishment and spanking of children, there is still considerable support in the United States, especially among conservative Protestants, for the idea that spanking is not only tolerable but also necessary for moral learning (Ellison & Sherkat, 1993). Most families use physical punishment with toddlers, and, while it declines with older children, nearly one-half of early adolescents in the United States experience corporal punishment from a parent (Turner & Finkelhor, 1996). Depression and other psychological distress is associated with teenagers experiencing such punishment. Straus (1994, 2001) presents both research and theoretical argument to refute this practice's efficacy and to show its link to later problems. Conservative religious and political beliefs do not always reflect the actual behavior of parents toward their children. In a recent qualitative study of a conservative religious group, parents gave a spirited defense of the importance of physical punishment of children as essential to Christian child-rearing, but in another part of the interview they said they did not spank their own children and discussed the positive physical and emotional responses they used to shape their children's behavior (Littles, 2003).

Family stress is related to adaptive strategies, not just to violence. In fact, violence, abuse, and neglect are not the primary responses to stressful events. Family members may pull together to problem-solve, to seek resources, and to initiate action that alleviates the stress. A complex documentation of families in economic, medical, and other stressful situations has shown many families to cope and to rise to a higher level of functioning.

7. DIVORCE, SEPARATION, AND REMARRIAGE

"No marriage or family lasts forever" (Sprey, 2000, p. 24), but there remains a tacit assumption that the natural ending for a family is death. Nevertheless, divorce is a common experience for both adults and their children, and it can be seen in the context of longer lifetimes as a phenomenon that continues to constitute a risk to those who marry. While one does not speak of divorce in the break-up of a cohabiting couple, the dissolution of such relationships is frequent (Seltzer, 2000). Divorce has shifted from an adversarial procedure to no-fault, but controversy still appears in the property settlement and sometimes custody. Divorce is often a pathway to economic disadvantage and even outright poverty for women and children. There has been some debate over the outcomes for men. Studies show gains for men in level of living after separation and divorce, but other studies suggest that there are leveling mechanisms that over the long term lessen this advantage (McManus & DiPrete, 2001).

Alimony shifted from a means of restoring property or giving support for those women who come to divorce court with little, to a practice for rehabilitating "the marriage-induced disability" (Shehan, Berardo, Owens, & Berardo, 2002). Separation and reconciliation may happen several times before a more complete break, but a first separation due to discord usually signals a likelihood of permanent breakdown (Binstock & Thornton, 2003). Mothers as custodial parents are affected by options for cohabitation, remarriage, or continuing in a single-parent household. Poorer women are more likely to cohabit than remarry, which continues the real difference in household resources (Morrison & Ritualo, 2000). Marriage stabilizes relationships in comparison to cohabitation, but the divorce rate for couples that have cohabited is higher than for those who moved directly to marriage (Seltzer, 2000). Living apart for other reasons than discord is more common for younger couples and suggests some higher risk of relationship breakdown.

In contrast to widowhood, divorce ends a marriage, but not a relationship. This is especially true when there are children and both parents remain in the same community with many occasions for further contact. Custody is one area where contact is encouraged, as more judges agree to a joint custody arrangements and listen to children's views when they are older and more articulate (Wallace & Koerner, 2003). Even when both parents are satisfied with the situation, many repeated contacts leave much opportunity for further negative interactions (Madden-Derdich & Arditti, 1999).

Remarriage has a higher likelihood of divorce than first marriages (Amato, 2000). Remarriage has many consequences for both the spouses and, where there are children, for the parenting experience (Thomson, Mosley, Hanson, & McLanahan, 2001). Remarrieds report a decrease in harsh discipline and improved quality of the mother–child relationship. Most such families can expect some increase in family economic well-being and social support for parenting and thus less stress. There is a change in support with the arrival of any new biological children in the remarriage household, although most fathers continue to support nonresident children (Manning & Smock, 2000). Remarrieds are slightly more likely to divorce than first-marrieds. Remarrieds work very hard at marital success, but they have already shown behaviorally that they are willing to use divorce as a solution to a bad marriage.

Parental rights to make decisions for their children have the protection of strict scrutiny when legal suits arise (Skinner & Kohler, 2002). The priority of biological ties, and the norm of exclusivity of one set of parents at a time has marginalized others who may be participating in the care and sponsorship of children as foster or stepparents. Stepparents are in a legal limbo, although in a few states there is a presumption of support as long as the marriage endures. In most cases there is no provision for foster or stepparents to manage medical care or give permission for school events or retain custody upon the death of the spouse. Stepparent adoption is seldom a solution, as it requires a voluntary relinquishment of parental rights by the nonresident parent or else a legal finding that the parent is unfit or that it is in the child's best interest to end the relationship with the biological nonresident parent and to grant adoption (Ganong, Coleman, Fine, & McDaniel, 1998).

Divorce, separation, and remarriage have penetrated U.S. society to the point that almost every extended family is affected. Breaking relationships is an ongoing risk that affects not just couples but everyone around them. Negotiating positive adaptations to the consequences of this reality remains problematic.

8. KINSHIP, PROPERTY, AND INHERITANCE

Kinship as Negotiated

Kinship beyond the household or nuclear family in America has been (1) dismissed as unimportant, (2) suggested as a latent resource activated by events, (3) seen as a field from which chosen individuals are included in the network of individuals and families, (4) thought to be a possible resource for preventing foster care or institutionalization of disabled or frail individuals, or (5) included when the individual sees others as family when queried. The Sussman rejoinder to Parsons' presentation of the stripped-down nuclear family has been widely accepted and the term *modified extended family* is used to characterize America's families. As Lee notes, both "Sussman and Adams demonstrated that interaction among kin is frequent and functional even in the most urbanized and industrialized areas in the United States and other Western societies" (1980, pp. 923–924). While extended family relationships may not be as central to U.S. families as in more agricultural societies, kinship ties are functional, and the ties between parents and children, especially between mother and daughter, are close (Adams, 1999). Relationships with secondary kin such as aunts, uncles, and cousins seem to be a matter of circumstance and variable as to the level of involvement.

Immigrant and subculturally different families have been handled as exceptions or else as on the way to assimilation as modified extended families. There is data to suggest that white families emphasize lineal kin and black families include more collateral kin and fluid boundaries. Another group of "relatives" who may prove supportive or fade into the distance are those who are relatives from earlier marriages or current remarriages (Adams, 1999). These potentially available kin are usually not included, although everyone knows someone who is still good friends with a former mother-in-law or with a "father" in a blended family.

Most families still provide a sibling, but few families have several siblings with whom to develop long-term ties. Stepsiblings are another source of such relationships. More emphasis on the generations is possible because of increasing longevity, giving children a greater likelihood that they will have living grandparents and great-grandparents even as young adults (Silverstein & Long, 1998). With communication and travel being relatively less expensive and difficult, some relationships may be nurtured and maintained at a distance, but many elders will outlive their children and even grandchildren, and may have few direct lineal kin (Bengtson, 2001).

> *Women are the unsung heroines of social integration:* As childrearers, caregivers, and kin keepers, women provide the glue that holds families and lineages together. In the highly urban societies of the 1990s with high social valuation of individualism, fragile ties to neighbors, and declining loyalties to the larger community, this fundamental axis of social integration takes on greater social and political significance than ever before. (Rossi, 1995, p. 275)

Blood Ties and Preferences

The preference in the United States for blood kin is much more pronounced than one would expect when choice is so possible in the kinship system. Wegar notes that "Americans still consider adoption as a 'second best' and suspect family form" (2000, p. 363). The current high interest in finding ones "real" parents if one is adopted, or informing putative fathers of the potential adoption of their child, highlights this romance with blood kin ties. Although mothers are presumed to have full parental rights, unwed fathers' rights often prevail over adoptive or prospective adoptive parents (Skinner & Kohler, 2002). In reorienting the welfare system, establishing legal paternity for children has become a priority, and in the literature it has become one of the marks of responsible fatherhood (Doherty, Kouneski, & Erickson, 1998). There is an assumption that stepfathers are not expected to be as involved as biological fathers with the mothers' children and that cohabiting fathers have even less clear roles (Hofferth & Anderson, 2003).

Adoption reunions with the "real parents" have become an important aspect of young adults' resolution of their adoption experience (Gladstone & Westhues, 1998). When the adoption occurred, the mother and father may have been promised privacy and confidentiality, but many reunions do take place and sometimes relationships are formed following the reunions. Whether there is some reciprocal filial responsibility for adult children in such situations is unclear. Open adoption in which some ties to the biological parents and their families exit is increasingly common, and the definition of these new boundaries is yet to be codified (Grotevant, Dunbar, Kohler, & Lash Esau, 2000).

Some changes in the foster-care system have led to adoption of older children, and questions about openness with biological parents and perhaps with the foster parent are now being explored (Frasch, Brooks, & Barth, 2000). In foster care, keeping siblings together is difficult, and children miss both siblings and their biological parents and are confused about their placement in care (Whiting & Lee, 2003). Society's ambivalence toward foster parents' motivations may be an indication of the primacy of blood kinship. Transnational and cross-racial adoptions leave families to face the question, "Are those kids really yours?" (Grotevant et al., 2000, p. 384). Judge (2003) reflects on the stress that adoptive parents of international children feel as they deal with the children's problems originating from previous conditions affecting their children's well-being and adaptability.

The genetic or biological underpinnings of family/kin relationships are challenged in many of the new alternatives for reproductive technology. The ambivalence that Americans have can be seen in their uncertainty over confidentiality issues in terms of whether sperm donors should remain secret, whether surrogate mothers may reclaim their child, and what to do with leftover frozen embryos (Moen & Forest, 1999). The choices available in terms of disabled or developmentally problematic fetuses and children are not clear for parents. Many special-needs children end up in foster care, and more are being placed for adoption with considerable success (Glidden, 2000).

Kin Support and Intergenerational Transfers

Kin support between parents and children across the life course is tied to beliefs and practices that parallel the principles of inheritance. Variations in state histories and legal reforms create a crazy quilt of possibilities. The primary guidelines are in each state's laws, with taxes at the national level also affecting inheritance. Sussman (1983) found in his study of intergenerational transfers that families who had written wills follow the general rules of distribution, but tailor specific legacies often in a sentimental way. Bilateral kinship is the normative equality of both sides of the family and is characteristic of much of American practice in terms of kinship and inheritance, with even the practice of wives taking the husband's name being less binding today (Adams, 1999).

While it is difficult for middle-class parents to leave a large inheritance, their help at earlier stages when young adults would benefit from their assistance—for purchases, education, or with grandchildren—has important advantages. Intergenerational transfers occur more frequently when the elder generation is still employed and active. Education is especially crucial in the initiation of occupational trajectories (Warren, Hauser, & Sheridan, 2002). The United States has become less of an agricultural economy, so that family property is now most often a house, some furnishings, and the remainder of investments and accumulated resources. Still, siblings and other relatives may be in conflict over small sums of money or property, or over vague instructions on how an estate is to be handled (Taylor & Norris, 2000). Occasionally a windfall does come through inheritance as families have savings, second homes, and other property, or as individuals do not live out their expected lifetime. With changing economic participation, more women have property of their own and are thus able to make intergenerational transfers.

Kinship has many latent functions, and broad choice is available among relationships in kin networks. The central core of parents and children receives the most attention, with maternal relatives more frequently included in everyday life. Within the foregoing descriptions there are many regional and subcultural differences in family involvement with kin.

9. AGING AND DEATH

Bengtson postulates that "[f]or many Americans, multigenerational bonds are becoming more important than nuclear family ties for well-being and support over the course of their lives" (2001, p. 5). In terms of family demography, the age structure has dramatically shifted from the pyramid to what is a more rectangular age structure. At the family level this resembles a "beanpole," with more family members alive, but fewer in each succeeding generation. Longer years of shared lives and potential caregiving may be the product of these changes. Not only good relationships may endure, but also "lousy" relationships. In families one can maintain conflict and grudges over many years. With increased marriage, divorce, and remarriage, relatives such as grandparents may play larger roles with grandchildren and in response to crisis. Silverstein, Chen, and Heller (1996) warn that the exchange of social support between elders and adult children may have costs in terms of the psychological moods of the elderly, especially as they become dependent or receive support. Pyke (1999) notes that adult children have an uncomfortable balancing act in handling their parents' desires for autonomy along with their need for care.

Aging grandparents are central to kin activity and involvement. The "kin-keeping" function, performed by women, is often played by a grandmother; in fact, her death frequently means the fragmenting of the kin network. Cherlin and Furstenberg (1986, pp. 70, 77) distinguish three styles of grandparenting: Fifty-five percent of their respondents are companionate, 29% are remote, and 16% are involved. The companionate is simply frequent enough contact, but without either services or much parenting behavior. The ones who are most likely to indicate a lot less time than they would like are, of course, the remote. For the "involved" role (that is, parenting and services) to be played, three conditions are necessary: proximity, being younger, and need (such as a divorce) (Cherlin & Furstenberg, 1986, p. 205).

The perception of grandparents in terms of the closeness and affection for their adult grandchildren appears first to decrease with less contact and proximity and to increase over the life course (Silverstein & Long, 1998). Grandfathers may be especially helpful to single mothers. While grandparents see gains from their youth in warmth, understanding, and love, and needs for more supportive roles because of unstable family life, they may overestimate the increasing strength of the grandparent–grandchild relationship. After all, the harsh reality of death rates 50 years ago meant that one-fourth of the current grandparents never knew a grandparent themselves (Cherlin & Furstenberg, 1986, pp. 47–48).

The extension of aging for many people today includes at least two major transitions, first to a postretirement phase beginning somewhere between 50 and 70 and ending with a transition to frailty, disability, or death. The projection from the Administration on Aging is that those age 65 and older will grow from 12.6% to 20% of the U.S. population by 2050. The fastest-growing population sector is the frail elderly group (85+), which is estimated to increase by 400% in the next 50 years (Siegel, 1996). This phase is characterized by loss of spouse, peers, and other relatives including children and lack of available caregivers (C. L. Johnson & Troll, 1996). While most people make some plans for the first phase of elder life, they are often surprised that new solutions are needed following an active retirement stage.

Caregiving is not limited to the period in which care is delivered in the home of the caregiver or recipient. Advocating and providing coordination of direct care continues into institutional placement and hospitalizations (Keefe & Fancey, 2000).

Quality of life is one of the standards for evaluating end-of-life decisions, and the concept of the "good death" has emerged from the impact of advanced technologies that may prolong length of life but not guarantee quality. The hospice movement has arisen to provide palliative care at the end of life (Carr, 2003). Advanced directives and the use of living wills are becoming more widespread. Dealing with issues of dependency and decision making in old age has drawn attention to how guardianship and advanced directives operate to protect or to ignore elders' opinions and desires. Assisted suicide is legal in Oregon and poses as set of questions about competency and conflicting interest in the elder person's decisions. Management of pain is one area in which there is greater consensus for responding to the individual's requests, but for which the financial limits of programs, such as Medicare's 6-month survival rule for hospice reimbursement, may interfere. Public guardianship has become an important legal voice for the dependent elderly, as relatives may not be available or appropriate. States often take a proprietary view that their borders are not permeable when it comes to possible guardians or those with power of attorney. Teaster (2002) estimates that nearly 1.5 million people are under private or public guardianship. Those elderly with public guardians may have no other family or friends in contact with them or who are concerned about how the guardian is interpreting his or her role.

Aging has a different feel in ethnic and racial communities. Black Americans, especially black men, often face early death (Hayward, Crimmins, Miles, & Yang, 2000). Hispanic young adults are also at higher risk (Bond Huie, Hummer, & Rogers, 2002). Race does not represent biology except as a nexus of social/political/economic forces interacting with this identifying label. A few diseases are correlated with race, but most health conditions have limited relationship to genetic differences but may be affected by the cumulative life course experiences especially as socioeconomic differences influence lifestyle and access to care. Ethnic families need policies and services that are fair and inclusive, but some professionals have difficulty in handling their own biases—or as Harriett McAdoo says so well: A great deal of "mental garbage" enters the picture (1999, p. 320).

Disease and death are taboo topics, with little clear communication among family members. Even awareness of the importance of different diseases and conditions in terms of risk and mortality is shaped by the attention given in the media (Adelman & Verbrugge, 2000). In their study of the coverage of six diseases with high mortality, high prevalence, and high public health concern—cancer, heart disease, AIDS, diabetes, Alzheimer's disease, and arthritis—investigations found that news coverage was related to mortality trends. Life expectancy had increased to 74.4 years for males and 79.8 for females in 2001 (Arias & Smith, 2003). But some deaths are "out of order," and this makes them more difficult to handle emotionally for those who grieve (Murray, 2000). When there is shared tragedy as in the 9/11 experience, there may be public support for those whose loss seems so out of place and time. But Gilbert (1995) investigated the experiences of pregnancy loss and stillbirth and found that these prospective parents receive little support from others. Funerals are a transition ceremony that is usually open to the public. A function of the funeral and "viewing" is that the death is recognized and faced by the family and support network.

10. FAMILY AND OTHER INSTITUTIONS: EDUCATION, HEALTH, ECONOMICS, AND RELIGION

Some peculiarly American features of the basic institutions of education, health, economy, and religion affect how families are treated and how these institutions complement or conflict with family processes. Families make many decisions with relatively limited information and support. Individual responsibility for coordinating one's economic support and access to services is assumed (Settles, 1999). The assumption that each family can muster and manage the resources to care for itself, with relatively little outside advice or support, is accepted, with families needing assistance seen as lacking in coping ability. Families are expected to be flexible and able to handle the expectations of work, school, and community, despite how uncoordinated the demands may be. Controversies about the quality and accessibility of education, health, and community services are newsworthy. Many families fall outside the service network, and many persons are unsuccessful in managing their family's integration with these institutions.

Education

United States public education is said to be in crisis, because much is expected of the system. Free education for all is seen as a right, but there is much concern that standards and outcomes from such a system may not provide the quality of education that private educational institutions offer. The concept that postsecondary education is critical to the nation's economic and political development has become a fundamental belief. Beginning with the founding of small private colleges in the 19th century and the Morrill Act signed by President Lincoln during the Civil War that provided for publicly funded agricultural and technical colleges and universities, postsecondary education has been available in every state. The result of having broadly available educational programs has been to create a demographic profile for age 25 or older in which over 80% of the population has at least a high school education and 24.4% are college graduates (Bauman & Graf, 2003). Postsecondary education is not free and the real cost even in publicly funded schools has risen significantly, more than doubling in real dollars in the last 20 years (GAO, 2000). The role of parents in sponsoring children's academic interests and

school achievement has received considerable interest and has recently focused on family process variables instead of simply looking at socioeconomic and family structural variables (Bowen & Bowen, 1998).

McCall (2000) calls attention to the need to be aware of regional differences in opportunities as they affect men and women in the labor market. The rising completion of high school and larger enrollment in postsecondary education has drawn attention away from the fact that many youth are employed while they are students in high school, and many in middle school as well, although minority youth may not be able to find and hold work as consistently (Entwisle, Alexander, & Olson, 2000). Some drop out and work and then return later or have intermittent work participation, but most attempt to do school and work at the same time. Many students manage both roles well, even if they work over 20 hours a week, but the limits of a 24-hour day demand compromises from everyone. For example, much is made of the lengthening time that students take to finish 4-year college programs, as though this were somehow an academic problem. For students who pay for their postsecondary education and accumulate large debt, work is not simply a means of affording luxuries.

Healthcare

Medical and healthcare systems in the United States have developed rapidly, increasing the scope of what is addressed (Clarke, Shim, Mamo, Fosket, & Fishman, 2003). While the transformation of medicine in the first half of the 20th century focused on professionalization and specialization, with the increasing production of medical knowledge and clinical services, the current transformation includes a broader attention "to more and more aspects of daily life and the lived experience of health and illness" (Clarke et al., 2003, p. 165). In this context, individuals and their families are made more responsible for tracking and managing their own health and medical coordination. Access to information is more open to patients and their families, but often the consumer has no way of sorting or vetting the quality or relevance of information. The need for families to adjust quickly and deal with systems and interventions with which they are unfamiliar is characteristic of many situations, such as childhood cancer (McCubbin, Balling, Possin, Frierdich, & Bryne, 2002). Extremely complex and challenging regimes may be proposed for home administration. Dismissal from hospitals has become quicker for birth, surgeries, and other treatments, and outpatient treatment has greatly expanded. While outcomes in terms of patient health have improved, the effects on family systems are less well documented (Smith & Soliday, 2001).

While there is care available for those who have access in the United States, many families are left outside this system. House states, "While the most advantaged portions of the US populations have levels of health that equal or exceed those anywhere, the least advantaged are little better off than people in the least developed nations of the world" (House, 2002, p. 138). Reducing the social inequities in health and healthcare is a major opportunity for improvement in the United States. Poverty in childhood is a substantial health risk, and over one-third (34%) experience at least a year below the poverty line by the time they are 17 years old and 23% by the time they are 6 years old (Rank & Hirschl, 1998). Specific risks are reflected in higher rates of poverty for African-American children (69%), nonmarried households (81%), and those with less than 12 years of education of the head (63%).

"Employer-based health insurance is one of the most important fringe benefits offered to workers as it affects not only their own access but also their families access to health care"

(Cubbins & Parmer, 2001, p. 45). Currently, 14.6% of the U.S. population has no health insurance of any kind (*U.S. Statistics in Brief*, 2003). Innovations in costs and in the way care is delivered and managed limit what care is available, and under what circumstances. Many families have adopted the strategy of dual employment with combined benefits. Cubbins and Parmer (2001) found in the 1990s that disadvantages by gender and race remain important, and not only did the breadth of health coverage decline, but so did the menu of medical options offered. Mental health services have been seriously affected by managed care, with shorter clinical interventions and use of medications. "Decreased use of long-term services may be beneficial to those who pay for that care, but it also may result in higher costs to families and communities (Scheid, 2003, p. 158). Employer-based health insurance was developed after World War II to tie a mobile work force to a company through benefits. Health plans restrict job mobility, because any existing medical condition in a family member may well be excluded from a new policy when the worker moves to another employer.

Some groups have access to other care. The elderly have Medicare and Medicaid, and some states have made available coverage for poor children through special subsidized insurance schemes, which require parents to be knowledgeable and proactive in getting the coverage. Of the $1,299 billion (or $4,615 per person) spent on national healthcare in 2000, $224 billion was covered by Medicare and $208 billion was in public assistance payments—more than double 1990 amounts (*U.S. Statistics in Brief*, 2003). Even though many of the dollars in these programs come from the federal level, states have much discretion in how to administer the programs. Healthcare reforms have altered access to care and services, with resulting public concern being voiced by the most vulnerable, who lack health insurance or are in poor health (Pescoscolido, Tuch, & Martin, 2001, p. 13). The future of health-care and its impact on families remains a serious problem in family policy.

Economics

To survive economically, Americans move around. Both spouses usually are employed, and education is seen as a key element in gaining and retaining employment. Two trends in governmental programs and regulation of business and services have been a commitment to privatize enterprises and to deregulate broadly. The government's role is mainly to monitor contract compliance. The assumption in deregulation is that market forces will lead to lower prices and better products and services. However, governmental oversight and regulation are needed to lessen inadequacies or gaps in the private administration of such family-sensitive issues as pensions, health insurance, workman's compensation for injury, disability access and accommodation, and children's and family's services. After World War II there was a period of 27 years of rapid real-wage growth across industries and jobs, followed by a period of real-wage stagnation (Levy & Michel, 1991). The wage gap between highest- and lowest-income families began to rise in the 1970s, intensified in the 1980s, moderated slightly during the boom of the 1990s (McCall, 2000), and has surged in the recent downturn. Often this is explained as an education or skills gap, with most attention to a college education as the crucial element in upward mobility. Both men and women are affected by wage structure changes, but women are affected more by insecure employment conditions. Susser suggests that in advanced capitalist societies "local poverty can be found side by side with mobile international wealth" (2001, p. 8). He also notes that the partial welfare state in the United

States has been under concentrated attack in recent decades (2001, p. 9) with a series of changes including less secure employment, less-assured public assistance, for-profit healthcare, privatized education, and lower investment in public needs.

Contractual labor, temporary workers, and other self-employment options are becoming more prominent (Kalleberg, Reskin, & Hudson, 2000). Nonstandard jobs may provide families with some flexibility while costing them fringe benefits. If one uses low wages and no health insurance or pensions as indicators of bad jobs, about one in seven jobs in the United States is bad on all three dimensions, nearly one-quarter is bad on two dimensions, and another one-quarter (more than one-half the total jobs) is bad on one dimension (Kalleberg et al., 2000). These jobs are likely to be held by women of any race, and by men of color and recent immigrants. Nonstandard jobs unlikely to provide job security often have highly variable work schedules and earnings outside the control of the employee, and usually are without any union protection. The practice of jobs being "exempt from fair labor practices" is seen in the avoidance of overtime compensation.

Managerial work has begun to include women in greater numbers, over 40% in 1995, with changes in recruitment and formalization of hiring—although the possibility of having these policies without really changing methods and outcomes still exists (Reskin & McBrier, 2000). The American norm is for a significantly limited vacation and holiday schedule compared with most other developed countries. In addition to the shorter length of time and difficulty of scheduling vacation, younger and newer workers have much more limited access to time off. While the Family and Medical Leave Act did not cover small employers and nonstandard workers, it was a crucial change in the national scene in expanding the fundamental and legitimate rights of workers for family support (Moen & Forest, 1999; Secret, 2000). Economic, and more specifically job, insecurity is seen at every level of the social structure and is a primary stressor for families.

Religious Fundamentalism, Commitment, and Free Thinking

While there is a wall between religion and government in our constitution and rhetoric, religious organizations and beliefs are quite politically influential. Visitors from abroad are struck by how much religious practice is referenced in everyday speech and attitudes and, according to Brooks (2002), characterized by exceptionally high levels of religious commitment and religious-organizational strength. It may be expressed as a Judeo-Christian ethos, more narrowly as a Christian Protestant evangelical value, and more broadly expanded to include Catholicism and Islam.

While it is not easy to formally reject religion in the United States, since the 1990s, those not expressing a religious preference have doubled from 7% to 14%, after remaining steady for two decades. Hout and Fischer (2002) note that most of those with no preference express some conventional religious beliefs, but suggest that the political growth of the religious right may push those who do not agree politically to withdraw and become alienated from organized religion. The lack of public recognition of the possibility that one could have no religious affiliation and still have some moral compass is a normative constraint to admitting or speaking of anyone's opposition to religious institutions. The fact that a few religious groups have taken the lead in interpreting family needs and values to policymakers and that secularists have been timid in proposing rational concepts (Jacoby, 2004) means a limited view

of families will govern the way families are supported by family service programs.

CONCLUSION

Having looked to the future in several publications, it is a good idea to close with a few comments on where U.S. families are headed (Settles, 1986, 1999, 2001c). Over the past decade the conservative agenda has continued to be an active voice in shaping family programs. A rich diversity among families seems likely to continue based on current diversity, continued immigration, and a wide economic disparity. There is also an emphasis on informal, small-scale, "family-like" substitutes such as foster and day-care programs for children, the disabled, and the elderly, except for the criminal justice system. Devolvement of programs to the state level is being accompanied by economic crises in state governments, with constraints in spending. A national menu of consumer goods and media influence counters diversity to some extent, although family privacy allows for different family paradigms.

It is not clear how privacy and individual rights will fare during the response to terrorism, though more surveillance of citizens and narrowing of the scope of individual freedom is one obvious outcome. "Families do not have a natural or mechanical collaboration with the international business or the nation-states' immediate goals" (Settles, 2001b, p. 162). Thus, globalization is a mixed experience, with many Americans being more involved in international travel, work, mobility, and communication. The belief that privatization and open trading will be a long-term benefit for U.S. families has been countered for many at the level of job loss and insecurity. While U.S. families are actively attempting to shape their own futures, they are having to adapt to changed governmental policies and a shrinking world.

REFERENCES

2000 Census Data Sampler. (2003). Retrieved July 21, 2003, from www.census.gov/prod/2003pubs/02statab/2000data.pdf.

Adams, B. (1999). Cross-cultural and U.S. kinship. In M. B. Sussman, S. K. Steinmetz, & G. W. Peterson (Eds.), *Handbook on marriage and the family* (2nd ed., pp. 77–92). New York: Plenum.

Adelman, R. C., & Verbrugge, L. M. (2000). Death makes the news: The social impact of disease on newspaper coverage. *Journal of Health and Social Behavior, 41*(3), 347–367.

Aidala, A. A., & Zablocki, B. D. (1991). The communes of the seventies: Who joined and why? *Marriage and Family Review, 17*(1/2), 87–116.

Aldous, J., Mulligan, G. M., & Bjarnason, T. (1998). Fathering over time: What makes the difference? *Journal of Marriage and the Family, 60*(4), 809–820.

Amato, P. R. (2000). The consequences of divorce for adults and children. *Journal of Marriage and the Family, 62*(4), 1269–1287.

Amato, P. R., & Gilbreth, J. G. (1999). Nonresident fathers and children's well-being: A meta-analysis. *Journal of Marriage and the Family, 61*(3), 557–573.

Amato, P. R., Johnson, D. R., Booth, A., & Rogers, S. J. (2003). Continuity and change in marital quality between 1980 and 2000. *Journal of Marriage and the Family, 65*(1), 1–22.

Anderson, E. A., Braun, B., Oravecz, L., & Kohler, J. K. (2003). Relations of rural low-income mothers: Implications for marriage-promotion policy initiatives. *Family Focus, 48*(1), 4–5.

Anderson, E. A., & Spruill, J. W. (1993). The dual-career commuter family: A lifestyle on the move. In B. H. Settles, D. E. Hanks III, & M. B. Sussman (Eds.), *Families on the move: Migration, immigration, emigration, and mobility* (pp. 31–54). Binghamton, NY: Haworth Press.

Anderson, M. J., & Fienberg, S. E. (2001). Who counts? The politics of census-taking in contemporary America. New York: Russell Sage Foundation.

Arias, E., & Smith, B. L. (2003, March, 14). *Deaths: Preliminary data for 2001.* National Vital Statistics Reports, *51*(5), March 14, 2003. Retrieved June 21, 2004, from http://www.cdc.gov/nchs/products/pubs/pubd/nvsr/51/51-12.htm.

Barber, J. S., Axinn, W. G., & Thornton, A. (1999). Unwanted childbearing, health, and mother-child relationships. *Journal of Health and Social Behavior, 40*(3), 231–257.

Barbour, C., & Barbour, N. H. (1997). *Families, schools, and communities: Building partnerships for educating children.* Upper Saddle River, NJ: Merrill/Prentice Hall.

Bauman, K. J., & Graf, N. L. (2003). *Educational attainment: 2000.* Retrieved October 8, 2003, from www.census.gov/prod/2003pubs/c2kbr-24.pdf.

Bengtson, V. L. (2001). Beyond the nuclear family: The increasing importance of multigenerational bonds. *Journal of Marriage and the Family, 63*(1), 1–16.

Berkner, B., & Faber, C. S. (2003). *Geographical mobility: 1995–2003.* Retrieved September 29, 2003, from www.census.gov/prod/2003pubs/c2kbr-28.pdf.

BIC. (2002a). *Legal Immigration, Fiscal Year 1999.* Retrieved October 6, 2003, from http://www.immigration.gov/graphics/shared/aboutus/statistics/IMM99AR.pdf

BIC. (2002b). *Legal Immigration, Fiscal Year 2000.* Retrieved October 6, 2003, from http://www.immigration.gov/graphics/shared/aboutus/statistics/IMM2000AR.pdf

BIC. (2002c). *Legal Immigration, Fiscal Year 2001*. Retrieved October 6, 2003, from http://www.immigration.gov/graphics/shared/aboutus/statistics/IMM2001AR.pdf.

Binstock, G., & Thornton, A. (2003). Separations, reconciliations, and living apart in cohabiting and marital unions. *Journal of Marriage and the Family, 65*(2), 432–443.

Bird, C. E. (1999). Gender, household labor, and psychological distress: The impact of the amount and division of housework. *Journal of Health and Social Behavior, 40*(1), 32–45.

Bogard, C. J., McConnell, J. J., Gerstel, N., & Schwartz, M. (1999). Homeless mothers and depression: Misdirected policy. *Journal of Health and Social Behavior, 40*(1), 46–62.

Bogenschneider, K. (2002). *Family policy matters: How policymaking affects families and what professionals can do.* Mahwah, NJ: Lawrence Erlbaum.

Bonczar, T. P. (2003). *Prevalence of imprisonment in the U.S. population, 1974–2001*. Retrieved October 11, 2003, from www.ojp.gov/bjs/pub/pdf/piusp01.pdf.

Bond Huie, S. A., Hummer, R. A., & Rogers, R. G. (2002). Individual and contextual risks of death among race and ethnic groups in the United States. *Journal of Health and Social Behavior, 43*(3), 359–379.

Bowen, N. K., & Bowen, G. L. (1998). The mediating role of educational meaning in the relationship between home academic culture and academic performance. *Family Relations, 47*(1), 45–51.

Boylan, A. M. (2002). *The origins of women's activism: New York and Boston, 1797–1840*. Chapel Hill: The University of North Carolina Press.

Braver, S. L., Cookston, J. L., & Cohen, B. R. (2002). Experiences of family law attorneys with current issues in divorce practice. *Family Relations, 51*(4), 325–334.

Brooks, C. (2002). Religious influence and the politics of family decline concern: Trends, sources and U.S. political behavior. *American Sociological Review, 67*(2), 191–211.

Budig, M. J., & England, P. (2001). The wage penalty for motherhood. *American Sociological Review, 66*(2), 204–225.

Carlin, P. S. (1999). Economics and the family. In M. B. Sussman, S. K. Steinmetz, & G. W. Peterson (Eds.), *Handbook on marriage and the family* (2nd ed., pp. 525–552). New York: Plenum.

Carr, D. (2003). A "good death" for whom? Quality of spouse's death and psychological distress among older widowed persons. *Journal of Health and Social Behavior, 44*(2), 215–232.

Cherlin, A., & Furstenberg, F. F. (1986). *The new American grandparent.* New York: Basic Books.

Chevan, A. (1996). As cheaply as one: Cohabitation in the older population. *Journal of Marriage and the Family, 58*(3), 656–667.

Christopher, F. S., & Sprecher, S. (2000). Sexuality in marriage, dating and other relationships. *Journal of Marriage and the Family, 62*(4), 999–1017.

Cicirelli, V. (2000). An examination of the adult child's caregiving for an elderly patient. *Family Relations, 49*(2), 169–175.

Clarke, A. E., Shim, J. K., Mamo, L., Fosket, J. R., & Fishman, J. R. (2003). Biomedicalization: Technoscientific transformation of health, illness and U.S. biomedicine. *American Sociological Review, 68*(2), 161–194.

Coleman, M., Ganong, L., & Fine, M. (2000). Reinvestigating remarriage: Another decade of progress. *Journal of Marriage and the Family, 62*(4), 1288–1307.

Coltrane, S. (2000). Research on household labor: Modeling and measuring the social embeddedness of routine family work. *Journal of Marriage and the Family, 62*(4), 1208–1233.

Cook, J. A., & Wright, E. R. (1995). Medical sociology and the study of severe mental illness: Reflections on past accomplishments and directions for future research. *Journal of Health and Social Behavior* (Extra Issue), 95–114.

Coontz, S. (1989). The pitfalls of "Family Policy." *Against the Current, 4*(4), 11–18.

Coontz, S. (2000). Historical perspectives on family studies. *Journal of Marriage and the Family, 62*(2), 283–297.

Cotton, S. R. (1999). Marital status and mental health revisited: Examining the importance of risk factors and resources. *Family Relations, 48*(3), 225–233.

Crowder, K. D., & Tolnay, S. E. (2000). A new marriage squeeze for black women: The role of racial intermarriage by black men. *Journal of Marriage and the Family, 62*(3), 792–807.

Cubbins, L. A., & Parmer, P. (2001). Economic change and health benefits: Structural trends in employer-based health insurance. *Journal of Health and Social Behavior, 42*(1), 45–63.

Daly, K. J. (2001). Deconstructing family time: From ideology to lived experience. *Journal of Marriage and the Family, 63*(2), 283–294.

Dellmann-Jenkins, M., Blankemeyer, M., & Pinkard, O. (2000). Young adult children and grandchildren in primary caregiver roles to older relatives and their service needs. *Family Relations, 49*(2), 177–186.

Demo, D. H., & Cox, M. J. (2000). Families with young children: A review of research in the 1990's. *Journal of Marriage and the Family, 62*(4), 876–895.

Doherty, W. J., Kouneski, E. F., & Erickson, M. F. (1998). Responsible fathering: An overview and conceptual framework. *Journal of Marriage and the Family, 60*(2), 277–292.

DOJ. (2003). *More than 5.6 million U.S. residents have or are serving time in state or federal prisons.* Retrieved October 11, 2003, from www.ojp.gov/press releases/BJS03119.htm.

DOT & DOJ. (1999). *Gun crime in the age group 18–20.* Retrieved October 11, 2003, from http://www.treas.gov/press/releases/reports/report.pdf.

Driscoll, A. K., Hearn, G. K., Evans, V. J., Moore, K. A., Sugland, B. W., & Call, V. (1999). Nonmarital childbearing among adult women. *Journal of Marriage and the Family, 61*(1), 178–187.

Edin, K., & Lein, L. (1997). *Making ends meet: How single mothers survive welfare and low wage work.* New York: Russell Sage Foundation.

Ehrenberg, M. F., Gearing-Small, M., Hunter, M. A., & Small, B. J. (2001). Childcare task division and shared parenting attitudes in dual earner families with young children. *Family Relations, 50*(2), 143–153.

Ellison, C. G., & Sherkat, D. E. (1993). Conservative Protestantism and support for corporal punishment. *American Sociological Review, 58*(1), 131–144.

Elo, I. T., King, R. B., & Furstenberg, F. F. (1999). Adolescent females: Their sexual partners and fathers of their children. *Journal of Marriage and the Family, 61*(1), 74–84.

Ennett, S. T., Bailey, S. L., & Federman, E. B. (1999). Social network characteristics associated with risky behaviors among runaway and homeless youth. *Journal of Health and Social Behavior, 40*(1), 63–78.

Entwisle, D. R., Alexander, K. L., & Olson, L. S. (2000). Early work histories of urban youth. *American Sociological Review, 65*(2), 279–297.

Fields, J., & Casper, L. M. (2001). America's families and living arrangements: Population characteristics. Retrieved October 2, 2003, from http://www.census.gov/prod/2001pubs/p20-537.pdf.

Foster, L. (1991). *Women, family and utopia: Communal experiments of the Shakers, the Oneida community and the Mormons.* New York: Syracuse University Press.

Fox, G. L. (1999). Families in the media: Reflections on the public scrutiny of private behavior. *Journal of Marriage and the Family, 61*(4), 821–830.

Fox, G. L., Bruce, C., & Combs-Orme, T. (2000). Parenting expectations and concerns of fathers and mothers of newborn infants. *Family Relations, 49*(2), 123–131.

Francoeur, R. T., & Hendrixson, L. L. (1999). Human sexuality. In M. B. Sussman, S. K. Steinmetz, & G. W. Peterson (Eds.), *Handbook on marriage and the family* (2nd ed., pp. 743–776). New York: Plenum.

Frasch, K. M., Brooks, D., & Barth, R. P. (2000). Openness and contact in foster care adoption: An eight year follow-up. *Family Relations, 49*(4), 435–446.

Friedman, D., Hechter, M., & Kanazawa, S. (1999). Theories of the value of children: A new approach. In R. Leete (Ed.), *Dynamics of values in fertility change* (pp. 19–50). New York: Oxford University Press.

Furstenberg, F. F., Jr., (2000). The sociology of adolescence and youth in the 1990's: A critical commentary. *Journal of Marriage and the Family, 62*(4), 896–910.

Furstenberg, F. F., Jr., & Kiernan, K. E. (2001). Delayed parental divorce: How much do children benefit? *Journal of Marriage and the Family, 63*(2), 446–457.

Furstenberg, F. F., Jr., Cook, T. D., Eccles, J., Elder, G. H., & Sameroff, A. (1999). *Managing to make it: Urban families and adolescent success.* Chicago: University of Chicago Press.

Ganong, L., Coleman, M., Fine, M., & McDaniel, A. K. (1998). Issues considered in contemplating stepchild adoption. *Family Relations, 47*(1), 63–71.

GAO. (2000). *GAO/HEHS-00-198R Cost of college.* Retrieved October 4, 2003, from www.nchelp.org/whats_new/2000_Archive/Oct/gaotuition.pdf.

Gelles, R. J. (1980). Violence in the family: A review of research in the seventies. *Journal of Marriage and the Family, 42*(4), 873–885.

Gelles, R. J., & Conte, J. R. (1990). Domestic violence and sexual abuse of children: A review of research in the eighties. *Journal of Marriage and the Family, 52*(4), 1045–1058.

Gilbert, K. R. (1995). Family loss and grief. In R. Day, K. Gilbert, B. H. Settles, & W. Burr (Eds.), *Research and theory in family science* (pp. 304–318). Pacific Grove, CA: Brooks/Cole.

Gladstone, J., & Westhues, A. (1998). Adoption reunions: A new side to intergenerational family relationships. *Family Relations, 47*(2), 177–184.

Glazer, N. (2001). American diversity and the 2000 census. *The Public Interest* (144/Summer), 3–18.

Glick, P. C. (1993). The impact of geographic mobility on individuals and families. In B. H. Settles, D. E. Hanks III, & M. B. Sussman (Eds.), *Families on the move: Migration, immigration, emigration, and mobility* (pp. 31–54). Binghamton, NY: Haworth Press.

Glidden, L. M. (2000). Adopting children with developmental disabilities: A long-term perspective. *Family Relations, 49*(4), 397–405.

Goldscheider, F. K., Hogan, D., & Bures, R. (2001). A century (plus) of parenthood: Changes in living with children 1880–1990. *The History of the Family, 6*(4), 477–494.

Goldstein, J. R., & Kenney, C. T. (2001). Marriage delayed or marriage forgone? New cohort forecasts of first marriage for U.S. women. *American Sociological Review, 66*(4), 506–519.

Greenstein, T. N. (1996). Husbands' participation in domestic labor: Interactive effects of wives' and husbands' gender ideologies. *Journal of Marriage and the Family, 58*(3), 585–595.

Grotevant, H. D., Dunbar, N., Kohler, J. K., & Lash Esau, A. M. (2000). Adoptive identity: How contexts within and beyond the family shape developmental pathways. *Family Relations, 49*(4), 379–387.

Gubrium, J. F., & Holstein, J. A. (1990). *What is family?* Mountain View, CA: Mayfield.

Haas, L. (1999). Families and work. In M. B. Sussman, S. K. Steinmetz, & G. W. Peterson (Eds.), *Handbook on marriage and the family* (2nd ed., pp. 571–612). New York: Plenum.

Haines, M. R. (1996). Long-term marriage patterns in the United States from colonial times to the present. *The History of the Family, 1*(1), 15–39.

Hardill, I. (2002). Gender, migration and the dual career household. New York: Routledge.

Hareven, T. K. (2000). *Families, history, and social change: Life-course and cross-cultural perspectives.* Boulder, CO: Westview Press.

Harris, D. R., & Sim, J. J. (2002). Who is multiracial? Assessing the complexity of lived race. *American Sociological Review, 67*(4), 614–627.

Hayward, M. D., Crimmins, E. M., Miles, T. P., & Yang, Y. (2000). The significance of socioeconomic status in explaining the racial gap in chronic health conditions. *American Sociological Review, 65*(6), 910–930.

Heaton, T. B., Jacobson, C. K., & Holland, K. (1999). Persistence and change in decisions to remain childless. *Journal of Marriage and the Family, 61*(2), 531–539.

Henderson, T. I., & Monroe, P. A. (2002). Introduction to the special collection on the intersection of families and the law. *Family Relations, 51*(4), 289–292.

Hernandez, D. J., with Myers, D. E. (1995). *America's children: Resources from family, government and the economy.* New York: Russell Sage Foundation.

Hofferth, S. L., & Anderson, K. G. (2003). Are all dads equal? Biology versus marriage as a basis for paternal investment. *Journal of Marriage and the Family, 65*(1), 213–232.

Hofferth, S. L., & Sandberg, J. F. (2001). How American children spend their time. *Journal of Marriage and the Family, 63*(2), 295–308.

Hong, J., Seltzer, M. M., & Krauss, M. W. (2001). Change in social support and psychological well-being: A longitudinal study of aging mothers of adults with mental retardation. *Family Relations, 50*(2), 154–163.

House, J. S. (2002). Understanding social factors and inequalities in health: 20th century progress and 21st century prospects. *Journal of Health and Social Behavior, 43*(2), 125–142.

Hout, M., & Fischer, C. S. (2002). Why more Americans have no religious preference: Politics and generations. *American Sociological Review, 67*(2), 165–190.

Hurtling, J. R., Grusky, D. B., & Van Rompaey, S. E. (1997). The social geography of interstate mobility and persistence. *American Sociological Review, 62*(2), 267–287.

Inglehart, R., & Baker, W. E. (2000). Modernization, cultural change and the persistence of traditional values. *American Sociological Review, 65*(1), 19–51.

INS. (2003). *Executive summary: Estimates of the unauthorized immigrant population residing in the United States: 1990 to 2000.* http://www.immigration.gov/graphics/shared/aboutus/statistics/2000ExecSumm.pdf.

Jacoby, S. (2004). Freethinkers: A history of American secularism. NY: Henry Holt.

Johnson, C. L., & Troll, L. (1996). Family structure and the timing of transitions from 70–103 years of age. *Journal of Marriage and the Family, 58*(1), 178–187.

Johnson, J. M. (1997). The changing concept of child abuse and its impact on family life. In M. Hutter (Ed.), *The family experience: A reader in cultural diversity* (pp. 404–416). Needham Heights, MA: Allyn & Bacon.

Johnson, M. P., & Ferraro, K. J. (2000). Research on domestic violence in the 1990's: Making distinctions. *Journal of Marriage and the Family, 62*(4), 948–963.

Jones, N. A., & Smith, A. S. (2001). *The two or more races population: 2000.* Census 2003 Brief C2KBR/01-6. Retrieved June 21, 2004, from http://www.census.gov/prod/www/abs/briefs.html.

Judge, S. (2003). Determinants of parental stress in families adopting children from Eastern Europe. *Family Relations, 52*(3), 241–248.

Jurich, A. P., Collins, O. P., & Griffin, C. (1993). Coping with the displaced farm family: The new migration. In B. H. Settles, D. E. Hanks III, & M. B. Sussman (Eds.), *Families on the move: Migration, immigration, emigration, and mobility* (pp. 77–98). Binghamton, NY: Haworth Press.

Kalleberg, A. L., Reskin, B. F., & Hudson, K. (2000). Bad jobs in America: Standard and nonstandard employment relations and job quality in the United States. *American Sociological Review, 65*(2), 256–278.

Kamerman, S. B., & Kahn, A. J. (2001, March). Child and family policies in the United States at the opening of the twenty-first century. *Social Policy and Administration, 35*(1), 69–84.

Keefe, J., & Fancey, P. (2000). The care continues: Responsibility for elderly relatives before and after admission to a long term care facility. *Family Relations, 49*(3), 235–244.

Kephart, W. M. (1982). *Extraordinary groups: The sociology of unconventional life-styles.* New York: St. Martin's Press.

Kiecolt, K. J. (2003). Satisfaction with work and family life: No evidence of a cultural reversal. *Journal of Marriage and the Family, 65*(1), 23–35.

King, V., & Heard, H. E. (1999). Nonresident father visitation, parental conflict, and mother's satisfaction: What's best for child well-being? *Journal of Marriage and the Family, 61*(2), 385–396.

Knudsen-Martin, C., & Mahoney, A. R. (1998). Language and processes in the construction of equality in new marriages. *Family Relations, 47*(1), 81–91.

Langman, L. (1987). Social stratification. In M. B. Sussman & S. K. Steinmetz (Eds.), *Handbook on marriage and family* (pp. 211–250). New York: Plenum Press.

Lee, G. (1980). Kinship in the seventies: A decade review of research and theory. *Journal of Marriage and the Family, 42*(4), 923–936.

Letiecq, B. L., Anderson, E. A., & Koblinsky, S. A. (1998). Social support of homeless and housed mothers: A comparison of temporary and permanent housing arrangements. *Family Relations, 47*(4), 415–421.

Levy, F., & Michel, R. C. (1991). *The economic future of American families: Income and wealth trends.* Washington, DC: The Urban Institute Press.

Lieberson, S., & Waters, M. C. (1988). *From many strands: Ethnic and racial groups in contemporary America.* New York: Russell Sage Foundation.

Linklater, A. (2002). *Measuring America.* New York: Walker.

Littles, J. A., Jr. (2003). *Theologically conservative parents' construction of parenting practices*. Unpublished doctoral dissertation, University of Delaware, Newark, DE.

Lloyd, S. A. (1991). The dark side of courtship: Violence and sexual exploitation. *Family Relations, 40*(1), 14–20.

Loftus, J. (2001). America's liberalization in attitudes toward homosexuality, 1973–1998. *American Sociological Review, 66*(5), 762–782.

Logan, J. R., Alba, R. D., & Zhang, W. (2002). Immigrant enclaves and ethnic communities in New York and Los Angeles. *American Sociological Review, 67*(2), 299–322.

Macklin, E. D. (1980). Nontraditional family forms: A decade of research. *Journal of Marriage and the Family, 42*(4), 905–922.

Madden-Derdich, D. A., & Arditti, J. A. (1999). The ties that bind: Attachment between former spouses. *Family Relations, 48*(3), 243–249.

Manning, W. D., & Smock, P. J. (2000). Swapping families: Serial parenting and economic support for families. *Journal of Marriage and the Family, 62*(1), 111–122.

Mapping census 2000: The geography of U.S. diversity. (n.d.). Retrieved September 4, 2003, from www.census.gov/population/www/ cen2000/atlas.html.

Marchand, J. F., & Hock, E. (2000). Avoidance and attacking conflict-resolution strategies among married couples: Relations to depressive symptoms. *Family Relations, 49*(2), 201–206.

Marsiglio, W., Hutchinson, S., & Cohan, M. (2000). Envisioning fatherhood: A social psychological perspective on young men without kids. *Family Relations, 49*(2), 133–142.

McAdoo, H. P. (1999). Family ethnicity: Challenges for the 21st century. In H. P. McAdoo (Ed.), *Family ethnicity: Strength in diversity* (2nd ed., pp. 319–320). Thousand Oaks, CA: Sage Publications.

McCall, L. (2000). Gender and the new inequality: Explaining the college/non-college wage gap. *American Sociological Review, 65*(2), 234–255.

McCubbin, M., Balling, K., Possin, P., Frierdich, S., & Bryne, B. (2002). Family resiliency in childhood cancer. *Family Relations, 51*(2), 103–111.

McManus, P. A., & DiPrete, T. A. (2001). Losers and winners: Financial consequences of separation and divorce for men. *American Sociological Review, 66*(2), 246–268.

Merkle, E. R., & Richardson, R. A. (2000). Digital dating and virtual relating: Conceptualizing computer mediated romantic relationships. *Family Relations, 49*(20), 187–192.

Moen, P., & Forest, K. B. (1999). Strengthening families: Policy issues for the twenty-first century. In M. B. Sussman, S. K. Steinmetz, & G. W. Peterson (Eds.), *Handbook on marriage and the family* (2nd ed., pp. 633–663). New York: Plenum.

Morris, A. (1994). International reform initiatives regarding violence against women: Successes and pitfalls. In S. Jagwanth, P. Schwikkard, & B. Grant (Eds.), *Women and the law* (pp. 351–380). Pretoria: HSRC Publishers.

Morrison, D. R., & Ritualo, A. (2000). Routes to children's economic recovery after divorce: Are cohabitation and remarriage equivalent? *American Sociological Review, 65*(4), 560–580.

Murray, C. I. (2000). Coping with death, dying and grief in families. In P. C. Mckenry & S. J. Price (Eds.), *Families and change* (pp. 120–153). Thousand Oaks, CA: Sage.

Nagel, J. (1995). American Indian ethnic renewal: Politics and the resurgence of identity. *American Sociological Review, 60*(6), 947–965.

National Research Council. (1995). *Integrating federal statistics on children: Report of a workshop.* Washington, DC: National Academy Press.

Oakley, A. (1974). *The sociology of housework.* New York: Pantheon Books.

Orloff, A. S. (1993). Gender and the social rights of citizenship: The comparative analysis of state policies and gender relations. *American Sociological Review, 58*(3), 303–328.

Osteen, S. R., & Auberle, T. (2002b). Homebuyer education: A doorway to financial literacy. *Journal of Family and Consumer Sciences, 94*(1), 29–32.

Palkovitz, R. (2002a). Involved fathering and child development: Advancing our understanding of good fathering. In C. Tamis-LaMonda & N. Cabrerra (Eds.), *Handbook of father involvement* (pp. 119–140). Mahwah, NJ: Lawrence Erlbaum.

Palkovitz, R. (2002b). *Involved fathering and men's adult development: Provisional balances.* Mahwah, NJ: Lawrence Erlbaum.

Patterson, C. J. (2000). Family relationships of lesbians and gay men. *Journal of Marriage and the Family, 62*(4), 1052–1069.

Perry-Jenkins, M., Repetti, R. L., & Crouter, A. C. (2000). Work and family in the 1990's. *Journal of Marriage and the Family, 62*(4), 981–998.

Pescosolido, B. A., & Rubin, B. A. (2000). The web of group affiliations revisited: Social life, postmodernism and sociology. *American Sociological Review, 65*(1), 52–76.

Pescosolido, B. A., Tuch, S. A., & Martin, J. K. (2001). The profession of medicine and the public: Examining Americans' changing confidence in physicians from the beginning of the "health care crisis" to the era of health care reform. *Journal of Health and Social Behavior, 42*(1), 1–16.

Pollard, M. S., & Morgan, S. P. (2002). Emerging parental gender indifference? Sex composition of children and the third birth. *American Sociological Review, 67*(4), 600–613.

Portes, A., Haller, W. J., & Guarnizo, L. E. (2002). Transnational entrepreneurs: An alternative form of immigrant economic adaptation. *American Sociological Review, 67*(2), 278–298.

Potuchek, J. L. (1997). *Who supports the family? Gender and bread winning in dual earner marriages.* Stanford, CA: Stanford University Press.

Powell, L. H., & Cassidy, D. (2001). Foundations of sexuality education. In *Family life education: An introduction* (pp. 129–145). Mountain View, CA: Mayfield.

Prewitt, K. (2002). Demography, diversity and democracy: The 2000 census. *Brookings Review,* (Winter), 6–9.

Price, C. A., & Rose, H. A. (2000). Caregiving over the life course of families. In S. J. Price, P. C. McHenry, & M. J. Murphy (Eds.), *Families across time: A life course perspective* (pp. 145–159). Los Angeles: Roxbury.

Pyke, K. (1999). The micropolitics of care in relationships between aging parents and adult children: Individualism, collectivism and power. *Journal of Marriage and the Family, 61*(3), 661–672.

Rank, M. R., & Hirschl, T. A. (1998). The economic risk of childhood in America: Estimating the probability of poverty across the formative years. *Journal of Marriage and the Family, 61*(4), 1058–1067.

Reskin, B. F., & McBrier, D. B. (2000). Why not ascription? Organizations' employment of male and female managers. *American Sociological Review, 65*(2), 210–233.

Robinson, J. R., & Milkie, M. A. (1998). Back to the basics: Trends in and role determinants of women's attitudes toward housework. *Journal of Marriage and the Family, 60*(1), 205–218.

Rogers, S. J., & White, L. K. (1998). Satisfaction with parenting: The role of marital happiness, family structure and parents' gender. *Journal of Marriage and the Family, 60*(2), 293–308.

Rosen, D. M. (1999). American families and American law. In M. B. Sussman, S. K. Steinmetz, & G. W. Peterson (Eds.), *Handbook on marriage and the family* (2nd ed., pp. 553–570). New York: Plenum.

Ross, C. E., & Mirowski, J. (2000). Family relationship, social support and subjective life expectancy. *Journal of Health and Social Behavior, 43*(4), 469–489.

Ross, C. E., & Van Willigen, M. (1996). Gender, parenthood and anger. *Journal of Marriage and the Family, 58*(3), 572–584.

Rossi, A. S. (1995). Commentary: Wanted: Alternative theory and analysis modes. In V. L. Bengtson, K. W. Schaie, & L. M. Burton (Eds.), *Adult intergenerational relations: Effects of societal change* (pp. 264–276). New York: Springer.

Scheid, T. L. (2003). Managed care and the rationalization mental health services. *Journal of Health and Social Behavior, 44*(2), 142–161.

Schwarzweller, H. K., Brown, J. S., & Mangalam, J. J. (1971). *Mountain families in transition: A case study of Appalachia.* University Park: Pennsylvania State University Press.

Secret, M. (2000). Identifying the family, job, and work-place characteristics of employees who use work-family benefits. *Family Relations, 49*(2), 217–225.

Seltzer, J. A. (2000). Families formed outside of marriage. *Journal of Marriage and the Family, 62*(4), 1247–1268.

Settles, B. H. (1986). A perspective on tomorrow's families. In M. B. Sussman & S. K. Steinmetz (Eds.), *Handbook on marriage and family* (pp. 157–180). New York: Plenum Press.

Settles, B. H. (1993). Expanding choice in long term planning for family futures. In B. H. Settles, R. S. Hanks, & M. B. Sussman (Eds.), *American families and the future: Analyses of possible destinies* (pp. 1–36). Binghamton, NY: Haworth Press.

Settles, B. H. (1995). Families in everyday life. In R. Day, K. Gilbert, B. H. Settles, & W. Burr (Eds.), *Research and theory in family science* (pp. 154–170). Pacific Grove, CA: Brooks/Cole.

Settles, B. H. (1998). Putting families in family policy and programs: Local, regional, national and international options. In K. Matthijs (Ed.), *The family: Contemporary perspectives and challenges* (pp. 263–283). Leuven, Belgium: Leuven University Press.

Settles, B. H. (1999). The future of families. In M. B. Sussman, S. K. Steinmetz, & G. W. Peterson (Eds.), *Handbook on marriage and the family* (2nd ed., pp. 143–176). New York: Plenum.

Settles, B. H. (2001a). Being at home in a global society: A model for families' mobility and immigration decisions. *Journal of Comparative Family Studies, 32*(4), 627–645.

Settles, B. H. (2001b). Conflicts between family strategies and state policy in a global society. *Journal of Comparative Family Studies, 32*(2), 147–166.

Settles, B. H. (2001c). The future of families in the 21st century: Hunches, probabilities and possibilities. *The Journal of the FRHD and FERM Divisions of the American Association of Family and Consumer Sciences, 4*, 1–14.

Settles, B. H., Davis, J. E., Grasse-Bachman, C., Janvier, K. A., & Rosas, S. R. (2000). Developing community and peer support for young parents: Process and outcome evaluation inputs in prevention programs. *Family Science Review, 13*(3&4), 182–196.

Settles, B. H., & Liprie, M. L. (1987). *Demography and the family: An interview with Paul C. Glick, Ph.D., Retired Senior Demographer, U.S. Census, Adjunct Professor, Arizona State University* [Video]. Newark: University of Delaware.

Settles, B. H., Steinmetz, S. K., Peterson, G. W., & Sussman, M. B. (Eds.). (1999). *Concepts and definition of family for the 21st century*. New York: Haworth Press.

Shehan, C., Berardo, F. M., Owens, E., & Berardo, D. H. (2002). Alimony: An anomaly in family social sciences. *Family Relations, 51*(4), 308–316.

Siegel, J. (1996). *Aging into the 21st Century. Administration on Aging*. Retrieved September 29, 2003, from www.aoa.gov/prof/Statistics/future_growth/aging21/table1.asp.

Silverstein, M., Chen, X., & Heller, K. (1996). Too much of a good thing? Intergenerational social support and the psychological well-being of older persons. *Journal of Marriage and the Family, 58*(4), 970–982.

Silverstein, M., & Long, J. D. (1998). Trajectories of grandparents' perceived solidarity with adult grandchildren: A growth curve over 23 years. *Journal of Marriage and the Family, 60*(4), 912–913.

Simmons, T., & O'Connell, M. (2003). *Married-couple and unmarried-partner households: 2000*. Retrieved Sept 29, 2003, from www.census.gov/prod/2003pubs/censr-5.pdf.

Skinner, D. A., & Kohler, J. K. (2002). Parental rights in diverse family contexts: Current legal developments. *Family Relations, 51*(4), 293–300.

Smith, S. R., & Soliday, E. (2001). The effects of parental chronic kidney disease on the family. *Family Relations, 50*(2), 171–177.

Sprecher, S., & Felmlee, D. (1992). The influence of parents and friends on the quality and stability of romantic relationships: A three wave longitudinal investigation. *Journal of Marriage and the Family, 54*(4), 888–900.

Sprey, J. (2000). Theorizing in family studies: Discovering process. *Journal of Marriage and the Family, 62*(1), pp. 18–31.

Stacey, J., & Biblarz, T. J. (2001). (How) does the sexual orientation of parents matter? *American Sociological Review, 66*(2), 159–183.

Straus, M. A. (1994). Should the use of corporal punishment by parents be considered child abuse? In M. A. Mason & E. Gambrill (Eds.), *Debating children's lives: Current controversies on children and adolescents* (pp. 196–203). Thousand Oaks, CA: Sage Publications.

Straus, M. A. (2001). Beating the devil out of them: Corporal punishment in American families and its effects on children. New Brunswick, NJ: Transaction.

Straus, M. A., & Gelles, R. J. (1986). Societal change in family violence from 1975 to 1985 as revealed by two national surveys. *Journal of Marriage and the Family, 48*(3), 465–479.

Susser, I. (2001). Cultural diversity in the United States. In I. Susser & T. Patterson (Eds.), *Cultural diversity in the United States* (pp. 3–15). Oxford, UK: Blackwell.

Sussman, M. B. (1983). Law and legal systems: The family connection. *Journal of Marriage and the Family, 45*(1), 11–34.

Sweeney, M. M. (2002). Two decades of family change: The shifting economic foundations of marriage. *American Sociological Review, 67*(1), 132–147.

Sweet, J. A., & Bumpass, L. L. (1987). *American families and households.* New York: Russell Sage Foundation.

Taylor, J. E., & Norris, J. E. (2000). Sibling relationships, fairness, and conflict over the transfer of the farm. *Family Relations, 49*(3), 277–283.

Teachman, J. D., Polonko, K. A., & Scanzoni, J. (1999). Demography and families. In R. Day, K. Gilbert, B. H. Settles, & W. Burr (Eds.), *Research and theory in family science* (pp. 39–69). Pacific Grove, CA: Brooks/Cole.

Teachman, J. D., Tedrow, L. M., & Crowder, K. (2000). The changing demography of America's families. *Journal of Marriage and the Family, 62*(4), 1234–1246.

Teaster, P. B. (2002). The wards of public guardians: Voices of the unbefriended. *Family Relations, 51*(4), 344–350.

Thompson, E. A. (2000). Mothers' experiences of an adult child's HIV/AIDS diagnosis: Maternal responses to and resolutions of accountability for AIDS. *Family Relations, 49*(2), 155–164.

Thompson, L., & Walker, A. J. (1995). The place of feminism in family studies. *Journal of Marriage and the Family, 57*(4), 847–865.

Thomson, E., Mosley, J., Hanson, T. L., & McLanahan, S. (2001). Remarriage, cohabitation, and changes in mothering behavior. *Journal of Marriage and the Family, 63*(2), 370–380.

Thornton, A., & Young-DeMarco, L. (2001). Four decades of trends in attitudes toward family issues in the United States: 1960's to 1990's. *Journal of Marriage and the Family, 63*(4), 1009–1037.

Tolnay, S. E., Crowder, K. D., & Adelman, R. M. (2002). Race, regional origin and residence at the beginning of the great migration. *American Sociological Review, 67*(3), 456–475.

Trost, J. (1998). LAT relationships now and in the future. In K. Matthijs (Ed.), *The family: Contemporary perspectives and challenges* (pp. 209–220). Leuven, Belgium: Leuven University Press.

Turner, H. A., & Finkelhor, D. (1996). Corporal punishment as a stressor among youth. *Journal of Marriage and the Family, 58*(1), 155–166.

Twenge, J. M., Campbell, W. K., & Foster, C. A. (2003). Parenthood and marital satisfaction: A meta-analytic review. *Journal of Marriage and the Family, 65*(3), 574–583.

Uggen, C., & Manza, J. (2002). Democratic contraction? Political consequences of felon disenfranchisement in the United States. *American Sociological Review, 67*(6), 777–803.

United States Summary. (1998). *Population: 1790 to 1990.* Retrieved July 21, 2003, from www.census.gov/population/censusdata/table-4.pdf.

U.S. Census Bureau. (2003). http://www.census.gov.

U.S. Statistics in Brief. (2003). Retrieved July 26, 2003, from www.census.gov/statab/www/part1.html#households.

Uttal, L. (1999). Using kin for child care: Embedment in the socioeconomic networks of extended families. *Journal of Marriage and the Family, 61*(4), 845–857.

Vanek, J. (1974). Time spent in housework. *Scientific American, 231*(5), 116–120.

Vlosky, D. A., & Monroe, P. A. (2002). Effective dates of no-fault divorce laws in the 50 states. *Family Relations, 51*(4), 317–324.

Voydanoff, P. (1990). Economic distress and family relations: A review of the eighties. *Journal of Marriage and the Family, 52*(4), 1099–1115.

Voydanoff, P. (1999). Gender and family relationships. In M. B. Sussman, S. K. Steinmetz, & G. W. Peterson (Eds.), *Handbook on marriage and the family* (2nd ed., pp. 439–474). New York: Plenum.

Walker, K. E., & Woods, M. E. (1976). *Time use: A measure of household production of family goods and services.* Washington, DC: American Home Economics Association.

Wallace, S. R., & Koerner, S. S. (2003). Influence of child and family factors on judicial decisions in contested custody cases. *Family Relations, 52*(2), 180–188.

Warren, J. R., Hauser, R. M., & Sheridan, J. T. (2002). Occupational stratification across the life course: Evidence from the Wisconsin longitudinal study. *American Sociological Review, 67*(3), 432–455.

Wegar, K. (2000). Adoption, family ideology, and social stigma: Bias in community attitudes, adoption research, and practice. *Family Relations, 49*(4), 363–370.

Weigal, D. J., & Ballard-Reisch, D. S. (1999). How couples maintain marriages: A closer look at self and spouse influences upon the use of maintenance behaviors in marriages. *Family Relations, 48*(3), 263–269.

Western, B. (2002). The impact of incarceration on wage mobility and inequality. *American Sociological Review, 67*(4), 526–546.

White, L., & Rogers, S. J. (2000). Economic circumstances and family outcomes: A review of the nineties. *Journal of Marriage and Family, 62*(4), 1035–1051.

Whiting, J. B., & Lee, R. E., III (2003). Voices from the system: A qualitative study of foster children's stories. *Family Relations, 52*(3), 288–295.

Wickrama, K. A. S., Conger, R. D., Wallace, L. E., & Elder, G. H. (1999). The intergenerational transmission of health-risk behaviors: Adolescent lifestyles and gender moderating effects. *Journal of Health and Social Behavior, 40*(3), 258–272.

Young, R. J. (1995). What kinds of immigrants have come to the Philadelphia area, where did they settle, and how are the doing? In M Hutter (Ed.), *The family experience: A reader in cultural diversity* (2nd ed., pp. 97–107). Boston: Allyn and Bacon.

Epilogue

The world in which families exist today is a world of economic *globalization*. It is a world of religious, racial, and economic *violence*. It is a world of the Internet and CNN, of mass communication, and—as Kerry Daly and Anna Dienhart remind us—of accelerated *time demands* (1998, p. 113). The effects of these factors are described by Michael Wallace in the following negative terms:

> The restructuring of the global economy has unleashed a tremendous torrent of technological and organization changes that are leaving in their wake broken careers, disheveled families, and shattered dreams. The affluent society is being divided into winners and losers, haves and have-nots, the jobbed and the dejobbed. (1998, p. 36)

Despite the changing world, Lynda Walters and her coauthors remind us that in many respects,

> the experience of living in a family is the same in all cultures. For example, relationships between spouses and between parents and children are negotiated; most relationships within families are still hierarchical; the work of the home is still primarily the responsibility of the wife;

financial support is the responsibility of both, but the wife's is seen as supplementary; conflict is damaging to children; and

> individuals and families change, or develop, in predictable ways. (Walters, Warzywoda-Kruszynska, & Gurko, 2002, p. 448)

While these may be constants in family experience, they obscure many broad and minute differences. An important cross-cultural change, described throughout this volume, is the increase in *women's education and employment* outside the home. This change, however, has hardly resulted in gender equality. The support mechanisms, such as childcare, have not materialized, equal opportunities are not available, and men may not see the necessity of taking an equal domestic role. An edited volume by Judith Mirsky and Marty Radlett describes the continuing struggles women face: In most of the world, marriage, divorce, and child custody still favor men; abuse against women still occurs; access to land, inheritance, and financial security is unavailable to most women; sexual harassment and discrimination occur in work and educational settings; and men's response to these issues and to their domestic responsibilities lag far behind (Mirsky & Radlett, 2000).

In addition to this incomplete revolution in gender roles, there are other changes occurring not just in the industrialized nations but in many others as well. Miller and Browning note that the patterns include "decreases in household size and fertility rates overall and increases in divorce and non-traditional living arrangements" (2000, p. 302).

Incidentally, it is most interesting that one can start with either increased women's employment, increased divorce, or decreased fertility, and explain the other two.

Lest we become overwhelmed with the language of change, it is a good idea to note that our view of *history* is often static or oversimplified. A good example is found in D'Cruz and Bharat's discussion of the joint family in India, explicated by Singh in this volume. D'Cruz and Bharat state that a

> systematic and comprehensive perusal of family literature in India at once breaks the deep-seated notion that the Indian family was basically joint and that the nuclear family has replaced it, following industrialization and urbanization. On the contrary, it has been demonstrated that a multiplicity of family patterns including joint families, nuclear families, single parent families, dual earner families, and adoptive families have always coexisted. (2001, p. 185)

In other words, plural or *multiple family forms* are found historically in India, China, Cuba, Israel, and many other societies in this volume. They are not new today.

As you have seen in the foregoing chapters, while comparisons can be made and similarities can be found, not all societies and cultures are changing at the same rate of speed or in exactly the same direction. One reason for the differences in change results from different *family policies*. For example, Chinese governmental intervention has affected not just fertility but also late marriage and household size (Yi, 2002, p. 31). Likewise, Sweden's parental-leave policy makes a difference in the fathering role. However, behavior lags behind government policy (Seward, Yeatts, & Zottarelli, 2002, p. 397). Lest one overstate the directive importance of public policy, one must note Kamerman and Kahn's (1997) important book on family change and policy in four English-speaking nations, none of which, they say, has a coherent family policy.

Change and lack of change, similarities and differences, and, as Walters et al. (2002) remind us, internal (often hidden) differences within societies are the essence of cross-cultural and cross-societal comparisons. Thus, we come to the end of this cross-cultural journey through families in 25 nations in the 21st century. We hope you have found the book as interesting and insightful as we did in putting it together.

REFERENCES

Daly, K., & Dienhart, A. (1998). Negotiating parental involvement: Finding time for children. In D. Vannoy & P. J. Dubeck (Eds.), *Challenges for work and family in the 21st century* (pp. 111–122). New York: Aldine de Gruyter.

d'Cruz, P., & Bharat, S. (2001). Beyond joint and nuclear: The Indian family revisited. *Journal of Comparative Family Studies, 32*, 167–194.

Kamerman, S., & Kahn, A. J. (1997). *Family change and family policies in Great Britain, Canada, New Zealand, and the United States.* New York: Oxford University Press.

Miller, R. R., & Browning, S. L. (2000). How constructions of ethnicity and gender contribute to shaping non-traditional family patterns. *Journal of Comparative Family Studies, 31*, 301–307.

Mirsky, J., & Radlett, M. (2000). *No paradise yet: The world's women face the new century.* London: The Panos Insitute and Zed Books.

Seward, R. R., Yeatts, D. E., & Zottarelli, L. K. (2002). Parental leave and father involvement in child care: Sweden and the United States. *Journal of Comparative Family Studies, 33*, 387–399.

Wallace, M. (1998). Downsizing the American dream: Work and family at century's end. In D. Vannoy & P. J. Dubeck (Eds.), *Challenges for work and family in the 21st century* (pp. 23–38). New York: Aldine de Gruyter.

Walters, L. H., Warzywoda-Kruszynska, W., & Gurko, T. (2002). Cross-cultural studies of families: Hidden differences. *Journal of Comparative Family Studies, 33,* 433–449.

Yi, Zeng. (2002). A demographic analysis of family households in China, 1982–1995. *Journal of Comparative Family Studies, 33,* 15–34.

Author Index

Subject Index

Abduction:
   Turkish brides, 368
   See also Argentinean families
Aboriginal Head Start, Canada, 540
Abortion, 333, 426, 448
Abuelas de Plaza de Mayo.
      See Argentinean families
Abuse. *See* Child abuse; Domestic abuse;
      Emotional abuse; Physical abuse;
      Sexual abuse
Act to Promote Family Counseling of 1974,
      Austria, 212
Adoption practices, 572, 581, 582-583
Aging. *See* Death; Elders
Agricultural activities:
   cash cropping, 15-16
   Kenya, 4, 15-16
   Nigeria, 26, 31-32
   non-resilient/fragile environments, 4
   Puerto Rico, 444-445, 449
   South Korea, 170
   subsistence farming, 15
   See also Land use
AIDS infection:
   Kenyan families and, 22
   Portuguese families and, 333
   South African families and, 58, 61
Alien's Control Act of 1991, 61
All India Democratic Women's
      Association (AIDWA), 146
Ancestor reverence:
   Iranian families and, 468
   South African families and, 48
   South Korean families and, 171, 173
Arabian society:
   family structures in, 513-514
   Israeli citizens, 488, 489, 491, 494, 499, 500
Argentinean families, 391-392
   abduction of children and, 408-410
   adolescent/child fertility and, 398
   cohabitation and, 394-395

detained/disappeared citizens and, 407-410
divorce and, 404-406
economic forces and, 403-404
education and, 396, 397-398, 399
employment and, 399-400
ex-nuptial births and, 393
family policy/law and, 393-394, 396, 397
fertility trends and, 395-399
gender roles and, 399-400, 405
household configurations and, 400-404,
   401 (table), 403 (table), 405 (table)
identity restitution and, 409-410
immigration trends and, 394, 396
kinship structures and, 401
marriage practices and, 393, 395, 405-406
mate selection/pairing systems, 394-395
military dictatorship, paternal
      authority/human rights crisis
      and, 406-410
national history, modernization and, 392-394
religious affiliation and, 393, 396
same-sex coupling and, 394, 404
sexual abuse and, 398-399
single-parent households and, 402-403,
   403 (table), 404
single-person households and,
   402, 403 (table)
Arranged marriages, 17
   Australian practices, 71
   Canadian practices, 541
   Chinese practices, 101-102
   Indian practices, 143-144, 161
   Israeli practices, 488
   Kuwaiti practices, 516
   Nigerian practices, 28-29
   South Korean practices, 170
   Taiwanese practices, 178
   Turkish practices, 367-368
Associação Portuguesa de Apoio à Vítima
      (APAV), 339
Australia, 67-68

About the Editors

Bert N. Adams is Professor Emeritus of Sociology at the University of Wisconsin, Madison, United States. He has published *The Family: A Sociological Interpretation* (5 editions) and *Sociological Theory*. He is a past president of the National Council on Family Relations, and still teaches 500 students in his Marriage and Family course.

Jan Trost is Professor Emeritus at Uppsala University, Department of Sociology, Sweden. He has published extensively in the fields of family studies and symbolic interaction. Dr. Trost is very active internationally and has been president of the Committee on Family Research (CFR) of the International Sociological Association (ISA), and has been president of the Nordic Family Research Network (NFRN) for 10 years. Since 1996 he has been honorary president of the CFR.

About the Contributors

Fausto Amaro, PhD, is Professor and Director of the Family Studies Centre at the Higher Institute of Social and Political Sciences, Technical University of Lisbon. His research has focused on family policy, child abuse, adoption, sexual behavior, and mental health. He is the author and coauthor of several books and articles on these subjects.

Taghi Azadarmaki, PhD, graduated from Maryland University in 1991 with a dissertation on Ibn-Khalduan's social theory. After returning to Iran, he has taught several courses on social theory, social and cultural changes in Iran, and cultural studies. He has conducted some survey research on values in Muslim countries and worked on some social and cultural issues in Iran. He has run the Social Science faculty at the University of Tehran since 1996 and was promoted to professor in sociology in 2003. During the last 10 years he has published 14 books on social theory, cultural and social changes, Iranian modernity, and family and culture in Iran, and has published 34 papers on different issues in academic journals.

Yu-Hua Chen is Assistant Professor of Rural Sociology at the National Taiwan University. She recently served as executive editor for the *Journal of Population Studies*, a leading demographic publication in Taiwan. Emphasizing the influence of demographic processes, her research focuses on women's well-being and their families over the life course. She is also interested in comparing the consequences of socioeconomic change for families and households among Chinese

societies. Her most recent publication is a chapter titled "The Impact of Co-residence on Marital Power: An Interplay Between Resources and Norms" (with Chin-Chun Yi) in Murray Rubenstein and Scott Simon (Eds.), *Engendering Formosa* (M. E. Sharpe, forthcoming).

Wilfried Dumon is Professor Emeritus at Katholijke Univeristeit Leuven, Department of Sociology, Belgium. He was secretary/treasurer of the Committee on Family Research (CFR) of the International Sociological Association (ISA) for many years. He was also awarded an honorary doctorate from Uppsala University, Sweden.

Elisa Facio is Associate Professor in Ethnic Studies at the University of Colorado at Boulder. Her research and teaching focus on racial-ethnic women and aging. She has been taking students to Cuba for over a decade. She also conducts research on gender inequality in Cuba during the Special Period.

Hannele Forsberg, PhD, is Assistant Professor of Social Work and vice-chair of the Childhood and Family Research Unit, University of Tampere. She has studied and written extensively about families, children, and the social construction of emotions in social problems work.

Carol D. H. Harvey, PhD, is a professor in the Department of Family Social Sciences, Faculty of Human Ecology, University of Manitoba, Winnipeg, Canada. She is a family researcher and teacher, with interest in family problem-solving among immigrant, refugee, and native families and among family caregivers with frail elderly members. She has worked in universities in the United States and Canada for 34 years; she has also had the opportunity to take sabbatical leaves in Finland, Scotland, and Australia.

Elizabeth Jelin is Senior Researcher at the National Council of Scientific Research, Argentina, Research Director at Instituto de Desarrollo Económico y Social, and Director of the Doctoral Program in the Social Sciences developed jointly at the Universidad Nacional de General Sarmiento and IDES. She is the author of numerous publications, including *State Repression and the Labors of Memory,* and editor of several volumes in the series "Memorias de la represión." She is also the author and editor of *Más allá de la nación: Las escalas múltiples de los movimientos sociales* and of *Pan y afectos: La transformación de las familias.* Her research interests are in human rights, the family, citizenship, and social movements.

Tomáš Katrnák is a research assistant in the Department of Sociology at the Faculty of Social Studies in Brno. His research concerns the sociology of family, demography, social inequality, and social stratification.

Ruth Katz received her PhD in sociology from Tel Aviv University. She is at the Department of Human Services, Faculty of Social Welfare and Health Studies, University of Haifa, and a senior researcher at the Center for Research and Study of the Family and at the Center for Research and Study of Aging. Her main fields of interest include family relations, gendered division of labor, alternative lifestyles, intergenerational relations, immigrant families, and family theory.

Daniela Klaus is employed as a scientific researcher at the Department of Sociology at the Technical University of Chemnitz, Germany. Her fields of interest are sociology of family and quantitative methods of empirical research. Currently, she is working in a cross-cultural study examining the value of children to their parents in Turkey, where she is doing her doctoral thesis on the subject of the demographic transition.

Thomas Klein is Professor of Sociology at Heidelberg University, Germany. His research interests are family and population sociology, comparative social stratification, and life course research. He has authored many publications on various topics in these fields.

Sandra Kytir received her MA in sociology at the University of Vienna and is currently undertaking a PhD at Lancaster University. She tutors in statistics and works in social indicator research with a special focus on family issues. Her current research interest is in transition processes from state socialism to a market economy, focusing on uneven development in Eastern European countries.

Yoav Lavee received his PhD in family studies from the University of Minnesota. He is at the School of Social Work, Faculty of Social Welfare and Health Studies, University of Haifa, and a senior researcher at the Center for Research and Study of the Family. His main fields of interest include family stress and coping, marital dynamics under stress, marital quality in a multicultural context, and family theory and methodology.

Kwang-Kyu Lee received a BA in history in 1960 from Seoul National University and a PhD in Cultural Anthropology in 1966 from the University of Vienna. From 1967 to 1998 Dr. Lee was a professor at Seoul National University, and became Professor Emeritus in 1998 at the same university. In 2003 Dr. Lee was president of the Overseas Koreans Foundation.

Irene Levin is a professor at Oslo University College, Graduate School of Social Work and Social Research. Her publications include books and articles on stepfamilies (including *Stepfamilies—Variations and Manifold* [Aventura, Oslo] and *Stepfamilies—History, Research and Policy* [The Howarth Press]), living apart together relationships (*LAT— One Couple Two Homes* [N. W. Damm, Oslo]), and symbolic interaction (*To Understand Everyday Life From a Symbolic Interactionist Perspective* [TANO, Oslo]).

Edward K. Mburugu is currently Associate Professor of Sociology and Associate Dean in the Faculty of Arts of the University of Nairobi, Kenya. Recent articles have focused on development and fertility in Africa and the changing family and kinship in African development. He is also a coeditor of *African Perspectives on Development* (James Currey Ltd. 1994).

Innocent Victor Ogo Modo is Nigerian. He holds a PhD in social anthropology. Currently, he is an associate professor of anthropology at the University of Uyo, Akwa Ibom State, Nigeria. He is a member of the committee of Family Research (RCO6) of the International Sociological Association.

Ivo Možný is Professor of Sociology and Social Philosophy and a senior researcher at the School for Social Studies, Masaryk University Brno Czech Republic. Dr. Mozny's scholarly interests include sociology of the family, poverty, social policy, social conflict and change, and higher education. Dr. Mozny has also published four books on family and social change and many papers in sociological journals, and is engaged in governmental advisory committees on the family and social policy.

Fahad Al Naser obtained his PhD in sociology of family from Michigan State University in 1986. Since his return to Kuwait, he has been teaching at Kuwait University. He has published many articles and has also authored textbooks related to marriage, family, divorce, mate selection, and the like, in both Arabic and English. While writing his contribution to this volume, he was just ending his term as chair of the Department of Sociology & Social Work, Kuwait University. After the liberation of Kuwait in 1991 (from the Iraqi occupation), Dr. Fahad was deeply involved with humanitarian projects that were related to rehabilitating the people of Kuwait who were affected by the crisis. He also serves on the board of several educational committees and institutions.

Bernhard Nauck is the founding Professor of the Department of Sociology at Chemnitz University of Technology, Germany. He received his PhD in 1977 from the University of Cologne, and habilitation in 1983 and 1987 (University of Bonn and Augsburg). His research interests include comparative family sociology, life course, and migration, and he has published some 150 scholarly pieces in German, English, French, Turkish, and Italian. Currently, he is president of the Committee on Family Research of the International Sociological Association.

Rudolf Richter, PhD, is University Professor of Sociology at the Institute of Sociology at the University of Vienna. He has been a member of the coordination team of the European Observatory on the Social Situation, Demography and the Family since 2000. He was a visiting professor at the University of Minnesota in 1985 and at Arizona State University in 1996. He is a member of several international sociological scientific organizations and is a past president of the Austrian Association of Sociology and a past vice president of the Committee of Family Research of the International Sociological Association. His main areas of research include sociology of family, sociology of the life course, political sociology, Eastern European studies, cultural sociology, and interpretative sociology.

Anne R. Roschelle is Associate Professor and Chair of Sociology at the State University of New York at New Paltz. Her teaching and research focus on the intersection of race, class, and gender, with a specialty in family poverty. She also conducts research on gender inequality in Cuba during the Special Period.

Barbara H. Settles, PhD, is Professor of Individual and Family Studies, University of Delaware, Newark. Her recent writings have focused on futures of families in the United States and internationally, immigration, migration and the concepts of home and society, prevention and family life and sexuality education, comparisons of the United States to China in family formation and intergenerational caregiving, and the scholarship of teaching and learning.

Xuewen Sheng worked as a research professor in the Department of Marriage and Family Studies, Institute of Sociology, Chinese Academy of Social Sciences, Beijing, China, from 1982 to 1997, with major research areas of comparative family studies and gender and aging issues. He received his MA on Human Development and Family Studies in 1999, and he is currently a PhD candidate on Human Development of Family Studies at the University of Delaware. His interest areas include comparative family studies, human development, and research methodology.

J. P. Singh is Professor in the Postgraduate Department of Sociology, Patna University, India. Earlier he was Reader in Research Methodology at the Tata Institute of Social Sciences, Mumbai. He obtained a PhD in demography from the Australian National University, Canberra. He held a UNDP Fellowship at the Institute of Social Studies, the Hague, and was a Professional Associate of the Institute of Population Studies, East-West Center, Hawaii. During the last three decades of his academic career, he has published eight books and over 50 research papers in books and leading professional journals from India and abroad.

Peter Somlai is Professor and Head of the Department of History of Social Theory in the Institute of Sociology at the Eötvös Loránd University, Budapest, Hungary. He taught on family and society in several universities in the United States, Germany, and Romania. His current research interest is theories of deviance. Recent publications include a chapter titled "Global Citizenship: An Essay on Its Ambiguities" in J. A. Myers-Walls & P. Somlai, with R. N. Rapoport (Eds.), *Families as Educators for Global Citizenship* (London: Avebury Press, 2001).

Maura I. Toro-Morn is Associate Professor of Sociology at Illinois State University. Her research and teaching focus on the intersection of race, class, and gender with a specialty in global migrations from a gendered perspective. She also conducts research on gender inequality in Cuba during the Special Period.

Olga Tóth is a senior researcher at the Institute of Sociology, Hungarian Academy of Sciences. She conducted a series of empirical studies on family and gender in recent decades. Her main research topics are family formations, violence in the family, and connections between generations. She also teaches courses for undergraduate students in different universities. She has published in Hungarian and in English.

David de Vaus is Professor of Sociology at La Trobe University in Melbourne, Australia. He has also worked as the director of research at the Australian Institute of Family Studies, where he has conducted research on cohabitation, intergenerational relationships, family values, mental health and families, and family disruptions as experienced by children. He is the author of many books including *Letting Go: Relationships Between Adults and Their Parents* (1994); *Australian Family Profiles: Social and Demographic Patterns* (1997) (with Ilene Wolcott); and *Diversity and Change in Australian Families* (2004).

Chin-Chun Yi is a research fellow at the Institute of Sociology, Academia Sinica, Taiwan. She is also teaching at the Department of Sociology, National Taiwan University. Her research interests include changing females' domestic status, youth study, and the transformation of private universities in Taiwan. Her recent publications are "Taiwan's Modernization Women's Changing Roles" (in Peter Chow [Ed.], *Taiwan's Modernization in Global Perspective* [Praeger, 2002]), "The Linkage Between Work and Family: Females' Employment Patterns in Three Chinese Societies" (in *Journal of Comparative Family Studies*, 2002), and "The Intergenerational Transmission of Family Values: Teenagers and Their Parents in Taiwan" (in *Journal of Comparative Family Studies*, in press).

Susan C. Ziehl is Associate Professor in the Department of Sociology and Industrial Sociology at Rhodes University, Grahamstown, South Africa. She holds an M.ECON degree from the University of Stellenbosch and a PhD from Rhodes University. She also spent 2 years at the University of Neuchatel, Switzerland. Her main research and teaching area is family sociology, with specific emphasis on household structures, marital status, and family law. She also teaches in industrial sociology, in particular, a course on gender and work. Her other areas of interest are infertility and modern reproductive technology, demography, affirmative action, and sexual harassment. Recent publications include *Population Studies* (Oxford University Press, 2002) and "Forging the Links—Globalization and Family Patterns" (in *Society in Transition, 34*[2], 2003).